FOUNDATIONS OF EMPLOYMENT DISCRIMINATION LAW

SECOND EDITION

FOUNDATIONS OF EMPLOYMENT DISCRIMINATION LAW

SECOND EDITION

JOHN J. DONOHUE III

Professor of Law, Stanford Law School

ISBN: 9781422498835

NOTE TO USERS

To ensure that you are using the latest materials available in this area, please be sure to periodically check the LexisNexis Law School web site for downloadable updates and supplements at www.lexisnexis.com/lawschool.

Editorial Offices
121 Chanlon Rd., New Providence, NJ 07974 (908) 464-6800
201 Mission St., San Francisco, CA 94105-1831 (415) 908-3200
www.lexisnexis.com

(Pub.3334)

PREFACE TO THE SECOND EDITION

This edition has drawn upon the considerable scholarly work over the last five years that addresses issues concerning employment discrimination law. The growing importance of discrimination on the basis of age and disability has prompted me to add new chapters on those topics, thereby expanding the examination of employment discrimination beyond the areas of race and sex discrimination that were the focus of the first edition. Moreover, the Civil Rights Act of 1991 for the first time established a potential federal remedy of compensatory and punitive damages for victims of sexual harassment, which has prompted an enormous increase in the filing of such cases, and in the amount of judicial and scholarly attention directed to this issue. As a result, the material on sex harassment has been expanded and made into a separate chapter. Finally, throughout I have updated the notes and questions to capture some of the important legal and scholarly developments in all areas of employment discrimination, which continues to be one of the most dynamic and growing areas of federal civil litigation.

In addition to the very helpful research assistance of Wade Pyun, I was also extremely fortunate to be aided in every aspect of this revision by Emily Ryo, whose scholarly talents and good judgment have been critical to this effort. I can't express my gratitude strongly enough.

FOUNDATIONS OF LAW SERIES

ROBERTA ROMANO, GENERAL EDITOR

Foundations of Administrative Law
Edited by Peter H. Schuck, Yale Law School

Foundations of Bankruptcy Law
Edited by Barry Adler, New York University Law School

Foundations of Commercial Law
Edited by Robert E. Scott, Columbia Law School and George G. Triantis, Harvard Law School

Foundations of Contract Law
Edited by Richard Craswell, Stanford Law School and Alan Schwartz, Yale Law School

Foundation of Corporate Law
Edited by Roberta Romano, Yale Law School

Foundations of Criminal Law
Edited by Leo Katz, Michael S. Moore and Stephen J. Morse, all of the University of Pennsylvania Law School

Foundations of the Economic Approach to Law
Edited by Avery Wiener Katz, Columbia Law School

Foundations of Employment Discrimination Law
Edited by John Donohue, III, Stanford Law School

Foundations of Environmental Law and Policy
Edited by Richard L. Revesz, New York University Law School

Foundations of Intellectual Property
Edited by Robert P. Merges, University of California Berkeley and Davis School of Law and Jane C. Ginsburg, Columbia University School of Law

Foundations of International Income Taxation
Edited by Michael J. Graetz, Yale Law School

Foundations of International Law and Politics
Edited by Oona A. Hathaway, Yale Law School and Harold Hongju Koh, Yale Law School

Foundations of Labor and Employment Law
Edited by Samuel Estreicher, New York University Law School and Stewart J. Schwab, Cornell Law School

Foundations of the Law and Ethics of Lawyering
Edited by George M. Cohen, University of Virginia School of Law and Susan P. Koniak, Boston University School of Law

Foundations of Tort Law
Edited by Saul Levmore, University of Chicago Law School and Catherine M. Sharkey, New York University School of Law

CONTENTS

Racial Discrimination

FOUNDATIONS OF EMPLOYMENT DISCRIMINATION LAW

SECOND EDITION

By

JOHN J. DONOHUE III

Professor of Law, Stanford Law School

FOUNDATION PRESS
New York, New York
2003

COPYRIGHT © 1997 FOUNDATION PRESS
COPYRIGHT © 2003 By FOUNDATION PRESS
      395 Hudson Street
      New York, NY 10014
      Phone Toll Free 1–877–888–1330
      Fax (212) 367–6799
      fdpress.com

TEXT IS PRINTED ON 10% POST CONSUMER RECYCLED PAPER

PREFACE TO THE SECOND EDITION

This edition has drawn upon the considerable scholarly work over the last five years that addresses issues concerning employment discrimination law. The growing importance of discrimination on the basis of age and disability has prompted me to add new chapters on those topics, thereby expanding the examination of employment discrimination beyond the areas of race and sex discrimination that were the focus of the first edition. Moreover, the Civil Rights Act of 1991 for the first time established a potential federal remedy of compensatory and punitive damages for victims of sexual harassment, which has prompted an enormous increase in the filing of such cases, and in the amount of judicial and scholarly attention directed to this issue. As a result, the material on sex harassment has been expanded and made into a separate chapter. Finally, throughout I have updated the notes and questions to capture some of the important legal and scholarly developments in all areas of employment discrimination, which continues to be one of the most dynamic and growing areas of federal civil litigation.

In addition to the very helpful research assistance of Wade Pyun, I was also extremely fortunate to be aided in every aspect of this revision by Emily Ryo, whose scholarly talents and good judgment have been critical to this effort. I can't express my gratitude strongly enough.

FOUNDATIONS OF LAW SERIES

ROBERTA ROMANO, General Editor

Foundations of Administrative Law
Edited by Peter H. Schuck, Yale Law School

Foundations of Contract Law
Edited by Richard Craswell, Stanford Law School and
Alan Schwartz, Yale Law School

Foundations of Corporate Law
Edited by Roberta Romano, Yale Law School

Foundations of Criminal Law
Edited by Leo Katz, Michael S. Moore and Stephen J. Morse,
all of the University of Pennsylvania Law School

Foundations of The Economic Approach to Law
Edited by Avery Wiener Katz, Columbia Law School

Foundations of Employment Discrimination Law
Edited by John Donohue, III, Stanford Law School

Foundations of Environmental Law and Policy
Edited by Richard L. Revesz, New York University Law School

Foundations of Labor Law
Edited by Samuel Estreicher, New York University Law School
and Stewart J. Schwab, Cornell Law School

Foundations of Tort Law
Edited by Saul Levmore, University of Chicago Law School

CONTENTS

Racial Discrimination

Sex Discrimination

Contents

*

FOUNDATIONS OF EMPLOYMENT DISCRIMINATION LAW

*

Racial Discrimination

Historical Background

The notion that discrimination in employment on the basis of race and sex is and should be prohibited by law is so deeply ingrained in the modern consciousness that challenges to this view may seem bizarre. Prior to World War II, however, the idea would have seemed equally strange that the federal government could tell private employers operating anywhere in the country that they must hire certain, albeit fully qualified, workers instead of some other preferred group of workers. Indeed, this profound shift in the public's conception of the appropriate role of law represents one of the major developments in legal consciousness since the Civil War. To understand modern employment discrimination law, one must comprehend the history that made such laws necessary.

Yet, in the study of history, W. E. B. DuBois wrote in 1935, one is constantly astonished by "the recurrence of the idea that evil must be forgotten, distorted, skimmed over." David Levering Lewis, ed., *W. E. B. DuBois: A Reader* 211 (New York: Henry Holt, 1995). With the possible exception of Native Americans, no racial or ethnic group in America has experienced such sustained and appalling mistreatment, and therefore has a stronger claim than blacks to compensatory and corrective governmental measures. The calculated oppression of black Americans by governmental bodies is not the product of some distant past but continued in a most virulent form at least until the mid to late 1960s, when the legislative and executive branches of the federal government finally joined the Supreme Court in trying to aid blacks with various antidiscrimination and affirmative action measures. In the current political debate over affirmative action, it is at times alarming to see how little of the appalling history is still remembered, and how quickly the notion has gained currency that the moral debt to a people enslaved and then oppressed and degraded has been paid by thirty years of relatively even-handed and in some cases preferential treatment.

Perhaps foreigners, untainted by the evil in the history of the treatment of blacks in America, have been able to document this mistreatment more candidly and accurately than those who have stood closer to the burning flames of injustice. The selections in this chapter, one by the famed French political theorist Alexis de Tocqueville and one by the Nobel Prize-winning Swedish economist Gunnar Myrdal, provide some background, some context to the ensuing analyses of the range of issues invoked by employment discrimination law.

And the history is unspeakably malevolent. The African slave trade delivered its first victims to North America some 375 years ago. From that point on, with the exception of two periods, governmental power in the United States has predominantly been arrayed to harm, oppress, or at best ignore the interests of black Americans. The two periods in which government authority has been actively marshalled in support of the welfare of African-Americans were during Reconstruction following the Civil War and during the last thirty years, beginning with the passage of the 1964 Civil Rights Act. Sadly, the perceived excesses of Reconstruction became the excuse for an egregious white backlash in the final decades of the nineteenth century that shattered the initial promise of the Civil War amendments to the United States Constitution. This post-Reconstruction backlash delivered a blow to black America from which it scarcely recovered over the next eighty years. Some fear that the potential for a similar overreaction to the second American Reconstruction is building in the United States today.

Writing in 1833 in his magisterial work *Democracy in America,* de Tocqueville describes how the unique character of a slavery premised on race delivered a particularly damaging wound to humanity. De Tocqueville perceptively comments on one of the critical aspects of the race problem in America—the role of law versus the role of customs and norms as the mechanism of black oppression. He also understood that, while the institution of slavery could not persist, its consequences would long endure.

Over one hundred years later, a second insightful foreigner, Gunnar Myrdal of Sweden, documented in his classic work *An American Dilemma: The Negro Problem and Modern Democracy* (New York: Harper and Brothers, 1944) the rise of the American apartheid and catalogued the discrimination, segregation, and violence that were imposed on black Americans. Myrdal also demonstrated that black economic welfare was often buffeted by major economic events in the first half of the twentieth century. For example, blacks were often the unintended victims of the increased enactment of progressive social legislation, which tended to elevate the costs of labor and thereby disproportionately displace the most marginal workers. In addition, the advent of World War II stimulated the demand for labor (although not uniformly across racial lines and geographic regions) and led to the first halting steps by the federal government to shield blacks from discrimination in defense industries and government. Although Myrdal wrote before the emergence of employment discrimination law, many of the issues that are addressed in Chapter 8 concerning the evaluation of the impact of such legislation are adumbrated in his exhaustive study of the myriad and conflicting influences on black economic welfare, for which analysts must control in assessing the effect of antidiscrimination law. The selection from Myrdal provides an overview of the legal forces—both constitutional and legislative, federal and state—that shaped the rights and lives of blacks from the end of the Civil War to the beginning of World War II.

Democracy in America*
ALEXIS DE TOCQUEVILLE

Generally speaking, it requires great and constant efforts for men to create lasting ills; but there is one evil which has percolated furtively into the world: at first it was hardly noticed among the usual abuses of power; it began with an individual whose name history does not record; it was cast like an accursed seed somewhere on the ground; it then nurtured itself, grew without effort, and spread with the society that accepted it; that evil was slavery....

Christianity has destroyed servitude; the Christians of the sixteenth century reestablished it, but they never admitted it as anything more than an exception in their social system, and they were careful to restrict it to one of the races of man. In this way they inflicted a smaller wound on humanity but one much harder to cure.

It is important to make a careful distinction between slavery in itself and its consequences.

The immediate ills resulting from slavery were almost the same in the ancient as in the modern world, but the consequences of these ills were different. In antiquity the slave was of the same race as his master and was often his superior in education and enlightenment. Only freedom kept them apart; freedom once granted, they mingled easily.

Therefore the ancients had a very simple means of delivering themselves from slavery and its consequences, namely, to free the slaves; and when they made a general use of this, they succeeded.

Admittedly the traces of servitude existed in antiquity for some time after slavery itself had been abolished.

A natural prejudice leads a man to scorn anybody who has been his inferior, long after he has become his equal; the real inequality, due to fortune or the law, is always followed by an imagined inequality rooted in mores; but with the ancients this secondary effect of slavery had a time limit, for the freedman was so completely like the man born free that it was soon impossible to distinguish between them.

In antiquity the most difficult thing was to change the law; in the modern world the hard thing is to alter mores, and our difficulty begins where theirs ended.

This is because in the modern world the insubstantial and ephemeral fact of servitude is most fatally combined with the physical and permanent fact of difference in race. Memories of slavery disgrace the race, and race perpetuates memories of slavery.

No African came in freedom to the shores of the New World; consequently all those found there now are slaves or freedmen. The Negro transmits to his descendants at birth the external mark of his ignominy. The law can abolish servitude, but only God can obliterate its traces.

The modern slave differs from his master not only in lacking freedom but also in his origin. You can make the Negro free, but you cannot prevent him facing the European as a stranger.

That is not all; this man born in degradation, this stranger brought by slavery into our midst, is hardly recognized as sharing the common features of humanity. His face appears to us hideous, his intelligence limited, and his tastes low; we almost take him for some being intermediate between beast and man.[1]

· · ·

Turning my attention to the United States of our own day, I plainly see that in some parts of the country the legal barrier between the two races is tending to come down, but not that of mores: I see that slavery is in retreat, but the prejudice from which it arose is immovable.

In that part of the Union where the Negroes are no longer slaves, have they come closer to the whites? Everyone who has lived in the United States will have noticed just the opposite.

Race prejudice seems stronger in those states that have abolished slavery than in those where it still exists, and nowhere is it more intolerant than in those states where slavery was never known.

1. To induce the whites to abandon the opinion they have conceived of the intellectual and moral inferiority of their former slaves, the Negroes must change, but they cannot change so long as this opinion persists.

It is true that in the North of the Union the law allows legal marriages between Negroes and whites, but public opinion would regard a white man married to a Negro woman as disgraced, and it would be very difficult to quote an example of such an event.

In almost all the states where slavery has been abolished, the Negroes have been given electoral rights, but they would come forward to vote at the risk of their lives. When oppressed, they can bring an action at law, but they will find only white men among their judges. It is true that the laws make them eligible as jurors, but prejudice wards them off. The Negro's son is excluded from the school to which the European's child goes. In the theaters he cannot for good money buy the right to sit by his former master's side; in the hospitals he lies apart. He is allowed to worship the same God as the white man but must not pray at the same altars. He has his own clergy and churches. The gates of heaven are not closed against him, but his inequality stops only just short of the boundaries of the other world. When the Negro is no more, his bones are cast aside, and some difference in condition is found even in the equality of death.

So the Negro is free, but he cannot share the rights, pleasures, labors, griefs, or even the tomb of him whose equal he has been declared; there is nowhere where he can meet him, neither in life nor in death.

In the South, where slavery still exists, less trouble is taken to keep the Negro apart: they sometimes share the labors and the pleasures of the white men; people are prepared to mix with them to some extent; legislation is more harsh against them, but customs are more tolerant and gentle.

In the South the master has no fear of lifting the slave up to his level, for he knows that when he wants to he can always throw him down into the dust. In the North the white man no longer clearly sees the barrier that separates him from the degraded race, and he keeps the Negro at a distance all the more carefully because he fears lest one day they be confounded together.

Thus it is that in the United States the prejudice rejecting the Negroes seems to increase in proportion to their emancipation, and inequality cuts deep into mores as it is effaced from the laws.

But if the relative position of the two races inhabiting the United States is as I have described it, why is it that the Americans have abolished slavery in the North of the Union, and why have they kept it in the South and aggravated its rigors?

The answer is easy. In the United States people abolish slavery for the sake not of the Negroes but of the white men.

The first Negroes were imported into Virginia about the year 1621. In America, as everywhere else in the world, slavery originated in the South. Thence it spread from one place to the next; but the numbers of the slaves grew less the farther one went north; there have always been very few Negroes in New England.

When a century had passed since the foundation of the colonies, an extraordinary fact began to strike the attention of everybody. The population of those provinces that had practically no slaves increased in numbers, wealth, and well-being more rapidly than those that had slaves.

The inhabitants of the former had to cultivate the ground themselves or hire another's services; in the latter they had laborers whom they did not need to pay. With labor and expense on the one side and leisure and economy on the other, nonetheless the advantage lay with the former.

This result seemed all the harder to explain since the immigrants all belonged to the same European stock, with the same habits, civilization, and laws, and there were only hardly perceptible nuances of difference between them.

As time went on, the Anglo-Americans left the Atlantic coast and plunged daily farther into the solitudes of the West; there they encountered soils and climates that were new; they had obstacles of various sorts to overcome; their races mingled, southerners going north, and northerners south. But in all these circumstances the same fact stood out time and again: in general, the colony that had no slaves was more populous and prosperous than the one where slavery was in force.

The farther they went, the clearer it became that slavery, so cruel to the slave, was fatal to the master.

But the banks of the Ohio provided the final demonstration of this truth.

The stream that the Indians had named the Ohio, or Beautiful River par excellence, waters one of the most magnificent valleys in which man has ever lived. On both banks of the Ohio stretched undulating ground with soil continually offering the cultivator inexhaustible treasures; on both banks the air is equally healthy and the climate temperate; they both form the frontier of a vast state: that which follows the innumerable windings of the Ohio on the left bank is called Kentucky; the other takes its name from the river itself. There is only one difference between the two states: Kentucky allows slaves, but Ohio refuses to have them.

So the traveler who lets the current carry him down the Ohio till it joins the Mississippi sails, so to say, between freedom and slavery; and he has only to glance around him to see instantly which is best for mankind.

On the left bank of the river the population is sparse; from time to time one sees a troop of slaves loitering through half-deserted fields; the primeval forest is constantly reappearing; one might say that society had gone to sleep; it is nature that seems active and alive, whereas man is idle.

But on the right bank a confused hum proclaims from afar that men are busily at work; fine crops cover the fields; elegant dwellings testify to the taste and industry of the workers; on all sides there is evidence of comfort; man appears rich and contented; he works.

The state of Kentucky was founded in 1775 and that of Ohio as much as twelve years later; twelve years in America accounts for as much as half a century in Europe. Now the population of Ohio is more than 250,000 greater than that of Kentucky.

These contrasting effects of slavery and of freedom are easy to understand; they are enough to explain the differences between ancient civilization and modern.

On the left bank of the Ohio work is connected with the idea of slavery, but on the right with well-being and progress; on the one side it is degrading, but on the other honorable; on the left bank no white laborers are to be found, for they would be afraid of being like the slaves; for work people must rely on the Negroes; but one will never see a man of leisure on the right bank: the white man's intelligent activity is used for work of every sort.

Hence those whose task it is in Kentucky to exploit the natural wealth of the soil are neither eager nor instructed, for anyone who might possess those qualities either does nothing or crosses over into Ohio so that he can profit by his industry, and do so without shame.

· · ·

What is happening in the South of the Union seems to me both the most horrible and the most natural consequence of slavery. When I see the order of nature overthrown and hear the cry of humanity complaining in vain against the laws, I confess that my indignation is not directed against the men of our own day who are the authors of these outrages; all my hatred is concentrated against those who, after a thousand years of equality, introduced slavery into the world again.

Whatever efforts the Americans of the South make to maintain slavery, they will not forever succeed. Slavery is limited to one point on the globe and attacked by Christianity as unjust and by political economy as fatal; slavery, amid the democratic liberty and enlightenment of our age, is not an institution that can last. Either the slave or the master will put an end to it. In either case great misfortunes are to be anticipated.

If freedom is refused to the Negroes in the South, in the end they will seize it themselves; if it is granted to them, they will not be slow to abuse it.

An American Dilemma: The Negro Problem and Modern Democracy*

GUNNAR MYRDAL

The Jim Crow Laws

Emancipation loosened the bonds on Negro slaves and allowed them to leave their masters. The majority of freedmen seems to have done some loitering as a symbolic act and in order to test out the new freedom. Reconstruction temporarily gave civil rights, suffrage, and even some access to public office. It also marked the heroic beginning of the Negroes' efforts to acquire the rudiments of education.

There is no doubt that Congress intended to give the Negroes "social equality" in public life to a substantial degree. The Civil Rights Bill of 1875, which, in many ways, represented the culmination of the federal Reconstruction legislation, was explicit in declaring that all persons within the jurisdiction of the United States should be entitled to the full and equal enjoyment of the accommodations, advantages, facilities, and privileges of inns, public conveyances on land and water, theaters, and other places of public amusement; subject only to the conditions and limitations established by law, and applicable alike to citizens of every race and color, regardless of previous condition of servitude. The federal courts were given exclusive jurisdiction over offenses against this statute. . . .

During Congressional Reconstruction some Southern states inserted clauses in their constitutions or in special laws intended to establish the rights of Negroes to share on equal terms in the accommodations of public establishments and conveyances. Louisiana and South Carolina went so far as to require mixed schools. From contemporary accounts of life in the South during Reconstruction, it is evident, however, that Negroes met considerable segregation and discrimination even during these few years of legal equality. It is also apparent that nothing irritated the majority of white Southerners so much as the attempts of Congress and the Reconstruction governments to remove social discrimination from public life.

After Restoration of "white supremacy" the doctrine that the Negroes should be "kept in their place" became the regional creed. When the Supreme Court in 1883 declared the Civil Rights Bill of 1875 unconstitutional in so far as it referred to acts of social discrimination by individuals—endorsing even in this field the political compromise between the white North and South—the way was left open for the Jim Crow legislation of the Southern states and municipalities. For a quarter of a century this system of statutes and regulations—separating the two groups in schools, on railroad cars and on street cars, in hotels and restaurants, in parks and playgrounds, in theaters and public meeting places—continued to grow, with the explicit purpose of diminishing, as far as was practicable and possible, the social contacts between whites and Negroes in the region.

We do not know much about the effects of the Jim Crow legislation. American sociologists, following the Sumner tradition of holding legislation to be inconsequential, are likely to underrate these effects. Southern Negroes tell quite a different story. From their own experiences in different parts of the South they have told me how the Jim Crow statutes were effective means of tightening and freezing—in many cases of instigating—segregation and discrimination. They have given a picture of how the Negroes were pushed out from voting and officeholding by means of the disfranchisement legislation which swept like a tide over the Southern states during the period from 1875 to 1910. In so far as it concerns the decline in political, civic, and social status of the Negro people in the Southern states, the Restoration of white supremacy in the late "seventies"—according to these informants—was not a final and consummated revolution but *the beginning of a protracted process which lasted until nearly the First World War. During this process the white pressure continuously increased, and the Negroes were continuously pushed backward.* Some older white informants have related much the same story.

Before the Jim Crow legislation there is also said to have been a tendency on the part of white people to treat Negroes somewhat differently depending upon their class and education. This tendency was broken by the laws which applied to *all* Negroes. The legislation thus solidified the caste line and minimized the importance of class differences in the Negro group. This particular effect was probably the more crucial in the formation of the present caste system, since class differentiation within the Negro group continued and, in fact, gained momentum. As we shall find, a tendency is discernible again, in recent decades, to apply the segregation rules with some discretion to Negroes of different class status. If a similar trend was well under way before the Jim Crow laws, those laws must have postponed this particular social process for one or two generations.

While the federal Civil Rights Bill of 1875 was declared unconstitutional, the Reconstruction Amendments to the Constitution—which provided that the Negroes are to enjoy full citizenship in the United States, that they are entitled to "equal benefit of all laws," and that "no state shall make or enforce any law which shall abridge the privileges and immunities of citizens of the United States"—could not be so easily disposed of. The Southern whites, therefore, in passing their various segregation laws to legalize social discrimination, had to manufacture a legal fiction of the same type as we have already met in the preceding discussion on politics and justice. The legal term for this trick in the social field, expressed or implied in most of the Jim Crow statutes, is "separate, but equal." That is, Negroes were to get equal accommodations, but separate from the whites. It is evident, however, and rarely denied, that there is practically no single instance of segregation in the South which has not been utilized for a significant discrimination. The great difference in quality of service for the two groups in the segregated set-ups for transportation and education is merely the most obvious example of how segregation is an excuse for discrimination. Again the Southern white man is in the moral dilemma of having to frame his laws in terms of equality and to defend them before the Supreme Court—and before this own better conscience, which is tied to the American Creed—while knowing all the time that in reality his laws do not give equality to Negroes, and that he does not want them to do so.

The formal adherence to equality in the American Creed, expressed by the Constitution and in the laws, is, however, even in the field of social relations, far from being without practical importance. Spokesmen for the white South, not only recently but in the very period when the segregation policy was first being legitimatized, have strongly upheld the principle that segregation should not be used for discrimination. Henry W. Grady, for instance, scorned the "fanatics and doctrinaires who hold that separation is discrimination," emphasized that "separation is not offensive to either race" and exclaimed:

> ... the whites and blacks must walk in separate paths in the South. As near as may be, these paths should be made equal—but separate they must be now and always. This means separate schools, separate churches, *separate accommodations everywhere—but equal accommodations where the same money is charged, or where the State provides for the citizen.*

Further, the legal adherence to the principle of equality gives the Southern liberal a vantage point in his work to improve the status of the Negroes and race relations. Last, but not least, it gives the Negro people a firm legal basis for their fight against social segregation and discrimination. Since the two are inseparable, the fight against inequality challenges the whole segregation system. The National Association for the Advancement of Colored People has had, from the very beginning, the constitutional provisions for equality as its sword and shield. Potentially the Negro is strong. He has, in his demands upon white Americans, the fundamental law of the land on his side. He has even the better conscience of his white compatriots themselves. He knows it; and the white American knows it, too.... It is commonly reported that white workers, if they become accustomed to working with Negro workers, tend to become less prejudiced, and consequently that the Negro workers become less suspicious and resentful. If, in later stages of the War, necessities in the nature of a national emergency should tend to open up new employment possibilities for Negroes in the war industries, this would probably have permanently beneficial effects on racial attitudes on both sides of the caste gulf. Our general hypothesis is that everything which brings Negro and white workers to experience intimate cooperation and fellowship will, on the balance, break down race prejudice somewhat and raise Negro status. The possibilities for Negroes to rise to the position of skilled workers have, therefore, not only economic significance but also a wider social import as this will tend to weaken the stereotype of the menial Negro.

Notes and Questions

1. De Tocqueville despaired of ever achieving equality of the races, especially in a democracy where "it is not possible for a whole people to rise, as it were, above itself." Do the civil rights movement and the passage of the major federal law prohibiting discrimination in employment—Title VII of the 1964 Civil Rights Act—reflect just such an effort? Do the events of the last ten to fifteen years confirm the insightfulness of de Tocqueville's concerns about the likelihood of elevated conduct by the body politic—at least with respect to sustained action?

2. While the primary victims of the brutal regime of slavery were obviously the enslaved, de Tocqueville believed that slavery also harmed the dominating class, both economically and spiritually. Does the admittedly lesser evil of employment discrimination impose similar if commensurately less acute harms on discriminators? A basic theme of Christianity, and of much modern psychology, is that hatred harms those who harbor such feelings. If this is true, and if government can do something to lessen the racial intolerance, then both victims and discriminators are potential beneficiaries of the government intervention.

3. It is sobering to contemplate how much pain and social strife might have been avoided had the Supreme Court pursued a different course—one that sought aggressively to eliminate race discrimination—beginning in the last quarter of the nineteenth century. Richard Epstein has argued that if the Supreme Court struck down as unconstitutional every *governmental* attempt at discrimination, such as the segregationist restriction imposed by law on railroad passengers that was upheld in *Plessy v. Ferguson,* 163 U.S. 537 (1896), the major social problems that followed from the Jim Crow regime would have been avoided. Epstein, *Forbidden Grounds: The Case against Employment Discrimination Laws* (Cambridge, Mass.: Harvard University Press, 1992). Certainly, eliminating governmental discrimination would have helped blacks tremendously, but does racial equality also require the elimination of *private* employment discrimination against blacks? How would present-day America be different if the Supreme Court in *The Civil Rights Cases,* 109 U.S. 3 (1883), had upheld the Civil Rights Act of 1875, which prohibited private acts of discrimination instead of striking it down? In that decision, the Supreme Court concluded that private refusals to deal with a black person do not "tend to fasten upon him any badge of slavery." Id. at 21. Would de Tocqueville and Myrdal agree with this conclusion?

4. Do you share Myrdal's general belief, which has been a motivating conviction underlying much of antidiscrimination law, that whatever brings

blacks and whites to experience intimate cooperation will diminish race discrimination? For a discussion of the psychological dimension of racial prejudice and the forces that lead to its expression or inhibition, see Chapter 5. Myrdal's discussion of the nature and extent of racial discrimination in the period up to World War II also provides a historical background that will be useful in considering which of the models of discrimination discussed in Chapters 5 through 7 is most persuasive.

5. Myrdal believed that policy measures, such as minimum wage laws, that raised the wages of marginal workers tended to throw blacks out of work. The same complaint has been leveled against laws that compel employers to pay equal wages to white and black workers, which generally elevate the wages of blacks. In Chapter 7, Judge Richard Posner uses the fact that the higher black wages can be achieved only at the cost of decreased black employment as an argument against antidiscrimination laws. Similarly, in Chapter 15, note 10, Edward McCaffery argues that the requirement of equal pay should be eliminated in order to enhance the employment prospects of women.

6. Myrdal was remarkably insightful in appreciating the powerful significance of World War II in highlighting both the lethal consequences of unchecked prejudice and the tension between the principles of equal protection of the laws and the treatment of American blacks. It is no coincidence that the pace of the legal response to the quest for racial justice quickened noticeably during the middle third of the decade of the 1940s. Thus, Southern states and school boards began consciously to equalize the salaries of black and white teachers at this time, and the first state antidiscrimination laws were passed in New York and New Jersey in 1945.

2

Freedom and Antidiscrimination Law: Philosophic Issues

In his classic essay "Two Concepts of Liberty," Isaiah Berlin raises a philosophic question of immense practical significance that has vexed great philosophers and political theorists for centuries: When should government curtail the freedom of some to secure the freedom of others? Berlin, *Four Essays on Liberty* 118 (New York: Oxford University Press, 1969). The answer that various societies have provided to this question, as reflected in the construction of differing political regimes, has often defined the difference between benign and moral governments and harsh and tyrannical ones. The question is of central importance to employment discrimination law because, to use Berlin's terminology, such laws necessarily use governmental coercion to curtail the negative freedom of employers to hire whomever they wish in order to promote the positive freedom of the intended beneficiaries of the law. The heart of an infringement of negative freedom is that "I am prevented by others from doing what I could otherwise do." Id. at 122. One lacks positive freedom, though, to the extent that the ability to attain one's goals and to lead a fulfilling life is impaired by something other than the coercive acts of others.

Liberal theorists such as John Locke and John Stuart Mill have argued that the state is entitled to use only the minimum coercion necessary to discourage behavior that limits the liberty of others. In Isaiah Berlin's terminology, Locke and Mill are most interested in maximizing the negative liberty of the citizenry, and *governmental*

14

interferences in freedom, such as the segregationist laws of the South, would clearly infringe the negative liberty of blacks. Berlin notes that others have argued that government should seek to enhance positive freedom by coercing "men in the name of some goal (let us say, justice or public health) which they would, if they were more enlightened, themselves pursue, but do not, because they are blind or ignorant or corrupt." Id. at 132–33. Using this rationale, one can rather easily fashion an argument for employment discrimination laws that additionally seek to prohibit *private* acts of discrimination. Indeed, some would contend that this rationale too easily justifies extensive government intervention. For further philosophic evaluation of negative and positive liberty, see Jeremy Waldron, "Liberal Rights: Two Sides of the Coin," in *Liberal Rights: Collected Papers, 1981–1991* 1 (New York: Cambridge University Press, 1993).

An earlier formulation of the concerns addressed by Berlin was provided by Immanual Kant, who offered the following paradox of freedom: the complete freedom of anarchy makes the weak unfree, but laws designed to protect the weak undermine freedom as well. In this view, the task confronting the United States in 1964 in defining the contours of employment discrimination law was to strike the correct balance of advancing the freedom of the weak by restraining the freedom of the powerful. Alternatively, one can formulate the rationale for the current law of employment discrimination as sacrificing the negative liberty of discriminators in order to advance the goal of equality. In the context of the debate over whether hate speech can permissibly be suppressed, Ronald Dworkin has argued that when liberty and equality really conflict "we should have to choose liberty because the alternative would be the despotism of the thought-police." According to Dworkin,

> Exactly because the moral environment in which we all live is in good part created by others . . . the question of who shall have the power to help shape that environment, and how, is of fundamental importance, though it is often neglected in political theory. Only one answer is consistent with the ideals of political equality: that no one may be prevented from influencing the shared moral environment, through his own private choices, tastes, opinions, and example, just because these tastes or opinions disgust those who have the power to shut him up or lock him up. Of course, the ways in which anyone may exercise that influence must be limited in order to protect the security and interests of others. People may not try to mold the moral climate by intimidating women with sexual demands or by burning a cross on a black family's lawn, or by refusing to hire women or blacks at all, or by making their working conditions so humiliating as to be intolerable.

> But we cannot count, among the kinds of interests that may be protected in this way, a right not to be insulted or damaged just by the fact that others have hostile or uncongenial tastes, or that they are free to express or indulge them in private. Recognizing that right would mean denying that some people—those whose tastes these are—have any right to participate in forming the moral environment at all.

Ronald Dworkin, "Women and Pornography," *The New York Review of Books,* 36, 41 (October 21, 1993).

Note that Dworkin specifically endorses employment discrimination laws, but given his belief in the preeminence of liberty over equality, the rationale for such an endorsement is unclear. Is Dworkin correct that the concern for equality should not enable government to prohibit private choices that indulge uncongenial tastes? Is the decision by a private employer not to hire a woman or a black something different from the expression of a private uncongenial taste?

Defining the scope and content of employment discrimination laws involves the task of trading off many highly prized philosophic and social values: negative freedom versus positive freedom, liberty versus equality, libertarian versus communitarian principles. Paul Brest provides a comprehensive and nuanced discussion in defense of the principle of antidiscrimination. He notes that this principle has the important function of limiting race-dependent decisions that purport to be rational and legitimate but which in fact rest upon assumptions of the differential worth of racial groups. Moreover, Brest argues that even when an employer refuses to hire black workers only for efficiency reasons, the great cumulative harm caused by the use of race as a proxy for productivity supports the adoption of the antidiscrimination principle. Indeed, Brest endorses a more relaxed standard of review in assessing benignly motivated race-dependent decisions that favor racial minorities precisely because they neither rest on a premise of differential worth of racial groups nor impose severe cumulative harm on the dominant racial group.

Richard Epstein is far less troubled by the concerns that Brest raises about the social harms derived from private race-dependent decisions. Epstein stresses that voluntary sorting in the workplace, in accommodations, and in social settings often takes place on racial, ethnic, religious, or sexual lines, and he contends that there are important advantages to allowing such sorting. Contrary to Brest, Epstein believes that, even when preferences for voluntary segregation are based on rabid hatred for other racial groups, such sorting can raise the "level of satisfaction for all workers in the workplace." Consequently, Epstein would jettison the antidiscrimination principle, except for governmental employers who, he believes, should be rigidly bound by a principle of color-blind decision making.

In Defense of the Antidiscrimination Principle*
PAUL BREST

By the "antidiscrimination principle" I mean the general principle disfavoring classifications and other decisions and practices that depend

* Excerpts from Paul Brest, "In Defense of the Antidiscrimination Principle," *Harvard Law Review,* The Supreme Court/1975 Term, vol. 90, copyright © 1976. Reprinted by permission of the author and publisher.

on the race (or ethnic origin) of the parties affected.... [This] principle rests on fundamental moral values that are widely shared in our society. Although the text and legislative history of laws that incorporate this principle can inform our understanding of it, the principle itself is at least as likely to inform our interpretations of the laws. This is especially true with respect to the equal protection clause of the fourteenth amendment. The text and history of the clause are vague and ambiguous and cannot, in any event, infuse the antidiscrimination principle with moral force or justify its extension to novel circumstances and new beneficiaries....

Stated most simply, the antidiscrimination principle disfavors race-dependent decisions and conduct—at least when they selectively disadvantage the members of a minority group. By race-dependent, I mean decisions and conduct (hereafter, simply decisions) that would have been different but for the race of those benefited or disadvantaged by them. Race-dependent decisions may take several forms, including overt racial classifications on the face of statutes and covert decisions by officials.

Rationales for the Antidiscrimination Principle

The antidiscrimination principle guards against certain defects in the *process* by which race-dependent decisions are made and also against certain harmful *results* of race-dependent decisions. Restricting the principle to a unitary purpose vitiates its moral force and requires the use of sophisticated reasoning to explain applications that seem self-evident.

Defects of Process

The antidiscrimination principle is designed to prevent both irrational and unfair infliction of injury.

Race-dependent decisions are irrational insofar as they reflect the assumption that members of one race are less worthy than other people. Not all such decisions are necessarily irrational, however. For example, if black laborers tend to be absent from work more often than their white counterparts—for whatever reason—it is not irrational for an employer to prefer white applicants for the job. If Americans of Japanese ancestry were more prone to disloyalty than Caucasians during World War II, it was not irrational for the United States government to take special precautions against sabotage and espionage by them. Regulations and decisions based on statistical generalizations are commonplace in all developed societies and essential to their functioning. And it is often rational for decisionmakers to rely on weak and even dubious generalizations. Consider, for example, a fire department's or airline's policy against employing overweight personnel, based on the rather slight probability that they will suffer a heart attack while on duty.

In short, the mere fact that most blacks are industrious and most Japanese-Americans loyal does not make the employer's or the Government's decision irrational. Indeed, if all race-dependent decisions were irrational, there would be no need for an antidiscrimination principle, for it would suffice to apply the widely held moral, constitutional, and practical principle that forbids treating persons irrationally. The antidiscrimination principle fills a special need because—as even a glance at history indicates—race-dependent decisions that are rational and purport to be based solely on legitimate considerations are likely in fact to rest on assumptions of the differential worth of racial groups or on the related phenomenon of racially selective sympathy and indifference.

Mr. Justice Black focused on the first of these dangers in *Korematsu v. United States,* the case in which the Government sought to justify its policy of interning Japanese-Americans, and in which the Court first enunciated the modern "suspect classification" doctrine. He wrote for the majority:

> [A]ll legal restrictions which curtail the civil rights of a single racial group are immediately suspect .... [C]ourts must subject them to the most rigid scrutiny. Pressing public necessity may sometimes justify the existence of such restrictions; racial antagonism never can.

Mr. Justice Black chose the word "suspect" advisedly. For, although a court often cannot ascertain the true motives underlying a decision, our history and traditions provide strong reasons to suspect that racial classifications ultimately rest on assumptions of the differential worth of racial groups. These racial value judgments appear in forms besides "racial antagonism"—for example in paternalistic assumptions of racial inferiority.

By the phenomenon of racially selective sympathy and indifference I mean the unconscious failure to extend to a minority the same recognition of humanity, and hence the same sympathy and care, given as a matter of course to one's own group.

Although racially selective sympathy and indifference (hereafter, just indifference) is an inevitable consequence of attributing intrinsic value to membership in a racial group, it may also result from a desire to enhance our own power and esteem by enhancing the power and esteem of members of groups to which we belong. And it may also result—often unconsciously—from our tendency to sympathize most readily with those who seem most like ourselves. Whatever its cause, decisions that reflect this phenomenon, like those reflecting overt racial hostility, are unfair; for by hypothesis, they are decisions disadvantaging minority persons that would not be made under the identical circumstances if they disadvantaged members of the dominant group. The unequal treatment could be justified only if one group were in fact more worthy than the other. This justification failing, such treatment violates the cardinal rule of fairness—the Golden Rule.

Harmful Results

A second and independent rationale for the antidiscrimination principle is the prevention of the harms which may result from race-dependent decisions. Often, the most obvious harm is the denial of the opportunity to secure a desired benefit—a job, a night's lodging at a motel, a vote. But this does not completely describe the consequences of a race-dependent decisionmaking. Decisions based on assumptions of intrinsic worth and selective indifference inflict psychological injury by stigmatizing their victims as inferior. Moreover, because acts of discrimination tend to occur in pervasive patterns, their victims suffer especially frustrating, cumulative and debilitating injuries.

The prevention of stigmatic harm played a major role in *Strauder v. West Virginia,* the first race discrimination case to reach the Supreme Court after the Civil War. On alternative grounds, the Court struck down a state law excluding blacks from juries. Although the first ground was the black defendant's right to a jury composed of a cross-section of the community, the second involved the rights of the members of the black community themselves. Mr. Justice Strong reasoned that the fourteenth amendment protects Negroes "from legal discriminations, implying their inferiority in civil society," and held that the West Virginia statute was "practically a brand upon them .... an assertion of their inferiority." Dissenting in *Plessy v. Ferguson,* Mr. Justice Harlan likewise observed that the segregation of railway passengers was a "badge of servitude" because it proceeded "on the ground that colored citizens are ... inferior and degraded."

Similarly, the essence of *Brown v. Board of Education* lay in Chief Justice Warren's observation that the segregation of black public school pupils "generates a feeling of inferiority as to their status in the community that may affect their hearts and minds in a way unlikely ever to be undone." As Charles L. Black noted, the Court could not properly have ignored "a plain fact about the society of the United States—the fact that the social meaning of segregation is the putting of the Negro in a position of walled-off inferiority—or the other equally plain fact that such treatment is hurtful to human beings."

Recognition of the stigmatic injury inflicted by discrimination explains applications of the antidiscrimination principle where the material harm seems slight or problematic. For example, it fully explains the harmfulness of de jure school segregation without the need to invoke controversial social science evidence concerning the effects of segregation on achievement, interracial attitudes, and the like, and thus explains the Supreme Court's casual extension of *Brown* to prohibit the segregation of public beaches, parks, golf courses and buses. It also explains how present practices that are racially neutral may nonetheless perpetuate the harms of past de jure segregation.

Racial generalizations usually inflict psychic injury whether or not they are in fact premised on assumptions of differential moral worth. Although all of us recognize that institutional decisions must depend on generalizations based on objective characteristics of persons and things rather than on individualized judgments, we nonetheless tend to feel unfairly treated when disadvantaged by a generalization that is not true as applied to us. Generalizations based on immutable personal traits such as race or sex are especially frustrating because we can do nothing to escape their operation. These generalizations are still more pernicious, for they are often premised on the supposed correlation between the inherited characteristic and the undesirable voluntary behavior of those who possess the characteristic—for example, blacks are less industrious, trustworthy or clean than whites. Because the behavior is voluntary, and hence the proper object of moral condemnation, individuals as to whom the generalization is inaccurate may justifiably feel that the decision-maker has passed moral judgment on them.

The psychological injury inflicted by generalizations based on race is compounded by the frustrating and cumulative nature of their material injuries. Racial generalizations are pervasive and have traditionally operated in the same direction—to the disadvantage of members of the minority group. A person who is denied one opportunity because he or she is short or overweight will find other opportunities, for in our society height and weight do not often serve as the bases for generalizations determining who will receive benefits. By contrast, at least until very recently, a black was not denied *an* opportunity because of his or her race, but denied virtually *all* desirable opportunities. As door after door is shut in one's face, the individual acts of discrimination combine into a systematic and grossly inequitable frustration of opportunity.

The cumulative disadvantage caused by the use of race as a proxy even for legitimate characteristics provides an independent ground for disfavoring nonbenign race-dependent decisions regardless of the integrity of the process by which they were made. To the unprejudiced employer who would prefer white applicants to blacks solely for reasons of efficiency, the antidiscrimination principle says in effect: "If you were the only one to do this, we would permit you to make efficient generalizations based on race. But so many other firms might employ similar generalizations that black individuals would suffer great cumulative harms. And, in the absence of an overriding justification, this cannot be permitted."

I have argued that the prevention of stigmatic and cumulative harms, as well as concerns for process, support the antidiscrimination principle. Individuals may, however, be stigmatized by *non*-race-dependent practices that *appear* to be discriminatory, and may also suffer cumulative disabilities from various non-race-dependent practices. Whereas the process rationales for the antidiscrimination principle apply only to race-dependent decisions, the result-oriented rationales seem to disfavor all practices that produce these harms and thus to support a doctrine broader than the antidiscrimination principle.

Nonetheless, these practices cannot automatically be presumed invalid. Race correlates so weakly with the legitimate characteristics for which it might be used as a proxy that, even if race-dependent decisions are sometimes rational, society loses little if they are presumptively forbidden. By contrast, a presumption prohibiting all decisions that stigmatize or cumulatively disadvantage particular individuals would affect an enormously wide range of practices important to the efficient operation of a complex industrial society. (Furthermore, a general doctrine disfavoring harmful results could not be administered by the judiciary.) Therefore, the law has tended to reflect the result-oriented concerns of the antidiscrimination principle, not by operating directly to scrutinize results, but by disfavoring particular classifying traits that tend to be especially harmful and have little social utility. This approach, as well as suspected defects of process, underlies the expansion of the antidiscrimination principle beyond race to encompass decisions based on ethnic and national origin, alienage, illegitimacy and sex. It also explains the occasional use of the cognate notion of "conclusive presumptions" to disfavor other classificatory traits.

. . .

Benign Decisions

The suspect classification standard was developed in response to traditional practices of racial discrimination when race-dependent decisions were seldom designed to benefit the members of disadvantaged minorities. The past decade has seen a significant increase in benignly motivated race-dependent practices, and their reconciliation with the antidiscrimination principle has become a matter of controversy.

Does the antidiscrimination principle disfavor race-dependent means for achieving ends such as preventing discrimination, remedying past discrimination, improving race relations, and ameliorating the status of traditionally disadvantaged minorities? To make the discussion more concrete, consider the effects of the following policies, adopted by white decisionmakers, upon whites and blacks. A school board remedies de facto segregation by assigning and busing pupils so that the racial proportion in each school approximately reflects the racial composition of the district. A firm preferentially employs black applicants in order to compensate for past discrimination against blacks. A legislature gerrymanders the lines of a political district to assure that blacks can elect a representative. A housing authority locates a low income project in a white neighborhood and sets both a minimum and maximum quota for black families, the maximum being short of a supposed "tipping point" at which whites will flee. A university or professional school preferentially admits black applicants to increase the diversity of the school and increase the number of blacks in high status occupations and professions.

From the point of view of the white individuals affected, it is highly improbable that decisions such as these are premised on assumptions that blacks are superior to whites or on the selective indifference of white decisionmakers to the humanity or aspirations of whites compared to blacks. With respect to results, each of these decisions may effectively deprive white individuals of a desired benefit—attendance at a neighborhood school, a place in a university, a job, a strong voice in the electoral process, an apartment. Yet in none of these cases is stigmatic injury likely to accompany the deprivation. Moreover, only preferential admissions and employment policies present any likelihood of cumulative disadvantage to whites based on race or of the frustration of being denied benefits because of an unchangeable trait. But, though reasonable people may differ, I doubt that "reverse discrimination" is likely to become so pervasive at any occupational level in our white-dominated society as to cause cumulative harms or frustrations approaching the magnitude of those inflicted by the malign discrimination to which the antidiscrimination principle fully responds.

. . .

Can apparently benign practices actually injure their supposed beneficiaries in ways cognizable by the antidiscrimination principle? It is conceivable, but not likely, that school desegregation and preferential employment and admissions policies might reflect assumptions that minorities are innately inferior and therefore in need of special aid. It is somewhat more likely that school desegregation may inflict stigmatic harm and reinforce feelings of differential worth in children of both races; that preferential admissions programs may foster the white community's belief that all minority students are preferentially admitted and, perhaps, graduated; and that preferential employment programs may induce or encourage white racial animus.

If, as I have argued, the antidiscrimination principle is concerned with harmful effects as well as invidious motives, these dangers cannot be ignored. Nonetheless, where the objective and immediate effect are to benefit minority persons, it seems inappropriate to subject the practice to the demanding criteria of the suspect classification standard. It should suffice for a policymaker to conclude that the probable benefits outweigh the harms, that the benefits cannot readily be gained by other than race-dependent means, and that the program is designed to minimize its possible adverse consequences.

Rational Discrimination in Competitive Markets*
RICHARD A. EPSTEIN

... [D]iscrimination in some contexts is a rational response to the frictions that necessarily arise out of long-term employment contracts.

The traditional conclusion, often repeated in the economic literature starting with Becker, that competitive markets will drive out all forms of discrimination, should hold in a world in which transaction costs do not matter. But once the analysis turns to the world of positive transaction costs, identified with Ronald Coase, that conclusion is no longer valid. It is now possible that some forms of discrimination could improve the ability of certain firms to compete. If so, then we should not expect to see all forms of discrimination driven out in unregulated markets. The arguments here are perfectly general, for they apply to employment contracts across the wide array of institutional settings. They indicate why *all* groups have some rational incentives to discriminate on the very grounds—race, creed, sex, age, religion—that Title VII prohibits. And if these cases of rational discrimination are the ones likely to persist, then the hidden costs of Title VII are higher than is ordinarily supposed. In order to organize the inquiry, I examine issues associated with governance and enforcement costs....

Collective Choice Within Groups

One question that every collective organization must face is how to make decisions that advance the overall welfare of the group without precipitating the defection of its key members. In the attempt to answer this question, most analytical work has been devoted to finding the kind of decision rule that best captures the sentiment of the various members of the collectivity. Does one use majority voting, or supermajority voting? Who sets the agenda? Should issues be considered separately or in bundles? Should compensation, in cash or kind, be provided to losers to keep them happy?

A second side to the inquiry, generally neglected, merits equal attention. How deep is the division of sentiment within the membership of the group in the first place? Here the answer depends critically on *who* is in the group, and on the distribution of tastes and preferences among the members. The group that can minimize differences in tastes will sometimes be ahead of the game, relative to one that has to rely on sophisticated decision rules to resolve deep-seated divisions of opinion. To see why, assume for the moment that all workers have identical preferences on all matters relevant to the employment relation. If the question is whether or not they wish to have music piped into a common

*Excerpts from Richard A. Epstein, *The Case Against Employment Discrimination Law*, copyright © 1992 by the President and Fellows of Harvard College. Reprinted by permission of the publishers.

work area, they all want music. If the question is what kind of music they wish to hear, the answer is classical—indeed, mostly Mozart. If the question is how loud, the agreement is perfect down to the exact decibel. In this employment utopia, decisions of collective governance are easy to make. The employer who satisfies preferences of any single worker knows that he or she has satisfied the preferences of the entire work force. It takes little effort and little money to achieve the highest level of group satisfaction. The nonwage terms of collective importance can be set in ways that unambiguously promote firm harmony.

The situation is quite different once it is assumed that there is no employee homogeneity in taste within the workplace. At this point the critical questions are two: First, what is the variation in preferences among the members of the firm? And second, how does individual dissatisfaction increase with increases in the distance between individual personal preferences and the collective outcome? The general proposition is clear: as the tastes within the group start to diverge, it becomes harder to reach a decision that works for the common good. If half the workers crave classical music, but loathe rock, and half like rock but disdain classical music, it is very difficult to decide whether music shall be placed in the workplace at all, and if so what kind.... The re-sorting that takes place as individual workers make voluntary decisions to quit thus has a social function: it reduces the pressure of decision rules by increasing the homogeneity within the group.

In the simplest model, then, the greater the variance in preferences, the greater the costs to the firm. Where the decisions on collective issues have yet to be made, there will be a tendency for the interested parties at each extreme to lobby for decisions in their favor, given the importance that they attach to the ultimate decision. If there is an all-or-nothing decision, then one group must lose while the other one wins, save in the unlikely event that people's preferences are transformed (from rock to classical or the reverse) after they hear arguments addressed to the merits of the opposing choice. The firm has to bear the cost of the internal conflict as well as the dissatisfaction that remains after the decision has been made ....

If voting procedures and internal rules are inadequate to control these problems, other methods may be explored. One way to cut these costs is to find means of reducing the level of variance in tastes among group members.... The partition of the market into specialized and well-defined niches should increase the satisfaction of all consumers. *Any* antidiscrimination law cuts against that commendable objective.

A sobering lesson follows. Any social policy that requires that membership in a private association should be randomly drawn from a subset of the larger whole is an invitation to trouble. Even the ideal set of contractual terms can go only so far toward buffering the problems and tensions of long-term legal relationships. In many senses the single most important contractual decision is a business decision: the selection of contractual partners. Choosing the right partners reduces the stresses on any set of legal relationships. Choosing the wrong partners exacerbates them. Governance costs are a function of the level of variation within the firm.... For any given type of relationship, the level of investment in legal governance must increase as the power of selection of contracting partners diminishes: that is why political bodies must limp along with elaborate and extensive safeguards. Private parties have strong incentives to minimize the sum of their selection and governance costs, and hence to decide when the costs of exclusion are lower than the costs of more extensive governance. In contrast, state regulation only reinforces the false impression that any governance structure is equally effective regardless of the composition of the group or the identities of parties to the contract....

Thus far it has been shown only that voluntary sorting can reduce the costs of making and enforcing group decisions. It remains to be noted that this sorting often takes place on racial, ethnic, religious, or sexual lines. The missing premise is that persons who are "the same" in some fundamental way are more likely to bring similar preferences to the workplace. In some cases the explanations are relatively benign. Workers may prefer to sort themselves out by language. It is easier and cheaper for everyone if Spanish-speaking workers work with Spanish-speaking workers and Polish-speaking workers with Polish-speaking workers, all other things held constant. Indeed, it seems quite possible that there are variations within the English language that make communication easier between blacks and other blacks than between blacks and whites. These language differences tend to lead to a prediction of voluntary segregation within the workplace, the intensity of which varies as a function of the level of separation between the languages....

In certain cases it may be that the preferences for voluntary segregation are based on ill will or other uglier sentiments. Nonetheless, the advantages of voluntary sorting cannot be ignored here either. If all persons who have a rabid hatred for members of different racial, ethnic, or other groups are concentrated within a small number of firms, then it makes governance questions easier for the remaining firms, as they do not have to contend constantly with dissidents and troublemakers. It follows, therefore, that voluntary sorting should (other skills being held constant) raise the level of satisfaction for all workers in the workplace....

There are, however, two sides to this question. Still to be considered are the benefits of diversity.... If all employees are exactly alike, then the firm may find it more difficult to establish bonds with some classes of potential customers. Diversity in a sales force may provide a benefit that offsets the costs of internal divisions on collective tastes. But the opposite conclusion may hold if the firm caters to a single class of customers. The problem for the firm is to find a way to maximize its profits, taking into account its total costs, including organizational costs. In some cases the gains from diversity will be rejected as too costly. But in others, firms will choose to maintain some degree of diversity and some degree of homogeneity, and expend resources (on retreats, picnics, intramural athletics, personnel departments) to foster a spirit of cooperation. In this type of environment, moreover, workers who are content to go along with most decisions offer a valuable asset their more eccentric colleagues lack: at the very least, they do not make waves, and they may help foster a communal spirit within the firm. As organizations grow and seek to serve broad national or international markets, it is highly doubtful that the firm itself could employ only members of one race, sex, or ethnic background. But it is quite possible even for large firms to maintain segregated divisions of workers in its various subdepartments or plants.

Informal Enforcement of Promises

. . . [B]usiness cannot be conducted if promises are kept only under the threat of lawsuits. Instead, business depends heavily on an informal set of sanctions that one market participant can bring to bear on the other. In this context, the concerns are often lumped together under the banner of reputation, that is, the ability to persuade other members of a trading community not to do business with any individual who has flouted its norms.

Generally speaking, the success of any system of informal enforcement is heavily dependent on the range of sanctions, legal and social, that can be brought to bear against wayward parties. Thus, one common complaint of tourists is that they have been cheated by local businessmen, who take advantage, for example, of their ignorance of exchange rates, general market prices, and local language and customs. Where there are repeated dealings between individuals on a variety of transactions, these abuses are far less likely to occur. Similarly, informal enforcement becomes more effective when members of a firm are all drawn from the same ethnic or racial group. The party who cheats at work now knows that he faces stricter sanctions, given the strong likelihood that the information will be brought home to him at play, at church, or in other business and social settings. The complex network of human interactions thus induces persons to honor their deals. . . .

Expanding Employment Opportunities

. . . Within voluntary markets we should expect to see, even in the long run, a wide divergence in the level of voluntary discrimination, but *not*, as it has sometimes been supposed, the total elimination of discrimination by competitive forces. Some firms will practice it widely; others will find it of little value.

These natural differences in firm profile count as a strong argument against the view, so common in modern legal and political thinking, that any deviation between the composition of the firm and the larger work force should be met with hostility and suspicion. In fact, quite the opposite is true. A perfect correspondence between the firm and the market demonstrates that the gains from trade available through specialization have not been realized; the identical structure and composition of all firms is a clear sign of underdeveloped markets, and of the dangerous effects of regulation. As long as a large number of firms operate within any market, persons can sort themselves out in the environment that they like best, free of external constraint. If thousands of prospective employers are offering different associational mixes, then the probability that any employee will find the ideal work setting is far greater than if all firms have to conform to some rigid state-established classification, which is driven not by consideration of the business pressures on the firm but by some independent ethical idea which the state, by majority rule or administrative order, is prepared to impose on those who refuse to accept it.

To put things another way, it is often said that any legal policy that allows all persons the right to select their contracting partners offends the principle of equal opportunity: every qualified person should be allowed to compete for every job. Therefore, as long as voluntary discrimination exists, there are necessarily some jobs for which qualified individuals cannot apply. At first blush this point has its undoubted emotional force, in large part because it is parasitic on a far more powerful sense of equality of opportunity, namely that all persons should be allowed to *offer* their services to whomever they see fit, free of state prohibition. Nonetheless, despite these apparent similarities the broader conception of equal opportunity—that all firms have a duty to consider every applicant—violates that principle because it denies to firms, and to the individuals who own and manage them, the very rights of autonomy and self-control that it confers on other individuals (or the same individuals in other capacities). The ostensible effort to legitimate the antidiscrimination law by the appeal to equal opportunity (as in the name of the EEOC—Equal Employment Opportunity Commission) is fundamentally unsound because it ignores the critical role freedom plays on both sides of the market. The costs of the error are not inconsiderable.

First, it is a mistake to assume that the number of opportunities available to workers is constant regardless of the external legal rules that govern the operation of the firm. The antidiscrimination provision places powerful limitations on firm structure, and should, like any tax, be expected to *reduce* the number of firms that enter the marketplace, and hence the number of employment opportunities. Some firms at the margin will not survive in an environment in which their costs are increased by regulation. At the very least, the ideal of equal access for all workers to all firms necessarily reduces the number of opportunities available in the aggregate, to the detriment of all potential employers ... who are closest to the margin. The antidiscrimination law may appear to place a limitation on firms for the benefit of workers, but in reality its effect is quite the opposite. The legal liabilities may fall on the firm, but the impact of the regulation (given compliance) falls on both firms and workers alike. Any restriction on the class of offers that a firm may make necessarily narrows the class of offers that workers are able to accept. The more gains from trade are shared by firms and workers, and the more effective the antidiscrimination norm, the greater the limitation on worker freedom. . . .

Second, the antidiscrimination policy, as I have noted, makes the problem of internal governance more difficult than would otherwise be the case. If workers who have strong preferences against any particular group are allowed to break off and form their own firms, it improves the value of the opportunities that other individuals enjoy in the firms that remain. If all the bigots and troublemakers are isolated in a small number of firms, other workers have a more attractive array of firms to choose from than they would if bigoted workers were distributed randomly across all firms. Thus, although the *number* of opportunities may go down, the *value* of the opportunities that do remain should increase.

Third, the argument for equal access presupposes some powerful notion of "legitimate" preferences that allows us to rule out of bounds the preferences of workers who do not have accepted or correct views on workplace arrangements. At a practical level that view is dangerous because it requires us to overlook the problems of governance that arise when persons with radically different tastes are forced into the same business against their will. Theoretically, moreover, there is no obvious reason why the preferences of any individuals should be excluded in determining the desirability of public regulation. Certainly there is no standard measure of *social* welfare that says the preferences of some persons are to be counted while the preferences of others are to be systematically ignored. . . .

Conclusion

. . . It is dangerous to assume that whatever conduct is thought to be wise or enlightened can and should be forced on society by the public speaking with one voice. There is little understanding of why the proscribed differences might matter, and little appreciation of the enormous political risks that come with concentrating power over employment decisions in the hands of a bureaucracy that operates under its own set of expansionist imperatives. There is also a failure to understand that the first question that should be asked in any public debate is *who* shall decide, not *what* should be decided. On the question of association, the right answer is the private persons who may (or may not) wish to associate, and not the government or the public at large. But having given the wrong collective answer to the "who" question, we find the "what" question receiving an extended elaboration that has resulted in the extensive and disruptive coercive structure that is civil rights enforcement today. More than I had anticipated, my study of the employment discrimination laws has persuaded me of the bedrock social importance of the principles of individual autonomy and freedom of association. Their negation through the modern civil rights law has led to a dangerous form of government coercion that in the end threatens to do more than strangle the operation of labor and employment markets. The modern civil rights laws are a new form of imperialism that threatens the political liberty and intellectual freedom of us all.

Notes and Questions

1.   Philosophic discussions on public policy issues often devolve into unhelpful attempts to assert that the position being advocated is based on a set of values universally deemed to be transcendent and absolute, inhering in the very essence of what it is to be human, and therefore ineluctable. The two conflicting sides both insist that their position rests on furthering values that are deeply embedded in culture or politics and which thus transcend mere personal preferences. For example, the libertarian asserts that the relevant transcendent value is the right freely to choose whom to hire and with whom to associate. The interventionist asserts that discrimination on the basis of race, sex, religion, color, and so on, violates the very essence of human dignity, and therefore it must be prohibited. For a good illustration of how short a distance one travels in this area when being driven by—even excellent—philosophic discussion, see Larry Alexander, "What Makes Wrongful Discrimination Wrong? Biases, Preferences, Stereotypes, and Proxies," 141 *University of Pennsylvania Law Review* 149 (1992).

2.   John Stuart Mill saw the resort to utilitarianism as the most viable alternative to this intractable battle of opposing assertion. But even if the shift to utilitarianism holds a greater promise of guiding public policy, the unyielding contention reemerges over what utilities should be counted in the utilitarian calculus. Do we include the utility the discriminator derives from his or her action, and do we include the utility that nonvictims of discrimination get from the elimination of discrimination? Much political ideology has been packed into the resolution of these questions.

3.   One possible answer is that both should be considered. Richard Epstein seems to advance this position in his provocative book *Forbidden Grounds: The Case Against Employment Discrimination Laws* (Cambridge, Mass.: Harvard University Press, 1992). He states that in trying to determine whether a given action will "lead to an increase or a decrease in overall levels of social satisfaction, subjectively measured for all persons," one should consider utilities rather than asking "whose preferences are legitimate and whose are not" Id. at 43. When the time comes to conduct the social calculus, however, Epstein jettisons the utility of the moralists (those who have not been direct victims of discrimination but are nonetheless offended by it): society should "exclude *all* instances of mere offense born of moral outrage or bruised sensibilities from the class of actionable harms, however deeply felt the hurt" Id. at 415.

While giving weight to the utility of discriminators but not to that of moralists might seem distorted, this position has many prominent proponents, such as Richard Posner and Ronald Dworkin. Dworkin, "Liberalism," in S. Hampshire, ed., *Public and Private Morality* (New York: Cambridge University Press, 1978). Moreover, the economist Paul Milgrom concludes that while altruistic values "have a role in the political part of public-policy considerations, [they] are not ... properly included in benefit-cost analyses, because including them obscures those analyses and prevents them from fulfilling their proper economic function" of identifying potential Pareto improvements. Paul Milgrom, "Is Sympathy an Economic Value? Philosophy, Economics, and the Contingent Valuation Method," in Jerry Hausman, ed., *Contingent Valuation: A Critical Assessment* 417, 422 (Amsterdam; New York: North-Holland, 1993). For a critique of this position, see Steven Shiffrin, "Liberalism, Radicalism, and Legal Scholarship," 30 *UCLA Law Review* 1103 (1983).

4. John Stuart Mill adopted a somewhat more refined view on this question. For Mill, an important dividing line in addressing the issue of what utilities should count is that between self-regarding behavior and otherregarding behavior, the latter being conduct that is aimed at and harms others. Thus, if I play my piano because of the joy I receive from hearing the music, my behavior is self-regarding, and my utility should count. If I play the piano because of the joy I receive from knowing that you dislike hearing me play, then my behavior is otherregarding, and my utility should not count. Although Mill's distinction is interesting, he has been criticized as an inconsistent utilitarian because he discounts the effects of selfregarding conduct on the utility of others. C. L. Ten, *Mill on Liberty* 10 (New York: Oxford University Press, 1980). Nonetheless, Mill's refinement might undermine Epstein's decision to count the utility of the discriminator. Certainly, the intense racial discrimination in the American South that led to the passage of Title VII might well be deemed to be otherregarding behavior, which under Mill's approach would disqualify the discriminator's utility from the social calculus. This would be the case if the rationale for the discrimination was primarily to obtain satisfaction by harming and subjugating blacks, which is the view of racial discrimination advanced by Richard McAdams in Chapter 5.

5. Mill also interjected an additional domain of uncertainty into the realm of his brand of utilitarianism when he argued that "I regard utility to be the ultimate appeal on all ethical questions, but it must be utility in the largest sense, grounded on the permanent interests of man as a progressive being." Mill, *On Liberty* 6 (New York: Longmans, Green & Co., 1913). This statement offers another rationale for ignoring the utility of the discriminator, since one could argue that this utility is not grounded in such exalted interests.

6. According to John Rawls, the first commandment of political liberalism is that individuals should not try to impose their private moral ideas on the basic institutions of society. Rawls, *Political Liberalism* (New York: Columbia University Press, 1993). If one conceives of Title VII as part of a larger federal governmental effort to prevent Southern whites from building

their segregationist beliefs into the basic institutions of the American South, then the law would appear to be advancing liberal values. On the other hand, the opponents of Title VII argue that antidiscrimination law is profoundly illiberal because it seeks to build the moral values of its proponents into the basic institutions of American life. These opponents of antidiscrimination law believe that even if Title VII is justified on some costbenefit calculusweighing either utilities or wealthit is still morally unjustified because liberalism trumps utilitarianism or wealthmaximization. Amartya Sen discusses the ultimate conflict between liberalism and utilitarianism, but he decidedly does *not* indicate which morally appealing principle should dominate in such clashes. Sen, "The Impossibility of a Paretian Liberal," 78 *Journal of Political Economy* 152 (1970).

7. An alternative view of liberalism might suggest that Title VII is a liberal intervention because it is the product of procedurally fair deliberation and enactment. Stuart Hampshire gives the example of the conflict over abortion where one side is convinced that it is immoral to prevent a woman from terminating a pregnancy in the first trimester, and the other side is convinced that morality demands just such an infringement of her liberty. He notes that in such a case,

> On the substantial nonprocedural issue of justice, there is outright conflict. In a just and perfectly liberal society the basic institutions will ensure that both sides have the opportunity to argue their case on equal terms, and this will mean to argue in Congress or parliament and in the Supreme Court if there is one. In a just society neither side can impose its moral convictions on the society by forceful domination and without following the recognized procedures of equal debate and of consistent and rulegoverned adjudication which are already established in that society.

Hampshire, "Liberalism: The New Twist," *The New York Review of Books* 43, 46 (August 12, 1993).

Since Title VII was enacted and has been amended in a procedurally fair manner, does this guarantee that it is just and liberal? During his famous debates with Abraham Lincoln, Stephen A. Douglas argued that, given the profoundly divergent moral positions on slavery, the people acting through their elected representatives in the individual states should be allowed to debate and determine the legality of slavery through the customary legislative procedures. Was Douglas's position just and liberal?

8. Note that the Supreme Court has recently rejected Paul Brest's suggestion that benign race-dependent practices, such as affirmative action, should not be subject to the extraordinary demands of the suspect classification standard under the Equal Protection Clause. Previously, the Court had held that Congress, acting under the broad remedial powers authorized by the Fourteenth Amendment, would be given considerable leeway in crafting affirmative action measures—*Fullilove v. Klutznick*, 448 U.S. 448 (1980) and *Metro Broadcasting, Inc. v. FCC*, 497 U.S. 547 (1990)—even though the race-based practices of other governmental entities would be strictly scrutinized. *City of Richmond v. J. A. Croson Co.*, 488 U.S. 469 (1989). In *Adarand*

Constructors, Inc. v. Pena, 515 U.S. 200 (1995), the Supreme Court announced that *all* racial classifications will be subject to strict scrutiny, whether imposed by federal, state, or local governmental authorities. For further discussion of the issues relating to affirmative action, see section 3.2 in Chapter 3.

9. Although Epstein offers an enthusiastic tribute to homogeneous workplaces, others have argued that the currently unequal distribution of power within society ensures that the Epsteinian world that exalts individual autonomy and freedom of association will turn out to be a world of dominance and subordination. Mari Matsuda has argued that, in defining what is preferable or "the norm," the dominant group destructively reinforces hierarchies among human beings. Matsuda, "Voices in America: Accent, Antidiscrimination Law, and a Jurisprudence for the Last Reconstruction," 100 *Yale Law Journal* 1329 (1991). She would interpret Title VII's antidiscrimination command as embodying an antisubordination principle, which would require toleration of linguistic diversity. Given the near-immutability of one's natural accent, Matsuda argues that "The promotion of individual personhood, the goal of human flourishing, and the procedural caution of noninterference with relatively harmless life choices suggest linguistic tolerance. The way in which we speak reflects self, personhood, identity. To tell people they cannot express themselves in the way that comes naturally to them is to tell them they cannot speak." Id. at 1388. Matsuda hopes to promote a "radically pluralistic re-visioning of our national identity."

10. Should a white employer be able to determine that, say, black English is unacceptable for a position as a receptionist? Is the employer's aversion to black English a productivity concern (based on the fact that it will raise the cost of communication within the firm)? Might this aversion be purely an aesthetic concern? If so, does it matter whether the preference is harbored by white employers, employees, or customers? Presumably, an employer's bona fide requirement that a worker speak standard English would not constitute intentional discrimination on the basis of race or national origin. Nonetheless, it could be unlawful if it fails to satisfy the disparate impact standard of Title VII, which, absent a sufficiently compelling business justification, prohibits neutral employment practices that have a disproportionate adverse effect on protected workers such as blacks and Hispanics. Could an employer successfully defend such a requirement as justified by business necessity?

11. Should an employer be free to discriminate against a New York accent, a Boston accent, a Southern accent, or a "low class" accent? There would seem to be no doctrinal basis for prohibiting such conduct, assuming that it did not have a disparate impact on protected workers. Does this suggest that Title VII does not really seek to protect the values of self-worth, identity, and autonomy that Matsuda argues are damaged by accent discrimination? Or is Title VII intended only to guard these values for the class of protected workers, which presumably would exclude poor whites from the Bronx or Boston or Mobile?

12. Matsuda's article is important because her comments about accents can be applied more broadly to cultural or ethnic differences in manners or styles of all conduct—both linguistic and behavioral. Should an employer's preference to be around those who like classical music and don't like rap music be a permissible influence in hiring decisions? Richard Epstein feels that society should honor such employer preferences, both to promote individual autonomy and to make the workplace more efficient, thereby expanding overall employment. Matsuda fears that, if white males hold most of the power in an unrestrained market economy, then their tastes will predominantly set the standard to which others must conform. While in general this fear is correct, one must not forget the power of competition. The Big Three automakers in the United States once held the dominant power in the U.S. automotive market, but they were taught a painful lesson by Japanese and German automakers who better catered to the demands of American consumers. Can similar competitive pressures work to the advantage of productive workers who happen to have nondominant accents or cultural styles?

13. Matsuda trumpets the benefits of linguistic variety and dismisses Epstein's contention that having a standard language enhances efficient communication. Isn't it clear that there are costs and benefits of diversity, which must be weighed to determine the efficient solution? Matsuda wants the government to make the decision for all firms; Epstein wants each firm to choose the efficient level of diversity itself.

Kevin Lang argues that linguistic barriers between different cultural groups hamper the productivity of integrated firms. Lang, "A Language Theory of Discrimination," 101 *Quarterly Journal of Economics* 363 (1986). As a result, Lang theorizes, "there will tend to be a single business language that will tend to be the language of the economically most powerful group. Economic life will be segregated by speech community in order to minimize transactions costs. Those transactions costs that cannot be eliminated will be borne by the minority group." If Lang is correct, should we give up some efficiency to reduce the costs borne by the minority group. Isn't the business justification defense designed to balance these interests?

14. Matsuda also argues that the barriers to effective communication are reduced when fear and prejudice are removed. Certainly, Title VII would generate enormous social benefits if it succeeded in reducing irrational fear and prejudice. Epstein argues, however, that the artificial pressures of governmentally enforced interaction are likely to accentuate fear and prejudice. Isn't this, too, ultimately an empirical question? Do you think Matsuda or Epstein has the stronger case on this point?

While Epstein's libertarian instincts underlie his desire to eliminate governmental restrictions on the exercise of personal preferences, Matsuda's communitarian values motivate her willingness to use government to promote more elevated preferences. The distinction was nicely captured by the economist Frank Knight, who wrote: "The chief thing which the common-sense individual actually wants is not satisfactions for the wants which he has, but more, and *better* wants." Quoted approvingly in Ronald Coase,

"Advertising and Free Speech," 6 *Journal of Legal Studies* 1, 10 (1977). Even if one accepts Knight's distinction, which Epstein and many economists do not (yet recall that Ronald Coase has won the Nobel Prize in Economics), one is still left with the question of whether the government in general, and employment discrimination law in particular, can effectively promote the better wants.

3

The Theory of Employment Discrimination Law

Public acceptance of the principle of equal employment opportunity has grown rapidly in the post-World War II period. As Paul Burstein noted: "The proportion of the population . . . stating that blacks should have equal opportunities for jobs rose from 42 percent in 1944 to 47 percent in 1946 and 1947, 83 percent in 1963, 87 percent in 1966, and 95 percent in 1972." Burstein, *Discrimination, Jobs, and Politics: The Struggle for Equal Employment Opportunity in the United States since the New Deal* 46 (Chicago: University of Chicago Press, 1985). The belief in equal employment opportunity for all races, religions, and both sexes is now virtually universal—at least as articulated in public opinion surveys. (See Chapter 5 for a discussion of the importance of this qualification.)

But what does the public want when it calls for equal employment opportunity? Given the oppressive legacy of slavery and Jim Crow legal restrictions, blacks as a group would have been at a severe disadvantage in 1965 even if Title VII of the 1964 Civil Rights Act immediately succeeded in ensuring that every employment decision was fully fair, color-blind, and meritocratic. Since the law in practice could not achieve such perfect equal opportunity, blacks had to overcome not only the historically generated disadvantages but also the continuing residual discrimination that the law had yet to eradicate. The net result inevitably was disappointment on the part of those who thought that Title VII would ensure equal treatment, and that equal treatment would lead to equal employment outcomes.

Owen Fiss correctly perceives the dichotomy between equal treatment and equal outcomes to be one of the central issues governing employment discrimination law. As we saw in the previous chapter, antidiscrimination law must strive to accommodate an array of conflicting governmental interests. Fiss asserts that, in adopting Title VII of the 1964 Civil Rights Act, the country endorsed the limited strategy of ensuring equal treatment, not because of the circumstances of politics, but because of the society's deep commitment to economic efficiency and individual fairness. While this viewpoint is now widely shared, it is forcefully attacked by both critical legal studies (CLS) scholars and critical race theorists. Alan Freeman, representing the CLS perspective, argues that equality of opportunity is a myth that obscures the reality of class domination in American society. In Freeman's view, the very concept of equal opportunity is unappealing because it generates a hierarchy of achievement instead of promoting true equality. As with many voices on the left, Freeman envisions employment discrimination law as a mechanism for promoting radical change in American society.

Kimberlé Crenshaw, a major critical race theorist, argues that CLS scholars have overlooked the fact that black subordination is due less to liberal legal consciousness, which has in fact supported some aspirations of blacks, than to the racist ideology that makes the present condition of underclass blacks appear fair and reasonable. Critical race theorists embrace subjectivity of perspective and seek to "confront and oppose dominant societal and institutional forces that [maintain] the structures of racism while professing the goal of dismantling racial discrimination." Mari Matsuda, Charles Lawrence, Richard Delgado, and Kimberlé Crenshaw, *Words That Wound: Critical Race Theory, Assaultive Speech, and the First Amendment* 3 (Boulder, Colo.: Westview Press, 1993). Crenshaw calls for the development of a distinct political thought that is informed by and focuses on the needs of blacks.

Those who believe that employment discrimination law must deliberately seek to generate economic equality for blacks as rapidly as possible are not content with the attainment of equal treatment for racial minorities. Instead, some "affirmative action" on behalf of certain protected groups is demanded. But the definition of affirmative action has changed over time, and the term is often used to describe preferential treatment for protected workers arising in very different contexts. Indeed, even as he embraces the equal-treatment goal of antidiscrimination law, Fiss argues in favor of departures from color-blind conduct in the form of measures to increase the pool of black applicants, albeit while ultimately retaining race-neutral selection criteria.

When President Kennedy signed the first executive order calling for federal government contractors to take affirmative action to ensure that they did not discriminate on the basis of race, his primary objective was to encourage just such an increase in the pool of black applicants. Later, presidents Johnson and Nixon expanded the obligations on federal government contractors, who now are required under Executive Order 11,246 to compare the racial composition of their workforces to the available supply of black labor in various major occupational categories and to determine whether there is any underutilization of blacks. If so, the contractor must devise an affirmative action plan that sets forth goals and timetables to correct any such underutilization. Firms that do not make good-faith efforts to address such imbalances face the loss of their government contracts. This "affirmative action" program, which applies only to major government contractors and their subcontractors, has generated substantial political battling. In fact, the Reagan Administration tried to kill the government contractors' compliance program in the early 1980s, but the effort failed as a result of support from within both political parties and from major business groups.

Affirmative action also refers to measures that private and governmental entities voluntarily adopt to correct past discrimination, as well as to remedial measures that are imposed by judicial order or through consent decrees that settle private or governmental litigation. Such measures, if appropriately tailored to avoid trammeling the rights of majority workers and if limited in duration, have been approved in a series of Supreme Court decisions, beginning with *United Steelworkers v. Weber*, 443 U.S. 193 (1979).

William Van Alstyne is distressed by the evolution in the concept of affirmative action from what he considers a legitimate policy of preventing discrimination to an insidious practice, encouraged and at times required by the government, of making employment decisions on the basis of a racial political spoils system. Randall Kennedy, on the other hand, confronts the arguments against affirmative action and argues that blacks and the nation as a whole have benefited from the black occupational gains derived from preferential treatment. A strong dissent from the left is offered by Richard Delgado, who sees affirmative action as a tool to preserve the status quo that exploits those whom it appears to help. Delgado argues that affirmative action provides employment to minorities not as a form of reparations or a vindication of their rights, but merely as a homeostatic device to control the level of social dissatisfaction.

3.1   Equal Treatment versus Equal Achievement

A Theory of Fair Employment Laws*
OWEN M. FISS

The Aims of the Law: Securing Equality for Negroes

Laws prohibiting racial discrimination in employment are inextricably linked to the goal of securing for Negroes a position of "equality." There

* Excerpts from Owen M. Fiss, "A Theory of Fair Employment Laws," *University of Chicago Law Review*, vol. 38, copyright © 1971. Reprinted by permission of the publisher.

are, however, two senses to "equality" in this context. One is equal treatment. Individual Negroes should be treated "equally" by employers in the sense that their race should be "ignored," that is, not held against them. This sense of equality focuses on the starting positions in a race: If color is not a criterion for employment, blacks will be on equal footing with whites. The second sense of equality—"equal achievement"—looks to the outcome of the race. It relates to the actual distribution of jobs among racial classes and is concerned with both the quantity and the quality (measured, for example, by pay level and social status) of the jobs. Jobs should be distributed so that the relative economic position of Negroes—as a class—is improved, so that the economic position of Negroes is approximately equal to that of whites. Disproportionate unemployment and underemployment of blacks should be eliminated or substantially reduced.

These two senses of equality are linked in fair employment laws, but it is not clear which is the goal of the law. Under one interpretation, the aim of a fair employment law is to secure equal treatment, and although equal treatment might alter the actual distribution of jobs and lead to equal achievement, such a result would be only incidental. Under an alternative interpretation, the aim is equal achievement, and the guarantee of equal treatment—the antidiscrimination prohibition—is the chosen method for equalizing the distribution of jobs among racial classes.

The distinction between these two views of the aim of the law is of little moment if it can be assumed that equal treatment will lead to equal achievement. But the assumption may be incorrect. It is conceivable, and indeed likely, that even if color is not given any weight in employment decisions, and in that sense equal treatment obtained, substantial inequalities by race in the distribution of jobs will persist in the immediate and foreseeable future.

Persistent inequalities in job distribution may be attributable in factors unrelated to particular employment decisions (that is, the conduct regulated by fair employment laws). For example, at any one point in time unemployment rates differ from industry to industry, from region to region, and from employer to employer; and disproportionate unemployment of blacks may be due to a heavy concentration of blacks in the industry, region, or business enterprise that has at any one moment the greatest unemployment. This unequal distribution may be due to custom, individual preference, or actual or imagined discrimination in areas other than employment, such as housing. It may simply be due to the fact that for blacks the starting point in the labor market was in the South and in agriculture. The concentration of blacks in non-growth industries and regions, or business enterprises, may be corrected over time as the unemployed relocate themselves; but that takes time, and whites will also be relocating.

Inequalities in the actual distribution of jobs between the races might also be due to the decisions of individual employers—the subject regulated by fair employment laws. One need not resurrect any notions of "innate inferiority" to explain this possibility. One need only be realistic about the historical legacy of blacks in America—one century of slavery and another of Jim Crowism. This legacy may result in inequalities in the actual distribution of jobs in several ways.

First, even if race is not used by an employer, his decisions may be based on criteria that do not seem conducive to productivity and that, because of the legacy, give whites an edge. In an industrial system where whites have a preexisting edge, rules that prefer relatives of the existing work force (nepotism) or those who started working for the firm at an earlier point in time (seniority) are examples of such criteria. The color-blind version of fair employment laws emphasizes the negative proposition that race is not a permissible basis for allocating jobs, but it does not purport affirmatively to catalog the permissible criteria, requiring that they all be conducive to productivity.

Second, even if the employer does not use race and uses criteria apparently conducive to productivity in his employment decisions, the historic legacy may have left blacks with several types of disabilities. One disability might be motivational. Conceivably, this legacy of slavery and discrimination has been responsible for the lessening of motivation of the class, making its members less willing to compete aggressively for the opportunities that are open or less willing to submit to industrial discipline. The legacy may have also made it more difficult for Negroes to acquire the references necessary to evaluate future promise. Finally, the legacy may have left the class without the qualities, abilities, skills or experience that efficiency-oriented employment criteria demand. This impact of the legacy need not be confined to the older members of the class. For younger blacks, not directly exposed to slavery or Jim Crowism, the disabilities might be "inheritable." The disabilities may have affected family structure, which in turn has an impact on a child's aspirations and on the guidance available. The disabilities also may have affected family wealth, which has an impact on the child's ability to acquire the training or credentials necessary to compete more successfully.

Thus the distinction between the two views of equality is real. The question that has to be asked is whether the goal of the antidiscrimination prohibition is equal treatment or equal achievement, and a great deal may turn on the answer to that question.... If equal achievement is the goal of the law, and, as may be the case, it is not obtained by color blindness, the desire to improve the relative economic position of blacks will create a greater temptation to construe the legal obligation arising from the command not to base employment decisions on race in a more and more "generous" fashion. There will be considerable pressure to construe the central regulatory device in a manner that would bring the law closer to the attainment of the alleged goal of equalizing the actual distribution of employment opportunities, and such a construction might well entail giving preferential treatment to blacks. On the other hand, the equal-treatment goal is more compatible with color blindness; it means that blacks are treated the same as whites and thus would seem to be achieved once all employment decisions are independent of the colors of the prospective employees.

. . .

The Equal-Treatment Concept: Responding to a Particularized Wrong

An employment decision is analyzable primarily as a decision to allocate a scarce opportunity—a job. The paradigm situation is one in which several individuals are competing for a limited number of opportunities. A choice among these individuals is required, and the question arises as to the appropriate criteria for that choice. A choice made on the basis of an improper criterion—classified by the law as "invidious" or "arbitrary"—is viewed as a particularized wrong. The rejected individual is not being treated fairly.

Two attributes of the racial criterion account for the sense of unfairness engendered by its use as the basis of an employment decision. The first is that an individual's race is not considered an accurate predictor of his productivity. Fair employment laws reflect a rejection of any views of innate inferiority and also a commitment to the principle that the choice among individuals for scarce opportunities should be on the basis of the individual's merit. In the employment context this commitment to the merit principle means that the individual businessman is expected to choose the most productive individual, that is, the best worker at any given wage rate. This will tend to maximize the businessman's own wealth, and it will foster society's interest in efficiency—producing the greatest number of goods and services at the lowest cost.

The second attribute is the absence of individual control. To judge an individual on the basis of his race is to judge him on the basis of his membership in a class where that membership is truly predetermined. Fair employment laws reflect not only a commitment to the merit principle but also a commitment to the principle that it is desirable to judge individuals on the basis of criteria that are within his reach. Each individual should, at least at some point in his life, have the power or capacity to put himself in the position of satisfying the criterion. Individual control is a value because it provides the prospect for upward mobility, an important incentive to self-improvement and efficient performance. Further, it is valuable because it rationalizes, and thus makes more tolerable, the unequal distribution of status and wealth among people in the society: failure is the individual's own fault. The principle that the individual should control his own fate also assumes that the allocation of scarce employment opportunities represents, to some extent, a reward. The reward may serve an instrumental purpose; it may be an incentive to develop the necessary qualities or skills or to perform well. Or the reward or allocation may be, for the individual, an end in itself. In either event, responsibility is a necessary condition for being rewarded, and individual control is a necessary condition for responsibility.

The Equal Achievement Concept: The Improvement of the Relative Economic Position of Negroes

The ethical basis for a law seeking equal treatment seems clear: Under the view that race is an arbitrary criterion, unequal treatment—disadvantaging Negroes because of their color—is one form of unfair treatment, a particularized wrong. However, the ethical basis for equal achievement—as an independent and distinctive goal of the law, and not merely as a possible incidental consequence of equal treatment—seems more uncertain to me. This uneasiness stems primarily from the redistributive quality of the equal-achievement goal. This goal not only entails an improvement in the position of Negroes from what it is now but also an improvement in comparison to that of other groups. "Equality" is a relative concept; it involves a comparison. Since whites are the economically dominant racial group, a concern with equal achievement is basically a concern with the relative economic position of Negroes as compared to whites. Moreover, because of scarcity, the achievement of one group will be at the expense of the other. There is a symmetry to each achievement: what one group gets, the other does not. Even assuming an expanding economic pie, the improvement of the relative position of Negroes means that they get a larger slice of the increment, that Negroes are benefited more from the expansion than whites. The redistributive aspect of this goal is even clearer assuming a static pie. And since neither the legal obligation nor the enforcement of fair employment laws is conditioned upon increasing demand for labor, due account must be taken of the situation where the pie is static. The ethical questions posed by the equal-achievement goal then are twofold. Why should society seek to obtain for Negroes a larger slice of the pie? How large should that slice be?

. . .

The Need for the Law: The Possibility of Self-Regulation

An interesting feature of the merit principle is that in a market economy it is to some extent self-enforcing. Employers have an obvious financial self-interest in making employment decisions on the basis of merit. And competition, if not greed, requires or leads them to pursue that self-interest with vigor. Hence, to the extent that a fair employment law does nothing more than prohibit businessmen from making employment decisions on the basis of a nonmerit factor—race—a question arises as to the need for the law.

The need for the law may be predicated on certain intangible values. For example, it may be valuable to reaffirm the principle of fair treatment. This affirmation may produce such nonquantifiable benefits as encouraging confidence in the legal system and encouraging those who believe themselves to be vulnerable to discrimination to compete aggressively for jobs. Reliance upon self-regulation entails a silence that may be pregnant with contrary implications for the likely victims.

The need for the law may also be more firmly rooted. Self-regulation may not materialize because of certain features of our market economy. In a number of situations the self-enforcing capacity of the merit principle is limited, and a risk is created that the employment decision will be based on a nonmerit criterion, such as race.

. . .

In a situation where the merit principle is self-enforcing, employers who deviate from the principle impose costs on themselves. In the other situations there is a need for the imposition of additional costs on the nonmerit employer, and the enforcement of fair employment laws supply these costs. Indeed, in some instances fair employment laws impose costs on those, such as the building trades unions, who in the short run might not otherwise feel the cost of using a nonmerit criterion in any direct fashion and who, in fact, would benefit because the labor supply would be restricted. Costs imposed by fair employment laws may take various forms—compensatory damages, punitive damages, the obligation to pay plaintiff's attorney's fees, the risk of losing customers (possibly the government), and the psychological or social impact of being adjudged guilty of violating a law that embodies an ethical norm. More drastic kinds of legal sanctions, such as fines and imprisonment, are not usually authorized; and because of continued nonuse, the fear of criminal contempt for disobedience of an injunction is not immediate. The softness of the available sanctions is one of the unique features of fair employment laws as a regulatory device. This may be a sign of society's less than full commitment to the antidiscrimination prohibition, or it may indicate either faith that compliance will be voluntary or a recognition that the legal obligation arising from the laws is so unclear that punitive sanctions would be inappropriate.

The Costs of the Law

All laws have costs, and fair employment laws are no exception. I do not identify these costs in order to determine whether there are less expensive alternatives. Rather, I am interested in further illuminating the theory underlying fair employment laws by making it clear what price society is willing to pay to achieve the purposes served by these laws.

Frustration of Personal Preferences

One set of costs arises from the frustration of personal preferences. A desire to exclude blacks from the work force because of antipathy, a desire to preserve a certain type of social structure, or a desire to associate only with whites, obviously is a personal preference. But, at a minimum, a fair employment law prohibits indulgence of preferences through exclusion of blacks, because of their color, from the work force or from better jobs. This frustration of desire, preference and choice not only has possible individual psychological consequences, but also runs counter to general principles in society insuring freedom of association and the freedom to act upon personal preferences.

Frustration of these personal preferences cannot be ignored on a theory of a political bargain—that the political majority is willing to trade the satisfaction of these personal preferences for the potential increase in total wealth. The view that the law will increase total wealth depends on estimations of the level of wealth without the law (where reliance is on self-regulation), the cost of enforcing the law, and the likelihood that increased use of other nonmerit criteria (for example, nepotism) might negate the effect of abolition of the race criterion. And even if it were possible to make these judgments and be assured that wealth would be increased by the law, it seems impossible to know *how much* that wealth would increase, that is, whether it would increase to a level at which the majority would be willing to engage in the trade-off. Instead, the frustration of these personal preferences must be acknowledged as one price society is willing to pay to achieve the aims of the law. The satisfaction of discriminatory personal preferences of whites entails particularized unfairness and continued relegation of Negroes to an inferior economic position. The law reflects the value judgment—the choice—that eradication of these evils is more "important" than preserving opportunities to vent discriminatory associational desires.

. . .

Economic Costs

Aside from frustration of personal preferences, fair employment laws, even under the regime of color blindness, involve economic costs. Once again, it would be disingenuous to ignore these costs on the ground that in the long run they will be offset or canceled by increased total wealth due to increased productivity. That view requires an estimate of the economic costs and benefits of the law, which seems, at least to me, unobtainable. The most that can be said is that the color-blind version of the fair employment laws, effectively and cheaply enforced, is consistent with increased productivity. This says very little. It seems more realistic to recognize the economic costs of the law and to assume that the justification for incurring these costs consists of the nonquantifiable value attached to the aims of the law.

The costs of enforcement. Initially, it may seem that the costs of enforcement are relatively insignificant because a fair employment law may be self-executing—almost like the nineteenth amendment. This can occur in four ways. First, the passage of the fair employment law communicates society's disapproval of race-based employment decisions. That general disapproval might be internalized, so that those responsible for the employment decisions conform their conduct to society's sense of moral propriety, if for no other reason than to avoid feelings of guilt. Second, the very existence of the law (perhaps coupled with a low-cost method of enforcement, such as consent decrees) enables an employer who previously discriminated only to avoid alienating customers, white workers or the community to explain to others that he is not "voluntarily" ending his discrimination and to assure them that his competitors are obliged to follow a similar policy. The mere presence of the law might enable him to pursue his self-interest vigorously and to apply scrupulously the merit principle without incurring the loss of sales, goodwill, or white workers that might otherwise flow from nondiscriminatory employment practices. Third, enforcement action against one employer, making him more merit-oriented, may make his competitors, through the operation of the market, more merit-oriented in their employment decisions. The effect of one enforcement action can be easily generalized. Fourth, a credible, but general, threat of enforcement may induce employers to conform their employment to the merit principle because satisfying the taste for discrimination becomes more expensive. The employer is exposed to the new risk of a successful enforcement action against him, with its attendant costs.

These four factors have operated with considerable efficacy in obtaining "voluntary compliance" with the antidiscrimination prohibition in another area of economic activity—public accommodations. The same phenomenon seems to be occurring in housing, where the extensive use of a low-cost enforcement method—consent orders—seems to be the rule rather than the exception. In employment, however, the discriminatory pattern seems, at least to the enforcement agencies, more intractable; the prospect of voluntary compliance slim; and the costs of enforcement higher.

The costs of enforcing a fair employment law may in part be viewed from the prospective of the plaintiff and the tribunal. Such costs would consist of the resources used by private and public agencies in investigating, prosecuting, adjudicating, mediating, or negotiating claims. There is a corresponding set of costs for the defendant—those actually consumed in defending against claims of racial discrimination. Of course, both sets of costs may be incurred whether or not the claim has merit, and their level may be independent of the outcome of the adjudication.

The risk of incurring litigation costs may, of course, result in nothing more than punctilious compliance with the law. On the other hand, the risk may also lead the businessman concerned with wealth maximization to insure himself against these costs. This insurance would minimize the risk of having to defend against a claim of discrimination and facilitate the defense against any such claim. The price of this insurance can be called an "anticipatory cost" and must be viewed as an economic cost arising from the risk of enforcement.

One form of insurance consists of racial-hiring—hiring, without regard to merit, some of those on behalf of whom claims are likely to be asserted. At least the appearance of compliance is established. The price of this insurance is the decrease in productivity attributable to the departure from the merit principle. This may be less than the price of defending (even discounted for the unlikelihood of an enforcement action). Another form of insurance may be the institution of a formalized selection system. Such a system would entail abandonment of subjective criteria (for example, "I liked him"), the substitution of so-called objective employment criteria (for example, the professionally-developed, standardized written test), and the establishment of a record-keeping system indicating why an applicant was rejected. The formalized system minimizes the risk of prosecution and reduces the cost of defending because the employer can easily point to performance under these objective criteria (for example, a score on a written test) as his basis for rejecting the individual who charges discrimination based on race. Here the price of insurance is the increased administrative costs of the formalized system, and these may be less than the discounted cost of defending.

The costs of the obligation: prohibiting efficient decisions based on race. Thus far the prohibition against racial discrimination has been viewed as consistent with greater productivity for the individual businessman and for society. One exception arises when a businessman must expend resources to defend against a bad claim or insure against the assertion of such claims. Perhaps these costs are inherent in any form of government regulation. However, there is another exception, which I find more problematic. It involves the costs imposed on the businessman by virtue of the obligation of the law itself. The mere fact that race itself is not a merit criterion does not mean that the efficient businessman cannot use it for purposes of increasing his productivity. There are at least four situations where the law's prohibition against the use of race precludes the good businessman from engaging in efficient conduct.

Race as a symptom of merit. Some businessmen may concede that race itself is an arbitrary criterion and yet use race in employment decisions on the theory that it is symptomatic of other qualities that are predictive of productivity. For example, they may think that black is a symptom of poor education or high turnover rate. They realize that the symptomatic use of race may not be free of error; obviously, not all Negroes have a poor education or change jobs frequently. But race is an easy criterion to apply, and the good businessman may decide accurately that the savings derived from applying this easy criterion (administrative costs) will offset the costs of occasional mistakes, that is, the loss of increased productivity that might result from excluding Negroes from his work force or from using them only for nonskilled jobs.

Catering to consumers' or clients' taste for discrimination. A second situation arises when increased productivity due to compliance with the antidiscrimination prohibition will be offset by decreased sales. This would be true under the following conditions: (a) Consumers or clients prefer a firm that discriminates against Negroes by either not hiring them at all or keeping them in inferior positions. (b) Consumers or clients are willing to pay enough to cover the increased costs of labor due to nonapplication of the merit principle. (c) Consumers or clients are able to police the performance of the particular employer to insure that he is discriminating against Negroes. (d) There are alternatives to the consumers or clients so that they need not do business with the complying employer. A decrease in sales would occur only if they are able not to consume or to switch to producers of the goods or services who would, for business or other reasons, satisfy their discriminatory preference by not complying. Mere coverage of the industry by a fair employment law will not insure industry-wide compliance, nor will the usual enforcement action directed against the single firm.

Personnel conflicts. The businessman may decide to limit the number of blacks working for him in preference to increasing the risk of costly personnel conflicts. His thinking is that hiring more blacks will cause the whites to be more antagonistic (because their prejudice has a tolerance level that may be exceeded), resulting in disputes and conflicts among the workers in the course of the workday. This might well be the judgment of the good businessman if three conditions are satisfied: (a) He is correct in his beliefs that increasing the number of blacks will increase the risk of personnel conflicts. (b) His productivity would be decreased if he had only blacks. (d) The costs in productivity due to the exclusion or limitation of blacks are offset by the decrease in costs that might otherwise arise because of the personnel conflicts or because it would be necessary to employ more supervisors to minimize the personnel conflicts generated by higher levels of black employment.

.   .   .

The flat ban against the use of race as a basis for the employment decision is not without its irony. The purported beneficiaries of the law—Negroes—may, as a class, suffer adverse practical consequences. The diseconomics we have been discussing may not stop at simply decreasing the wealth of the businessman. The supply of goods may be restricted because the incentive to the businessman is diminished or the businessman may be able to pass on, through higher prices, some significant portion of the increased costs due to the ban against efficient decisions based on race. Negroes occupy a low economic position in our society and thus are likely to feel the brunt of diseconomics that result in higher prices or shortages of goods and services. Moreover, a prohibition on racial wage differentials—a requirement of "equal pay for equal work"— may lessen Negro employment. Under the ban, the businessman loses some of the incentive to hire equally qualified black workers (that is, the savings due to paying them lower pay), for he will have to pay them the same as white workers. And if his costs are higher, he will hire fewer workers, black and white, and the reduction in employment opportunities is likely to hit blacks harder. The paternalism is clear. Some whites, and some blacks, are telling those blacks who might actually benefit from a differential-wage structure that they will not be allowed to accept that benefit because of concerns or interests of the remainder of the class or society as a whole.

Racism, Rights, and the Quest for Equality of Opportunity: A Critical Legal Essay*

ALAN FREEMAN

. . .

[W]hen I teach antidiscrimination law, [m]ore and more students (armed with more cases each year) announce that the key principles are "rationality" and "color blindness" and that affirmative action programs utilizing racial criteria are clear violations of settled norms. In the face of such complacency, my painstaking response is to demonstrate that the development of antidiscrimination law is an ongoing dialogue ... between the concrete historical reality of oppression and the principles generated by that experience. The abstract principles may end up contradicting reality and history when they are permitted or encouraged to take on lives of their own. Thus, to claim that the affirmative use of "blackness" as a criterion violates "principle" stands in tragic contradiction to the fact that for over 350 years blacks in America have been categorically oppressed by whites on account of the very same "blackness."

. . .

Equality of opportunity has been the only clearly acceptable goal of the legal battle against racial discrimination. Temporary deviations from the procedural matter of making sure all can enter the game have been treated as just that—matters of expediency to be tolerated no longer than absolutely necessary to get the game working. Thus the law has allowed remedial standards of racial balance: limited uses of affirmative action quotas, race-conscious subsidies and minority admissions programs. All of these were treated as hard-to-justify exceptions. They were

* Excerpts from Alan Freeman, "Racism, Rights, and the Quest for Equality of Opportunity: A Critical Legal Essay," *Harvard Civil Rights–Civil Liberties Law Review*, vol. 23, copyright © 1988. Reprinted by permission of the President and Fellows of Harvard College.

accompanied by reminders, usually in other cases which followed, that a pure quest for racially proportional results was unthinkable, as was viewing racially disproportionate results as presumptively discriminatory against the minority. In retrospect, the most radical of all antidiscrimination cases, *Griggs v. Duke Power Co.*, was not an attack on the equality of opportunity assumption, but expressed a belief that it could be made to work better.

.   .   .

Most questionable is why we (as detached, moral, analytic philosophers) might find equality of opportunity desirable at all. Even if it works efficiently, it replaces in the name of equality, oblige, with a new hierarchy of "achievement," "ability," self-importance, and graduated ostentation in material display. Like property rights themselves, which are thought by some economists to come into being to reduce "externalities" of over-consumption and conflict-avoidance costs, but instead may themselves generate enormous externalities of alienation, the real cost of the inequality produced by equality of opportunity may be in excess alienation. Most economists and moral philosophers, however, do not account for alienation as a social cost. The world of perfectly realized meritocracy might well be an unhappy one for many if not most of its residents.

Nevertheless, given its rhetorical and experiential intensity, as well as its prominent role in our history, there must be a philosophical basis for the notion. From a dynamic, or historical perspective, equality of opportunity seems a fine rallying cry for have-nots seeking to displace haves whose positions rest not on achievement or ability but on mere status conferred by tradition. Once the have-nots take over, however, they must resort to timeless and static rationalizations that may serve as well to justify their own newly won roles as haves. At this point the arguments of moral philosophy enter. Let us imagine a world of individuals bearing "talents" or "abilities." Such persons seek individually to maximize personal satisfactions in life, but, lacking incentive by way of rewards, might lazily do no more than minimally necessary to sustain themselves in their hammocks. Such individuals would in their indolence remain unfulfilled, incomplete human beings. Moreover, "society," which values and seeks to maximize the useful productions of their talents, would suffer from losses of production, and a smaller mass aggregate of satisfactions than would otherwise be possible.

Equality of opportunity theory rests upon a peculiar blend of many philosophical concepts: "Kantian" individualism (the rights of "free" and "autonomous" beings), personality and desert theories of property (you realize yourself through your action upon the external world and deserve to keep what you have fashioned from it), pessimistic behaviorism (people, like laboratory animals, will exert themselves only for rewards, and exert themselves even more for even bigger rewards), and some kind of utilitarian aggregation theory (more is better, and "we" want more). That some abilities, or achievements, are valued more highly and are also rewarded more highly, simply reflects our strong preferences for those scarcely available goods or services.

A key assumption for equal opportunity theory is that "abilities" and "talents" are widely distributed in our "classless" society, so that any enterprising individual possessing a socially desirable talent can reap rewards through will, hard work and perseverance in educational endeavor. Viewed from the standpoint of social mobility, equality of opportunity simply does not work as it claims to.

. . .

[T]he basic point about equality of opportunity is its failure, historically and presently. To be sure, there have been times of economic expansion when significant numbers became wealthier or even made marginal crossings of class borders. If the opportunity for upward mobility ever was a reality, it has not been so for some time. If you are born of the lower class, you are much more than likely to stay there, and if you are nonwhite and of the lower class, the odds are considerably worse. The assumption of "classlessness" presupposed by equal opportunity theory is belied by the reality of our class structure, with its insidious and disempowering reality of racism. And the reality of class seems to be getting worse.

. . .

What, then, is wrong with equality of opportunity in theory and practice in the context of our time and culture? For one thing, we have never even given it a try. British liberals in the early twentieth century recognized the obvious truth that equal opportunity necessarily required the abolition of all inherited wealth, otherwise those who already possess it will deploy it to gain immediate distance from the pack....

Property itself raises the same problem, inhibiting the equality of opportunity in much the same way as wealth, especially when compounded by the fact of its inheritance. John Locke not only undercut, but made a mockery of, his labor theory of property by automatically legitimating existing holdings, imagining that they must have been originally the fruit of authentic labor. The one move that might have given American ex-slaves even a chance in the equal opportunity game—confiscation of Confederate landholdings followed by wide-scale redistribution to former slaves (the "forty acres and a mule" movement)—was quickly discarded as, among other things, too radically at odds with that most American of all institutions—property rights.

Beyond the problem that equality of opportunity has never been tried and has thus far failed, in other numerous yet equally significant ways, the ideology of equal opportunity belies itself. Is it really "talent" that enables particular young people to advance? Or is it the dynastic impulse of elite schools to admit children of their graduates; the advantages in connection and status that can simply be bought for cash; the pre-existing networks of power that make for the availability of positions; or, the differential self-images internalized by the children of the poor and those of the rich in their daily contacts and interactions with teachers, as well as family members, who have already internalized their own position in the equal opportunity game?

The aggregate of these institutional realities is probably sufficient to undercut any claim that equal opportunity exists in practice, despite the few and exceptional cases pointed out to prove the opposite. The more difficult question is whether without some game such as equality of opportunity people will be willing to achieve their potentials. Assuming that question involves notions of incentive, differential reward, and, especially, "talent." That without material incentive people will avoid work as much as possible presupposes our sorry culture as the natural human condition. It is contradicted by examples from other cultures, by communities of caring, and, on reflection, by our own sense of the lonely, empty, vision of our humanity. Any politics worth their name must take on and challenge that premise. Differential reward, however, assumes both the incentive problem and an additional notion that in the "natural" distribution of talents, some are worth more than others.

If we're talking about objective human differences, there may be some talents of more value than others, at least in theory. Market theory would then imply that the more sought after talents would be more rewarded through competition. Given the flawed assumptions of market theory, one could end the discussion here. That critique has been done well before. The point here is to understand how "talents" come to be valued and how that relates to a supposed natural and objective distribution of same.

For one thing, there is no such thing as a natural and objective "talent." All such skills are socially and historically contingent, the ones a particular culture needs and wants in its time. That they are socially contingent means also that they may be socially constructed (e.g., playing the violin), having little to do with basic or objective human need even allowing for social and historical contingency.

The more distorted the power relations within a culture (call it a class structure if you like) the more likely the valued talents will have their value distorted by those power relations. Consider, for example, the ways in which doctors and lawyers are obscenely overvalued in our culture, because they have had rich constituencies ready to bid for their services, while legitimating harsh monopolistic screening practices to reinforce their excessive self-importance and control of their numerical membership.

. . .

The gap between an authentic effort to seek out and identify the myriad human skills that might contribute to the social well-being of a community on the one hand, and the test-dominated search for a hierarchy of "intelligence" or "talent" in our culture, on the other, is in fact the distance between real and imagined human need. The latter becomes a way of transforming class-based domination into "natural" hierarchy.

. . .

Every one of us who has internalized meritocratic norms is complicit in the subtle reproduction of relations of domination through the "neutral" machinery of "equality of opportunity." It has been a presumption of Western culture, at least going back to Ancient Greece, that there exists a Universal Rationality. The intersection of that presumption with the deployment by the dominant classes of their "cultural capital" makes the dominant culture, with all of its attendant forms, the universal one. Meritocracy at its base is an inquiry as to whether a particular subject does or does not possess any of the cultural capital already more or less possessed by the powerful (hierarchy is not either-or, but graduated and overlaid with oppression in its many forms).

In such a "meritocracy," historical access to and acquisition of such cultural capital may be much more important than wealth itself. Other forms of knowledge or practice, deviant from the one that claims universality, are silenced, marginalized, dismissed, or simply ignored. If we cannot change the credentials enforced by reliance on equality of opportunity, we must effect a redistribution of cultural capital itself or devalue it by validating a multiplicity of cultures and knowledges and, accordingly, transforming most of our institutionalized occupational practices. What seems clear is that more "inputs" into our existing educational system in the name of equal opportunity cannot begin to compensate for the disempowerment of those lacking the correct cultural capital as against those who already control it.

Race, Reform, and Retrenchment: Transformation and Legitimation in Antidiscrimination Law*
KIMBERLÉ WILLIAMS CRENSHAW

The Hegemonic Role of Racism: Establishing the "Other" in American
  Ideology

Throughout American history, the subordination of Blacks was rationalized by a series of stereotypes and beliefs that made their conditions appear logical and natural. Historically, white supremacy has been

* Excerpts from Kimberlé Williams Crenshaw, "Race, Reform, and Retrenchment: Transformation and Legitimation in Antidiscrimination Law," *Harvard Law Review*, vol. 101, copyright © 1988. Reprinted by permission of the author and publisher.

premised upon various political, scientific, and religious theories, each of which relies on racial characterizations and stereotypes about Blacks that have coalesced into an extensive legitimating ideology. Today, it is probably not controversial to say that these stereotypes were developed primarily to rationalize the oppression of Blacks. What *is* overlooked, however, is the extent to which these stereotypes serve a hegemonic function by perpetuating a mythology about both Blacks *and* whites even today, reinforcing an illusion of a white community that cuts across ethnic, gender, and class lines.

As presented by Critical scholars, hegemonic rule succeeds to the extent that the ruling class world view establishes the appearance of a unity of interests between the dominant class and the dominated. Throughout American history, racism has identified the interests of subordinated whites with those of society's white elite. Racism does not support the dominant order simply because all whites want to maintain their privilege at the expense of Blacks, or because Blacks sometimes serve as convenient political scapegoats. Instead, the very existence of a clearly subordinated "other" group is contrasted with the norm in a way that reinforces identification with the dominant group. Racism helps create an illusion of unity through the oppositional force of a symbolic "other." The establishment of the "other" creates a bond, a burgeoning common identity of all non-stigmatized parties—whose identity and interests are defined in opposition to the other.

.   .   .

The Role of Race Consciousness in a System of Formal Equality

The previous section emphasizes the continuity of white race consciousness over the course of American history. This section, by contrast, focuses on the partial transformation of the functioning of race consciousness that occurred with the transition from Jim Crow to formal equality in race law.

Prior to the civil rights reforms, Blacks were formally subordinated by the state. Blacks experienced being the "other" in two aspects of oppression, which I shall designate as symbolic and material. Symbolic subordination refers to the formal denial of social and political equality to all Blacks, regardless of their accomplishments. Segregation and other forms of social exclusion—separate restrooms, drinking fountains, entrances, parks, cemeteries, and dining facilities—reinforced a racist ideology that Blacks were simply inferior to whites and were therefore not included in the vision of America as a community of equals.

Material subordination, on the other hand, refers to the ways that discrimination and exclusion economically subordinated Blacks to whites and subordinated the life chances of Blacks to those of whites on almost every level. This subordination occurs when Blacks are paid less for the same work, when segregation limits access to decent housing, and where poverty, anxiety, poor health care, and crime create a life expectancy for Blacks that is five to six years shorter than for whites.

Symbolic subordination often created material disadvantage by reinforcing race consciousness in everything from employment to education. In fact, the two are generally not thought of separately: separate facilities were usually inferior facilities, and limited job categorization virtually always brought lower pay and harder work. Despite the pervasiveness of racism, however, there existed even before the civil rights movement a class of Blacks who were educationally, economically, and professionally equal—if not superior—to many whites, and yet these Blacks suffered social and political exclusion as well.

It is also significant that not all separation resulted in inferior institutions. School segregation—although often presented as the epitome of symbolic and material subordination—did not always result in inferior education. It is not separation *per se* that made segregation subordinating, but the fact that it was enforced and supported by state power, and accompanied by the explicit belief in African–American inferiority.

The response to the civil rights movement was the removal of most formal barriers and symbolic manifestations of subordination. Thus, "White Only" notices and other obvious indicators of the societal policy of racial subordination disappeared—at least in the public sphere. The disappearance of these symbols of subordination reflected the acceptance of the rhetoric of formal equality and signaled the demise of the rhetoric of white supremacy as expressing America's normative vision. In other words, it could no longer be said that Blacks were not included as equals in the American political vision.

Removal of these public manifestations of subordination was a significant gain for all Blacks, although some benefited more than others. The eradication of formal barriers meant more to those whose oppression was primarily symbolic than to those who suffered lasting material disadvantage. Yet despite these disparate results, it would be absurd to suggest that no benefits came from these formal reforms, especially in regard to racial policies, such as segregation, that were partly material but largely symbolic. Thus, to say that the reforms were "merely symbolic" is to say a great deal. These legal reforms and the formal extension of "citizenship" were large achievements precisely because much of what characterized Black oppression was symbolic and formal.

Yet the attainment of formal equality is not the end of the story. Racial hierarchy cannot be cured by the move to facial race-neutrality in the laws that structure the economic, political, and social lives of Black people. White race consciousness, in a new form but still virulent, plays an important, perhaps crucial, role in the new regime that has legitimated the deteriorating day-to-day material conditions of the majority of Blacks.

The end of Jim Crow has been accompanied by the demise of an explicit ideology of white supremacy. The white norm, however, has not disappeared; it has only been submerged in popular consciousness. It continues in an unspoken form as a statement of the positive social norm, legitimating the continuing domination of those who do not meet it. Nor have the negative stereotypes associated with Blacks been eradicated. The rationalizations once used to legitimate Black subordination based on a belief in racial inferiority have now been reemployed to legitimate the domination of Blacks through reference to an assumed cultural inferiority.

Thomas Sowell, for example, suggests that underclass Blacks are economically depressed because they have not adopted the values of hard work and discipline. He further implies that Blacks have not pursued the need to attain skills and marketable education, and have not learned to make the sacrifices necessary for success. Instead, Sowell charges that Blacks view demands for special treatment as a means for achieving what other groups have achieved through hard work and the abandonment of racial politics.

Sowell applies the same stereotypes to the mass of Blacks that white supremacists had applied in the past, but bases these modern stereotypes on notions of "culture" rather than genetics. Sowell characterizes underclass Blacks as victims of self-imposed ignorance, lack of direction, and poor work attitudes. Culture, not race, now accounts for this "otherness." Except for vestigial pockets of historical racism, any possible connection between past racial subordination and the present situation has been severed by the formal repudiation of the old race-conscious policies. The same dualities historically used to legitimate racial subordination in the name of genetic inferiority have now been adopted by Sowell as a means for explaining the subordinated status of Blacks today in terms of cultural inferiority.

Moreover, Sowell's explanation of the subordinate status of Blacks also illustrates the treatment of the now-unspoken white stereotypes as the positive social norm. His assertion that the *absence* of certain attributes accounts for the continued subordination of Blacks implies that it is the *presence* of these attributes that explains the continued advantage of whites. The only difference between this argument and the older oppositional dynamic is that, whereas the latter explained Black subordination through reference to the ideology of white supremacy, the former explains Black subordination through reference to an unspoken social norm. That norm—although no longer explicitly white supremacist—remains, nonetheless, a white norm. As Martha Minow has pointed out, "[t]he unstated point of comparison is not neutral, but particular, and not inevitable, but only seemingly so when left unstated."

White race consciousness, which includes the modern belief in cultural inferiority, acts to further Black subordination by justifying all the forms of unofficial racial discrimination, injury, and neglect that flourish in a society that is only formally dedicated to equality. In more subtle ways, moreover, white race consciousness reinforces and is reinforced by the myth of equal opportunity that explains and justifies broader class hierarchies.

Race consciousness also reinforces whites' sense that American society is really meritocratic and thus helps prevent them from questioning the basic legitimacy of the free market. Believing both that Blacks are inferior and that the economy impartially rewards the superior over the inferior, whites see that most Blacks are indeed worse off than whites are, which reinforces their sense that the market is operating "fairly and impartially"; those who should logically be on the bottom are on the bottom. This strengthening of whites' belief in the system in turn reinforces their beliefs that Blacks are *indeed* inferior. After all, equal opportunity *is* the rule, and the market *is* an impartial judge; if Blacks are on the bottom, it must reflect their relative inferiority. Racist ideology thus operates in conjunction with the class components of legal ideology to reinforce the status quo, both in terms of class and race.

To bring a fundamental challenge to the way things are, whites would have to question not just their own subordinate status, but also both the economic and the racial myths that justify the status quo. Racism, combined with equal opportunity mythology, provides a rationalization for racial oppression, making it difficult for whites to see the Black situation as illegitimate or unnecessary. If whites believe that Blacks, because they are unambitious or inferior, get what they deserve, it becomes that much harder to convince whites that something is wrong with the entire system. Similarly, a challenge to the legitimacy of continued racial inequality would force whites to confront myths about equality of opportunity that justify for them whatever measure of economic success they may have attained.

Thus, although Critics have suggested that legal consciousness plays a central role in legitimating hierarchy in America, the otherness dynamic enthroned within the maintenance and perpetuation of white race consciousness seems to be at least as important as legal consciousness in supporting the dominant order. Like legal consciousness, race consciousness makes it difficult—at least for whites—to imagine the world differently. It also creates the desire for identification with privileged elites. By focusing on a distinct, subordinate "other," whites include themselves in the dominant circle—an arena in which most hold no real power, but only their privileged racial identity. Consider the case of a dirt-poor, southern white, shown participating in a Ku Klux Klan rally in the movie *Resurgence,* who declared: "Every morning, I wake up and thank God I'm white." For this person, and for others like him, race consciousness—manifested by his refusal even to associate with Blacks—provides a powerful explanation of why he fails to challenge the current social order.

. . .

Conclusion

For Blacks, the task at hand is to devise ways to wage ideological and political struggle while minimizing the costs of engaging in an inherently legitimating discourse. A clearer understanding of the space we occupy in the American political consciousness is a necessary prerequisite to the development of pragmatic strategies for political and economic survival. In this regard, the most serious challenge for Blacks is to minimize the political and cultural cost of engaging in an inevitably co-optive process in order to secure material benefits. Because our present predicament gives us few options, we must create conditions for the maintenance of a distinct political thought that is informed by the actual conditions of Black people. Unlike the civil rights vision, this new approach should not be defined and thereby limited by the possibilities of dominant political discourse, but should maintain a distinctly progressive outlook that focuses on the needs of the African–American community.

Notes and Questions

1.   Freeman complains about the hierarchy of achievement that results from a system that is based upon "equality of opportunity." Would these same problems still exist if only whites lived in the United States? If so, does this imply that, to Freeman, capitalism is as much a problem as racism? Can the substantial disparities in wealth and income that exist in the United States be justified according to the Rawlsian ethical mandate that the inequality, which presumably provides incentives to create wealth that will expand the nation's resources, enhances the well-being of the least well-off members of society? John Rawls, *A Theory of Justice* (Cambridge, Mass.: Harvard University Press, 1971).

Are the social and economic disadvantages resulting from low intelligence as unjust and personally damaging as systematic racial discrimination? For a bitter satire of an imagined governmental effort to reduce what Freeman calls "the enormous externalities of alienation" that result from inequality, see Kurt Vonnegut's story "Harrison Bergeron" in *Welcome to the Monkey House* 7 (New York: Delacorte Press, 1968), in which George Bergeron, whose "intelligence was way above normal, had a little mental handicap radio in his ear. He was required by law to wear it at all times. It was tuned to a government transmitter. Every twenty seconds or so, the transmitter would send out some sharp noise to keep people like George from taking unfair advantage of their brains."

2. Freeman notes that many Americans do not in fact have privacy, autonomy, liberty, and freedom to choose, even if they have formal rights to such freedoms. Would the number of Americans actually enjoying such rights increase or decrease given Freeman's vision of a highly interventionist state that would restrict the choices of the dominant class? Have countries that have tried such programs prospered? Freeman calls for steeply progressive taxation and radical redistributions of wealth to promote racial equality. Would these measures be successful? What costs would they impose on society?

3. In an earlier article, Freeman attacked the tendency of antidiscrimination laws to limit racial preferences favoring blacks to cases of obvious individual fault:

> The fault concept gives rise to a complacency about one's own moral status; it creates a class of "innocents," who need not feel any personal responsibility for the conditions associated with discrimination, and who therefore feel great resentment when called upon to bear any burdens in connection with remedying violations. This resentment accounts for much of the ferocity surrounding the debate about so-called "reverse" discrimination, for being called on to bear burdens ordinarily imposed only upon the guilty involves an apparently unjustified stigmatization of those led by the fault notion to believe in their own innocence.

Freeman, "Legitimating Racial Discrimination through Antidiscrimination Law: A Critical Review of Supreme Court Doctrine," 62 *Minnesota Law Review* 1049, 1055 (1978). Who is personally responsible for the "conditions associated with discrimination?"

4. Thomas Sowell argues in *Race and Culture: A World View* (New York: Basic Books, 1994) that a group's economic success is primarily the product of long-standing, deeply rooted cultural patterns. These patterns of culturally driven economic success or failure are not significantly affected by discriminatory attitudes, nor are they readily influenced by governmental intervention. Is Sowell's view consistent with the evidence presented by George Borjas that blacks suddenly started a process of economic advance (relative to whites) sometime after World War II? (See note 4 in section 3.2 of this chapter.) Was there a sudden shift in black culture that spurred this economic success? For the view that governmental antidiscrimination and affirmative action efforts improved black economic welfare starting in 1965, see the selection by John Donohue and James Heckman in Chapter 8.

Crenshaw criticizes Sowell's view that culture, rather than race, can explain the difficult economic circumstances of most black Americans. She states that black culture has been shaped by centuries of black oppression, so that racism is the problem in either event. Gunnar Myrdal similarly saw black culture as the product of social pathology, for which he was sharply criticized by Ralph Ellison for failing to recognize that black culture represented an authentic and conscious adoption of different values. Ellison, "An American Dilemma: A Review," in *Shadow and Act* 303 (New York: Random

House, 1964). Does Ellison's criticism of Myrdal as a scholar clinging "to the sterile concept of 'race' " apply with equal force to Crenshaw?

Note that the sociologist Elliot Liebow has argued against the view that the low levels of achievement of poor blacks is the product of a distinct culture of poverty. Liebow, *Tally's Corner: A Study of Negro Streetcorner Men* (Boston: Little, Brown, 1967). Writing prior to the passage of the 1964 Civil Rights Act, Liebow asserted that the "inability of the Negro man to earn a living and support his family [is] the central fact of lower-class Negro life." "If there is to be a change in this way of life, this central fact must be changed; the Negro man, along with everyone else, must be given the skills to earn a living and an opportunity to put these skills to work." Id. at 224. Liebow was convinced that blacks shared the goals of the larger society, and that those lower-class blacks who appeared to reject these goals did so only to conceal their inability to achieve them.

5. After articulating the equal treatment—equal outcome dichotomy in antidiscrimination law, Owen Fiss concludes that equal treatment is what the federal law of employment discrimination commands. In contrast, Freeman and Crenshaw argue forcefully that equal achievement must be the goal of Title VII if we are to eradicate the effects of racial oppression. While the text of the statute is not dispositive, the congressional debates over Title VII strongly suggest that equal treatment was in fact the goal of Title VII. It seems highly unlikely that a congressional guarantee of equal outcomes could have passed in 1964, or any time since. For evidence on the public opposition to affirmative action, see note 6 in section 3.2 of this chapter. Even though there is ambiguity in the meaning of a legislative command not to discriminate, is there uncertainty concerning the intent of the supporters of Title VII in 1964? Is there uncertainty about what the legislature would do today if it were forced to resolve the textual indeterminacy?

According to Christine Jolls, important aspects of disparate impact liability under Title VII are not premised on a principle of equal treatment; rather, they are accommodation mandates that require employers to incur special costs to meet distinctive needs of certain groups. Such mandates can apply regardless of whether an employer has treated a protected group with discriminatory intent. Jolls, "Antidiscrimination and Accommodation," 115 *Harvard Law Review* 642 (2001). Based on this view, is disparate impact liability in conflict with the likely congressional intent to require only equal treatment (not equal achievement) in enacting Title VII?

6. Of course, a discussion about the correct interpretation of a statute says nothing about the entirely distinct question of whether the law should be based on some larger conception of social welfare. Here Freeman and Crenshaw are on much stronger ground in saying that until there is far greater equality of outcome, the problem of racial conflict and tension in America will continue to be a divisive and corrosive issue. But would a more radical interpretation of Title VII be able to achieve far greater equality? At what cost? Would racial harmony be enhanced? If Congress will not act, is it permissible for the Court to do so?

3.2   Affirmative Action

Affirmative Action and Racial Discrimination Under Law: A Preliminary Review*

WILLIAM W. VAN ALSTYNE

The purpose of this paper is to identify the several usages of "affirmative action" that can be distinguished in our conduct and in our laws. It is also to disentangle varieties of affirmative action that do not encourage or require racial discrimination from those that do.

The latter kinds of action, although not now regarded as unconstitutional, nonetheless tend to divide ... the people of the United States. The former are, in contrast, overwhelmingly ameliorative and vastly more in keeping with our mutual commitment to equal protection under law. The dividing line between them is that the object of appropriate affirmative action is to protect every person from racial discrimination even while expanding opportunities, whereas the object of inappropriate programs is to determine each person's civil rights, either in whole or in part, by race. To be sure, this too is sometimes also called affirmative action. But for reasons that will become clear during the course of this review, I do not believe the description to be warranted....

My [position] is that affirmative action is generally welcome while racial discrimination is never welcome....

There are, in fact, not less than four distinct usages of affirmative action that do not involve racial discrimination. We may understand each and distinguish each from that which involves racial discrimination, in the following way:

The most obvious use of affirmative action is nontechnical and purely personal. It is not enmeshed in legal structures or even in constitutional principles. It is, rather, fundamentally a matter of attitude and of character. It is a personal disposition to think well of people, to welcome their company, and to treat each as their own person "unjudged" by race.

Affirmative action, in this sense, is Kantian. It is a way of living as well as of teaching, by personal example. It acts out one's belief that individuals are not merely social means; i.e., they are *not* merely examples of a group, representatives of a cohort, or fungible surrogates of other human beings; each, rather, is a person whom it is improper to count or to discount by race. The friendship of a person should not be less valued than another because of race, for it is not friendship at all if,

---

* Excerpts from William W. Van Alstyne, "Affirmative Action and Racial Discrimination under Law: A Preliminary Review," *Selected Affirmative Action Topics in Employment and Business Set-asides*, vol. 1, copyright © 1985. Reprinted with permission of the author and publishers.

indeed, race provides its contingency. A brightness with numbers or an athletic grace the rest of us lack are talents by which we are all, nonetheless, enriched. We impoverish ourselves and we cheat the human beings whom we refuse equally to admire when we measure these things only more or less, depending upon who has them, by what race they are. Affirmative action is, thus, the antithesis of schemes that sponsor race ways. Affirmative people do not, in fact, share race ways of thinking or race ways of acting. Genuine affirmative action internalizes and enacts a personal resolve and a personal attitude. It measures no one person by race, and it is appalled by a government that does....

Affirmative action of this sort is, of course, frequently difficult. One's society and its laws may make race count. They may insist that race be used, one way or another, but used nonetheless. A resolve not to do so either disables one from work in any environment where those racial decrees must be obeyed, or puts one at risk (insofar as one explicitly refuses those racial decrees), or presses one into covert violations of the law such that one feels oneself a hypocrite.

Whether the particular racial decree is one from South Africa, forbidding a person from using a black contractor unless no white contractor applies, or a decree from the United States, with its opposite racially ordered preference, the difficulty for the affirmative individual is the same: to quit the field thus occupied by a race law; to act out your unwillingness to yield regardless of what others may do and the penalties that you will be subject to; or to dissemble by pretending to comply while, in fact, not complying. Which course each of us pursues necessarily tells us something crucial about ourselves—how much we are committed to affirmative action and how much we care.

Each society that gives us only these choices, however, and sets its own laws against the freedom to banish racism and racial ordering from our own lives, has also said something crucial about itself as well—whether in South Africa or in the United States. It says it does *not* want affirmative action. What it wants is racial discrimination. Currently, the laws of the United States both require and encourage a considerable amount of racial discrimination....

In an additional and equally correct usage, however, affirmative action may go beyond the definition respecting personal conduct. Rather, it may also extend to taking special steps (i.e., affirmative steps) to ensure that discrimination does *not* occur within an enterprise that is subject to one's own power of management and control. These measures are taken to show that you mean what you say. A merely literal application of the original Executive Order 11246 ... provides an excellent illustration.

The order requires of each contractor an assurance that the contractor will engage in *no* racial discrimination and that the contractor will, moreover, take meaningful affirmative action to ensure that such discrimination does not occur. Note exactly what is required and note how the phrase "affirmative action" is used:

> The contractor will not discriminate against *any* employee or applicant for employment because of race, color, religion, sex, or national origin. The contractor will take *affirmative action* to ensure that applicants are employed, and that employees are treated during employment, *without* regard to their race, color, religion, sex or national origin. [Emphasis added.]

These steps are "race conscious" in the specific sense of steps that are taken from a consciousness that racial discrimination might otherwise occur and yet go undetected and/or uncorrected. These affirmative actions, moreover, may be quite expensive. And none is required, strictly speaking, by a standard of nondiscrimination, as such. Examples include such decisions as: to provide special personnel to whom complaints of suspected discrimination may be carried; to provide also for the posting of admonitory notices regarding civil rights laws and the wrongfulness of discrimination, inclusive of information respecting modes of redress individuals are advised are available to them; to make provision for records to be maintained in the employment office and elsewhere, for periodic review to ensure that applicants and employees are, in fact, treated fairly and without discrimination—all to the end of ensuring the integrity of business practices from the vices of racial discrimination.

This is affirmative action (i.e., action of a positive character, discriminating against none, dispreferring no one, involving neither quotas nor queues nor targets nor presumptions of what is the "right" mix or "proper" share of each according to race). It has nothing to do with such a philosophy and, indeed, represents quite the opposite of that philosophy. It seeks the better protection of *each* person from racial discrimination that might otherwise occur, whether in a white-owned enterprise against blacks, in a black-owned enterprise against whites, or whatever. It takes a strong national policy seriously. It is action undertaken consciously (and sometimes at considerable expense) to vindicate more effectively a commitment opposed to racial discrimination in *all* its forms.

Affirmative action to avoid *gratuitous* discrimination is related to affirmative action of the kind just described, but it goes considerably further than even a scrupulous resolve to prevent discrimination. Even so, it, too, is wholly consistent with a common resolve to make no disadvantaging use of *any* person's race. Rather, its aim is the removal of gratuitous barriers to each person's opportunity to be treated the same as others, without fear or favor of their being white or black, Hispanic or Oriental, or however the charts of racism would seek to identify people and allocate racial shares by racism's ingenious and derogatory indexes.

Gratuitous discrimination is that which occurs *not* by design, but indeed quite contrary to one's best resolve. Rather, it is the unintended consequence of unexamined practices or habits that create unnecessary headwinds or hardships. It is the tendency of habit or custom to assume the need or appropriateness of certain things without realizing that: (a) these things may, in fact, be quite unnecessary (i.e., they are gratuitous); and (b) they, nonetheless, do not even affect everyone similarly. They ought, therefore, to be reexamined to determine whether they might be abandoned or changed. The process that pursues this course is itself one of affirmative action—action undertaken to reduce gratuitous differential treatment of persons not necessary to distinguish in the manner one's customary practice did distinguish them. One acts affirmatively by being sensitive to this possibility, and by acting affirmatively to avoid it.

. . .

In respect to affirmative action and race, one portion of Title VII . . . forbids ways of classifying applicants or employees that tend to affect their chances although not meant to do so. The law imposes an obligation to review employment criteria to take care that they are, in fact, job related (rather than the mere residue of custom or habit, like unnecessary curbs obstructing sidewalk access). It may also reach customs of advertising and job notices, to take care that able people are not overlooked by the limits of one's rather narrow recruiting patterns, as relying solely on a union hiring hall.

The *extent* to which this kind of affirmative action is required, on the other hand, is genuinely controversial. It is controversial at whatever point it becomes questionable as to whether the practice in question is gratuitous. The easiest cases are not numerous. It is hardly surprising that this is so, for ordinarily the exigencies of competition will discipline an employer who is inattentive to the actual relevance of employment criteria. Whenever the cost of altering the business practice will be less than the gain in production resulting from the change, the resulting economic advantage will compel the change under genuinely competitive circumstances. The harder cases raise substantial questions, e.g., how great an expense is it reasonable to assume to change from one practice to another when the former practice may, in fact, have been reasonably efficient and the new one, moreover, may produce very little gain in expanded chances for additional persons? The extent to which a demonstration of job necessity may be demanded may, in fact, simply drive the person on whom it is imposed into a practice of racial discrimination in order to forestall the demand itself.[1] He or she may be, thus, furtively directed to do whatever appears necessary to generate the right num-

---

1. In fact, it may operate with the reprehensible consequence of compounding racial discrimination. *See, e.g.,* Connecticut v. Teal, . . . (acts of gratuitous discrimination against some persons were sought to be offset by the employer by acts of outright discrimination against other persons, and then defended on the grounds that the overall resulting work force was of approximately the same racial mix as it would have been in the absence of any discrimination of either kind). The *Teal* case is of pivotal importance. . . . It rejects the view that an individual's personal opportunities may be measured by race, i.e., that an individual may be discriminated against because of that person's race so long as the racial group has been granted its fair share as a racial group. . . .

bers, including racial discrimination against others, in order to avoid the threat of suit by the EEOC or by others concerned only to secure better racial results. There is no doubt that such actions themselves violate Title VII.

But in the clear case, there is surely nothing objectionable to this form of affirmative action and, indeed, there is much to commend it. The elimination of gratuitous barriers to equal opportunity disadvantages no one by race. It is conscious of those whom it will benefit, and conscientious of those with whom they are then treated identically, without indexing or allocating by the quotas or stratagems of racism.

A fourth form of affirmative action is similarly race conscious as were the two forms just examined. But, like them, it too never asks persons their race and never measures what they receive according to the answer they are invited or required to furnish.

This species of affirmative action operates at a political level of social choice. Specifically, it selects a preferred program partly in anticipation of those expected to benefit disproportionately by race. It measures the comparative worth of one program as more urgent than another partly because of the comparatively greater racial group advantage some programs will provide vis-a-vis other programs. Even so, whatever the program, it never divides by race those otherwise eligible for benefits or participation. It establishes no racial classifications of any kind. Its administration never, therefore, seeks to treat one person as less deserving than another, or less desirable than another, as racism is wont to do.

This form of affirmative action is, however, also quite distinct from those we have already examined. Unlike either of them, it goes substantially beyond (a) providing substance and enforcement to a clear policy that forbids racial discrimination, and (b) removing all gratuitous barriers or inadvertently created headwinds. Rather, it deliberately makes choices based partly on what proportion of persons most immediately eligible for (or benefiting from) a proposal are likely to be black (or Hispanic or Native Americans, etc.), and elects the program thought most likely and most appropriate to do greater good according to this deliberately *racial* preference. A single example may be helpful to illustrate the general idea.

A municipality may consider itself as having a budget choice between $1 million for downtown street improvements or $1 million for the improvement of the public library's reading program. It may be obvious in a given circumstance, moreover, that given the location of the library, a larger proportion (and/or number) of the community's black population than of its white population may take advantage of the proposed library program. The decision to fund the reading program may be preferred to the decision to spruce up the downtown area. It may even be thought to constitute the better choice partly because of (rather than despite or with indifference to) the likely racial characteristic of many, perhaps most, who may use it. It is thus, in fact, at least partly a racially driven choice. It is regarded as affirmative action, nonetheless, for although it was done to advance the quality of life principally for black residents (because they are expected to be its principal users and because the decision was made in anticipation of that fact), it does not tolerate any discrimination in its operation or execution. Under no circumstances would any *further* use of race be involved. Under no circumstances, for instance, would one issue black and white cards, reserving all books on call for a white only if no black wants it, or allocating enrollment in reading classes by racial share (such that one becomes "ineligible by race" if one's racial share has already been "subscribed"), or the like.

This species of affirmative action is tremendously sensitive, despite what might appear to be the modest and uncontroversial example I have just provided. In its favor, there are the two obvious and strong features: (a) It is well designed to be of significant benefit (indeed, even of disproportionate benefit) to ethnic minority families; and (b) it nonetheless does not involve any racial discrimination in its operations—the books and the reading program are made a part of the public library which does not measure eligibility by race. Rather, it operates as always, with no race cards, no race quotas, no race preferences of any kind. . . .

Despite these strong and genuinely compelling features, this form of affirmative action can raise troubling questions. The difficulty can be seen merely in considering two variations on the example already provided. In the case we have supposed, the alternative object for the $1 million expenditure was for downtown street improvements. In a given community, such an expenditure might be seen as much more beneficial to whites than to blacks, perhaps even disproportionately beneficial to them. It might be seen as such, for instance, if the majority of business establishments likely to benefit from the street improvements are predominantly white-owned establishments. Similarly, if disproportionately more whites than blacks tend to frequent the city's business center rather than the library, which is mostly used only by blacks, spending for such street improvements as make their activities easier might well be seen for that reason as the better choice than to spend the same sum on library improvements unlikely to benefit whites so favorably.

Yet, as a matter of constitutional law, if it could be shown that the street improvement plan was approved in order to benefit whites disproportionately and that the library expenditure would have been approved instead but for the city council's preference solely for white-favoring expenditures, a Federal court injunction may be secured against this race-driven preference, and rightly so. Where such a race-favoring effect is not simply the indifferent consequence of the action, but is rather the very reason why the action was taken and why alternative proposals were rejected, it may properly be enjoined under 42 U.S.C. 4057 1983. . . . The taint is in the racially driven motivation of the city council's social preference plus the sought-after, disparate impact of its action. Its problem is that it embraces a view of the political process that the 14th amendment does not countenance, namely, that political control properly entitles one to use that control as a racial spoils system. The 14th amendment meant to drive out, rather than to entrench, such uses of public and governmental power.

Presumably the same conclusion would follow equally if a library expenditure were favored over downtown street improvements, assuming the decision were, nonetheless, made on the same improper basis—that the location of the library indicates predominantly white library traffic so that white interests will be preferred over street improvements less helpful to whites albeit more helpful to blacks.

If this is correct, however, then the original affirmative action case also rests less comfortably as well. The implicit assumption in affirmative action of this sort is that it is merely appropriate for government to acknowledge the special circumstances of ethnic minorities, at least in its selection of social priorities and programs and expenditures. Thus, *at least insofar as the programs themselves involve no racial discrimination in their administration,* a compassionate resolve to grant priority to such expenditures precisely because they will be of disproportionate assistance to ethnic minority groups must surely be an acceptable form of affirmative action.

There is, nonetheless, considerable naivete to this view, despite its obvious force. It assumes that the determination of social preference on racial grounds, so long as it is racially minority favoring, rather than racially majority favoring, will be wholly ameliorative and healing. It assumes also that the vast majority of uses to be made of such affirmative action will tend principally to benefit underprivileged persons in general, and not merely certain politically favored, racially dominant segments within a given community. It is unclear that either of these outcomes is necessarily the case, however, because we cannot deceive ourselves into thinking these sort of decisions are right or lawful only when undertaken unselfishly (i.e., only when undertaken by allegedly benign majorities attempting thus to offset such abuses of power as may have occurred in the past). The problem is that there is nothing inherent in the mechanism we have been reviewing to keep it harmless, from extremely selfish and altogether racially meanminded capture and use.

As a logical and political proposition, what we affirm here as a general proposition can scarcely be denied the very first moment new black majorities and/or other purely self-serving ethnic coalitions suddenly capture urban government and at once resolve to vote for nothing not emphatically conducive solely to their own racially targeted self-interests. Yet, it is surely doubtful whether such varieties of racial spoils are rightly described as affirmative action. And it is surely odd, is it not, to hold that the 14th amendment flatly forbids controlling white majorities to enact only disproportionately white-favoring regulations or expenditures, but to see no equivalent constitutional wrong in permitting or even encouraging precisely such racist exercise of power by others. Whatever its virtues, then, what we have been discussing is probably not a proposal that is, in fact, a proper feature of a mature and compassionate community. That such communities should be attentive to the less fortunate regardless of race and that they should act affirmatively in selecting among priorities those particularly helpful to disadvantaged neighborhoods or families is entirely unobjectionable. But that they should instead sedulously cultivate the different question (Who will racially benefit?) is emphatically not affirmative action at all. The resulting demoralization, polarization, bitterness, fight, and intrinsic race hatreds that must come under these new circumstances are all obvious. The reintroduction of fears and of anxieties, to think in terms of "us" (racially) and of "them" (racially), is altogether predictable.…

Before stating a fifth kind of affirmative action, it may be useful very briefly to recapitulate the four kinds we have already reviewed. The reason for doing so is principally for clarity. The four we have briefly reviewed were these:

1. Acting affirmatively toward each human being as a person and as an individual entitled to one's regard unbounded by his or her race.

2. Acting affirmatively to ensure that racial discrimination does not occur anywhere within one's field of control.

3. Acting additionally to eliminate gratuitous obstructions otherwise tending to limit each person's eligibility or opportunities.

4. Electing among alternative nondiscriminatory political choices those likely to be of most significant use to ethnic minority persons.

A fifth thing is also called affirmative action, but in my view it is not—not affirmative action at all. On occasion, it is also called reverse discrimination, but it is not that either. These are but euphemisms for a new racial order. They are today's demagogic terminology for an acceptable legal order of direct racial discrimination.

Racial discrimination consists of indexing individuals by race and then measuring their civil rights according to that racial index. In the simplest terms, it is the practice of requiring each person to be identified racially, precisely for the purpose of distinguishing that person's civil rights from those of others.

The distinction may be in respect to whom one may marry. It may as readily be the determination of the life insurance premium one must pay, different from the premium charged others. The distinction may be in respect of the school to which one is assigned. It may as readily be the determination of job eligibility. The distinction may be in bidding on government contracts, or in the determination of one's eligibility for housing. It could be in determining which military unit one serves with, or it might as well be in determining in which ballot box one's vote shall be placed, whether one is subject to a curfew, or whether one is admitted to a Head Start program, a medical school, or, for that matter, a concentration camp, or a cemetery. As such, racial discrimination is indifferent to its own uses, how it is used, or whom it hurts or helps. Irrespective of those considerations, it has one persistent, ineradicable, and essential characteristic: It assigns a person's race, and it makes each such person's civil rights differ in some respect from those of others according to that assignment. . . .

. . .

Racial discrimination that the government currently requires or encourages (one need not say "or," however, since the government does both), it accordingly wants desperately to describe as affirmative action in order to give a bad thing a good name. It indexes people according to racial categories and allocates to them different civil rights by their race. It adopts quotas; it prescribes queues; it provides set-asides; it designates targets, goals, subsidies, and guidelines by race, deliberately and willfully prescriptive of racial discrimination. In its own practices, it inquires about one's race and computes one's civil rights by a racial index. In its regulatory capacity, it requires others to demand racial identification and demands that one's racial identity be used to fix a different set of rights than others are to have. . . .

The vision of a new racial order, to each according to his race, is thus fast upon us. . . . And it is so obvious to anyone that these incessant varieties of racial discrimination are fundamentally not desired by the vast majority of Americans as to make one tremendously angry with a government that will not stop its own weaknesses. . . .

Persuasion and Distrust: A Comment on the Affirmative Action Debate*

RANDALL KENNEDY

The controversy over affirmative action constitutes the most salient current battlefront in the ongoing conflict over the status of the Negro in American life. . . .

Opponents of affirmative action maintain that commitment to a nonracist social environment requires strict color-blindness in decision-making as both a strategy and a goal. In their view, "one gets beyond racism by getting beyond it now: by a complete, resolute, and credible commitment *never* to tolerate in one's own life—or in the life or practices of one's government—the differential treatment of other hu-

* Excerpts from Randall Kennedy, "Persuasion and Distrust: A Comment on the Affirmative Action Debate," *Harvard Law Review,* vol. 99, copyright © 1986. Reprinted by permission of the author and publisher.

man beings by race." Proponents of affirmative action insist that only *malign* racial distinctions should be prohibited, they favor *benign* distinctions that favor blacks. Their view is that "[i]n order to get beyond racism, we must first take race into account" and that "in order to treat some persons equally, we must treat them differently." ...

The Efficacy and Lawfulness of Affirmative Action

. . .

The Claim That Affirmative Action Harms Blacks

In the face of arguments in favor of affirmative action, opponents of the policy frequently reply that it actually harms its ostensible beneficiaries. Various interrelated claims undergird the argument that affirmative action is detrimental to the Negro. The most weighty claim is that preferential treatment exacerbates racial resentments, entrenches racial divisiveness, and thereby undermines the consensus necessary for effective reform. The problem with this view is that intense white resentment has accompanied every effort to undo racial subordination no matter how careful the attempt to anticipate and modify the reaction. The Supreme Court, for example, tried mightily to preempt white resistance to school desegregation by directing that it be implemented with "all deliberate speed." This attempt, however, to defuse white resistance may well have caused the opposite effect and, in any event, doomed from the outset the constitutional rights of a generation of black school children. Given the apparent inevitability of white resistance and the uncertain efficacy of containment, proponents of racial justice should be wary of allowing fear of white backlash to limit the range of reforms pursued. This admonition is particularly appropriate with respect to affirmative action insofar as it creates vital opportunities the value of which likely outweigh their cost in social friction. A second part of the argument that affirmative action hurts blacks is the claim that it stigmatizes them by implying that they simply cannot compete on an equal basis with whites.... I do not doubt that affirmative action causes some stigmatizing effect. It is unrealistic to think, however, that affirmative action causes most white disparagement of the abilities of blacks. Such disparagement, buttressed for decades by the rigid exclusion of blacks from educational and employment opportunities, is precisely what engendered the explosive crisis to which affirmative action is a response. Although it is widely assumed that "qualified" blacks are now in great demand, with virtually unlimited possibilities for recognition, blacks continue to encounter prejudice that ignores or minimizes their talent. In the end, the uncertain extent to which affirmative action diminishes the accomplishments of blacks must be balanced against the stigmatization that occurs when blacks are virtually absent from important institutions in the society....

A third part of the argument against affirmative action is the claim that it saps the internal morale of blacks. It renders them vulnerable in a dispiriting anxiety that they have not truly earned whatever positions or honors they have attained. . . .

[B]lack beneficiaries do not see their attainments as tainted or undeserved—and for good reason. First, they correctly view affirmative action as rather modest compensation for the long period of racial subordination suffered by blacks as a group. Thus they do not feel that they have been merely *given* a preference; rather, they see affirmative discrimination as a form of social justice. Second, and more importantly, many black beneficiaries of affirmative action view claims of meritocracy with skepticism. . . . Overt exclusion of blacks from public and private institutions of education and employment was one massive affront to meritocratic pretensions. . . .

Finally, and most importantly, many beneficiaries of affirmative action recognize the thoroughly political—which is to say contestable— nature of "merit"; they realize that it is a malleable concept, determined not by immanent, preexisting standards but rather by the perceived needs of society. Inasmuch as the elevation of blacks addresses pressing social needs, they rightly insist that considering a black's race as part of the bundle of traits that constitute "merit" is entirely appropriate.

A final and related objection to affirmative action is that it frequently aids those blacks who need it least and who can least plausibly claim to suffer the vestiges of past discrimination—the offspring of black middle-class parents seeking preferential treatment in admission to elite universities and black entrepreneurs seeking guaranteed set-asides for minority contractors on projects supported by the federal government. This objection too is unpersuasive. First, it ignores the large extent to which affirmative action has pried open opportunities for blue-collar black workers. Second, it assumes that affirmative action should be provided only to the most deprived strata of the black community or to those who can best document their victimization. In many circumstances, however, affirmative action has developed from the premise that special aid should be given to strategically important sectors of the black community—for example, those with the threshold ability to integrate the professions. Third, although affirmative action has primarily benefitted the black middle class, that is no reason to condemn preferential treatment. All that fact indicates is the necessity for additional social intervention to address unmet needs in those sectors of the black community left untouched by affirmative action. . . .

Does Affirmative Action Violate the Constitution?

The constitutional argument against affirmative action proceeds as follows: *All* governmental distinctions based on race are presumed to be illegal and can only escape that presumption by meeting the exacting requirements of "strict scrutiny." Because the typical affirmative action program cannot meet these requirements, most such programs are unconstitutional. Behind this theory lies a conviction that has attained its most passionate and oft-quoted articulation in Alexander Bickel's statement:

> The lesson of the great decisions of the Supreme Court and the lesson of contemporary history have been the same for at least a generation: discrimination on the basis of race is illegal, immoral, unconstitutional, inherently wrong, and destructive of democratic society. Now this is to be unlearned and we are told that this is not a matter of fundamental principle but only a matter of whose ox is gored.

.   .   .

Professor Bickel suggests that a proper resolution of the affirmative action dispute can be derived from "the great decisions of the Supreme Court." Certainly what Bickel had in mind were *Brown v. Board of Education* and its immediate progeny, the cases that established the foundation of our post-segregation Constitution. To opponents of affirmative action, the lesson of these cases is that, except in the narrowest, most exigent circumstances, race can play no legitimate role in governmental decisionmaking.

This view, however, is too abstract and ahistorical. In the forties, fifties and early sixties, against the backdrop of laws that used racial distinctions to exclude Negroes from opportunities available to white citizens, it seemed that racial subjugation could be overcome by mandating the application of race-blind laws. In retrospect, however, it appears that the concept of race-blindness was simply a proxy for the fundamental demand that racial subjugation be eradicated. This demand, which matured over time in the face of myriad sorts of opposition, focused upon the *condition* of racial subjugation; its target was not only procedures that overtly excluded Negroes on the basis of race, but also the self-perpetuating dynamics of subordination that had survived the demise of American apartheid. The opponents of affirmative action have stripped the historical context from the demand for race-blind law. They have fashioned this demand into a new totem and insist on deference to it no matter what its effects upon the very group the fourteenth amendment was created to protect. *Brown* and its progeny do not stand for the abstract principle that governmental distinctions based on race are unconstitutional. Rather, those great cases, forged by the gritty particularities of the struggle against white racism, stand for the proposition that the Constitution prohibits any arrangements imposing racial subjugation—whether such arrangements are ostensibly race-neutral or even ostensibly race-blind.

This interpretation, which articulates a principle of antisubjugation rather than antidiscrimination, typically encounters two closely related objections. The first objection is the claim that the constitutional injury done to a white whose chances for obtaining some scarce opportunity are diminished because of race-based allocation schemes is legally indistinguishable from that suffered by a black victim of racial exclusion. Second, others argue that affirmative discrimination based on racial distinctions cannot be satisfactorily differentiated from racial subjugation absent controversial sociological judgments that are inappropriate to the judicial role.

As in the first objection, the injury suffered by white "victims" of affirmative action does not properly give rise to a constitutional claim, because the damage does not derive from a scheme animated by racial prejudice....

As to the second objection, I concede that distinctions between affirmative and malign discrimination cannot be made in the absence of controversial sociological judgments. I reject the proposition, however, that drawing these distinctions is inappropriate to the judicial role. Such a proposition rests upon the assumption that there exists a judicial method wholly independent of sociological judgment. That assumption is false; to some extent, whether explicitly or implicitly, *every* judicial decision rests upon certain premises regarding the irreducibly controversial nature of social reality. The question, therefore, is not whether a court will make sociological judgments, but the content of the sociological judgments it must inevitably make.

·   ·   ·

The Question of Racism

The Need for Motive Analysis

·   ·   ·

... Whether racism is partly responsible for the growing opposition to affirmative action is a question that is virtually absent from many of the leading articles on the subject. These articles typically portray the conflict over affirmative action as occurring in the context of an overriding commitment to racial fairness and equality shared by *all* the important participants in the debate.... This portrait, however, of conflict-within-consensus is all too genial.... It obscures the emotions that color the affirmative action debate and underestimates the alienation that separates antagonists. It ignores those who believe that much of the campaign against affirmative action is merely the latest in a long series of white reactions against efforts to elevate the status of the Negro in American society....

The conventional portrait also implicitly excludes from consideration those whose opposition to affirmative action stems from racism. It concedes the presence of prejudice "out there" in the workaday world of ordinary citizens. But it assumes that "in here"—in the realm of scholarly discourse and the creation of public policy—prejudice plays no role....

Why have scholars consistently avoided scrutinizing the motives of policymakers and fellow commentators? ... One objection centers on the evidentiary difficulties involved in ascertaining someone's motives. If the devil himself knoweth not the mind of man, how can mortal commentators know the motivation of officials and fellow analysts? A second objection is that the cost of the inquiry, including the inevitable possibility of error, outweighs any gains. A third objection is that, whatever the propriety of motive review in adjudication, it is an improper mode of analysis within intellectual discourse because it strongly tends toward ad hominem attacks on honesty that are impossible to disprove.... A fourth objection is that motive-centered inquiries are irrelevant: after all, a policy stemming from bad motives can nevertheless turn out to be a positive contribution to the public good, fully justifiable on the basis of sound reasons unrelated to covert and evil motives.

These objections serve a useful cautionary function. They fail, however, to show that motive analysis is misplaced in intellectual discussion and policy analysis. First, awkward problems in assembling evidence regarding the suspected objectives of a scholar or public official need not justify a wholesale rejection of the inquiry. Such problems merely indicate that a motive-centered analysis is difficult—not that it is improper or unfruitful. Second, although motive analysis does entail the possibility that a person or institution may be wrongly accused of harboring racist sentiments, forgoing such inquiry also imposes a high cost: loss of information regarding the nature of our society....

Third, the danger that concern with motive will overshadow attentiveness to ideas is simply another of the many dangers of excess that adhere to *any* methodology. The proper reaction is not wholesale rejection, but rather a disciplined use of the methodology that is informed by the limits of any one particular line of inquiry. Finally, to suggest that a policy is completely distinct from the motive from which it arises simply distorts reality. The animating motive is an integral aspect of the context in which a policy emerges, and there is no such thing as a policy without a context.

Affirmative Action as a Majoritarian Device: Or, Do You Really Want to Be a Role Model?*
RICHARD DELGADO

. . .

The Affirmative Action Mystique: Let the Bandwagon Roll Right On

Scholars of color have grown increasingly skeptical about both the way in which affirmative action frames the issue of minority representation

* Excerpts from Richard Delgado, "Affirmative Action as a Majoritarian Device: Or, Do You Really Want to be a Role Model?" *Michigan Law Review*, vol. 89, copyright © 1991. Reprinted by permission of the author and publisher.

and the effects that it produces in the world. Affirmative action, I have noticed, generally frames the question of minority representation in an interesting way: Should we as a society admit, hire, appoint, or promote some designated number of people of color in order to promote certain policy goals, such as social stability, an expanded labor force, and an integrated society? These goals are always forward-looking; affirmative action is viewed as an instrumental device for moving society from state *A* to state *B*. The concept is neither backward-looking nor rooted in history; it is teleological rather than deonto-logical. Minorities are hired or promoted not because we have been unfairly treated, denied jobs, deprived of our lands, or beaten and brought here in chains. Affirmative action neatly diverts our attention from all those disagreeable details and calls for a fresh start. Well, where are we now? So many Chicano bankers and chief executive officers, so many black lawyers, so many Native American engineers, and so many women physicians. What can we do to increase these numbers over the next ten or twenty years? The system thus bases inclusion of people of color on principles of social utility, not reparations or *rights*. When those in power decide the goal has been accomplished, or is incapable of being reached, what logically happens? Naturally, the program stops. At best, then, affirmative action serves as a homeostatic device, assuring that only a small number of women and people of color are hired or promoted. Not too many, for that would be terrifying, nor too few, for that would be destabilizing. Just the right small number, generally those of us who need it least, are moved ahead.

Affirmative action also neatly frames the issue so that even these small accomplishments seem troublesome, requiring great agonizing and gnashing of teeth. Liberals and moderates lie awake at night, asking how far they can take this affirmative action thing without sacrificing innocent white males. Have you ever wondered what that makes *us*—if not innocent, then ... ? Affirmative action enables members of the dominant group to ask, "Is it fair to hire a less-qualified Chicano or black over a more-qualified white?" This is a curious way of framing the question, as I will argue in a moment, in part because those who ask it are themselves the beneficiaries of history's largest affirmative action program. This fact is rarely noticed, however, while the question goes on causing the few of us who are magically raised by affirmative action's unseen hand to feel guilty, undeserving, and *stigmatized*.

Affirmative action, as currently understood and promoted, is also ahistorical. For more than 200 years, white males benefited from their own program of affirmative action, through unjustified preferences in jobs and education resulting from old-boy networks and official laws that lessened the competition. Today's affirmative action critics never characterize that scheme as affirmative action, which of course it was. By labeling problematic, troublesome, and ethically agonizing a paltry system that helps a few of us get ahead, critics neatly take our eyes off the system of arrangements that brought and maintained them in power, and enabled them to develop the rules and standards of quality and merit that now exclude us, make us appear unworthy, dependent (naturally) on affirmative action. . . . We should reformulate the issue. Our acquiescence in treating it as "a question of standards" is absurd and self-defeating when you consider that we took no part in creating those standards and their fairness is one of the very things we want to call into question.

Affirmative action, then, is something no self-respecting attorney of color ought to support. We could, of course, take our own program, with our own goals, our own theoretical grounding, and our own managers and call it "Affirmative Action." But we would, of course, be talking about something quite different. My first point, then, is that we should demystify, interrogate, and destabilize affirmative action. The program was designed by others to promote their purposes, not ours.

The Role Model Argument

In this Part, I address an aspect of affirmative action mythology, the role model argument, that in my opinion has received less criticism than it deserves. This argument is a special favorite of moderate liberals, who regard it as virtually unassailable. Although the argument's inventor is unknown, its creator must have been a member of the majority group and must have received a prize almost as large as the one awarded the person who created affirmative action itself. Like the larger program of which it is a part, the role model argument is instrumental and forward-looking. It makes us a means to another's end. A white dominated institution hires you not because you are entitled to or deserve the job. Nor is the institution seeking to set things straight because your ancestors and others of your heritage were systematically excluded from such jobs. Not at all. You're hired (if you speak politely, have a neat haircut, and, above all, can be trusted) not because of your accomplishments, but because of what others think you will do for them. If they hire you now and you are a good role model, things will be better in the next generation.

Suppose you saw a large sign saying, "ROLE MODEL WANTED. GOOD PAY. INQUIRE WITHIN." Would you apply? Let me give you five reasons you should not.

Reason Number One. Being a role model is a tough job, with long hours and much heavy lifting. You are expected to uplift your entire people. Talk about hard, sweaty work.

Reason Number Two. The job treats you as a means to an end. Even your own constituency may begin to see you this way. "Of course Tanya will agree to serve as our faculty advisor, give this speech, serve on that panel, or agree to do us *X, Y,* or *Z* favor, probably unpaid and on short notice. What is her purpose if not to serve us?''

Reason Number Three. The role model's job description is monumentally unclear.... If you are a role model, are you expected to do the same things your white counterpart does, in addition to counseling and helping out the community of color whenever something comes up? Just the latter? Half and half? Both? ...

Reason Number Four. To be a good role model, you must be an assimilationist, never a cultural or economic nationalist, separatist, radical reformer, or anything remotely resembling any of these. As with actual models (who walk down runways wearing the latest fashions), you are expected to conform to prevailing ideas of beauty, politeness, grooming, and above all responsibility. If you develop a quirk, wrinkle, aberration, or, heaven forbid, a vice, look out! ...

Reason Number Five (the most important one). The job of role model requires that you *lie*—that you tell not little, but big, whopping lies, and that is bad for your soul. Suppose I am sent to an inner city school to talk to the kids and serve as role model of the month. I am *expected* to tell the kids that if they study hard and stay out of trouble, they can become a law professor like me. That, however, is a very big lie: a whopper. When I started teaching law sixteen years ago, there were about thirty-five Hispanic law professors, approximately twenty-five of which were Chicano. Today, the numbers are only slightly improved. In the interim, however, a nearly complete turnover has occurred. The faces are new, but the numbers have remained the same from year to year. Gonzalez leaves teaching; Velasquez is hired somewhere else. Despite this, I am expected to tell forty kids in a crowded, inner city classroom that if they work hard, they can each be among the chosen twenty-five. Fortunately, most kids are smart enough to figure out that the system does not work this way. If I were honest, I would advise them to become major league baseball players, or to practice their hook shots. As Michael Olives points out, the odds, pay, and working conditions are much better in these other lines of work....

Suppose I told the ghetto kids these things, that is, the truth.... What would happen? I would quickly be labeled a poor role model and someone else sent to give the inspiring speech next month.

Why Things Are the Way They Are and What Can Be Done

The role model theory is a remarkable invention. It requires that some of us lie and that others of us be exploited and overworked. The theory is, however, highly functional for its inventors. It encourages us to cultivate nonthreatening behavior in our own people. In addition, it provides a handy justification for affirmative action, which, as I have pointed out, is at best a mixed blessing for communities of color.

As with any successful and popular program, I think we need only examine the functions served by the role model argument to see why our white friends so readily embrace it. Demographers tell us that in about ten years, Caucasians will cease to be the largest segment of California's population. In approximately sixty years, around the year 2050, the same will happen nationally. While this radical demographic shift is occurring, the population also will be aging. The baby boomers, mostly white, will be retired and dependent on social security for support. These retirees will rely on the continuing labor of a progressively smaller pyramid of active workers, an increasing proportion of them of color. You see, then, why it is essential that we imbue our next generation of children with the requisite respect for hard work. They must be taught to ask few questions, pay their taxes, and accept social obligations, even if imposed by persons who look different from them and who committed documented injustices on their ancestors.

If you want the job of passing on *that* set of attitudes to young people of color, go ahead. You will be warmly received and amply rewarded.... But to the ad, ROLE MODEL WANTED, the correct answer, in my view, is: NOT ME!

Notes and Questions

1. William Van Alstyne draws a sharp distinction between desirable affirmative action that prevents racial discrimination and undesirable racial preferences, which he considers to be wrongful discrimination, regardless of the intended beneficiary. Van Alstyne's position is consistent with the initial conception of affirmative action as used in President Kennedy's executive order calling for government contractors to take affirmative action to prevent racial discrimination in their employment practices. Is Van Alstyne concerned only with governmental conduct, as the title of his essay suggests? If so, then he would be in agreement with those, such as Richard Epstein, who contend that only governments should be prohibited from engaging in discrimination. For Epstein, malign racial discrimination or benign racial preferences are equally acceptable—as long as they are freely chosen by *private* actors.

On the other hand, many of Van Alstyne's comments about the harm of racial discrimination, and a number of his examples, seem to involve cases of private conduct. For example, he objects to the voluntarily adopted racial preference for the private job training program that the Supreme Court endorsed in *Weber*. See Chapter 4, section 4.1 for a discussion of the genesis and rationale for the affirmative action program in *Weber*. Does Van Alstyne object to this racial preference only because the government encouraged its adoption, or, unlike Epstein, would Van Alstyne think it wise to prohibit purely private acts of (benign) racial discrimination?

2. In *Connecticut v. Teal*, 457 U.S. 440 (1982), the Supreme Court explored whether the State of Connecticut violated the disparate impact doctrine of Title VII when it relied on a written test that screened out black

candidates for promotion at a disproportionately high rate, even though the entire multipart promotion process had no disparate impact on blacks. Van Alstyne embraces the Kantian aspect of this decision on the grounds that, in rejecting the bottom-line defense, the Supreme Court fostered individualized treatment of workers. Van Alstyne was concerned that the state's unintended discrimination against blacks through the use of the written test was prompting a corrective effort to discriminate in favor of blacks in the next stage of the promotion process. But as Richard Epstein has noted,

> By opening the components up to separate examination, we ... create the possibility that any multistage employee selection procedure discriminates against applicants of all groups simultaneously—the legal equivalent of squaring the circle.... Using the tests, the state made an effort to select the best candidates within the black applicant pool, to whom it then gave a systematic advantage in the rest of the selection process relative to whites. After the invalidation of the test, the employer can still obtain exactly the same ratio of blacks to whites, but average quality will be lower than when the written test was used. [*Teal*] is one of those rare decisions that should be condemned by supporters and opponents of affirmative action alike.

Epstein, *Forbidden Grounds* 227–229 (Cambridge, Mass.: Harvard University Press, 1992).

3. One of the tragic lessons of the twentieth century is that racial and ethnic tensions have an explosive character that can lead to enormous bloodshed and unspeakable cruelty. Indeed, the horrible racial, religious, and ethnic mass killings of World War II vividly confirmed this danger and proved to be a catalyst to the American civil rights movement. Employment discrimination law is one mechanism for containing the dark passions of racial hatred that always seem to be simmering in modern America. The question is whether these passions can best be dampened by maintaining a policy of pure color-blind employment practices, which reduces some of the selfish haggling and tensions of a racial spoils system, or whether the unredressed injustices of the past along with the benefits from breaking down perceived or real employment barriers counsel in favor of a policy of preferential treatment.

According to Linda Krieger, color-blindness will not adequately control intergroup bias and hostility inherent in diverse societies. Drawing on various empirical findings from social psychology (see also the excerpt from Linda Krieger in Chapter 5), she points out that because cognitive intergroup bias occurs automatically and without intention or awareness, it can be controlled only through deliberate *color-conscious* "mental correction." Thus her recommendation is to preserve affirmative action, not because it is the best policy to address problems of past and current racial discrimination, but because no other adequate alternative exists—least of all, a color-blind policy. Krieger, "Civil Rights Perestroika: Intergroup Relations after Affirmative Action," 86 *California Law Review* 1251 (1998).

Moreover, according to David Schwartz, color-blindness is not a coherent theory of antidiscrimination law because it does not correctly articulate why race discrimination is fundamentally wrong. Color-blindness, which embraces reverse discrimination and eschews affirmative action, is premised on the assumption that all differential treatments are equally wrong. In Schwartz's view, however, race discrimination is wrong not simply because it is differential treatment per se, but because it is "differential treatment that arises from, and perpetuates, a caste system, a history of oppression, or exclusion of groups based on their group characteristics." Schwartz, "The Case of the Vanishing Protected Class: Reflections on Reverse Discrimination, Affirmative Action, and Racial Balancing," 2000 *Wisconsin Law Review* 657 (2000).

4.   There can be no dispute that African Americans have been subject to appalling discrimination that was endorsed and perpetuated by racist governmental entities. This history of officially sanctioned racial oppression provides the foundation of the argument for affirmative action. Indeed, as Paul Brest and Miranda Oshige have written, "[N]o other group compares to African Americans in the confluence of the characteristics that argue for inclusion in affirmative action programs." Brest and Oshige, "Affirmative Action for Whom?" 47 *Stanford Law Review* 855 (1995). But a policy justified by an historical wrong raises the question: "How long must we give blacks preferential treatment in hiring and in education?"

To get a sense of roughly how long it will take blacks to achieve economic convergence with whites, consider the research of George Borjas, who analyzed the thirty-two national origin groups that made up the bulk of the "Great Migration" to the United States during the period 1880–1910. In 1910 there were enormous differences in literacy rates, education, and earnings among the various ethnic groups, and after three generations in the United States these differentials had narrowed considerably but had not been eliminated. Borjas finds that, on average, it takes about four generations, or about one hundred years, for the economic disadvantages of relatively deprived groups to be eliminated. Interestingly, when Borjas compared the economic status of black Americans in 1940 and 1980, he found that their pattern of economic improvement over that forty-year period was roughly similar to that experienced by the white ethnic immigrants starting in 1910. This evidence reveals that as soon as blacks were able to step on the economic escalator from which they previously had been excluded, they began to advance economically at the same rate that the ethnic immigrants of the Great Migration had advanced. But note that because the prior oppression of blacks restrained their progress, Borjas's work suggests it will take another fifty to seventy years before they achieve economic equality. Borjas, "Long–Run Convergence of Ethnic Skill Differentials: The Children and Grandchildren of the Great Migration," 47 *Industrial and Labor Relations Review* 553 (1994). Should the society take stronger measures to speed up the point at which blacks reach their rightful place, or are fifty to seventy more years of equal treatment the best solution?

5.   Cheryl Harris has argued that nothing less than vigorous affirmative action can achieve the self-realization of oppressed minorities in America. Harris, "Whiteness as Property," 106 *Harvard Law Review* 1707 (1993). Harris notes that there are two difficulties with a corrective justice rationale

for affirmative action for blacks. First, she states that the beneficiaries of preferential treatment today are not the victims of the past misconduct. But is that true in light of Borjas's confirmation of the only slowly decaying intergenerational transmission of economic disadvantage? The wrongs committed through the mid-1960s have imposed continuing burdens on the blacks of today, and their children and grandchildren. Second, Harris observes that those who bear the burden of today's preferential treatment of blacks were not the wrongdoers. But neither were the American taxpayers who recently paid compensation to the Japanese–Americans who were wrongfully incarcerated and stripped of their property during World War II. (See note 12.) Are the practical obstacles to a corrective justice argument for affirmative action compelling? For the view that they are, see Terry Eastland, "The Case Against Affirmative Action," 34 *William and Mary Law Review* 33 (1992), and Paul Carrington, "Diversity!" *Utah Law Review* 1105, 1156–1160 (1992).

Nonetheless, Harris argues that considerations of distributive justice support a policy of affirmative action that will redistribute wealth toward blacks. She contends that affirmative action must be used to challenge the sanctity of the present distribution of power and resources by undermining the prevailing notion that there is a protectable and inviolable property interest in "whiteness." For an argument that affirmative action for blacks cannot be justified on the basis of distributive justice, but can be justified only on the basis of social utility, see Thomas Nagel, "Equal Treatment and Compensatory Discrimination," 2 *Philosophy and Public Affairs* 348 (1973).

6. Public opinion evidence—despite its uninformed nature, high volatility, and admittedly uncertain reliability—suggests that most white Americans oppose policies specifically designed to aid blacks in securing jobs. For example, in 1990, some 61.4 percent of surveyed whites were "strongly against" such affirmative action for blacks and another 21.1 percent were "against" such a policy. Although the strength of this opposition had declined somewhat from 1986, and other surveys suggest a less universal opposition, it seems that whites are quite antagonistic to affirmative action. Among blacks, support for affirmative action in employment was rising over this same period, with 63.4 percent "strongly in favor" and 11.4 percent "in favor" in 1990. Lawrence Bobo and Ryan Smith, "Antipoverty Policy, Affirmative Action, and Racial Attitudes," in Sheldon Danziger, Gary Sandefur, and Daniel Weinberg, eds., *Confronting Poverty: Prescriptions for Change* 365, 381 (Cambridge, Mass.: Harvard University Press, 1994).

One of the most disturbing findings about affirmative action is reported by Paul Sniderman and Thomas Piazza, who conclude that the intense dislike of affirmative action seems to engender ill-will toward blacks:

> What we found was that merely asking whites to respond to the issue of affirmative action increases significantly the likelihood that they will perceive blacks as irresponsible and lazy.... 43 percent of those who had just been asked their opinion about affirmative action described blacks as irresponsible, compared with only 26 percent of those for whom the subject of affirmative action had not yet been raised.

Sniderman and Piazza, *The Scar of Race* 103 (Cambridge, Mass.: Harvard University Press, 1993). Does this imply that affirmative action prompts racial antagonism, or does it suggest that, given the legitimacy afforded to principled opposition to affirmative action, this issue can draw out existing racist attitudes?

As between the categories of "African Americans" and "women," it would seem indisputable that the principled arguments on behalf of affirmative action apply with greater force to the former group than to the latter. For example, the degree of deprivation and stigmatization for blacks has clearly been greater than it has for women, and on many measures of well-being, black men are clearly worse off than black or white women. (See the Human Development Index, discussed in Chapter 11, note 6.) Yet, public opinion polls conducted in 1995 show greater support for affirmative action for women than for blacks: A USA Today/CNN/Gallup poll showed that 50 percent of Americans favor affirmative action for women but only 40 percent favor such programs for minorities. A CBS News/New York Times poll found that 44 percent favored hiring preferences for women while only 29 percent favored such preferences for minorities. Lisa Anderson, "Women Escape Affirmative Action Feud," *Chicago Tribune* A1 (May 16, 1995). Does this show racism, or just greed (since virtually everyone gains something from preferences that help a mother, sister, daughter, or wife, but, owing to the lack of economic integration between blacks and nonblacks, nonblacks see little gain to their narrow self-interest from preferences that aid blacks)?

Is there an alternative explanation for these public opinion data? Perhaps affirmative action for women is deemed more acceptable than for blacks because (1) women are not at a disadvantage vis-à-vis men in terms of schooling, so the productivity losses associated with affirmative action for women may be smaller than those generated by affirmative action for blacks; and (2) women make a contribution to society in terms of childbirth and childrearing, for which they are not fully compensated. If the second factor were a concern, wouldn't stipends and child care for mothers be a more targeted and effective policy than affirmative action for women generally, regardless of their childbearing contributions to society? (See Chapter 15, note 7.)

7. Randall Kennedy asks whether the bitter opposition to affirmative action is fueled by racism. While there are certainly legitimate arguments for a clear rule of color-blind governmental conduct, it is very hard to explain the intensity of the opposition to affirmative action as a product of rational evaluation. As Nobel Prize-winning economist Gary Becker has noted, there are many governmental subsidies and regulations—such as tax breaks to the housing industry and import quotas on cars, textiles, and computer chips— that pose far greater social costs than affirmative action does, but one rarely hears impassioned debate over these programs. Becker states that "I don't like group quotas and other aspects of affirmative-action programs, but I am puzzled by the handwringing and anger of those who are opposed, especially some intellectuals." Becker, "How Is Affirmative Action Like Crop Subsidies?" *Business Week* 18 (April 27, 1992).

Moreover, those who argue loudest that affirmative action conflicts with our nation's traditional commitment to meritocracy seem strangely unaware of the fact that our society is far more meritocratic today than it has ever been. Indeed, Richard Herrnstein and Charles Murray recently indicated that one of the great transformations in American education is that, over the last thirty-five years, the elite institutions have for the first time become filled with intellectually elite students. As an illustration of the rapidity and extent of this change, Herrnstein and Murray note that "the average Harvard freshman in 1952 would have placed in the bottom 10 percent of the incoming class by 1960." Herrnstein and Murray, *The Bell Curve* 30 (New York: Free Press, 1994). It also seems distressingly clear that many of those who are most opposed to affirmative action for blacks today were remarkably quiet about the need to eliminate racial preferences when whites were the beneficiaries in the decades before 1965.

No doubt, racism explains some opposition to affirmative action, but fear also plays a role, since many whites feel economically insecure and worry that affirmative action will harm their prospects. Roger Wilkins tells the story of how, after being named a distinguished professor of history at George Mason University, he was shown an article by a white historian who claimed that he was passed over for that very job because it went to an unqualified black. In fact, the white historian was far down the list of potential candidates and would not have gotten the job anyway, but "his 'reverse discrimination' story is out there polluting the atmosphere" in which the affirmative action debate is conducted. Wilkins, "The Case for Affirmative Action: Racism Has Its Privileges," 260 *The Nation* 409 (March 27, 1995). It may well be the case that when, for example five whites and two blacks compete for a job and one of the blacks gets it, all five whites feel that they have been a victim of affirmative action even though at most only one of them could have been displaced. While there are only about 18.2 million employed blacks in the United States, my guess is that there are substantially more than that many whites who feel displaced by some supposedly lesser qualified affirmative action candidate. Since a large number of blacks are in rather poor jobs that are not highly coveted, the anomaly is even more puzzling.

Does this reveal irrationality on the part of the complaining whites? Might it suggest the presence of a deeper rationality—that it is psychologically and at times practically useful to blame one's failures on others? Do blacks ever fall victim to this syndrome? For a controversial assertion by a black academic that blacks depend on their status as victims, see Shelby Steele, *The Content of Our Character: A New Vision of Race in America* (New York: St. Martin's Press, 1990). Sorting out self-interested from principled claims can be extraordinarily difficult. Do these considerations cut against any sort of preferential hiring and in favor of a strong antidiscrimination principle?

According to David Oppenheimer, fears of reverse discrimination may be partly based on whites' exaggerated view of the number of nonwhites in the United States. According to a recent survey he cites, white respondents substantially underestimated the white population (deeming it to be under

50 percent, as opposed to the actual 82 percent according to 2000 Census data) and overestimated the black population (23.8 percent, as opposed to the actual 12.8 percent). Oppenheimer, "Understanding Affirmative Action," 23 *Hastings Constitutional Law Quarterly* 921 (1996). If Oppenheimer is correct, then presumably the white fear would be greater in certain parts of the country where rapid demographic changes are making nonwhites the majority.

8.   To pick up on Becker's point about the puzzling intensity of the antagonism to affirmative action, let us consider the burdens of affirmative action on those who are not its beneficiaries. Assume that one million blacks have been advanced over apparently more qualified nonblacks by affirmative action programs. (See Chapter 8, note 7. Note the tension between the position that affirmative action has not advanced black welfare, and the position that it has massively displaced more qualified nonblack workers. The conflicting points can be reconciled only if the productivity losses imposed by affirmative action are so large that black welfare falls because the shrinking economic pie offsets the greater share of it going to blacks. This seems unlikely.) This implies that one million nonblacks would be in less attractive jobs than they otherwise would have obtained. If one generously estimates the earnings reduction suffered by the nonblacks at $10,000 per year, then the loss to nonblacks would be in the neighborhood of $10 billion per year. In other words, affirmative action might be thought of as aiding one million blacks at the expense of one million whites who bear a cost of perhaps $10 billion per year. Additional losses in terms of lowered productivity associated with these programs are probably spread fairly widely, particularly for the government contract compliance program that imposes such costs on taxpayers generally. Note that it can hardly be the magnitude of the affirmative action subsidy that is problematic. In 1986, agricultural price supports cost more than $30 billion to aid perhaps one million largely white farmers without generating anywhere near the bitter opposition that affirmative action programs stimulate.

Why then is one transfer payment so vilified when another more costly transfer payment having no apparent social justification has little ability to galvanize public discontent? One possible answer is that, although the overall cost of affirmative action is not high, it falls disproportionately on a small number of individuals. Moreover, while only a relatively small number of whites bear this burden, it is a high one and one that other whites could fear that they might have to bear in the future—thus generating more widespread discontent beyond the actual number of losers from affirmative action. This fact has led some to suggest that the whites who are adversely affected by affirmative action should be compensated by the federal government. Gertrude Ezorsky, *Racism and Justice: The Case for Affirmative Action* 86–88 (Ithaca, N.Y.: Cornell University Press, 1991). Such compensation would clearly be fairer because the burden of affirmative action would then be shifted from a small number of rejected candidates to society as a whole through the tax system. Would this increase or decrease the political acceptance of affirmative action?

9. Is it clear that more aggressive affirmative action—as opposed to greatly expanding and improving prenatal care, drug treatment facilities, inner-city child-enrichment programs and schools, and job training opportunities—would be the best approach to promote greater equality of outcome? Katha Pollitt writes:

[T]o eradicate the opportunity-diminishing effects of poverty, we would have to eradicate poverty itself. Affirmative action is thus a good example of the right hand not caring what the left hand is doing: American society generates inequality in every conceivable way, which affirmative action then palliates for a handful of lucky people.

Pollitt, "Subject to Debate," 260 *The Nation* 552 (April 24, 1995).

In *Reflections of an Affirmative Action Baby* 71 (New York: Basic Books, 1991), Stephen Carter contends that affirmative action is "racial justice on the cheap" in that it doesn't really address the serious social problems but signals an effort to at least do something when the political will to provide the resources needed for real solutions is lacking.

10. Richard Delgado attacks affirmative action as a ploy to preserve the status quo by reducing the destabilizing consequences that would flow from wholly ignoring the plight of minorities. Do you agree with his claim that affirmative action tends to advance those minorities who need it the least? Is there any value to hiring racial minorities to serve as role models, or is this a purely exploitive act as Delgado suggests? Doesn't the conspicuous presence of racial minorities in positions of significant authority help to break down negative stereotypes, and therefore promote equal opportunity? See the discussion concerning these negative stereotypes in Chapter 5.

11. Whether affirmative action is inefficient because more qualified nonblack workers are being displaced by less qualified black workers is a complex and controversial question. See Chapter 8, note 8. Based on their recent meta-analysis of empirical data on the effects of affirmative action, Harry Holzer and David Neumark find that there is virtually no evidence of weaker educational qualifications or job performance among female beneficiaries of affirmative action in employment. The evidence is more mixed for minority beneficiaries of affirmative action, but it is weak enough to allow Holzer and Neumark to generally conclude: "affirmative action offers significant redistribution toward women and minorities with relatively small efficiency consequences." Holzer and Neumark, "Assessing Affirmative Action," 38 *Journal of Economic Literature* 483, 559 (2000). For a helpful review of four major books engaging in broader discussions about the costs and benefits of affirmative action, see Deborah C. Malamud, "Values, Symbols, and Facts in the Affirmative Action Debate," 95 *Michigan Law Review* 1668 (1997).

For a discussion of the benefits and likely costs of the major affirmative action program in the country, the federal government contractor compliance program, see Chapter 8, notes 6 through 8, and Chapter 9, section 9.1, notes 1 and 2. Chapter 4, section 4.2 discusses one mechanism for achieving affirmative action—the race-norming of employment examinations—which is now banned by federal law.

12. One alternative to a policy of affirmative action is to pay reparations to black Americans for the centuries of oppression their race has suffered. Charles Krauthammer has written that this approach would involve "a one-time cash payment in return for a new era of irrevocable color blindness." Krauthammer, "Reparations for Black Americans," *Time* 18 (December 31, 1990). See also Boris I. Bittker, *The Case for Black Reparations* (New York: Random House, 1973); Mari Matsuda, "Looking to the Bottom: Critical Legal Studies and Reparations," 22 *Harvard C.R.-C.L. Law Review* 323 (1987); Vincene Verdun, "If the Shoe Fits, Wear It: An Analysis of Reparations to African Americans," 67 *Tulane Law Review* 597 (1993); Rhonda Magee, "The Master's Tools, from the Bottom Up: Responses to African–American Reparations Theory in Mainstream and Outsider Remedies Discourse," 79 *Virginia Law Review* 863 (1993).

In recent years, the reparation movement has grown strong, culminating in the filing of the first federal class-action lawsuit in New York in March of 2002 against a number of national corporations that allegedly profited from slave labor and slave trade. Charles J. Ogletree, "Litigating the Legacy of Slavery," *New York Times* (March 31, 2002). The reparation movement in general and the reparation litigation in particular, raise many thorny questions. Who should be compensated? The federal class-action lawsuit names all black descendants of slaves, but as Charles Ogletree points out, the damage has not been done equally within the group. How high a payment is appropriate?

Consider in this regard that the internment of 120,000 West Coast Japanese Americans during three years of World War II was followed forty-six years later by a national apology and the payment of $20,000 to 80,000 former internees (a total cost of $1.6 billion). Leslie Hatamiya, *Righting a Wrong: Japanese Americans and the Passage of the Civil Liberties Act of 1988* (Stanford, Calif.: Stanford University Press, 1993). Is the reparation of Japanese American internees an appropriate precedent for the slavery reparation litigation, given that in the former case, the compensation was awarded to the actual internees and not their descendants? Comparing the slavery reparation to the recent (successful) Holocaust survivors' litigation also runs into the same problem. Robert F. Worth, "Companies Are Sued for Slave Reparations," *New York Times* B2 (March 27, 2002). As a matter of principle and not mere practicality, should it matter that slavery was abolished more than 140 years ago in providing restitution?

4

The Evolution of the Law

When Title VII took effect on July 2, 1965, it became the duty of courts, aided by the Equal Employment Opportunity Commission (EEOC) and litigants, to give meaning to the broad but undefined prohibition against employment discrimination. As we will see in Chapter 8, the first decade of federal employment discrimination law was one of substantial economic gains for blacks relative to whites. Importantly, these relative gains in black wages occurred only in the South—the region of the country where most blacks lived, and the one in which no state fair employment practice laws had yet been enacted. The predominant congressional purpose behind the enactment of Title VII was to protect blacks in the South, and, of all categories of workers, Southern blacks benefited most visibly during the first ten years of federal employment discrimination law.

Alfred Blumrosen, a key figure in formulating employment discrimination strategy during the first years in the life of the EEOC, discusses how Title VII was used to open up to blacks entire industries that had previously been closed to them. This achievement was encouraged and facilitated by the strong support of the Southern federal judges who played a particularly important role in developing a very pro-plaintiff body of Title VII law. As Blumrosen documents, the federal appellate court judges of the South were the primary architects of a doctrinal framework that aided the efforts of Title VII litigants to secure relief. But while this developing framework was vitally important in attacking and removing wholesale barriers to black employment, it was ultimately attacked and scaled back in many respects by subsequent decisions of

the United States Supreme Court. Interestingly, the large black economic gains over the period 1965–1975 began to stall as the Supreme Court
began to curtail the most aggressively pro-plaintiff decisions. Blumrosen's insightful essay sheds light on the difficult question of whether this
doctrinal retrenchment was appropriate because the law had succeeded
in eliminating the egregious forms of exclusions, or whether the retrenchment itself contributed to the cessation of a decade of relative
progress for blacks.

Certainly by 1980, as judicial and then executive enthusiasm for
employment discrimination law waned, many of the factors that had led
to relative gains for blacks in the first decade were no longer present.
For example, as John Donohue and Peter Siegelman document in
Chapter 9, class-action lawsuits and "failure to hire" cases—the most
promising weapons against racially discriminatory barriers to employment—were becoming increasingly rare. The Reagan and Bush adminis-
trations were not zealous supporters of employment discrimination law,
and indeed major initiatives of the Reagan Administration attacked
affirmative action by calling for an end to the contract compliance
program and by seeking to prohibit the race-norming of general ability
tests as a form of reverse discrimination against whites. With the
increasing influence of Reagan-appointed justices, the Supreme Court in
1989 issued a series of rulings that were designed to trim the scope of
employment discrimination law—for example, by shifting the burden of
proof to plaintiffs in Title VII disparate impact cases, and by limiting the
applicability of section 1981, the other major federal statute forbidding
intentional race discrimination, only to disputes over refusals to hire.
Somewhat ironically, the congressional response to these decisions resulted in the passage of a stronger employment discrimination law.
Indeed, the Civil Rights Act of 1991 provided the first unequivocal
legislative endorsement of the disparate impact theory of discrimination,
and extended to all Title VII litigants the right, previously available only
in employment discrimination cases brought under section 1981, to trial
by jury and to compensatory and punitive damages in disparate treatment cases. The Act did prohibit the race-norming of employment tests,
and the Republican sweep of Congress in 1994 has led to a rekindling of
the failed Reagan efforts to end affirmative action by the federal government, efforts that the Clinton Administration has been steadfastly
resisting. (See the Administration's *Affirmative Action Review* [July 19,
1995].)

Thus, the law of employment discrimination has undergone an
interesting process of evolution, as competing political forces and judicial
philosophies, and the efforts of employers to comply with the perceived
dictates of the law, have shaped and transformed its doctrinal core. For
example, the early conception of objective employment testing was that

it provided an important protection to minority workers who had long been victimized by the unbridled discretion of discriminatory managers, and employers increased their reliance on testing after the passage of Title VII (see Chapter 9, section 9.2). It soon became apparent, though, that, given the appallingly bad schooling conditions that had been available to blacks, employment testing would present more of an obstacle than an opportunity to black advancement. The Supreme Court partially addressed this concern in the landmark case of *Griggs v. Duke Power Co.*, 401 U.S. 424 (1971), which held that neutral practices, such as employment tests, could run afoul of Title VII if they had a substantial disparate impact on black employees and could not be justified by a strong showing of business necessity. Many employers responded to *Griggs* by adjusting the scores of their employment tests to eliminate the disparate impact. Yet, as noted, the Reagan Administration tried to fight race-norming as a form of reverse discrimination, and this position ultimately prevailed when Congress specifically prohibited the use of race-norming in the otherwise decidedly pro-plaintiff Civil Rights Act of 1991.

Paul Sackett and Steffanie Wilks discuss some of the difficult scientific, legal, and political issues that are raised by the use of general ability employment tests, given that whites tend to outperform blacks on these tests. In the mid-1980s, the National Academy of Sciences assembled a distinguished panel, of which Sackett was a member, to address these issues, and the panel concluded that racial adjustments to general ability test scores were necessary to avoid unfairness to blacks. The panel's report sparked enormous controversy, as indicated in the selection by Jan Blits and Linda Gottfredson attacking the panel's recommendations as political rather than scientific. Although the tests appear to be equally valid for white and black test takers, their use results in a lower acceptance of productive workers who happen to score poorly on the test. While this fact is true regardless of race, more blacks are in this disadvantaged category of low test scorers. The interesting scientific finding is that an equally valid test that is not biased against blacks can still have a racially disparate impact that disfavors blacks.

While the debate over testing is largely framed in the language of statistics and psychometrics, the ultimate resolution of this controversy turns on many important legal and philosophical issues. In an interesting and broad-ranging essay, Mark Kelman probes the appropriate conception of discrimination that should be used in addressing the thorny issues surrounding the use of weakly predictive employment testing. He recommends that employment discrimination law should be interpreted to encompass a theory of distributive justice that prohibits employers from relying on such tests, given their tendency disproportionately to exclude capable blacks.

4.1 Constructing the Doctrinal Framework

The Law Transmission System and the Southern Jurisprudence of Employment Discrimination*
ALFRED W. BLUMROSEN

. . .

The Law Transmission System and Title VII

Formulating Title VII Policies: The Steel Industry and EEOC

Title VII did not take effect until one year after its passage. This "grace period" was designed to allow compliance with the law's requirements. The statute established a five-member Equal Employment Opportunity Commission (EEOC or "Commission") to investigate and conciliate complaints and it provided for civil actions where conciliation failed.

. . .

In the fall of 1965 the EEOC began what proved to be nearly ten years of negotiation between the federal government and the steel industry concerning discriminatory seniority practices. At one early meeting, the Steelworkers' initial response to Title VII became apparent. One union attorney declared that *Whitfield v. United Steelworkers of America, Local No. 2708* was controlling.[1] *Whitfield* had held that a

---

* Excerpts from Alfred W. Blumrosen, "The Law Transmission System and the Southern Jurisprudence of Employment Discrimination," *Industrial Relations Law Journal,* vol. 6, copyright © 1984. Reprinted by permission of the author and publisher.

1. Prior to 1956, the Armco Steel Company and the Steelworkers Union had maintained strict job segregation by race at the plant in Houston, Texas. Jobs were organized in lines of progression, or job ladders. "Black" jobs and black lines of progression were openly acknowledged. Blacks could not obtain any white jobs.

In 1956, the company and the union decided to end their rigid job segregation. Black employees were allowed to enter the previously white line of progression at the bottom, as if they were new employees. They were not given seniority credit for their prior service in "black" jobs. They contended that this new opportunity did not satisfy the union's "duty of fair representation." (In 1944, the Supreme Court had held that unions had a duty to bargain fairly and without racial discrimination on behalf of employees whom they represented). The Court invalidated a "quota" which would have eliminated blacks from desirable jobs. Steele v. Louisville & N.R.R., 323 U.S. 192 (1944). The "duty of fair representation" was sparingly enforced in the next twenty years.

The *Armco* case came before the Fifth Circuit as Whitfield v. Steelworkers, 263 F.2d 546 (5th Cir.1959). In an opinion by Judge Wisdom, the court upheld the Armco agreement, stating:

The problem before us is not unique. It is bound to come up every time a large company substitutes a program of equal job opportunity for previous discriminatory practices. In such case it is impossible to place Negro incumbents holding certain jobs, especially unskilled jobs, on an absolutely equal footing with white incumbents in skilled jobs. In this situation, time and tolerance, patience and forebearance, compromise and accommodation are needed in solving a problem rooted deeply in custom.

We attach particular importance to the good faith of the parties in working toward a fair solution. It seems to us that the Union and the Company, with candor and honesty, discriminatory seniority system was cured if senior black employees were allowed to enter previously "white" jobs as new employees, even though they received no credit for their prior service in "black" jobs. If *Whitfield* applied under Title VII, the outlook for major improvement in black employment opportunities was bleak. Under *Whitfield,* the most senior black employee would be permanently locked in behind the most recently hired white worker.

The EEOC finally decided to seek remedies for discriminatory seniority systems beyond that provided for in *Whitfield.* The Commission . . . insisted that the steel industry both afford black workers "the opportunity to fill vacancies anywhere in the line on the basis of their company seniority," and agree that "company seniority would govern their status in the line for layoff purposes." The EEOC, the toothless tiger of equal employment opportunity law, in a classic low-visibility administrative decision, thus rejected the effort to engraft the *Whitfield* doctrine into Title VII and insisted on greater relief for the senior black employees, including the establishment of training programs.

Implementation of Title VII Policies: Training Programs

The need for training programs to enable black workers to take advantage of newly opened opportunities was recognized in the early days of Title VII. . . .

The major success story of 1966, however, was the Newport News Agreement. This agreement was the first detailed plant-wide revision of industrial relations systems under Title VII and the executive order program. Akin to a collective bargaining agreement in breadth and depth, it specifically provided for enhanced black participation in apprenticeship programs:

> As the Company's last report to the Government (Form 40) showed that only 6 of the 506 apprentices enrolled in the apprenticeship program were Negroes, the Company agrees that, to provide affirmatively for equal employment opportunity, apprenticeship classes shall henceforth be filled as follows:
>
> . . . .
>
> d.   In filling vacancies in the apprenticeship classes, the Company agrees to exercise its utmost efforts to see that substantial numbers of Negroes are included in such classes. To this end the Company agrees, (1) to include in its recruitment efforts the predominantly Negro schools in the labor market areas; and (2) to notify civil rights organizations in said area of this Agreement and to solicit such organizations to send qualified applicants for such programs. . . .

acknowledged that in the past Negroes were treated unfairly in not having an opportunity to qualify for skilled jobs. . . . The Union and the Company made a fresh start for the future. We might not agree with every provision but they have a contract that *from now on* is free from any discrimination based on race. Angels could do no more.

The Newport News agreement had been negotiated during the suspension of government contracts with the shipyard. The various federal agencies involved cooperated with each other in the negotiations. After the agreement, however, the agencies disagreed on the question of credit for the agreement. As a result, the Department of Labor, the Department of Justice, and the EEOC independently developed policies concerning remedies for seniority discrimination. The courts finally resolved the ensuing confusion. Despite this bureaucratic bickering, the EEOC, the Department of Labor, and the Department of Justice, by the close of 1966, had laid the foundation for those principles which would prove important as the courts began to interpret Title VII. These principles were:

(1) A "fresh start for the future," the *Whitfield* solution, was not a sufficient remedy for seniority discrimination. Senior blacks could not be treated as junior employees in white jobs. Further relief for senior black workers confined to low-paying jobs because of their race was necessary;

(2) Training programs to equip minorities to handle the jobs from which they had been traditionally excluded were an essential part of a major settlement package correcting the historic exclusion of minorities and;

(3) The training opportunities should be allocated by reference to the proportion of blacks and whites in the labor market.

The EEOC pressed these positions in the limited forms which were open to it, including conciliation proposals, publication of sanitized reasonable cause decisions, amicus briefs and guidelines, and speeches by Commissioners and staff. Some employers did not accept the EEOC's broad interpretations of Title VII. Thus, in the late 1960s, the issues moved to the courts.

Reinforcing Title VII Policies in the Courts

The principles which the EEOC formulated were asserted in many Title VII class actions brought primarily by private plaintiffs, often supported by the NAACP Legal Defense and Educational Fund, Inc.... In one particularly influential decision, Judge Butzner, in the Eastern District of Virginia, concluded that "Congress did not intend to freeze a generation of Negro employees into discriminatory patterns that existed before the Act." The Fifth Circuit adopted the view that senior black employees were entitled to advance to their "rightful place" measured by overall length of service; these employees should not remain behind junior white workers, as they would be compelled to do under the *Whitfield* rule. The court later squarely held the *Whitfield* doctrine inapplicable to Title VII in a case arising from the same facility which had been involved in the *Whitfield* case.[2]

2. Taylor v. Armco Steel Corp., 429 F.2d 498 (5th Cir.1970). The case dealt with the same plant and the same contractual provision which had been upheld in *Whitfield*. Judge

In *United States v. Bethlehem Steel Corp.* the Second Circuit went further, sweeping away not only the *Whitfield* defense, but also many other legal objections that the steel industry employers and unions had raised to a revision of the seniority system. *Bethlehem Steel* involved a fact pattern of "classic job discrimination in the north." One issue was whether black employees who transferred into white lines of progression could carry their plant seniority with them for bidding purposes. The court answered the question in the affirmative thus joining the Fifth Circuit in rejecting the *Whitfield* doctrine.

. . .

In 1973, two more blows were dealt the steel industry's seniority systems. First, the Secretary of Labor found the system at Bethlehem Steel's Sparrows Point plant in violation of the executive order proscribing discrimination by government contractors. Second, the district court in Birmingham in *United States v. United States Steel Corp.*, rejecting both the *Whitfield* analysis and the "bona fide seniority" defense, found discriminatory the seniority systems of the nine plants of U.S. Steel's Fairfield Works. Judge Pointer's order required revisions in the seniority systems and associated promotional opportunities for *all* employees. The Second Circuit and the Secretary of Labor had required that blacks be allowed to use plant-wide seniority in competing with whites. But the seniority rights of whites vis-à-vis each other were left on a departmental basis. The results were dual-seniority systems, which created considerable tensions. The union cited these tensions in its argument for even-handed plant-wide seniority for all workers, black and white. Judge Pointer agreed, ordering a complete change in the seniority system. His decision was the final event leading to the industry-wide settlement.

The Steel Industry Response

After Judge Pointer's decision, steel industry employers and the United Steelworkers sought to settle the seniority discrimination issues being raised throughout the industry. They decided to alter the departmental seniority system and give decisive weight to plant seniority. The modifications would provide long term black employees with seniority credit for time spent in black jobs. Plant seniority would be applied to blacks and whites alike, thus avoiding the dual-seniority systems which had

---

Wisdom, the author of the *Whitfield* decision, wrote the opinion. In contrast to his conclusion in *Whitfield* that "[a]ngels could do no more," he wrote:

> Eleven years ago this Court gave its blessing to the revision of ... a system ... that improved the lot of many black employees but still fell short of cleansing progression lines of past racial discrimination.... Within the context of the NLRA ... *Whitfield* is defensible. Today, however, the court must reverse and remand this case ... for proceedings consistent with Title VII....

429 F.2d at 499.

Seven years later, Judge Wisdom was to apply his understanding of Title VII in a powerful dissent to the Fifth Circuit's decision in *Weber*. That dissent influenced the Supreme Court's ultimate disposition of the case.

emerged under some early court orders. The decision to change the nature of the seniority systems was based on the case law, which included many decisions invalidating "small unit" seniority. This law, uniform throughout the circuits, suggested that the employers and the union would lose many of the discrimination cases which had been filed against them.

After the union and the employers reached this agreement, they sought to negotiate governmental approval. In intricate and exhausting negotiations, the government demanded back pay and increased minority participation in the trade and craft jobs in exchange for its approval. The companies earmarked some thirty million dollars for settlement payments to nearly 50,000 black workers. The union and the employers also agreed to create specific promotional opportunities for minority workers into trade or craft jobs on a 50–50 basis, despite their preference for a color-blind program.... The agreement ... is the precise precursor of the Kaiser Plan approved by the Supreme Court in *Weber*. The specificity of language in the steel industry settlement was the result of programs under EO 11,246 requiring government contractors to establish "goals and timetables" to correct underutilization of minorities and women.

A comparison of the 1966 Newport News agreement with the Kaiser-Steelworkers agreement of 1974 involved in *Weber* reflects important developments in the intervening years under EO 11,246 in the Labor Department. The Newport News agreement concerning apprentices contained only a general provision:

> [A]s a natural result of this recruitment effort ... the ratio of Negro to white apprentices in any given year should approach the ratio of Negro to white employees and the ratio of Negro to whites in the labor market area but this provision shall not be construed to require or permit the rejection of any qualified applicant on the basis of his race or color.

The Kaiser-Steelworkers agreement was far more specific, requiring fifty percent minority placements in craft training programs until the minorities reached their work-force proportion.

Other Sources of Anti-Discrimination Values: The Executive Order Program and "Plans for Progress"

This increased specificity resulted from efforts of the Labor Department to find a formula to increase minority hiring under EO 11,246. In the 1960s, the Labor Department attempted to address the virtual exclusion of minorities from some building construction unions. After a series of experiments, the Department established the "Cleveland Plan," which required contractors to agree to meet unspecified minority hiring goals as a condition of obtaining government contracts. After the Comptroller General held this obligation too vague to be enforceable, the Department of Labor decided to adopt more specific standards. It developed a plan for Philadelphia which set specific goals and timetables in those skilled trades where minorities were underrepresented. Once again, contractors appealed to the Comptroller General, this time claiming that the specificity which his earlier decision required had produced preferential treatment for minorities, in violation of the Constitution, EO 11,246, and Title VII.

The Comptroller General ruled that the specific goals and timetables were unconstitutional. Both the Department of Labor and the Justice Department viewed this ruling as a usurpation of authority. The Justice Department, supported by the Labor Department, issued an Attorney General's opinion upholding the constitutionality of the "Philadelphia Plan," after which the contractors and unions in Philadelphia sought to enjoin the program. In *Contractors Association v. Secretary of Labor,* a 1971 case, the Third Circuit upheld the goals and timetables aspect of the "Philadelphia Plan."

In 1970, Senator Fannin proposed a rider to an appropriations bill which would have abolished such goals and timetables. The Nixon Administration, prompted by Secretary of Labor Shultz and Assistant Secretary Fletcher, opposed the rider. The rider was defeated. Thus in the crucible of the construction industry and its history of exclusion of minorities from skilled crafts was born the goals and timetables approach which the Department of Labor, under Order No. 4, expanded to all government contractors in 1970.

. . .

[B]y the end of 1971 the Labor Department's program to require specific performance of the affirmative action obligation was in place, and had been upheld by the Third Circuit in the "Philadelphia Plan" case. Major efforts made during the 1972 Congressional review of Title VII to knock out the "Philadelphia Plan" concept of goals and timetables failed. By the time that the steel industry and the steelworkers sat down to negotiate their settlement of seniority discrimination issues, the use of specific goals and timetables had been upheld in the courts, and had survived the rigors of Congressional review.

The steel industry settlement was the product of three strands of enforcement activity under the equal employment opportunity laws and orders. The seniority discrimination cases created the pressure for settlement between the union and the companies; the government's challenge to discrimination in the construction trades produced the focus on skilled jobs; and the evolution of the goals and timetables under EO 11,246 provided the formula which was incorporated into the agreement. Through this gradual institutionalization, the concept of specificity in hiring goals became a viable option for the steel industry in 1974, in contrast to 1966, when the Newport News agreement relied on general statements of objectives.

An Increase in Voluntary Compliance

The industrial relations specialists in the aluminum industry were aware of the negotiations in the steel industry. After observing the agonies which the steel industry had endured for nearly a decade, the aluminum industry and the steelworkers decided to improve minority employment opportunities without waiting for the plethora of suits and administrative proceedings which had preoccupied the steel industry. The aluminum industry's agreement with the steelworkers, which was involved in *Weber,* tracked several aspects of the steel settlement, including its 50–50 training program.[3] The Supreme Court in *Weber* upheld this imitative approach, even though the circumstances at the Kaiser plant in *Weber* differed from the circumstances in the steel industry which gave rise to the 50–50 training program.

In the steel industry large numbers of black workers had not been promoted into skilled positions. The 50–50 training program allowed *senior* black employees to enter skilled jobs, thus addressing problems of discrimination in promotions. Kaiser, on the other hand, had employed few blacks as unskilled workers and virtually none as skilled workers. Because there were few senior blacks, the 50–50 program became a method by which junior blacks (some themselves the beneficiaries of affirmative action in hiring) could advance to skilled jobs.

The inclusion of junior blacks in the program precipitated the litigation in *Weber;* senior white employees claimed "reverse discrimination." The Supreme Court, in an opinion authored by Justice Brennan, held that the social purpose which the training program served, which mirrored the purpose of Title VII, justified the program.

Justice Brennan's opinion took judicial notice of the traditional exclusion of blacks from craft unions and concluded that the employers' preference for previously trained craftsmen severely limited the number of blacks in those positions because of the history of discrimination in craft unionism. This situation, the court held, warranted an agreement between the union and employer to create a program to provide skills training for blacks. The court noted with approval that the program was not limited to blacks in concluding that it did not "unnecessarily trammel" the interests of white employees, that its duration was limited to "correcting racial imbalance," and that it could not be continued to "maintain a racial balance" once the imbalance had been corrected. Justice Rehnquist's dissent argued that the legislative history of Title VII required a color-blind interpretation of the statute.[4]

---

3. *United Steelworkers v. Weber,* 443 U.S. 193 (1979).

4. The history of the program involved soundly distinguished *Weber* from the decision of the Court in Regents of the University of California v. Bakke, 438 U.S. 265 (1978). In *Bakke,* the Court had invalidated, under the fourteenth amendment, a program which set aside for minorities a specific number of seats in a medical school class. On the facts concerning a "set aside" on specific racial grounds, *Weber* and *Bakke* are identical. The major factual difference in the cases is that the program in *Weber* was the product of years of intensive development under the strictest scrutiny by various groups interested in the matter, while the program in *Bakke* apparently reflected the judgment only of the medical school faculty. The course of development and testing of the plan in *Weber* provided not

The operation of the law transmission system in the *Weber* case—the fact that the program in *Weber* had been hammered out in the crucible of the steel industry settlement, and was based on a decade of developments among employers, unions, courts, and agencies—gave the program a stamp of legitimacy. The consent decrees, conciliation agreements and affirmative action programs, which many other companies in a wide variety of fields had adopted, attest to the degree to which Title VII values had become embedded in American industry. The American Telephone and Telegraph (AT&T) consent decree, for instance, incorporated goals and timetables, training programs, and a "seniority override."

Although one could argue that any action taken in anticipation of possible adverse legal consequences is not "voluntary," such an argument disregards the key role of the law transmission system in modern regulation. Voluntarism in modern regulation does not mean "done of charitable motives from the goodness of the heart." Rather, it means choosing from among options available after considering institutional and legal pressures. Voluntary collective bargaining, for example, means bargaining within the framework of legal and economic pressures which the parties can impose on each other. The concept of voluntarism is best understood as allowing the regulated institutions to exercise options and choices within the framework of law, not as justifying a disregard for legal norms.

In this sense, the course of industrial relations described in this paper represents voluntarism at its most useful. The various institutions involved—employers, unions, administrative agencies, and the courts—all participated to produce a workable result which comported with congressional objectives. The court and administrative decisions striking down the existing seniority system and requiring affirmative relief for black workers were the anvil on which the settlement was forged. Title VII suits and executive order proceedings provided the hammer.

. . .

The Rise and Fall of "Southern Jurisprudence" of Title VII

The Emergence of "Southern Jurisprudence"

To understand the role of courts in the transmission of the policies of equal employment opportunity, one must examine the corpus of Title VII law which underlay the steel settlement and its progeny. This body of Title VII law was developed in important part by the circuit courts of appeal for the southern states, and confirmed in a crucial aspect by the Supreme Court in *Griggs v. Duke Power Co.* The key holdings in *Griggs* were (1) that under Title VII, employment practices which had an adverse effect on blacks were illegal unless justified by business necessi-

only assurance that it had met the test of acceptability among tough-minded institutions, but also that it was likely to be limited to situations where that test had been met.

ty, (2) that the "good intent" of the employer was no defense, and (3) that the "present effects of past discrimination" constituted illegal behavior without a "new act" of discrimination.

These holdings confirmed, and thus laid a foundation for the expansion of, a series of southern courts of appeals decisions apparently based on the assumption that a black plaintiff in a Title VII action had probably been discriminated against. In this way, *Griggs* broadened the substance of Title VII beyond previous expectations and provided the legal foundation for the changes in employment practices which followed. Numerous important decisions concerning Title VII from circuits other than those located in the south also interpreted the statute sympathetically. The decisions of the Fourth and Fifth Circuits, however, were particularly influential in the overall development of the law, as reflected by extensive citation to them in the opinions of the other circuits. The judges in the other circuits seemed to defer informally to their counterparts in the south who had intimately experienced the relationship between racial prejudice and employment practices. The southeastern states had "open and notorious" job segregation, dual lines of seniority and officially segregated school systems which tended to assure inferior education and employment for minorities. The district judges sitting in those states, with some notable exceptions, were unsympathetic to Title VII. With almost monotonous regularity, they adopted a narrow construction of the statute and made findings of fact in favor of defendants. Thereupon the Fourth and Fifth Circuit Courts of Appeal wrote a remarkable chapter in the history of statutory interpretation. They created a jurisprudence of Title VII which was calculated to simplify the attack on segregated employment systems.

A 1968 Fifth Circuit decision on a procedural point foreshadowed the new jurisprudential approach. The issue in *Oatis v. Crown Zellerbach* was whether the beneficiaries of Title VII were limited to those who had filed charges with the EEOC or whether a class action could include minorities who had not filed charges. The court concluded that a Title VII suit could benefit all such minorities, basing its decision on the premise that "[r]acial discrimination is by definition class discrimination, and to require a multiplicity of separate, identical charges before the EEOC, filed against the same employer, as a prerequisite to relief through resort to the court would tend to frustrate our system of justice and order."

. . .

In *Local 189 Papermaker v. United States,* the Fifth Circuit determined "how to reconcile equal employment opportunity *today* with seniority expectations based on *yesterday's* built in racial discrimination." The court required the employer and the union to give seniority credit to blacks for time worked in "black jobs" when they competed with whites, until they reached their "rightful place." In its opinion, the court emphasized Judge Butzner's comment in *Quarles* that "Congress did not intend to freeze an entire generation of Negro employees into discriminatory patterns that existed before the act," and adopted his view that the "bona fide seniority" clause in Title VII did not protect seniority systems which had that effect.

In *Jenkins v. United Gas Corp.*, the court sustained a class action suit against a charge of mootness even though the plaintiff had been offered the job he sought: "Whether in name or not, the suit is perforce a sort of class action for fellow employees similarly situated." On this premise, the court later permitted "across the board" class actions reaching many employment practices of the employer, on the theory that the facts concerning the policies and practices of racial discrimination were the common questions required by Federal Rule 23. Furthermore, the court, in *Baxter v. Savannah Sugar Refining Corp.*, developed the bifurcated burden of proof in class actions, which permitted the general facts about discriminatory policies of the employer to be established *prior* to careful scrutiny of individual cases of discrimination. These two rulings required the district courts to determine the legality of employer discriminatory practices even though the claims of individual plaintiffs might be weak. A liberal interpretation of the attorney fee provision of Title VII supported this type of "private attorney general" litigation.

For individual cases of discrimination, the Fifth Circuit developed a presumption of discrimination upon a showing that a vacancy existed, and that the plaintiff had applied, been rejected, and was qualified for the job. After the plaintiff had made such a showing, the employer had to persuade the judge that the rejection had been for nondiscriminatory reasons.

To insure that the district courts would apply this body of law vigorously, the court took at least three unusual actions. First, it enhanced its authority to reverse a district court by emphasizing that the clearly erroneous rule did not apply to the ultimate fact of whether discrimination had occurred. In this way, the court could control those district court findings of fact based on a narrow interpretation of Title VII. Second, the court decided class certification questions which district courts had erroneously neglected rather than remand to lower courts which had not carried out their obligation under Rule 23. Third, the court set forth the terms of a decree after reversing a district judge rather than remand to the district court.

The knowledge of traditions of racial discrimination shaped the judges' attempt to provide a body of substantive and procedural law that would give a "glimmer of hope" to the intended beneficiaries of Title VII. The premise that discrimination permeated employment patterns in the South lay at the heart of the line of cases discussed above. The way to cut through this fabric of discrimination was to simplify the plaintiff's case while making it difficult for employers to rely on denials of discriminatory intent. These decisions helped prompt both the steel industry consent decree and the nationwide settlement between the EEOC and AT&T.

The Repudiation: 1977–1982

In 1977, the Supreme Court rejected the course of decision not only of the Fourth and Fifth circuits but of all the circuits which had subjected previously segregated seniority systems to judicial review. In *International Brotherhood of Teamsters v. United States,* the Court held that the bona fide seniority systems exemption of Title VII protected seniority systems which perpetuated past discrimination. Concluding that Congress *did* intend to exempt an otherwise "bona fide" seniority system under Title VII even if that system perpetuated pre-Act discrimination, the Court held that such a system was lawful unless it was the product of an intent to discriminate.[5] *Teamsters* was extended in 1982 in *Patterson v. American Tobacco Co.,* which held that even a seniority system which reflects post-Act job segregation does not violate Title VII unless it is the result of "discriminatory intent."

The Court has repudiated many of the procedural as well as substantive aspects of the southern jurisprudence. The Supreme Court first cast doubt on the Fifth Circuit's practice of allowing widespread "across-the-board" class actions in 1977, then made its reservations explicit five years later in *General Telephone Co. v. Falcon,* requiring specificity in pleading individual harm and its connection with class harm as a predicate for Title VII class actions. The court expressly rejected the presumption that a minority plaintiff was an appropriate representative of minority applicants and employees.

In 1981, the Supreme Court rejected the Fifth Circuit rule requiring an employer in an individual discrimination case to bear the burden of persuasion that there existed a nondiscriminatory reason for an action adverse to a minority plaintiff who had established a prima facie case. The burden of persuasion in employment discrimination cases was held never to shift from the employee.

---

5. This intention had not been proved in pre-*Teamsters* cases because the issue did not appear open. The southern jurisprudence had concluded that the "bona fide seniority" provision did not insulate a seniority system which perpetuated pre-act discrimination.

Therefore, plaintiffs simply produced either statistical or "live" proof of pre-Act discrimination (which was not seriously controverted), demonstrated how the system carried forward the effect of pre-Act discrimination (which was easy), and prevailed. Thus, it could be argued that the pre-*Teamsters* discrimination cases on which the steel industry settlement was based may have been wrongly decided. The Supreme Court suggested in *Teamsters* that these cases might have been properly decided the same way even if evidence of discriminatory intent had been required. If the issue of pre-Act intent had been litigated, the outcome would have been predictable. The lines of progression in the steel industry in the south had been structured around racially segregated job assignments. In the *Whitfield* case, for example, the lines of progression had been openly established and maintained by race. This situation is as well known and as well documented as the discrimination in the construction industry of which the Supreme Court took judicial notice in *Weber....*

Finally, the Supreme Court in 1982 rejected the special superintending power over district courts which the Fifth Circuit had exercised.

Thus, by 1982, the Supreme Court had rejected much of the edifice of Title VII law which the southern courts of appeals had developed around an underlying assumption that a black person denied employment had probably been discriminated against along with all other black prospective employees. Despite its repudiation, this line of cases left its mark on American society, including the south, because of the operation of the law transmission system and the regulated community's of the values represented by this body of law, which the steel industry settlement exemplifies.

The Impact of Southern Jurisprudence

The strong medicine of southern jurisprudence profoundly affected southern discrimination in employment. The steel industry settlement had signaled the acceptance by employers and unions of the responsibility for abolishing job segregation. This task had been accomplished to a significant extent before the Supreme Court repudiated much of the southern jurisprudence. Half of the work force in 1964, the year Congress passed the Civil Rights Act, had retired by 1980, and half of the work force had entered a system which by the mid-1970s no longer reflected the segregation of the past.

. `. .

A distinction between first and second generation Title VII cases is important in understanding this conclusion. The first generation cases were based on situations which existed in the late 1960s, where many employment or promotion standards carried forward the previous pattern of explicit segregation and discrimination. Southern judges who had lived with the traditional practices and were committed to implementing the national policy requiring its change deemed proof of the discriminatory legacy unnecessary.

But second generation cases are different. The facts of those cases arose in the 1970s, after employers and unions had implemented changes. The discrimination pattern is no longer so clear. The precise practices which were easily identified as discriminatory in first generation cases are now difficult—or impossible—to locate. Plaintiffs' cases are therefore less substantial, and less winnable under any standard.

Furthermore, the statistics concerning minority employment demonstrate that the presumption of discrimination which southern jurisprudence developed is no longer as valid a social fact in either the south or the nation as a whole. The sharp alteration in patterns of employment over the past fifteen years has made statistically vivid what personal impression suggests. Judges are bound to sense this change just as they once recognized the pervasive quality of discrimination.

. . .

In assessing the Supreme Court decisions cutting back on the southern jurisprudence, one should recognize how significant a part of the underlying evil which Title VII addressed has been corrected. The system of seniority in basic steel, the heavy industry of Alabama, and the paper industry, which so heavily dominates Mississippi, has been changed. The pattern of employment in the textile industry in the Carolinas has changed. The segregated systems in the petrochemicals industry in Texas and in Louisiana have been altered.

At this point, the questions become political. How much of a change is "enough" is a basic value judgment which cannot be made through rational processes alone. Considering the improvement in assessing whether the Supreme Court should have continued the presumption of discrimination of the southern jurisprudence is not akin to supporting the repeal of the civil rights law, or the abandonment of affirmative action. The statistics presented suggest that the Court rightly rejected the web of rules which assumed that blacks were usually the victims of discrimination. The changes reflected in the statistics are sufficient to vitiate the assumption that minorities are being "kept in their place" because of race in the way that they were in 1965. Therefore, demanding proof beyond that which the southern jurisprudence required is appropriate.

Even those who accept the assertion that more than two million minority workers were in improved circumstances in 1980 when measured by 1965 standards, however, may not view this difference as indicating a major improvement in employment opportunity. Minorities are still predominantly employed in the lower blue collar jobs. High unemployment rates and lower income levels persist, and in some instances have worsened. In addition, there is a serious concern that once the Supreme Court has narrowed the scope of Title VII, a resurgence of discrimination could resegregate the work force. This will probably not happen. Any attempt to change back to a segregated system would of course create new acts of intentional discrimination. But there is a deeper reason why the work force will not be resegregated. This lies in the widespread recognition that the "southern pattern" of discrimination was wrong. The new generations of workers, managers and union officials will not seek to revive the old system. The work of legal rules developed by the southern circuits and the passing of the generations have destroyed it. . . .

Having allowed the southern circuits to dismantle the fabric of segregation which gave rise to Title VII, the Supreme Court decisions which limit the manner in which the law controls employment decisions may have expressed a deeper wisdom: that the law should withdraw when the industrial relations system operates fairly without such extensive judicial or administrative supervision.

This conclusion does not offend democratic principles. The key decision of Congress in passing Title VII was to repose authority not in a regulatory agency, but in the federal courts *sitting in equity*. The confidence of Congress in the flexibility of equity justifies the course of decision described here. The need for the massive judicial intervention of southern jurisprudence had substantially lessened by 1982. The success of the law in changing the patterns of discrimination was a sufficient reason for the Supreme Court to reject the presumption of discrimination which underlay the edifice of southern jurisprudence. Given the vast changes in the south—and in the nation—since 1965, this presumption, having done its work, should be put aside. The strong medicine of the southern jurisprudence should be replaced by more traditional, if less potent, ways of the law.

. . .

Notes and Questions

1. Southern congressmen aggressively fought the passage of the Civil Rights Act of 1964, but the law was passed over their intense opposition. One of the great dilemmas facing the congressional architects of Title VII was how to ensure that the legal right to be free of employment discrimination would be protected in judicial hearings. Given the nature of Southern justice at the time, there was little confidence that Southern blacks alleging discrimination in employment would be treated fairly by white juries. While this fact counseled against having jury trials in employment discrimination cases, the Seventh Amendment confers a right to jury trial in civil cases at law. Congress resolved this problem by deciding that Title VII would be enforced only with the equitable remedy of reinstatement with back pay. As a result, white employers could not opt for a jury trial, and Title VII cases would be decided by federal judges.

But while Congress feared that the hostility of white juries would subvert the ban on employment discrimination, federal appellate judges were also concerned about the hostility of federal trial judges to the mandate of the law. As a result, the Southern federal courts of appeal developed an array of legal strategies to assume greater authority over cases and to limit the power of unsympathetic district court judges to undermine the protections of Title VII by making biased findings of fact, which were ordinarily subject only to a deferential standard of review. The Southern appellate judges also formulated a presumption of discrimination against blacks that applied once a rather weak factual threshold was met, and they also broadly assumed the power of certifying racial class actions.

2. Given this supportive legal environment, many formerly discriminatory firms in the South changed their discriminatory policies, and some even succumbed to pressure from the EEOC or private litigants and implemented broad-ranging "voluntary" affirmative actions plans. With the egregious

pattern of discrimination broken after more than a decade of strenuous legal efforts, the Supreme Court finally entered the fray and in many respects cut back on the aggressively pro-plaintiff legal doctrine that had emerged in the Southern courts of appeal. Blumrosen describes the unusual evolution of a body of legal doctrine that emerged through interpretation of a single unvarying legal command not to discriminate on the basis of race. Given the pervasive racial discrimination at the time of the passage of Title VII, aggressive corrective measures were needed and the Southern court of appeals judges provided them. Once the extreme discriminatory patterns were broken, and the rejection of particular black candidates was no longer strongly indicative of discrimination, the Supreme Court stepped in and weakened the power of the law to presume discrimination and provide broad classwide relief.

Was this pattern that Blumrosen finds so appealing the product of foresight, or happenstance? Might it be that the aggressively pro-plaintiff decisions of the Southern judges were not reviewed by the Supreme Court so long as the basically liberal majority was in power, but when the more conservative appointments of President Nixon were made, they were quite happy to cut back on the law? If so, does this suggest that if Nixon rather than Kennedy had been elected in 1960, the decade of black progress beginning in 1965 that is discussed impressionistically by Blumrosen and more systematically in Chapter 8 by John Donohue and James Heckman might never have occurred? In this view, even if an employment discrimination law could have been enacted at that time with a Republican in the White House, the judicial appointments to the Supreme Court would have provided a more grudging interpretation of the legal prohibition against discrimination on the basis of race.

3.   One indication of the amazing improvements in race relations that have occurred in the last thirty years is the shift in the attitudes of juries toward employment discrimination against blacks. As mentioned previously, the authors of Title VII were so wary of Southern juries, who were largely white because of the massive exclusion of Southern blacks from civic and political life, that Congress eliminated the jury trial from Title VII cases, thereby preventing black plaintiffs from seeking compensatory or punitive damages (other than back pay). By the late 1980s, there was much greater integration of blacks into Southern political and civil life, and the civil rights community's fear of Southern juries had considerably lessened. Indeed, such fears had by then become much less significant to supporters of Title VII plaintiffs than the burden of not being able to seek greater financial damages for discriminatory acts. Thus, the great compromise of 1964 was quietly undone in 1991, as pro-plaintiff forces were able to secure the right to trial by jury and the ability to secure compensatory and punitive damages for intentional discrimination. Is this further evidence of Blumrosen's point that the benefits generated by civil rights law have made subsequent changes in the law more likely? At least in this regard, though, the later development involved a strengthening of, rather than a retrenchment from, early Title VII law.

4.2   The Battle over Testing

Within-Group Norming and Other Forms of Score Adjustment in Preemployment Testing*

PAUL R. SACKETT AND STEFFANIE L. WILK

Civil Rights Act of 1991: Origins and Effects

Case of the GATB

The recent history of the Department of Labor's GATB [General Aptitude Test Battery] illustrates the complicated interplay of scientific and policy issues that surround employment testing. The GATB is a general test of cognitive functioning that includes a number of psychomotor subtests to assess manual and finger dexterity. It is administered by the USES [United States Employment Service], an agency created in the 1930s by an act of Congress expressly to help the disadvantaged job seeker. Until 1980 the GATB was used primarily as an aid to vocational counseling. In an atmosphere of declining American competitiveness and in response to the business orientation of the Reagan administration, the Department of Labor proposed that the GATB be adopted throughout the USES system to screen applicants for virtually all jobs.

Approximately 19 million people pass through the 1,800 local offices annually, and approximately 3.5 million of them are actually placed in jobs. If even one third to one half of all registrants were given the GATB, this would be by far the largest testing program in the country.

In order to get the greatest possible economic benefit from testing, the program was set up so that people would be referred to jobs in order of test score. Because the probability is that the higher test scorer will also be the better performer on the job, this top-down method of choosing from among the applicants on file would give the employer that subset of available job seekers with the greatest expected performance.

However, USES recognized that referral in strict order of test score would also make the employer—and USES—vulnerable to charges of discrimination under Title VII of the Civil Rights Act of 1964. The research staff had evidence that the mean GATB score for Black applicants falls about one standard deviation below the mean score in the White group. In practical terms, this meant that if 25% of the White group were referred, only 5% of the Black group would be referred to a typical job handled by the USES.

To prevent this from happening, USES sought a compromise between the governmental interest in promoting economic productivity and the equally compelling interest, given the USES mission, in helping disadvantaged minorities into the economic mainstream. The solution used was to compute each registrant's GATB score as a percentile score within his or her own racial or ethnic group (Black, Hispanic, and other). In other words, the USES used the within-group norming approach. . . .

This strategy retains the top-down approach to referral, but in a qualified way. It effectively wipes out the average score differences among the groups because Black, Hispanic, and White candidates assigned a given percentile—say, the 70th percentile—would be referred at the same time, even though their raw scores on the GATB would be substantially different. In the new system, those referred from the available pool of applicants would be the Black, Hispanic, and White applicants with the highest predicted performance in their respective groups. At the same time, minority applicants would be referred, on average, in numbers proportionate with their presence in the applicant pool, thus avoiding the exclusionary effect that testing would otherwise cause.

In the fall of 1986, William Bradford Reynolds, then Assistant Attorney General for Civil Rights in the U.S. Department of Justice, challenged the GATB referral system because of the within-group scoring strategy. In Reynolds's view, computing test scores by racial and ethnic groups constituted an illegal and unconstitutional violation of an applicant's right to be free from racial discrimination. And because the effect of the score adjustments is to raise the scores of Blacks and Hispanics, Reynolds found that it advances the interests of one group at the expense of another and as such constitutes intentional racial discrimination, in this instance what is commonly called *reverse discrimination.*

Officials of the Departments of Labor and Justice agreed to disagree until a study could be conducted by the National Research Council (NRC), the working arm of the NAS [National Academy of Sciences], and a report presenting the study committee's findings and recommendations was published under the title *Fairness in Employment Testing Validity Generalization, Minority Issues, and the General Aptitude Test Battery.*

The publication suggested that the two goals of simultaneously increasing work force efficiency and bringing Blacks into the economic mainstream are not mutually exclusive. The crucial issue is to find a way to use the GATB so that it will not screen out virtually all Black and Hispanic job seekers on the one hand and unduly abridge the rights of majority-group job seekers on the other.

It is important to note the context in which the committee endorsed score adjustments, namely, one in which the GATB would be used by the USES as a screening device. The top-scoring applicants on this device would be referred to the hiring organization, which would then further screen the applicants using any of a wide variety of selection techniques.

The committee was concerned about the exclusion of a high proportion of the minority applicant pool on the basis of a single factor—GATB scores—when it is very clear that other factors are also relevant for job success. In endorsing referral on the basis of adjusted scores, the committee sought to extend to minority applicants the opportunity to have their job-relevant characteristics recognized and to reserve to the employer the capacity to look at minority and majority job seekers in terms of the specific characteristics that are important in the employer's firm. For example, in some jobs punctuality and regular attendance are critical; in many firms the ability to work in small, interactive groups is critical; in many jobs sociability is fundamental. The GATB does not purport to measure any of these characteristics. Does this mean that the GATB is of no value? Obviously not. GATB abilities, however imperfectly measured, are also related to successful job performance. Adjusting scores so that a greater proportion of minorities are referred means that GATB information can inform the employer's decision but will not overwhelm it to the exclusion of consideration of other relevant factors when majority and minority candidates are considered for employment.

Aftermath of the National Academy of Sciences Report

The above discussion focused on the issue of the role of testing in balancing the competing objectives of minority employment and productivity enhancement. What became very clear in the year following the release of the NAS committee's report was that such discussions were too abstract. In the mind of the general public, score adjustment was "cheating."

. . .

The precursor to the Civil Rights Act of 1991, at that time the Civil Rights Act of 1990, was under debate at the same time and was labeled a "quota bill" by then-president George Bush. Although the act made no reference to quotas, it was argued that the provisions of the bill were so difficult to comply with that employers would be forced into quota hiring. The ban on score adjustment that became Section 106 of the Civil Rights Act of 1991 was introduced in response to claims that the GATB referral system constituted a quota system and that supporting such a system constituted supporting quotas. Members of Congress supported the language of Section 106 virtually without exception. While denying that the Act was a quota bill, supporters of the Act did not want to be tagged as supporters of quotas.

Thus the ban on score adjustment was a direct response to the USES GATB system. There is no evidence that there was broader consideration of the implications of the Act for any other setting than the use of cognitive ability testing.

Consequences of Score Adjustment for Different Types of Tests

In this section we review group differences and their relationship to job performance for a variety of types of tests, including cognitive ability, personality, physical ability, biodata, and vocational interest measures.

Cognitive Ability Tests

The phrase *cognitive ability tests* encompasses a variety of conceptually distinct domains, the most prototypic of which are verbal, numerical, and reasoning ability. A characteristic that has long been noted is the substantial positive correlation among measures of various cognitive abilities. Resulting from this observation is the notion that underlying the various cognitive abilities is a common factor, identified around the turn of the century by Spearman and referred to as g, for general cognitive ability.

It has been hypothesized that g is the factor that accounts for the relationship between cognitive ability tests and performance in various jobs. An extensive body of literature shows that g is related to performance across a wide range of jobs and that specific ability tests explain little additional variance in job performance over that accounted for by g.

Black-White differences of approximately 1.0 standard deviation [SD] units and Hispanic-White differences of approximately 0.6–0.8 standard deviation units have been widely and consistently reported for measures of cognitive ability. Efforts to find ways to reduce these differences through the use of different item formats (e.g., formats not reliant on mastery of the English language) have not been very successful. Note that the issue is not merely whether a test can be devised that reduces group differences, but whether group differences can be reduced while retaining the same levels of reliability and criterion-related validity. Gender differences are not generally found on composite measures of g. Although differences may be found in individual subtests, the pattern of results does not consistently favor men or women.

The implications of these differences for personnel selection have long been recognized. The Black-White difference on a cognitive ability test was a central feature in *Griggs v. Duke Power Co.* (1971), the first testing case to be considered by the Supreme Court after the passage of the Civil Rights Act of 1964 and the case that gave credibility to the concept of adverse impact as a basis for challenging employment tests. As a means of reducing adverse impact, a number of test publishers made use of separate norm tables for different groups. All of these, however, left the choice of whether and how to adjust scores to the employer. To our knowledge, the within-group norming of the GATB was the first instance of score adjustment of a cognitive ability test in which the adjustment was done automatically by the test provider, with the test user receiving only adjusted scores.

The crucial question is whether adverse impact reflects real differences in the characteristic under investigation or whether the differences reflect some form of bias so that a given test score has different meanings if obtained by a member of one group than if by a member of another group. [T]here is a well-accepted mechanism for examining whether there is predictive bias in the use of tests, namely, the comparison of regression lines relating test scores to job performance. If regression slopes and intercepts are the same for the groups under consideration, there is no predictive bias. Scores have the same meaning for individuals regardless of group membership. If the regression lines differ, a finding that use of the reference group regression line underpredicts the job performance of members of the minority group would indicate predictive bias against the minority group. Although a finding of overprediction would also indicate bias, the bias would operate to the advantage of the minority group.

There is an extensive literature examining the question of predictive bias in the use of cognitive ability tests. . . . This literature does not show evidence of underprediction of Black or Hispanic performance. Although regression slopes do not differ more frequently than would be expected by chance, intercepts frequently differ. The differences, however, indicate overprediction, rather than underprediction, of minority group performance.

In summary, research on cognitive ability tests for personnel selection has documented consistent predictive validity for a wide range of jobs, a lack of predictive bias against Blacks and Hispanics, and large and consistent adverse impact by race.

. . .

Rationales for Score Adjustment

Score adjustment takes a number of forms, including converting scores to percentiles within race or gender groups, adding a fixed number of points to the scores of members of particular groups, and others.

. . .

In some settings score adjustment on the basis of group membership is done without much apparent controversy. The legally mandated practice of adding points to the scores of veterans in some public sector settings is a well-known example. In other settings, particularly when the issue involves score adjustment on the basis of race or gender, score adjustment practices have been an incendiary issue. Debate has tended to deal with two settings: physical ability tests, which produce substantial adverse impact against women, and cognitive ability tests, which produce substantial impact against some racial and ethnic minority groups, particularly Blacks and Hispanics (these findings are documented in the section on consequences).

Disputes about score adjustment can be argued on legal, technical, and social grounds. Legally, before the passage of the Civil Rights Act of 1991, various commentators differed strongly as to the permissibility of the practice. On technical grounds, score adjustment may be offered as a mechanism to eliminate biased measurement. On social grounds, arguments tend to be cast in terms of individual merit versus general societal good. Opponents of score adjustment tend to argue for the sanctity of individual merit and the inappropriateness of minority group membership as a factor in selection decisions. Arguments about attaching social stigma to members of the aided minority group are also common.

We find it useful to separate the rationales offered for score adjustment into three categories. The first is purely philosophical: Increased minority representation is argued to be of such value that minority preference is warranted to achieve it. The second is that score adjustment is needed because of bias measurement in the test. If a given test score does not carry the same meaning for members of all groups, then score adjustment is needed. The third is that score adjustment is needed when a particular way of using a test is at odds with an espoused position as to what constitutes fair test use. We will explore the rationales offered for score adjustment in some detail.

Position 1:   Adjust Scores to Attain Business or Societal Goals

One common theme in arguments for minority preference is that of righting a social wrong. The long history of social inequities endured by members of racial and ethnic groups in this country is viewed as a wrong so grave as to warrant strong measures, including minority preference in job allocation. A second common theme is an appeal to pluralism: All groups deserve a fair and proportional share of the society's benefits, and jobs are among those benefits. A third theme that has emerged strongly in the last few years is that workforce diversity contributes to a firm's success. The term *diversity* is used with varying degrees of inclusiveness, ranging from a narrow focus on groups protected by civil rights law to concerns for issues such as sexual orientation.

Proponents of minority preference to increase diversity argue for a variety of benefits. First, examinations of demographic trends suggest that increasing proportions of new entrants to the workforce over the next several decades will be women and minority group members. Firms will find themselves competing for a limited applicant pool, and actions taken today to increase diversity will make the firm more attractive to job applicants in the future. Second, as their customer base becomes increasingly diverse, firms may find that their customers view diversity as a factor in deciding where to take their business. Third, as the structure of work is increasingly team oriented, appeal is made to the group problem-solving and group creativity literatures, which some interpret as suggesting that heterogeneous groups may produce better solutions to problems.... Thus the value to the firm of increased diversity can be offered as a rationale for minority preference.

Opponents of minority preference in general argue that by making preferences for certain groups to correct past inequalities, society is essentially trying to make the proverbial right out of two wrongs. Given that it is the social inequalities suffered by certain minority groups that score adjustment is attempting to alleviate, making preferences for one group (minority) over another (majority) is simply shifting the burden to the majority. Therefore, supporters of this view believe that the solution is to make no preferences toward one group or the other.

Arguments in this category are a matter of personal values. People can disagree both as to whether minority representation is a valued outcome and as to whether score adjustment is an appropriate means of attaining the goal. There is no technical or scientific basis for taking either side regarding these positions. These positions are not dependent on the technical merits of the selection system in question, which is the focus of the next section.

Position 2:   Adjust Scores to Alleviate Test Bias

Test critics routinely assert that tests are biased against members of various groups. Various causes of test bias are offered. Among the most common are that tests use language specific to majority groups, that tests use item formats that give advantage to majority groups, and that test-taking skills have no link to real-world job behavior....

Whatever the causal mechanism, the arguments boil down to assertions that the regression line relating test scores to measures of the job-relevant criterion of interest has a different slope for one group than for another (the test predicts performance well for the majority group, but less well for the minority group), has a different intercept for one group than for another (minority group members get lower scores than majority group members equal in ability), or differs in both slope and intercept. As a result, regression analysis has become accepted as the mechanism for investigating claims of test bias. According to the *Standards for Educational and Psychological Tests* (1985): "The accepted technical definition of predictive bias implies that no bias exists if the predictive relationship of two groups being compared can be adequately described by a common algorithm (e.g., regression line)."

Two caveats are in order concerning this approach. First, it is dependent on the quality of the measure of the job-relevant criterion of interest: If that measure is systematically biased against the minority group in question, then the method cannot be used to identify the presence or absence of predictive bias. Second, the approach requires larger sample sizes than will be available for the vast majority of organizations. Conclusions about predictive bias will commonly come from cumulating data across organizations, rather than from a single organization. It is imperative that firms be permitted to draw on data other than that from their own organization in order to draw conclusions about predictive bias.

Although a finding of a common slope and intercept is a refutation of claims of test bias, it is useful to consider the implications of finding group differences in slope or intercept. *Figure 4.1 illustrates several examples.* (Note that Figure 4.1 is intended to illustrate concepts of slope and intercept differences rather than to represent actual research results.) Consider first the findings of markedly different slopes by group. As the slope of the regression line indexes the predictive validity of the test for the group under consideration, differing slopes indicate differential validity: The test is, in fact, a more effective predictor of performance in one group than in another. Such a finding would be particularly disturbing should the slope approach zero for one group, as in Figure 4.1a. Predicted performance for majority group members is positively related to test scores; that is, the higher test scores correspond to higher predicted performance. The performance of minority group members, however, is predicted to be the same across all possible test scores. Such an occurrence would certainly preclude further use of the test unless and until subsequent research demonstrates that the finding was artifactual. Empirically, however, there is little evidence for differential validity in the domains where it has been investigated. Extensive research with cognitive ability tests suggests that differential validity by race and gender is found no more frequently than would be expected by chance (see the section on consequences for a review). However, the issue has not been investigated extensively in other domains such as personality assessment.

Turning to the implications of intercept differences by group, we see two possibilities: a larger intercept for the comparison group, indicating that the use of the majority group regression line (or a common regression line) would underpredict the performance of minority group members, and a lower intercept for the minority group, indicating that the use of the majority group regression line would overpredict the performance of minority group members. In the case of underprediction as in Figure 4.1b, the minority group is disadvantaged by amount z_1, and score adjustment would be a technically appropriate solution. After such score adjustment, a common regression line would apply to both majority and minority groups. In the case of overprediction, the use of the majority group regression line is to the advantage of the minority group and thus is not likely to be challenged by the minority group. Score adjustment would again be a technically appropriate solution, but the adjustment would involve a reduction in the scores of minority group members. The social and political consequences of such a course of action make such adjustments an unattractive course of action for many organizations.

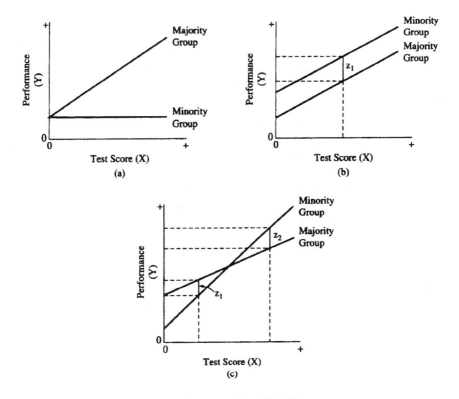

Figure 4.1. Examples of Test Bias

Finally, Figure 4.1c gives an example of both slope and intercept differences between groups. Both of the previous issues apply: There is differential validity, evidenced by the slope differences, and there is an intercept difference. As the regression lines cross, the minority group's performance is overpredicted for part of the score range and underpredicted for part of the score range, as Figure 4.1c illustrates. No simple score adjustment could remedy this situation, and the use of separate regression lines for each group would be the technically appropriate thing to do.

Thus conceptually there is a situation in which score adjustment is technically justified, namely, a finding of a common regression slope but a higher intercept for a minority group. In the area of cognitive ability tests, overprediction, rather than underprediction, is the consistent finding when intercept differences are found. However, differences in regression slopes and intercepts have not been extensively examined in domains other than cognitive ability (e.g., personality assessment).

Position 3: Adjust Scores When Justified by a Particular Perspective on Fairness

This category refers to rationales for score adjustment that pair the observation that selection systems are imperfect predictors of job performance with the assertion that the burden of these imperfections should not fall disproportionately on minority groups.

A variety of criteria for assessing the impact of imperfect selection systems on minority group members have been put forward under the rubric of "models of selection system fairness." As one example, Thorndike proposed an approach in which the success rate (i.e., the proportion of job applicants who would exceed a specified level of job performance if hired) is determined for each group. For a selection system to be fair, the rate of selection from each group must be proportional to these success rates. Top-down selection will meet this standard only when majority-minority differences on the selection device used are equal in magnitude to majority-minority differences in job performance. A variety of models of test fairness were put forward in the late 1960s and early 1970s....

In the 1970s, approaches such as Thorndike's were grouped with the regression model of test bias discussed above under the rubric "models of test fairness." A key insight of that era was the recognition that models such as Thorndike's were qualitatively different from the regression model. The regression model deals directly with the meaning of individual test scores: It addresses the question, Does a given score have the same meaning (i.e., predict the same level of job performance) across groups? and it has come to be viewed as the means of assessing predictive test bias. In contrast, it has been demonstrated that models such as Thorndike's do not deal directly with flaws in the test. Rather, violations of the Thorndike model are inevitable when a test that predicts performance with less than perfect accuracy and on which group differences exist is used in a top-down fashion.

It is important to distinguish between the phrase "test that predicts performance with less than perfect accuracy" used in the previous paragraph and the phrase "flawed test." Conceptually, we can show that even if we had an absolutely perfect measure of a particular job-relevant construct, the test could have less than perfect predictive validity and could violate a Thorndikian model of fairness. For example, assume (a) a simple model of the determinants of performance in which performance within groups is a perfectly determined function of cognitive ability and work group support, defined as the amount of coaching and social support provided by one's supervisor and peers; (b) that cognitive ability, work group support, and job performance are measured without error; (c) a large organization in which the work group to which the individual will be assigned is not known at the time of selection; (d) that the two determinants of performance are uncorrelated and that each contributes equally to the prediction of performance; and (e) that there are no majority-minority differences in work group support and that there is a 1 *SD* majority-minority difference in cognitive ability.

Under these assumptions, the majority-minority difference in job performance would be 0.71 *SD*. The question is whether the use of a top-down selection system based solely on cognitive ability would be unfair in this setting. It would be unfair according to the Thorndike model. Fewer minority group members would be selected than the model would require because majority-minority job performance differences would be smaller than majority-minority differences in cognitive ability. However, there is clearly nothing an employer can do to design a better selection system. In the scenario under consideration here, sole reliance on the ability test is the optimal selection system: No other attributes knowable before hire contribute to performance.

Thus fairness models such as Thorndike's cannot be viewed as models of test bias. They can be offered as models of selection system fairness, with fairness viewed as a socially constructed standard to which selection systems should be held, but not as a characteristic of a test.

The NAS committee on the GATB based its endorsement of score adjustment on such a perspective on selection system fairness. As this has proved to be controversial, we will discuss the committee's approach in more detail. We will describe here how and why this approach differs from approaches commonly taken by psychologists.

As a starting point, note that Black-White differences in measured job performance are much smaller than Black-White differences in scores on cognitive ability tests. Observed differences in job performance are approximately 0.3–0.4 *SD*. Similar differences are found for both subjective and objective performance measures. Observed differences in performance are smaller than true differences in performance because of measurement error. However, even if correcting for measurement error produces Black-White differences in the 0.5–0.6 *SD* range, this is still much smaller than the 1 *SD* difference in ability test scores. From this Black-White difference in job performance, we can determine the number of White and Black applicants who would be hired under different scenarios (e.g., size of applicant pool and proportion of Blacks and Whites in the applicant pool) if one were able to select on the basis of actual job performance. What emerges clearly is that selecting on the basis of job performance will result in the hiring of more Blacks than would be the case if hiring were on the cognitive ability test (because the Black-White difference in on-the-job performance is smaller than the Black-White difference in cognitive ability). If one gave all applicants a job tryout and kept the highest performers (i.e., hiring on the basis of what is the criterion in the typical validity study), one would retain considerably more Blacks than would be hired using the present test. This observation is at the heart of the committee's adoption of an approach that focuses on the probability of selection given a specified level of job performance, rather than the focus on the probability of a specified level of job performance given selection.

In contrast to the committee's approach is the position that because only test performance is known before hire, it is appropriate to focus on success given selection, rather than selection given success. Some have also argued that because the phenomenon of smaller job performance differences than test differences is not explicitly racial (with a less than perfectly valid test, any lower scoring group with a larger difference from the majority group on the predictor than the criterion will produce this result), it is not appropriate to remedy the situation for a racially defined group. In other words, proponents of this position can accept that all low scorers will be subject to disproportionate rates of false rejection in order for employers to enjoy the benefits of testing, but not that some low scorers (i.e., Blacks) should be spared the effects of imperfect prediction, as would be the case if score adjustment is used.

The NAS committee's thinking also incorporated two additional ideas: the consequences of using an incomplete predictor set and the consequences of using one test as an initial hurdle to determine who will continue for additional screening. We will further explore these ideas regarding test use.

Imagine the following hypothetical scenario: Two uncorrelated traits (cognitive ability and conscientiousness) are each found to have a squared correlation of .50 with performance within groups. Thus these two factors completely explain performance within groups. Assume Blacks and Whites differ by 1 SD in cognitive ability and by 0 SD in conscientiousness; thus the Black-White difference in job performance is 0.71 SD. Now assume a researcher sets out to develop a selection system for this job. The researcher attempts to measure only cognitive ability. No attempt is made to measure conscientiousness. The researcher finds that the cognitive ability test is valid, finds that Black performance is not underpredicted, and concludes that the test lacks predictive bias. The NAS committee's approach, however, would find this unfair, as the Black-White difference in job performance is much smaller than the Black-White difference in test performance.

The researcher's approach is appropriate in determining whether there is something wrong with his or her measure of cognitive ability. The researcher has properly determined that the cognitive ability measure is not biased in the sense of being a more accurate predictor for one group than another. Yet by failing to include other aspects of the predictor domain that are also important for job performance and on which Black-White differences are smaller, the end result is a system in which Blacks who would have been high performers if hired are less likely to be hired than are Whites who would be high performers if hired. As the committee's report concludes, the burden of the limitations of testing technology falls more heavily on Blacks than on Whites, hence the recommendation of score adjustment.

One encounters the same problem when an ability test is not the sole basis for the selection decision but is simply the first hurdle. This is a very common scenario: A test is used to screen a large pool down to a smaller number of candidates who are then further screened using some additional selection device. Let us continue to use the above example in which two uncorrelated predictors—cognitive ability and conscientiousness—are being used. By administering the device with the large Black-White difference (cognitive ability) as the initial screening device, candidates (both Black and White) scoring high on the conscientiousness dimension but below whatever cutoff is set on the ability test do not have the opportunity for their high standing on the conscientiousness measure to compensate for their lower standing on the ability measure. It can be shown that the order in which the two measures are used influences the outcome: Reversing the process and administering the conscientiousness screen first results in the selection of a larger number of Blacks under a number of common selection scenarios. . . .

As an example, consider the case of the GATB. The top-scoring applicants on the GATB would be referred to the hiring organization, which would then further screen the applicants using any of a wide variety of selection techniques. The NAS committee was concerned about the exclusion of a high proportion of the minority applicant pool on the basis of a single factor—ability test scores—when the committee believed that other factors are also relevant for job success. Thus the committee did not endorse hiring on the basis of adjusted scores but rather endorsed referral for further screening. Score adjustment gives the employer the opportunity to determine whether any minority applicants with lower unadjusted scores have other compensating qualities that would lead to a favorable decision. For example, might an employer prefer an applicant with a good attendance record over one who is chronically absent, even if the chronically absent employee scores 10 points higher on a valid ability test? If the higher scoring applicant is a member of the majority group and the lower scoring applicant is a member of the minority group, score adjustment gives the employer the opportunity to decide if work habits compensate for lower ability. Without score adjustment the lower scoring minority applicant might never be considered by the employer. Clearly, the preferred solution would be to assess attendance records and other relevant characteristics for all applicants; in many cases, however, cost or logistic constraints lead to the use of a multistage sequential selection system.

Thus the position that score adjustment is justified on the basis of violation of the requirements of a particular model of selection system fairness is one that is informed by empirical data about test-criterion relationships. It does, however, require judgment about the appropriateness of the particular fairness standard that is offered. Consider the question, Is score adjustment scientifically justified? The NAS committee on the GATB answered yes and relied on the approach to selection system fairness discussed above, focusing on the observation that a selection system that overemphasizes the role of a selection device on which majority-minority differences are large will lead to lower rates of minority group selection than actual group differences in job performance would lead one to expect. The committee's position might best be described as a value judgment informed by scientific data about the consequences of different approaches using the GATB. The committee, in essence, focused on the "informed by scientific data" phrase in the previous sentence in presenting their recommendation that score adjustment is scientifically justified. Critics of the committee in essence focus on the phrase "value judgment" in the same sentence as the basis for rejecting the conclusion that score adjustment is scientifically justified.

Employment Testing & Job Performance*
JAN H. BLITS AND LINDA S. GOTTFREDSON

. . .

[The Report of the National Academy of Sciences (NAS)] panel, headed by Yale statistician John Hartigan, confirms that the GATB's validity for predicting job performance is strong enough to enhance worker productivity; but it recommends that the tests not be used unless the results are race-normed. The panel was unable to justify race-norming on the grounds of racial bias—it confirms that tests like the GATB may even slightly overpredict the performance of blacks, particularly in higher level jobs; in this sense the tests are slightly biased in favor of blacks. Nor did it find that the tests were irrelevant—the panel found a 0.3 correlation between test scores and job performance, which means that employers can realize 30 percent of the gains in work-force productivity that a perfectly valid test would yield. Undeterred, the panel looked elsewhere and found—or at least claimed to find—justification for race-norming in the very nature of a selection system that favors people with high scores over those with low scores.

   Any selection system that selects higher scorers over lower scorers necessarily favors those who are above a cut-off rather than those who are below it. However, some candidates who score below a cut-off may in fact be able to perform the job at least at a minimally acceptable level; such candidates are called "false negatives." Others, "false positives," score above the cutoff but are nonetheless unable to perform at a minimally acceptable level. The lower a test's validity, the more such false predictions are likely to occur. Now, more blacks than whites fall in the category of "false negatives," and more whites than blacks are "false

   * Excerpts from Jan H. Blits and Linda S. Gottfredson, "Employment Testing and Job Performance," *The Public Interest,* no. 98, copyright © 1990 by National Affairs, Inc. Reprinted with permission of the authors and publisher.

positives." The reason for these disproportions has nothing to do with race *per se,* but arises from the fact that more whites have scores above the cut-off and more blacks below it. "[T]hese effects," the panel agrees, "are a function of high and low test scores, not racial or ethnic identity." Yet even as it emphasizes that the effect is the same for all low-scoring individuals, regardless of their race, the panel nevertheless claims that "the disproportionate impact of selection error provides scientific grounds for the adjustment of minority scores." It concludes, in other words, that the disproportions in false predictions provide a "scientific justification" for benefiting test takers whose scores—if anything—*over*predict their job performance.

The central failing of the NAS panel is that it recommends a race-based solution to what it concedes is not a race-based problem; thus it seeks a scientific justification for what is scientifically unjustifiable. The panel evidently set out to endorse race-norming; to do so, it had to make slanted analytic assumptions, to choose a questionable criterion for determining the tests' fairness, to disregard technical distinctions, and to frame policy considerations one-sidedly.

For example, the panel consistently interprets its data in ways that minimize the GATB's validity. Repeatedly choosing what it acknowledges to be the most "conservative analytic assumptions," it is able to limit the tests' estimated validity to 0.3. (Labor Department technical reports place it at 0.5 or higher.) Time and again the panel then belittles this correlation as "imperfect" or "only modest," despite admitting that it is strong enough to increase productivity. Since the tests' validity poses a stumbling block to any attempt to offer "scientific justifications" for race-norming, the panel is forced to disparage it. The better a test predicts job performance, the more "deceptive" (the panel's word) race-norming becomes.

Even as the panel chooses analytic assumptions that limit the tests' validity, it also sets a standard of perfect validity. The panel shows that the unadjusted GATB scores meet the only widely accepted criterion of fairness in testing—that a test predict equally well for all groups; it then drops that criterion, however, and adopts another—that the test's false predictions not adversely affect minorities—that the unadjusted scores fail to satisfy. In fact, though, any test that meets the commonly accepted criterion must necessarily fail to meet the panel's criterion. (Conversely, any test that meets the panel's criterion must necessarily fail to meet the commonly accepted one.) Only a perfectly valid test could meet both criteria; and perfectly valid tests do not exist. Most experts reject the panel's chosen criterion, viewing it as internally inconsistent; but the panel adopts it without reviewing the scientific literature critical of it or even acknowledging that serious criticism exists.

The panel also draws attention only to the crudest distinctions in job performance, ignoring differences between minimally competent and highly productive workers. For example, when asserting the unfairness of using unnormed test scores, the panel indiscriminately groups together as "able" all workers whose job performance is above a minimum level. This procedure has the effect of exaggerating the significance of false predictions, providing specious strength to the panel's "scientific justification" for race-norming. Similarly, the panel recommends reporting a second, unnormed score for all candidates already referred on the basis of race-norming; the second score would indicate the probability that a candidate will perform "above average." Although ostensibly meant to reveal intergroup distinctions that race-norming (admittedly) conceals, the unnormed score in fact conceals the full extent of differences in expected job performance because it makes no distinctions among higher levels of performance. Its sole standard is "above average" performance.

· · ·

What the panel in fact shows is not that race-norming is scientifically justified, but that the decision to race-norm is not a scientific issue. The panel confirms that testing's adverse impact is not caused by defects in the tests themselves. Hence the adverse impact has no technical solution, let alone one that requires adjusting minority scores to compensate for "the inadequacies of the technology [of testing]." Nor is race-norming an issue on which scientists are in a special position to make policy recommendations. Instead, race-norming is a political question that ought to be answered politically. Whether the nation should adopt race-norming should be decided by public officials and ultimately by the citizens; to pretend that science can supply an answer is only to pervert science by politicizing it.

Concepts of Discrimination in "General Ability" Job Testing*
MARK KELMAN

Introduction

As a group, blacks score significantly lower on "general ability" tests than do whites and will thus obtain employment less frequently than white applicants if employers use such tests as a basis for hiring decisions. Proponents of testing believe that the tests accurately predict on-the-job performance and exclude only those people who would perform less capably. Testing proponents therefore argue that the disadvantage blacks suffer when an employer uses tests is justified, not discriminatory. Whether testing proponents convincingly prove this claim depends in part on the degree to which tests do in fact predict perfor-

* Excerpts from Mark Kelman, "Concepts of Discrimination in 'General Ability' Job Testing," *Harvard Law Review,* vol. 104, copyright © 1991. Reprinted by permission of the author and publisher.

mance. The persuasiveness of their claim depends as well on how we answer a less familiar conceptual question—what do we mean by "discrimination"?

. . .

The Input Cost vs. Employee Output Distinction: Individual-Output-Centered Discrimination

... A profit-maximizing employer comparing two applicants' impact on firm profitability judges each in terms of his "net value added." That is, each employee contributes to output, and each employee requires the employer to make expenditures on items such as wages and benefits and marginal capital costs associated with production. In some cases, no one would deny the legitimacy of the employer's focus on the marginal capital costs associated with employing a particular worker. It would appear ironic for an applicant for a typing pool to claim that he is as productive as another typist because he can type the same amount, with the same accuracy, in the same amount of time, as long as he is given a machine that is twice as expensive.

There are, however, title VII, disability discrimination, and age discrimination cases in which courts have permitted employers to screen out employees only if their output is lower, not if the input costs inevitably associated with their employment are higher. These cases suggest that it may not be legitimate for employers to pay workers in accord with net value added; instead, this limited attack on market distributive norms demands that employers ignore differential inputs and treat applicants differently only insofar as their capacity to produce output is different. Thus, one might view these cases as examples of the courts accepting a mild version of what are typically considered more politically radical distributive invalidity theories.

It might be helpful in conceptualizing the difference between cases in which the employee's output is lower and those in which the employee's input costs are higher to think of the distinction between costly capital equipment that is universally helpful and costly equipment that aids only the disadvantaged person. A hearing aid, for instance, may enable a hearing-impaired employee to respond more readily to supervisor's commands, but it would not give a non-hearing-impaired worker any advantage over another non-hearing-impaired worker. On the other hand, one could imagine an employer providing aids to a protected group member that would help *any* worker's relative productivity. If, but perhaps only if, a worker requires only equipment that helps her in ways that would not help the bulk of workers, courts may, and perhaps should, prohibit employers from screening her out. Courts may treat the costly equipment as simply providing her an opportunity to demonstrate her capacity, not as specially boosting her capacity relative to other workers.

One might also want to differentiate between cases in which the employer seeks to avoid privately shouldering a social cost that will be borne in any event from cases in which the employer legitimately claims that screening out the employee will eliminate a needless social cost. Assume, for instance, that whether or not they take the job some applicants are predisposed to contract an illness that is especially expensive to treat. Assume, further, that an atypically high proportion of such applicants are members of protected groups. Finally, assume that the employer self-insures so that she will bear the costs of such an applicant's medical care. In such a case, the employer's selfish profit interests dictate screening out the applicant, even though doing so will not reduce the social costs of health care. The screening shifts costs; it does not eliminate them.

· · ·

General Ability Job Tests: Are They Consistent With the Demands of Meritocracy and Antidiscrimination Principles?

Are General Ability Job Tests Statically Discriminatory?

The question whether general ability job tests discriminate is of great current concern.

· · ·

... I contend that, as an empirical matter, the tests have only modest statistical validity as predictors of productivity. I argue that the use of such low-validity screening devices, rather than what I will hypothesize to be more expensive ex post screening systems based on retaining only competent workers and discharging those who prove to be inadequately competent, may prove both privately rational for employers and socially cost minimizing. Nonetheless, such devices do not reward people in accord with their productivity and should thus be suspect if we adopt the individual output view of discrimination.

· · ·

The validity of general ability tests. The claim that tests are highly valid predictors of productivity is problematic.... First, when test validators correlate a predictor (the screening test) with a criterion (performance on the job), the information they produce is useful only if the criterion they measure is a reasonable surrogate for actual productivity. Industrial psychologists, however, do not correlate test scores with pay, the best presumptive measure of worker productivity in a market system. Economists have generally found quite low correlations between the "ability" that the tests purportedly measure and earnings. Unless employers cannot observe productivity or observe productivity but do not pay in accord with it, these findings cast grave doubt on testing advocates' claims that ability test scores predict output. Nevertheless, test validators typically correlate the predictor with performance on job sample tests or with supervisor ratings.

Using job sample tests as an indicator of productivity is conceptually problematic, because the capacity to perform well on the sorts of highly individualized tasks that job sample tests can measure may correlate only weakly with the capacity to contribute to the product of the group in which production occurs. The existing job sample tests on which Hunter and Schmidt rely in extolling ability tests do not even do a particularly good job of measuring individualized skills. Positive correlations between ability tests and job sample tests may simply reflect shared methods variance (people proficient at one type of test will do well on other, similar tests) rather than a correlation between predictor and output.

· · ·

Second, even if the chosen criteria are in fact accurate measures of productivity, the critical question is whether the use of cognitive tests can be justified on the basis that such tests have a significantly higher validity than alternative screening devices such as education, job experience, peer evaluations, and interviews. In fact, observed mean validities (correlations between test and criterion) for general ability job tests, while positive, are not demonstrably higher than those for many of these other screening devices. Although Hunter and Schmidt state that mean validities are typically higher than the observed validities for alternative screening devices, other analysts have found mean validities for cognitive tests that are either barely distinguishable from, or actually lower than, validities for alternative screening devices.

· · ·

Individualistic arguments against using low-validity tests that have disparate impact on identifiable social groups. Because in reality those who fail to get the same economic rewards as others with equal job performance capacity often constitute a socially identifiable group (women or blacks) rather than a "group" that one can identify only by reference to members' specific disadvantaging factor (poor test taking), the use of the sort of facially "fair" but inaccurate test we have been considering may seem problematic....

... There is little doubt that, when people identify themselves as members of discrete groups, the success of other members of the group affects them. Whether one tends to emphasize the more immediate self-esteem effects on individuals or the more long-term benefits of successful role models is not pertinent to the ultimate argument. As long as people are more affected by the achievements of people in their group than by the achievement of people in general, the relative status of each group, as a whole, has significant consequences in the lives of particular people.

Racial subgrouping may be particularly appropriate in the American context. Given the enormous historical disparities in the life circumstances of blacks and whites both during and after slavery, social practices that disadvantage blacks as a group will inexorably both confirm blacks' sense of exclusion from the larger community and create or reinforce self-doubt. A message of inferiority is inevitably reinforced because one aspect of blacks' cultural subjugation by the white majority has been the attempt by whites to suggest that black failure is both natural and inevitable.

Notes and Questions

1.   Assume that an employer hires workers on the basis of a test that is weakly predictive of true productivity on the job. Since the test is imperfect, some capable workers will fail the test, and some incapable workers will pass. Assume that 67 percent of the capable whites and 40 percent of the incapable whites pass the test, but at the same time only 38 percent of the capable blacks and 30 percent of the incapable blacks pass the test. In other words, regardless of which category of true productivity blacks fall into, they are screened out at a higher rate than whites falling in the same category of actual underlying productivity. Should the use of such a test be lawful?

One's first response might be to think that the test must be biased against blacks: perhaps it is less accurate at predicting true productivity for blacks than for whites. In fact, this example is based on a simulation in which the test is equally predictive for blacks and whites. For both racial groups, there is a .3 correlation between their test scores and their true productivity—exactly the National Academy's assessment of the predictive validity of the GATB.

In this example, the observed lower pass rates for blacks result not from bias but from the statistical property of regression to the mean. For any test that has a specific cutoff, the following will be true: those who tend to score low will have their true productivity understated, and those who tend to score high will have their true productivity overstated. This result has nothing directly to do with race. But since it turns out that, on average, blacks score lower than whites, the statistical property means that blacks can be adversely affected by the use of such a test. It is this feature that concerned the National Academy of Sciences panel: given the long history of oppression suffered by blacks, a neutral practice that imposes an additional burden on blacks raises serious equity considerations.

2.   Blits and Gottfredson simply point out that the test, however imperfect, is the best predictor of performance and has no racial bias. Nonetheless, the use of the test disadvantages blacks (and other low scorers) to an even greater extent than their own average lower true productivities. Blits and Gottfredson claim that the GATB's predictive validity of .3 implies that the use of such a test generates 30 percent of the increase in productivity that would be garnered from using a perfectly valid test. But this should not be taken as evidence that the use of the test is necessarily desirable.

To illustrate how the use of such an imperfect test could be more harmful than using no test at all, consider a diagnostic medical test that generates the score results given earlier for whites and blacks. Assume that "passing the test when you are capable" means "being correctly identified as in need of certain medicine." The rub is that for whites, failure to take the medicine when needed means getting a bad cold, whereas for blacks, failure to take it when needed leads to death. Note what this implies: 67 percent of the whites who needed the medicine were actually determined to have such need by the test, which implies that 33 percent of those who needed the medicine will get a bad cold (because despite their need the test incorrectly categorized them as not in need of the medicine—i.e., the test produced a false negative). At the same time, 38 percent of the blacks who needed the medicine were identified by the test and thus saved, while 62 percent died (the false negatives). If the medicine were cheap and harmless, providing it to everyone would prevent all the colds among whites and the deaths among blacks. If the medicine were expensive or scarce, however, the relative nature of the harm from failing to correctly identify who needs the medicine suggests that the test should be disregarded and the medicine directed toward blacks. The reason for this result is that the consequences of false negatives are far more serious for blacks than for whites (and also far more serious than false positives).

Is the social cost of a black being wrongfully rejected on an employment test greater than the social cost of an equal-scoring white being wrongfully rejected? The belief that it is provides the rationale for Kelman's argument against relying on general ability tests to make significant employment decisions when such tests are only weakly predictive of actual productivity and disproportionately exclude capable blacks. Just as the example above illustrates a case in which it might be sensible to give everyone a certain medicine because reliance on a certain medical test leads to serious harm, Kelman would like to move in the direction of hiring more workers and letting on-the-job performance more accurately reveal the capable workers in order to reduce the harm of adverse impact on blacks.

3. While Blits and Gottfredson are correct in stating that the National Academy panel attacked the test on scientific grounds when the true grounds for the attack should have been on equity grounds, are they being obtuse in failing to comprehend fully the fairness issue? If the social calculus could be based on a full and accurate assessment of all of the costs and benefits of using tests like the GATB, would some test score adjustment to aid blacks be appropriate?

4. Kelman also addresses the interesting questions of what constitutes a lower productivity worker and when should an employer be obliged by antidiscrimination law to hire a legally protected worker who, from a strict profit-maximization perspective, is less productive than a legally unprotected worker. Title VII clearly has been interpreted not to defer to an employer's goal of pursuing the highest profits when profit maximization would lead a firm to adopt discriminatory practices to please discriminatory customers. Kelman speculates more generally that the impact of a practice on employer profits may not be a reliable guide to assessing when courts will impose

burdens on employers to promote the employment prospects of protected workers.

To illustrate some of the relevant issues, consider two cases. In case I, by incurring a onetime expense with a present value of $2000, an employer could train or accommodate a protected worker and equalize that worker's productivity with the work of an unprotected worker. In case II, no productivity-equalizing training opportunity exists, and the employer must simply decide whether to hire an unprotected applicant or a protected applicant who is only slightly less talented. The employer estimates that the present value of the lost profits that would result from hiring the less talented protected worker is $1000. Kelman speculates that courts would be more likely to order the hiring of the protected worker in case I than in case II—even though the economic burden on the employer is greater in case I—because the court would view case I as imposing "a one-time cost of remedying past discrimination."

If profit maximization were the guiding principle, in neither case would the protected worker be hired. If courts were more likely to order the hiring of protected workers in inverse proportion to the magnitude of the burden thereby imposed on the employer, then the protected worker in case II would be more likely to be hired than the protected worker in case I—exactly the opposite of Kelman's intuition. Might there be a greater *social* cost in hiring the less productive protected worker in case II because in that case, unlike in case I, fellow workers and customers would be constantly exposed to a less productive protected worker, which might generate friction and harden negative stereotypes about the productivity of protected workers?

5. Note that the issue about whether an employer is required by antidiscrimination law to incur added costs to make particular workers more productive is a central concern of the Americans with Disabilities Act (ADA). This Act, which was adopted in 1991, specifically directs employers to shift from a single-minded focus on worker productivity—what John Donohue has called the guarantee of intrinsic equality—to a focus on what fairness requires to assist a statistically less productive worker—the guarantee of constructed equality. The ADA requires employers to take reasonable measures to accommodate disabled workers, and prohibits discrimination against those disabled workers who will become equally productive by virtue of such reasonable accommodation. As John Donohue has indicated:

> Clearly, given a choice between two equally productive workers, one requiring the expenditure of significant sums in order to accommodate him and one requiring no such expenditures, the profit-maximizing firm would prefer the worker who is less costly to hire. Thus, the transformation that has occurred in the realm of civil rights is that the ideal nondiscriminatory market solution, which previously was the benchmark of intrinsic equality and what the law demanded, is now regarded as an obstacle to social justice. . . .

> The ADA has imposed perhaps the greatest demand of constructed equality by explicitly requiring that employers take reasonable measures to make the disabled equal. Rather than the early Title VII insistence

that employers disregard the traits of protected workers, the ADA requires employers to identify the traits of the disabled that undermine their productivity and to seek whenever possible to overcome these traits.

Donohue, "Employment Discrimination Law in Perspective: Three Concepts of Equality," 92 *Michigan Law Review* 2583, 2609, 2612 (1994).

Has the ADA paved the way for economically disadvantaged minorities to argue that the effects of the factors that have undermined their productivity—including poor schooling and broken families—are now to be corrected by employers? Would employers be able to remedy these problems through reasonable expenditures?

5

The Nature and Extent of Racial Prejudice

Over an extended period of time, researchers have asked white Americans questions about their racial attitudes, such as, "Do you believe that blacks are inferior to whites?" The primary finding to emerge from this survey literature exploring the level of antiblack prejudice is that racism declined steadily in the second half of this century. But how valid is survey evidence? Although simple surveys of racial attitudes can provide some insight into the degree of racial prejudice, the likelihood of truthful reporting diminishes as racial bias becomes less socially acceptable. This is not to suggest that the survey evidence is not interesting and important. Indeed, the increase in nonprejudiced responses to survey questions may confirm a highly significant phenomenon—the development of a dominant, egalitarian ideology. What the surveys cannot reveal, however, is the extent to which survey respondents have internalized the egalitarian values or simply learned to disguise their true feelings.

As a result, researchers have sought a number of indirect ways to observe discriminatory behavior as a means of inferring the presence of prejudiced attitudes. Faye Crosby, Stephanie Bromley, and Leonard Saxe review a wide array of the unobtrusive studies of racial discrimination and demonstrate that racial prejudice is more widespread than survey results suggest. These studies show that whites tend to be more likely to provide help to other whites as opposed to blacks, and to manifest more aggression toward blacks than whites—particularly if the costs of indulging in this conduct are low. Crosby, Bromley, and Saxe conclude that "whites still discriminate against blacks in terms of behaviors that lie largely out of awareness," and they suggest that overt expressions of racial bias have been replaced by more subtle and covert expressions of prejudice.

While there is disagreement over how much racism exists in the world, even greater controversy exists over the origins and functions of racism. Is it purely a learned trait, or does racial antagonism represent an innate fear of the "other" that must be deliberately unlearned? Are discrimination and stereotyping inevitable elements of information processing, or dysfunctional traits that burden their possessor? Does racism enhance the self-esteem or material well-being of those who harbor such views?

Linda Krieger summarizes some of the new psychological theories concerning the factors that contribute to the development of negative stereotypes and their automatic activation by the presence of blacks. The disturbing conclusion of cognitive bias theory is that the very nature of cognitive functioning can negatively influence the perception of and behavior toward blacks, even among those who consciously reject racial bias. According to this view, stereotyping is neither aberrant nor indicative of discriminatory motivation, but is simply an element of perceiving and interpreting a complex reality.

While Charles Lawrence is alert to the possibility of cognitive biases, he also attributes much discriminatory treatment to unconscious discriminatory motivations. He attempts to clarify the nature of American racism by arguing that it is largely the product of a historical and cultural heritage that now unconsciously influences our beliefs about and actions toward blacks. Scarred by a common history, we all share the malady of racism, says Lawrence, and therefore its ubiquity causes racism to be seen as normal. Lawrence contends that the self-protective psychological response to the discomfort and guilt caused by the conflict between our culture of racism and the more recently adopted ideal of equality results in excluding racism from one's consciousness. Moreover, this psychological phenomenon makes racism particularly difficult to counteract through legal intervention because even rigorous investigation into the conscious motives of an employer may be incapable of uncovering the racist stereotypes that unconsciously motivate personnel decisions.

The economist Gary Becker has championed the very different view that racism is simply a taste for avoiding contact with certain racial or ethnic groups, not unlike a taste for tart apples or red wine. Becker, *The Economics of Discrimination* (Chicago: University of Chicago Press, 2d ed., 1971). But Becker's associational preference model is unsatisfying in that it offers no explanation for the emergence of the particular taste or the fact that some embrace this associational preference tightly while others reject it completely. Indeed, Becker and his colleague and fellow

Nobel laureate George Stigler later wrote: "[N]o significant behavior has been illuminated by assumptions of differences in tastes. Instead, they, along with assumptions of unstable tastes, have been a convenient crutch to lean on when the analysis has bogged down." Stigler and Becker, "De Gustibus Non Est Disputandum," 67 *American Economic Review* 76, 89 (1977).

Motivated by the deficiencies of the Becker model, Richard Mc-Adams has developed an alternative model of racism, which he calls the status-production model of race discrimination. According to this model, racism emerges because it can serve the interests of those who practice it. McAdams argues that race discrimination is the avenue by which members of a group seek to raise their self-esteem by lowering the status of the group against which they discriminate. McAdams uses the status-production model to answer questions such as "Who will discriminate?"—whites with the most limited abilities to produce status in other ways. Furthermore, the status-production model gives insights into the nature of racial stereotypes and the persistence of race discrimination.

Recent Unobtrusive Studies of Black and White Discrimination and Prejudice: A Literature Review*
FAYE CROSBY, STEPHANIE BROMLEY, AND LEONARD SAXE

. . .

Unobtrusive Studies of Racism

[It is] difficult to determine whether recent decreases in expressed racial prejudice reflect an underlying change in attitudes. Questionnaires and opinionnaires are notoriously reactive. Perhaps the shift toward liberalism is simply a function of changing social desirability effects and does not yet reflect any real change in underlying attitudes. In view of the complex relationship between verbally expressed attitudes toward general attitude objects on the one hand and specific overt behaviors on the other, one wonders if the decrease in prejudiced attitude statements necessarily means that discriminatory behavior has declined or will decline. What, then, do less reactive measures show?

Helping Behavior Studies

Most of the recent unobtrusive literature on discriminatory behavior consists of experiments in which subjects are presented with an opportunity to aid another individual (sometimes a confederate of the experimenter who is either black or white). In such studies, the principal dependent variable is the differential amount of aid given to whites and

* Excerpts from Faye Crosby, Stephanie Bromley, and Leonard Saxe, "Recent Unobtrusive Studies of Black and White Discrimination and Prejudice," *Psychological Bulletin*, vol. 87, copyright © 1980 by the American Psychological Association. Reprinted by permission of the authors and publisher.

blacks. Discrimination exists when individuals from one group (e.g., whites) receive significantly more help than individuals from the other group (e.g., blacks).

[T]he helping behavior studies [are separated into] experiments that involved face-to-face contact between the potential helper and helped person from those that did not. In a few of the studies within the face-to-face category (Type 1), an explicit request for aid (e.g., change for a quarter) was made, but in the majority of the studies, no explicit request for aid was made. The situation was usually merely one in which it was made obvious that the target person needed assistance. In Lerner and Frank's experiment, for example, white and black experimenters dropped their grocery parcels.

Four of the remote studies (Type 2 . . .) involved telephone contact. In Gaertner and Bickman's experiment, for instance, white and black experimenters pretended to have dialed the wrong telephone number. Under the pretext of having used their last dime, they asked the subjects to make a telephone call for them. A fifth remote study used the lost letter technique. This technique involved leaving a completed application to graduate school in an airport telephone booth. Half of the time, the applicant (shown in a photograph) was white; half of the time the applicant was black. In all cases, a stamped, addressed envelope and a note asking "Dad" to mail the form were attached. The context made it obvious that Dad had already left the airport on an earlier flight. Differential rates of posting the lost letter constituted the measure of racism in this experiment.

The final set of laboratory experiments, classified as remote . . . , used Latané and Rodin's lady in distress paradigm. Subjects believed that they were receivers in an ESP experiment, communicating with a black or white sender. In Experiment 1 subjects believed that they were alone or were part of a group of receivers when they heard chairs fall on the sender and heard the sender call for help. In Experiment 2 the ambiguity of the emergency situation was manipulated.

The vast majority of [these] experiments . . . were performed in field settings. Thus, the results are obviously applicable to life outside the experimental laboratory. Furthermore, because less than a third of the studies used college students as subjects, the results are more generalizable than is usually the case with social psychological studies.

Three observations [emerge from this review]. First, discriminatory behavior is present, but it is not extreme. In 19 of the 43 cases (44%), subjects gave more aid to their own race than to the opposite race. In the remaining 56% of the cases, no discrimination or reverse discrimination was observed. Second, whites and blacks are nearly equally likely to discriminate against the opposite race. Of the cases involving white subjects, 40% showed antiblack discrimination, whereas 46% of the cases involving black subjects showed antiwhite discrimination.

Finally, and most interestingly, it is clear from Table 5.1 that whites exhibit discrimination much more often in remote situations (Type 2) than in face-to-face situations (Type 1)....

The finding that whites discriminate more often in situations in which they do not have actual contact implies that whites today hold prejudiced attitudes but that they inhibit expression of this prejudice when the possibility of negative consequences is great. In the more removed and anonymous situations (Type 2), discrimination is much more likely to emerge. The proposition that social desirability strongly affects behavior in face-to-face helping situations is indicated, furthermore, by Wispé and Freshley's observation that white female subjects in their field experiment offered aid to blacks and whites equally often but gave only perfunctory aid to blacks and real aid to whites.

Table 5.1.   Helping Behavior Studies With White Subjects

Type	No. of cases		
	More help to whites	More help to blacks	No difference
Face-to-face	7	4	11
Remote	6	0	2

Note. Face-to-face studies are Type 1 studies; remote studies are Type 2 studies.

Also consistent with the proposition that covert antiblack racism exists is the finding that whites respond more favorably to blacks in stereotypically subordinate or nonassertive roles than to blacks in equal roles, Clark found that whites were more willing to assist black females than black males over the telephone.... I. Katz, Cohen, and Glass found that black experimenters who identified themselves as Negro and who sounded submissive elicited more help from whites during a telephone encounter than did black experimenters who identified themselves as black and sounded aggressive. Finally, Dovidio and Gaertner found covert racism in a laboratory situation. White male subjects were told that they would be a supervisor or a subordinate to a black or white partner on a dyadic task. The partner, who was a confederate of the experimenters and was described as having either low or high ability, "accidently" knocked over a container of pencils. The main dependent measures were whether the subject helped and how many pencils he picked up. The results showed that low-ability black subordinates were helped more than low-ability white subjects. Subjects also tended to help black supervisors less than black subordinates. That is, subjects responded more favorably to blacks when they were in the "correct" stereo-typic role.

Aggression Studies

A second method for studying racism unobtrusively has been developed by the Donnersteins and others. In these experiments, subjects are provided with a legitimate or socially acceptable chance to aggress against a white or black target. The basic procedure in these experiments has been to bring white male subjects into a laboratory under the guise that they are participating in an experiment on learning. Subjects are then assigned the role of teacher by a rigged drawing, and another individual is assigned the role of learner. The learner is actually a confederate of the experimenter, but the subjects believe him to be another subject. In the course of the supposed learning experiment, subjects, seated at a Buss shock machine, administer bogus electrical shocks to the learner each time the learner makes a mistake on the learning task. The pattern of mistakes is preprogrammed. The subject is free to select the level of shock (shock intensity) and may depress the shock button as long as he wishes. Shock intensity is taken to be a measure of direct aggression, whereas shock duration is taken to be a measure of indirect aggression.

Variations in the basic procedure primarily involve additional independent variables. Four experiments manipulated potential retaliation. Half of the time, it was understood that the teacher and learner would exchange roles so that retaliation by the erstwhile target was possible. The other half of the time, no retaliation was possible, or the subject learned of the possibility of retaliation only after the shocks had been delivered. In other experiments, censure or anonymity were manipulated. Half of the subjects were told that their behavior would be recorded and could therefore be open to censure, or half of the subjects believed that their responses would be anonymous. A final variation of interest here was the nature of the outcome. In several experiments, subjects administered rewards rather than punishments to the black or white target.

One may inspect the Donnersteins' program of research for two indicators of antiblack racism among whites. First, there might be main effects for the race of the learner, with black targets receiving more intense or longer shocks than did white targets. Second, there might be interaction effects involving race of learner so that, for instance, potential retaliation influences the subjects' behavior toward black targets but not toward white targets. The second indicator of racism is obviously more subtle than the first.

Over the series of experiments, race of learner has not consistently emerged as a main effect. Some of the experiments showed that aggression was not a function of the race of the target. However, in several studies the white college students aggressed more against blacks than against whites. One experiment revealed that white subjects delivered both more intense and longer shocks to blacks than to whites. In another experiment, black targets elicited more indirect aggression than did white targets. A third experiment showed that whites delivered more intense shocks (direct aggression) to blacks than to whites. It is interesting to note that this last study occurred shortly after a race riot at the university at which the subjects were students.

An independent researcher, Schulman, also failed to find a main effect for race of learner. Schulman examined aggression as a function of the subjects' scores on a four-item Sexual Security Index that had been embedded in a larger questionnaire months prior to the experiment. Schulman found that sexually insecure white males delivered more intense shocks to black targets than to whites but that sexually secure subjects delivered an equal amount of shocks, on the average, to blacks and whites.

When one looks at the interaction effects in the Donnersteins' program of experiments, a striking pattern emerges: Retaliation, censure, and anonymity all affect the behavior of white subjects toward black targets but not toward white targets. In three studies, a significant interaction between race of target and potential retaliation was obtained. When the learner was black, subjects exhibited less direct aggression and more indirect aggression in the retaliation condition than in the no-retaliation condition; but when the learner was white, the potential for retaliation did not affect either direct or indirect aggression. The effect of potential retaliation on aggression against a black target was replicated in a fourth study, in which the learner was always black and the teacher was always white.

A similar pattern of results obtained when potential censure or anonymity replaced potential retaliation. When the target was black, direct aggression was lower in the censure (nonanonymous) conditions than in the noncensure (anonymous) conditions, whereas indirect aggression was higher in the censure condition than in the noncensure condition. Neither censure nor anonymity affected the level of aggression toward white targets.

Finally, when the experimental situation involved administering rewards, the findings were consistent with the data on punishments. Potential reciprocation elevated the rewards given to blacks but did not affect the rewards given to whites.

The findings that retaliation, censure, and anonymity all affect aggression against black targets but fail to affect aggression against white targets is important. The data imply that antiblack hostility was pervasive, but subtle, in the white college students who served as subjects in the Donnersteins' series of experiments. Assuming that these subjects are representative of the general population, we may conclude that whites today harbor covert hostility toward blacks. When the conditions are "safe" (i.e., no retaliation, no censure, anonymous), the hostility emerges in the form of direct aggression, so that more intense shocks are delivered to blacks than to whites. When the conditions render the direct expression of aggression unsafe, the expression of hostility becomes indirect, such that longer shocks are delivered to blacks than to whites.

The proposition that whites inhibit the behavioral expression of their attitudinal prejudice is further supported by data indicating that whites fear retaliation from blacks more than from other whites. In one study, the subjects indicated on the Buss shock machine the shocks that they anticipated from their partners. Subjects who had been paired with black learners expected to receive more intense and longer shocks after the teacher—learner roles were reversed than did subjects who had been paired with white learners.

Less disheartening than the findings that have emerged from the original series of experiments with black or white targets are the results of two recent studies by the Donnersteins in which a white male subject was always presented with a black male target. In the first study, half of the subjects were exposed to a model prior to their own performance as teacher in the bogus learning experiment. The model either delivered consistently high rewards to the black learner or delivered consistently low shocks to the black learner. Subjects exposed to the model delivered less intense shocks to the black learner than did the control group (no exposure to model). More importantly, subjects in the model condition did not increase the duration of the shocks delivered. Thus, exposure to a nonracist model helped to decrease overt discrimination without effecting a compensatory increase in covert discrimination.

The most recent study explored the relative effectiveness of two strategies for controlling white aggression toward blacks. White male college students either saw or did not see another white student receive censure for shocking a black learner. In addition, they were told either that their own responses would be videotaped (potential censure) or that they would be anonymous (no direct censure). The results indicated that both types of censure effectively reduced direct aggression. Indirect aggression was virtually unaffected by either manipulation. When observed censure was paired with potential direct censure, however, indirect aggression decreased substantially.

. . .

All of the unobtrusive aggression studies (unlike the majority of the helping studies) have been performed in laboratory settings. One may wonder, therefore, if the findings obtained under these artificial conditions would generalize widely to the world outside the laboratory. A field experiment by Dertke, Penner, and Ulrich bears some similarity to the aggression studies and indicates that the findings obtained by the Donnersteins have direct real-world applicability. In Dertke et al.'s study, a white or black female shoplifted some items in a retail store in the presence of white shoppers. Using as subjects those shoppers who were rated by an independent observer as having noticed the crime, the results reveal race discrimination. The subjects spontaneously reported and confirmed (when questioned) the crime more often when the shop-lifter was black than when she was white. If one assumes that reporting or confirming the crime is likely to result in punishment to the offender, these data indicate that whites exhibit more aggression (albeit, socially sanctioned aggression) against blacks than against whites.

.   .   .

In a . . . laboratory study, white undergraduates viewed an interaction on a monitor that they believed was live. The interactions involved two males and culminated in one of the males (harm doer) shoving the other (victim). When the harm doer was black, subjects perceived the shove as violent; but when the harm doer was white, subjects labeled the shove as "playing around" or "dramatizing." Furthermore, black harm doers elicited personality attributions, whereas white harm doers elicited situational attributions. . . .

Interpretations: Explanatory Models

The unobtrusive studies of racism reviewed here reveal two points: First, white discrimination appears to be a function of the characteristics of the situation and of the behavior under study. In the helping behavior studies, discrimination was more marked in the relatively anonymous situations than in the face-to-face encounters. In the aggression studies, potential retaliation and censure decreased the amount of direct aggression and increased the amount of indirect aggression against blacks. Aggression against whites seems to be unaffected by potential retaliation or censure. . . .

The second point is that discriminatory behavior is more prevalent in the body of unobtrusive studies than we might expect on the basis of survey data. If we assume (a) that verbal reports are valid indicators of people's actual or privately held sentiments, and (b) that overt behavior is consistent with actual sentiments, then we ought to find few instances of racial discrimination in the literature reviewed here. In fact, we find a lot of discrimination.

Where does this lead? One alternative is to reevaluate our assumptions. Perhaps privately held sentiments are not a good indicator of discriminatory behavior; or perhaps verbal statements are not a good indicator of actual sentiments. Our own position has been to question the assumption that verbal reports reflect actual sentiments, and we inferred from the literature that whites today are, in fact, more prejudiced than they are wont to admit. This inference closely parallels the conclusions drawn by Baxter, Gaertner, Gaertner and Dovidio, Linn, and Weitz all of whom found that verbally reported sentiments failed to predict overt behavior in interracial situations.

.   .   .

[Based on] the data we have reviewed, we may infer that whites today are complying with the norms of nondiscrimination but that they have not yet internalized unprejudiced values. In the helping studies, discrimination is relatively low in those situations in which surveillance is high and in which the costs and rewards for nondiscriminatory behavior are obvious and immediate. Discrimination emerges with a vengeance in the non-face-to-face helping situations, in which surveillance is low or absent and a refusal to help is not potentially costly. In the aggression studies, whites exhibit less direct aggression against blacks when the potential costs are high. The finding that potential cost does not affect aggression toward other whites is consistent with the view that whites have internalized a positive image of whites.

The Content of Our Categories: A Cognitive Bias Approach to Discrimination and Equal Employment Opportunity*

LINDA HAMILTON KRIEGER

. . .

In 1963, social psychologists Henri Tajfel and A. L. Wilkes performed a series of simple experiments, asking subjects to estimate the relative lengths of lines that differed in length by a constant ratio of 5 percent. In one condition, eight lines had not been presented as belonging to several groups. In a second condition, the longer four of the eight lines had been previously presented as belonging to "Group A," the shorter four lines as belonging to "Group B."

Tajfel and Wilkes found that once they introduced the concept of "groupness" into the situation, subjects perceived objects in different groups as more different from each other, and objects in the same group as more similar to each other, than was in fact the case. In the second condition, where the lines were previously presented as belonging to one of two groups, subjects consistently overestimated the variation between lines belonging to different groups and underestimated the variation between lines belonging to the same group. Similar distortions were not observed in the "unclassified" condition. In other words, subjects tended to "stereotype" lines based on their group membership.

Tajfel and Wilkes' findings replicated those of another social psychologist, Donald Campbell, who in 1956 had performed a series of similar experiments using groups of nonsense syllables located along a spatial continuum. Campbell's results, like Tajfel and Wilkes', demon-

* Excerpts from Linda Hamilton Krieger, "The Content of Our Categories: A Cognitive Bias Approach to Discrimination and Equal Employment Opportunity," *Stanford Law Review*, vol. 47, copyright © 1995 by the Board of Trustees of the Leland Stanford Junior University. Reprinted by permission of Stanford Law Review and Fred B. Rothman & Company.

strated that when subjects were led to think about objects as belonging to separate groups, they systematically exaggerated the variation between objects from different groups. Nonsense syllables, like lines of varying lengths, can fall prey to human stereotyping.

Experiments such as these represented the earliest empirical investigation of a theoretical claim made by psychologists such as W. E. Vinacke, who argued that stereotypes should be understood as cognitive structures no different from other categorization-related constructs. Vinacke also suggested that principles derived from the investigation of human cognition be applied to the study of intergroup perception and judgment.

Campbell, Tajfel, and Wilkes interpreted their findings along these lines. In his 1956 study, Campbell suggested that what he termed the "bias of enhancement of contrast," is, in either person or object perception, "a natural, automatic, and inevitable aspect of imperfect learning about the individual members of overlapping groups." Similarly, Tajfel wrote in 1969 that intergroup bias was not necessarily motivational in origin. It may result, he suggested, from the same processes of categorization, assimilation, and search for coherence that underlie all human cognition, whether the objects judged be persons of different races or lines assigned to different groups. Campbell, Tajfel, and Wilkes' findings lent the first empirical support to what became known as the cognitive approach to intergroup bias, or social cognition theory.

The emergence of social cognition theory represented a profound shift in psychologists' thinking about intergroup bias. [U]ntil well into the 1970s, intergroup prejudice was generally understood as stemming from motivational processes. Stereotypes of members of "outgroups" were seen as developing out of prejudice, and as serving to rationalize it. While psychologists such as Gordon Allport recognized that stereotyping was functionally similar to categorization, stereotypes were seen as something "special," discontinuous with "normal" cognitive process. Before the 1970s, few psychologists seriously entertained the notion that normal cognitive processes related to categorization might *in and of themselves* produce and perpetuate intergroup bias.

This is a central premise of social cognition theory—that cognitive structures and processes involved in categorization and information processing can in and of themselves result in stereotyping and other forms of biased intergroup judgment previously attributed to motivational processes. The social cognition approach to discrimination comprises three claims relevant to our present inquiry. The first is that stereotyping, as Vinacke suggested in 1957, is nothing special. It is simply a form of categorization, similar in structure and function to the categorization of natural objects. According to this view, stereotypes, like other categorical structures, are cognitive mechanisms that *all* people, not just "prejudiced" ones, use to simplify the task of perceiving, processing, and retaining information about people in memory. They are central, and indeed essential to normal cognitive functioning.

The second claim posited in social cognition theory is that, once in place, stereotypes bias intergroup judgment and decisionmaking. According to this view, stereotypes operate as "person prototypes" or "social schemas." As such, they function as implicit theories, biasing in predictable ways the perception, interpretation, encoding, retention, and recall of information about other people. These biases are *cognitive* rather than *motivational*. They operate absent intent to favor or disfavor members of a particular social group. And, perhaps most significant for present purposes, they bias a decisionmaker's judgment long before the "moment of decision," as a decisionmaker attends to relevant data and interprets, encodes, stores, and retrieves it from memory. These biases "sneak up on" the decisionmaker, distorting bit by bit the data upon which his decision is eventually based.

The third claim follows from the second. Stereotypes, when they function as implicit prototypes or schemas, operate beyond the reach of decisionmaker self-awareness. Empirical evidence indicates that people's access to their own cognitive processes is in fact poor. Accordingly, cognitive bias may well be both unintentional and unconscious.

· · ·

For example, in 1980, H. Andrew Sagar and Janet Schofield conducted a study demonstrating the effect of social schemas on the interpretation of ambiguous information. In the study, school-age children were presented cartoonlike drawings of two children and a verbal description of the scene, read by the experimenter. One drawing showed two students sitting in a classroom, one behind the other. The verbal description of the scene was: "Mark was sitting at his desk, working on his social studies assignment, when David started poking him in the back with the eraser end of his pencil. Mark just kept on working. David kept poking him for a while, and then he finally stopped." In one condition, David was depicted as black, in the other condition, white. Subjects were asked to rate David's behavior on four scales, evaluating the extent to which they thought it was playful, friendly, mean, or threatening.

The results demonstrated that the race of the actor had a significant impact on the manner in which subjects categorized his actions. If the actor was black, subjects judged his behavior to be more mean and threatening and less playful and friendly. The opposite result obtained when the actor was white. Thus, subjects interpreted the same behavior differently depending on the race of the actor performing it.

Sagar and Schofield's results replicated the finding of a similar experiment conducted by Birt Duncan in 1976. In Duncan's study, white college students watched one of four videotapes in which two males discussed alternative solutions to a particular problem. Subjects were told they were watching a live interaction happening in another room, and that its purpose was to develop a new system for rating interpersonal behavior. While the videotape played, a buzzer rang at specified intervals, signalling subjects to categorize the behavior they were then viewing in one of ten categories and to indicate its intensity on an 8-point scale.

As the videotaped discussion progressed, the dialogue became increasingly heated. Finally, one of the participants (the protagonist) shoved the other (the victim). At that point, the buzzer rang—not for the first time—and subjects were asked to characterize and rate the intensity of the protagonist's behavior.

As in the Sagar and Schofield study, the protagonist's race significantly affected how subjects characterized the shove. If the protagonist was white, his behavior was characterized as "playing around" or "dramatizes." If he was black, it was characterized as "aggressive" or "violent."

Once behavior has been interpreted and encoded into memory, its meaning is in a sense "fixed," for once a person has constructed an explanation of an event, it is this construction, not the raw information that stimulated it, that is used in making subsequent judgments or predictions. Indeed, once a behavior has been encoded as a trait, its effect on subsequent judgments increases over time. It then supports and validates the preexisting stereotypic expectancy. So, for example, when a female or Asian cadet performs a particular behavior we may characterize it as "passive," yet characterize the same behavior as "prudent" or "restrained" when performed by a male Caucasian cadet. One might invoke "racism" or "sexism" to describe this discrimination. Less dramatically, but perhaps more informatively, one could describe it as one way that social schemas subtly distort information processing about other people and result in intergroup bias.

· · ·

The decisionmaker may be wholly unaware that the employee's gender in any way influenced his decisionmaking. As he sees it, the two employees simply are not similarly situated.

· · ·

The causal attribution of success and failure plays a critical role in performance evaluation, promotion, compensation, and discharge decisions. Absent corrective measures, systematic biases in causal attribution can be expected to disadvantage members of stereotyped groups or individuals who are socially "distant" from the decisionmaker or who, for whatever reason, the decisionmaker has grouped in a different cognitive category. [T]hese biases operate largely outside of the realm of decisionmaker self-awareness, and can be expected to contaminate interpersonal judgment even in the absence of any intent to discriminate.

The Id, The Ego, and Equal Protection: Reckoning With Unconscious Racism*

CHARLES R. LAWRENCE III

Psychoanalytic Theory: An Explanation of Racism's Irrationality

The division of the mind into the conscious and the unconscious is the fundamental principle of psychoanalysis. Psychoanalytic theory explains the existence of pathological mental behavior as well as certain otherwise unexplained behavior in healthy people by postulating two powerful mental processes—the primary and the secondary—which govern how the mind works. The primary process, or Id, occurs outside of our awareness. It consists of desires, wishes, and instincts that strive for gratification. It follows its own laws, of which the supreme one is pleasure. The secondary process, or Ego, happens under conscious control and is bound by logic and reason. We use this process to adapt to reality: The Ego is required to respect the demands of reality and to conform to ethical and moral laws. On their way to gratification, the Id impulses must pass through the territory of the Ego where they are criticized, rejected, or modified, often by some defensive measure on the part of the secondary process. Defensive mechanisms such as repression, denial, introjection, projection, reaction formation, sublimation, and reversal resolve the conflicts between the primary and secondary processes by disguising forbidden wishes and making them palatable.

Several observations about the nature of racial prejudice give credence both to the theory of repression and to the suggestion that racial antagonism finds its source in the unconscious. For example, when we say that racism is irrational, we mean that when people are asked to explain the basis of their racial antagonism they either express an instinctive, unexplained distaste at the thought of associating with the out-group as equals or they cite reasons that are not based on established fact and are often contradicted by personal experience. In one study on racial prejudice, E. L. Hartley included in his survey three fictitious groups he called the Dariens, the Praneans, and the Wallonians. A large portion of respondents who expressed a dislike for blacks and Jews also disliked these nonexistent groups and advocated restrictive measures against them.

In psychoanalytic terms, this irrational behavior indicates poor "reality-testing." When people of normal intelligence behave in a way that rejects what they experience as real, it requires some explanation. Psychoanalytic theory assumes that inadequacy in reality-testing fulfills a psychological function, usually the preservation of an attitude basic to the individual's makeup. If adequate reality-testing threatens to undermine such a functionally significant attitude, it is avoided. In such cases, the dislike of out-groups is based on rationalization—that is, on socially acceptable pseudoreasons that serve to disguise the function that the antagonism serves for the individual.

Of course, not all inadequate reality-testing is a rationalization of hidden motives. The occasion for reality-testing is not always available, and all of us make prejudgments based on insufficient evidence. But when these prejudgments become rigidly stereotyped thinking that eschews reality even when facts are available, there is reason to search for a psychological function that the rigidity of the prejudgment fulfills.

An examination of the beliefs that racially prejudiced people have about out-groups demonstrates their use of other mechanisms observed by both Freudian and nonFreudian behavioralists. For example, studies have found that racists hold two types of stereotyped beliefs: They believe the out-group is dirty, lazy, oversexed, and without control of their instincts (a typical accusation against blacks), or they believe the out-group is pushy, ambitious, conniving, and in control of business, money, and industry (a typical accusation against Jews). These two types of accusation correspond to two of the most common types of neurotic conflict: that which arises when an individual cannot master his instinctive drives in a way that fits into rational and socially approved patterns of behavior, and that which arises when an individual cannot live up to the aspirations and standards of his own conscience. Thus, the stereotypical view of blacks implies that their Id, the instinctive part of their psyche, dominates their Ego, the rationally oriented part. The stereotype of the Jew, on the other hand, accuses him of having an overdeveloped Ego. In this way, the racially prejudiced person projects his own conflict into the form of racial stereotypes.

The preoccupation among racially prejudiced people with sexual matters in race relations provides further evidence of this relationship between the unconscious and racism. Taboos against interracial sexual relations, myths concerning the sexual prowess of blacks, and obsessions with racial purity coexist irrationally with a tendency to break these taboos. Again, psychoanalytic theory provides insights: According to Freud, one's sexual identity plays a crucial role in the unending effort to come to terms with oneself. Thus, the prominence of racism's sexual component supports the theory that racial antagonism grows in large part out of an unstable sense of identity.

Another piece of evidence that supports the contention that racism originates in the unconscious is the fact that racially discriminatory behavior usually improves long before corresponding attitudes toward members of the out-group begin to change. Again, this is to be expected in light of the underlying psychological processes. Behavior is more frequently under Ego control than is attitude. Attitude reflects, in large part, the less conscious part of the personality, a level at which change is more complex and difficult. It also seems reasonable for a change in behavior to stimulate a change in attitude, if for no other reason than that flagrant inconsistency between what one does and what one thinks is uncomfortable for most people.

Thus far we have considered the role the unconscious plays in creating overtly racist attitudes. But how is the unconscious involved when racial prejudice is less apparent—when racial bias is hidden from the prejudiced individual as well as from others? Increasingly, as our culture has rejected racism as immoral and unproductive, this hidden prejudice has become the more prevalent form of racism. The individual's Ego must adapt to a cultural order that views overtly racist attitudes and behavior as unsophisticated, uninformed, and immoral. It must repress or disguise racist ideas when they seek expression.

Joel Kovel refers to the resulting personality type as the "aversive racist" and contrasts this type with the "dominative racist," the true bigot who openly seeks to keep blacks in a subordinate position and will resort to force to do so. The aversive racist believes in white superiority, but her conscience seeks to repudiate this belief or, at least, to prevent her from acting on it. She often resolves this inner conflict by not acting at all. She tries to avoid the issue by ignoring the existence of blacks, avoiding contact with them, or at most being polite, correct, and cold whenever she must deal with them. Aversive racists range from individuals who lapse into demonstrative racism when threatened—as when blacks get "too close"—to those who consider themselves liberals and, despite their sense of aversion to blacks (of which they are often unaware), do their best within the confines of the existing societal structure to ameliorate blacks' condition.

There is considerably less research and literature concerning the aversive racist than there is concerning the self-conscious racist. This is hardly surprising. Our culture has only recently rejected the morality of white supremacy; the repression of racist ideas is a relatively new phenomenon. It is also a more difficult phenomenon to discern and observe than is self-conscious racism. The researcher's subjects no longer readily admit their membership in the group to be studied. Also, those who would observe and document unconscious racism are not themselves immune from its blight . . . .

Unconscious Racism in Everyday Life

. . .

A crucial factor in the process that produces unconscious racism is the tacitly transmitted cultural stereotype. If an individual has never known a black doctor or lawyer or is exposed to blacks only through a mass media where they are portrayed in the stereotyped roles of comedian, criminal, musician, or athlete, he is likely to deduce that blacks as a group are naturally inclined toward certain behavior and unfit for certain roles. But the lesson is not explicit: It is learned, internalized, and used without an awareness of its source. Thus, an individual may select a white job applicant over an equally qualified black and honestly believe that this decision was based on observed intangibles unrelated to race. The employer perceives the white candidate as "more articulate," "more collegial," "more thoughtful," or "more charismatic." He is unaware of the learned stereotype that influenced his decision. Moreover, he has probably also learned an explicit lesson of which he is very much aware: Good, law-abiding people do not judge others on the basis of race. Even the most thorough investigation of conscious motive will not uncover the race-based stereotype that has influenced his decision.

This same process operates in the case of more far-reaching policy decisions that come to judicial attention because of their discriminatory impact. For example, when an employer or academic administrator discovers that a written examination rejects blacks at a disproportionate rate, she can draw several possible conclusions: that blacks are less qualified than others; that the test is an inaccurate measure of ability; or that the testers have chosen the wrong skills or attributes to measure. When decisionmakers reach the first conclusion, a predisposition to select those data that conform with a racial stereotype may well have influenced them. Because this stereotype has been tacitly transmitted and unconsciously learned, they will be unaware of its influence on their decision.

If the purpose of the law's search for racial animus or discriminatory intent is to identify a morally culpable perpetrator, the existing intent requirement fails to achieve that purpose. There will be no evidence of self-conscious racism where the actors have internalized the relatively new American cultural morality which holds racism wrong or have learned racist attitudes and beliefs through tacit rather than explicit lessons. The actor himself will be unaware that his actions, or the racially neutral feelings and ideas that accompany them, have racist origins.

. . .

Cooperation and Conflict: The Economics of Group Status Production and Race Discrimination*
RICHARD H. MCADAMS

A New Economic Theory of Race Discrimination

Nobel Laureate Gary Becker pioneered what is now the prevailing economic theory of race discrimination. He began with the simple claim that people who discriminate act as if they have a "taste" for avoiding contact or association with members of other races. Discrimination is thus defined as an act by which one seeks to avoid this undesired association. Although there are alternative economic explanations for discriminatory behavior, this "associational preference" model has dominated the law and economics discussion of discrimination. Based on this model, Becker argued that unfettered market competition would tend to drive out discrimination. In turn, other economic theorists contend that, within a free market, laws prohibiting race discrimination are unnecessary and inefficient.

. . .

As an alternative to the associational preference model, I propose that we understand race discrimination as an especially virulent and pathological form of status production. Discrimination and racist behavior generally are processes by which one racial group seeks to produce esteem for itself by lowering the status of another group. The key to understanding this behavior is to perceive its subordinating quality. Status comes about by disparaging others, by asserting and reinforcing a claim to superior social rank. Under this view, the associational preference model is partly, but only partly, correct. One obvious way to express disrespect toward others is to refuse to associate with them. But non-association is over-and underinclusive because one can subordinate those with whom one associates and because, when non-association is used, it does not exhaust the means of subordination.

. . .

Using Status Production to Explain Who Discriminates

The associational preference model has little to say about why some people discriminate more than others, except for the circular claim that some people have stronger discriminatory tastes than others.

. . .

The status-production model . . . explains the shape of contemporary attitudes on race. For instance, among whites, there is a strong inverse

* Excerpts from Richard H. McAdams, "Cooperation and Conflict: The Economics of Group Status Production and Race Discrimination," *Harvard Law Review,* vol. 108, copyright © 1995. Reprinted by permission of the author and publisher.

relationship between social status and discriminatory racial attitudes. The poorest and least educated whites, for example, were the most likely to participate in lynching blacks. Sociologist Judith Caditz summarizes: "For decades social scientists have tried to understand reasons people affirm prejudicial attitudes and engage in discriminatory behavior. Much social science literature supports the thesis that status-threatened people will exhibit prejudicial attitudes toward minorities." Caditz adds that those who think their membership in ethnic, religious, occupational, and other social groups or classes is important are more likely to hold ambivalent or negative attitudes about blacks. These findings are the most direct contemporary evidence supporting the status-production model. Whites with the most limited opportunities for producing status will predictably be prepared to engage in more discrimination, because lowering the status of others is one of their last remaining mechanisms of status production. Similarly, the more closely one identifies with one's racial or ethnic group—that is, the more one's status depends on the status of racial traits, the more one can produce status by subordinating (or being willing to subordinate) others on racial grounds.

                                   . . .

The desire for status can systematically distort beliefs. The conventional assumption is that false beliefs are costly because mistakes impede the individual's effort to satisfy her preferences. This approach mistakenly assumes that beliefs are useful only as a means of determining what behavior will serve one's interests. To the contrary, casual observation confirms that people derive pleasure from merely *expressing* their beliefs. Indeed, the act of voting is expressive, and many rational choice theorists have abandoned any attempt to explain political voting except as an expressive activity enjoyable in and of itself.

Once we understand that people gain utility from expressing their beliefs, we can identify a category of beliefs not subject to the usual economic constraints. We can now imagine, for example, why people bother to form beliefs about so many things that do not seem instrumentally important, such as who is the best goalie in professional hockey, whether a celebrity is guilty or innocent of criminal charges, or which of two films is better. People form such beliefs for the pleasure that comes from expressing them. The novelty of these otherwise non-instrumental beliefs is that the normal economic correctives to false belief formation do not apply. For expressive purposes, a "good" belief is not necessarily an accurate belief, but rather one that is pleasurable to express. Of course, even if a category of beliefs serves only expressive ends, there are some constraints on belief formation....

Most important for our purposes, however, is the constraint of self-esteem. Some beliefs are more pleasant than others. For expressive purposes, people are more likely to adopt beliefs that enhance, rather than degrade, their self-esteem.... If esteem can influence expressive belief formation in this manner, esteem can also affect conventionally instrumental beliefs—beliefs concerning how best to satisfy one's preferences. As long as the gain in esteem from the bias toward esteem-producing beliefs is larger than any instrumental loss from the bias, then such a bias serves the individual's overall interests. There is considerable evidence to support this claim: research shows, for example, that people tend systematically to overevaluate their own performance and characteristics. Such a bias may even be essential to mental well-being. Self-evaluation is clearly an instrumental belief—one needs to know what one's talents and abilities are—yet the need for self-esteem is sufficient to create some deviation from strictly impartial beliefs about oneself.

If esteem production favorably biases one's self-evaluations, esteem production may also cause a positive bias toward the social groups to which one belongs. One may gain pleasure from believing positive things about one's groups. Moreover, groups will reward status to those who hold beliefs that are conducive to group welfare. A favorable bias regarding group members may strengthen intra-group cooperation by increasing the apparent material advantage available from transacting with members rather than non-members.

But groups may encourage and reward beliefs more complex than simple bias. For example, although he does not explain how belief distortion occurs, Richard Posner has invoked such distortion to explain how certain cartels solve collective action problems. According to Posner, the distinguishing feature of certain successful cartels—which he terms "guilds"—is their having an "ideology." A guild is a social as well as an economic institution in which members have adopted a common "personal morality" of loyalty, conformity, and craftsmanship, and which has achieved a certain "mystique" involving the idealization of quality over quantity. The "mutually reinforcing combination" of this morality and mystique comprises "the *ideology* of guild production," which serves the "the self-interest of producers in the cartelization of production."

. . .

Return now to racial beliefs. In Posner's terms, negative stereotypes are part of a racial "guild's" efforts to monopolize production of esteem. Even for beliefs that serve an instrumental purpose (such as evaluating potential employees), the desire for esteem will cause an individual to adopt distorted beliefs about racial groups as long as the esteem benefit exceeds the instrumental cost. . . .

If one assumes that this analysis correctly explains the existence and direction of racial bias, the question remains how to explain the *evolution* of white attitudes regarding race. Recall that status production commonly involves the denial that one's motive is status production. When one seeks to gain status by lowering the status of others, it is all the more important to deny that one is degrading others in order to look better by comparison. Consequently, "guild ideology" never acknowledges its self-serving nature. Members of Posner's representative guild do not openly declare, even among themselves, that they desire to restrain competition in order to charge higher prices and earn monopoly profits. Similarly, whites never explain their discriminatory behavior as serving the function of status production. Even in the Jim Crow South, whites attempted to justify segregation not by reference to naked self-interest but by claims that blacks ere inherently inferior, that blacks preferred segregation, or that segregation somehow reflected the natural order of things. Toward this end, the Jim Crow doctrine of "separate but equal" was ideal. Separation was a means of expressing contempt; the pretense of equality served to deny the status motivation.

When proponents of a status-driven ideology can no longer confidently deny the status motivation of their beliefs, the ideology fails and proponents must search for another ideology. This insight may explain the evolution of white attitudes toward segregation. Although the exact causal strands are difficult to disentangle, events leading up to and including the modern civil rights movement undermined the ability of whites to believe that their existing racial beliefs were anything other than a self-serving ideology. World War II provided one ideological shock, as revulsion to Nazi claims of racial superiority was difficult to square with rationalization of southern racial practices. Rising levels of black education and job skills put a material strain on racial ideology by raising the attractiveness of black labor and thus the cost of absolute racial exclusion. I suspect the most immediate cause of ideological breakdown occurred during the civil rights movement, when photographs captured segregation extremists using violent means, often against women and children, to suppress peaceful protests. Violence against peaceful demonstrators was, even for some southern supporters of Jim Crow, irrefutable evidence that whites were not (at least morally) superior, that blacks were indisputably unhappy with segregation, and that segregation was not a naturally ordained moral order. One of the constraints I have suggested for non-instrumental beliefs is "palpable falsity"; the events of the 1950s and 1960s made salient to whites the falsity of the belief that intentional racial segregation is something other than selfishly hurtful.

Whatever the causal mechanism, many whites have come genuinely to believe that segregation is wrong. This shift does not mean, however, that a psychological veil of prejudice has simply been lifted from their eyes. The expressive beliefs whites adopt about race can no longer be of the crude form needed to justify segregation, but the quest for the production of status continues. Having abandoned the older ideology, whites still tend to oppose policies and candidates that would increase the social status of blacks. Whites can give up old, extreme stereotypes and still embrace negative views of blacks. Unless one consciously scrutinizes the statistical validity of one's generalizations about other groups—an unlikely scenario—even false stereotypes will rarely be *pal-*

pably false. Thus, one may acknowledge the good faith and intellectual integrity of conservative arguments on political issues concerning race— like busing, affirmative action, and welfare—and still worry that the same status-maximizing bias that first rationalized slavery and then segregation infects much of the public thinking on these matters. It is more pleasant to believe that one lives in a society in which everyone (or at least everyone else) is being treated as well as she deserves, that past transgressions have been righted, and that fairness and justice require no further sacrifice. The evolution of white attitudes, therefore, reflects an ideological adjustment to status production under changed circumstances. The final descriptive virtue of the status-production theory is that it offers some insight into this otherwise puzzling evolution of white attitudes.

Implications of the Status Production Model of Discrimination

. . .

The Persistence of Race Discrimination

. . .

Under the status-production model, discrimination is not the result of costs that discriminators incur from contact with members of other groups, but is a means of producing status. The discriminator does bear a cost in discriminating—forgoing otherwise beneficial trade with the objects of the discrimination—but that cost is an *investment* in the production of status. As long as such investments are cost-effective for the discriminator, the status-production model predicts that race discrimination will persist in the face of market competition.

. . .

The Stability of Discriminatory Norms

. . .

One might object that discriminatory norms do not exist if any whites are willing to act against them. That some whites will boycott discriminators merely reflects, however, the fact that American whites do not constitute a single group. "Whites" include various ethnic, religious, political, regional, and class subgroups. How much a particular subgroup invests in subordination as a means of producing status will depend on what its various status options are. Low-status whites have fewer options and tend to discriminate more than high-status whites. Further, white condemnation of the blatant racial discrimination common in an earlier era is consistent with a more subtle discriminatory norm. Subordination works only as long as one can deny that one is acting for the purpose of producing status. Whites are less able to deny this function of racial derogation now than in the past; consequently, overt discrimination is no longer as productive of status as it once was. Just as a "nouveau riche" may undermine her own status by engaging in ostentatious and wasteful consumption, a "redneck" or bigot undermines her own status by expressing contempt solely on the basis of race. But, there is still status in wealth if one displays it more deftly, with the appearance of not calculating to make a display. Likewise, there is status to be gained from race discrimination of a more subtle form, especially when one can plausibly deplore its more flagrant manifestations.

One might nevertheless assert that there are significant numbers of whites who oppose even subtle forms of discrimination. One interpretation of this behavior is that high-status whites who condemn low-status whites for their discrimination may gain more by distinguishing themselves from other whites than by investing in the subordination of blacks or other minorities. In fact, certain classes of whites may enjoy free-riding on the status that other whites secure and then further increase their status by subordinating those whites for being discriminatory.

. . .

The Power of Esteem-Producing Racial Biases

A final factor that contributes to the persistence of discrimination is racially biased beliefs or stereotypes. As noted above, discriminatory norms invoke rationalization mechanisms; discriminators prefer to have reasons for discriminating other than a bare interest in status production. Indeed, because status production is inconsistent with an overt strategy of subordination, it is important that discriminators have an explanation—an "ideology"—apart from status production. Such an explanation can most easily take the form of negative stereotypes—that the failure of blacks to succeed is their own fault, due to their own shortcomings in ability, integrity, or dependability. This ideology buttresses discriminatory norms. Whatever the social cost of violating the norm, biased evaluations of blacks make it appear that the material benefits of norm violation are less than they are. Self-deception prevents cheating that would undermine the cartel.

. . .

Notes and Questions

1. Crosby, Bromley, and Saxe express a healthy skepticism about the value of survey data showing a long-term decline in racial prejudice. One interesting finding is that much of this apparent improvement is explained by a cohort effect: those born in the 1940s and 1950s were less prejudiced than those born before 1940. Apparently, then, the factors that have caused younger individuals to articulate less-prejudiced sentiments have not been brought to bear on, or have been less effective in changing the survey responses of, older individuals. Since in the late 1960s and early 1970s when this survey evidence was collected, most businesses were being run by

individuals who were born before 1940, one would think that the legal pressures on such individuals not to discriminate in employment would be at least as great as the legal pressures falling on younger individuals. Does the fact that those who most feel the legal pressure are also most likely to express biased opinions suggest that the law is not an important force in molding opinions? Or does this suggest that any beneficial effect generated by the law in reducing discrimination is likely to emerge only in younger cohorts, whose beliefs are less likely to be so thoroughly crystallized? Does the presence of the cohort effect indicate that the baleful effects of parental influence in the development of prejudice can be offset by benign societal factors? Is law one of these social forces? To the extent that government and law can, at reasonable cost, generate attitudinal changes that diminish racial prejudice, an unambiguous gain in social welfare will result (See the selection by Donohue in Chapter 7.)

David Oppenheimer's analysis of opinion survey data also suggests that individual survey answers should not be considered in isolation, as they can lead to misleading conclusions. For example, in 1972 one survey showed overwhelming white support for equal employment opportunity (97 percent), which seemed to indicate that racial prejudice was no longer salient. Interestingly, however, a survey of 600 non-blacks in 1989 found that a majority of the respondents (65 percent) believed that average blacks have worse jobs, income, and housing than white people either because blacks have less in-born ability to learn or because they lacked motivation. Oppenheimer, "Understanding Affirmative Action," 23 *Hastings Constitutional Law Quarterly* 921, 952–953 (1996).

2. Social psychological studies have found that, regardless of their personal beliefs, individuals are often heavily influenced in exercising discriminatory behavior by the expectations of relevant reference groups. Specifically, when faced with considerable social pressure to act in a racially discriminatory manner, individuals are more likely to conform to this pressure regardless of their personal attitudes. Patricia Devine, "Automatic and Controlled Processes in Prejudice: The Role of Stereotypes and Personal Beliefs," in Anthony Pratkanis, Steven Breckler, and Anthony Greenwald, eds., *Attitude Structure and Function* 181, 200–203 (Hillsdale, N.J.: Lawrence Erlbaum Associates, 1989). Conversely, the imposition of social constraints on the exercise of discriminatory behavior—and antidiscrimination law would seem to be one such constraint—can dampen discriminatory conduct even among the racially prejudiced. The social welfare implications of such legal constraints are not unambiguous in this case, since the burden on the discriminator conflicts with the benefit from the reduction in discriminatory conduct. If the antidiscrimination law speeds a change in attitudes, however, this conflict between attitude and behavior will diminish over time.

3. There is evidence that employers discipline and discharge black workers at significantly higher rates than white workers. See Craig Zwerling and Hilary Silver, "Race and Job Dismissals in a Federal Bureaucracy," 57 *American Sociological Review* 651 (1992); Stephen Barr, "Minority Workers Discharged at Higher Rates than Whites," *The Washington Post* A21 (December 15, 1993). Kingsley Browne has argued that the fact that blacks

commit crimes at far higher rates than whites makes it unsurprising that they would be more likely to commit sanctionable infractions in the workforce. Browne, "Statistical Proof of Discrimination: Beyond 'Damned Lies,' " 68 *Washington Law Review* 477, 509 n. 97 (1993). An alternative explanation is suggested by the social psychological studies described in this chapter showing that (1) whites are more likely to notice and report shoplifting when committed by blacks, (2) are more likely to punish blacks for mistakes in a learning experiment, and (3) are more likely to interpret an ambiguous shove as hostile or violent when given by a black but as playful when given by a white.

In light of this evidence, Linda Krieger argues that disparate treatment doctrine should be reformulated "to reflect the reality that disparate treatment discrimination can result from things other than discriminatory intent. To establish liability ... a Title VII plaintiff would simply be required to prove that his group status *played a role* in causing the employer's action or decision. Causation would no longer be equated with intentionality." Krieger, "The Content of Our Categories: A Cognitive Bias Approach to Discrimination and Equal Employment Opportunity," 47 *Stanford Law Review* 1161, 1242 (1995).

4. Similarly, Charles Lawrence argues that "requiring proof of conscious or intentional motivation as a prerequisite to constitutional recognition that a decision is race-dependent ignores much of what we understand about how the human mind works. It also disregards both the irrationality of racism and the profound effect that the history of American race relations has had on the individual and collective unconscious." Lawrence, "The Id, the Ego, and Equal Protection: Reckoning with Unconscious Racism," 39 *Stanford Law Review* 317, 323 (1987). On the basis of such considerations, David Oppenheimer has proposed that an employer should be found liable under Title VII for negligent discrimination when it fails to take reasonable care to prevent discrimination that it knows or should know is occurring. Oppenheimer, "Negligent Discrimination," 141 *University of Pennsylvania Law Review* 899 (1993).

5. If discrimination were purely the product of malign intent or cognitive bias, one would imagine that the market would tend to eradicate it by rewarding employers who harbored no such intent or who were less hampered by distorted thinking. McAdams sees discrimination quite differently, as a rational—that is, effective—means of elevating one's own status. Which view of discrimination seems more plausible? McAdams's status-production model of racial discrimination posits that whites can form socially connected groups that elevate their self-esteem by investing in the subordination of blacks. This model raises the question of how this process can avoid the free-rider problem: whites have an incentive to enjoy the benefits of the higher esteem afforded to whites but not to bear the costs of subordinating blacks. In other words, in the presence of widespread discrimination, a white employer can make added profits by hiring the productive black workers that other whites have shunned. McAdams responds that the desire for esteem in a socially connected group both motivates individuals not to violate the primary norm of racial subordination of blacks and generates a secondary

norm that requires sanctioning those who violate the primary norm. Consequently, the profit-seeking entrepreneur who attempts to hire the shunned black workers will face sanctions from other whites. In this way, the desire for intragroup status diminishes the free-rider problem. The enforcement of racist norms was undoubtedly an important force in the pre-1964 South. Is it likely to be a significant factor in America today? For an attack on Mc-Adams's article that claims "The time has come to stop beating the dead horse of Jim Crow," see Richard Epstein, "The Status–Production Sideshow: Why the Antidiscrimination Laws Are Still a Mistake," 108 *Harvard Law Review* 1085, 1108 (1995).

6. If much of today's discrimination is due to unconscious bias, as the cognitive bias theory suggests, what is the appropriate remedy? In Amy Wax's view, unconscious bias should be treated as a form of workplace "accident" because it is "an inadvertent and unpredictable event that inflicts an undesirable and costly injury on employees as the side effect of the otherwise useful activity of employing a workforce in a productive enterprise." Wax, "Discrimination as Accident," 74 *Indiana Law Journal* 1129, 1132 (1999). Applying the principles of accident law, Wax argues that antidiscrimination statutes do not serve the principle goals of liability schemes—deterrence, compensation, and insurance—in a cost effective way. Thus, she favors not holding employers liable, since "[t]he nature of the phenomenon of unconscious bias is such that there are no known steps that employers can reliably take to control biases that may distort ... judgments that must inevitably be made in the course of managing personnel in the modern workplace." Id. at 1133.

Moreover, Wax suggests that the workers themselves may be the cheapest cost avoiders because they can reduce their chances of becoming the target of unconscious discrimination by improving their credentials or becoming model employees. Consider Michael Selmi's vigorous critique of this view:

> This kind of argument suggests that most discrimination is largely deserved or trivial: if women and minorities would work harder and become more like the dominant worker, presumably a white male, then they would find that discrimination will recede. But this argument ignores everything we know about discrimination, including the very concept of discrimination itself. As Wax well knows, discrimination befalls strong as well as weaker employees. More to the point, her analysis also fails to grapple with the very meaning of disparate treatment. Even if it were somehow true that African Americans or women could avoid some discrimination by becoming a model employee, the law clearly states that it would still be unequal, and thus unlawful, treatment if African Americans or women were required to perform at a level that exceeds that required of their white male counterparts as a way of avoiding discrimination.

Selmi, "Response to Professor Wax Discrimination as Accident: Old Whine, New Bottle," 74 *Indiana Law Journal* 1233, 1246 (1999).

6

The Nature and Extent of Racially Discriminatory Conduct

The interpretive lens through which one views employer conduct heavily influences one's assessment of the existence and prevalence of labor market discrimination. If the Becker model of employer discrimination provides the theoretical framework, then one is apt to believe that the ultimate economic impact of discrimination on blacks is likely to be small. If, in a competitive labor market, one or even many employers refuse to hire blacks or systematically underestimate their productive potential, then other employers can make handsome profits from stepping in and hiring the shunned or undervalued black workers. This is a powerful theoretical critique that is designed to blunt the force of seemingly plausible theories of discrimination such as those raised by Charles Lawrence or Linda Krieger in the previous chapter. The view that unconscious psychological forces or cognitive biases prompt employers to discriminate against blacks runs into the theoretical buzz saw of the Becker model of employer discrimination—as long as some employers can be found who prefer profits to prejudice. In a capitalist society such as the United States, one would imagine that many entrepreneurs would be driven by the bottom line, to the benefit of all victims of nonproductivity-based discrimination by employers.

This chapter attempts to examine actual employer conduct to provide some empirical evidence with which one can evaluate the various abstract theoretical conceptions of racial discrimination that were explored in the preceding chapter. We begin with the rather remarkable recent story of race discrimination at Shoney's, a major fast-food restaurant chain. Apparently, the Chief Executive Officer of Shoney's was a racist, who frequently expressed considerable hostility toward blacks. What is less clear is whether this case represents an example of Beckerian employer discrimination, or one of customer discrimination, where consumers respond positively to the absence of black employees. The distinction is crucial, since in the first case, the market tends to punish the discriminator, and in the second, the market unfailingly rewards the discriminator.

An interesting methodological issue exists over the best way to find out whether employers are discriminating on the basis of race. Joleen Kirschenman and Kathryn Neckerman try to answer this question by surveying 185 Chicago employers concerning their views about black workers. In contrast, the Urban Institute tried to ascertain whether employers discriminate not by asking them, but by examining their conduct in field experiments in which black and white "audit pairs" were sent to apply for similar jobs in a number of cities, including Chicago. Both studies examined the process of selection in the same type of low-skilled jobs, although the Urban Institute testers were limited to pursuing job openings that were advertised in newspapers. James Heckman and Peter Siegelman evaluate the evidence from the Urban Institute studies and demonstrate that the difficulties in trying to test for discrimination are far greater than one might expect. (For additional critique of the logic and assumptions of the audit method, see James J. Heckman, "Detecting Discrimination," 12 *Journal of Economic Perspectives* 101 (1998)). In reading these selections, it is helpful to consider whether their findings are in conflict or reconcilable, whether the evidence they provide supports any of the theories of discrimination that we have discussed, and how they both can contribute to our understanding of the complex issue of race discrimination.

Racism Du Jour at Shoney's*
STEVE WATKINS

Billie Elliott wants to get a spot on *Oprah*.... She wants civil rights lawyer Tommy Warren on as well so he can talk about the five hard years he has spent as the principal attorney on her case, *Haynes et al. v. Shoney's Inc.*, which started when Billie and her husband, Henry, white managers of a Captain D's seafood restaurant in Marianna, Florida, were fired because they wouldn't obey orders to "lighten up" their store—a company euphemism for reducing the number of black workers—and hire "attractive white girls" instead. The black workers they tried to protect lost their jobs; among them were Madeline Herring, with whom

Billie had worked for years at the Union 76 diner before they came to Captain D's, and Lester Thomas, whom Henry had promoted to assistant manager because Lester had worked hard and deserved it.

Billie wants to get on *Oprah* and tell people how she and her husband fought back against Captain D's parent company, Shoney's Inc., one of the largest family restaurant chains in the country, with its 1,800 stores in thirty-six states and its billion-and-a-half-dollar-a-year business. It's also a chain whose unwritten but clearly racist policies in hiring and promotions are now costing it $132.5 million as it is forced to enact a sweeping affirmative action plan and pay off claims to tens of thousands of former workers and job applicants—with $19 million going to the plaintiffs' lawyers—in the country's largest class-action settlement ever for racial job discrimination.

Tommy Warren's voice trembles in anger sometimes when he talks about the case that has consumed him for the past five years—about the Elliotts and other white managers who were fired because they wouldn't get rid of black workers, and about the thousands of black workers themselves who were cut out of jobs: people like Josephine Haynes, one of the nine named plaintiffs in the class-action suit, who never got a response to repeated applications at two Shoney's in Pensacola, Florida; and Carolyn Cobb, another plaintiff, who spent more than twenty years at a South Carolina Shoney's and has seen a steady stream of white employees advance past her into management. Warren is angry for a lot of reasons—the lost opportunities, the damaged lives—but one of them is the failure of the E.E.O.C. to recognize the blatant pattern of discrimination in the Shoney's empire—or to do anything about it. Workers filed hundreds of complaints against Shoney's and its various divisions over the years, Warren says, but little came of them beyond some small individual settlements, all in keeping with what for some time has been the commission's chamber-of-commerce approach to discrimination complaints. Before Reagan, Bush, and Thomas, the E.E.O.C. was settling 32 percent of the cases it closed; that figure has dropped to less than 14 percent. Those "Merit Resolutions," or settlements, fell from 26,507 in 1981 to 11,032 in 1991, while complaint dismissals rose from 21,097 to 38,369.

The E.E.O.C. did manage to file an amicus brief in support of class certification—two years after the Shoney's suit was filed. However, the federal judge handling the case said he already had "too much paperwork" and dismissed the government's brief as irrelevant.

Warren wasn't aware of the E.E.O.C. complaints or the number of individual suits against Shoney's when he heard the Elliotts' story in April 1988. When he started interviewing other Shoney's and Captain D's employees, though, the stories they told convinced him that the Marianna Captain D's case fit a racist pattern that ran throughout the company. He found a former manager at a Tallahassee Shoney's who said that he too had been pressured to get rid of blacks and to hire white workers instead. The manager said that once, when two black employees were late for work, a Shoney's division director who was visiting the store took him into a cooler, grabbed him by the tie and yelled in his face, "This is how you talk to them: 'Listen you black bastard, get to work on time or get the fuck out.'" The manager was later fired.

With the Elliotts' case bolstered by stories such as these, Warren hired an investigator to visit 250 Captain D's and Shoney's in ten other states and check out their racial composition. The investigator came back with a report that echoed the Elliotts': few black managers or cashiers; few blacks in "customer contact" positions; garden-variety restaurant racism; blacks in the back.

Warren dug through old court records, contacted other civil rights attorneys scattered around the country and tracked incidents of discrimination in ever-widening circles to other stores in other states. One of the most troubling, because it might have blown the lid off the Shoney's secret years before, was a 1985 lawsuit in Montgomery, Alabama. In that case, two black Shoney's employees said they were ordered by their manager to hide in a restroom because some company executives had shown up for a surprise visit and there were "too many" blacks at work that day. The women complained and subsequently lost their jobs, but they sued. Shoney's settled out of court. The manager for the Montgomery restaurant said later in a deposition that he got a call from the company president when the settlement was announced. "You're not going to believe this," the manager said he was told, "but the stupid fucking bitch has decided to settle the suit for about $25,000."

The case spiraled upward as Warren continued his investigation through 1988 and gathered evidence implicating company officials all along the corporate chain of command, including particularly damming testimony against Ray Danner, the co-founder, longtime C.E.O. and board chairman of Shoney's. Everyone, it seemed, had a Danner story— about a racial epithet, a joke, a threat, an order to terminate—and when Warren traced some of those tales to former upper-level managers in Nashville, "in the belly of the monster," where Shoney's has its national headquarters, he knew he was onto something big.

Warren discovered zero minority representation at the upper levels of Shoney's management, and virtually none at *any* level in the central office in Nashville. He learned that well-built black men at some stores might be referred to as "Arnold Schwarzenigger," that too many blacks meant a restaurant was "too cloudy" or that someone must be "shooting a jungle movie" or that it was "Little Africa." He learned that hiring blacks back after you'd just "lightened" your store was known as "re-nigging." He learned that "nigger stores" in predominantly black neighborhoods might have black managers, but that otherwise the place for many minority applications was "File 13," the trash can. But there were other ways to note the race of black job applicants so they could be rejected: a simple "A," for instance, which stood for "Ape"; or a colored-in "O" in the Shoney's name on the application form.

When the NAACP Legal Defense Fund agreed to help out with the case near the end of 1988, one of the first things it did was publicize an 800 number for complaints. The calls poured in from black workers and job applicants who said they had been victims of Shoney's discriminatory policies, and from white employees as well, many of whom had worked in supervisory positions and said they had been forced to carry out those policies in order to keep their jobs. These witnesses described a corporation where there was no affirmative action plan; where there was no job posting, formal application process or objective criteria for promotions; where racial slurs and specifications on the "right" number of blacks were common; where officials charged with discrimination were rarely, if ever, punished; and where all the decision makers were white. Plaintiffs' attorneys filed more than a hundred depositions from these witnesses in the class action.

Nineteen eighty-nine was not a good year for class actions in job discrimination cases. With an increasingly conservative federal judicial system, class certification requests had been in freefall for more than a decade, down 96 percent from 1,106 in 1975 to 51 in 1989. The Supreme Court punctuated that decline in 1989 with half a dozen new rulings that severely restricted the ability of workers to bring and win discrimination suits. But Warren and Barry Goldstein, who was the N.A.A.C.P.'s attorney on the case—and who had been the principal attorney in one of those Supreme Court cases, *Lorance v. AT & T Technologies*—were confident that they had overwhelming evidence of "the most easily understood type of discrimination," evidence that fundamentally challenged the E.E.O.C.'s smug and often-repeated assertion that "demographic diversity" had been achieved in the workplace and that systematic discrimination no longer existed.

The class action that Warren and Goldstein filed in April 1989 alleged massive discrimination in hiring, firing, and promotion in the Shoney's corporate empire; they had depositions from job applicants, cooks, waitresses, store managers, area supervisors, division directors, regional vice presidents, personnel directors and even a former C.E.O. implicating seventy restaurant managers, 104 midlevel supervisors and thirty-six senior executives.

No name came up more often in the class action complaint than Captain D himself, Ray Danner, as senior corporate officials got in line to confess their sins and tell their Danner tales. Dave Wachtel, the former C.E.O. who had worked his way up over a twenty-year career beginning as a Shoney's busboy, said in a deposition that his boss's racial attitudes were common knowledge in the company, and that Danner once discussed contributing money to the Ku Klux Klan and matching dollar-for-dollar any senior employee's contributions.

Another high-level Shoney's executive, a former division personnel director named Thomas Buckner, said Danner apparently thought the company's discriminatory policy made good business sense. "Danner would say that no one would want to eat at a restaurant where 'a bunch of niggers' were working," he reported.

Royce Browning, a former Shoney's vice president, echoed Buckner, Wachtel, and dozens of others. Everyone, he said, knew Ray Danner's laws: "Blacks were not qualified to run a store. Blacks were not qualified to run a kitchen of a store. Blacks should not be employed in any position where they would be seen by customers."

And the personnel statistics prior to the lawsuit bore this out. Only 1.8 percent of the store managers in the Shoney's restaurant division were black. Out of 441 employees at the supervisory or supervisory-trainee level in the corporation, only seven, or 1.6 percent, were black. Out of sixty-eight division directors, a position at the low end of out-of-store management, only one was black. And at the higher levels of corporate management, at the end of 1989, the year *Haynes et al. v. Shoney's Inc.* was filed, there were no blacks at all. Instead, more than 75 percent of black Shoney's restaurant workers held jobs in three low-paid, non-customer-contact positions: bus-person/dishwasher, cook/prep person and breakfast bar attendant.

In his deposition Danner himself denied everything—or almost everything. He admitted to having used the word "nigger," but repeatedly answered "I do not recall" when confronted with a long list of employee accusations. And there was one other incredible admission: "In looking for anything to identify why is this unit under-performing," Danner said, "in some cases, I would have probably said that this is a neighborhood of predominantly white neighbors, and we have a considerable amount of black employees and this might be a problem."

Indeed, the smoking gun in the case came in the form of a letter Danner wrote complaining about the performance of a Jacksonville, Florida, Captain D's and comparing the racial makeup of that store, which had several black employees—some of whom were later fired—to the all-white, or nearly all-white, composition of other fast-food restaurants Danner visited in the area.

The *Haynes* case won class certification in July 1992 for as many as 75,000 black workers, former employees and job applicants in all company-owned stores in the corporation's Shoney's and Captain D's divisions. The white plaintiffs—including Billie and Henry Elliott—were dropped from the suit, not because their complaints lacked merit but because they didn't meet court standards for class recognition. The Elliotts did win $175,000 in a separate settlement with their franchise owner, which was about what they would have earned had they stayed with the company.

Four months later, in November 1992, Shoney's—without admitting guilt—agreed to the record $132.5 million settlement. Ray Danner, who refuses to comment on any aspect of the case or his involvement in it, was forced to pay half that amount out of his own pocket; insurance covered most of the rest. The company also agreed to a comprehensive affirmative action plan that includes a commitment to hire increased numbers of black workers at all levels in company restaurants, with the targets for those hired based on area demographics. Shoney's is also required to place black managers in 20 to 23 percent of its restaurants within the next five or six years; to have at least three black regional directors by 1998; and to test equally qualified job applicants of different races against each other regularly to see if the company's restaurants are selecting employees fairly. The settlement even gave plaintiffs' attorneys veto power over candidates for senior jobs in some departments, including personnel and recruiting.

Danner wasn't quite through, though. Shortly before the settlement was finalized in January 1993, the Danner-controlled board of directors—unhappy with the imposed settlement, according to an article in *The Wall Street Journal,* and with the company's zealous approach to implementing the affirmative action plan—forced out the progressive C.E.O. they had brought in to handle the lawsuit and counter the negative publicity. When Shoney's stock dropped after that, however, in reaction to what analysts said were fears that the tainted Danner still controlled the corporation, the board initiated a buyout of all Danner's remaining shares to finally sever his ties to the company.

In a *Washington Post* Op–Ed piece shortly before he left office last year, Evan Kemp, Clarence Thomas's replacement as E.E.O.C. chairman, suggested that the idea of diversity in the workplace is being used to cover what he called "a regime of quotas" that threatens to tear the country apart along ethnic, racial and gender lines. "Hiring by the numbers," he said, has become our de facto civil rights policy, and since there are 106 ethnic groups in the American labor force, how can we possibly provide group entitlements for them all?

Kemp repeated the conservative lament about these "group entitlements" wrecking our happy workplace, where businesses would hire the right people for the right jobs—regardless of race, gender and ethnicity—if only they were left alone to do it.

"We'd Love to Hire Them, But ...": The Meaning of Race for Employers*

JOLEEN KIRSCHENMAN AND KATHRYN M. NECKERMAN

Race and Employment

In research on the disadvantages blacks experience in the labor market, social scientists tend to rely on indirect measures of racial discrimination. They interpret as evidence of this discrimination the differences in wages or employment among races and ethnic groups that remain after education and experience are controlled.

· · ·

[D]espite intense interest in the relation of race to employment, very few scholars have ... queried employers directly about their views of black workers or how race might enter into their recruitment and hiring decisions.

· · ·

This research is based on face-to-face interviews with employers in Chicago and surrounding Cook County between July 1988 and March 1989.... Our overall response rate was 46 percent, and the completed sample of 185 employers is representative of the distribution of Cook County's employment by industry and firm size.

Interviews included both closed-and open-ended questions about employers' hiring and recruitment practices and about their perceptions of Chicago's labor force and business climate. Our initial contacts, and most of the interviews themselves, were conducted with the highest ranking official at the establishment....

Most of the structured portion of the interview focused on a sample job, defined by the interview schedule as "the most typical entry-level position" in the firm's modal occupational category—sales, clerical, skilled, semiskilled, unskilled, or service, but excluding managerial, professional, and technical.... In effect, what we have is a sample of the opportunities facing the Chicago job-seeker with minimal skills....

Race and Ethnicity

When they talked about the work ethic, tensions in the workplace, or attitudes toward work, employers emphasized the color of a person's skin. Many believed that white workers were superior to minorities in their work ethic....

When asked directly whether they thought there were any differences in the work ethics of whites, blacks, and Hispanics, 37.7 percent of the employers ranked blacks last, 1.4 percent ranked Hispanics last, and no one ranked whites there. Another 7.6 percent placed blacks and Hispanics together on the lowest level; 51.4 percent either saw no difference or refused to categorize in a straightforward way. Many of the latter group qualified their response by saying they saw no differences once one controlled for education, background, or environment, and that any differences were more the result of class or space. . . .

Blacks are by and large thought to possess very few of the characteristics of a "good" worker. Over and over employers said, "They don't want to work." "They don't want to stay." "They've got an attitude problem." One compared blacks with Mexicans: "Most of them are not as educated as you might think. I've never seen any of these guys read anything outside of a comic book. These Mexicans are sitting here reading novels constantly, even though they are in Spanish. These guys will sit and watch cartoons while the other guys are busy reading. To me that shows basic laziness. No desire to upgrade yourself." When asked about discrimination against black workers, a Chicago manufacturer related a common view: "Oh, I would in all honesty probably say there is some among most employers. I think one of the reasons, in all honesty, is because we've had bad experience in that sector, and believe me, I've tried. And as I say, if I find—whether he's black or white, if he's good and, you know, we'll hire him. We are not shutting out any black specifically. But I will say that our experience factor has been bad. We've had more bad black employees over the years than we had good." This negative opinion of blacks sometimes cuts across class lines. For instance, a personnel officer of a professional service company in the suburbs commented that "with the professional staff, black males that we've had, some of the skill levels—they're not as oriented to details. They lack some of the leadership skills."

One must also consider the "relevant nots": what were employers not talking about? They were not talking about how clever black workers were, they were not talking about the cultural richness of the black community, nor were they talking about rising divorce rates among whites. Furthermore, although each employer reserved the right to deny making distinctions along racial lines, fewer than 10 percent consistently refused to distinguish or generalize according to race.

These ways of talking about black workers—they have a bad work ethic, they create tensions in the workplace, they are lazy and unreliable, they have a bad attitude—reveal the meaning race has for many employers. If race were a proxy for expected productivity and the sole basis for statistical discrimination, black applicants would indeed find few job opportunities.

Class

Although some respondents spoke only in terms of race and ethnicity, or conflated class with race, others were sensitive to class distinctions. Class constituted a second, less easily detected signal for employers. Depending somewhat on the demands of the jobs, they used class markers to select among black applicants. The contrasts between their discourse about blacks and Hispanics were striking. Employers sometimes placed Hispanics with blacks in the lower class: an inner-city retailer confounded race, ethnicity, and class when he said, "I think there's a self-defeating prophecy that's maybe inherent in a lot of lower-income ethnic groups or races. Blacks, Hispanics." But although they rarely drew class distinctions among Hispanics, such distinctions were widely made for black workers. As one manufacturer said, "The black work ethic. There's no work ethic. At least at the unskilled. I'm sure with the skilled, as you go up, it's a lot different." Employers generally considered it likely that lower-class blacks would have more negative traits than blacks of other classes....

[A]lthough many employers assumed that black meant "inner-city poor," others—both black and white—were quick to see divisions within the black population. Of course, class itself is not directly observable, but markers that convey middle-or working-class status will help a black job applicant get through race-based exclusionary barriers. Class is primarily signaled to employers through speech, dress, education levels, skill levels, and place of residence. Although many respondents drew class distinctions among blacks, very few made those same distinctions among Hispanics or whites; in refining these categories, respondents referred to ethnicity and age rather than class.

Space

Although some employers spoke implicitly or explicitly in terms of class, for others "inner-city" was the more important category. For most the term immediately connoted black, poor, uneducated, unskilled, lacking in values, crime, gangs, drugs, and unstable families. "Suburb" connoted white, middle-class, educated, skilled, and stable families. Conversely, race was salient in part because it signaled space; black connoted inner city and white the suburbs....

The skepticism that greets the inner-city worker often arises when employers associate their race and residence with enrollment in Chicago's troubled public education system. Being educated in Chicago public schools has become a way of signaling "I'm black, I'm poor, and I'm from the inner city" to employers. Some mentioned that they passed over applicants from Chicago public schools for those with parochial or suburban educations. If employers were looking at an applicant's credentials when screening, blacks in the inner city did not do well. As one employer said, "The educational skills they come to the job with are

minimal because of the schools in the areas where they generally live."
. . .

Employers were clearly disappointed, not just in the academic content and level of training students receive, but in the failure of the school system to prepare them for the work force. Because the inner city is heavily associated with a lack of family values, employers wished the schools would compensate and provide students the self-discipline needed for worker socialization. . . .

Employers readily distinguished among blacks on the basis of space. They talked about Cabrini Green or the Robert Taylor Homes or referred to the South Side and West Side as a shorthand for black. But they were not likely to make these distinctions among whites and Hispanics. They made no reference to Pilsen (a largely immigrant Mexican neighborhood), Humboldt Park (largely Puerto Rican), or Uptown (a community of poor whites and new immigrants).

For black applicants, having the wrong combination of class and space markers suggested low productivity and undesirability to an employer. The important finding of this research, then, is not only that employers make hiring decisions based on the color of a person's skin, but the extent to which that act has become nuanced. Race, class, and space interact with each other. Moreover, the precise nature of that interaction is largely determined by the demands of the job.

They Don't Have What It Takes

This section provides evidence about what race and ethnicity signal for different types of employers, and how they seem to respond. We compare three categories of occupations with distinctive sets of hiring criteria: sales and customer service jobs, clerical jobs, and semiskilled, unskilled, and other service jobs. Race enters into hiring decisions in different ways, depending on the observability of key job requirements and particular occupational demands.

Sales and Customer Service Jobs

For sales and customer service jobs, employers' key criteria are appearance, communications skills, and personality. When asked about the most important qualities for the sample job, one said, "Probably the ability to communicate, you know. Can they communicate with you. That's very important. And their appearance is very important also. As far as qualities, that's really about everything." Honesty and simple mathematics skills were occasionally mentioned, as were intelligence, flexibility, and aggressiveness. But . . . job skills and specific work experience were relatively unimportant. How workers look, talk, and interact with customers or clients were clearly more important. . . .

Given the significance of interaction with the public for sales and service employers, one might expect to have found some discussion of "black" styles of interaction and speech, as we found among clerical employers. But sales and service employers' discussions of race made little reference to customers. The two respondents who made specific references to "black English" or black culture spoke in terms of interaction with supervisors or coworkers rather than with the public.... A florist, describing a black male employee who did not get along with coworkers, said, "He did not speak really white English American. He spoke black American English. And there's a big discrepancy there. A lot of black people are very bright and speak both black and white, but some don't speak white, and that makes it very hard."

Evidence of consumer discrimination appeared in a more direct form. One city restaurateur acknowledged that he discriminated by race because his customers did: "I have all white waitresses for a very basic reason. My clientele is 95 percent white. I simply wouldn't last very long if I had some black waitresses out there." ...

Although most important qualities for sales and customer service workers are observable in the hiring interview, race, class, and space might also function as signals for at least one unobservable characteristic: honesty. A suburban drug store manager said,

> It's unfortunate, but, in my business I think overall [black men] tend to be known to be dishonest. I think that's too bad but that's the image they have.
>
> (Interviewer: So you think it's an image problem?)
>
> Yeah, a dishonest, an image problem of being dishonest men and lazy. They're known to be lazy. They are [laughs]. I hate to tell you, but. It's all an image though. Whether they are or not, I don't know, but, it's an image that is perceived.
>
> (Interviewer: I see. How do you think that image was developed?) Go look in the jails [laughs]....

Clerical Jobs

Clerical jobs are the most highly skilled of the jobs we consider here. When asked what qualities were most important to them, employers of clerical workers emphasized job experience and skills, communications skills, and specific skills such as mathematics or typing but also mentioned personal qualities such as appearance.

Language ability and other clerical skills can readily be tested, and in fact two-thirds of clerical employers administered some kind of basic (language and mathematics) skills test. A few tested for writing, asking applicants to write brief essays or letters. Informal "tests" were also common; one insurance company solicited letters from job applicants to get a sense of their writing skills. A law firm employer scanned the format of the resume. Requiring a high school degree was common, although the poor reputation of the Chicago public schools was reflected in significant differences between city and suburb: 90.9 percent of suburban employers required a high school diploma, compared with only 61.2 percent of city employers.

But clerical employers looked for other qualities as well. [E]mployers are often concerned with interpersonal skills such as the ability to deal with the public or cooperate with coworkers. Employers in law firms, public relations agencies, and similar businesses emphasized the need for secretaries to get along with the hard-driving and demanding professionals they worked for....

Some white-collar employers told us that they felt blacks' styles of presentation and speech were inappropriate. The placement director quoted earlier complained that "a lot of the blacks still will wear their hair in tons and millions of braids all over their head. They're sort of hostile. They will [say] 'I never wear make-up.'" A black personnel officer said, "Unfortunately, there is a perception that most of [Chicago public high school] kids are black and they don't have the proper skills. They don't know how to write. They don't know how to speak. They don't act in a business fashion or dress in a business manner, in a way that the business community would like." Black speech patterns were an immediate marker of an undesirable job candidate; a former counseler [sic] said that one of the first things job seekers were taught was "you don't 'ax' nobody for a job, you'll *ask* them." ...

Clerical employers were notable for their sensitivity to class distinctions among blacks, and their responses were often framed in terms of speech patterns:

> I think it's primarily what I mentioned—the cultural thing. We have a couple of black workers—a friend of mine, one of the black secretaries who's been here several years, said, "Well, they're black but their soul is white" and, because culturally, they're white. They do not have black accents. They do not—I think the accent is a big part of it. If someone—it doesn't matter—if someone is black but they speak with the same accent as a Midwestern white person, it completely changes the perception of them. And then dress is part of it. So, you're dealing with what is almost more socioeconomic prejudice than purely racial prejudice....

Less common was reference to inner-city residence. One respondent described her interview with an applicant from the projects:

> The person came in, made a very, very poor impression physically.... I mean she was already for the interview in a state of pretty bad disarray. And I just did not feel she would mix in with the people that I already had, and I didn't want to start explaining that she'd have to show up for work in the morning and you go home at this time, and I think this company gives our clerical employees a fair amount of latitude.... I didn't really want to explain these small nuances of behavior to somebody like that....

[I]t is likely that most inner-city applicants are screened out by the education and skill requirements of clerical jobs. So while the category "inner city" may be familiar from newspaper accounts, it is not one that is prominent in their hiring and recruitment decisions, other than through its correlation with lower class. Rather, the primary criteria that distinguish appropriate black clerical applicants are those based on class.

Low-Skilled Blue-Collar and Service Jobs

Like sales and customer service employers, most employers of low-skilled blue-collar and service workers do not require job skills....

In fact, several employers said explicitly that they valued trainability over experience. One looked for a "bright" job applicant, one with an attitude that "I don't have any of the basic skills but I can learn them in a hurry." ...

What is crucial in these jobs is dependability: "Every day coming to work on time." Common complaints about low-skilled workers focused on those who were hired and never showed up, or quit without warning. Respondents tended to use terms such as "stability," "dependability," "good work history," and "attendance record" interchangeably, and many said explicitly that they saw an applicant's work record as an index of stability: "As far as dependability, and that's why I said earlier that past work record, that's important, so I almost automatically disqualify someone who has moved from position to position, numerous positions within a very short period of time." ...

Closely related to dependability in employers' discussions were work ethic, "willingness to work," or "desire to have a job." This phrasing almost never occurred in interviews with other types of employers, but these respondents took its meaning for granted when discussing the most important qualities of a worker with few skills: "Desire to have a job and do a good job, willingness to come to work." ...

> Willingness to cooperate with others and take instructions were other crucial characteristics for low-skilled workers. Employers were concerned not with brief interactions with the public but with day-to-day working relations over the long term. Some respondents said they would use the interview to "get a fix on" how well someone worked with others. But one employer stressed the difficulty of assessing this quality:

You know they have to be able to get along with the other employees that we have up there. We've had in the past years people who just cannot get along, they're always arguing with each other and so forth and so on and we try to avoid that type of thing where possible. But, of course, you never know until after they are hired. When you are interviewing them, everybody is on good behavior.

· · ·

Only a few respondents made an explicit connection between racial heterogeneity and workplace tensions. But those employers of low-skilled workers who valued teamwork were twice as likely to have racially and ethnically homogeneous work forces in the sample job—37.8 percent versus 16.4 percent.[1]

. . .

Because the most desired traits in low-skilled workers are unobservable, employers of such labor seemed more likely to engage in statistical discrimination. According to some of our respondents, the widespread perception that black workers were unreliable or had a poor work ethic hurt them in the labor market:

> In talking about reasons black men don't get jobs, you know, I think a lot of people see that group as being quote lazy unquote, which is a stereotypical image that you would have, and a lot of employers have had experience with hiring people like that and if they get enough of them who tend to make that a reality—that yes, they are. They're not reliable. They're not dependable. They don't show up. When they do show up they don't do a good job. They're just going to say, "Well, I'm not going to hire anybody like that anymore." And that's human nature.

An inner-city manufacturer reported that "when we hear other employers talk, they'll go after primarily the Hispanic and Oriental first, those two, and, I'll qualify that even further, the Mexican Hispanic, and any oriental, and after that, that's pretty much it, that's pretty much where they like to draw the line, right there."

. . .

Like those cited above, some employers talked only in terms of race and ethnicity. But in most cases race did not disqualify a job applicant: many employers praised their "good" black employees, often speaking in terms of their long tenure at the firm. Rather, employers perceived the black labor force as relatively heterogeneous. The significance of race for them was that black job applicants were scrutinized more carefully. As one manufacturer said, "I meet people who look at the black males with a little more finely tuned eye than they would someone else."

In contrast to employers of clerical workers, who were concerned with class and paid little attention to space, employers of low-skilled workers were most concerned with characteristics associated with the distinction between inner-city blacks and other blacks. Some drew this distinction explicitly, as one responded to the question about "address discrimination": "If you take a perceived bigoted position that black males are lazy, which I probably unfortunately did earlier, then how do you sort through that and find those who are not? Well, you sure as hell don't go to the projects to look for someone who is not. Now a lot of great people come out of the projects, but you know, that's not where I'd go looking for the exception."

---

1. Homogeneous work forces were defined as those in which 90 percent or more of sample job workers were either white, black, or Hispanic.

Conclusion

Chicago's employers did not hesitate to generalize about race or ethnic differences in the quality of the labor force. Most associated negative images with inner-city workers, and particularly with black men. "Black" and "inner-city" were inextricably linked, and both were linked with "lower-class."

Regardless of the generalizations employers made, they did consider the black population particularly heterogeneous, which made it more important that they be able to distinguish "good" from "bad" workers. Whether through skills tests, credentials, personal references, folk theories, or their intuition, they used some means of screening out the inner-city applicant. The ubiquitous anecdote about the good black worker, the exception to the rule, testified to their own perceived success at doing this. So did frequent references to "our" black workers, as opposed to "those guys on the street corner."

And black job applicants, unlike their white counterparts, must indicate to employers that the stereotypes do not apply to them. Inner-city and lower-class workers were seen as undesirable, and black applicants had to try to signal to employers that they did not fall into those categories, either by demonstrating their skills or by adopting a middle-class style of dress, manner, and speech or perhaps (as we were told some did) by lying about their address or work history.

The Urban Institute Audit Studies: Their Methods and Findings*

JAMES J. HECKMAN AND PETER SIEGELMAN

Audit studies are a potentially promising method for extending our understanding of hiring discrimination. Although such studies can overcome some of the limits inherent in traditional analyses of discrimination, they also pose a number of important and subtle challenges. Both the generation of the audit pair and its interpretation need to be conducted with extreme care if the potential usefulness of hiring audits is to be realized.

· · ·

This chapter critically examines the methods and findings of two recent Urban Institute studies and a study of the Denver labor market patterned after them. For brevity, the Urban Institute black/white study will henceforth be denoted UIBW, the Urban Institute Anglo/Hispanic

* Excerpts from James J. Heckman and Peter Siegelman, "The Urban Institute Audit Studies: Their Methods and Findings," in Michael Fix and Raymond J. Struyk, eds., *Clear and Convincing Evidence: Measurement of Discrimination in America,* copyright © 1993 by The Urban Institute Press. Reprinted by permission of Fix and Struyk.

study will be denoted UIAH, and the Denver study will be called just
that.

. . .

Using a variety of tests, and the measure of discrimination that
seems most satisfactory, we find little evidence of discrimination against
Denver blacks and Denver Hispanics. For Chicago blacks, the evidence in
support of discrimination is at best marginal. For Washington, D.C.
blacks and Chicago and San Diego Hispanics, our tests reveal evidence of
what might be termed discrimination.

. . .

How Audits Work

Audits have been adopted by social scientists from techniques employed by legal activists, who pioneered their use in the enforcement of
fair-housing laws during the late 1960s. The audit procedure can be
conveniently divided into two parts. First is the selection and training of
auditors. Groups of two individuals, one white or Anglo and one black or
Hispanic, are selected from a group of applicants to resemble each other
as closely as possible except for race. Testers are typically matched on
such attributes as age, education, physical appearance (subjective level of
attractiveness), physical strength, and level of verbal skills, as deemed
relevant. The goal is to produce pairs of testers who are identical in all
relevant characteristics so that any systematic difference in treatment
within each pair can be attributed only to the effects of race. In addition
to their outward similarities, testers are given training about how they
are supposed to behave during the course of the audits. Such training
typically includes developing synthetic biographies (current and past
employment, references, education, and so on), behavioral alignment
(e.g., level of aggressiveness and overall "presentation of self"), and
experience in role-playing, simulating the kind of transaction being
audited.

An important element of subjective judgement enters at this stage.
Audit pair analysts assume that they know which characteristics are
relevant to employers, and when such characteristics are "sufficiently"
close to make majority and minority audit pair members "indistinguishable." Audit pair members must be matched on each of the relevant
characteristics. Alternatively, audit analysts assume that they know how
employers trade off characteristics....

Given the current low level of factual knowledge about which
characteristics employers value and how attributes trade off in productive content, and given the likely heterogeneity among employers in
making these assessments, it is not obvious that audit analysts would
possess the relevant information required to make perfect matches.
There is a presumption of knowledge about "what is really important"

that is difficult to demonstrate objectively. This inability to defend, or even fully enunciate, the criteria used to match audit pair members constitutes the Achilles heel of the audit pair methodology. In the UIBW study five audit pairs were chosen in Chicago and Washington from a group of male college students between the ages of 19 and 24 at the major universities in those environments (excluding junior colleges and community colleges) who applied to perform the audits. Job announcements were mailed to university employment and placement offices, social science departments, minority affairs offices, and selected professors. There were 23 applicants in Washington and 31 in Chicago, who were winnowed to five audit pairs in each site. The choice among potential audit pair partners was thus rather limited.

· · ·

Payment was made to applicants for a fixed sum of $3,000 for six weeks of work. It was not made contingent on performance in the audit study. Each audit pair partner applied without knowledge of the employment outcomes of the other partner.

The second phase of an audit study is the generation of the data. Job openings to be audited are selected at random for certain types of entry level jobs sampled from help-wanted advertisements in local newspapers. Members of an audit pair are then sent in random order to apply for the job, typically within a few hours of each other. (If the first member of a pair is offered a job, he is instructed to turn down the offer so as to leave the vacancy available for his teammate.) Each pair typically conducts many tests, so repeated observations are available for each person in each pair. However, in these studies, the same firms are not visited by more than one audit pair.

One ... major advantage of the audit technique is that it allows more control over the characteristics that are thought to be relevant to the employment decision than is possible in conventional ex-post regression analyses. For example, regression studies typically use years of education as a control variable in explaining wage discrimination. But this is an extremely crude control, ignoring as it does differences in educational quality and performance between workers with the same number of years of education. In an audit, by contrast, the two testers can be matched exactly on certain characteristics (by giving them identical educational histories, including schools attended, GPA, and so forth), providing a much cleaner measure of the demand-side response to race and ethnicity than techniques based on passive observation. In addition, by sending pairs of auditors to the same firms, one gains partial control over idiosyncratic differences in firm valuations of common bundles of characteristics that plague ordinary observational studies.

· · ·

Table 6.1 presents summaries of outcomes for each black/white audit pair in Washington, D.C., and Chicago. Table 6.2 presents comparable summaries from the UIAH study, in which similar definitions are used. Table 6.3 presents the aggregate data from Denver. See Table 6.4 for the disaggregated data.

.   .   .

[O]ne of the most striking features of all three tables is the relatively high proportion of trials in which there was no difference in treatment by race/ethnicity—roughly 80 percent by the get-a-job measure. The Denver Hispanic/Anglo study showed the smallest proportion of equal treatment, but in that study Hispanics were actually favored over Anglos. Compared with the housing audit studies of Yinger or the car negotiations tested by Ayres and Siegelman, the proportion of tests in which applicants received equal treatment is very high. By focusing on the disparities between the treatment of majority and minority group members, the Urban Institute studies deemphasize the high proportion of audits in which equal treatment of both partners was found. An appropriate question, therefore, is "whether the glass is one-quarter empty or three-quarters full?" In all of the audit pair studies it seems quite full to us.

.   .   .

Table 6.1.   Outcomes in the Urban Institute Black/White Study
in Chicago and Washington, D. C. (Get Job or Not)

Number of Audits	Pair	(a) Both get job	(b) Neither gets job	a + b	White yes, black no	White no, black yes
Chicago						
35	1	(5) 14.3%	(23) 65.7%	80%	(5) 14.3%	(2) 5.7%
40	2	(5) 12.5%	(25) 62.5%	75%	(4) 10.0%	(6) 15.0%
44	3	(3) 56.8%	(37) 84.1%	90.9%	(3) 6.8%	(1) 2.3%
36	4	(6) 16.7%	(24) 66.7%	83.4%	(6) 16.7%	(0) 0%
42	5	(3) 7.1%	(38) 90.5%	97.6%	(1) 2.4%	(0) 0%
197	Total	(22) 11.2%	(147) 74.6%	85.8%	(19) 59.6%	(9) 4.5%
Washington						
46	1	(5) 10.9%	(26) 56.5%	67.4%	(12) 26.1%	(3) 6.5%
54	2	(11) 20.4%	(31) 57.4%	77.8%	(9) 16.7%	(3) 5.6%
62	3	(11) 17.7%	(36) 58.1%	75.8%	(11) 17.7%	(4) 6.5%
37	4	(6) 16.2%	(22) 59.5%	75.7%	(7) 18.9%	(2) 5.4%
42	5	(7) 16.7%	(26) 61.9%	77.6%	(7) 16.7%	(2) 4.8%
241	Total	(40) 16.6%	(141) 58.5%	75.1%	(46) 19.1%	(14) 5.8%

Note. Results are percentages; figures in parentheses are the relevant number of audits.

Table 6.2. Outcomes in the Urban Institute Anglo/Hispanic Study
in Chicago and San Diego (Get Job or Not)

Number of Audits	Pair	(a) Both get job	(b) Neither gets job	a + b	Anglo yes, Hispanic no	Anglo no, Hispanic yes
Chicago						
33	1	(9) 27.3%	(16) 48.5%	75.8%	(7) 21.2%	(1) 3.0%
32	2	(4) 12.5%	(18) 56.3%	68.8%	(9) 28.1%	(1) 3.1%
39	3	(9) 23.1%	(20) 51.3%	74.2%	(7) 17.9%	(3) 7.7%
38	4	(4) 10.5%	(19) 50.0%	60.5%	(10) 26.3%	(5) 13.2%
142	Total	(26) 18.3%	(73) 51.4%	69.7%	(33) 23.2%	(10) 7.0%
San Diego						
39	1	(5) 12.8%	(24) 61.5%	74.3%	(6) 15.4%	(4) 10.3%
37	2	(8) 21.6%	(18) 48.7%	70.3%	(9) 24.3%	(2) 5.4%
44	3	(14) 31.8%	(17) 38.6%	69.4%	(11) 25.0%	(2) 4.6%
40	4	(9) 22.5%	(18) 45.0%	67.5%	(8) 20.0%	(5) 12.5%
160	Total	(36) 22.5%	(77) 48.1%	70.6%	(34) 21.2%	(13) 8.1%

Note. Results are percentages; figures in parentheses are the relevant number of audits.

Table 6.3. Outcomes in the Denver Study (Aggregate Data)

Total	Pair	Majority favored	Minority favored	Neither favored
140	Hispanic/Anglo	(26) 18.6%	(36) 25.7%	(78) 55.7%
145	Black/White	(17) 11.7%	(15) 10.3%	(113) 77.9%

Notes: Results are percentages; figures in parentheses are the relevant number of audits.

Table 6.4. Disaggregated Denver Data: "Get a Job" Measure

| | Black/White | | | | |
Pair	Both get job	Neither gets job	White yes, lack no	White no, Black yes	Total
1	(2) 11.1	(11) 61.1	(0) 0.0	(5) 27.8	(18)
2	(2) 3.8	(41) 77.4	(10) 18.9	(0) 0.0	(53)
3	(7) 21.2	(25) 75.8	(0) 0.0	(1) 3.3	(33)
4	(9) 60.0	(3) 20.0	(2) 13.3	(1) 6.7	(15)
9	(3) 11.5	(23) 88.5	(0) 0.0	(0) 0.0	(26)
Total	(23) 15.8	(103) 71.1	(7) 4.8	(12) 8.3	(145)

| | Hispanic/Anglo | | | | |
Pair	Both get job	Neither gets job	Anglo yes, Hispanic no	Anglo no, Hispanic yes	Total
5	(0) 0.0	(11) 91.7	(0) 0.0	(1) 8.3	(12)
6	(4) 7.8	(30) 58.8	(3) 5.9	(14) 27.5	(51)
7	(1) 2.8	(35) 97.2	(0) 0.0	(0) 0.0	(36)
8	(2) 4.9	(30) 73.2	(6) 14.6	(3) 7.3	(41)
Total	(7) 5.0	(106) 75.7	(18) 12.8	(9) 6.5	(140)

Note. Results are percentages; figures in parentheses are the relevant number of audits.

Qualifying the Urban Institute Conclusions: Some Limitations of the Evidence

This section addresses [three] aspects of the audit methods used in the employment discrimination studies. The first is the question of the proper sampling frame for selecting the firms and jobs to be audited. The second is the possibility of "experimenter effects." The third . . . is the possible problem posed by the presence of facial hair and accents among the Hispanic testers.

Sampling Frame

The Urban Institute studies presented persuasive reasons for sampling jobs from newspaper advertisements. Employers seeking applicants through this route clearly signal the availability of jobs. For audit studies with limited budgets and operating over limited time frames, it is clearly much more cost-efficient to sample firms with jobs than it is to sample the universe of all firms to determine subsamples of firms that are hiring.

An important drawback to the use of newspaper advertisements in constructing the sampling frame, however, is that relatively few actual jobs are obtained through this route, even for youth participating in the unskilled labor markets analyzed in the Urban Institute and Denver studies. Recent evidence by Holzer, . . . indicates that friends and relatives and direct contact of firms by applicants are much more common sources of jobs in searches by both employed and unemployed youth. For employed youth, only 26 percent of search time is spent on contacts generated by newspaper advertising. For unemployed youth, the corresponding figure is only 18 percent. [Holzer] documents that job acceptances from newspaper-generated searches are much less common than acceptances from other sources. In sum, youths' job searches are characterized by primary use of informal networks. Sampling from these networks poses a major challenge to the audit pair methodology.

Holzer's evidence suggests that the sampling frame adopted in the UI studies is not representative of the job search process followed by most workers. The UI studies claim that this lack of representativeness leads to an understatement of the extent of labor market discrimination as measured by their studies. Their argument is that discriminatory firms are more likely to use informal employment sources, rather than publicly advertising for applicants, in an effort to conceal their discriminatory practices and avoid prosecution under employment discrimination laws.

The claim that firms that hire through networks are inherently more discriminatory than firms that hire from newspaper advertisements must be treated with caution, however. The use of informal networks may simply be an efficient means of screening prospective workers, in that firms may prefer to rely on the information and reputation of existing workers when considering new applicants. In light of the great gains made by minority workers in unskilled markets in the past 25 years, it is not obvious that informal networks now act to exclude minorities. Indeed, in unskilled markets like those studied by the Urban Institute, it seems likely that there are both majority and minority networks that certify applicants by word of mouth.

Nevertheless, Holzer reports that the fraction of blacks using each search method is virtually identical to that of whites but that job offers from friends and relatives and direct contacts are greater for whites than for blacks. Whites spend more time searching by direct application and through leads generated by friends and relatives than do blacks (397 minutes vs. 252 minutes, respectively, for searches via friends and relatives). Blacks spend more time on searches at state agencies (292 minutes vs. 187 minutes), newspaper searches (292 minutes vs. 223 minutes) and other methods (266 minutes vs. 205 minutes). Assuming rational search behavior by both blacks and whites, this pattern provides indirect support for the UI claim that firms advertising in newspapers are less discriminatory. . . .

Experimenter Effects

By experimenter effects, we mean that "the experimenter is not simply a passive runner of subjects, but can actually influence the results" of an experiment. When it exists, such influence is not exerted by any deliberate or conscious actions on the part of the experimenter but, rather, occurs because of unconscious motivations or because subjects may have a desire to conform to (what they perceive as) the experimenter's wishes. . . .

Anyone who doubts the importance of experimenter effects need only consider the importance of controls in the testing of new drugs. According to one expert, "it is not at all unusual to find placebo effects that are more powerful than the actual chemical effects of drugs whose pharmacological action is fairly well understood." Studies evaluating the effects of drugs are always double blind (neither the patient nor the experimenter knows whether the drug being administered is a placebo or the real drug) precisely to minimize such effects.

Both of the Urban Institute studies, as well as the Denver audits, are potentially subject to experimenter effects. All three studies made a point of stressing the nature of the experiment and its expected findings to the testers in several days of training. This was done in part to minimize the psychological impact of discriminatory treatment on minority auditors, but it may have had perverse unintended effects. (However, the performance of the other testers in the project was not revealed to any tester, so at least there was no contamination from direct feedbacks.) An explicit part of the training of auditors was a general discussion of the pervasive problem of discrimination in the United States.

In the UIBW study, part of the first day of the five-day auditor training session included an introduction to employment discrimination and equal employment opportunity and a review of project design and methodology. Similar protocols were used in UIAH. In both studies, participants were warned about the employer bias they might encounter and how they should react to it. We would prefer an experimental design in which the testers themselves were kept ignorant of the hypothesis being tested (discriminatory hiring) and the fact that they were operating in pairs.

Facial Hair and Accents

In the Urban Institute study, all the Hispanic testers in San Diego had facial hair and strong Hispanic accents. The presence of accents, facial hair, or any other characteristic across *all* testers of one type is unfortunate because it means that the hypotheses of discrimination against "accents" or "hair" are observationally equivalent to (indistinguishable from) the hypothesis of discrimination against Hispanics per se. There is some evidence that employers are sensitive to the general appearance or "attractiveness" of applicants. Thus, it is interesting and important to know whether Hispanic men without beards and/or accents do better relative to whites than do those with these characteristics. The fact that in Denver, Hispanic men were more like Anglo men in these characteristics, and did not experience discrimination, indicates that this problem is potentially serious.

Using the presence of facial hair or an accent—rather than race/ethnicity itself—to make hiring decisions could constitute discrimination that would subject an employer to "disparate impact" liability under Title VII of the 1964 Civil Rights Act. Since effect, not intent, is what is at issue in such cases, if Hispanics were disproportionately hurt by a "no beards" or "no accents" rule, one might be able to mount a legal challenge to such a rule. Still, it makes an important difference to policy whether employers are using ethnicity directly in making hiring decisions, or are instead relying on apparently neutral rules that disproportionately hurt minorities. Moreover, in the context of the audit pair methodology, in which Anglo and Hispanic testers were virtually identical in all other observable productivity-related characteristics, slight differences in accents (or facial hair) could have ended up being more important in employers' decisions than they ordinarily are. In other words, employers might have used accents or facial hair only to "break a tie" between candidates who were otherwise identical. This kind of behavior might well constitute discrimination, but it is probably an unusual kind of discrimination compared to what typically occurs in the market, with very different policy implications.

·   ·   ·

Evidence on Reverse Discrimination

Those who see reverse discrimination as a more serious problem than discrimination against racial/ethnic minorities will find no support in any of these findings. In virtually no dimension did white and Anglo auditors consistently do worse than their black and Hispanic partners.

·   ·   ·

Comparing the Denver and Urban Institute Studies

An interesting problem posed by the collection of audit studies considered here is the apparent disparity in the results between the two Urban Institute studies on one hand and the Denver studies on the other. While the Urban Institute studies based on large sample testing methods apparently find evidence of discrimination against Hispanics in San Diego and Chicago, and in Washington, D.C. against blacks, the Denver study suggests virtually no discrimination against either of these groups.

Two explanations for these divergent results should be considered. One possibility is that the differences are simply artifacts of methodological differences between the two groups of studies. Although the methodology used in Denver was patterned after that of the Urban Institute studies, there were some differences that may have had an effect on the results. The second possibility is that there is actually less discrimination (against both blacks and Hispanics) in Denver than in Chicago, San Diego, or Washington, D.C.

Of course, these are not mutually exclusive explanations—both could be operating at the same time. In fact, our view is that the differences between Denver and the other cities seem small enough to be explained by either of the two sources, or both together.

The disaggregated data from the Denver experiments are presented in table 6.4. While we do not resolve this issue definitively in this paper, the data strongly suggest that the pairs of Denver auditors were much more heterogeneous (diverse) than are the pairs in either UIBW or UIAH. Thus, while the aggregate experience for *all* Denver audit pairs reveals little evidence of discriminatory treatment, this aggregation conceals large differences in the way certain pairs were treated. A Fisher exact test rejects the hypothesis of across-pair homogeneity, as does a large sample test.

Table 6.4 reveals that overall, black auditors got a job when their white partner did not in 7 out of 145 audits (4.8 percent); white auditors were favored in 12 audits (8.3 percent). [T]his relatively small difference does not provide statistically significant evidence of the existence of discrimination at the aggregate level or at the individual level.

The aggregate results conceal a widely disparate set of outcomes among the different pairs of testers, however. For example, consider pairs 1 and 2. In pair 1, the black tester was favored over his white partner in 5 out of the 18 tests, while the white tester was never favored. For pair 2, the results are dramatically opposite: the white tester was favored in 10 of the 53 tests, while the black tester was never favored. Roughly similar patterns can be observed for Hispanic/Anglo pairs 6 and 8. In the notation developed earlier, the quantity (P_3-P_4) ranges from 28 percent to −19 percent for the black audit pairs, and from 21.6 percent to −7.3 percent for the Hispanic pairs. There are large differences among the different audit pairs that are masked when the experiences of all the pairs are aggregated.

The heterogeneity found in the Denver data raises three important issues. First, it demonstrates the importance of providing data at the disaggregated (pair-by-pair) level. Aggregation of audit pair results by city can obscure some important differences in the way individual pairs were treated, which can in turn influence the interpretation of the aggregate results. . . .

Second, both the Denver and UI studies show how difficult it is to draw inferences about the homogeneity of pairs from verbal descriptions of the selection and matching procedures by themselves. Looking only at the *descriptions* of the rigorous and careful procedures used in the Denver (or UI) studies, one would naturally be inclined to assume that the pairs were all quite homogeneous. In fact, however, we reject homogeneity in three of the six race/city sites (Denver blacks, Denver Hispanics, and Chicago blacks). In spite of the extremely careful efforts made by all of the researchers to ensure that all the pairs of testers resembled each other, the pairs appear to have been treated quite differently in their respective labor markets.

This raises a final problem. Why should the audit pair analysts have found it relatively difficult to control for heterogeneity across pairs? The answer must rest on the difficulty of comparing and matching large numbers of auditor characteristics, many of which are intangible or difficult to describe. If mismatching in characteristics occurs in half of the city/race sites despite the best efforts of the testers to prevent it, it would seem that our knowledge of the hiring process being audited is rife with uncertainty. One should be wary of assuming that much is known about how hiring decisions are actually made. The burden of proof that audit pairs are properly aligned must be assumed by audit pair analysts. More objective demonstrations of the matching methods actually used would increase the value of audit pair evidence.

Notes and Questions

1. Was some of the racial discrimination committed at Shoney's potentially profit maximizing? Was all of it? Note in this regard that one of the employers interviewed in Chicago by Kirschenman and Neckerman stated that, with a 95 percent white clientele, it was necessary for the survival of his business not to hire black waitresses. Assuming that this belief was sincerely held, could it be influenced by the type of unconscious racism and cognitive biases that were discussed in Chapter 5?

2. In Chapter 7, John Donohue argues that Title VII adds a legal penalty to whatever market penalty already exists for engaging in employment discrimination, and therefore Title VII should more rapidly achieve the goal of eliminating discriminatory owner-managers. Does the Shoney's case illustrate this point? What, if any, were the social costs of eliminating Ray

Danner from his position of control in Shoney's? Does the affirmative action plan that Shoney's agreed to in order to end the litigation seem appropriate and just? Do you expect it will have any effect on the company's profitability?

3. Does the Kirschenman and Neckerman study indicate that Chicago employers are primarily concerned with worker productivity? Does it reveal that the main problem confronting black job applicants is the need to conform to mainstream expectations of appearance, language, punctuality, motivation, and courtesy? In light of the evidence discussed in Chapter 5 concerning the results of the survey literature on race discrimination, are you confident that interview answers are honest and meaningful?

4. The Urban Institute study of Chicago employers, discussed by Heckman and Siegelman, found that 85.8 percent of the time, black and white job testers either both got the job or both were rejected for the job to which they were applying. In 9.6 percent of the audits, the white tester got a job and the black did not, and in the remaining 4.5 percent of the audits the black tester got the job and the white did not. Is this degree of discrimination in low-skilled jobs in Chicago surprisingly low given the finding by Kirschenman and Neckerman that, when asked about the work ethics of whites, blacks, and Hispanics, 37.7 percent of the Chicago employers ranked blacks last, 51.4 percent thought they were the same, and no one ranked whites last?

Can you explain the apparent gulf between the degree of discrimination found in the two studies? Recall that the evidence in Chapter 5 suggests that, given the current norms and legal pressures fostering equality, survey evidence is likely to *understate* true discriminatory attitudes, which lends added credence to Kirschenman's and Neckerman's finding of widespread discriminatory attitudes. But the Urban Institute study appears to find that the percentage of employers who will turn down apparently attractive minority workers is far smaller than the percentage of employers found by Kirschenman and Neckerman to hold these prejudiced beliefs. Does this imply that employers' discriminatory tendencies are being checked either by antidiscrimination law or by the market?

Perhaps because of the status-producing benefits stressed by Richard McAdams or the unconscious racism or cognitive biases noted by Charles Lawrence and Linda Krieger in Chapter 5, many employers harbor the belief that, in general, blacks are unattractive workers, yet they view their task in selecting a workforce to be finding the "unusual" blacks that do not conform to their stereotypes. In this view, employment decisions might be made on the merits more often than one would expect, given the underlying degree of prejudice, because employers can secure the enhanced self-esteem from holding negative judgmental beliefs about another group without sacrificing the profits that would be lost from failing to hire attractive workers from this group. Indeed, one might imagine that the employer who ferrets out the "good" black workers takes pride in having unusual perspicacity. This may explain the finding by Kirschenman and Neckerman that many employers drew strong distinctions between "their" black workers, who were deemed to be "good," and blacks in the abstract, who were deemed to be "bad." Since the audit pair study was designed to make the testers conform to mainstream expectations of appearance and conduct, the Urban Institute may have presented to employers exactly the type of "good" workers they are willing to hire. Therefore, a possible reconciling interpretation of the Kirschenman and Neckerman and Urban Institute studies is that they reveal the willingness of employers in the large majority of cases—90.3 percent—to treat black applicants who conform to these mainstream expectations as well as, or occasionally better than, white applicants.

5.   The Urban Institute audit pair studies involved tests of discrimination against young applicants applying for low-skilled jobs. Would discrimination be greater or lesser if the jobs were higher skilled? Richard Epstein speculates in *Forbidden Grounds* that evidence of reverse discrimination would more likely have been found in the case of higher-skilled jobs or government employment. Epstein, *Forbidden Grounds* 57 (Cambridge, Mass.: Harvard University Press, 1992).

6.   Remember that the employers who were audited in the Urban Institute study operated in an environment in which employment discrimination was unlawful. The fact that discriminatory conduct, although present, was somewhat limited does not indicate that the law is unnecessary. The law may be effectively deterring discrimination. Epstein, however, argues that the discrimination against blacks that was observed, rather than being the residual that was not deterred by Title VII, may actually be *caused by Title VII*. Epstein at 58. The rationale for this contention is that antidiscrimination laws potentially can increase the likelihood of discrimination if the risk of being sued for firing an employer is far greater, as it is, than the risk of litigation over the failure to hire a minority worker. See the discussion of this issue by Donohue and Siegelman in Chapter 9.

7

Are Antidiscrimination Laws Efficient?

In the absence of market failure, the outcome generated by the operation of competitive labor markets is generally taken to be "efficient." Efficiency in this sense implies the inability to improve the well-being of one or more individuals without making anyone else worse off. When this definition is met, the economy is said to be Pareto efficient, since no Pareto-improving moves (those benefiting at least one person without harming anyone) are possible. But no Pareto-improving moves would exist if one individual owned everything; therefore, efficiency alone is not indicative of a socially desirable allocation of resources. On the other hand, there are important benefits that flow from having an efficient economy. First, greater efficiency generates more goods and services that will then be available for satisfying the wants and needs of the citizenry. Second, important nonmaterial benefits seem to emerge from greater economic productivity. For example, all of the economically developed countries have stable democracies, and a large body of literature supports the view that democracy is the product of economic development. In other words, because affluence tends to reduce the intensity of distributional conflicts and generates the education needed to support democratic institutions, there are significant political advantages from having an efficient and productive economy. Adam Przeworski and Fernando Limongi, "Political Regimes and Economic Growth," 7 *Journal of Economic Perspectives* 51, 62 (Summer 1993); Evelyne Huber, Dietrich Rueschemeyer, and John Stephens, "The Impact of Economic

179

Development on Democracy," 7 *Journal of Economic Perspectives* 71 (Summer 1993).

The preceding statements are the basis for a powerful syllogistic argument to which many conservatives—Milton Friedman, Richard Posner, and Richard Epstein to name a few—would subscribe: unrestricted labor markets are efficient; efficiency promotes highly desirable political, social, and economic benefits; antidiscrimination laws restrict labor markets; therefore antidiscrimination laws are inefficient and inimical to the attainment of these benefits.

Before accepting this syllogism, though, one must address whether the premise of a competitive labor market with no market failure is correct and whether the particular definition of efficiency is appropriate. The resolution of these issues turns on many formidable philosophic, historical, economic, and empirical judgments. For example, unlike Friedman, Becker, and Posner, who believe that Southern labor markets have been perfectly competitive throughout the twentieth century, Richard Epstein has accepted the empirical reality that the market was not driving out the extreme discriminatory practices of the Jim Crow South as evidence of a major market failure—which Epstein attributes to the collusive influence of racist Southern governments. Accordingly, Epstein concludes that Title VII was needed to destroy the racist governmental power in order to create the competitive labor market that is the guarantor of efficiency and all its attendant benefits. Therefore, at its inception Title VII was efficiency enhancing, according to Epstein; now, however, with the power of racist government in check, Title VII serves only to shackle the unrestrained competitive market that can guarantee efficiency. Epstein, *Forbidden Grounds* (Cambridge, Mass.: Harvard University Press, 1992). But Epstein's argument rests on establishing that private actors, through the cultivation of pervasive racist norms and social sanctioning mechanisms, were not capable in the Jim Crow South, or in America today, of effectively restricting the employment opportunities of blacks.

In one sense, Epstein has adopted John Donohue's view that Title VII promoted efficiency because it moved the society to a nondiscriminatory equilibrium more quickly than market forces acting alone would have. Posner, believing that the market was competitive all along, is willing to entertain the possibility that Title VII could achieve the nondiscriminatory equilibrium more quickly. But he would still maintain that since a competitive market will secure such an outcome at the most efficient rate, Title VII, to the extent it is successful at achieving its goals, would inefficiently reduce discrimination too quickly.

Robert Cooter carries the efficiency question one step further by applying the economic critique of regulation to antidiscrimination law. If the goal of Title VII is to promote the employment of blacks or other groups, one can achieve these goals at lower cost by relying on market incentives rather than a universal prohibition of employment discrimination. Thus, Cooter argues that, if market-like instruments replace bureaucratic rules wherever possible, the cost and coercion of achieving policy goals will be reduced, while efficiency and liberty will be advanced.

Is Title VII Efficient?*
JOHN J. DONOHUE III

Title VII of the Civil Rights Act of 1964 is widely regarded as one of the most important pieces of legislation enacted in this century.

. . .

Despite its undoubtedly heroic ambitions and unrivaled legislative prominence, however, the Act is not without its critics. In fact, some view it as the most conspicuous example of a legislative effort to shape private preferences—an endeavor that is thought to be "at best misguided and more likely tyrannical." The neoclassical economic model, which rests so heavily on the desirability of aggregating private preferences expressed in the marketplace, has long provided the theoretical foundation for the argument against this antidiscrimination legislation. Indeed, coupled with the normative principle of wealth maximization, the neoclassical economic model might appear to serve as the basis for unrelenting opposition to any form of government interference in free market outcomes. But, as is now well recognized, legal intervention can also serve to facilitate or enhance the operation of the market, thereby furthering the objective of wealth maximization.

If one looks beyond the traditional static analysis of Title VII and instead evaluates the law in a dynamic context, one finds that the logic of the attack on Title VII is incomplete. As this paper shows, legislation that prohibits employer discrimination may actually enhance rather than impair economic efficiency.

The Neoclassical Model of the Labor Market

Consider the market for labor in a nondiscriminatory world. For a given capital stock, firms have a downward sloping demand for laborers, while the supply curve for laborers slopes upward. The intersection of these two curves, as shown in Figure 7.1, determines the equilibrium wage (the vertical axis) and quantity of labor hired (the horizontal axis).

For those unfamiliar with demand and supply curves, it may be helpful to discuss how they are derived and what they represent. The demand curve for labor is predicated on the assumption that capital is fixed in the short run. The first worker hired by a firm will then have a certain capital stock at her disposal, which is used to generate a certain

* Excerpts from John J. Donohue III, "Is Title VII Efficient?," *University of Pennsylvania Law Review*, vol. 134, copyright © 1986. Reprinted by permission of University of Pennsylvania Law Review and Fred B. Rothman & Company.

physical product. The value to the employer of the worker's product is represented by the vertical distance from the horizontal axis up to the firm's demand curve and will depend on both the amount of the particular product produced and the price at which the product sells. One can therefore think of the vertical distance to the demand curve as representing the marginal benefit associated with hiring an additional worker.

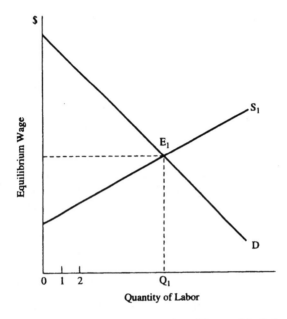

Figure 7.1. The Short-Run Supply and Demand for Labor

Of course, to obtain this benefit the employer must incur the expense of hiring that worker. The wage that must be paid to hire an additional worker is given by the vertical distance to the supply curve. The supply curve, therefore, represents the cost to society of employing one extra worker. Put differently, it represents the worker's monetary valuation of the cost of working.

Accordingly, so long as the demand curve lies above the supply curve, society will gain by employing an additional worker. This is because the benefit to the employer of the value of the worker's production is greater than the cost to the worker of working—obviously a mutually beneficial transaction. It is important to recognize a central tenet of the neoclassical economic model: in a world without externalities, market-determined private costs and benefits will equal social costs and benefits. It is this assumption that allows one to conclude that, if the *private* benefit to the employer of receiving the worker's output exceeds the worker's *private* cost of toiling, *social* welfare is increased by hiring the worker.

. . .

This process can be repeated until the intersection of the supply and demand curves at E_1 is reached-the point of maximum social welfare. If fewer than Q_1 workers are hired, the demand curve lies above the supply curve, which indicates that the benefits of additional hiring are greater than the accompanying social costs. On the other hand, if more than Q_1 workers are hired, the costs will exceed the benefits and social welfare would be reduced. Because E_1 represents the point of maximum social welfare it is, by definition, the economically efficient outcome.

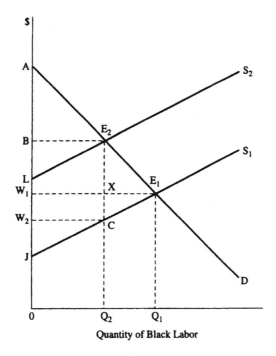

Figure 7.2. The Short-Run Supply and Demand for Black Labor Given Employer Discrimination

Introducing Discrimination

Thus far, it has been assumed that no discrimination exists in the labor market. Gary S. Becker's pioneering work, however, has shown that the neoclassical model can readily be extended to analyze labor market discrimination. Following Becker, discrimination is now introduced in the form of an aversion by employers to certain groups even though all groups of workers are equally productive.

If, for example, employers have an aversion to black workers, the consequence of this discrimination is, in effect, to shift the supply curve for black labor from S_1 up to S_2, as shown in Figure 7.2.[1] This upward parallel shift in the supply curve due to employer distaste for black workers is exactly analogous to a tax of amount E_2C on each black worker hired. The benefits derived from hiring additional black workers are still given by the same demand curve, but now there is a cost associated with hiring black workers in addition to the previously specified monetary cost embodied in the wage. Thus, to hire the first worker, a discriminatory employer must pay not only the monetary wage but also a psychic or nonmonetary cost associated with hiring a worker for whom she has personal distaste. The analysis then proceeds exactly as before. Employers will evaluate the benefits of increased production from hiring black workers and will offset them against the total costs, both monetary and nonmonetary, of hiring these workers.

The effect will be to reduce the number of blacks hired from the previous level Q_1 to a lower level Q_2. At the same time, the wage of black workers will fall from the previous level W_1 to a lower level W_2. The model therefore generates two plausible predictions: (1) discrimination leads to a reduction in the hiring of black labor, and (2) discrimination causes a decrease in black wages.

The effect of discrimination on the welfare of employers is an important and controversial issue. With capital fixed in the short run, employers are interested in maximizing "profits," which are determined by subtracting the total labor cost from the total value of production. In the nondiscriminatory case, profits were given by the area of the triangle W_1AE_1 in Figure 7.2. The total value of production is the area under the demand curve from zero to Q_1 workers, or area $0AE_1Q_1$. Employers, however, have paid a wage of W_1 to their Q_1 workers, an amount represented by the area $0W_1E_1Q_1$. The difference between what is produced and the cost of production represents short-run profits, W_1AE_1.

The introduction of discrimination changes the wage and hiring levels for black workers. Because the number of black workers has declined to Q_2, total production now falls to $0AE_2Q_2$ and the total wage cost falls to $0W_2CQ_2$. But, in addition to the monetary cost imposed by the wage bill, discriminatory employers will also have to bear a nonmonetary cost associated with the hiring of black laborers—a type of "discrimination" tax—given by the area W_2BE_2C. As a result, the net profits earned by discriminatory employers fall to the amount represented by the area of the triangle BAE_2. The triangle BAE_2 necessarily encompasses a lesser area than the triangle W_1AE_1. Therefore, not only does the

---

1. Intuitively, employer discrimination against blacks reduces the demand for black labor. The supply curve in Figure 7.2 is shown shifting upward rather than the demand curve shifting downward, however, simply for heuristic convenience, as both approaches are identical. . . .

black labor force suffer but discriminatory employers are also harmed by the discrimination.

Interestingly, in this partial equilibrium analysis of the black labor market, Figure 7.2 depicts a situation in which the *monetary* profits of the discriminatory employers have risen. The reason for this increase in monetary profits is that the reduction in the hiring of black labor has driven the black wage down to such a degree that monetary profits to the discriminators, represented by W_2AE_2C, are greater than the profits of the nondiscriminatory firms, represented by W_1AE_1.[2] Consequently, the uniform pattern of discrimination has caused employers to make more money but to be less profitable in an economic sense.

The implication that employers may earn more money but be less profitable is not as perplexing as it might first appear. This phenomenon occurs in many contexts throughout the economy, because, quite simply, money is not the only thing that people value. For example, consider a professor who applies for a position at Elite University that pays a salary of $30,000 and for a similar position at Podunk University, which offers $40,000. If the professor would prefer to work at Elite in spite of its lower salary, this can be restated in economic terms to say that the difference in prestige is worth more than $10,000 to the professor. If she receives an offer only from Podunk, she will earn more money, but will be less satisfied and less well off in economic terms. Just as the prestige-conscious professor has an incentive not to go to Podunk, the discriminatory employers in the Becker model have an incentive not to hire blacks and thereby bear the associated psychic costs. Therefore, Becker's point is that, even though employers may earn more money because of their discriminatory practices, it is not economic self-interest that prompts employer discrimination.

Consider what would happen if discriminatory employers did not really dislike blacks but merely acted as if they did in the hopes of raising their monetary incomes. At first glance, it would appear that such employers could end up at point E_2 in Figure 7.2, earning higher monetary profits without suffering any discriminatory cost. But while nondiscriminatory employers would have an economic incentive to restrict the hiring of black workers to arrive at point E_2, they would have no power to do so in a competitive market. Indeed, employers could only arrive at the E_2 outcome if they could collude or gain the backing of government. Thus, in this model, it is the government—which may resort to pernicious legislation such as the apartheid laws in South Africa—not the free market, that stands as the potential enemy of the victims of discriminatory conduct.

2. This is true because W_2W_1XC is greater than XE_2E_1. In Figure 7.2, W_2W_1XC is approximately 1.5 times as large as XE_2E_1. This relationship is not invariable, however.

The Impact of Title VII

Although no one disputes that an unwise or pernicious government can produce socially harmful consequences through interference in labor markets, a more interesting question is whether the government can play a positive role as well. Landes alludes to the traditional view that if one's objective is wealth maximization then the passage of antidiscrimination legislation can only be harmful: "[I]f the benefits [of such legislation] are viewed as the added net (monetary plus psyche) income to the community, then the benefits would be negative, because net income is maximized in the absence of fair employment laws."

The rationale for this contention can be readily illustrated by reference to Figure 7.2. Suppose that, by enacting Title VII, the government succeeds in restoring the nondiscriminatory equilibrium E_1. Short-run social welfare would fall according to this model because the hiring of any workers beyond the Q_2 level would impose greater social costs (represented by the S_2 supply curve) than social benefits (represented by the D demand curve). The location of E_2 represents the point of wealth maximization, and any attempt to move to E_1 will simply lower total social welfare. Consequently, if one accepts both the Becker model of employer discrimination and the goal of wealth maximization, then the short-run effect of introducing Title VII into a discriminatory environment is clear: to the extent that Title VII has any effect on the labor market, it will be socially harmful.

Opponents of antidiscrimination legislation urge that government action is not necessary because, in the long run, the operation of the competitive market will return the equilibrium level to E_1. The basic argument is that discriminatory firms are not maximizing profits and therefore eventually will be driven out of the market. The short-run analysis had assumed that the level of capital was fixed. In the long run, however, capital will flow to more profitable enterprises, and any employer that has shunned discrimination will earn higher profits. Such a firm would be willing to hire more black workers at the depressed market wage of W_2 (in Figure 7.2) and would be able to expand production and profits beyond the levels of its competitors. As long as there is a single nondiscriminatory employer, all discriminators will be driven out of the market. Therefore, in the long run the nondiscriminatory equilibrium E_1 will be restored.

The traditional view thus can be summarized as follows: in the short run, antidiscrimination legislation is harmful because it will reduce total social welfare; in the long run, it is unnecessary because the market will restore the nondiscriminatory equilibrium by disciplining discriminators. Within the framework of the neoclassical economic model, this argument has a certain elegance and logical appeal. Nonetheless, it is incorrect. A more discerning dynamic analysis reveals that there is no a priori basis for assuming that Title VII reduces total social welfare.

A Dynamic Analysis of Title VII

The previous discussion has provided only a static analysis of Title VII. This analysis demonstrated that the total social welfare associated with the nondiscriminatory equilibrium (labeled SW_1) is necessarily greater than net social welfare associated with the short-run discriminatory equilibrium (labeled SW_2). It will now be useful to consider explicitly how net social welfare will change over time both with and without antidiscrimination legislation.

First consider the case in which Title VII does not exist. Figure 7.3 depicts the changing level of net social welfare, beginning at time 0, with SW_2 representing the initial short-run net social welfare associated with the discriminatory equilibrium E_2. As time passes, more and more discriminatory employers will be driven from the market by nondiscriminatory employers, thereby increasing social welfare. Ultimately, when all the discriminatory firms have been driven out, net social welfare will rise to the level of SW_1 associated with equilibrium E_1—where it presumably will remain. The time path of social welfare in the laissez-faire state begins at SW_2 and rises to SW_1 at time 2t, as shown in Figure 7.3.

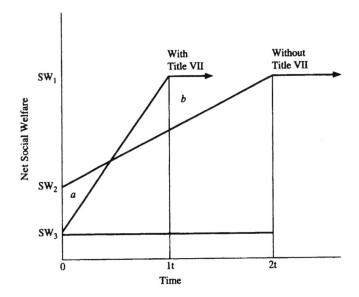

Figure 7.3. The Time Path of Social Welfare With and Without Title VII

The dynamic pattern of net social welfare would look different if Title VII were adopted at time 0. Initially, as discussed [above], net social welfare would be reduced by virtue of the imposition of Title VII. Thus, at time 0, total net social welfare associated with Title VII (labeled

SW$_3$) would be less than the unrestrained market outcome (i.e., SW$_3$ < SW$_2$).

To dissect the impact of Title VII, however, its effects on the profits of employers as well as on the earnings of black labor must be examined. Figure 7.4 replicates Figure 7.2 in showing the supply and demand curve for black labor. Once again, the shifted-up supply curve S$_2$ reflects the total—monetary and psychic—cost of hiring black workers when employers are prejudiced against blacks. Figure 7.4 can be used to illustrate that discriminatory firms necessarily will earn lower net profits under Title VII than they would earn without this legal constraint. Imposition of Title VII requires employers to hire Q$_1$ units of black labor at the nondiscriminatory wage W$_1$. The total cost associated with hiring a black worker under the legal constraint of Title VII is 0F = 0W$_1$ + W$_1$F, wherein the first term (0W$_1$) represents the wage cost and the second term (W$_1$F) represents psychic cost of discrimination. Therefore, the total value of production is given by 0AE$_1$Q$_1$ and the total cost is given by 0FHQ$_1$. As a result, the net profit to the discriminator under the Title VII regime is FAG – GHE$_1$, which is less than the profit of BAE$_2$, which is generated in the absence of a legal requirement of nondiscriminatory behavior.

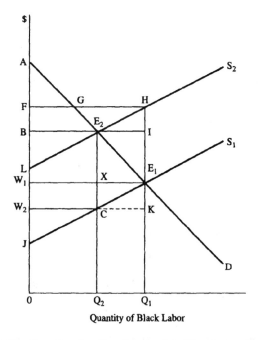

Figure 7.4. The Short-Run Supply and Demand for Black Labor Given Employer
Discrimination: Effect of Title VII

The fact that Title VII causes a reduction in the profits of discriminators has an important implication for the time path of net social welfare: one can assume that discriminators will be driven from the market more rapidly with Title VII than without it. In the long run, the Becker model predicts that discriminators will be driven from the market, thereby elevating net social welfare to the level SW_1 shown in Figure 7.3. But the stochastic nature of the economic environment suggests that for some discriminators the long run will be reached more quickly than it will be for others. Some firms will soon realize that they will be unable to compete and therefore will exit more rapidly, whereas others will try to ward off the inevitable and succumb more slowly to the ineluctable market forces.

Accordingly, the rate of exit ... can be viewed as a stochastic process that is a function of the profit level of the discriminatory firms.... [B]ecause profits for discriminating firms are lower with Title VII, these firms will exit from the market more quickly with Title VII than without it.

Consequently, the return to the point of highest social welfare where all discriminators have been driven from the market (SW_1) would be far more rapid with the antidiscrimination legislation than in the free market scenario, as shown in Figure 7.3. Thus, while Title VII imposes a short-run cost in net social welfare (i.e., $SW_3 < SW_2$), it will drive out discriminators more rapidly, thereby elevating net social welfare to the higher level (SW_1) more rapidly. So long as area b is greater than area a in Figure 7.3, net social welfare would be enhanced by the imposition of Title VII.

Various factors will determine the relative sizes of triangles a and b. The smaller the initial net social welfare loss associated with Title VII ($SW_2 - SW_3$) and the faster Title VII accelerates the exit of the discriminators ..., then the larger area b will tend to be relative to area a. The size of $SW_2 - SW_3$, which will always be positive, will depend upon how much Title VII helps blacks and injures discriminatory employers. [Title VII-induced] injuries to discriminatory employers will drive them out of business. At the same time, such injuries also yield a lower SW_3. But note that there is an important offsetting factor at work: although Title VII harms white employers it aids black workers. Thus, $SW_2 - SW_3$ (the reduction in total social welfare caused by Title VII at time 0) is less than ... (the reduction in profits of discriminatory employers). The cost imposed by Title VII, therefore, is properly focused to achieve greater dynamic efficiency; the greater the burden on discriminatory employers, the faster welfare rises to the optimal level SW_1.

The Efficiency and the Efficacy of Title VII*

RICHARD A. POSNER

... John Donohue argues that Title VII of the Civil Rights Act of 1964, which forbids employment discrimination on racial and other invidious grounds, may well be an efficient intervention in labor markets, even if efficiency is narrowly defined as maximizing social wealth. His argument is of considerable interest. Social welfare legislation, notably including legislation designed to help minority groups, is usually thought to involve a trade-off between equity and efficiency, or between the just distribution of society's wealth and the aggregate amount of that wealth. If Donohue is right and equity and efficiency line up on the same side of the issue, these laws are considerably less problematic than they have seemed to some observers.

Donohue's argument builds on Gary Becker's theory of racial discrimination. For Becker, discrimination by whites against blacks is the result of an aversion that whites have to associating with blacks. This aversion makes it more costly for whites to transact with blacks than with other whites. Becker likens this additional transaction cost to transportation costs in international trade. The higher those transportation costs are, the less international trade there will be. Countries such as Switzerland that are highly dependent on such trade because their internal markets are small will suffer more than countries that, by virtue of the large size of their internal markets, are more nearly self-sufficient. Similarly, blacks will be hurt more than whites by the whites' aversion to associations with them because the white community is more nearly self-sufficient than the black.

Just as there are potential gains from measures that lower transportation costs, so there are potential gains from measures that lower the costs of association between whites and blacks. One of these measures is competition. White employers who are not averse to such associations will have lower labor costs and will therefore tend to gain a competitive advantage over their bigoted competitors. Hence competition should, over time, erode the effects of discrimination, not by changing preferences, to be sure, but by shifting productive resources to firms that are not handicapped by an aversion to associating with blacks.

Donohue's argument is simply that this process can be accelerated by a law against employment discrimination, such as Title VII. By adding a legal penalty to the market penalty for discrimination, Title VII accelerates the movement toward the day when discrimination has been squeezed out of markets and the gains from trade have thereby been

* Excerpts from Richard A. Posner, "The Efficiency and the Efficacy of Title VII," *University of Pennsylvania Law Review*, vol. 136, copyright © 1987. Reprinted by permission of University of Pennsylvania Law Review and Fred B. Rothman & Company.

maximized. In his analysis, Title VII is like an innovation that reduces the costs of transportation—to zero.

The obvious objection to Donohue's argument is that he has failed to balance the costs of administering Title VII against the gains from lowering the costs of transacting between blacks and whites. In the year ending June 30, 1986, more than 9,000 suits charging employment discrimination, the vast majority under Title VII, were brought in federal court. The aggregate costs of these cases, and of the many more matters that are settled without litigation, must be considerable. However, I want to emphasize two more subtle points. The first is that, to the extent it is effective, Title VII may generate substantial costs over and above the costs of administering the statute. The second point is that Title VII may not be effective, in which event its administrative costs are a dead weight loss.

The Efficiency of Title VII

An analogy in the international-trade sphere to Donohue's argument would be to advocate passage of a law requiring a nation's industries to increase their exports and imports. Such a law would increase the amount of the nation's international trade, but not by lowering the cost of transportation. It might bring the nation to a level of international trade that it would not otherwise have reached for another fifty years through falling costs of transportation, but there would be no gain in efficiency because those costs had not yet fallen.

In Becker's analysis, the costs to whites of associating with blacks are real costs, and a law requiring such associations does not, at least in any obvious way, reduce those costs. Of course, it makes blacks better off, but presumably by less than it makes whites worse off; for if both whites and blacks were made better off, there would be net gains from association and the law would not be necessary.

Another analogy to international trade may help to clarify my disagreement with Donohue's argument. Consider a law that requires the international maritime industry to adopt a newly developed, more efficient technology; and suppose someone has just invented a type of hull design that enables a ship to sail faster on less fuel. If adopted, the design would lower the costs of international transportation. Donohue's argument implies that a law requiring the adoption of the new technology as soon as possible would increase economic welfare by accelerating attainment of the new, more efficient equilibrium made possible by the invention. The difficulty is that such a law is likely to distort the optimal path to the new equilibrium. It is rarely efficient to scrap an existing technology the minute a superior one is developed. We usually leave it to competition to determine the rate at which the new displaces the old.

The basic difficulty with Donohue's analysis should now be plain. He argues for the efficiency of government intervention in a market not marked by externalities, monopoly or monopsony, high costs of information, or any other condition that might justify such intervention on economic grounds. It might of course be the case that the labor markets likely to be affected by Title VII had one or more of these conditions but that is not his argument. It might equally be the case that the costs to whites of being forced to associate with blacks are morally unworthy of consideration in the formulation of public policy. Stated differently, it might be that a tax on those whites for the benefit of blacks would be justifiable on grounds of social equity. But that would not be an *efficiency* justification in the wealth-maximization sense that Donohue employs.

Moreover, it is not altogether plain that a reluctance by white employers to employ blacks *at the same wage as whites* (an essential qualification, as we shall see) must reflect nothing more than an inexplicable aversion, whether by the employer itself or by its white employees, to associating with blacks. Suppose that, because of past exclusion of blacks from equal educational opportunities or for other reasons, the average black worker is less productive than the average white, and suppose further that it is costly for an employer to determine whether an individual worker deviates from the average for the worker's group. Then an unprejudiced employer might nonetheless decide to pay blacks less than whites. This would be unfair to blacks who were in fact above average, yet might still be an efficient method (in the presence of high information costs) of compensating black workers. If Title VII comes along and forbids this method of classifying workers, as it assuredly does, then the employer will either incur additional information costs or, by lumping all workers together regardless of productivity, depart even further from the optimum wage, which is the wage equal to a worker's marginal product. Either way, efficiency will be reduced. Again, gains in social equity may trump losses in efficiency. But Donohue is not concerned, at least in the article under discussion, with equity.

The Efficacy of Title VII

I have assumed thus far, as does Donohue, that Title VII is effective—that it improves the employment prospects of black people. If it does not, then its administrative costs yield no gains, either in efficiency or in equity. One's intuition is that a law, which imposes sanctions on employers who discriminate and which is enforceable not only by a federal agency (the Equal Employment Opportunity Commission) but by the victims of discrimination in private suits, *must* improve the employment opportunities of members of a group that, at the time the law was passed, was a frequent target of employment discrimination. But this may be incorrect ... Suppose that, for whatever reason, the market wage rate of blacks is lower than that of whites. Title VII forbids the use of race as a ground for pay differentials. Because this part of the law is difficult to evade, and because (as I mentioned earlier) employers find it difficult to measure the marginal product of the individual worker, we can assume that blacks and whites will be paid the same wage by the same employer for the same job. This means, however, that the employer will be paying some or many of its black workers more than their marginal product. The employer will therefore have an economic incentive to employ fewer blacks. The law also forbids making hiring or firing decisions on the basis of race, but this part of the law is very difficult to enforce. To see this, however, it is necessary to get more deeply into the structure of the law than Donohue attempts to do in his article.

There are two basic approaches that plaintiffs can use to make out a case under Title VII. The first, the "disparate treatment" approach, requires proving intentional discrimination. This turns out to be exceptionally difficult in practice. No employer of even moderate sophistication will admit or leave a paper record showing that it has refused to hire, or has fired, a worker because of the worker's race. In the absence of such evidence, the worker may try to eliminate alternative explanations, but this usually is impossible. There are, it is true, some workers who are so superior that no cause other than racial animus could explain a refusal to hire them or a decision to fire them. But even a bigoted employer is unlikely to take out his racial animus against a perfect worker. Most workers are not perfect. As to them, it is usually easy to supply a plausible reason why they were not hired or why they were let go. The plaintiff may try to rebut the reason by showing an overall pattern of racial hiring or firing, but this type of proof is expensive and will rarely be cost-justified....

Occasionally, a group of workers will band together in a class action, or the EEOC will bring suit against a company or even an industry on behalf of a large group of workers who have been discriminated against. But there are few such cases relative to the vast labor market in the United States, and the threat of such a suit may not have much deterrent effect because the available sanctions are so mild.

The second basic approach under Title VII is the "disparate impact" approach. If a firm uses a screening device such as an aptitude test or requiring a high-school degree that has the effect of excluding a disproportionate number of blacks, the device is unlawful unless the firm can show a strong business justification for it, even if the device is not intended to keep out blacks. The crux of the problem is identifying disproportionate exclusion. The usual solution is to compare the percentage of blacks employed by the firm with the percentage in the labor pool from which the firm draws. This method of proof makes it more costly for a firm to operate in an area where the labor pool contains a high percentage of blacks, by enlarging the firm's legal exposure. Therefore, when deciding where to locate a new plant or where to expand an existing one, a firm will be attracted (other things being equal) to areas that have only small percentages of blacks in their labor pools.

This incentive exists even if the firm is not worried about disparate-impact suits. Title VII makes it more costly to employ black workers; it also makes it more costly to fire them because the firm may have to incur the expense of defending a Title VII disparate-treatment suit when a black employee is discharged. These costs operate as a tax on employing black workers and give firms an incentive to locate in areas with few blacks.

Thus Title VII can be expected to have several effects: to increase the wages of those blacks who are employed by wiping out racial pay differentials; to eliminate some discrimination in hiring and firing; but, in the case of some employers, to reduce the number of blacks who are employed. When the wages of black workers are averaged over all blacks, both those who are employed and those who are not, the average black wage may not have increased (or increased much) as a result of Title VII, and may even have decreased. Any net loss of wealth might be offset by a gain in self-esteem from being freed from direct (though not, if the foregoing analysis is correct, indirect) racial discrimination, but that gain would be outside the scope of the analyses that Donohue and I are making.

·   ·   ·

To conclude, I am not persuaded by Donohue's argument that Title VII can be defended on strictly economic grounds, as overcoming the transaction-cost barrier to market interactions between white and black people that Gary Becker identified in his economic study of racial discrimination. Title VII, to the extent effective, ignores, rather than reduces, the costs of undesired associations between whites and blacks. It may be correct on moral grounds to do so, but that is not Donohue's argument. Furthermore, it is an open question whether Title VII has improved the net welfare of black people, directly or indirectly. If it has not, then the costs of administering the law are a dead weight social loss that cannot be justified on grounds of social equity.

Further Thoughts on Employment Discrimination Legislation: A Reply to Judge Posner*

JOHN J. DONOHUE III

Will Title VII End Discrimination Too Quickly?

While Judge Posner would certainly agree that we are better off if employers who harbor racial animus are squeezed out of the market, he offers two reasons for believing that the cost of moving to this happy

* Excerpts from John J. Donohue III, "Further Thoughts on Employment Discrimination Legislation: A Reply to Judge Posner," *University of Pennsylvania Law Review*, vol. 136, copyright © 1987. Reprinted with permission of University of Pennsylvania Law Review and Fred B. Rothman & Company.

condition through government intervention may be too great. In essence, Judge Posner argues that my assessment of the efficiency of Title VII would be altered if I explicitly considered the costs of administering the Act and the added costs of adjustment that it imposes in driving discriminators from the market more quickly than would occur under laissez faire.

.   .   .

The Added Costs of Adjustment Under Title VII

... Adhering to Becker's analogy that discrimination can be thought of as similar to the transportation costs that deter nations from engaging in international trade, Judge Posner contends that a law forbidding discrimination would be as ill-advised as a law requiring two nations to engage in trade when the transportation costs between them made such trade inefficient. But this analogy is flawed. In Judge Posner's international trade example, the level of trade is assumed to be at some equilibrium level based on the existing size of transportation costs. Unless these costs changed, there would be no economic force that would induce changes in the level of international trade, nor would there be any advantage in the government trying to depart from this equilibrium condition. In the Beckerian world, however, discrimination is a disequilibrium phenomenon: over time, discriminators would be driven from the market because they failed to minimize costs. In this case, government intervention is potentially useful because it can speed up this process.

Judge Posner next analogizes Title VII to a law requiring the international maritime industry to adopt a new and more efficient technology. This is a more appropriate analogy because, by assumption, the new technology will ultimately replace the old technology just as nondiscriminators will ultimately replace discriminators. Judge Posner properly questions whether the government would do a better job than business enterprises at determining the optimal rate at which the new technology should supplant the old. While I think the analogy is useful to illustrate Judge Posner's point—that is, that with frictionless competitive markets even the speed at which the economy moves towards a new equilibrium will be optimal—there are important distinctions between a law that tries to encourage a new transportation technology and one that tries to eradicate discrimination in employment.

For example, assume that all trans-Atlantic shipping is being carried by boat when the invention of the cargo plane provides a lower cost method of shipping. Ultimately, all trans-Atlantic shipments will be by plane. This does not mean that we should immediately scrap the existing boats, which may have no other use than for ocean freight transportation. Since the boats have already been built, they represent "sunk" costs. As a result, the variable cost of continuing to use the boats may be less than the full cost of using a plane to carry the cargo. In this case, the boats will be used until they wear out, and the proportion of freight sent by air will constantly expand. A law that taxed the use of the old boats would generate a quicker conversion to plane cargoes but at the cost of wasting valuable resources.

Similarly, Judge Posner argues that the market, rather than the government, should determine the rate at which discriminators are eliminated, noting that adjustment costs are higher if the process occurs too quickly. But we have already noted that the case of employment discrimination is unlike the case of an old technology that should not necessarily be immediately scrapped if it still retains sufficient value. The reason is that a company that owns outmoded machines cannot suddenly be transformed into an efficient operation by simply transferring the assets to another party. But this is precisely the case for a discriminatory firm: if a nondiscriminator buys out a discriminator, the psychic costs of discrimination immediately disappear. Therefore, an upper bound estimate of the cost needed to eliminate employer discrimination is simply the cost of transferring the assets to nondiscriminators. But the Becker model tells us that this transfer will take place ultimately even without Title VII. Indeed, the assurance that the discriminators will be eradicated absent legislation is one of the strongest arguments against Title VII, so the costs of adjustment associated with driving discriminators out of the market will presumably be faced whether the Act is passed or not. Consequently, the only *additional* burden imposed by the Act results from the fact that these adjustment costs are borne earlier—and are thus larger in present value terms—under Title VII.

To summarize: merely transferring ownership to a nondiscriminator automatically yields an immediate benefit since the psychic costs of discrimination would thereby be eliminated. Moreover, while there are no sunk costs to consider in the case of discrimination, there are transaction costs incurred in transferring ownership. But, Judge Posner can be heard to say, if there are immediate benefits to be had at little cost, one would expect the market to generate these benefits. Clearly, if every employer were ruthlessly maximizing profits, then we would not need Title VII because there would be no animus-based discrimination in the first place. If there are enough enterprising individuals who either exploit the possibility of hiring cheap black labor or who simply buy out discriminatory firms, then there still may be no role for the government, for in this event the path to the new equilibrium will indeed be optimal. In essence, at every point in time these actors would be calculating whether the benefits from undermining a discriminator are sufficient to justify the costs of such competition. If the costs are too great, it would not be efficient for government to encourage this behavior. If the benefits exceed the costs at any given moment, the discriminators should be flushed from the system by the operation of market forces.

But why doesn't the process occur more quickly? Perhaps the answer lies in the fact that some types of departures from profit-maximization are punished far less quickly and thoroughly than we might have thought. As long as there is some rigidity in the market, there is no reason to believe that the market will generate the optimal path to the nondiscriminatory equilibrium. And, as Kenneth Arrow has noted, the persistence of discrimination for decades suggests that either Becker's model is wrong in predicting the demise of employer discrimination, or there is some rigidity in the market that may justify government intervention. . . .

Is It Inefficient to Prohibit Statistical Discrimination?

In my original Essay and thus far in the present Essay, I have followed Becker in explicitly assuming that discrimination is caused by employers' animus against the disfavored minority. . . . In his rebuttal to my Essay, however, Judge Posner raises the possibility that employment discrimination could have a different genesis, in which the disciplinary role of the market as the ally of the victims of discrimination is absent. He notes that "a reluctance by employers to employ blacks at the same wage as whites" may be the product of "statistical discrimination," in which discrimination against, for example, blacks is not the result of racial animus, but rather stems from a realization that, for whatever reasons, black workers are on average less productive than white workers. If this generalization is accurate, and if it is costly to ascertain individual abilities, then statistical discrimination, unlike Beckerian discrimination, may be profit-maximizing.

Since statistical discrimination can be profit-maximizing, it tends to be stable while Beckerian discrimination tends to be eroded by competitive markets. Consequently, if we are dealing with a case of statistical rather than Beckerian discrimination, then the effect of Title VII is indeed different from that presented in my initial Essay. Nonetheless, the conclusion that I reached with respect to animus-based discrimination may also apply in the case of statistical discrimination: specifically, while prohibiting employers from discriminating may be inefficient in the short run, it may be efficient in the long run.

. . . At first glance, it might seem that statistical discrimination will necessarily be efficient whenever it is profit-maximizing. Nonetheless, it is possible that discrimination could be profit-maximizing for the firm, yet inefficient for society as a whole.

The basic argument is that statistical discrimination will distort the incentives for individuals to invest in human capital since they will simply be treated as the average member of their class whether or not they make such investments. By divorcing an employee's individual productivity from the wage that the employee receives, statistical discrimination introduces inefficiencies into the human capital investment decisions of workers. If the concomitant costs are large, statistical discrimination may be harmful from a social perspective, although

beneficial to individual employers. By discouraging workers from investing in their own human capital, society is deprived of all of the benefits
that flow from these investments. Therefore, while we should recognize
that, unlike animus-based discrimination, statistical discrimination is
presumably profit-maximizing, a *full* cost-benefit analysis of Title VII
would include the benefits from proscribing statistical discrimination as
well as the costs. . . .

Market Affirmative Action*
ROBERT COOTER

Economic Critique of Regulation

. . . Economists reached a consensus in the 1970s concerning the framework for analyzing government regulations. According to this framework, a prima facie case for regulation requires demonstrating a market
failure and a policy to correct it. Tests for market failure are developed
in general equilibrium theory; corrective policies are evaluated by cost-
benefit techniques. A conclusive case for regulation requires a further
demonstration that the proposed remedy would succeed politically, rather than being subverted by interest groups. Tests for political failure are
developed in collective choice theory.

This consensus over the framework of debate obviously did not end
disagreements among economists over regulation. Left-liberal economists
stress market failures, and conservative economists stress political failures. However, the arguments between the two sides join because they
proceed within the same general framework. The joining of the arguments focuses research on questions that both sides consider decisive.

. . .

[M]ost economists agreed in the 1970s and 1980s that government
officials were retarding the economy with heavy-handed regulations.
While agreeing about the necessity of reform, economists disagreed over
its direction and scope. Thus, George Stigler wanted to repeal most
regulations and Charles Schultze wanted to improve them. The diversity
of views among economists provided intellectual sanction for reforming
politicians who repealed some regulations and reformed others. However, few economists found anything good to say about "command and
control" regulations.

Contrary to these trends, legislatures, courts, and administrators
have imposed new "command and control" regulations since 1964 for
the stated purpose of eliminating current discrimination or undoing its
past effects upon various social groups, including racial minorities,

* Excerpts from Robert Cooter, "Market Affirmative Action," *San Diego Law Review,*
vol. 31, copyright © 1994 by the San Diego Law Review Association. Reprinted by
permission of the *San Diego Law Review.*

women, the elderly, and handicapped people. These regulations apply to hiring and promoting ("employment discrimination"), and the sale of goods and services ("refusal to deal"). Although complex and uncertain in application, the effect of the laws are far-reaching. New rights have been created for employees, job applicants, and consumers. Many organizations have adopted targets for the social mix of employees and implemented procedures to handle disputes and complaints.

. . .

Discrimination As Inefficiency

... Performance in economic life is usually measured by productivity. Consequently, discrimination in economic life usually consists in sorting people according to traits rather than productivity. When people are sorted by traits rather than productivity, industrial efficiency diminishes. Consequently, discrimination as defined here necessarily reduces efficiency in production. Conversely, nondiscrimination maximizes the productivity of organizations.

. . .

Organizations mix people by traits in various ratios, with some organizations being relatively homogeneous and others being relatively heterogeneous. As defined above, discrimination occurs when mixing in an organization does not go far enough to maximize production. People who are willing to sacrifice productivity and lose income in order to reduce mixing have "a taste for separation." Economists often take the satisfaction of preferences as the appropriate goal of public policy. However, there is much dispute about whether satisfying the taste of people for separation is an appropriate policy goal.

Equal opportunity to compete in economic transactions conflicts with freedom of contract. Complete freedom of contract implies the right to deal or not to deal with anyone for whatever reason, including their personal traits. In contrast, antidiscrimination laws attempt to prohibit certain motives from affecting economic transactions. Antidiscrimination laws necessarily interfere with freedom of contract. In general, liberty rights conflict with equality rights, because the former create a sphere of individual autonomy and the latter intrude into it.

Promoting Mixing By Targets, Taxes and Transferable Rights

Many markets are "workably competitive," which means that they function much like the ideal type of a perfectly competitive market. Suppose that politicians and policy makers wish to achieve more mixing than workable competition yields, or to achieve it very quickly. One way to pursue such a goal is by imposing "targets" or "quotas" on organizations.... What happens under workable competition if government imposes targets upon all organizations in order to achieve uniform mixing? For example, what happens if government requires fifty percent of the workers in each organization to be male and fifty percent to be female? Like any quota system, employment targets are insensitive to underlying differences in costs, which causes inefficiencies.

. . .

In contrast, "market-like instruments" of regulation [can achieve employment goals more efficiently. For example, a] tax-subsidy solution requires each firm to pay a tax on "excess" workers of the disfavored type and receive a subsidy for "surplus" workers of the favored type. To illustrate . . ., assume that policy makers adopt the target of fifty percent female workers in the combined professions of law and economics. Each firm would receive a target of fifty percent females in its work force in these professions. A firm that fell short of the target would be charged a tax on its excess male workers, and a firm that exceeded the target would receive a subsidy for its surplus female workers. For example, if Firm A is an economic forecasting company that employs one hundred economists and thirty of them are female, then it must pay a tax on its twenty "excess" male economists. If the tax is high enough, Firm A will respond by replacing male economists with females. In general, the higher the tax-subsidy, the more male employees will be replaced with females. It is not hard to see that a tax-subsidy rate exists, and can be identified easily, which achieves any target for increased female employment at the least cost to society.

. . .

An alternative policy that achieves the same results in principle is to create a transferable right to employ disfavored workers. Firms would be required by law to own as many legal rights as they employ workers of the disfavored type. To illustrate by our previous example, assume that policy makers adopt the target of fifty percent female workers in the combined professions of law and economics. Thus, the regulators must create a total number of rights to employ male lawyers or economists equal to fifty percent of the current workers in those jobs. These rights must be allocated initially, say by gift or auction. It matters little from an efficiency perspective how they are initially allocated. Once allocated, firms would buy and sell the rights.

. . .

Discriminatory Power

I have discussed discrimination in markets with perfect competition and the achievement of affirmative action targets in perfectly competitive labor markets. Although the perfectly competitive model describes powerful forces at work in the economy, part of the historical differences in wages between blacks and whites, or between women and men, are usually attributed to discrimination. Rather than confirming the prediction that discriminators paid for it, empirical studies suggest that the targets of discrimination in the United States historically received lower wages than others with equivalent skills, and that civil rights laws helped raise the income of blacks. Given the evidence, discriminatory practices in this country cannot be explained fully by the model of perfect competition.

In subsequent sections of this Article, I will consider several market failures that might explain how discriminators shift the burden of segregation to its victims. First I develop a model of discrimination based upon power, not competition. Just as producers collude to fix prices and obtain monopoly profits, so social groups sometimes collude to obtain the advantages of monopoly control over markets. To enjoy the advantages of monopoly, a social group must reduce competition from others by excluding them from markets. In this way, the more powerful social group can shift the cost of segregation to its victims, and more costs besides, so that the victims of discrimination are worse off and the discriminators are better off.

. . .

Anti-Discrimination as Antitrust

In general, a group with the power to reduce competition from others can benefit itself, whether the group is defined by race, religion, gender, or industry. Discriminatory social groups are much like cartels, and a discriminatory norm is analogous to a price-fixing agreement. Thus, the analysis and attack upon discriminatory market power can borrow much from monopoly theory and antitrust law. I will develop this parallel.

Cartels are unstable because each member can increase its profits by defecting from the group. For example, the Organization of Petroleum Exporting Countries (OPEC) tried to fix prices, but countries like Algeria secretly discounted oil in order to sell more of it. As a cartel becomes large, detecting and preventing such "cheating" by members becomes harder. Without legal backing and formal enforcement of their agreements, large cartels like OPEC collapse.

Similarly, social groups can exert power to increase their wages by restricting competition in the labor market, but individuals can profit from violating the restrictions.... In general, sustaining discriminatory norms requires the collusion of many people, which presupposes sanctions to enforce the discriminatory norms. Informal sanctions such as gossip, ostracism, and boycotts can operate spontaneously, especially when a culture stresses group solidarity. In the past, many Americans used informal sanctions to punish individuals who failed to keep the races separate or women "in their place." However, the informal sanctions were probably not enough to sustain segregation without being buttressed by formal laws.

Although cartels are inherently unstable, the U.S. antitrust framework does not merely withhold enforcement from contracts to create cartels. In addition, the original U.S. legislation, which was enacted at the end of the nineteenth century, outlaws cartels and other "conspiracies against trade." ... These prohibitions greatly increase the difficulty of sustaining a cartel. Similarly, U.S. civil rights laws prohibit business practices involving "disparate treatment" of those persons belonging to any one or more protected classes. The illegality of conducting certain business transactions with the intent to discriminate greatly increases the difficulties involved in explicit discrimination, especially in large organizations.

Over the years, the effective scope of antitrust law expanded from banning cartels to suppressing monopolies. A monopoly can arise even without collusion or engaging in practices that are illegal per se. For example, monopoly power can be "thrust upon" a producer due to economies of scale in production. Such monopolies are evaluated for their legality in the United States according to a balancing test. The balancing test is intended to determine whether the savings in cost from scale economies outweigh the risk to the public of having only one or two producers. Balancing tests have their own history that I cannot discuss in detail, but a relevant episode is the rise and fall of the "structural approach." In the 1970s, the antitrust authorities prosecuted some very large manufacturers with the intention of restructuring whole industries in order to increase the number of producers. However, this approach was deemed a failure and abandoned in the 1980s for a variety of reasons.

Antidiscrimination law has a history with some similarity to antitrust law. At first the government focused its prosecutorial efforts upon explicitly discriminatory practices. In these cases, the plaintiff had to prove the existence of disparate treatment by the employer. In 1971, however, the law evolved further and the U.S. Supreme Court developed the concept of "disparate impact." A practice can have an illegal disparate impact in the absence of discriminatory intent. The illegality of the outcome is identified by a pattern suggesting that a protected group has been unreasonably disadvantaged by a business practice. Thus, the concept of disparate impact in antidiscrimination law bears a certain resemblance to "monopoly structure" in antitrust law. Whether the courts and the political process will deem the past twenty-three years of disparate impact analysis a success or a failure remains to be seen.

When antitrust laws block cartels, the industry may try to circumvent the law through the help of regulators. For example, airlines are forbidden to collude in setting prices, but they had much influence with the Civil Aeronautics Board and apparently used it to impose the cartel price upon many routes. Similarly, southern whites actively used the power of state and local government to reduce competition from blacks through the "Jim Crow" legislation that was enacted in the closing decades of the nineteenth century.

Antidiscrimination laws can also be used to benefit a social group by reducing competition from others. To illustrate ..., suppose ... the historic victims of discrimination ... acquire legislative power and enact laws mandating preferential hiring.... For example, the law might mandate filling job openings in various categories with [workers from the previously victimized group] until [a target percentage is reached]. In job categories where the target binds, [competition is thwarted to the advantage of the former victims of discrimination.] These arguments underlie the claim that affirmative action is reverse discrimination.

The phrase "rent seeking" refers to the efforts of people to secure laws that convey monopoly power and profits upon themselves. A standard prescription for preventing rent-seeking is to remove the issue from ordinary politics by constitutionalizing it. For example, constitutional guarantees of private property inhibit politically influential people from using the state to appropriate the property of others for themselves. Similarly, constitutional guarantees against discrimination can reduce rent-seeking by social groups. On the other hand, the creation of vague and uncertain constitutional rights by courts can unleash extensive rent-seeking through litigation.

I have shown that social groups, including racial and ethnic groups, are paradigmatic interest groups in many respects. Like other interest groups, they seek to collude and redistribute wealth to themselves by inefficient restrictions on competition. However, self-interest and morality often prompt individuals to evade these restrictions. So discriminatory social groups suffer the same problems of instability as any other cartel. To sustain discriminatory norms, evaders must be punished by a combination of informal sanctions and formal laws. By repealing these laws and undermining these sanctions, law can cause the discriminatory norms to disintegrate. Constitutional protection against discrimination, like constitutional guarantees of property, can facilitate competition and preclude wasteful efforts to redistribute income among social groups by political means.

Discriminatory Signals and Asymmetrical Information

I first considered discrimination in the context of competition, and then I considered market power. Now I consider a different kind of market imperfection, specifically, imperfect information on the part of buyers and sellers. To understand the problem of imperfect information, I begin with a familiar example concerning insurance against automobile accidents. Insurance companies classify drivers into broad groups and set premiums according to the probability that the average driver will have an accident. For example, young drivers cause more accidents on average than old drivers, and young males cause more accidents on average than young females. The gender and age of policy holders, which are cheap for insurance companies to discover, predict the riskiness of drivers with sufficient accuracy to be useful for setting insurance rates. So insurance companies charge higher premiums for being young and male.

"Good signal" is the name economists give to a characteristic that predicts accurately on average and is cheap to observe. In transactions with imperfect information, the parties search for good signals to reduce their uncertainty....

Now I turn to signaling in labor markets. Just as insurance companies know little about individual policy holders, so employers know little about job applicants. In choosing among them, employers rely upon signals to predict performance. For example, a job applicant with a college degree can easily provide the employer with a copy of his transcript. The college degree may signal traits like intelligence that the employer values. Education effectively signals intelligence because more intelligent people can acquire education more easily and cheaply than less intelligent people.

The original models of job-market signaling concerned the "rat-race" that could arise when the signal had no intrinsic value. For example, suppose that certain employers value native intelligence but not education. Students might over-invest in education, not to learn anything useful, but merely to signal their intelligence ("credentials race"). In the rat-race models, people over-invest in an observable variable to signal a fixed trait.

Discriminatory signaling inverts the "rat-race" models. In discriminatory signaling, a fixed trait like gender or race signals an unobserved variable. To illustrate, men are physically stronger than women on average, so some employers reject all female applicants for jobs requiring strength. By adopting such policies, an employer will often make mistakes like rejecting a strong woman and accepting a weak man, just as an automobile insurance company sometimes over-charges safe males and undercharges dangerous females. If these mistakes cost less than gathering more individualized information, the use of the signal maximizes profits, and competition will reinforce the discriminatory practice. Conversely, if the cost of these mistakes exceeds the cost of gathering more individualized information, then the use of the signal is inefficient and competition will eliminate it.

People cannot acquire a fixed trait. To illustrate, few people will alter their race or sex in order to improve their job prospects, even with modern surgery. Consequently, discriminatory signals cannot produce a wasteful rat-race. Instead, sorting by traits can produce the opposite effect: under-investment in human capital. If employers attribute to each individual the average productivity of members of the group having his traits, then the benefit of investments that increase an individual's productivity will accrue in part to the group. Consequently, each individual will have a tendency to under-invest in acquiring productivity-increasing skills. The tendency to under-invest may be strongest in groups that are the victims of discrimination.

Although discriminatory signals can cause inefficiency, the usual objection to them is that they are unfair. The unfairness consists in judging individuals by averages. Suppose that government prohibits employers from using certain signals. For example, a statute might give strong women the right to sue employers who hire men exclusively for jobs that require strength. If the prohibited signals are inefficient, the law bans what competition will eliminate anyway. If the prohibited signals are efficient, the law augments the cost of production, which someone must bear.

. . .

Notes and Questions

1. As we have discussed, Gary Becker, writing in 1959, argued that employers who discriminate against a class of workers for a reason unrelated to productivity tend to be driven from the market. Remarkably, many economists accepted this theory as dispositive proof that no legal prohibition on employment discrimination would be needed, since the market would fully protect blacks against discrimination. This naive assertion—so obviously detached from the reality of the American South in the period before 1964—has tarnished the reputation of economists, even though many talented economists were highly critical of the Becker model. Indeed, Nobel economist Kenneth Arrow chided Becker for developing a theory of employment discrimination that "predicts the absence of the phenomenon it was designed to explain." Arrow, "Some Mathematical Models of Race in the Labor Market," in A. H. Pascal, ed., *Racial Discrimination in Economic Life* 187, 192 (Lexington, Mass.: Lexington Books, 1972). Becker tried to salvage his model by arguing that the shortage of entrepreneurial skill prevented the competitive elimination of discriminatory cost differentials. He therefore acknowledged in 1968 that "discrimination exists, and at times even flourishes, in competitive economies, the position of Negroes in the United States being a clear example." Becker, "Discrimination, economic," in D. L. Sills, ed., *International Encyclopedia of the Social Sciences* vol. 4, 208, 210 (New York: Macmillan and Free Press, 1968). But Becker's speculation about the shortage of entrepreneurs is highly unconvincing for the Southern labor market. No special skill was needed to know that hiring black workers in the textile industry would be profitable—unless the scarce skill was knowing how to do this without having one's mill burned down by the Ku Klux Klan.

2. The widespread acceptance of the Becker model of employer discrimination is understandable given that the model required only two assumptions, both of which seemed reasonable and the second of which economists were well primed to believe: first, the source of discrimination is the purely individualistic racial animus of the employer, and second, the labor market is perfectly competitive. If both of these assumptions hold, then the Becker

model is almost definitionally true, as long as profit-maximizing firms exist who can hire the undervalued black workers.

But although the *assumptions* of Becker's model might have seemed reasonable when he initially wrote this work in 1959, the *predictions* of the Becker model diverged sharply from reality: the market was showing little sign of disciplining discriminators in the South, as evidenced by the enormous gap between black and white wages in that region, even after controlling for human capital attributes like education and experience. In fact, the large earnings gap was not being eroded by nondiscriminatory Southern employers snapping up black workers at bargain wages. To the extent there was any black progress in the South before the mid-1960s, it resulted from increasing black education and from black outmigration to higher-paying jobs in the North. (See the selection by Donohue and Heckman in Chapter 8.)

In other words, there was a powerful theoretical prediction that the market would protect blacks, and there was very obvious evidence that the prediction was not true. Why then did theory win out over evidence? There are probably two reasons. First, the profession hands out its highest rewards to theorists—Becker himself garnered a Nobel Prize—and the culture of the discipline grooms its adherents to value elegant theory over messy empiricism. The assumptions of Becker's employer discrimination model appeared reasonable, and the elegant model led to strong and understandable theoretical predictions.

Second, some economists liked Becker's employer discrimination model because they were philosophically antagonistic to employment discrimination law and the model seemed to fortify this predisposition. Thus, Milton Friedman, writing in 1962, announced:

> [Antidiscrimination] legislation involves the acceptance of a principle that proponents would find abhorrent in almost every other application. If it is appropriate for the state to say that individuals may not discriminate in employment because of color or race or religion, then it is equally appropriate for the state, provided a majority can be found to vote that way, to say that individuals must discriminate in employment on the basis of color, race or religion. The Hitler Nuremberg laws and the laws in the Southern states imposing special disabilities upon Negroes are both examples of laws similar in principle to [antidiscrimination legislation].

Friedman, *Capitalism and Freedom* 113 (Chicago: University of Chicago Press, 1962).

While one is tempted to reject as utterly absurd Friedman's equation of Nazi laws and Jim Crow legislation with a law *banning* discrimination, the equation follows from his acceptance of the view, discussed in Chapter 2, that government should be concerned only with promoting negative freedom. Put differently, while many see a trade-off between the two important values of liberty and equality, Friedman values only liberty, and therefore governmental restrictions that curtail liberty are equally pernicious whether they are designed to promote equality (Title VII) or to inflict greater inequality (the Nuremberg laws). With two giants of economics marshalled behind the theory of employer discrimination—for Becker, out of love for elegant abstraction; for Friedman, out of love for libertarianism—this theory flourished in the fertile soil prepared by academic economists. Interestingly, though, alternative assumptions that the racial discrimination in the South was fostered either by white employees or by customers would have led to very different conclusions from those of the model of employer discrimination, for in these alternative cases, competitive markets would encourage employers to discriminate. In some ways, the left discouraged the acceptance of these alternative models by blaming the existence of discrimination on malicious employers rather than on fellow workers or customers. See Michael Reich, "The Economics of Racism," in D. Gordon, ed., *Problems in Political Economy,* 2d ed., 183 (Lexington, Mass.: Heath, 1977).

In retrospect, it is now clear that the assumptions of the Becker model of employer discrimination, however plausible they may have seemed, were either incorrect or incomplete. First, the conception of discrimination as an individualized taste, like the taste for apples, missed the significance of Southern race discrimination as a social phenomenon. Whether a person likes or dislikes apples will have an impact only on a trivial dimension of that person's behavior. Whether a Southerner decided to discriminate against blacks was a decision that involved an acceptance or rejection of an entire social system built on the ideology of white supremacy. Second, Becker's associational preference model disregards one of the most salient facts of American racism in the South—that whites were frequently and intentionally in close contact with blacks, but only in very specific settings. Blacks commonly were hired to raise white children, but they were prohibited from entering the front door of a white Southerner's house. White employers were happy to have black workers—but only in jobs where their subordinate status was constantly reaffirmed.

Third, even if employment discrimination was in part motivated by employer animus, it was also caused by the animus of fellow workers and customers, and by the desire to use race as a proxy for productivity—so-called statistical discrimination. Fourth, the Southern labor market was at best not as highly competitive as a modern efficient capital market, and was undoubtedly mired down by the cartel-like influence of racist governmental restrictions and the enforcement mechanisms of racist norms and racially motivated violence that Richard McAdams emphasized in Chapter 5. (For a discussion of the differences between labor markets and highly efficient capital markets, and the significance thereof, see Donohue, "Employment Discrimination Law in Perspective: Three Concepts of Equality," 92 *Michigan Law Review* 2583 (1994).) As Robert Higgs observed, Becker's conception of discrimination was more applicable "to a kind of tea party discrimination than to the blood and steel of the southern racial scene." Higgs, *Coercion and Competition: Blacks in the American Economy, 1865–1917* (New York: Cambridge University Press, 1977).

Given these real-world complexities, the model of employer discrimination was an inadequate theoretical guide to race discrimination in the early 1960s and before. Whether the world has changed in such a way that its

assumptions are now more accurate is an important question that merits
further examination. Moreover, the Becker model may be more useful in
dealing with other types of discrimination where the employer distaste—
perhaps against the disabled, the elderly, or other ethnic or religious
groups—emanates from an individualistic feeling rather than from a complex
social structure that is reinforced by strong community norms. Thus, there
is evidence in the labor market that physically unattractive individuals earn
less than more attractive individuals, and that this effect is stronger for men
than for women. Daniel Hamermesh and Jeff Biddle find that "The 9
percent of working men who are viewed as being below average or homely
are penalized about 10 percent in hourly earnings," while the earnings
penalty for the least attractive women is only 5 percent. Hamermesh and
Biddle, "Beauty in the Labor Market" 84 *American Economic Review* 1174
(1994). See also Susan Averett and Sanders Korenman, "The Economic
Reality of the Beauty Myth" 31 *Journal of Human Resources* 304 (1996).

3.   The introduction to this chapter observed that the justification for
promoting efficiency is that increased societal wealth seems to translate into
a number of important political, social, and economic benefits. In general,
productive efficiency will tend to be greatest when firms do not discriminate.
As Donohue shows, prohibiting discrimination will increase certain psychic
losses, but it may stimulate total production. Indeed, Figure 7.2 from the
first selection in this chapter shows that the passage of an antidiscrimination
law will increase the number of blacks hired from Q_2 to Q_1. Under reasonable assumptions, employers will respond by decreasing the number of
nonblack workers, but this decrease will be smaller in magnitude than the
mandated increase in black employees. In other words, the antidiscrimination law may increase total production and overall employment (even
though static net welfare falls because of the psychic cost borne by the
discriminator). Therefore, if the collateral benefits that are associated with
economic development are stimulated more by the magnitude of the gross
value of goods and services than by their net value (i.e., net of psychic costs
to discriminators), then employment discrimination law would stimulate the
attainment of the various collateral benefits, such as improved education.
Put differently, we may wish to consider whether the overall market efficiency that comes with a free market—which will give greater weight to the
psychic well-being of discriminators—will promote the collateral benefits
associated with enhanced overall wealth, such as strengthened democratic
institutions, to the same degree as an antidiscrimination policy that generates greater material wealth.

4.   According to the economic framework that Cooter describes, a
necessary but not sufficient condition for government intervention in the
labor market is that there is some market failure. What is the market failure
that justifies antidiscrimination law? This is a complicated question that
invokes many issues discussed throughout this book. Posner argues that
there is no market failure, and therefore there is no need for antidiscrimination law. Consider the following four arguments that discrimination does
constitute a market failure that justifies the existence of federal legislation.

First, Richard McAdams conceives of racial discrimination as a mechanism to enhance the status of whites by subordinating blacks (see Chapter 5). The attempt to transfer wealth and status from blacks to whites through racial subordination is costly for both groups, creating a mutual effort to manifest disrespect for each other that produces no positive social product. In general, economists disfavor the expenditure of real resources purely for the purposes of transferring, as opposed to creating, wealth. A prohibition of racial discrimination, like that of theft, will hopefully shift individuals from engaging in a socially wasteful competition toward conduct designed to advance their interests by creating wealth—such as securing more education and working harder.

Second, Donohue points to the empirical evidence, discussed at length in Chapter 8, that over a long period of time the Southern labor market failed to elevate the wages of blacks to reflect their true productivity, which suggests that some market failure was operating. Epstein identifies the market failure to be the pernicious involvement of racist Southern governments, and others, such as Richard McAdams, have noted the influence of strong racist customs. In either event, federal legislation appears to have substantially aided Southern blacks beginning in the mid-1960s. Of course, it now matters greatly whether the need for the Title VII intervention was generated by racist government or racist attitudes. In Epstein's view, Title VII, having tamed the racist state governments, has served its purpose and can now be repealed. For discussion of the historical issues, see Donohue, "Advocacy versus Analysis in Assessing Employment Discrimination Law," 44 *Stanford Law Review* 1583 (1992).

Third, in Chapter 13 Donohue proposes that a form of market failure exists when the market is incapable of generating certain seemingly beneficial transactions. He offers an example in which terminating discrimination would enhance the productivity of the workforce to such a degree that, in theory, a Pareto-improving agreement to end the discrimination would be possible. Implementing such a contract, however, would in essence require the victims of discrimination to pay the discriminator not to discriminate. But the very act of making such a payment would establish the presence of what the contract was designed to eliminate.

Fourth, Donohue has argued that discrimination can be thought of as causing an external harm to those who view such conduct as a breach of one of the moral bases of our democracy. Id. Given the widespread objection to private discrimination in the employment sphere, one could liken such discrimination to the external harm caused by pollution. This claim has two important implications. First, because discrimination imposes externalities, which is one of the major causes of market failure, the presumption that the market will generate the wealth-maximizing outcome is theoretically impaired. Second, it provides an efficiency justification for employment discrimination law if the value to the discriminator of discriminating is less than the burden on those, including both victims and moralists, who dislike the discrimination.

Interestingly, the Coase theorem offers insight into whose utility should be included in evaluating the efficiency of a ban on employment discrimination. The theorem assumes that, in a world of zero transaction costs, parties will come together and agree contractually to arrange their affairs in an efficient—or wealth-maximizing—manner. Ronald Coase, "The Problem of Social Cost," 3 *Journal of Law and Economics* 1 (1960). As a result, lawmakers in the real world who are trying to promote efficiency should mimic the wealth-maximizing solution that would emerge in the zero-transaction-cost world. The Coase theorem yields an obvious resolution to the problem of employment discrimination: such discrimination would be banned by the agreement of all parties if the benefits to discriminators were outweighed by the costs it imposed on victims *and moralists,* since this defines the wealth-maximizing outcome. Yet Richard Posner, who takes wealth maximization as the appropriate measure of social welfare, argues against considering the utility of moralists in evaluating a ban on discrimination. (For the argument that the welfare of strangers to a transaction should not be considered in the moral calculus, see Chapter 2, notes 2 through 5). This view puts Posner in the conceptually awkward position of opposing an employment discrimination law that would be adopted by the agreement of all parties in a zero-transaction-cost world. Nonetheless, Posner's unwillingness to consider the utility of moralists may be justified by pragmatic considerations: can one really weigh the utility of moralists in light of the difficult problems of accurate preference revelation? What would stop a moralist, who is opposed to discrimination, from vastly exaggerating the disutility it imposes? Note that the difficulty is not symmetric for the discriminator, since one can often observe what a discriminator is willing to give up to effectuate discriminatory preferences.

The primary problem is that there is no observable market that identifies the value of the reduced discrimination that is provided by an antidiscrimination law. Therefore, we do not know how much the public would be willing to pay to secure this reduction in discrimination. While one can survey the population to determine what they say they are willing to pay for such a law—this is called the contingent valuation method—this approach raises intractable issues concerning the truthfulness and reliability of such responses. For an excellent introduction to the problems of contingent valuation, see volume 8 of the Fall 1994 issue of the *Journal of Economic Perspectives:* Paul Portnoy, "The Contingent Valuation Debate: Why Should Economists Care?" 9; Michael Hanemann, "Valuing the Environment through Contingent Valuation," 19; and Peter Diamond and Jerry Hausman, "Contingent Valuation: Is Some Number Better Than No Number?," 45.

But not knowing the value of the external cost of discrimination is not a basis for concluding that the value is zero. Donohue shows that for plausible values of this external harm, an employment discrimination law could satisfy a cost-benefit analysis: "If the average adult American would [be willing to] forego $100 per year to maintain the basic Title VII regime, then the benefit of the statute would be $17.5 billion"; "If the annual costs of litigation and government expenditures are $1 billion, the compliance costs are $6.5 billion, and the productivity losses are $7.5 billion, the total cost of EEO law and regulation would be $15 billion." Donohue, "Advocacy versus Analysis in Assessing Employment Discrimination Law," 44 *Stanford Law Review* 1583, 1602, 1605 (1992). If one accepts these plausible, but highly speculative, estimates of the costs and benefits of Title VII, then the law would be efficiency enhancing, since the yearly benefits would exceed the yearly costs.

5. The suggestions of economists that the problem of pollution could be more cheaply addressed by using market incentives to reduce emissions was at first viewed as outlandish but is now well accepted. Indeed, the Clean Air Act Amendments of 1990 provided a statutory foundation for a system of tradable emission rights. Cooter suggests that a similar transformation may occur in the arena of employment discrimination. In fact, Germany has a tax-subsidy scheme designed to encourage the employment of disabled workers. See Martin Pfaff and Walter Huber, "Disability Policy in the Federal Republic of Germany," in Robert Haveman et al., eds., *Public Policy toward Disabled Workers: Cross-National Analyses of Economic Impacts* 193 (Ithaca, N.Y.: Cornell University Press, 1984).

The tax-subsidy scheme that is employed in Germany to encourage the hiring of handicapped workers would probably work better to deal with discrimination against the handicapped, women, or the elderly, since one would expect them to be rather uniformly spread around the country. Blacks, however, are highly concentrated in certain geographic locations, which suggests that either different targets would have to be set throughout the country (which increases administrative burdens) or certain areas would find it quite difficult to meet quotas and therefore would pay taxes disproportionately (which is politically infeasible).

Cooter's point is that moving to a regime of market incentives to further equal employment opportunity goals could reduce the productivity losses imposed by the more rigid prohibition of Title VII. This prospect suggests that Title VII is inefficient compared with the more flexible market-based regulation. But would a shift toward setting a price on discrimination rather than prohibiting it substantially reduce the symbolic *benefits* of Title VII? If so, Cooter's proposed regulation might lower both the costs and benefits of EEO regulation, with uncertain consequences for the overall cost-benefit calculation.

Ideally, we would like individuals to be motivated to adhere to the norm of antidiscrimination by an appreciation of the unfairness of and social harm imposed by employment discrimination. To the extent that the blanket prohibition of such discrimination that is embodied in Title VII underscores and buttresses the acceptance of the moral principle of antidiscrimination, the law serves an important symbolic function. This instructional impact would be dampened if the blanket prohibition were replaced by a market-based regulatory scheme. Such a scheme would be particularly unattractive if the market-based approach would be less effective than a universal condemnation in inducing Americans to change their prejudiced attitudes, since benign attitudinal shifts cause the great costs of discrimination to shrink.

6.   Derrick Bell satirizes an imagined Racial Preferencing Licensing Act that would enable whites to purchase permits allowing them to discriminate against blacks in business. Do you agree with Bell that relying on market incentives to reduce discrimination would be tantamount to "the legalized reincarnation of Jim Crow"? See Derrick Bell, *Faces at the Bottom of the Well: The Permanence of Racism* 47, 59 (New York: Basic Books, 1992). Are the obvious benefits of the market-based approach to dealing with employment discrimination large relative to the sacrifice in the symbolic impact of Title VII that would be needed to achieve them? Is the symbolic value of a legal prohibition of discriminatory conduct in the workplace so great that we value it more highly than improving the employment prospects of black Americans? Note that any desired degree of stimulation to black employment is achievable at least cost through the market-based approach—unless the law is an effective technology for diminishing prejudiced attitudes, as adumbrated in the previous note.

7.   Title VII protects a black worker's interest in securing a particular job in two ways: a qualified worker has the right to be installed (or reinstated) in any job that has been discriminatorily denied (a property rule), and has the right to receive back pay damages (liability rule). Cooter's proposed market-based scheme, like the contract compliance program, would lead to greater levels of black employment, but his scheme would afford no protection against a discriminatory refusal to hire to a worker whose heart is set on a particular job. How important is it that the law protect such idiosyncratic losses that are imposed by racially discriminatory rejections? Would Cooter's scheme adequately protect against racial harassment on the job?

8.   Citizens commonly seek to use governmental power to confer special benefits on themselves. This process of "rent seeking," which is socially wasteful, can be restrained when there are clear theoretical limits on the appropriate extent of governmental largesse. A prohibition on intentional racial discrimination provides a relatively clear limit on governmental power. But Cooter's proposed scheme to use explicit market incentives to increase black employment has no obvious theoretical constraint, which implies that parties would rent seek by vying to raise or lower the target employment of blacks. The rent-seeking problem is likely to be acute for any policy of affirmative action, and perhaps even in the case of a prohibition of disparate impact discrimination, since groups may try to argue, on the basis of ostensibly compelling moral justifications, that higher and higher quotas or targets are needed to achieve true equality.

9.   Might a nondiscriminatory employer be inclined to pay a fixed sum to be free to discriminate simply as a means of avoiding the risk of the imposition of substantial monetary damages? Indeed, some employers do pay just such an ex ante fee, by purchasing insurance that covers them in the event of being sued for employment discrimination. Should such insurance contracts be deemed in violation of public policy, or is it useful to have insurance companies monitoring employer conduct to limit instances of employment discrimination? How does an insurance scheme differ from the market-based scheme that Cooter proposes and that Bell ridicules?

8

Are Antidiscrimination Laws Effective?

One of the most important issues in evaluating governmental antidiscrimination policy is the effectiveness of employment discrimination law. The primary goal of employment discrimination laws is to eliminate or reduce discriminatory behavior. Achieving this goal should stimulate the demand for black workers and those in other protected categories, thereby expanding employment and elevating wages. Therefore, the first step in assessing the effectiveness of the law is to examine the historical trends in employment and wages to see if any positive gains have been made. This chapter looks primarily at the effects of civil rights law on black men, and Chapter 13 explores the effects on white and black women.

There is so much media focus on the high rate of unemployment, poor education, and high crime rate of the black community that many Americans incorrectly believe that the economic condition of blacks has improved little, or has even gotten worse, over the last fifty years. Although there have been some adverse trends, it is important not to overlook the many dimensions in which considerable progress has been made. James Smith and Finis Welch carefully document the substantial improvements in income and education that American blacks have experienced in the postwar period. Recall that in note 4 of section 3.2, Chapter 3, we discussed the evidence presented by George Borjas that sometime after 1940 blacks were finally able to get on the economic escalator and start the ride up. While knowledgeable authorities agree that substantial economic progress has been made, we still have the difficult task of identifying the causal factors that explain this progress.

Smith and Welch attribute black economic progress to two main factors: improved skills resulting from increasing education, and migration out of the South in search of higher paying jobs. Viewing these long-run historical forces to be of primary importance in explaining black economic gains, Smith and Welch doubt that federal civil rights initiatives played a significant role. John Donohue and James Heckman, who focus more sharply on the precise periods during which blacks made greater economic gains than whites, find that long-run historical factors have not acted mono-lithically to advance relative black economic welfare throughout this century. Rather, Donohue and Heckman argue that the periods of black advance are episodic and seem to coincide with important antidiscrimination initiatives.

Evaluating the impact of a law such as Title VII is particularly difficult, since its near-universal coverage reduces the opportunity for making comparisons between similar firms that are and are not subject to the legal command. Moreover, while Donohue and Heckman document an apparent discontinuous jump in black wages beginning in the mid-1960s, it is difficult to determine the gains resulting from Title VII. To do so, one must also account for the influence of the government contractor compliance program, increased black political influence due to the Voting Rights Act, and the general diminution in discrimination that both prompted these legislative efforts and resulted from them, not to mention changes in the overall economy caused by the tight labor markets induced by the Vietnam War effort and the Great Society programs.

Nonetheless, an impressionistic story that black progress follows from strong governmental antidiscrimination and affirmative action measures can be teased from the data. A study by James Heckman and Brook Payner—described in the excerpt from Donohue and Heckman—examines black employment in the South Carolina textile industry throughout the twentieth century and provides the most cogent illustration of Title VII dramatically impacting employment in an important manufacturing industry. Heckman and Payner, "Determining the Impact of Federal Antidiscrimination Policy on the Economic Status of Blacks: A Study of South Carolina," 79 *American Economic Review* 138 (1989). There is now a body of evidence showing significant gains in black employment from the government contract compliance program, and we know that direct hiring of blacks by governmental entities has grown sharply over the last thirty years (and much of this growth in governmental employment of blacks has come outside of the South, and is therefore not the product of Voting Rights Act pressures).

Black Economic Progress After Myrdal*
JAMES P. SMITH AND FINIS R. WELCH

Introduction

Forty-five years ago, Gunnar Myrdal published his masterwork on race relations in America, *An American Dilemma*. He begins his chapter on the economic situation of blacks with the following summary:

> The economic situation of the Negroes in America is pathological. Except for a small minority enjoying upper or middle class status, the masses of American Negroes, in the rural South and in the segregated slum quarters in Southern cities, are destitute. They own little property; even their household goods are mostly inadequate and dilapidated. Their incomes are not only low but irregular. They thus live from day to day and have scant security for the future. Their entire culture and their individual interests and strivings are narrow.

In the 45 years since Myrdal's bleak assessment, this country has undergone a series of dramatic and far-reaching changes—economically, demographically, and politically. These changes have had important implications for the economic status of blacks, especially relative to the status of whites. This essay presents a reassessment of the relative long-term economic progress of black men, focusing on trends over those 45 years and the reasons for them.

The Issues and the Research

During the time period we cover, the American economy grew rapidly. It also shifted from its traditional agricultural and manufacturing base to one that is service and technology oriented. Part of this shift was the elimination of black sharecropping in cotton, which had been the primary economic activity of Southern blacks since the Civil War. This change motivated large numbers of Southern rural blacks to migrate into the inner cities of the North, eventually transforming the black population from predominately rural to largely urban.

During the 1970s, the American economic structure suffered additional shocks. Increased international competition hit the older industrialized sectors of the Northeast and North Central states particularly hard. And these were the areas where blacks had made hard-won advances.

Black-White Male Wages 1940–80

Since 1940, the American economy has enjoyed substantial economic growth, and inflation-adjusted incomes of all its citizens have risen dramatically. Table 8.1 lists yearly incomes of men of both races. To

---

* Excerpts from James P. Smith and Finis R. Welch, "Black Economic Progress after Myrdal," *Journal of Economic Literature*, vol. 27, copyright © 1989. Reprinted by permission of the authors and publisher.

adjust for the sevenfold inflation that has occurred since 1940, all incomes are expressed in constant 1987 dollars.

Table 8.1. Mean Male Income by Race, 1940–80 (In Constant 1987 Dollar)

Census Year	White Men	Black Men
1980	28,212	20,480
1970	28,075	18,078
1960	21,832	12,561
1950	15,677	8,655
1940	11,441	4,956

Note. Yearly incomes are weekly wages multiplied by an assumed workyear of 50 weeks.

Real incomes of white men expanded two-and-one-half-fold between 1940 and 1980—but earnings growth was even more rapid among black men. Real incomes of black men have more than quadrupled over these 40 years. In 1940, the typical black male employed for a full workyear earned almost $5,000; by 1980 he earned over $20,000.

The standard of living of today's black men has improved not only as measured against earlier black generations, but also relative to their white contemporaries. While incomes of white men were growing at a 2.2 percent rate throughout these 40 years, black men were enjoying an income growth of 3.5 percent per year. Table 8.2 depicts our estimates of black-white male weekly wage ratios from each of the decennial Census tapes. The final row in this table contains relative wages aggregated across all experience classes. In addition, ratios are listed for five-year intervals of years of work experience.

Table 8.2 points to a very impressive rise in the relative economic status of black men over this 40–year time span. Between these 40 years, black male wages increased 52 percent faster than those of whites. In 1940, the typical black male worker earned only 43 percent as much as his white counterpart. By 1980, the average black man in the labor force earned 73 percent as much as the typical white man.

Table 8.2. Black Male Wages as a Percentage of White Male Wages, 1940–80

Years of Market Experience	Census Years				
	1940	1950	1960	1970	1980
1–5	46.7	61.8	60.2	75.1	81.2
6–10	47.5	61.0	59.1	70.1	76.6
11–15	44.4	58.3	59.4	66.2	73.5
16–20	44.4	56.6	58.4	62.8	71.2
21–25	42.3	54.1	57.6	62.7	67.3
26–30	41.7	53.2	56.2	60.6	66.9
31–35	40.2	50.3	53.8	60.0	66.5
36–40	39.8	46.9	55.9	60.3	68.5
All	43.3	55.2	57.5	64.4	72.6

The pace at which blacks were able to narrow the wage gap was far from uniform. The largest improvement occurred during the 1940s, a decade that witnessed a 24–percent expansion in the relative wages of black men. These advances slowed considerably during the 1950s, but the pace picked up again in the years after 1960. During both the 1960s and 1970s, the rise in black wages was more than 10 percent higher than for whites.

Obviously, there has been impressive improvement in the relative economic status of blacks since 1940. It is largely an untold story that belies widely held views of black stagnation. However, one must remember that even today black male incomes still lag well behind those of whites. We are left then with a dual message: Considerable progress has been made in narrowing the wage gap between the races—but race is still an important predictor of a man's income.

· · ·

Causes of the Closing Wage Gap: Education

Causes of the Convergence in Racial Wage Ratios

In this section and the next, we examine reasons for the substantial narrowing of the racial wage gap over time. Our aim here is to quantify how much of the closing was due to gains in education, and in the next section how much should be attributed to migration and the resurgence of the Southern economy.

· · ·

The Role of Education

· · ·

[The] consensus of early research implied that even if blacks got more and better education, the racial wage gap would persist. The historical record now strongly challenges this view: It shows that black education has risen relative to white education, that the wage return on black educational investment has risen over time. These factors, together, have significantly narrowed the racial wage gap.

Trends in Educational Differences

The first step in documenting this claim involves tracking racial trends in years of school completed. The number of grades completed is a crude summary index of the amount of learning and skill acquired in American classrooms. But if education plays a significant role in closing the racial wage gap, the most elementary evidence must rely on monitoring the extent to which black educational accomplishments are catching up to those of whites. . . .

Not surprisingly, the education levels of each new generation of workers increased between 1940 and 1980, but the increase was much greater for black men. Educational differences still persist between the races, but they are far less today than at any time in our history. Between 1940 and 1980, 40 percent of the racial education gap disappeared.

A simple way of depicting how these changes transformed the educational makeup of the work force is to examine racial disparity in the schooling of male workers at 20–year intervals. Begin this examination in 1980, when the majority of all workers of both races were high school graduates. Three-quarters of younger male workers (those aged 26–35) of both races were high school graduates in 1980, but blacks lagged more than a year behind whites. For the first time in our history, a sizable number of young black men were college graduates. One in nine blacks aged 26–35 completed college, compared to three in ten young white men.

It is easy to forget how little schooling the average black male worker had, even as late as 1960, and how large black-white education differences were in that year. Across the full age distribution, white men had a 2.7 year educational advantage over black men in 1960. If a high school graduate typified the 1980 black male worker, our average 1960 black worker competed in the labor market with only his elementary diploma. Fully 80 percent of the 1960 black male work force had not finished high school, and less than 3 percent of all black male workers had college degrees. The average level of schooling of young black workers in 1960 was about 9 years; the typical older black worker had not even completed the sixth grade. In contrast, the majority of white workers in 1960 still had completed high school, and one in ten were college graduates.

As dismal as these 1960 numbers seem, they represent substantial improvement over those for 1940. In that year, 80 percent of the 1940 black male work force had only elementary schooling and 40 percent had less than five years of education. Only 1 in 14 black men in 1940 had graduated from high school and 1 in 100 received a college degree. Matters were little better among younger blacks in that year. Among black men 26 to 35 years old, four out of five failed to go beyond elementary school and the mean schooling level was less than six years.

While the 1940 education credentials of white workers were far less than those of today's workers, white men had a decidedly larger educational advantage over their black contemporaries. In that year, the average white worker completed 9.4 grades, 3.7 more than their black rivals. The majority of white men had at least some high school training and one in four were high school graduates.

· · ·

Among men born in this century, there has been a substantial narrowing of racial difference in years of school completed. Moreover, this convergence has accelerated as each new cohort arrived in the labor market.

The Wage Gains From Schooling

In examining the role of education, the key issues are (*a*) whether blacks have been able to translate better schooling into higher incomes and (*b*) whether blacks realize the same return as whites on educational investment. Our analyses indicate that education has translated into higher incomes for blacks and has helped narrow the racial wage gap. However, the interracial payoff for education has not been equal until very recently and even then only for younger workers.

Black-White Wage Ratios by Education.... Black men earned 50 to 55 percent as much as comparably educated whites in 1940. While these racial wage differences narrowed substantially over time, they remained at levels of 70 to 80 percent in 1980. These within-education wage ratios should be contrasted to the aggregate ratios of 43 percent in 1940 and 73 percent in 1980 (see Table 8.2). The difference informs us that education does play a significant role in explaining the racial wage gap. However, it also warns us that simply equalizing the number of years of schooling alone would leave a sizable racial wage gap.

. . .

Estimated Increase in Wages Associated With Increased Schooling

To understand the historical trend, we need to know how much another year of schooling has raised labor market earnings over time. We obtained estimates for each race of schooling coefficients—the proportionate increase in weekly wages associated with an additional year of schooling.

. . .

Alternative explanations can be offered for this racial convergence in education coefficients. One obvious candidate is the civil rights movement (and its associated legislation) during the 1960s. A number of studies, including our own, demonstrated that black male college graduates were among the primary beneficiaries of affirmative action pressures. This view is supported by a racial convergence in education coefficients that was twice as large in the 1970s as in the 1960s.

However, this cannot be the whole story nor, for that matter, a very large part of it.... [T]he general pattern of rising relative returns to black schooling emerged long before the civil rights activism of the 1960s. The root cause of the improvements in relative black returns apparently lies within long-term improvements across birth cohorts that enabled blacks to translate an incremental year of schooling into more income. The evidence we have accumulated in earlier research clearly points to improving quality of black schools as the most plausible explanation for this cohort improvement. We found dramatic changes in such basic indices as number of days attended, pupil-teacher ratios, the education accomplishments of teachers. This evidence ... suggests why blacks were able to translate a year of schooling into increasingly higher incomes over time.

. . .

Causes of the Closing Wage Gap: Geographic Location

Americans have always tried to improve their economic lot by moving to places where prospects for their economic advancement were better. Since the end of slavery, large numbers of black men exercised their freedom to choose the place where they lived and worked. For many decades, most of this black migration took place within the South. Beginning in 1910, the great black migration northward started, a movement that accelerated after 1940.

While migration has been changing residential patterns, the regional structure of the American economy has also changed—to the point that it bears little resemblance to that of 1940. The agriculture-based economy of the South, for example—characterized by low productivity and little technological advance—was viewed as a drag on black economic progress in 1940. The situation now is far different. Today, the smokestack industries of the North Central and Northeastern states are in decay while the restructured Southern economy is booming.

In this section, we investigate the impact of these changing patterns of regional location on trends in black-white male wage ratios. We will concentrate on the three regional issues that loom most important in the economic literature—the large-scale black South to North migration, the increasing urbanization of the black population, and differential interregional economic growth.

Changing Patterns of Residential Location

Two geographic factors stand out in shaping the economic status of blacks: their concentration in the Southern states and their increasing urbanization. During the period that we are studying, important changes were occurring across both dimensions that would radically transform the geography of the black population.

. . .

Throughout American history, the economic welfare of blacks has been tied closely to events in the South. Fully nine out of ten blacks were Southerners in 1790, a proportion that changed but little over the next 120 years. Since 1910, the fraction of blacks living in the South has steadily declined. Spurred in part by the cutoff in European immigration, the great Northern black migration spanned the next two decades, 1910–30. When completed, it transformed the geographic and economic character of black America.

Even so, three-quarters of all blacks still lived in the Southern states in 1940 ..., but with the end of the Depression, the movement North resumed with renewed force. During each decade between 1940 and 1970, a million and a half Southern blacks migrated to the North. The end result was to leave only slightly more than half of all black men Southern residents in 1970. The flow then reversed during the 1970s: As it did for white Americans, the net movement of blacks turned southward. A slightly larger proportion of blacks lived in the South in 1980 than lived there ten years earlier.

. . .

The great northern migration had profound effects. The culture, laws, and economy of the South would no longer play so exclusive a role in shaping the economic position of blacks. However, it is also easy to exaggerate the extent of this change. Even today, the majority of blacks remain citizens of the South. Compared with the situation for whites, black economic well-being is still closely tied to the robustness of the Southern economy.

Moreover, geographical shifts in the place where blacks currently live shroud the continuing legacy of the South. Place of birth being immutable, the effects of migration on place of birth appear with a generational lag when the Northern-born children of migrants finally enter the labor force.... Three-quarters of all black men were Southern-born by as late as 1970—another reminder that black roots in the South still run deep.

Besides migration, the geography of black people altered in another fundamental way. After the Civil War, nine of ten blacks lived in rural farm areas, especially in the rural counties of the Southern black belt. This century has witnessed the transition of the black people from largely rural to predominately urban. Although it began in the early decades of the twentieth century, this transition was completed during the 40–year period after 1940.

Whites were still more urbanized than blacks in 1940.... Urbanization affected both races, but blacks far more so than whites. By 1980, four out of every five men of both races lived in urban areas. Today, the principal difference between them is where they live within urban areas: whites in the suburban fringes, blacks in the central cities. Fully 75 percent of all black SMSA residents resided in the central cities, compared with only 38 percent of whites.

. . .

In summary, our work identifies two geographic sources of long-term relative black economic improvement: the direct wage gains received from migration, and the erosion of the Southern racial wage gap during the 1970s. Migration raised black wages 11 to 19 percent between 1940 and 1980; the closing of the Southern wage gap added another 4 to 10 percent. While the decline of central cities had negative consequences for blacks, and the resurgence in the Southern economy positive ones, the overall net effect of these regional developments was small.

· · ·

Affirmative Action

The next issue we address is affirmative action, which still dominates the debate over government labor-market policy regarding race. Modern efforts at affirmative action began with the 1964 Civil Rights Act, aimed at eliminating employment discrimination against minority groups. Because of the historically intense discrimination against them, American blacks were the principal group this legislation was meant to protect. In the last two decades, an extensive legal and federal administrative enforcement structure has been set up to enforce affirmative action. Title VII of the Civil Rights Act of 1964 established the Equal Employment Opportunity Commission (EEOC) to monitor compliance with its provisions. These provisions prohibited discrimination on the basis of race and sex—in pay, promotion, hiring, training, and termination.

The second major federal enforcement agency was the Office of Federal Contract Compliance Program (OFCCP). This agency was established by a 1965 executive order (No. 11246) that prohibited discrimination by race among government contractors (amended in 1967 by No. 11375 to include sex).

Our discussion of affirmative action focuses on two questions: First, has affirmative action significantly altered the types and locations of jobs that blacks can obtain? Second, how has affirmative action affected the incomes of black men?

Employment effects. To detect discriminatory behavior, EEOC has set up an extensive monitoring system. Since 1966, all firms in the private sector with 100 or more employees, and federal contractors with $50,000 contracts and with 50 or more employees, have been required to report annually on their total employment in each of nine broad occupation categories, reporting separately for each race-sex group. Firms are also required to indicate their federal contractor status on their EEO–1 reports. These reports give enforcement agencies their initial opportunities to detect employment deficiencies.

Because of these reporting requirements, only about half of the nongovernment, noneducation work force is directly covered by affirmative action. Federal contractors employed 35 percent of all nongovernment, noneducational institution workers in 1980, and 70 percent of all EEOC-covered workers.

We test for employment effects by measuring whether affirmative action has altered the location of black employment. If affirmative action is effective and is adequately enforced, minority representation should expand more among firms that are required to report to EEOC than among firms that are not. Because federal contractors have more to lose, the greatest relative gains in employment and wages should occur among those EEO–1—reporting firms that are federal contractors.

While such relocation of black workers should be discernible in total employment figures, the largest minority gains should appear within certain occupation groups. We anticipate that the greatest black gains should occur in professional and managerial jobs for firms that are reporting to EEOC. Once again, these changes should be even larger among those firms that are federal contractors.

Table 8.3 lists the relative probability that blacks are employed in EEOC-covered employment, and strongly supports the employment-response hypothesis.

The basic test of affirmative action is its effect on employment trends in minority representation over time. On these grounds, the message of Table 8.3 is unambiguous. Black men were almost 10 percent less likely than white men to work in covered firms in 1966. By 1980, they were 25 percent more likely to work in EEOC-reporting firms. Compared with the 48 percent in 1966, fully 60 percent of all black men worked in covered firms by 1980.

As large as those changes in total employment seem, they pale next to changes within the managerial and professional jobs. Black managers and professionals were half as likely as white managers and professionals to work in covered firms in 1966. By 1980, black managers and professionals were equally likely to be found in covered firms.

Table 8.3. Representation of Black Men and Women in Covered EEOC Employment Compared with White Men (In Percent)

Occupation	1966	1970	1974	1978	1980
Total Employment					
Black men	91.8	112.5	123.1	128.4	126.4
Black women	91.5	118.7	141.2	144.8	154.4
Officials and Managers					
Black men	53.3	80.8	104.0	101.1	106.8
Black women	61.4	10.5	142.3	178.5	154.4
Professional and Technical					
Black men	62.8	82.9	137.8	117.2	97.6
Black women	74.5	63.4	84.3	104.3	118.7

The biggest employment changes clearly occurred between 1966 and 1970 (the first four years of reporting). Among black men, the trend continued at a diminished pace until 1974, and then apparently stabilized. The growth was greater for black women and persisted throughout the 1970s.

Wage effects. The economic literature has now reached a consensus that affirmative action significantly altered the industrial location of minority employment. But have these shifts been accompanied by an improvement in the incomes of blacks? Here there exists much less consensus.

. . .

To avoid exaggerated claims about the wage effects of affirmative action, we need to place them in historical perspective. The Civil Rights Act was passed in 1964 and the powers of two enforcement agencies, EEOC and OFCCP, were slowly put into place during the next decade. As a result, affirmative action is only relevant as an explanation for any post-1965 closing of the racial wage gap.

Table 8.4 helps illustrate our point. It lists the percentages by which the wage gap for black males narrowed between 1940 and 1960 and between 1960 and 1980. Wage effects attributed to affirmative action must occur in the second 20–year interval. The lesson of Table 8.4 is clear. While some experience groups were favored in one 20–year period and some in the other, the general pattern reveals that the racial wage gap narrowed as rapidly in the 20 years prior to 1960 (and before affirmative action) as during the 20 years afterward. This suggests that the slowly evolving historical forces we have emphasized in this essay— education and migration—were the primary determinants of the long-term black economic improvement. At best, affirmative action has marginally altered black wage gains around this long-term trend.

. . .

The key impact on wages relates to timing. During the initial phases of affirmative action, there was a remarkable surge in incomes of young black males. The abrupt jump in relative wages for young black men from 1967–68 to 1971–72 . . ., especially for college graduates, is remarkable. According to our estimates, the racial wage gap for young college graduates jumped from 76 percent in 1967–68 to complete wage parity by 1971–72. A similar, but less sharp, surge exists among young high school graduates. In this group, black men earned 82 percent as much as comparable whites in 1967–68; four years later, they earned 91 percent as much.

Table 8.4   Percentage Narrowing of the Racial Wage Gap by Years of Schooling, 1940–80

	Years of Experience				
Period	1–10	11–20	21–30	31–40	All
16+ Years of Schooling					
1940–60	6.8	31.3	29.0	29.0	21.2
1960–80	23.5	26.3	29.7	31.3	23.5
12 Years of Schooling					
1940–60	3.3	15.7	34.5	53.3	15.8
1960–80	13.1	15.3	13.7	23.1	17.4
8–11 Years of Schooling					
1940–60	3.9	14.0	19.8	24.0	20.6
1960–80	23.4	22.0	15.3	17.5	20.8

These black wage gains, however, did not prove to be permanent. By mid-1975–76, ... the racial wage gap had returned to more normal levels. Wages of young black college graduates were now 89 percent of those of whites, compared with the 1971–72 peak of 101 percent. Similarly, young black high school graduates in 1975–76 earned 83 percent as much as whites, a wage gap little different from the one that prevailed in 1967–68. The timing pattern, resembles a wage bubble, with a sharp increase in black male incomes from 1967 to 1972, followed by the bursting of the bubble during the next five years.

In our view, affirmative action is the most plausible cause of this wage bubble. First, the timing of the wage bubble is consistent with the timing of the employment effects. The large shift in black employment was concentrated during the years 1966–70 and was largely completed by 1974. During these early years, EEOC-covered firms rapidly increased their demand for black workers, bidding up their wages. However, once the stock of black workers had reached its new equilibrium, this short-run demand increase was completed and wages returned to their long-run levels.

. . .

Continuous Versus Episodic Change: The Impact of Civil Rights Policy on the Economic Status of Blacks*

JOHN J. DONOHUE III AND JAMES HECKMAN

The Improvement in Black Relative Economic Status

The simplest depiction of the changes in black relative economic status since 1953 is provided in Figure 8.1, which presents the time series of the median earnings of full-time black male workers relative to the same measure for white males for the entire country. The graph reveals that significant black progress has occurred, but the early data are sufficiently noisy to obscure the precise starting point of the upward trend. It is clear, though, that a decade of unbroken black progress begins in 1965,

* Beginning in 1979 these figures reflect consolidation of 11 agency offices with OFCC to form OFCCP.

followed by a period of decline. Thus, the aggregate black/white earnings ratio rose from .62 in 1964 to .72 by 1975, but then fell with the 1987 figure at .69.

While the existence of the sustained post-1964 growth of the black/white earnings ratio is revealing, its cause is uncertain. Conceivably, the booming economy during the second half of the 1960s or relative improvements in education might help to explain the black economic advance. Richard Freeman demonstrated, however, that the pattern of post-1964 acceleration in black male relative earnings persists in aggregate Current Population Survey (CPS) data time-series regressions that control for the state of aggregate demand (business cycle effects) and relative educational attainment going back to 1948. Three subsequent analyses that extend the time series forward have confirmed Freeman's original finding[.]

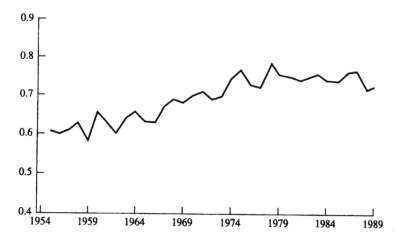

Figure 8.1. Ratio of Non-white to White Total Money Income of Year-Round Full-time
Male Workers, 1955–1989
—United States

But while the evidence for discontinuity is clear using the standards of modern time-series analysis, the reliance on aggregate national data obscures some important features in the improvement of black relative economic status.

· · ·

[M]icro evidence on this question is given in a recent paper by John Bound and Richard Freeman. Using CPS annual March Demographic Files, they estimated wage equations for males age 20–64 for every year from 1963–1984 controlling for race, region, urban status, age (using separate dummy variables for each year of age), and years of education. Bound and Freeman then computed a time series of estimated racial differentials (the coefficient on a race dummy variable equal to one if a person is black) for both log annual and weekly earnings. While there is some danger in estimating wage equations under the assumption that the effect of factors such as education, age, and race will be the same across diverse sectors of the economy, the results are dramatic. In both cases, black relative economic status improves dramatically until the mid-1970s and then stagnated thereafter. Moreover, Bound and Freeman also disaggregate the CPS data into South and non-South, and demonstrate that the truly dramatic relative economic gain for blacks came in the South.

In Figure 8.2, we graph our estimates of the racial differentials in hourly earnings for male workers for every other year over the period 1963–1987. This graph once again underscores the importance of regional disaggregation. For the non-South, there is virtually no improvement in the earnings deficit of black men over the twenty-four year period. In contrast, Southern blacks experienced sharp relative wage gains over the decade 1965–1975, with virtual stagnation thereafter. Note that in 1987 the adjusted black earnings shortfall, which had historically been far greater in the South, for the first time became equal at about 19 percent in both regions.

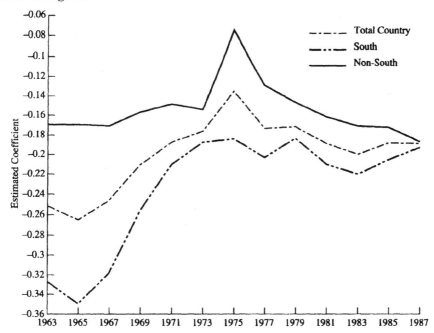

Figure 8.2. Estimated Percentage Black Male Deficit in (hourly wage) Relative to White Male

Do Migration and Increased Education Explain post-1964 Black Gains?

The evidence of episodic as opposed to continuous black economic progress is in apparent conflict with the story of secular black improvement summarized in the following quotation from Smith and Welch:

> The racial wage gap narrowed as rapidly in the 20 years prior to 1960 (and before affirmative action) as during the 20 years afterward. This suggests that the slowly evolving historical forces we have emphasized . . .—education and migration—were the primary determinants of the long-term black economic improvement. At best, affirmative action has marginally altered black wage gains around this long-term trend.

This statement raises two questions: (1) was the post-1964 relative black improvement simply part of a longer historical trend of black progress? and (2) do migration and increased education explain post-1964 black gains?

[We first demonstrate] that the evidence of sustained economic advance for blacks over the period 1965–1975 is not inconsistent with the fact that the racial wage gap declined by similar amounts in the two decades following 1940 as in the two decades following 1960. The long-term picture from at least 1920–1990 has been one of black relative stagnation with the exception of two periods—that around World War II and that following the passage of the 1964 Civil Rights Act.

Nonetheless, if migration and black relative educational advances fully explain relative black economic progress after 1960, then Smith and Welch are correct that the impact of Federal civil rights policy must be minimal. But, in fact, . . . the pattern of black migration from the South buttresses the view of episodic black progress, and, at least by 1965, migration ceased to be an important contributory factor to relative black economic progress. [We then show] that, while black relative educational gains do contribute significantly to increased black earnings, they explain only a small portion of the post-1964 relative black advance. Together, the combined effect of migration and educational improvements on post-1964 black relative gains is small. We will discuss these issues in turn.

Was the Post-1964 Relative Black Improvement Simply Part of a Longer Historical Trend of Black Progress?

Donald Dewey notes that in the South:

> In the fifty years before World War II the relative position of Negro workers in Southern industry actually deteriorated; they did not share proportionately in the expansion of urban employment and they were not upgraded as individuals into jobs previously held by whites.

Stability in the racial status quo in the South is the conclusion of Dewey's work. Both Dewey and Gunnar Myrdal document that blacks were excluded from new industries and occupations in the South over the period 1890–1940. To the extent there was any black advance, it occurred because of migration to the North. Secular trends of improving relative education and advancing industrialization in the South coincided with the stagnant economic status of Southern blacks in the pre-World War II period.

Recent studies of the economic history of South Carolina blacks support the pre-World War II stagnation hypothesis of Dewey and Myrdal as well as the hypothesis of post-1964 sustained advance. Figure 8.3 presents the share of black employment by sex in the textile industry of the state over the period 1910–1977 taken from the study by James Heckman and Brook Payner. Textiles has long been the major manufacturing employer in the state, accounting for 80 percent of all manufacturing employment in 1940 and more than 50 percent in 1970. Through two World Wars, the Great Depression and the Korean War, the share of blacks remained low and stable, despite the fact that the industry was expanding in employment throughout this period. Even when young white men left their manufacturing jobs to fight in World War II, they were replaced not by older black men but by white women. The breakthrough in black employment occurred only after 1964. Black male and female wages (relative to those of white males) accelerated in the industry after that date. The breakthrough in textiles occurred primarily in the nonurban South Atlantic region which is documented by Smith and Welch to have been the region of the greatest black relative wage gains over the period 1968–1974.

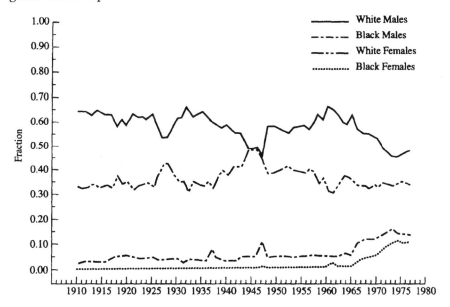

Figure 8.3. Employment in the South Carolina Textiles Industry

Gavin Wright similarly corroborates Myrdal by documenting the long-term stability in the Southern industrial division of labor by race. The pre-World War II position of blacks was rigidly maintained in the South despite increases in their relative educational levels and the quality of their schooling. Blacks were systematically excluded from new industries during this period. Heckman and Payner demonstrate that black progress in South Carolina after World War II occurred in new firms and new sectors of the economy that were not bound by the rigid racial practices of the prewar South.

.   .   .

In summary, it is universally acknowledged that blacks failed to gain relative to whites in the 1920s. In the 1930s, the Great Depression and New Deal acreage restriction policies which encouraged capital intensive agricultural methods in the South had a disproportionately adverse impact on blacks. Blacks rebounded economically in the 1940s with the tight labor markets induced by World War II. Relative stagnation for blacks characterizes the 1950s and 1980s, leaving the periods around World War II and following the passage of the 1964 Civil Rights Act as the only significant spells of relative black progress over the seventy year span from 1920 through 1990. Even though black relative gains were of comparable size in the periods from 1940–1960 and from 1960–1980, this equality does not imply a forty-year trend of unbroken progress. It is questionable whether the 1940 Census provides an appropriate benchmark from which to measure black progress given the extraordinarily poor state of the economy during the 1930s and the immense stimulus to aggregate demand provided by the War. Clearly, black progress in this period was generated far more by demand forces than by schooling effects. Focusing purely on the five Census years of 1939, 1949, 1959, 1969, and 1979 can create the illusion of a stable pattern when a more encompassing effort to correlate periods of improvement with specific causal factors would suggest far more episodic change.

If migration and black relative educational advances fully explain relative black economic progress after 1960, then Smith and Welch are correct that the impact of Federal civil rights policy must be minimal. But, in fact, the pattern of black migration from the South buttresses the view of episodic black progress, and, at least by 1965, migration ceased to be an important contributory factor to relative black economic progress. Moreover, while black relative educational gains do contribute significantly to increased black earnings, they represent only a small portion of the post-1964 relative black advance.

.   .   .

The Unimportance of Migration after 1965

The story of black migration between 1940 and 1980 is both dramatic and revealing: 14.6 percent of the black population of the South left during the 1940s, 13.7 percent more departed during the 1950s, and an additional 11.9 percent exited during the 1960s. Such immense population shifts—close to a quarter of young black men left the South *each decade* between 1940 and 1970—are readily explained by the substantial wage disparities across regions. For example, in 1960 Southern black men age 30–40 earned 57 percent less than their white Southern counterparts, while the comparable earnings disadvantage for non-Southern black men was only 32 percent. Interregional differentials of this magnitude existed across all cohorts for much of the period from 1940–1965, prompting an immense number of blacks to flee the South. This Southern outmigration provided a powerful stimulus for black relative economic gain.

The 1970s experienced a reversal of this flow since there was actually net black migration to the South during that decade. But an important fact to note is that the abrupt shift in the pace of migration began in the mid-1960s. Of the net outmigration of 1.4 million blacks from the South during the 1960s, only 15.7 percent left after 1965. In other words, the period of 1960–1965 was one of black migration from the South at a pace considerably higher than the average rates of the 1940s and 1950s, while in the period 1965–1970 migration slowed to a near trickle. This sharp curtailment of black migration further buttresses the thesis of sustained economic advance concentrated in the South because it is quite likely that perceived improvements in economic opportunities would staunch the outflow of Southern blacks.

There is uniform agreement that prior to 1960 black migration out of the low-wage South significantly elevated black relative economic status. But the timing of the drop in black migration also demonstrates that black migration cannot explain the improvements in black economic status beginning in 1965. The vast bulk of any benefits occurring from migration during the 1960s had already been achieved by 1965. If the long-term historical factors emphasized by Smith and Welch are to explain the sustained improvement in black relative earnings beginning in 1965, the story must rest with relative black educational advance.

The Relative Improvement of Black Education

Smith and Welch have examined the growth of the years of education for blacks and whites, and changes in the labor market returns to this education, in order to determine the contribution of educational advance to increasing black relative earnings. It is useful, in considering their analysis, to note three factors that would tend to elevate relative black earnings: (1) greater relative increases in the number of years of education accumulated by blacks; (2) greater relative improvements in the quality of schools attended by blacks; and (3) greater relative increases in the labor market valuation of black education. Although, as we shall see, the analysis presented by Smith and Welch cannot distinguish the individual effects of factors (2) and (3), new evidence by Card and

Krueger does attempt to quantify the relative contributions of these two factors.

The Modest Impact of Relative Increases in the Quantity of Schooling

Smith and Welch reveal that black relative earnings rose from 18 to 35 percent across experience categories in the period from 1960 through 1980. Particularly for younger cohorts, Smith and Welch contend that education is the overwhelmingly dominant factor in explaining this relative advance....

Smith and Welch [document] how much of this education effect is caused by the greater quantities of black education (measured in years of schooling) and how much results from greater returns to this schooling. [Remarkably, more than 80 percent of the black gains in closing the racial gap in earnings over the period 1960–1980 is explained by the higher relative returns to black education.] *The contribution of measured changes in years of schooling is small in comparison.* Smith and Welch [attribute the higher black returns to education to] improvements in the quality of black schooling relative to that of white schooling, and indeed any such relative quality improvements will be reflected in this term. But black gains [generated by higher returns to education] may also be caused by reductions in market discrimination against black schooling (i.e., differences in prices paid to schooling by race).... [B]lack economic progress through education has come more from changes in the *rewards* to black education (compared to that of white education) than from increases in the relative quantity of education. The question left unresolved ..., though, is the relative importance of increases in the relative quality of black education (the supply side) and of lessening labor market discrimination (the demand side) in generating these changing returns to education.

· · ·

Improving Relative Schooling Quality or Reduced Discrimination?

· · ·

[T]he previously noted decline in black/white earnings differentials over time for cohorts of workers who have completed their schooling is inconsistent with [the simple quality improvement hypothesis advanced by Smith and Welch]. First, in their analysis of 1967–1974 CPS data, Smith and Welch acknowledge that within education cohorts there is secular improvement in black/white wage ratios by age—in later years black/white wage ratios rise. In other words, over time labor markets priced black skills more favorably, presumably reflecting demand-side changes favoring blacks.

Second, ... Smith and Welch document the sharp decline in the penalty that blacks incurred by living in the South. In a subsequent paper in 1989, they state that two explanations are possible for the rapid movement toward the national norm in the Southern racial wage gap during the 1970s:

> First, black-white skill differences may have converged in the South as the post-World War II cohorts entered the labor market. To illustrate this point, assume that Southern schools were effectively desegregated in 1960, six years after the Brown decision. The first class of Southern black children who had attended entirely desegregated schools would have first entered the labor market in the early to mid-1970s. Some of the improvement in black incomes during the 1970s may have been due to the skills acquired through this improved schooling. However, that is unlikely to be the whole story because there was a substantial erosion in racial wage disparities even among older workers in the 1970s.... *A more plausible explanation may well be that racial discrimination is waning in the South.*

As Smith and Welch observe, an explanation for black relative progress based on improvement in the quality of black schooling relative to white schooling must contend with the dramatic black economic advance across all experience groups. Moreover, one ordinarily thinks of changes in schooling quality as occurring at a continuous, slowly evolving pace, with wage gains being experienced only by each graduating cohort. Yet the relative wage improvement that we have documented throughout this paper occurs abruptly and across all age groups.

The potentially attractive feature of the desegregation story, though, is that it appears to offer a basis for a discontinuous advance in schooling quality that could translate into a discontinuous improvement in black economic welfare. It is to this issue that we now turn.

The Schooling Quality Hypothesis

Thus far, we have demonstrated that there is ample evidence of substantial change in black relative status over the period 1965–1975, that this change is concentrated in the South, and that it cannot be explained by migration or the relative black increases in the number of years of education. In addition, we noted that the schooling quality argument could not explain across-the-board increases in black relative earnings for cohorts that had previously finished their education. But it is clear, as Smith and Welch have stressed, that for much of this century there have been substantial relative improvements in the quality of education that blacks have received ..., as measured by three variables: the student-teacher ratio, the length of the school term, and teacher salaries. The trend is in the direction required to support the increase in the estimated schooling coefficients for successive cohorts (or "vintage" effect) reported by Smith and Welch.

· · ·

By linking schooling quality data by race to microdata on earnings, Card and Krueger have been able to extend the pioneering work of Smith and Welch. Their ultimate conclusion is that schooling quality improvements do contribute significantly to future earnings growth, and that between 15 and 20 percent of the overall growth in black-white relative earnings between 1960 and 1980 was attributable to these relative schooling quality gains.

Note that we have already alluded to one difference in the studies of Smith and Welch versus that of Card and Krueger: the former select the weight for the effect of relative increases in years of education in a way that enlarges the impact of this factor, which explains why Smith and Welch find that this factor did play a small but significant role in narrowing the black/white wage gap while Card and Krueger find no role. A number of other points about these two studies should be noted. First, the regressions are specified differently in the two studies and estimated on different populations. Smith and Welch control for location within a central city while Card and Krueger do not, and Card and Krueger employ a quadratic term for experience, and a marital status dummy while Smith and Welch do not. Smith and Welch control for Southern residence while Card and Krueger additionally control for residence in three other Census regions. Smith and Welch segment their regressions into separate intervals based on years of potential experience (1 to 5 years, 6 to 10 years, etc.). Card and Krueger estimate their regressions on broader ten-year birth cohorts, and such pooling may be problematic given the different results found across experience intervals by Smith and Welch. These differences in specification and population interval undoubtedly explain the rather large differences in the educational coefficients obtained in the two studies. Second, neither the Smith and Welch nor the Card and Krueger regressions generate accurate predictions of the actual relative wage changes across each ten-year interval. For example, for the youngest experience category, Smith and Welch predict relative black wage gains of 63 percent between 1970 and 1980 when the actual wage gain was 8 percent and they predict relative wage gains of 15 percent between 1960 and 1970 when the actual wage gain was 27 percent. Similarly, for the 21–30 age group, Card and Krueger report that the actual change in the wage gap was 12 percent during the 1960s and .7 percent during the 1970s, but the predicted effect attributable to education were 19 percent and 35.7 percent for these two periods. Since all explanatory variables are being evaluated at their means, such discrepancies can occur only if the differences in intercepts of the fitted regressions are shifting sharply. Such shifts undermine confidence in the functional forms of the earnings functions employed in both studies and suggest the possibility of potentially serious problems of misspecification.

One might wonder why the rather dramatic relative improvement in measures of schooling quality ... would play such a modest role in explaining black gains in the period from 1960–1980. Three factors should be noted. First, the dramatic growth in the ratio of black/white teacher salaries in the 1940s was a consequence of successful teacher salary equalization cases brought by the NAACP that substantially eliminated teacher pay inequities. Prior to this NAACP campaign, the disparities in expenditure partly reflected discrimination in salaries, and the rapid elimination of such discrimination may create the illusion of rapidly growing schooling quality. But rather than reflecting a higher average level of black school teachers, the evidence indicates that the existing stock of black school teachers received higher salaries. Any improvement in real teacher quality was likely to have taken considerably more time and been far more gradual in its effects. As late as 1965, the Coleman report found substantial racial disparity between the quality of teachers in Southern black schools and the quality of teachers in Southern white schools. John Owen concludes his analysis of the Coleman data with the remark that the data:

> demonstrate the rather dismal prospects for the gains in teacher quality that could have been expected for blacks within a segregated system in spite of salary equalization. The racial gap in verbal competence [was] larger for newer than for older teachers and still larger among high school and college students planning to enter teaching.

Second, the long-term continuous improvement in the relative educational quality enjoyed by blacks is an unlikely source of the secular improvement in black economic welfare that occurred in the decade from 1965–1975. Any claim of improved schooling quality based on the effective desegregation of Southern schools by 1960 is demonstrably false. Despite the *Brown* decision in 1954, virtually no desegregation of schools in the Deep South had occurred by 1960. In 1963, when President Kennedy asked Congress to pass a civil rights bill that would grant greater federal powers to attack segregation, 99 percent of black students in 11 Southern states attended all black schools. Real desegregation began to occur only after the passage of Titles IV and VI of the 1964 Civil Rights Act, which threatened segregated school districts with cutoffs of federal funds and enforcement actions by the Department of Justice. Still, the proportion of blacks in segregated schools had only fallen to 78 percent by 1968 (see Table 8.5). In the landmark decisions of *Green* and *Alexander* in 1968 and 1969, however, the Supreme Court forcefully declared that the command of *Brown* that states must desegregate "with all deliberate speed" finally meant "Now!" The results were dramatic: the number of blacks students attending segregated schools dropped from 78 percent in 1968 to 25 percent in 1972. Since desegregation in the 11 Southern states occurred roughly ten years after Smith and Welch claimed, any benefits from this desegregation would occur in the early 1980s rather than the early 1970s, as they asserted. Desegregation simply comes too late to explain black economic progress over the decade from 1965–1975.

Table 8.5. Percentage of Black Students in 90–100% Minority Enrollment Schools

Region	1968	1972	1976	1980
South	77.8	24.7	22.4	23.0
Border	60.2	54.7	42.5	37.0
Northeast	42.7	46.9	51.4	48.7
Midwest	58.0	57.4	51.1	43.6
West	50.8	42.7	36.3	33.7
U.S. Average	64.3	38.7	35.9	33.2

Finally, it is well documented that the post-*Brown* era (1954–1972) was a period of turmoil in Southern education. Opposition to desegregation led to bombings in Tennessee and riots throughout the South. In perhaps the most extreme case, black children in Prince Edward County, Virginia were left without formal education for years following the closure of the county's public schools in 1959. Whites were able to afford private schools while blacks were not. While there is evidence of greater increases in expenditures for black Southern schools than for white Southern schools between 1953 and 1957, the disruptive effects of Southern opposition to forced desegregation may have been serious enough to offset at least some of the relative schooling quality gains for blacks in the post-1954 era until integration was completed in the late 1960s or early 1970s.

Where does this leave us in our effort to account for black relative advance in the decade following the effective date of Title VII in 1965? We have noted that migration had no effect and increases in the years of education had small effects on black relative progress after 1965. Given Card and Krueger's estimate for the period 1960–1980 of 15–20 percent as the contribution of relative black schooling gains to black relative earnings advances, it would seem that a considerable portion of the black economic progress enjoyed in the post-1964 era cannot be explained by the long-term forces of migration and educational improvement.

We should also note that attachment to the labor force has been dropping faster for blacks than for whites over much of the last three decades. If labor force drop-outs tend to be relatively low earners, this selection effect would bias upward the measured growth in black relative earnings. The studies reviewed in Heckman suggest that the selective attrition of low wage blacks from the labor force likely accounts for 10–20 percent of the black measured wage gains. Conceivably, selective attrition of low-wage blacks could have been concentrated in the South accounting for some of the improvements in the relative wages of Southern blacks over the decade beginning in 1965 and creating the impression of greater economic gains for blacks in the South than in the North. This view receives little support.... [T]he pattern of declining relative labor force participation rates is similar in both the South and non-South over the period in question. The relative drop-out rates in the non-South are actually greater than in the South....

If one accepts the Card and Krueger estimates of 15–20 percent as the contribution of relative black schooling gains and the virtually zero role of migration after the mid-1960s, we have perhaps explained between 25 and 40 percent of the measured black gains. Even granting a 25 percent contribution from relative black gains in years of education leaves a sizable unexplained residual. Combining this evidence with the evidence aligning black gains in the South with the focus of the multi-pronged federal assault on racial discrimination in that region lends considerable credence to the argument that government played a considerable role in elevating black economic welfare.

A more expansive conception of Federal action would commensurately increase the proportion of black relative gains attributable to governmental action. For example, at least some of the relative black school quality gains ... were the product of federal court action in response to NAACP lawsuits seeking to enforce the constitutional mandate of separate but equal in the pre-*Brown* era. Moreover, when educational benefits for black students did come in the form of forced desegregation of Southern schools in the late 1960s and early 1970s, they were the direct product of a massive effort of the legislative, executive, and judicial branches of the Federal government. To a significant degree, the "schooling quality" argument relies on schooling quality engineered by Federal action.

Demand-Side Influences on Black Economic Progress

· · ·

Title VII Litigation and the EEOC

The available evidence on the impact of Title VII and EEOC enforcement activities is ... meager.... Because the entire country is covered by the law (except for firms with fewer than fifteen employees), there is no natural comparison group against which to measure the impact of the law. One is forced to use notoriously fragile aggregate time-series methods to ferret out EEOC effects from numerous other changes that affected the post-1964 American economy. Freeman uses cumulative EEOC expenditure—basically a post-1964 time trend—to estimate the impact of this agency using aggregate time-series data. His variable reproduces the aggregate shift already discussed. Freeman's measure is essentially a reparameterization of the shift in the trend that remains to be explained.

· · ·

Leonard offers a more favorable assessment of the impact of Title VII. On the basis of a cross-section study, he reports that the number of Title VII class action lawsuits per corporation is correlated with significantly greater increases in the percentage of black workers over the period from 1966 to 1978.

An indirect argument against strong government policy effects has been advanced by Butler and Heckman and Smith and Welch. These authors point to data of the sort summarized in Table 8.6. During the crucial period 1965–1975, enforcement budgets were low during the time black advance was so rapid. Few federal contractors lost their contracts because of OFCC actions. Knowledgeable observers such as Phyllis Wallace, James Jones, and Gregory Ahart write about understaffed EEOC and OFCC offices. Ahart notes that EEOC and OFCC did not coordinate their enforcement efforts. See Arvil Adams for detailed study of EEOC policies.

From these accounts, the federal effort appears weak during the period in which black breakthroughs in employment and wages took place. As enforcement budgets grew, black relative gains fell off and actually receded in some sectors. These well-documented features of the Federal enforcement effort pose an apparently enigmatic pattern for proponents of the view that federal policy mattered.

Table 8.6.   Summary Statistics for the Equal Employment Opportunity Commission (EEOC) and Office of Federal Contract Compliance (OFCC)

Year	Budget (1,000 of 1982$)	EEOC Resolved Cases (1,000s)	Employment Discrimination Cases Filed in Federal Courts
1966	9,680	6.4	NA
1970	32,954	8.5	336
1975	98,796	62.3	3,772
1979	148,100	81.7	5,032
1981	149,899	61.8	5,714
1982	144,739	57.2	7,015

Year	OFCC Budget (1,000 of 1982$)	Positions
1970	1,418	34
1975	8,072	201
1978	10,642	216
1979*	57,440	1,021
1981*	51,158	1,232
1982*	43,150	979

* Beginning in 1979 these figures reflect consolidation of 11 agency offices with OFCC to form OFCCP.

A More Refined View of Federal Policy

But the enigma is resolved if one adopts a more refined view of Federal policy that is at once broader in its conception of the Federal tools that were brought to bear in attacking racial discrimination and narrower in its geographic focus concerning the targeting of this Federal action. We have stressed throughout that much of the black improvement in the decade following enactment of Title VII of the 1964 Civil Rights Act came in the South, and it strengthens the case for the importance of the governmental effort to note that most of the Federal activity was directed toward that region. First, Title VII was primarily intended to combat discrimination against blacks in the South—virtually the only area of the country where state laws forbidding racial discrimination had not yet been enacted. Although the law did prohibit sex discrimination in employment, women were covered by the Act only as a result of an unsuccessful ploy by Southern congressmen to defeat the law by widening its mandate. Second, a substantial portion of the complaints filed with the EEOC and federal employment discrimination litigation occurred in the South. Table 8.7 reveals that roughly half of all charges filed with the Equal Employment Opportunity Commission over the period 1966–1972 originated in the South. Over this same period, more than half of all employment discrimination cases filed in federal court were brought in the South.

Furthermore, the view that initially enforcement was weak and that it became strong much later is exaggerated. Although Table 8.6 indicates that the number of employment discrimination cases filed in federal court is very low during the period of considerable black progress and very high during the period of black stagnation, these raw figures create an inaccurate impression of the intensity of civil rights activity for a number of reasons. First, almost all of the growth in employment discrimination cases since the early 1970s has come from cases alleging wrongful discharge, yet it is cases of hiring and wage discrimination, which predominated in the early days of Title VII, that are more likely to generate positive employment and wage effects for blacks. Second, the dramatic decline in the number of class action lawsuits at the same time that the number of individual suits rose exponentially once again indicates that the degree of Federal pressure was greater at a time when the number of cases brought was far smaller than the current level. Third, case filings and resolutions probably lag behind effective enforcement, and in general are noisy indicators of enforcement efforts. Employers (even those who are entirely innocent) commonly respond to the threat of litigation or the filing of the lawsuit with some remedial action, thereby obscuring the causal link between the onset or resolution of litigation and favorable employment outcomes for minority workers.

Table 8.7.   Charges Filed with the EEOC by Year

	1966	1967	1968	1969	1970	1971	1972
South	3,011	4,058	5,103	8,188	10,044	12,571	42,975
Total	6,133	8,512	11,172	14,471	17,780	28,609	86,677
Percentage in South	.491	.476	.456	.565	.564	.439	.496

Moreover, the South was the target of Federal civil rights policy in many areas in addition to employment, and it severely understates the magnitude of the Federal effort to focus purely on discrimination in the workplace. The 1954 *Brown v. Board of Education* decision was an attack on de jure school segregation—a practice that was most prevalent in Southern states and the District of Columbia. The 1962 and 1965

Voting Rights Acts were also focused on the South where blacks had been excluded from political life for over 70 years. In other words, Federal employment discrimination policies were imposed on a pre-existing larger Federal agenda designed to undermine the rigid racial segregation of the South.

There is ample evidence that Federal voting rights and school desegregation policies were effective in the South, especially during the crucial years 1965–1975. Table 8.8 presents the percentage of voting age Southern blacks registered to vote by year. There is a sharp jump in black voter registration during the period 1962–1970. The preceding rise in registration between 1952 and 1962 can be attributed in part to both the private and Federal civil rights activism that is documented by Steven Lawson and Garrow. Similarly, as we discussed above, the period of greatest desegregation of Southern schools came between 1968 and 1972 as the Federal courts strictly interpreted the mandate of the Constitution and Federal law to call for affirmative integration of Southern schools. Over this short period of time, Southern schools went from being the most segregated to the least segregated in the country (see Table 8.5). Federal desegregation efforts were directed toward the North only after 1973.

This evidence indicates the magnitude of the Federal activity on behalf of blacks in the South and reveals its success, at least in the area of school desegregation and voting rights. Even if the South had not been the intended target of Federal legislation and administrative decrees, any rational enforcement strategy would initially have concentrated attention on the South. The wholesale exclusion or segregation of blacks in employment, accommodations, schooling, and voting was easy to document and prove in court cases.

Table 8.8.   Black Registration in Southern States, 1940–1984

Year	Registration Rate (percentage)
1940	3.1
1946	12.2
1952	20.0
1956	25.0
1958	26.1
1960	28.7
1962	28.8
1964	41.9
1966	51.6
1968	58.7
1970	66.9
1972	55.8
1974	58.6
1976	59.9
1978	—
1980	55.1
1982	53.3
1984	66.9
1986	64.7
1988	63.7

Moreover, in certain ways the South was ripe for change. There is evidence that some Southern employers were eager to employ blacks if given the proper excuse. In their study of the dramatic breakthrough in the employment of blacks in the South Carolina textile industry that began in 1965, Butler, Heckman, and Payner document that employment of blacks slowed down the growth of labor costs and kept the industry competitive in the period 1965–1975 in the face of rising foreign competition. Integration of geographically isolated textile mills was aided by integration of housing, schooling, and employment, and therefore the results of the multipronged Federal effort in all of these areas were mutually reinforcing. Integration occurred rapidly and without major incidents. After 55 years of near total exclusion, blacks became a significant fraction of total industry employment, and black wages rose relative to white wages.

The rapid progress of blacks in the South in the crucial period 1965–1975 is consistent with the multiple equilibria explicit in the tipping models of T. C. Schelling and George Akerlof. Specifically, Akerlof's model of social custom provides a coherent interpretive framework for the experience of the South in the late 1960s and early 1970s, as an example from the history of Southern school desegregation shows. Southern school districts frequently responded to the 1954 decision in *Brown* by enacting "freedom of choice" plans that enabled white and black children to elect to attend either of the historically racially segregated schools in their area. The customary response to these plans was that 15–20 percent of the black students would select the formerly all-white school and none of the whites would select the black school. The effect, then, was to keep 80–85 percent of the black students in completely segregated schools. The firmly entrenched custom of segregation, enforced through pressures from neighbors and employers, made further integration impossible even as the attitudes that gave rise to the custom began to change. Enforcement of the law in the wake of the previously discussed Supreme Court decisions in 1968 and 1969 may have been necessary to break the log jam even when a substantial majority was no longer opposed to desegregation.

Similarly, community norms may have made marginal experimentation in hiring black workers privately costly. Unlike the school desegregation situation, there were monetary benefits to be obtained by employers if they could tap the black workforce without incurring the wrath of their communities. Federal pressure may have tipped the balance and led to a new equilibrium that employers collectively embraced but were individually unable to initiate. In the particular case of the textile industry—where integration of employment mutually reinforced integration of housing and schooling—the multipronged nature of the Federal effort may have been particularly effective.

In sum, the "enigma" of rapid black advance during a period of low Federal enforcement budgets may not be enigmatic at all. The early success of Federal policy occurred because it was targeted toward the South where racial exclusion was blatant. A multipronged Federal effort enlisted willing employers who needed an excuse for doing what they wanted to do anyway. post-1975 evidence of growing enforcement budgets with weaker employment and wage effects for black workers may largely be a manifestation of the triumph of the initial Southern initiative and diminishing returns to a Federal enforcement effort that turned Northward, and began focusing on sex and age discrimination in addition to racial discrimination.

Notes and Questions

1. Isn't it clear that Title VII was one of the primary weapons in the effort to dismantle the egregious system of apartheid that dominated the American South until the mid to late 1960s? Does this successful elimination of such an obvious evil suggest that the law was effective and beneficial, even without regard to whether it stimulated the demand for black labor?

2. Donohue and Heckman show that, relative to white wages, black wages jumped sharply over the decade beginning in 1965 but stagnated thereafter. Does this suggest that weakened affirmative action pressure and the legal retrenchments discussed in the selection by Blumrosen in Chapter 4, section 4.1, are responsible for the halt in progress? The argument that black welfare is strongly aided by governmental civil rights initiatives and impaired by governmental retrenchment is set forth in Martin Carnoy, *Faded Dreams: The Politics and Economics of Race in America* (New York: Cambridge University Press, 1994), and in Gary Orfield and Carole Ashkinaze, *The Closing Door: Conservative Policy and Black Opportunity* (Chicago: University of Chicago Press, 1991).

Conversely, might the post-1975 stagnation in relative black economic gains imply that the major benefits of antidiscrimination law have been achieved, and that further efforts to intensify enforcement would bring diminishing returns and increasing costs? This view is consistent with the opinion of Dave and June O'Neill, who contend that current earnings differentials between blacks and whites reflect differences in labor market skills rather than discrimination. They write:

> Substantial differences between blacks and whites have been found in scores on tests measuring school achievement. For example, at the same age and schooling level, black men score well below white men on the Armed Forces Qualification Test (AFQT). It has been demonstrated that the earnings of both blacks and whites are positively associated with AFQT scores. It follows that, on average, blacks and whites with the same education level may not be viewed as equally productive by nondiscriminating firms.

> How much of the racial differential in earnings between blacks and whites with the same educational level can be explained by the AFQT

differential? Results derived from analysis of data on individual black and white male earners in 1987 show that after controlling for AFQT differentials by race—as well as years of schooling and region—the earnings ratio increases from 83 percent to 90–96 percent. Among those with college training, the ratio rises above 100 percent. These results suggest that deprivation related to school, home, and neighborhood are more serious obstacles to the attainment of black-white equality in earnings than current labor market discrimination.

O'Neill and O'Neill, "Affirmative Action in the Labor Market," 523 *Annals of the American Academy of Political and Social Science* 88, 102 (1992). In other words, O'Neill and O'Neill contend that blacks still have an earnings disadvantage of roughly 5 to 10 percent after one controls for AFQT scores and education, except for college-educated blacks who now experience no earnings shortfall.

This evidence raises three possibilities. First, O'Neill and O'Neill believe that the unexplained gap in earnings between blacks and whites is now small, and the modest gap that remains is most likely the product of unobservable differences in productivity or motivation. Under this view, further efforts to improve blacks' earnings should focus not on antidiscrimination policy but on improving the skills of black workers. See also James J. Heckman, "Detecting Discrimination," 12 *Journal of Economic Perspectives* 101 (1998) for arguments in favor of this view.

Second, the unexplained earnings gap between blacks and whites after controlling for education and AFQT score may in fact be the product of racial discrimination. For example, we know that increased education is associated with a greater willingness to pursue Title VII litigation. See the selection by John Donohue and Peter Siegelman in Chapter 9, section 9.1. This might suggest that, when aggressively enforced, the law is effective in eliminating discrimination: college-educated blacks are more likely to sue, and they now appear to suffer no discrimination, while less educated blacks are less likely to sue, and they may therefore suffer an earnings disadvantage of from 5 to 10 percent. Indeed, as indicated in note 7 below, when the pressure to hire black college men declined in the 1980s, the economic status of recent graduates began to decline significantly.

Third, as John Ogbu has argued, the forces that lead to blacks scoring lower on AFQT tests, and other measures of intelligence or scholastic achievement, are themselves the product of a discriminatory culture. In this view, O'Neill and O'Neill have the direction of causation backward: while they contend that the lower schooling achievement scores explain the lower earnings, Ogbu asserts that the discriminatory culture itself causes the poorer school performance. If one could remove the burden of discrimination from blacks, their schooling achievement and economic performance would rise. In support of this position, Ogbu notes that a disfavored minority in Japan, the Buraku, who have no physical or cultural differences from majority Japanese, are widely thought by majority Japanese to be wasteful, parasitic, and irresponsible. In the face of such prejudice and discrimination, the Buraku in Japan do indeed perform poorly in school and on IQ tests relative to majority Japanese. Ogbu notes, however, that when the Buraku are transplanted from this culture of discrimination to the United States, they perform at the same level as majority Japanese in the United States. See Ogbu, "Immigrant and Involuntary Minorities in Comparative Perspective," in Margaret Gibson and John Ogbu, eds., *Minority Status and Schooling* 3 (New York: Garland, 1991). Although Ogbu's findings are intriguing, one would want to be certain that they are not explained by differential migration to the United States by the most talented Buraku.

Recent research by Claude Steele and Joshua Aronson tends to support the basic Ogbu thesis that stress induced by racism may be a factor in the observed lower test scores of blacks. Steele and Aronson have found that when black and white Stanford undergraduates took tests drawn from the verbal portion of the Graduate Record Exam, the results were heavily influenced by the black students' assumptions about the nature of the test. For example, blacks did much worse on the exam if they were told the test was diagnostic of ability than if they were told it was a laboratory problem-solving task unrelated to ability. In another experiment, blacks did much worse if they were asked to fill out a demographic identifier just before taking the test. Kathleen O'Toole, "Stereotypes Found to Affect Performance on Standardized Tests," 37 *Stanford University Campus Report 1* (1995).

3.   What would happen if Title VII and the counterpart state employment discrimination laws were now repealed? Would the gains of the past be lost? Do you think the black-white earnings differential would grow for the first time this century? Isn't it likely that most firms would try to avoid discriminating, some would be happy to discriminate (or at least not care if they did) while trying to keep it secret, and a small few would gain satisfaction by openly discriminating against blacks? Would it be wise to tolerate the public racial slights caused by such open discrimination, even if they did not diminish the overall economic opportunity available to blacks? Would such a situation divert talented blacks into private action designed to stamp out discrimination, when an effective governmental antidiscrimination policy would free them to pursue more personally productive endeavors?

4.   In evaluating the data on black and white relative wages, note the importance of the claim advanced by Posner that employment discrimination laws have elevated black wages but have lowered overall employment, and thus have operated much like an increase in a minimum wage law. As Donohue and Heckman document, over the last thirty years, employment rates and labor force participation rates have indeed dropped more for blacks than for whites. Would Title VII be an attractive policy if it improved the lot of 90 percent of blacks but harmed the remaining, and most disadvantaged, 10 percent? Is it clear that Title VII has contributed to the declining rates of employment and labor force participation? There are many possible explanations for this phenomenon—higher social service spending on welfare and disability, increases in the minimum wage, the loss of manufacturing jobs, the beneficial increase in black postsecondary education, the growth of the

illegal drug trade—that have nothing to do with employment discrimination law.

For recent empirical evidence on this issue, see David Neumark and Wendy A. Stock, "The Effects of Race and Sex Discrimination Laws," NBER Working Paper No. W8215, April 2001, which concludes:

> Overall, we interpret the evidence as corroborating the general conclusion that race discrimination laws positively impacted the relative employment and earnings of blacks, although the evidence is less dramatic than that reported in other research, and there are some cases (in particular, earnings effects for black males) and periods for which we find little positive impact. We find some evidence that sex discrimination/equal pay laws boosted the relative earnings of black and white females. Finally, we find that sex discrimination/equal pay laws reduced the relative employment of both black women and white women.

5. Note that while workers are obviously immensely concerned with the availability of employment and the wages of such employment, they are also concerned with the conditions of employment. Do you think that Title VII has improved the conditions of employment for blacks? Was black welfare enhanced simply by virtue of the creation of a federal cause of action for such discriminatory misconduct? Did the law reduce the incidence of low-level and more serious forms of racial harassment? Each year, a relatively small, but in aggregate not trivial, sum of money is paid to blacks to resolve or avoid employment discrimination litigation. What bearing does this have in assessing the law's effectiveness?

The issue of whether Title VII has improved the conditions of employment for women, and what impact such improvement might have on female wages and employment, is discussed in Chapter 13 generally (particularly in the excerpt from Donohue).

6. For almost thirty years, the government contractor program has required major government contractors and their subcontractors to take affirmative action to ensure that they do not have gross underutilization of minority employees in any of their broad occupational categories. The genius of the program is that the public pays for any lost productivity or training costs that are needed to implement the affirmative action program, since the contractors pass the costs on to the government purchasers. In other words, the costs of the contract compliance program are designed to be borne by government—which makes sense given the nature of the moral debt owed to black Americans. This approach contrasts with one in which the government imposes burdens on private employers by requiring all firms to have affirmative action plans.

7. But does the affirmative action program work? Studies show that this pressure did benefit blacks, at least through 1980, when the Reagan Administration drastically reduced oversight of the program. Still, those interested in burying the program frequently misstate the results of the empirical research. For example, the *Wall Street Journal* recently reported "three separate studies of the federal contract compliance programs between 1966 and 1980 found that job growth for blacks at contractors forced to

comply with government-hiring guidelines was only .8% to 1.2% higher than at similar companies where such plans were voluntary." Robert Frank and Eleena de Lisser, "Research on Affirmative Action Finds Modest Gains for Blacks over 30 Years," *The Wall Street Journal* (February 21, 1995). This quote suggests a minute improvement over a fourteen-year period when in fact the gain is in the *annual* growth rate, which is quite substantial. For example, if one started out with 5 million blacks in the contract sector and 5 million blacks in the noncontractor sector, and the annual percentage growth in black employment were 2.82 percent in the contractor sector and only 2 percent in the noncontractor sector, then after fourteen years you would end up with 7.4 million blacks in the contract sector and 6.6 million blacks in the noncontractor sector—a difference of 800,000 jobs!

The Smith and Welch suggestion that black employment may have only shifted away from the noncontractor sector to the government contractor sector suggests the possible flaw in the program: the fluid nature of labor markets may have undermined the desired stimulative effect on overall black employment, if the law has only served to influence the location of black employment, without elevating overall black wages. This shuffling could occur if a modest increase in wages among the government contracting firms induces a large shift in employment to that sector—that is, if the intersectoral elasticity of supply of black labor is high. Nonetheless, even if blacks simply shifted their location of employment, the presumption is that they were induced to do so by the lure of higher wages. In other words, when enforced, the program seems to have benefited blacks to at least some degree.

John Bound and Richard Freeman have noted that some recent adverse trends in the economic well-being of black males correspond with slackening antidiscrimination and affirmative action pressure:

> Evidence that Equal Employment Opportunity and Affirmative Action help explain the huge improvements in relative earnings of the late 1960s–early 1970s ... implies by symmetry that weakened pressure would have the converse effect. The large decline in the relative earnings and downgrading of the occupational position of young black college men found in our data is what one would expect from firms no longer facing an affirmative action gun, since young college men were the major beneficiaries of the previous decades' pressures.

Bound and Freeman, "What Went Wrong? The Erosion of Relative Earnings and Employment among Young Black Men in the 1980s," 107 *Quarterly Journal of Economics* 201, 229 (1992).

Bound and Freeman also note how young blacks were hit particularly hard over the last two decades by the decline in union manufacturing jobs— the very jobs that so much time and litigation effort on the part of the EEOC and NAACP was devoted to opening up to blacks, as documented in the Blumrosen selection in Chapter 4, section 4.1.

8. Thus far we have spoken only of benefits; we must also inquire about costs of the contract compliance program. Here again, the opponents of affirmative action are prone to enormous exaggeration. Figures of $100

billion or more are trumpeted as the *annual* productivity and compliance costs associated with advancing black workers. But a cost of this magnitude would leap out in an empirical assessment, and Jonathan Leonard has concluded that "direct tests of the impact of affirmative action on productivity find no significant evidence of a productivity decline." Leonard, "The Impact of Affirmative Action Regulation and Equal Employment Law on Black Employment," 4 *Journal of Economic Perspectives* 47, 61 (1990). Admittedly, there are pecuniary costs, but they are likely to be in the neighborhood of $5 billion to $10 billion, only a fraction of what the critics assert. Donohue, "Advocacy versus Analysis in Assessing Employment Discrimination Law," 44 *Stanford Law Review* 1583 (1992).

Other more subtle costs may exist. Does the program stigmatize blacks? Does a continuing program of this type undermine worker initiative and responsibility by encouraging blacks to coast and whites to complain about and justify their own failures? O'Neill and O'Neill speculate that "its main impact may have been to generate divisiveness and ill will." O'Neill and O'Neill, "Affirmative Action in the Labor Market," 523 *Annals of the American Academy of Political and Social Science* 88, 103 (1992). These are difficult questions that go to the issue of remedy. Linda Krieger examines a number of empirical studies that address these questions. Krieger, "Civil Rights Perestroika: Intergroup Relations after Affirmative Action," 86 *California Law Review* 1251 (1998). Krieger concludes that the evidence concerning the degree to which beneficiaries of affirmative action suffer from feelings of stigma is complex and contradictory. Conversely, Krieger finds that the evidence suggests that affirmative action reinforces negative stereotypes, citing a substantial body of research that documents how affirmative action negatively affects people's evaluations of the beneficiaries' qualifications. Next, on the issue of whether affirmative action undermines the beneficiaries' work motivation and commitment, Krieger's concludes that the existing research data shows that results are inconclusive at best. Finally, as to whether affirmative action generates racial divisiveness and hostility, Krieger contends that in some contexts (for example, where intergroup competition is already present), affirmative action may exacerbate intergroup tensions. See Chapter 3, section 3.2, for further discussion on affirmative action.

9. According to Michael Selmi, the failure of civil rights laws, such as Title VII, to bring about more effective social changes is not due to any inherent weaknesses in the legislation, but the government's refusal to effectively enforce the law. Based on an analysis of EEOC discrimination cases in the 1990s, Selmi finds that the government generally chose to litigate small and routine claims while avoiding substantial class action cases. Selmi contends that government attorneys are reluctant to pursue controversial and hard to win cases and proposes making civil rights cases more lucrative in order to attract private attorneys. Selmi, "Public vs. Private Enforcement of Civil Rights: The Case of Housing and Employment," 45 *University of California Los Angeles Law Review* 1401 (1998). Will such a change encourage more frivolous litigation? If so, is a more appropriate remedy to change the incentive structure of government lawyers?

9

The Responses of Litigants and Employers to Antidiscrimination Law

Employment discrimination law creates a complex regulatory regime that is designed both to prevent employers from using certain traits—such as race, sex, age, disability, and religion—in making their employment decisions and to aid certain traditionally disadvantaged groups in their pursuit of employment opportunities. Federal court litigation has been one of the major tools to enforce the rights created under federal employment discrimination law, and the pattern of federal litigation is shaped by the conduct and decisions of Congress, courts, employers, and employees—and the economic and social forces that act upon them. Interestingly, as we saw in Chapter 8, federal employment discrimination law began having an impact on the economic welfare of blacks almost immediately, which is perhaps surprising given how little federal litigation was brought in the early days of the statute. For example, in 1970, five years after effective date of Title VII, fewer than 350 employment discrimination cases were filed in federal court. By 1983, the number reached 9000. John Donohue and Peter Siegelman try to explain this explosive growth, which occurred over a period in which by most accounts discrimination was declining, or at least not rising significantly.

Donohue and Siegelman examine the role of various legal changes in contributing to the rapid growth in federal employment discrimination litigation, and also show that this litigation is heavily influenced by the business cycle, with periods of high unemployment causing major increases in federal court case filings. Not only has the volume of cases grown enormously, but the nature of the litigation has shifted sharply from a regime dominated by class action lawsuits attacking the failure to hire protected workers to one in which the large majority of cases are brought by single plaintiffs claiming they were discharged because of their race, sex, or age. Somewhat paradoxically, Donohue and Siegelman suggest that this transformation has occurred in part because of the success of Title VII, but that the success of the law is now threatened to some degree by the transformation.

While Donohue and Siegelman analyze the nature of employment discrimination litigation and its growth and changing composition, the authors of the other two selections in this chapter focus on the behavior of the potential litigants. Kristin Bumiller examines a small number of individuals who claimed to have experienced employment discrimination, and probes their frequent decision not to pursue litigation. In general, she shares the judgment of many on the right that Title VII is a generally wasteful and ineffective statute that tends to create victims out of its intended beneficiaries. Bumiller, however, reaches this conclusion from a critique from the left that sees victim-initiated litigation as an ineffectual weapon against the systematic processes of discrimination, and one that is likely to divert effort from more promising politically generated structural changes.

Frank Dobbin, John Sutton, John Meyer, and Richard Scott explore how the passage of employment discrimination laws has influenced the behavior of employers. The existence of this body of law means that employers must develop strategies for selecting a productive labor force that are reasonably cost effective and that reduce any potential civil liability. Blatantly racist and sexist policies tended to disappear rather quickly under the threat of large damage awards. Racial epithets have largely been purged from the managerial lexicon at the time of adverse personnel decisions. But the recruitment and selection of workers is a complex task that is carried out through the implementation of an array of personnel practices, and the invocation not to consider race or sex in making employment decisions does not resolve many questions about how a firm's workforce should be selected. Until a set of judicial precedents developed to inform and guide employer decisions, there was considerable uncertainty about the best set of procedures for avoiding employment discrimination litigation.

For example, in Chapter 4, section 4.2, we alluded to the conflicting pressures on employers with regard to the use of employment tests. Should employers resort to rigorous, objective testing to be sure that their employment decisions are not based on race, sex, religion, or other prohibited characteristics? Or would reliance on testing create greater risks of liability for employers? Firms were also uncertain whether the adoption of racial quotas—as in the voluntary consent decrees challenged in *United Steelworkers v. Weber,* 443 U.S. 193 (1979)—would insulate employers from liability or guarantee reverse-discrimination lawsuits. As Dobbin, Sutton, Meyer, and Scott demonstrate in this chapter, employers and personnel professionals struggled over many such questions, and over time certain practices were either rewarded or discouraged by the judiciary and the market. On the whole, they find that antidiscrimination law has contributed to the formalization and bureaucratization of personnel decision making. As a result, more resources are spent on the process of employee selection, but in consequence, both the quality of the workers relative to the demands of the particular job and the fairness with which applicants and employees are treated tend to be higher than they would otherwise be.

9.1   The Growth and Composition of Litigation

The Changing Nature of Employment Discrimination Litigation*

JOHN J. DONOHUE III AND PETER SIEGELMAN

The Growth in Volume of Employment Discrimination Cases

Distinguishing Long-Term Trends from Cyclical Fluctuations

As Figure 9.1 (on page 251) illustrates, the volume of employment discrimination litigation has grown substantially over the last twenty years—from less than 350 cases filed per year in FY 1970 to a peak of about 9,000 in FY 1983. Figure 9.2 (on page 252) compares the pattern of employment discrimination filings with all other federal civil litigation and reveals two phenomena: First, employment discrimination case filings have grown far faster than the general federal civil caseload, which rose by only about 125 percent between FY 1970 and FY 1989, as compared with the 2166 percent growth in the employment discrimination caseload; and second, the variation around the general upward trend is far greater for employment discrimination cases than for the general civil caseload. In other words, the volume of employment discrimination cases filed has grown much more rapidly than the overall civil caseload, but this growth has also been much more erratic, with periods of substantial decline and spurts of exceptional growth.

· · ·

The equation in Table 9.1 presents a simple way of quantifying this distinction by regressing the quarterly volume of employment discrimination cases filed in federal district courts on a time trend (TIME and TIME^2) and lagged values of the unemployment rate (UNEM$_{-1}$ and UNEM$_{-2}$).

The estimated coefficient on the time trend is meant to capture the average growth in the volume of cases while holding the state of the economy constant; the coefficient on the unemployment rate shows how the volume of cases responds to ups and downs in economic activity. Table 9.1 reports the results from our regression.

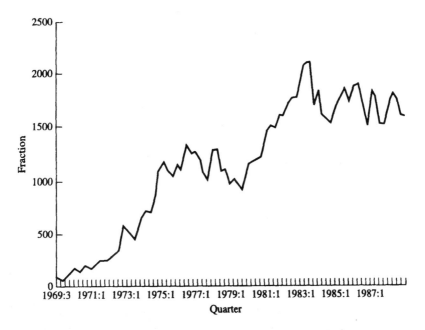

Figure 9.1. Number of Employment Discrimination Suits Filed in Federal District Court

The coefficients on the TIME and TIME^2 variables suggest that employment discrimination cases increase at an underlying trend rate of 344 cases per year. It must be emphasized that the time trend only measures any persistent upward (or downward) movement in the number of cases filed, and does not identify the cause of the observed trend. The significant coefficients on the lagged unemployment rates reveal that a decrease of one percentage point in the unemployment rate would cause the number of case filings to fall by roughly 103 in the next quarter and by 48 in the following quarter. In other words, good economic conditions will lead to fewer employment discrimination lawsuits, presumably because the greater availability of alternative employment serves as an attractive alternative to litigation....

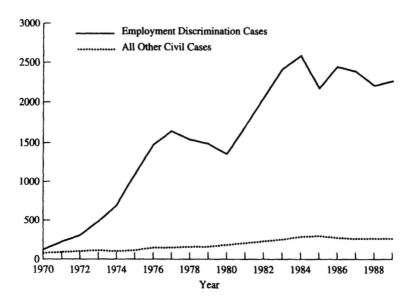

Figure 9.2. Employment Discrimination and Other Civil Suits Filed in Federal District
Court, Index Numbers, 1970 = 100

The explanatory power of the regression, as measured by its R^2 coefficient, is quite high, even for a time-series estimate: 96 percent of the variance in the number of suits filed is explained by the time trend and the lagged unemployment rates. The relatively sparse model of Table 9.1 therefore serves the useful functions of both approximating the size of the underlying growth rate in the number of employment discrimination cases and explaining the variation around this upward trend.

Table 9.1 Maximum Likelihood Estimates of Quarterly Volume of Employment Discrimination Cases (Corrected for Autocorrelated Disturbances)

$$\text{CASES} = -692.5 + 28.7\,(\text{TIME}) -0.09\,(\text{TIME}^2) + 102.9\,(\text{UNEM}_{-1}) + 48.3\,(\text{UNEM}_{-2})$$
$$\phantom{\text{CASES} = } (-5.63) \quad (4.32) \qquad (-1.14) \qquad\quad (5.58) \qquad\qquad (6.64)$$

Adjusted R^2 = 0.96

T-statistics are in parentheses.
Number of observations = 80.

Decomposing the Long–Term Trend Growth in Employment Discrimination Litigation

Thus far we have demonstrated the existence of a positive time trend in the volume of litigation and briefly discussed why the number of employment discrimination cases bounces around this long-term trend. But we have not yet offered any explanation for the existence of the trend itself. This section attempts to quantify the importance of several factors that are likely to have played a role in the growth of employment discrimination litigation. Our results are summarized in Table 9.2 and are discussed at greater length below.

. . .

In Table 9.2 we draw a distinction between "legal or policy" and "economic or demographic" sources of growth in the employment discrimination caseload. Such a distinction is necessarily somewhat artificial. Nevertheless, we make it in order to highlight a fundamental difference between the sources of growth in litigation. Litigation prompted by new laws, changes in judicial interpretation of statutes, or governmental decisions to bring suit is subject to control by policy makers. In contrast, litigation arising from exogenous events such as changes in the size of the labor force or a rise in the unemployment rate is largely beyond the government's scope of influence.

In brief, Table 9.2 suggests that the single most important factor explaining the growth in the employment discrimination caseload over the period from FY 1970–1989 is the increase in the unemployment rate. This factor explains roughly 20 percent of the growth in litigation. The increase in the protected work force generated by both the Age Discrimination in Employment Act (ADEA) and the 1972 Title VII amendments account for about another 20 percent of the growth in litigation between FY 1970 and 1989. Other doctrinal developments, and the direct role of the federal government, are noticeably less important factors. Moreover, even given the likelihood of double counting, which would inflate the "explained" portion of the increase, we are still left with a substantial unexplained residual—roughly one-third of the caseload growth is unaccounted for by the factors set forth in Table 9.2.

Table 9.2   Sources of Growth in the Volume of Federal Employment Civil Rights Cases, 1970–1989

		Cases	% of Line 3
1.	Number of Employment Civil Rights Cases, 1989	7613	
2.	*Less* Number of Cases, 1970	336	
3.	*Equals* Total Case Increase to be Explained	7277	
		(2166%)	
4.	*Less* Increase in Volume of Cases Due to Economic or Demographic Factors	2121	
	Of which, increase due to effects of:		
5.	Growth in unemployment	1416	19.5
6.	Demographic increase in "protected" work force	544	7.5
7.	Replacement of older by younger cohorts	161	2.2
8.	*Less* Increase in Volume of Cases Due to Legal or Policy Changes:	2700	
	Of which, increase due to effects of:		
9.	Cases brought by U.S. Government as plaintiff	383	5.3
10.	Cases brought under ADEA	829	11.4
11.	Cases challenging discrimination on basis of pregnancy, reverse discrimination, or under §1981	703	9.7
12.	Cases brought under *Griggs vs. Duke Power* (disparate impact theories)	101	1.4
13.	Cases due to 1972 changes in Title VII coverage	684	9.4
14.	"Explained" Increase (line 4 + line 8)	4822	66.3
15.	*Equals* "Unexplained" Increase (line 3 – line 14)	2455	33.7

Growth Attributable to "Economic" or "Social" Factors

The rise in unemployment. We have already noted the effect of unemployment on the cyclical variation in the number of suits. But unemployment has also contributed to the long-run upward trend in the volume of cases. Between 1969 and 1989, there has been roughly a 2.31 percentage point increase in the unemployment rate. [We estimate] the effect of this long-term rise in unemployment on the number of employment discrimination cases filed [in 1989 to be] ... 1416 extra cases for the final year of our data.

"Demographic" growth in the protected work force. The population of workers eligible to sue under federal employment discrimination statues has been rising throughout the period in question. Our Table 9.2 decomposition of the factors generating the growth in employment discrimination accounts for the effects of demographic/economic forces expanding the protected work force (line 6) separately from policy-induced expansions (line 13). Most of the growth in the eligible population since 1973 arises from demographic or economic factors—population growth as a whole and the increased participation of women in the labor force. Legislative decisions (the ADEA and changes in Title VII coverage) also expanded the population of workers protected by civil rights legislation, especially in the period between 1966 and 1973. The effect of these legislative actions are estimated in the following section.

As is apparent from Figure 9.3, the steady increase in both the female labor force and the total work force clearly accounts for most of the rise in the protected work force after 1973. The effects of the 1972 Title VII amendments (which took effect in 1973) also appear. Overall, the protected population rose from 45.84 million in 1969 to 89.70 million in 1989, an increase of 95.7 percent (roughly 3.4 percent per year). However, 15.45 million (one-third) of this growth in population arises from the 1972 Amendments. Thus, the population increase attributable to demographic factors is 28.41 million, or 62 percent. This implies that demographic growth in the population of protected workers contributed about 544 suits to the volume of employment discrimination litigation.

The cohort effect.... To raise a bona fide claim of employment discrimination, a worker must first perceive that discrimination has occurred. Clearly, the ability to detect violations of one's rights—and, once detected, to categorize such violations as legally actionable—depends not only on the grossness of the violation but also on one's education, legal sophistication, and general perceptions of one's rights. Younger women and minorities may experience less wage discrimination (measured as the difference between marginal product and actual wages) than their older counterparts. Yet their higher levels of education and greater expectations of equal treatment make them more able and willing to categorize their experiences as discriminatory.

We calculate that the replacement of older by younger workers between 1969 and 1989 increased the volume of employment discrimination suits by about 161 suits.

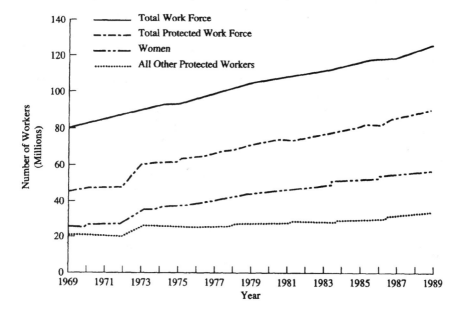

Figure 9.3. Protected Population Under Federal Antidiscrimination Legislation

. . .

Growth Attributable to "Legal" or "Policy" Changes

In the previous section we discussed some social or economic forces that contributed to the growth of the employment discrimination caseload. This section focuses on the caseload growth induced by government action—administrative, legislative, and judicial.

U.S. Government cases. We distinguish cases brought by the U.S. Government as plaintiff (most of which the Equal Employment Opportunity Commission (EEOC) files) from those brought by private citizens, since different factors usually motivate the two kinds of litigation.

The increase in government-plaintiff litigation was derived in a straightforward fashion by simply taking the difference between the volume of government-plaintiff suits in FY 1970 (140) and FY 1989 (523)—yielding an increase of 383 suits. This figure represents only 5.3 percent of the 7277 additional cases in 1989.

. . .

Innovations in selected legal doctrines. We next seek to derive estimates for the increases in cases filed due to: (1) the enactment of the ADEA and the Congressional prohibition of differential treatment on the basis of pregnancy; and (2) judicial decisions expanding the reach of Section 1981, permitting reverse discrimination cases, and creating the disparate impact standard. The following method was used to estimate lines 10 through 12 of Table 9.2: For each of the legal innovations, we assumed that no cases were brought under that theory prior to FY 1970, since the vast bulk of the cases generated by all the legal innovations came during the 1970s. Using data from the American Bar Foundation's (ABF) Survey of Employment Civil Rights Litigation, we calculated the proportion of all cases at the end of our sample period that stated a claim based on the legal innovation. Applying this share to the total volume of cases filed in 1989 produces the estimate of the effect of the legal change. Since by assumption no such claims were brought until 1970, the increase in litigation attributable to the legal innovation is the entire estimated volume of suits.

Consider first the Age Discrimination in Employment Act (ADEA). The Act took effect in 1968, and, by the end of the ABF sample period, 15.1 percent of the Employment Civil Rights cases were based on age discrimination. Thus, we estimate that the ADEA increased litigation by 829 additional cases filed in 1989.

. . .

A number of other important innovations in the law of employment discrimination also contributed to the caseload growth over the last two decades. In 1975 and 1976, the Supreme Court expanded Section 1981's prohibition of discrimination against racial minorities in the "making and enforcement of contracts" to provide damages to those who proved employment discrimination. Also in 1976, the Supreme Court first recognized a cause of action for reverse discrimination, and in 1978, Congress authorized a cause of action for women who were treated discriminatorily due to pregnancy. Using the same technique described to estimate the effects of the ADEA, we found that together, these new doctrines generated an increase in litigation of 703 suits.

Table 9.3   Volume of Employment Civil Rights Cases
Raising a §1981 Claim

	1972–1976	1977–1981	1982–1987
Number of Cases that:			
1. Raised a §1981 Claim	112	151	147
2. Raised only a §1981 Claim	1	9	9
3. Line 1 as a Percent of All Employment Discrimination Claims	46.5	34.4	27.0

In evaluating the contribution of Section 1981, we assume that any case that raised a Title VII claim in addition to the Section 1981 count would have been brought even if the Section 1981 remedy were unavailable. Table 9.3 shows that the number of employment discrimination cases raising only a Section 1981 claim is quite small. A less restrictive assumption would enhance the significance of the contribution of Section 1981 to the employment discrimination caseload growth. Somewhat surprisingly, Table 9.3 demonstrates that the percentage of cases that raised a Section 1981 claim (either alone or in conjunction with a Title VII claim) diminished after the 1975 and 1976 expansions by the Court.

The disparate impact definition of discrimination, first recognized by the Supreme Court in the landmark case of *Griggs v. Duke Power Co.*, is generally considered to be the most important innovation in the legal doctrine defining employment discrimination. Indeed, one commentator has recently suggested that "[Title VII originally] banned what civil-rights lawyers call 'disparate treatment'; by now, *most litigation is instead about 'disparate impact'*." Yet whatever its effects on labor market performance by firms and workers, it appears to have had only an extremely modest influence on the volume of litigation. We estimate that the disparate impact doctrine generated only 101 additional cases in 1989.

The 1972 amendments to Title VII. Title VII was amended in 1972. Besides expanding the EEOC's enforcement powers, the major impact of the amendment was to increase the population covered by Title VII to include those working in firms with 15 to 25 employees, employees of state and local governments, and employees of educational institutions, all of whom had formerly been outside of Title VII's protection. We estimate that these changes created an additional 684 cases in 1989.

. . .

Findings

Despite the broad brush with which Table 9.2 is painted, it does reveal some important facts about the growth in employment discrimination. Perhaps the most important conclusion we draw from our analysis of the growth in the volume of employment discrimination litigation is that a healthy economy is a strong ally of those whom the antidiscrimination laws are designed to protect. When unemployment rates are low and labor markets are tight, workers probably encounter less discrimination and are certainly better positioned to seek remedies outside the litigation process for any discrimination they do encounter. The link between macroeconomic performance and the number of employment discrimination filings is therefore a strong one. For example, the results in Table 9.1 imply that if the unemployment rate had remained at its 1969 low of 3.9 percent, 33,600 (32.5 percent) fewer employment discrimination cases would have been filed in federal courts and 537,600 fewer charges would have been filed with the EEOC between 1969 and 1989. The increase in the unemployment rate has had a major effect on the volume of litigation, by itself explaining 19.5 percent of the growth in cases since 1969. Other exogenous economic factors seem less significant in explaining the rising caseload.

Second, the ADEA and the 1972 Title VII Amendments have clearly had an important influence on the volume of litigation. Without the expansion of protection offered by these laws, roughly 20 percent less litigation would have occurred in 1989. In contrast, relatively little growth in litigation arises from changes in judicial doctrines. This finding contradicts those who have argued that changes in legal doctrine can explain almost all growth in employment litigation.

Finally, we conclude from our analysis that the EEOC has played an essentially passive role in the growth of employment discrimination suits. First, it has brought relatively few cases. Second, it seems not to have been responsible for the growth in private litigation. . . . [T]he ratio of EEOC cases to federal district court cases has remained fairly constant during the period from 1975 to 1986. If roughly the same proportion of EEOC charges turns into federal court complaints each year, then the EEOC's processing of such charges cannot be responsible for the growth in litigation. Rather, it makes more sense to think of the Commission as a screening device that has consistently filtered out about 95 percent of the charges filed with it. This view is substantiated by the fact that the composition of charges heard by the EEOC is virtually identical to the makeup of cases filed in federal court: Both sets of cases contain the same proportion of hiring and firing disputes, race versus sex discrimination claims, and so on.

Even given the potential double-counting problems discussed earlier, roughly one-third of the growth in litigation is not attributable to any of the factors analyzed in Table 9.2. This implies considerable work is still needed to explain the growth in the caseload, a topic to which we now turn.

Explaining the Residual

This section begins by confronting several popular explanations for the growth in employment discrimination litigation: first, an actual increase in discrimination; second, promotion of litigation by lawyers; and third, changes in the propensity to sue. We conclude that none of these explanations is supported by the evidence. We then offer two explanations that are consistent with increasing litigation in an era of declining discrimination. The movement of minorities and women into better and more integrated jobs may explain some of the residual growth not accounted for in the analysis underlying Table 9.2. We demonstrate a positive relationship between a worker's wage and her propensity to sue for employment discrimination. This relationship arises because the benefits of a successful suit are proportional to the worker's wage, while the costs of bringing suit contain an important fixed element. In addition, we argue that integrated work forces are more likely to produce litigation because minorities or women who work by themselves have no benchmarks (whites or males) against whom they can measure their treatment and determine whether or not it is discriminatory.

Although neither of these effects can be tested or measured directly, we do produce evidence that they are consonant with the observed progress of minorities and women into better and more integrated jobs.

Dismissing Some Traditional Explanations for the Growing Volume of Litigation

Growth in discrimination. Although the rising volume of employment discrimination litigation could conceivably be explained by increasing levels of race and sex discrimination, the social science and survey literature suggests that, by most measures of attitudes towards women and minorities in the work place, prejudice has been declining for decades. Two 1985 surveys on racial attitudes concluded that racist beliefs have been steadily declining over the past forty years. A number of surveys have also suggested that inhospitable attitudes toward women in the work place have softened over the last twenty years. While these studies document changes in articulated beliefs and external conduct, they cannot, of course, answer the important question whether this trend represents true behavioral change or merely increased hypocrisy.

Additional evidence from fair housing audits—in which teams of black and white "testers" attempt to buy houses in certain neighborhoods—indicates that housing discrimination against blacks has followed a pattern of decline similar to that reflected in the attitudinal surveys. Finally, there is indirect evidence that the amount of discrimination in labor markets—as measured by earnings regression equations and the trends in the black-white and male-female earnings ratios—has decreased since 1970, particularly for blacks in the South. In sum, while the evidence is scattered and of varying quality, it does suggest that discrimination has almost certainly not increased over the period from 1969–1989.

Litigation promoted by lawyers. Another popular explanation for the increase in all federal civil litigation is that the increasing supply of lawyers spawns more litigation. But the percentage growth in the number of attorneys is far smaller than the percentage growth in the employment discrimination caseload. Therefore, if changes in the legal profession have contributed to the caseload growth it must be due to increased efficiency of law firms in processing complaints. Lawyer advertising may alert potential litigants to the possibility of lawsuits as well as reduce their search costs in finding representation. Legal clinics and prepaid legal services also may have increased the probability of suing about an unfavorable experience in the labor market. On the other hand, the increase in the number of lawyers and clinics handling employment discrimination could simply represent a response to an independent increase in litigant demand.

Changes in propensity to sue. One readily accepted explanation for the increase in litigation is that workers are simply more willing to sue today than in the past. The literature on the so-called litigation explosion suggests that Americans have generally become more litigious over the past twenty years, and one might imagine that this phenomenon is at work in the area of employment discrimination. In our view, this argument ... fails to consider the difference in magnitude between the growth in employment discrimination litigation and that of other federal civil suits. Since the size of the growth in the employment discrimination caseload is vastly greater, it would appear to represent a qualitatively different phenomenon.

Despite [this] reservation, the argument that there has been an increase in propensity to sue by potential employment discrimination plaintiffs merits serious consideration. A recent survey conducted for the *National Law Journal*, for instance, found an apparent increase in the likelihood that an individual will sue if he or she experiences employment discrimination. We evaluate some of the available data to determine whether such an increase constitutes a plausible explanation for the observed increase in litigation.

The Curran report on the legal needs of the American public, based on interviews conducted in March 1974, showed that while perceived instances of job discrimination were not uncommon, the number of individuals perceiving the problem who then consulted a lawyer was trivial compared with other types of common legal problems. Figure 9.4, which is reprinted from the Curran report, demonstrates that of twenty-nine commonly encountered legal problems, the one least likely to lead to consultation with an attorney was job discrimination: Only 1 percent of those experiencing this problem consulted a lawyer upon the most recent occurrence. People overlook many perceived instances of discrimination when they retain their jobs, because the costs of suing a present employer can be high. Nonetheless, the Curran report shows that all growth in the federal employment discrimination caseload since March 1974 could be explained if the willingness to pursue legal remedies for perceived employment discrimination had risen to 2.33 percent, one-third the level of the next lowest item on the list—problems with municipal services (7 percent).

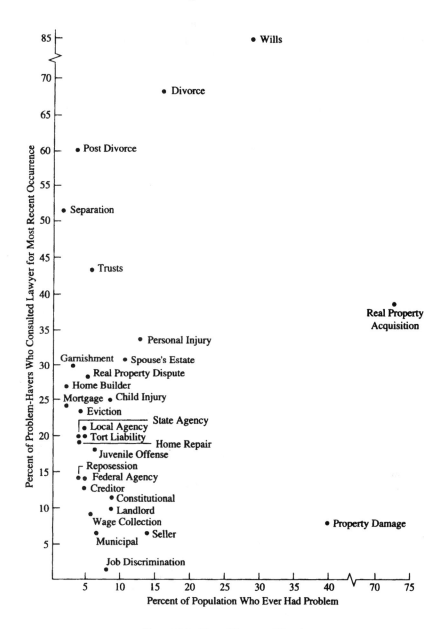

Figure 9.4. Use of Lawyers' Services

Two Explanations for the Residual Increases in Litigation

The "better jobs" effect. The propensity of a rejected worker to sue will typically be a positive function of the wage in the job from which she is rejected. To see why, take the case of a fired employee who is considering filing suit under Title VII. If she wins, damages under Title VII are limited to backpay for the time she was unemployed. Thus, we can approximate the award to a prevailing plaintiff by the product of her wage in her former job and the duration of her unemployment. The costs of bringing suit, by contrast, are generally fixed. Now define

w = weekly wage

D = duration of unemployment

p = probability of plaintiff victory if there is a suit

C_p = plaintiff's cost of bringing the suit.

A risk-neutral potential plaintiff who maximizes expected utility will bring suit only if the expected benefits exceed the expected costs. Thus, under Title VII rules in which prevailing plaintiffs receive their costs from defendants (but not vice versa, unless the suit is found to be frivolous), the rule for bringing suit translates to

$$pwD > (1 - p) \times C_p.$$

Notice that the left side of the equation is a function of the wage rate, but the right side is not. Holding other things (including p and D) constant, an increase in the wage rate will increase the expected benefits of litigation, while leaving the expected costs unchanged, thereby encouraging potential plaintiffs to sue. We can rearrange the equation to get an expression for the critical value of the wage rate, w^*, below which rejected workers will not sue

$$w^* = (1 - p) \times C_p/pD.$$

As an example, consider a worker who is fired from her minimum-wage job because of discrimination by her employer. Presumably, w is less than w^* for such a worker. If she sues and wins, she stands to collect a backpay award (at minimum wage) for the period between her firing and her next job. Since her wage is low and since minimum-wage jobs are relatively easy to find, she is unlikely to be unemployed for very long. Her total award, wD, will probably be small. If she loses, moreover, she will have to pay costs of C_p, which might easily exceed her expected gains if she wins. In sum, the better paying the job, the more likely the job-holder or applicant is to sue if rejected.

The better-jobs effect can explain an increase in employment discrimination suits, despite a constant or falling level of discrimination. As the number of "protected" workers in (or applying for) jobs that pay more than w^* increases, with a constant amount of discrimination, more suits will be filed, since more workers now have "good" jobs that are worth suing for. Even if discrimination is decreasing, the number of suits can nevertheless rise if a higher proportion of the discriminated-against workers find it worthwhile to sue.

If we assign plausible values for p, D, and C, in the critical value wage rate equation of .15, 12.5 weeks, and $1,000, the value of w^* is about $450 per week. Any worker earning more than this amount should find it worthwhile to sue (given the other parameter values). If the plaintiff's probability of recovery rises to .2, w^* drops to $320. About 22 percent of all full-time wage and salary workers earned more than $450 per week in 1986; slightly more than 60 percent of such workers earned more than $320 per week. Clearly, these values are not absolute thresholds—some potential plaintiffs will have a higher likelihood of victory if they sue; some may mistakenly conclude that their odds of winning are greater than they actually are; and some plaintiffs will experience longer unemployment durations, or have lower legal costs. In general, however, the better-jobs effect predicts that higher-wage workers will be over-represented among plaintiffs.

Although it is difficult to test this theory directly, the ABF survey provides some evidence. Table 9.4, which compares the occupational distribution of the general labor force with that of employment discrimination plaintiffs, shows that nonwhite plaintiffs in the sample were far more likely to be managerial/professional workers or technical/sales workers than nonwhite workers nationally. Conversely, the relatively low-paid service and agricultural workers were substantially under-represented in the sample of nonwhite employment discrimination plaintiffs.

Table 9.4 Occupational Distribution of Nonwhite Labor Force and Nonwhite Plaintiffs in the ABFs Survey of Employment Discrimination Litigation, 1972–1987 (Column percent in parentheses)

Occupation	Nonwhite Labor Force	Nonwhite Employment Discrimination
Managerial/Professional	6341	138
	(15.9)	(24.0)
Technical, Sales	8590	139
	(21.5)	(24.1)
Service	9153	91
	(23.0)	(15.8)
Agriculture	934	3
	(2.3)	(0.5)
Precision Production	3693	52
	(9.3)	(9.0)
Operator, Laborer	11,157	153
	(28.0)	(26.6)
Total	39,868	576
	(100.0)	(100.0)

The better-jobs effect thus attributes the rise in discrimination litigation to the increasing numbers of racial minorities and women in (or applying for) jobs paying more than the "threshold" wage necessary to bring suit. The threshold itself need not be constant over time, moreover. As the equation demonstrates, the threshold wage is a negative function of the plaintiff win rate (p) and the duration of unemployment (D). For example, the average duration of unemployment has risen substantially over the last twenty years, thereby depressing the threshold wage. The lower threshold wage increases the number of employees who earn more than the threshold wage, and therefore increases the number of workers who find it in their interests to sue if they perceive discrimination in hiring or firing.

Some sense of the increasing access to good jobs enjoyed by minorities and women is provided in Table 9.5, [which] reveals that from 1970 through 1980 the number of nonwhite managerial and professional workers rose 144 percent, and the number of female managerial and professional workers rose by 71 percent. The dramatic progress of female workers continued throughout the 1980s, although that of minorities did not.

· · ·

The "integration" effect. Job upgrading not only increases the incentives for bringing an employment discrimination suit, but it also significantly affects the ability of workers to detect discrimination in the first place. White males have historically held better-paying jobs than both minorities and women. But as

Table 9.5 Number of Female and Nonwhite "Managerial, Professional, and Technical" Workers, Selected Years, 1960–1988 (In Thousands)

Year	Nonwhites	Women	All M, P & T Workers
1960	485	3,587	12,825
1970	802	5,721	18,024
	(65.36%)	(59.49%)	(40.54%)
1980	1,958	9,767	26,532
	(144.14%)	(70.72%)	(47.2%)
1988	2,112	14,735	32,711
	(7.87%)	(50.87%)	(23.29%)
Change since 1970	163.4%	157.9%	81.4%

Numbers in parentheses are percent changes over preceding period.

women [and minorities] are more likely to be in occupations that contain [white] men, a larger number of them [women and minorities] will . . . have a readily accessible [white] male against whom they can measure their labor market success, particularly in dimensions not measured in [data on wage differences]. Thus they will have more nonstatistical evidence of discrimination without necessarily being more discriminated against according to the standard statistical measures.

Both the legal and the common sense definitions of discrimination are relative: Discrimination occurs when blacks are treated differently from whites, or women differently from men. Without reference groups against which blacks or women can judge their own treatment by employers, discrimination is more difficult both to detect and to prove.

Our review of a number of employment discrimination cases reveals a common fact pattern: A worker is fired as part of a reduction in force or because of some alleged individual misconduct such as tardiness. The worker then alleges that workers of the opposite race or gender were either less productive or even more guilty of the alleged offense but were not fired. If the firm had been completely segregated, this comparative evidence of discrimination would not have been available. Integrating the work force by race and gender, then, is likely to produce more evidence and allegations of discrimination, even if the incidence of discrimination itself is falling. Due to the increased awareness of relative mistreatment, discrimination in an integrated firm may be more personally harmful than general discrimination against an entire group in a segregated firm.

. . .

Conclusion. In conclusion, the better-jobs and integration effects have an ironic aspect: The attainment of better and more integrated jobs for minorities is clearly a major goal of antidiscrimination laws, but society's very success in meeting this goal has contributed to a sizable increase in employment discrimination lawsuits. Improvements in the workplace have spawned strife in the courtroom.

But one might challenge our observations as reversing cause and effect: Rather than the increased access of minorities and women causing an increase in Title VII lawsuits, perhaps it is the increased litigation that has catalyzed employment gains for minorities and women. While Title VII did initially open many areas to minorities that previously had been foreclosed, the nature of Title VII litigation has shifted dramatically over time, indicating that the subsequent explosion in Title VII cases is caused by and not the cause of improved labor market experience.

The Shift in the Nature of Employment Discrimination Litigation

Assuming that concrete improvements have occurred, one might expect to see a significant shift in the nature of employment discrimination cases as minorities and women no longer need to complain about blanket exclusions from good jobs—that battle has, by now, largely been won—but now complain more commonly of being fired from these better jobs. Indeed, the evidence suggests that just such a shift has occurred. Figure 9.5 charts the number of hiring and termination charges brought before the EEOC. The figure shows a dramatic divergence in the pattern of hiring and termination charges. Hiring charges outnumbered termination charges by 50 percent in 1966, but by 1985, the ratio had reversed by more than 6 to 1. The ABF survey results illustrated in Figure 9.6 confirm the EEOC data: 19 percent of suits alleged discrimination in hiring, while 59 percent alleged discrimination in discharge. Moreover, the pattern of allegations over time is consistent with that observed in the EEOC data. The volume of hiring and termination charges was roughly similar in the early years but diverged sharply by 1986.

What accounts for this dramatic change in the composition of litigation? No divergence in the legal standards for proving discrimination in hiring as opposed to firing cases occurred during this period. Nor were there any differences in the calculation of damages for the two kinds of discrimination.

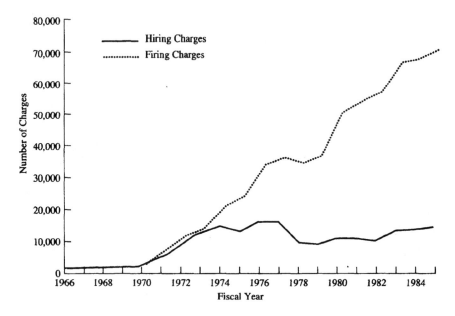

Figure 9.5. Hiring and Termination Allegations in Complaints Filed with the EEOC Against
Private Employers

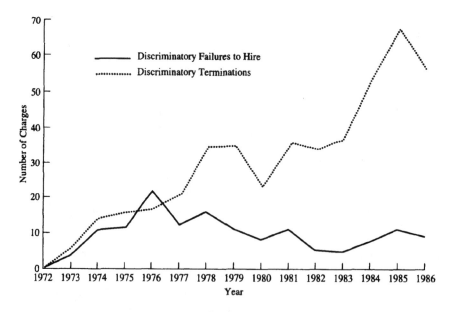

Figure 9.6. Bases of Employment Discrimination Complaints in the ABF Survey

. . .

The Decline of the Class Action Lawsuit

Figure 9.7 demonstrates another important change in the nature of employment discrimination litigation. The class action lawsuit, once a mainstay in the effort to enforce civil rights in the workplace, has virtually vanished from the scene. Only 51 requests for class certification in employment discrimination cases were filed during FY 1989, down nearly 96 percent from a peak of 1106 in FY 1975.

Figure 9.7. Class Actions Requested, Certified, and Denied in Federal Employment Civil Rights Cases

While changes in legal rules have been responsible for only about 30 percent of the total increase in employment discrimination litigation, they probably explain a far greater proportion of the decline in class actions. Evidence comes from both the timing and the magnitude of the decline. If a fall in hiring discrimination were responsible for the drop in class action requests, the drop would have occurred earlier and more gradually than Figure 9.7 indicates. One possibility is that the pattern is an artifact of the Administrative Office's coding scheme, although extensive discussions with those involved do not support this hypothesis. An alternative is that the falloff reflects changes in legal doctrine that occurred in 1977 and 1982, when the Supreme Court considerably tightened the standards for class action certification in employment discrimination cases. This too is only a partial explanation since the changes in doctrine occurred after the downward trend in the volume of filings had already begun. Finally, developments outside of the employment discrimination context (such as changes in the rules governing attorneys' fees, notification, etc.) may have been responsible for some of the decline. Paul Carrington, official reporter of the Federal Rules of Civil Procedure, remarked recently that "class actions had their day in the sun and kind of petered out." This explanation is supported by Figure 9.8, which plots the annual volume of non-U.S. Government plaintiff class actions in employment civil rights cases and in all other federal civil cases. A clearly apparent parallel decline in both kinds of litigation suggests that the declining use of class actions in employment discrimination suits is part of a larger trend in the use of class actions in all contexts.

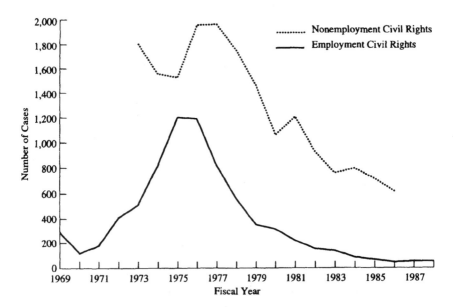

Figure 9.8. Class Action Requests by Non-U.S. Government Plaintiffs Employment Civil Rights and All Other Categories

Conclusion: Legal and Policy Implications

The Deterrent Effect of Private Litigation

The efficacy of Title VII and many other federal antidiscrimination laws depends primarily on the willingness and ability of workers to bring private suits challenging discriminatory employment practices. The law provides an incentive to end discriminatory behavior by making such behavior costly to employers; but if discrimination victims never sue, then employers have no economic incentive to comply. More generally, if enforcement is left in the hands of private litigants, and if private and social incentives to bring suit differ, the system may fail to produce the optimal amount (and perhaps the optimal composition) of litigation. Thus, one might question whether relying on individual citizens to bring suits is the most effective enforcement strategy. On one hand, Paul Burstein and others have pointed out that civil rights opponents intended the private enforcement mechanism as a deliberate road-block to plaintiffs' effective pursuit of their rights, especially given that "many of those discriminated against would be poor and legally unsophisticated." On the other hand, Alfred Blumrosen offers a substantially different interpretation. Writing in 1971, Blumrosen claimed that

> The crucial innovation in the 1964 Civil Rights Act was the enlargement of the role of the individual right to sue in the federal courts, rather than the enhancement of administrative agency powers.... The decision to prefer the courts over the administrative process was sensible, in light of the quarter century of failures by state and federal administrative agencies....

> The decision to establish an individual right to sue rather than to expand the role of administrative agencies was a political compromise between "liberals" who wished to create an all-powerful administrative agency and "conservatives" who objected to the creation of such a bureaucracy. *The compromise ... may have created the most effective possible arrangement for reducing employment discrimination.*

But a regime in which hiring cases predominate may differ substantially from one in which discharge cases do. Such a shift in the nature of Title VII litigation may alter the deterrent effect of the statute in a way that generates some perverse consequences. Consider first an employer who is thinking about whether to hire a worker in a "protected" category. If the worker is hired, the employer will realize some additional output, which constitutes the benefit to the employer. Of course, the employer must also pay wages. If the employer feels animus toward women or minorities, he must in addition bear some psychological costs of associating with the worker. Absent any law prohibiting discrimination, then, the employer will make his hiring decision by comparing the value of the applicant's output if hired with the economic and psychological costs of hiring her. If the first quantity is larger than the second, the employer will decide to hire; otherwise, he will reject the applicant.

When discrimination is illegal, the employer must also take into account the potential costs of rejecting the applicant. These costs include the possible litigation costs if the applicant decides to sue and the damage award if the suit is successful, all weighted by their respective probabilities of occurrence.

The equation becomes more complicated when the possibility of discriminatory firing suits is introduced. A worker who is not hired in the first place is obviously in no position to bring a future firing suit.

Thus, an employer must consider the *increase* in expected costs when he hires a female or minority worker, because some probability exists that the worker will be fired and will sue. Whether the increase in expected costs from hiring outweighs the savings realized by preventing a hiring discrimination suit depends on a number of factors. The greater the likelihood that the worker will ultimately be fired, and the higher the probability of a firing suit, the greater are the expected costs imposed by hiring. With the enormous increase in discharge cases, the probability that a worker will bring a discriminatory firing suit is now substantially higher than the probability that a worker will bring a failure to hire suit. Consequently, antidiscrimination laws may actually provide employers a (small) net disincentive to hire women and minorities.

[A] sensitivity analysis ... suggests that for a range of seemingly reasonable parameter values, the net effect of antidiscrimination litigation on hiring may now indeed be negative. As explained in more detail below, this ironic result stems from two facts: first, workers are much more likely to sue when fired from a job they already have than when their application for a new job is rejected; and second, the involuntary turnover rate is relatively high.

· · ·

[Our analysis assumes] that firing cases are six times more likely than hiring cases. Moreover, we assume that the average prospective worker files five job applications. These two assumptions imply that the likelihood of suit when an employer fires a protected applicant is thirty times greater than the likelihood of suit if the employer simply fails to hire the worker. Thus, the changing nature of employment discrimination litigation to primarily firing cases has had a profound effect on the monetary incentives that employers face. When hiring cases outnumbered firing cases by 50 percent, the likelihood of suit when an employer fired a protected applicant was only 3.3 times greater than the likelihood of suit if the employer simply failed to hire the worker. When we [conducted our analysis] using the 3.3 to 1 ratio instead of the 30 to 1 ratio, [the expected cost of failing to hire a protected worker] became positive. In other words, given the smaller likelihood of firing suits in the immediate aftermath of the passage of Title VII, the costs of failing to hire a protected worker outweighed the costs of possibly having to risk a firing lawsuit at some later time. The dramatic shift to firing cases has greatly increased the likelihood that Title VII will create a drag on the hiring of protected workers rather than the positive inducement it originally provided.

While the implications of [this analysis] are intriguing, one should interpret this table with care. First, [we] evaluate the effect of Title VII at the margin; presumably, firms have already spent considerable sums in avoiding Title VII litigation, for example, through affirmative action plans and validation of employment tests. These inframarginal precautionary expenditures partially explain both the low probability of a hiring suit and the low probability of plaintiff victory. Thus, the conclusion that Title VII's penalties are too small to have had any effect in the past would be grossly wrong. Any employer who failed to hire qualified blacks in the late 1960s or early 1970s would probably have faced a lawsuit. Moreover, the suit could well have been a class action. Thus, a total flouting of the law would have vastly escalated both the probability of a suit and the likely penalty. This explains why Title VII produced some important changes in employment practices during its first decade. The estimates do suggest, however, that antidiscrimination laws no longer provide employers with much additional incentive to avoid discriminatory conduct, especially in hiring. But that does not imply that eliminating the law entirely would increase total employment of blacks.

[Our analysis] should be viewed with caution for a second reason: The results assume that the probability a discharged worker will sue is constant regardless of the reasons the worker lost her job. The model does not distinguish between "individual-specific" and "macroeconomic" job terminations. But most workers who lose their jobs do so because of economic recession, not because of anything they might have done (for instance, absenteeism, poor job performance, or theft). In contrast, most litigation arises from individual-specific terminations. If most litigation arises from individuals who lost their jobs due to inadequate performance, and if such individuals constitute, say, one-fifth of all job losers, then the correct "probability of firing" figure [might well be far smaller than we have estimated]. This would naturally tend to reduce the disincentive effects of firing protection.

What Has Title VII Wrought?

We are left with a paradox: Over twenty times more employment discrimination cases were filed in FY 1989 than in FY 1970, while the amount of bias against women and minorities and exclusions from jobs and occupations has almost certainly fallen. If there were so many fewer suits twenty-five years ago, how can we argue that federal antidiscrimination policy was actually more effective then than it is now? The answer is fourfold. First, the flagrant and obvious violations of the pre-Title VII era—systematic refusal to hire women or minorities for certain jobs, gross disparities in pay for identical jobs, segregated work place facilities—were much more likely to produce plaintiff victories than the subtler and less-frequent forms of discrimination practiced today. A rational employer in 1965 need not have waited until he was actually sued to change his employment practices. Thus, the mere threat of litigation would probably have induced an employer to change his behavior. But this is increasingly less true.

Second, we note that class action suits are well-suited to attacking gross violations of the law, as many discriminators learned. When gross violations are eliminated, the possibilities for bringing class action suits should fall. This is precisely what has happened, as we demonstrated earlier.

Third, the vast preponderance of the rise in litigation has come from allegations of discriminatory firing. Such suits actually provide employers with a disincentive—perhaps even a net disincentive—to hire minorities and women. Thus, we would expect less of an improvement per suit now than in the earlier phase.

Finally, we have ignored the other components of the federal antidiscrimination effort, including affirmative action programs for federal contractors. These programs constitute an important complement to private litigation under Title VII and other statues. Indeed, if the thrust of this paper is correct, such programs are especially important in encouraging hiring, given that private litigation may no longer have a strong pro-hiring effect.

In summary, the effects of Title VII have changed from the opening up of access to jobs for traditional victims of discrimination to the protection of those who already have jobs. We may now have a sort of implicit tort of wrongful discharge—absent the potential for punitive damages—for virtually all workers except white males under age 40. In large measure, this result has not come about through direct changes in the law itself or the ways that courts have interpreted it. Rather, the nature of the protection provided by antidiscrimination legislation has been shaped by the behavior of plaintiffs, defendants, and the economy at large.

Victims in the Shadow of the Law: A Critique of the Model of Legal Protection*

KRISTIN BUMILLER

Contemporary antidiscrimination policies are based on a model of legal protection. From this perspective, the law is a powerful and effective instrument. The law provides victims with a tool by which they can force perpetrators of unlawful conduct to comply with socially established norms. The model of legal protection assumes that those who have suffered harms will recognize their injuries and invoke the protective measures of law. Since most antidiscrimination laws rely primarily on victims to identify violations, report them to public authorities, and participate in enforcement proceedings, these laws tacitly assume that such behavior is reasonably unproblematic. In other words, because protective laws place responsibility on the victim to perceive and report

* Excerpts from Kristin Bumiller, "Victims in the Shadow of the Law: A Critique of the Model of Legal Protection," *Signs: Journal of Women in Culture and Society,* vol. 12, copyright © 1987 by the University of Chicago Press. Reprinted with permission of the author and the publisher.

violations, they assume that those in the protected class can and will accept these burdens.

Research on antidiscrimination policies has often relied on the model of legal protection, and, as a consequence, it has been uninformed by the social-situational viewpoint of women and men of color.... [This] study examines the choices discrimination victims make in light of the perceived social constraints and the vision of protective law. Unlike conventional legal analysis that magnifies the authority of legal rules vis-à-vis other social constructions, these in-depth portrayals of responses to discrimination illustrate how the link between economic, social, psychological, sexual, and legal roles creates an ethic of survival that precludes the protective role of law.

The Research Project

The initial source of data for this study was a household survey designed to measure the incidence of civil disputes. In the survey, conducted by the Civil Litigation Research Project (CLRP) in 1980, a sample of 560 discrimination claims was obtained from approximately 5,000 households. Respondents were asked if they had experienced "illegal or unfair treatment" because of their "race, age, sex, handicaps, union membership, or other things." In this way, it was possible to obtain a sample of discrimination grievances that had not reached courts or public agencies. Preliminary analysis indicated that approximately half of the aggrieved individuals did not make a claim to the other party, nearly two-thirds did nothing further to rectify their perceived mistreatment, and only a very small percentage had achieved successful resolution of their claims. Discrimination grievances had a significantly lower rate of escalation into court cases than civil matters such as contract disputes or landlord-tenant problems. The size of the gap is indicative of the more problematic relationship between victims and the law in discrimination cases compared to other civil cases. This study began with the anticipation that to bring the complaint into the realm of public action forced victims to encounter deeper and more encompassing conflicts of racial, gender, and social identity than complaints arising from relationships defined by legal roles (i.e., landlord/tenant)....

A subsample of eighteen persons in Milwaukee and Los Angeles were selected for in-depth interviewing. The format of the interviews was unstructured but directed at probing for interpretations of the discrimination incident, people's attitudes about themselves and their social status, and their justifications for their beliefs and actions. The interviews were conducted from April to October 1982. Each face-to-face interview was two to four hours long. The participants in the interviews are representative of those affected by the social inequalities and the pattern of discrimination in American society: six black and Hispanic women, nine white women, and three black and American Indian men.

The Response to Discrimination

In the civil litigation research project survey on incidence of civil disputes, each individual who perceived they experienced discrimination and made no protest was asked to explain their decision with the question "Why didn't you complain?" In response to this question, participants denied the worthiness of their own interests in comparison to their opponents'....

Some respondents accounted for their inaction in terms of the harm their opponent could impose on them.... Others acknowledged they should have done something, yet either blamed themselves for not pursuing the dispute or accepted the inevitability of the situation.... The explanations focus on an interpretation of immediate circumstances rather than norms or rights; for example, the expense of legal action and the inability to prove discriminatory motives....

These persons were not rejected by unresponsive agencies, deterred by the unavailability of lawyers, or barred from pursuing legal claims by technicalities. Although the anticipation of these factors played a role in their decision making, they did not take action primarily because they legitimized their own defeat. For the most part, the problem is never conceptualized in terms of public action. In this universe of discrimination problems far removed from legal fora, the labeling of acts as discriminatory and the eventual deflation of the conflict by apology or self-blame serve as coping mechanisms for suppressing burgeoning discontent....

The Creation of Illegitimate Bonds

Discrimination conflicts usually occur in situations where there are asymmetrical power relations. In most instances of discrimination the perpetrator acts in an authoritative role (employer, landlord, or teacher, e.g.)....

The authority figures described by [the] participants behave according to Machiavelli's instructions to *The Prince:* they control by fear and simplification of reality. As tyrants the perpetrators are brutal simplifiers of the situation through appearances that disguise realities....

The potential for explosion reinforces the inviolable bonds of the victim/oppressor relationship. Since the expression of anger is unacceptable in bureaucratic settings, there are no minor infractions within normal ranges of behavior: there is only rebellion and submission. The victims of discrimination, therefore, perceive their own reactions to injustice as explosive and extreme. Most of the individuals admitted to extreme anger (often violent in intent), which persisted for long periods of time. A seventy-two-year-old woman involved in an age discrimination dispute said in reference to her employer: "I wanted to punch her. I was angry for a couple of weeks. I would like to take a good swing at her and teach her a couple of things.... I'd still [two years later] like to punch her." ... In only one case did anger lead to physical violence: when a black woman slapped a white, fellow employee who had made a racist comment.

These people seem to respond to the violation of their dignity within these power relations with intense anger, expressed in the very terms that had been prohibited—immediate physical retaliation—but the result was that anger silenced the victims. They were intimidated by the social unacceptability of their anger; therefore, they confronted their emotions by exercising control. As Patricia explains, she can only remain angry if it is "vital," otherwise if she let herself get angry, "then I'd be angry all the time." Others admit they "don't know how to fight," they "stay quiet," "calm down," or "absorb a lot of anger before [they] let go." These rationalizations about the desirability of control may stifle the expression of injustice in any form.

An Ethic of Survival

The attitude about their successes and failures of those individuals who confronted discrimination is best described in Virginia's words: "The main measurement of success [was] basically survival." The ethic of survival means different things to different people, depending on how they define their responsibilities and their bases for self-respect and how they view their struggles and needs.

Carmen, for example, considers her encounter with discriminatory treatment an inevitable event in the life of a woman of color. Carmen, who worked as a clerk in a discount department store for almost ten years, discovered that after a promotion to a more responsible position as an area supervisor her salary was lower than those of men in the same position. Carmen chose not to make a formal complaint. She made this decision because of a complex set of constraints that reveals that her powerlessness in obtaining equal pay is linked to her powerlessness in other domains. She needs the job because she has responsibilities as a single parent for four children. She also recognizes that in any dispute it would be "me against a large corporation," and then it becomes "your word against [a more powerful] somebody else's...."

The Discrimination Victim's View of the Law

Claiming Discrimination

In order for an individual to press a claim that unfavorable treatment stems from discriminatory practices she must assume the role of the victim. This transforms a social conflict into a psychological contest to reconcile a positive self-image with the image of the victim as powerless and defeated. Deciding whether or not to make a public claim of discrimination thus becomes intertwined with the process of reconciling these self-images.

In this study, those interviewed discussed the discrimination they experience in qualified terms. Some approached it by denying self-involvement: "Sometimes I don't even feel like I was personally being discriminated against, as if they did not know who I was or saw who I was." Another approach characterized acts of discrimination as the result of personal likes and dislikes: "You come across it so often it is really ridiculous." ...

The Intruding Presence in Everyday Life

Despite the fact that victims are reluctant to use the law, they cling to the belief that it benefits them.... All the respondents, when asked if they felt the law was on their side in the dispute, suggested that, at least in principle, the law would have supported their position....

Their assumption that there are absolute guarantees in the law seems to contradict their attitudes toward the law once it is employed. After they engaged the apparatus of law or even considered invoking it, the respondents saw legal resolution as a risky course of action. They feared legal intervention would worsen their situation.

The prospect of legal intervention heightened a sense of powerlessness and produced a fear of loss of control. Nora believed that the decision to go to court was like opening up a "Pandora's box...."

Victims of discrimination also fear that their powerlessness will be accentuated in the legal forum because the legal disposition will address only a part of the problem. As one respondent reasoned, the law will "not represent personality: it is cut and dry—there [is] not room for emotion." Behavior and loyalties may change when allies are asked to participate in legal proceedings: "[Going to court] would mean that people would have to speak up. In the lounge they might say you are really getting screwed. To say that in a court of law is different. When your neck is on the chopping block, you ain't going to start talking...."

Several respondents revealed that when they were confronted with the prospect of initiating a legal action they worried about their own guilt, as if they were charged with criminal offenses. Delma, while considering whether to file a complaint, mused, "Maybe it is me, maybe I am doing something wrong...."

More generally, these discrimination victims felt it was necessary to prevent law from aggravating their situations. Often this meant blocking the law from taking over the relative normalcy of day-to-day life. As Carmen said, "What was important to me at the time was trying to erase the situation. I was split between the idea of pursuing it in court and just letting it die. I couldn't stand the stress." Another woman explained, "The situation is really blocked out, because I don't want them to take action against me...."

Conclusion

These descriptions of the social reality of victims explain why only an exceptional few who perceive they have experienced discrimination achieve successful resolution of their problems. This study offers three explanations for victims' reluctance to assert the worthiness of their interests and their acceptance of defeat as inevitable. First, the bonds between the perpetrator and the discrimination victim drive the conflict to self-destructive or explosive reactions. Second, these individuals are guided by an ethic of survival that encourages self-sacrifice rather than action. And third, the potential for legal remedies is diminished by a view of the law that engenders fear of legal intervention. Injured persons reluctantly employ the label of discrimination because they shun the role of the victim, and they fear legal intervention will disrupt the delicate balance of power between themselves and their opponents.

The hostile image of the law held by respondents considering legal recourse is a harsh reality compared to the spirit of protective law that promises to give purpose and justice to its beneficiaries' lives. In contemporary American society it is typically assumed that the "rule of law" is strengthened by the increase in enforcement powers, the clarification of goals, or the removal of discretion, so that the right-bearer is protected. Yet when people contemplate invoking the right of "equal treatment under law," they find themselves in a position with only undesirable alternatives. The invocation of antidiscrimination law does not enable the victim to overcome power differentials in situations where she or he is pitted against the more powerful opponent. The bonds of victimhood are reinforced rather than broken by the intervention of legal discourse.

The civil rights movement has produced numerous lessons about the limits of the law. Evaluations of doctrinal development and policy implementation have demonstrated the limited role of courts in restructuring social and economic relations. Champions of litigation may misrepresent the problem by ignoring the complexity of systematic processes of discrimination that operate throughout society and then misrepresent the solution by creating the impression that the elimination of legal barriers is sufficient to achieve racial equality. Litigation thus becomes the focal point of activism at the cost of possibly more dynamic attacks on the root causes of racial and sexual subordination. Moreover, legal ideologies can constrain the social vision of the victim and promote self-blame. The mythologies which perpetuate racism and sexism are reflected in both the benevolent policies of legal reformers and the self-image of those who experience discrimination.

The inaction of discrimination victims is problematic from the vantage point of the ideology of legal protection. From the social reality of the victim, however, we find that "survival is a form of resistance." In this study, the majority of these individuals view protest as contrary to their well-being and livelihood. The situation creates a paradox of irrationality, in which people engaged in discrimination conflicts believe they are better off if they decide not to pursue their interests. To act aggressively and battle for a principle requires "irrational" sacrifices and defeats the individual's ethic of survival.

Notes and Questions

1. According to Paul Oyer and Scott Schaefer's recent empirical analysis, there is no evidence that the Civil Rights Act of 1991 created a quota effect, which would have increased the employment of protected workers. Instead, Oyer and Schaefer conclude that this legislation, by increasing the costs of firing protected workers, merely sorted these employees to firms that are least susceptible to discrimination litigation. Thus Oyer and Schaefer suggest that the Civil Rights Act of 1991 did not lead to an opening up of new opportunities for protected workers. Oyer and Schaefer, "Sorting, Quotas, and the Civil Rights Act of 1991 Who Hires When It's Hard to Fire?," 45 *Journal of Law and Economics* 41 (2002).

Ian Ayres and Peter Siegelman further explore the effects of antidiscrimination law by extending Donohue and Siegelman's (1991) analysis of the tradeoff between disparate treatment hiring and firing protections to the effects of disparate impact liability. Ayres and Siegelman conclude that disparate impact firing liability promotes hiring discrimination against minorities by making these workers more costly and thus less attractive at the hiring stage. According to this analysis, disparate impact firing liability reduces average inequality between black and white workers as more blacks than whites are kept longer on the job (leading to an increase in earnings for blacks), but at the same time, it increases inequality within the black community as fewer blacks are hired overall. Ayres and Siegelman, "The Q–Word as Red Herring: Why Disparate Impact Liability Does Not Induce Hiring Quotas," 74 *Texas Law Review* 1487 (1996). Given these considerations, should policymakers be concerned about the transformation in the focus of employment discrimination litigation from opening up new job opportunities to challenging allegedly discriminatory discharges? Does the relative frequency of these types of claims now result in Title VII acting as an impediment to black employment? If so, would it make sense to encourage class-action lawsuits and to authorize increased damage awards in "failure to hire" cases?

The possible inhibitory effect of Title VII on black employment might suggest another reason for retaining the government contract compliance program, which is basically focused on expanding the level of black employment. Indeed, if the choice were between a regime that mandated or effectively encouraged higher levels of black employment and one that was less successful at maintaining high employment but that provided substantial damage awards to those who were wrongly dismissed for racial reasons, which policy option would you favor? Do these options now reflect the distinction between the contract compliance program and Title VII?

These issues once again raise the fundamental question of what is the most important element of employment discrimination law? (Recall the discussion in Chapter 7 about whether the market-based affirmative action requirement discussed by Robert Cooter could achieve any given level of stimulus to black employment at lower cost than would a general prohibition on discrimination.) Is the function of employment discrimination law to elevate the level of black employment and wages, or is it to assert the wrongfulness of discriminatory conduct and provide remedial relief to those who have been victimized? Would Cooter's market-based affirmative action and the contract compliance program be preferable if it were clear that the intended beneficiary of employment discrimination law was a single group or a limited number of groups, in which case the welfare of that class of beneficiaries could be most directly enhanced? If the law starts seeking to protect blacks, Hispanics, Asians, Native Americans, women, those over forty years of age, the disabled, gays and lesbians, and so on, then a market-incentive policy to stimulate employment for the entire class of beneficiaries starts to become unworkable. It would be easier simply to put a tax on the employment of heterosexual, white males under age forty who are not disabled. Might such a tax encourage white men to conceal their heterosexuality and claim that they were older and more infirm than they appeared? Doesn't the fact that society clearly prefers the prohibitory approach of Title VII to such a soulless tax scheme reveal (1) the importance of the legal symbolism that attaches to any law designed to address the problem of discrimination in employment, and (2) that a legal command to act fairly in making employment decisions is a goal that can be achieved, at least in theory, regardless of the number of groups seeking to claim the law's solicitude?

2. One of the advantages of the Title VII regime over both Cooter's suggested approach and the contract compliance program is that it provides the potential for monetary and injunctive remedies to all individuals who have been harmed by discrimination. By so doing, Title VII might be thought to empower individuals against discriminatory or harassing wrongdoers. But this benefit may come at a high price, since the private enforcement component of Title VII places on victims the burden of recognizing their injury and pursuing legal remedies. Yet many of the people who might be most in need of legal protection are not particularly well equipped to invoke the protective measures of the law. As a result, only a small percentage of those who perceive themselves to be victims of discrimination actually sue. Is this another reason to think that the contract compliance program is likely to be more effective than Title VII? The contract compliance program does not rely on individual complaints to generate legal redress but instead calls for audits by public officials to see if protected workers are "underutilized" relative to their numbers in the relevant labor market, and if so, to evaluate the adequacy of the efforts to eliminate any such shortfall.

Bumiller contends that antidiscrimination law reinforces the bonds of victimhood. Is this because the law makes those who experience discrimination reflect on the fact that the mistreatment they have received is improper, making them conscious that they are victims of misconduct? Or is it because legal redress is unlikely, and therefore the promise of justice that the law holds out is illusory, making the initial insult all the more bitter? Others have argued that antidiscrimination law fosters a victim mentality because protected workers who fail can always claim they are victims of discrimination. Do you believe that any of these effects are significant? Would Bumiller prefer the approach of the contract compliance program to that of Title VII?

3. Donohue and Siegelman (1991) note that relatively few perceived instances of discrimination lead to EEOC complaints in part because employees do not like to sue their current employer. This conforms with Bumiller's statement that some respondents to her survey "feared legal intervention would worsen their situation." Are all of Bumiller's findings explained by two facts: first, it is potentially costly to a worker to sue, or aid another's suit, against one's current employer; and second, most victims of any type of mistreatment tend to be those who are less adept at asserting and enforcing their legal rights?

Where workers have greater protections against retaliation—for example, in the federal government—they are far more likely to sue their employer. See Donohue and Siegelman, "Law and Macroeconomics: Employment Discrimination Litigation over the Business Cycle," 66 *Southern California Law Review* 709, 729 (1993), noting that over a twenty-year time span, federal workers sued their employers alleging violations of their civil rights at about 3.25 times the rate at which other employees sued their employers.

4. Bumiller laments that the law does not enable victims of discrimination to overcome their relative lack of power vis-à-vis their employer. Are the protections of substantive employment discrimination law, and the existence of the right to attorney's fees in the event of victory at trial, beneficial to covered workers? Would these workers be better off if Title VII were repealed, since, according to Bumiller, the focus on litigation diverts activists from "more dynamic attacks on the root causes of racial and sexual subordination?" What measures would constitute such dynamic attacks? Could Title VII be amended in a way that would address Bumiller's concerns?

5. Bumiller, who interviewed fifteen women and three men for her study, states that "there was a disproportionate number of women in the intensive interview sample because they had a higher response rate" Bumiller at 425, n. 12. Is this sample sufficiently large and representative to draw meaningful conclusions about responses to discriminatory conduct?

6. Bumiller indicates that several respondents started to question their own conduct when considering the alleged discrimination, which she considers to be a sign of victimization. In many cases, Bumiller's concern could be legitimate, but let us say that a worker is fired for alleged misconduct and she suspects that the discharge may be discriminatory. Wouldn't it be sensible and mature for the discharged worker in such a case to examine her own conduct to see if it played a role in the events that led to the discharge?

7. Bumiller states that employment discrimination law "creates a paradox of irrationality, in which people engaged in discrimination conflicts believe they are better off if they decide not to pursue their interests"—by which she seems to mean pursue litigation. As Donohue and Siegelman (1991) note, the remedies that were available in most employment discrimi-

nation cases before the enactment of the Civil Rights Act of 1991 were limited to reinstatement and back pay. This meant that if you were a desirable employee, you might well be able to get a new job readily, and thus not be entitled to any monetary award from litigation. If you were indifferent between the old and new jobs, or even preferred the change so as to be away from the discriminators, then rejecting litigation would make perfect sense. Why go through the hassle so that your lawyer can collect attorney's fees?

8.   In this regard, it is worth noting that the lure of higher damages to successful plaintiffs posed by a lengthier spell of unemployment after the alleged discriminatory act does correlate with substantially more employment discrimination lawsuits being filed. Thus, Donohue and Siegelman have found that when the economy goes into recession, employment discrimination suits rise because spells of unemployment, and thus potential back pay damages, rise. This effect is rather powerful: "A relatively modest rise in the unemployment rate from, say, 5% to 6.5% (which is a 30% increase) would generate a 21% increase in the number of employment discrimination cases." Donohue and Siegelman at 717 (1993). This certainly suggests that a significant number of employment discrimination litigants are making very rational assessments about whether to bring suit.

9.   While the observed cyclical pattern of case filings seems to conform with one's intuitions that in bad times more employment discrimination lawsuits would be filed, the particular pattern is not inevitable and the reasons for its emergence are not immediately obvious. For example, if damages rise during recessions because spells of unemployment last longer, potential plaintiffs would have a greater incentive to sue, but employers would have a greater incentive to avoid discriminating. Donohue and Siegelman (1993) conclude from the observed cyclical pattern that workers are more sensitive than employers to the higher potential damages induced by recession, which seems plausible given that the bulk of litigation is brought by individual discharged workers.

It is conceivable that the cyclical pattern would have nothing at all to do with the higher potential damages but rather would simply be the product of the greater number of unpleasant employment events that occur during recessions—what Donohue and Siegelman (1993) term an incidents effect. They reject this theory, noting that it is not consistent with the actual patterns of case filings in the EEOC (which is not cyclical), or with the lag time from the start of the economic downturn until the jump in district court filings (given the administrative hurdle of having to file with the EEOC, the cases get into federal court faster than would be possible if the incidents effect were driving the increased federal court litigation). Moreover, Donohue and Siegelman (1993) find the identical cyclical pattern of case filings for discrimination suits against the federal government, even though there is no such cyclical pattern in the untoward employment events experienced by federal workers.

Donohue and Siegelman summarize their findings as follows:

The evidence suggests that the most important connection between macroeconomic performance and employment discrimination litigation is not that the number of litigation-generating incidents rises during recessions. Rather, the key link is what we have termed the worker benefits effect, which is based on the fact that potential victims of employment discrimination receive higher damage awards when they have been out of work for longer periods of time. Because business downturns are associated with longer average spells of unemployment, damages tend to rise during such periods. Higher potential damage awards cause an increase in the number of suits filed. The prospect of greater awards for successful complaints also encourages some less meritorious (or less easily proved) discrimination claims to be brought, which is reflected in the data as lower plaintiff win rates for cases brought during recessions.

Donohue and Siegelman (1993) at 761–62.

Donohue and Siegelman have also found that the marginal cases induced by the economic downturn settle at substantially higher rates and are won at trial at significantly lower rates than other employment discrimination cases. These findings are consistent with predicted litigant behavior of plaintiffs with weak cases in terms of probability of success at trial. Donohue and Siegelman, "The Selection of Employment Discrimination Disputes for Litigation: Using Business Cycle Effects to Test the Priest–Klein Hypothesis," 24 *Journal of Legal Studies* 427 (1995).

9.2   Changing Personnel Practices

Equal Opportunity Law and the Construction of Internal Labor Markets*

FRANK DOBBIN, JOHN R. SUTTON, JOHN W. MEYER, AND W. RICHARD SCOTT

. . .

... We will argue that equal employment opportunity law led organizations to formalize promotion mechanisms to undermine managerial discrimination. How do we know that organizations did not simply adopt these measures in response to the civil rights and women's movements? Of course these movements were important, but their broad effects do not explain the fact that organizational antidiscrimination policies converged on a set of personnel practices that were isomorphic with the procedurally oriented, quasi-judicial administrative configuration of the federal government—formal, merit-based, employment and promotion conventions complete with an internal system of grievance adjudication. Once sanctioned by the courts, this approach eclipsed all competing strategies for redressing discrimination. It is clear that, even if social

* Excerpts from Frank Dobbin, John R. Sutton, John W. Meyer, and W. Richard Scott, "Equal Opportunity Law and the Construction of Internal Labor Markets," *American Journal of Sociology*, vol. 99, copyright © 1993 by the University of Chicago Press. Reprinted with permission of the authors and the publisher.

movements encouraged organizations to end discrimination, public policy shaped the particular approach organizations would embrace.

Equal employment opportunity law. We hypothesize that two major changes in the legal environment increased the popularity of internal labor market [ILM] mechanisms. First, the passage of the Civil Rights Act of 1964 prompted employers to experiment with various antidiscrimination approaches, including (1) formal hiring and promotion procedures to depersonalize employment decisions, (2) sophisticated employment and promotion tests to create objective selection criteria, and (3) numerical quotas for the employment of disadvantaged groups. Second, in the early 1970s legislative changes and court decisions required more employers to be attentive to the issue of discrimination, but discouraged the testing and quota solutions while reinforcing the ILM strategy. More generally, because ILM procedures operate on a classificatory logic in which certain categories of employees are afforded specified protections against firing and promises of consideration for promotion, they were particularly well suited to protecting rights for new classifications based on gender and minority status.

. . .

[M]any organizations responded to Title VII and EO 11246 by designating affirmative action officers, and establishing affirmative action offices, between 1964 and 1970.

In the early 1970s several judicial and administrative clarifications of EEO compliance criteria discouraged the use of tests and quotas and encouraged the adoption of formal ILM mechanisms. First, in *Griggs v. Duke Power Company,* the Supreme Court outlawed employment tests that were not demonstrably related to the work to be performed if those tests had the effect of excluding blacks. In ruling that employment tests must be relevant to job tasks the Supreme Court spurred firms to specify job prerequisites, in written job descriptions, and discouraged them from using general employment tests. In 1974 EEOC guidelines explicitly stated that education, experience, and test scores could not be used as selection criteria unless they could be shown to be related to job performance. Few employers were able to convince the courts that their tests could predict job performance and, as a result, many ceased using testing to achieve EEO goals.

Second, in the early 1970s, discrimination and reverse-discrimination suits increased in number. Between 1965 and 1970 only three reverse-discrimination suits reached appellate courts, yet in the next six-year period 24 such suits were heard. These suits made employers reluctant to follow compliance strategies, such as quotas, that explicitly gave an edge to disadvantaged groups. Voluntary quotas (i.e., those not mandated by courts) had never been the favored EEO compliance strategy and now several well-publicized judgments found them to be illegal. In addition, the General Accounting Office's interpretation of the

Equal Employment Opportunity Act of 1972 rejected the use of quotas in the federal Civil Service on the grounds that quotas would undermine the merit system. This interpretation caused both public and private employers to retreat from voluntary quotas and to expand the formalization of hiring and promotion.

Third, in December 1971 the OFCCP issued Revised Order 4, which set out specific affirmative action guidelines for federal contractors. The order required federal contractors to file annual EEO reports detailing employment in each job category by gender, race, and ethnicity. The order also called for affirmative action plans to identify areas of minority and female "underutilization," to develop numerical goals and timetables for enlarging job opportunities in those areas, and to specify mechanisms for evaluating program effectiveness.

Fourth, the 1972 Equal Employment Opportunity Act gave the EEOC the authority to bring suit in federal court under Title VII; the act also extended Title VII coverage to private employers with 15 or more employees, to educational institutions, and to state and local governments. This legislation simultaneously expanded the scope of federal EEO law and strengthened the capacity for active enforcement. Finally, the EEOC's 1974 guidebook for employers, *Affirmative Action and Equal Employment,* suggested that employers could avoid litigation by formalizing hiring and promotion procedures and expanding personnel record keeping so that they would be able to prove that they did not discriminate.[1]

Personnel Professionals

Personnel professionals played a central role in constructing formal ILM practices as EEO compliance mechanisms. Personnel departments typically implement and administer ILMs, and they have promoted ILMs to serve a series of management problems since early in this century. We argue that personnel departments provided the path through which ILM mechanisms diffused in the years after the Civil Rights Act.

Personnel professionals responded to the ambiguity of the 1964 legislation by developing the three principal antidiscrimination strategies we have discussed: quota systems, tests designed to objectively evaluate the qualifications of job candidates, and rules to formalize hiring and promotion. The personnel and business management journals published articles advocating all three strategies between the mid-1960s and mid-1970s. Personnel managers also came to extol affirmative action-related formalization as a way to rationalize personnel allocation: open bidding for jobs would undermine favoritism and periodic, written, performance evaluations would encourage promotions based on objective criteria.

1. The report argued that if an EEO survey shows that women and minorities are not employed in an organization "at all levels in reasonable relation to their presence in the population and the labor force, the burden of proof is on ... [the employer] to show that this is not the result of discrimination, however inadvertent."

Personnel managers sold their bosses on formal evaluation and promotion systems with two arguments: these systems thwarted discrimination and, at the same time, rationalized the allocation of human resources. Their rhetoric coupled the ideas of equity and efficiency.

Job descriptions, performance evaluations, and salary classification. In the early 1970s, in response to the OFCCP's Revised Order 4 and the 1972 expansion of the EEOC's authority, the major practitioner journals began publishing articles that promoted a specific set of ILM practices to improve federal accountability and to redress discrimination. For instance, in 1974 the *Harvard Business Review* published "Make Your Equal Opportunity Program Court–Proof," which emphasized "the need for positive action against the risk of prolonged and serious litigation or crippling financial judgments." It specifically encouraged firms to establish nondiscriminatory job descriptions and salary classification systems and to "ensure that prescribed qualifications and pay scales can be justified on business grounds and that inadvertent barriers have not been erected against women and minorities." In the same year, the journal *Personnel* published "A Total Approach to EEO Compliance," which argued that affirmative action programs must begin with a census of minority and women employees in each department and within each major job classification—which required having a salary classification system in place—and encouraged employers to implement periodic performance evaluations for all categories of employees to make all employees eligible for promotion. Written performance evaluations were also thought to be essential to the successful defense of discrimination suits involving promotions. In brief, the personnel journals promoted salary classification systems, job descriptions, and formal performance evaluations as EEO compliance mechanisms. These articles noted that salary classification systems, and expanded record keeping in the areas of hiring and promotion, were now virtually mandatory for federal contractors who were required to file annual EEO reports. Evidence that federal contractors expanded black male employment in response to federal oversight leads us to predict that these contractors were also likely to adopt ILM mechanisms.

Many of these articles treated EEO law as an opportunity to increase the efficiency of personnel decisions. Executives soon recognized that by requiring middle managers to justify hiring and promotion decisions, they could undermine favoritism and ensure that jobs would be filled by the best-qualified applicants. As Robert J. Samuelson argued in 1984, "Many firms have overhauled personnel policies.... Promotions are less informal. When positions become open, they are posted so anyone (not just the boss's favorite) can apply. Formal evaluations have been strengthened so that, when a manager selects one candidate over another ... there are objective criteria." By 1979 some two-thirds of top corporate executives favored government efforts to increase female and minority participation in the labor force, and a decade later the

Harvard Law Review argued that managerial support for EEO had become widespread because EEO was seen as a force promoting rational personnel practices. Alternative economic analyses reinforce this view by suggesting that EEO encourages employers to match employees with jobs on the basis of their abilities rather than on the basis of irrelevant ascribed characteristics. Thus while neoclassical economists argued that antidiscrimination laws were inefficient because they disrupted market mechanisms and unnecessary because discriminatory practices would eventually die under the weight of their own inefficiency business executives came to see EEO as a source of increased efficiency.

Job ladders, testing, and quotas. By contrast, personnel journals suggested that formal job ladders, testing, and quota schemes could lead to problems with the EEOC and OFCCP. Formal job ladders had not been part of any of the three main EEO compliance strategies devised in the 1960s, and in the 1970s they were found to produce unnecessary barriers to advancement by making only certain groups of employees eligible for promotion. Giblin and Ornati counseled that firms should examine whether their promotion ladders "create unwarranted restrictions to minority mobility" and, in particular, whether "women or minorities are concentrated in certain jobs *outside* any line of progression or in jobs that dead-end." DiPrete argues that the problem with job ladders was quite simple: most organizations had different, discontinuous, upper-and lower-tier job ladders. Employees in the lower tier, frequently dominated by women and minorities, were generally ineligible for promotion to upper-tier jobs even if they held the necessary educational qualifications. Federal agencies responded to EEO legislation by creating bridges between job ladders in different tiers, but the personnel journals urged private employers to switch to open bidding systems that allowed any employee to bid for a vacant job—such systems had already substituted for formal job ladders in several industries. Thus after about 1973 job ladders were incorporated into some government EEO programs, but were less likely to be used in private-sector programs.

A number of personnel administrators initially believed that employment and promotion testing could solve their EEO problems. Since the time of Frederick Taylor, testing had been viewed as a way to ensure that workers would be allocated to "the highest class of jobs" that they were capable of performing, thereby maximizing both their own rewards and their utility to the organization. Personnel managers reacted to the 1971 *Griggs* decision, which required them to demonstrate the relevance of tests, in two ways: some saw this ruling as a chance to expand their departments by developing more sophisticated tests that would predict job performance and stand up to EEOC guidelines, while others advocated the abandonment of testing. The second camp came to prevail. A study conducted in 1973 and reported in *Personnel* found that 15.1% of sampled firms had already abandoned employment tests in reaction to the *Griggs* decision. Similarly, in our sample, 15% of the organizations using employment tests abandoned them during the period under study, and 11% of the organizations using promotion tests abandoned them. By contrast, no other practice was abandoned by more than 2% of the organizations using it.

The reverse-discrimination suits of the early 1970s led personnel managers to repudiate schemes, such as quotas, that explicitly advantaged protected groups. While court orders and consent decrees had required some companies to conform to specific black-white or female-male hiring ratios, the voluntary establishment of quotas had led to a number of legal fights. By 1974 personnel experts were advising their colleagues that voluntary quotas could "render them liable to legal attack." In 1978 the widely publicized *Bakke* case led personnel managers who had not yet done so to excise the word "quota" from their personnel guidelines.

Finally, public and nonprofit organizations were most susceptible to these trends because these organizations (*a*) depend on public opinion for legitimacy and resources and (*b*) are subject to evaluation on the basis of their use of up-to-date procedures and structures because they cannot, in most cases, be judged on the basis of profitability. Other studies have shown such organizations to be most likely to install formal affirmative action offices and procedures. To the extent that organizations adopt ILM mechanisms to symbolize their commitment to equality, rather than to retain firm-specific skills as labor economists suggest, we should find that the likelihood of adoption is highest among public and nonprofit organizations, rather than among technically complex organizations.

. . .

Data and Methods

The Sample

We selected a stratified random sample of public, for-profit, and nonprofit organizations in 1985–86, collecting retrospective data from 279 organizations on the history of their personnel practices. We generated the sample in three states—California, New Jersey, and Virginia—that have varying legal environments. We concentrated on a limited number of sectors, which represent different parts of the economy, so that we would be able to examine arguments about sectoral effects. In each state we selected an equal number of organizations from each of 13 sectors.

. . .

Measurement and Model Specification

Dependent variables. We examine the rate of adoption of six personnel practices: job descriptions, performance evaluations, salary classification systems, job ladders, employment testing, and promotion testing. Formal *job descriptions* outline the work to be performed in each job and the prerequisites for job applicants; they thereby enable the organization to identify a pool of internal candidates for each vacant position. Periodic, written *performance evaluations* are conducted by supervisors and results are kept on record for use in promotion decisions. *Salary classification systems* arrange jobs in a series of hierarchical wage categories based on requisite duties and skills; the creation of categories that are consistent across departments enables managers to determine which job shifts constitute lateral moves and which constitute vertical moves. Each formal *job ladder* specifies a succession of jobs in a sequence that constitute an expected promotion pattern. Written *employment tests* are designed to evaluate applicants' intelligence, experience, and personal character in order to match them with jobs, and *promotion tests* are used to judge current employees for promotion....

To code each practice in event-history format, we asked respondents whether their organization had ever used the practice. For each affirmative response, we coded the year in which the practice was first used; if the practice had been abandoned we coded the year in which that occurred.

Independent variables. Table 9.6 lists the independent variables. All vary over time, and all but the time periods, time trend, and density are measured at the organizational level.

. . .

Table 9.6   Variable List

Variable	Description
Log employment	Natural logarithm of the number of employees reported in the current year
Personnel office	Binary variable for presence of a personnel office in the current year
Member of personnel association	Binary variable for membership in a personnel association in current year
Period 2	Binary variable for spells occurring between 1964 and 1973, inclusive
Period 3	Binary variable for spells occurring between 1974 and 1985, inclusive
Time trend	Linear variable representing years since 1954 (1–30)
Chemicals, machinery, electrical, non-profit	Binary variable for organization operating in the sector
City, county, federal government	Binary variable for government agency
Density (for each ILM practice)	Percentage of firms in the sample reporting the use of the practice in current year
Federal contractor	Binary variable for federal contracts in current year (limited to private organizations)
EEO reporting status	Binary variable for organizations that filed an EEO report with the EEOC or the OFCCP in current year (limited to private organizations)
AA office/officer	Binary variable for presence of affirmative action office, or designated officer, in current year
Union contract,	Binary variable for presence of union contract in current year

Estimation

Before turning to methods and modeling, we show changes in the prevalence of the six personnel practices. Figure 9.9 reports the proportion of existing organizations that used each of the practices in each year. Changes are dramatic over time. While a small proportion of organizations used performance evaluations, job descriptions, and salary classification systems in 1955, a majority of sampled firms used these three practices by 1985. It is evident that these first three practices grew more quickly between 1964 and 1973 than they did before 1964; they grew even more quickly between 1974 and 1985. By contrast, employment tests, which were at first more prevalent than any other practice, diverge notably from the first three practices after the early 1960s. Promotion tests and job ladders rise very slowly in absolute terms. Table 9.7 reports the average annual hazard rate for each of the six outcomes, in each of the three policy periods.[2] These figures tell a similar story about the positive effects of legal changes on the first three variables in both periods 2 and 3. They also support our hypothesis that job ladders should increase in period 3, and that employment testing should increase between periods 1 and 2 but not between periods 2 and 3.

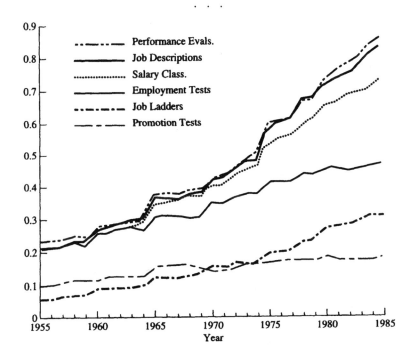

Figure 9.9. Proportion of sample with ILM practices

2. [The hazard rate measures the rate of adoption of the six studied labor market practices. Table 9.7 reveals how the rate of adoption varied across three time periods: (1) prior to Title VII; (2) the early years of Title VII, which was enacted in July 1964 and went into effect a year later; and (3) the period beginning a decade after Title VII's enactment.— ED.]

Over the 30–year time frame we cover, the 279 organizations sampled yield 6,701 annual spells of observation. In the models, organizations are excluded from the at-risk pool before their birth, and after they have adopted a practice. The number of at-risk spells ranges from 3,400 to 5,396 for the five modeled outcomes. The number of transitions modeled ranges from 61 to 164.... For each outcome we [estimate] equations that include, in addition to other variables, (1) the two binary time-period variables representing changes in EEO law, (2) a time-trend variable, and (3) the time-period variables as well as the time trend. Our aim here is to discern either a linear increase in the likelihood of adopting ILM practices, which might be caused by any number of factors, or stepwise increases that correspond to legal changes.

Table 9.7 Average Annual Hazard Rate for Each
Internal Labor Market Practice

ILM Practice	Period 1 (1955–63)	Period 2 (1964–73)	Period 3 (1974–85)
Job descriptions	.015	.036	.095
Performance evaluations	.011	.039	.099
Salary classification	.013	.031	.061
Job ladders	.005	.009	.017
Employment testing	.009	.024	.023
Promotion testing	.006	.007	.004

· · ·

Findings

· · ·

Contrary to rationalist arguments that size is the most important cause of the formalization of organizational personnel practices, employment size shows significant effects for only two of the outcome variables.... On the whole, public and nonprofit organizations were most likely to adopt these practices, as institutional theory predicts. The density measures representing the proportion of the sample with the specified practice in the current year, which operationalize the argument that organizations install ILM mechanisms to compete for labor, performed well in bivariate analyses, but their effects disappeared in multivariate models.

· · ·

Legal changes show strong effects. The time periods, which represent changes in the legal environment, were important in all of our models. In accord with our predictions, the period effects are consistently positive, and the period 3 coefficients exceed the period 2 coefficients for job descriptions, performance evaluations, and salary classification systems.

. . . Very similar findings are presented for performance evaluations and salary classification. For job ladders, only period 3 shows a significant effect; this supports DiPrete's argument that civil service systems bridged job ladders to conform to EEO guidelines after the early 1970s. For employment tests, the parameters for the two later periods are roughly equal, which supports our argument that personnel professionals responded to the Civil Rights Act by encouraging adoption of such tests but that the legal precedents of the early 1970s made testing difficult to support in court. Some organizations undertook studies to demonstrate that tests predicted job performance, but many avoided testing altogether.

. . .

. . . [I]ncreases in the likelihood of adoption were stepwise and dramatic rather than incremental. While these general measures of legal change show robust effects, the direct measures of whether organizations come under federal EEO scrutiny—federal contractor status and EEO report filing status—showed weak effects that did not hold up in multivariate models. . . .

The presence of a personnel office shows a positive effect on the adoption of job descriptions, performance evaluations, and salary classification, which were ultimately approved by the personnel profession and the courts as EEO compliance strategies, but not on job ladders or employment tests, which were generally discouraged by the profession and the courts. For one outcome, salary classification, membership in a personnel association also shows a weak net effect. In bivariate analyses the presence of an affirmative action office or officer showed a significant positive effect for four of the outcomes, but the fact that this measure washed out in multivariate analyses suggests that personnel networks, not affirmative action networks, were the most important interorganizational conduits of these practices.

Location in the "institutional" (nonprofit and government) sector showed an effect for every outcome despite the fact that many state and federal agencies used civil service systems, which incorporate our outcome variables, before 1955; the at-risk group includes relatively few state or federal agencies.

. . .

The practice of promotion testing showed the slowest growth over the period and was the least prevalent of all of these practices by 1985; this supports our hypothesis that EEO case law discouraged employers from using tests to evaluate employees.

We believe that, taken together, these results demonstrate that since 1955 particular ILM practices diffused largely in response to shifts in the legal environment. They diffused through networks of personnel professionals who collectively devised organizational formulas for inoculation against EEO litigation.

.   .   .

Conclusion

Our findings concern the relationship between the state and organizations.... Ambiguous public policies invite organizations to experiment with solutions that will withstand legal tests, and in turn the courts and Congress affirm certain strategies and veto others. This process contributed to the evolving understanding of what constitutes discrimination and how to guard against it. In the case of EEO law, the courts discouraged the use of formal testing and made it clear that organizations that used voluntary quotas would open themselves up to reverse-discrimination litigation. But they approved the formalization of hiring and promotion through the use of traditional ILM practices. This procedural strategy became the favored approach to pursuing nondiscrimination. The process was diffuse and normative, rather than targeted and coercive, and this showed up in our finding that being a federal contractor, or coming under EEOC or OFCCP scrutiny, had no net effect. In short, public policy helped to create broad models of organizing that were embraced as just and rational by all sorts of organizations; it did not force a narrow range of targeted organizations to adopt specified practices in order to avoid sanctions.

.   .   .

Since 1964 federal EEO law has caused personnel managers to view formal selection and promotion practices as ways to protect employee rights and, simultaneously, rationalize the allocation of workers. One result is that management came to see affirmative action in a positive light—as a force for equity and efficiency. Legal changes also encouraged managers to treat all employees as career oriented and self-actualizing by creating organizational structures that would allow all classes of employees to pursue promotions, including groups employers previously took to have naturally low aspirations and weak needs for ego gratification (e.g., minorities and women).

.   .   .

We have suggested that organizational employment practices are driven by evolving conceptions of the individual, and of individual rights, that become institutionalized in public policy. Employment practices, in turn, feed back into these conceptions. To wit, ILM practices that make promotion available to all categories of employees portray ambition and

achievement orientation as characteristics of *all* individuals—as inherent
in individualism.

. . .

We view the legal and organizational concern with guarding the
integrity of workers (e.g., sexual harassment policies), with participative
management and work-group identification (e.g., quality circles), and
with transforming all jobs into rungs on career ladders to make advancement available to all (e.g., open job bidding and formal promotion
mechanisms) as integral to today's organizational representation of the
individual. However, evidence that, since the mid-1980s, firms have
moved away from long-term employment and toward short-term contracting suggests that the future of the organizational embodiments of
individualism that we have depicted is uncertain.

. . .

Notes and Questions

1. Dobbin, Sutton, Meyer, and Scott examine how the rise of the
organized personnel department has routinized and bureaucratized personnel decisions in major firms. Does this development raise another doubt
about the applicability of the Becker model of employment discrimination,
since hiring and firing decisions would no longer be directly in the hands of
the employer? Wouldn't a principal-agent model better describe the problem
of discrimination? In this view, the employer-principal would like to maximize profits by not discriminating, but the agents staffing the personnel office
could within some limits exercise their discriminatory preferences without
paying a financial penalty for doing so.

2. Although their own data show a substantial increase in the proportion of firms that relied on employment tests over the period 1955 through
1985 (see Figure 9.9), as well as a jump in the rate of adoption of testing
starting in 1964, Dobbin, Sutton, Meyer, and Scott contend that the evolving
law of employment discrimination has discouraged the use of objective
employment tests. They base this conclusion on the fact that, beginning
around 1965, the increase in the use of testing was smaller than the increase
in the implementation of other personnel practices, such as performance
evaluations, salary classifications, and formal job descriptions. Note that the
legal developments after 1985 that were discussed in section 4.2 of Chapter 4
will likely further inhibit the use of testing for two reasons: (1) the Civil
Rights Act of 1991 affirmed and strengthened the disparate impact doctrine,
which is the typical basis for a legal attack on testing, and (2) the Act also
prohibited race-norming, which had become the primary mechanism for
maintaining testing while circumventing the problem of disparate impact.

3. Dobbin, Sutton, Meyer, and Scott analyze three time periods: before
1964, 1964 through 1973, and 1974 through 1985. The choice of 1964 was
clearly made to coincide with the passage of the 1964 Civil Rights Act,
although it is worth noting that Title VII did not take effect until July 2,

1965. The authors do not indicate what legal changes characterize the final period that begins in 1974. Does their assessment of the pattern of legal change correspond with the description of doctrinal change discussed by Blumrosen in section 4.1 of Chapter 4 and with the development of employment discrimination litigation described by Donohue and Siegelman in section 9.1 of this chapter?

4. Dobbin, Sutton, Meyer, and Scott assert that the development of the employment procedures that they refer to as internal labor market practices "reflect and embody the expanding Western conception of the individual that is central to the process of modernity." But in the last sentence of the excerpt from their article they note that there is movement away from the internal labor market practices toward short-term contracting. Could this development be a response to the pressures of antidiscrimination law and the growing regulatory burdens governing the employment relationship? Does this development imply that the modern Western conception of the individual may be shrinking?

5. In what can be thought of as a sequel to the project that Dobbin, Sutton, Meyer, and Scott began in the early 1990s, Susan Sturm, in examining what she calls "second generation" employment discrimination, provides an insightful evaluation of the personnel practices that emerged in response to the changing nature of workplace discrimination in the 1990s. Sturm, "Second Generation Employment Discrimination: A Structural Approach," 101 *Columbia Law Review* 458 (2001). According to Sturm, smoking guns in employment discrimination—deliberate exclusion or subordination of minorities (what she calls "first generation" patterns of bias)—are largely things of the past; now "second generation" discrimination, which is defined as patterns of complex interactions among groups that have the effect of excluding minorities over time, has taken the center stage.

Sturm examines three companies (Deloitte & Touche, Intel Corporation, and Home Depot) that implemented innovative personnel practices in an effort to address broader problems of structural, relational, and situational biases that result in inequalities. Because these problems cannot be traced solely or directly to the sexism or racism of a single "bad actor," the approaches these employers have adopted are comprehensive and multifaceted. For example, according to Sturm, Intel adopted a problem-solving system that systematically gathers and analyzes data about overall patterns of employee complaints. Integral to the system are independent specialists within the company who act as "intermediaries and cross-boundary problem solvers." Unlike traditional human resources managers whose interests are essentially aligned with management, these independent specialists enjoy a high degree of investigative freedom and are perceived by employees as such. More importantly, their task is not only limited to resolving individual complaints, but analyzing broader data in order to uncover patterns and trends of bias within the company.

While Sturm is optimistic about the benefits of such internal dispute resolution and problem solving system, some commentators fear that the newly emerging dispute resolution systems are essentially liability-avoidance tools with more symbolic than practical meaning. They are also highly skeptical of what appears to be a trend towards deregulation and privatization of discrimination law. Are courts the best institutional actors to address the problems of second generation discrimination? Consider Michael Selmi's argument that the Supreme Court has never moved beyond its initial recognition of blatant forms of discrimination in the 1960s. Selmi, "Proving Intentional Discrimination: The Reality of Supreme Court Rhetoric," 86 *The Georgetown Law Journal* 279 (1997). Moreover, according to Sturm, the traditional rule enforcement approach is misguided, as it "superimpos[es] universal solutions over an area where culture and context are key to effective problem solving and normative elaboration." Sturm at 539.

*

10

Using Statistical Evidence to Prove Discrimination

In the past, some employers publicly declared their unwillingness to hire women or members of certain racial or ethnic groups, for instance, in signs indicating "No Irish Need Apply." Under such circumstances, one has direct and indisputable evidence of labor market discrimination. The passage of antidiscrimination legislation and the growing social disapproval of overtly discriminatory behavior have eliminated such proclamations far more thoroughly than they have eliminated discriminatory conduct on the part of employers. As a result, plaintiffs in employment discrimination cases are frequently confronted with the difficult task of proving that certain decisions were made *because* of race or sex or national origin, despite the lack of explicit evidence that any of these factors influenced the employer's conduct. In such cases, the plaintiffs must turn to statistical evidence to establish the existence of actionable disparate treatment. Moreover, the development of the disparate impact theory of discrimination also elevates the importance of statistical evidence because of the need to show that a neutral employment practice actually has an adverse impact on a protected class of workers. Consequently, statistical evidence is often a central feature of disparate treatment claims of discrimination, and it nearly always is in disparate impact cases.

But the entry of statistics into the courtroom can be problematic, because lawyers and judges are often asked to resolve difficult quantitative issues that lie far from their area of expertise. The readings in this chapter convey a sense of some of the intractable issues surrounding the statistical proof of discrimination. Paul Meier, Jerome Sacks, and Sandy Zabell discuss the assumptions that underlie the random sampling model of nondiscriminatory hiring adopted by the Supreme Court in *Hazelwood School District v. United States,* 433 U.S. 299 (1977), and the dangers of erroneous implementation of this now widely used methodology. When is it appropriate to assert that a disparity between the percentage of workers hired from a protected group and their percentage in some relevant labor market establishes a prima facie case of intentional discrimination? Meier, Sacks, and Zabell offer a cautious evaluation of this question, while Kingsley Browne supplies an irate answer, "Never— or hardly ever." Browne argues that "a proper amount of skepticism ... where the proof is largely statistical would result, in virtually all cases, in a judgment for the defendant" (p. 557).

The increasing reliance on statistical proof in employment discrimination cases has not been limited to the simple statistical methods examined in the first two selections. The more complex method of multiple regression has become a major statistical tool in employment discrimination litigation, and the notes at the end of the chapter illustrate the use of multiple regression in examining the question of affirmative action in law school hiring. This example reveals that a question that is the subject of extreme and polar viewpoints, such as the existence and magnitude of racial and gender preferences in hiring law professors, can be addressed more profitably through the collection and careful analysis of the appropriate data than through animated and eloquent, but ultimately uninformed, speculation.

What Happened in Hazelwood: Statistics, Employment Discrimination, and the 80% Rule*

PAUL MEIER, JEROME SACKS, AND SANDY L. ZABELL

The One-Sample Model: Proportion in Sample Compared to Proportion in Population

In *Hazelwood School District v. United States,* the United States had brought suit against the Hazelwood School District alleging that it had engaged in a "pattern or practice" of employment discrimination in violation of Title VII. Hazelwood was a largely rural area in the northern part of St. Louis County, with few blacks in its student body and a corresponding dearth (under 2%) of black teachers on its staff. The government based its statistical case on the small proportion of black teachers in the district compared with the surrounding area in which the percentage of black teachers was substantially higher (St. Louis County

* Excerpts from Paul Meier, Jerome Sacks, and Sandy L. Zabell, "What Happened in Hazelwood," *American Bar Foundation Research Journal,* copyright © 1984 by the University of Chicago Press. Reprinted with permission of the authors and the publisher.

and the City of St. Louis, the latter being encompassed by, but not included in, the former).

The district court found the approximate parity between the percentage of black staff and black students in the district an adequate defense, and found for defendant. On appellate review, the court of appeals ruled that the appropriate comparison was instead that of staff with the labor force in the St. Louis area, and reversed. The Supreme Court granted certiorari and vacated and remanded, holding that the court of appeals had erred in "disregarding the statistical data in the record dealing with Hazelwood's hiring after it became subject to Title VII" and in "disregarding the possibility that the prima facie statistical proof in the record" might be rebutted by those statistics. The opinion notes that of 405 teachers hired by the defendant in the two years 1972/73 and 1973/74, 15 were black, or 3.7%. This proportion was judged against the proportion of black teachers in St. Louis County, namely, 5.7%. The comparison is based on the implicit (and, as discussed below, highly questionable) assumption that, in the absence of discrimination, the percentage of blacks hired would not be significantly different from the percentage of blacks in the teacher population.

The random sampling model for nondiscriminatory hiring used by the Court rests on two implicit assumptions: (a) the chance that any particular teacher hired will be black is the same as the overall percentage of black teachers—5.7%, and (b) the racial outcomes of the 405 hires are "statistically independent." With these two assumptions it can be shown mathematically that the sample proportion (i.e., the proportion of blacks hired) should be near the population proportion of 5.7% and will deviate from it only to an extent described by the binomial probability distribution. Such a distribution permits one to calculate the probability that a sample proportion in a properly drawn random sample will deviate from the population proportion to as great an extent as actually found in the observed sample. The greater the observed deviation, the smaller this probability will be. If the probability is found to be very small, one might then reasonably conclude that the random selection model is not credible.

Calculations directly using the binomial distribution are often tedious, but can usually be well approximated by use of the *normal distribution,* the familiar bell-shaped curve. Use of the normal approximation requires only calculation of a statistical quantity called the *standard error; in Hazelwood* this is readily computed to be

$$\sqrt{(.057 \times .943)/405} = .0115 = 1.15\%$$

The Court's statement that "a fluctuation of two or three standard deviations would undercut the hypothesis" of randomness is based on the mathematical fact that there are fewer than 5 chances in 100 that a deviation from 5.7% as large as 2 standard errors will occur (i.e., 5.7% ±

2.3%), and less than 3 chances in 10,000 that a deviation as large as 3 standard errors will occur. In *Hazelwood,* the difference between sample and population proportions is 3.7% – 5.7% = –2%, or 1.74 standard errors (= 2%/1.15%), and under the assumption of random selection, a discrepancy this large has more than 8 chances in 100 of occurring. Because the discrepancy was less than 2 standard errors, the Court concluded that the disparity between the observed sample proportion, 3.7%, and the standard of comparison, 5.7%, might be "sufficiently small to weaken the Government's other proof, while the disparity between 3.7% and 15.4% [the standard advanced by the plaintiff] may be sufficiently large to reinforce it."

. . .

The Two-Sample Binomial Model: Comparison of Two Samples with Each Other

In *Connecticut v. Teal* a test used to determine eligibility for promotion was challenged on the ground of adverse impact. Of 48 blacks who took the test, 26 passed (54%), while of 259 whites who took the test, 206 passed (80%). In this case, there is no standard pass rate for comparison. There being no external standard, the only question is whether the pass rate for black applicants is different enough from the pass rate for white applicants to indicate a substantial disparity. The sampling model for the testing situation, analogous to that used in *Hazelwood,* presumes that, absent discrimination, applicants in both groups have the same chance of passing and that the outcomes, pass or fail, for the 307 candidates (48 blacks plus 259 whites) are statistically independent. In such a case, the difference in the observed proportions can be expected to be small but subject to random fluctuation whose magnitude can again be gauged by an appropriate standard error. As in the one-sample model, an observed difference of magnitude greater than 2 standard errors creates a presumption against the random selection model, *possibly* indicative of a discriminatory mechanism. In *Teal* the difference in hire rates is 25%, or 3.76 standard errors, well above the "2 or 3 standard errors" benchmark enunciated in *Hazelwood.*

Here again, there is a single exact test, commonly referred to as the "Fisher exact test" which is appropriate for determining whether a difference in hire or promotion rates is statistically significant.

. . .

Interpretation of significance level. Unless an employer were hiring by quota, we would not expect *exactly* equal hire or promotion rates for two different groups. Thus we always expect to see some disparity due merely to chance or random fluctuation, and what is needed is a tool to enable us to distinguish between minor disparities resulting from such fluctuations on the one hand, and substantial disparities due to intentional or unintentional discriminatory practices on the other. Absolute certainty being seldom attainable, the most we will be able to arrive at will be a so-called *conditional probability* that the practice in question was fair or nondiscriminatory, based on (or "given") the evidence of the observed disparity and all other available information; symbolically, this probability is written as

P(nondiscrimination/observed disparity and other evidence)

It is a serious but very frequent error to confuse this conditional probability with the level of significance or "P-value" that results from a test of significance. The level of significance, it will be recalled, is the chance that, assuming one is hiring or promoting at random, a disparity at least as large as the one observed would occur; symbolically this is

P(observed disparity/random selection)

The first conditional probability is what would be most relevent for evaluating whether there is discrimination; but the second conditional probability is all that classical statistical theory is able to provide. Note that there are three major differences between the two:

1. The first conditional probability refers to whether there is nondiscriminatory or fair selection, the second to whether there is *random* selection, where random is used in its technical statistical sense. It is a major point of this paper, discussed at length in the next section, that there is no reason to expect nondiscriminatory employment practices to closely resemble the outcome of a random sample of employees from a specified pool of applicants.

2. The first conditional probability refers to the total evidence available (the observed disparity *and* all other evidence), the second only to the evidence of the observed disparity. The remaining evidence in an employment discrimination case will often be nonstatistical, perhaps of an anecdotal and individual nature, and it is hardly surprising that it does not enter into the calculation of the level of statistical significance.

Despite the first two reservations, one might pragmatically decide to proceed, keeping these distinctions in mind, and substitute in the first conditional probability "random" for "fair" or "nondiscriminatory," and "observed disparity" for "observed disparity and other evidence;" the result would be

P(random selection/observed disparity)

The sole difference between *this* conditional probability and the second,

P(observed disparity/random selection)

is that

3. The two terms, what is taken as given and what is in question, are juxtaposed.

It is this third difference, that between $P(A/B)$ and $P(B/A)$, which is crucial. The two conditional probabilities are not unrelated, but the relationship between them is complex and not easily stated, requiring the introduction of subjective probabilities. Perhaps a simple example, provided by John Maynard Keynes, will best make the distinction clear. Suppose the Archbishop of Canterbury were playing in a poker game: the probability that the Archbishop would deal himself a straight flush, given honest play on his part, is *not* the same as the probability of honest play on his part given that the prelate dealt himself a straight flush. (The first conditional probability may be calculated to be 40 in 2,598,960 and is quite small; the second conditional probability would be, at least for most Anglicans, much larger, indeed quite close to 1.) The first of the two probabilities is a frequency or so-called "objective" probability, stating what proportion of hands will, in the long run, give rise to straight flushes; the second probability is an epistemic or "subjective" probability, stating one's degree of belief or personal evaluation of the odds for the event in question. The first probability has a unique, statistically calculable value; the second will vary from person to person depending on his opinions and knowledge.

Consider a hypothetical example in the employment discrimination context. Suppose a statistical expert witness testifies that an observed hiring disparity is statistically significant at the 25% level. If this meant that there were a 75% probability that the employer had engaged in discriminatory practice, then under the preponderance of evidence standard we would be warranted in finding against him. But what the 25% in fact means is that *a company which hired at random would produce disparities this large 25% of the time.* That is, if we confine our attention to the stratum of random (or "fair") employers, we would, *by definition,* find that fully one out of every four such employers would exhibit disparities which were statistically significant at the 25% level. And if one were to look at different divisions within a single large company that hired randomly, one out of every four divisions would exhibit disparities significant at the 25% level.

Choice of significance level. Using statistical tests of significance to assess disparity requires not only strong assumptions about the sampling model (for the most part invalid or unverifiable, as discussed below ...), but also the choice of an appropriate probability level or level of significance at which a disparity will be considered substantial.

The Supreme Court's introduction of tests of significance in *Castaneda* and *Hazelwood* leaves a large measure of ambiguity about the significance level thought to provide convincing evidence (its reference to "2 or 3 standard errors" corresponds to a significance level between 5% and 1/4%). There is good reason for this. Courts ordinarily consider far more than statistical evidence, and in one case a difference not "significant" at the 5% level may combine with collateral evidence to make a convincing case of discrimination, while in another case a stronger statistical finding, say, a result significant at the 3% level, might be overcome by contrary evidence pointing to fair and nondiscriminatory practices. However, in light of the impact of the *Hazelwood* opinion on the lower courts, we have reason to wish for more specific guidance. Thus far that additional guidance has not been forthcoming, and therefore some review of the statistical tradition to which the Court alludes in *Castaneda* may prove helpful.

The tradition of choosing a specific "level of significance," and discounting evidence that fails to reach that level is due to the eminent British statistician and geneticist, R. A. Fisher. The method is presented most clearly, but almost solely by example, in his classic work *Statistical Methods for Research Workers*. An examination of Fisher's examples discloses that he regards any test of significance that results in a larger than 5% significance level (i.e., less than 1.96 standard errors) as unpersuasive, a difference with significance level between 5% and 2% (i.e., between 1.96 and 2.33 standard errors) as credible, and a difference with significance level more extreme than 2% (i.e., greater than 2.33 standard errors) as clearly indicative of a real, underlying difference. (Note that the *greater* the disparity, the *smaller* the probability that it would result from random selection, hence the *greater* the evidence it provides against the so-called null hypothesis of random selection. For this reason, a 2% level of significance is sometimes said to be "greater" than a 5% level; that is, the evidence against the null hypothesis is greater.)

Fisher thus thought of attained levels of significance as providing evidence against a hypothesis (in the present context, the assumption of random selection), smaller levels providing stronger evidence. He did not regard them, nor should the courts, as decision rules on which to alone accept or reject a hypothesis. As is the case with scientific questions, employment discrimination cases involve other types of evidence, and the extent or severity of relief granted by the court will, as a practical matter, depend on how clear or well established a case of discrimination is. The level of significance is therefore best thought of as but one item of evidence, rather than as the sole basis for a decision. Even though later approaches can also accommodate such considerations, we shall adopt Fisher's view with its attendant simplicity.

Extending the above ideas, some have argued that no magic resides in the conventional 5% level of significance; that, say, a 6% level of significance has very nearly the same persuasiveness as 5%; and that a useful mode of statistical presentation is simply to state the attained level of significance, however weak it may be. Thus, a result significant at the 20% level would be viewed as having some persuasive power, even though it would be far from convincing. Such a variant procedure departs markedly from Fisher's usage and seems more likely to confuse than clarify in the legal setting. The key point is to recognize that variation is pervasive, and that what is required is a means of avoiding distraction by inessential differences which have little or no probative value. Although an inherent arbitrariness obviously resides in the particular choice of the 5% (or any other) level as a universal minimal standard, such arbitrariness is unavoidable if one is to adopt a minimal standard, and *some* minimal standard is clearly necessary. The 5% level is the conventional choice. If a difference does not attain the 5% level of significance, it does not deserve to be given weight as evidence of a disparity. It is a "feather."

One- and two-sided tests. Implicit in our discussion of the simple models and their associated statistical tests is the premise that disparity would be recognized not only when the difference is negative but also when it is positive. Thus, even if blacks are favored in the sample data, disparity would be found. If one is asking whether the selection process treats blacks and whites equally, this "two-sided" view is natural enough. But if the appropriate question is whether the proportion of blacks hired is substantially *less* than some standard, then the disparity would be worthy of note only if, as in *Hazelwood,* it reflected less favorable treatment of blacks. The probability of a given disparity in a specified or "one-sided" direction is half the significance level provided by the "two-sided" perspective indicated above, and it is this one-sided formulation that is at the heart of Justice Stevens's statistical analysis in his dissent to the *Hazelwood* opinion.

The question whether to adopt a "one-sided" or a "two-sided" view has an ambiguous history in the statistical literature. Fisher, in his concern for scientific research, regarded one-sided tests as largely inappropriate for statistical inference; but some later commentators admit and employ one-sided tests in a prominent way. The matter is confounded with the choice of significance level, since the one-sided significance level is typically half the two-sided level. A simple rule, which we adopt here, is to take a one-sided 2½% level criterion (equivalent to a two-sided 5% level) and assert that an observed disparity could not have plausibly arisen from purely random fluctuations if the magnitude of the difference is more than 1.96 standard errors.

Critique of the Use of Statistical Models

With this statistical background in mind, we turn to a more detailed examination of the appropriateness of the statistical models used by the courts. There are two key assumptions required to permit unambiguous interpretation of the results of statistical testing, and neither is ordinarily capable of direct verification. We will discuss these two assumptions under the headings of *random selection* and *relevance.* Under *random selection* we deal with the issues of statistical independence and stratification; under *relevance,* we deal with the relationship of the models and statistical tests to the concept of discrimination. Because both these assumptions are likely to be violated to some degree in typical employment processes even in the absence of discrimination, a careful assessment of the applicability of these assumptions is essential to decide the extent to which statistical analysis should be used as evidence of discrimination.

Random Selection

[The statistical] models discussed [above] assume that (*a*) the sample(s) under review are produced by an effectively random process of sampling from the "relevant group(s)" and (*b*) that each such group is essentially equivalent to the population of appropriately qualified individuals. Thus, in judging the statistical significance of the disparate hiring in *Hazelwood,* the Court states explicitly that a large deviation from the given standard of black teachers, $p = 5.7\%$, "would undercut the hypothesis that decisions were being made *randomly* with respect to race." In other words, the hypothesis being tested is that each hire has probability 5.7% of resulting in the selection of a black and that choices are statistically independent, each being unrelated to the race outcome of any other choice or set of choices. A consequence of this assumption is that the probability of any particular sequence of hires will be a product of terms involving either $p = 5.7\%$ or $q = 1 - p = 94.3\%$. For example, the probability for the sequence WWBBW is $q \times q \times p \times p \times q = p^2q^3 = (.057)^2 (.943)^3 = .0027$. This algorithm for calculating probabilities is known as the "product rule," and it leads directly to the binomial probability distribution specified by the *Hazelwood* court. The product rule is often applied, almost as a matter of course, in circumstances in which there is no clear basis for the assumption of independence.

In fact, however, random sampling, which gives rise to the applicability of the product rule, is rarely present in nature or human affairs. Indeed, statistical sampling practitioners find they must go to great lengths to achieve it.

The Court is correct in its assertion that the recommended statistical procedure tests "randomness" in hiring to the extent that "randomness" is read to mean random selection from a specified pool of teachers. However, the Court then appears to equate "randomness" with "fairness" or "nondiscrimination" in employment. The latter concepts are relevant to the legal issue, but only the former is tested statistically; since hiring will seldom be truly "random" even if it *is* fair or racially nondiscriminatory, the nexus between the two sets of concepts is more problematic than is usually recognized.

Indeed, there is a long history in the legal literature of misconceived notions about the applicability of the assumptions of statistical independence and random sampling. Thus, in the context of employment testing, Shoben states: "Independence in performance can be assumed if no person is allowed to take the test more than once and there are no opportunities for cheating or passing on information about the test to later test takers." While these are certainly necessary conditions for independence, they are by no means sufficient, since they provide no constraints on the origin of the sample of applicants being tested. Two relevant issues here are the effects of *clustering* and *stratification*.

Clustering effects. As Smith and Abram aptly point out, varying recruitment procedures inevitably cause departures from the simple random sampling model:

> Actual hiring practices, however, rarely approximate a random process. For instance, an employer may vary its recruitment practice over time. The employer might recruit in the suburbs one month and the inner city next, or advertise job openings in a Spanish-language newspaper one week and a newspaper with a predominantly black readership the next. Thus, the selection of applicants resulting from these recruitment efforts may not, for any given time period, be truly random because the applicants may not be representative of the population in terms of ethnicity or socio-economic background. Because an employer's selection process cannot, by definition, be a random procedure, statistical inference cannot play as decisive a role in employment discrimination cases as it has in jury selection decisions. That an employer's selection process may not be random for any particular time period underscores the fact that economic concepts of labor supply and demand apply to employment patterns developed over the long term. Reliance on evidence from a narrow time period may be misleading, precluding reliable inferences about the nature of an employer's behavior.

It is easy to suggest other scenarios as well: a person recruited may recommend or otherwise bring along friends into the company; success with applicants from a given school or other organization may set up a short-term "pipeline" of future applicants. Any of these scenarios might be entirely compatible with nondiscriminatory hiring and even with overall long-term equality of selection rates for whites and blacks. However, they are not compatible with the binomial model on which the statistical tests are based. The problem is that this type of "clustered sampling" effect is the rule in real world hiring, not the exception.

In some circumstances it might be possible to take clustering into account in the statistical analysis. Since the allowance for error (the standard error) is inversely proportional to the sample size, it should be intuitively clear that clustering, by lowering the *effective* sample size, will necessarily increase the magnitude of the proper allowance for error. The resulting difference in sample sizes can have a profound effect because, as a general rule, *the smaller the sample size, the larger the disparity in rates can be without reaching statistical significance.*

To be specific, consider a hypothetical example: 100 blacks and 100 whites apply for jobs and do so in clusters; for example, groups of classmates apply together. For simplicity, suppose each cluster has 4 individuals, leading to 25 clusters of 4 blacks and 25 clusters of 4 whites, and that clusters are hired or rejected as a group. Thus, if there are 10 black clusters hired, then 40 blacks are hired, and if 15 white clusters are hired, then 60 whites are hired. Supposing that hiring decisions are made entirely at random, we have a random sample from the 25 clusters for each of the two groups. It follows that we should compare the cluster rates, which are 10/25 and 15/25 for blacks and whites, respectively, to determine if a significant disparity exists. Even though the individual hire rates themselves (40/100, 60/100) are equivalent to the cluster rates (10/25, 15/25), the sample size of the cluster data is only one-quarter as large as the number of individuals. Since decisions were made by clusters, not by individuals, comparison of the individual hire rates could not properly be based on the theory of random sampling of individuals. In this example, the smaller cluster sample doubles the standard error that would result if the analysis were made using individual data. Thus, what might appear to be a significant difference in the individual rates assessed using the binomial standard error can (and in this example does) turn out to be a nonsignificant difference in cluster rates if clustering effects are taken into account.

Where clustering is measurable and can be taken into account in the analysis, or where it is a result of illegal practice (e.g., if only the sons of existing union members are admitted to apprenticeship), the strain on the assumption of random sampling as a standard for judgment is not a critical matter. However, the existence of undetected and "natural" clustering, which is bound to exist to some degree and which can rarely be measured or modeled, substantially diminishes the credibility of the random selection assumption.

Stratification. A second source of variability not accounted for in the simple random sampling model results from the aggregation of several distinct but related job categories into a single broader one. Thus the category of "craft" worker might include carpenters, plumbers, and electricians, as well as other specialties, but data on the racial composition of the pool of craft workers may not provide so much detail. If there are different proportions of blacks in the several subgroups, or strata, an employer operating "fairly" in his hiring from each stratum separately might nonetheless appear to be hiring a substantially lower proportion of blacks overall than the proportion of blacks in the combined employment pool.

An example of this effect is provided by an analysis of graduate admission rates for men and women at the University of California in Berkeley. Overall, the percentage of male applicants admitted in 1973 was significantly higher than the percentage of admissions among female applicants, but a survey of the admissions to individual departments showed that for virtually all departments the admission rate for male applicants was lower than the admission rate for females.

This paradoxical situation, sometimes referred to as *Simpson's paradox,* actually has a very simple explanation. At Berkeley, women had applied preferentially to departments such as English and History, with large numbers of applicants and correspondingly low rates of admission, while men had applied preferentially to departments such as Mathematics and Physics with fewer numbers of applicants and hence much higher rates of admission. Simpson's paradox should not be thought of as a rare or freakish event: instances can easily be found. To cite another example in perhaps a more familiar setting, it will come as no surprise that from 1976 to 1979 the overall rate of personal income paid out as federal income tax increased, although surprisingly, the rate in each bracket actually decreased. The explanation: because of inflation, taxpayers had been pushed into higher brackets.

Stratification can occur when different divisions of a firm make hiring decisions independently of one another. Such decisions may appear fair at the divisional level but unfair when viewed in the aggregate. Like clustering, stratification (i.e., aggregation of relevant strata), may occur in nondetectable ways or, even when detectable, in ways not amenable to appropriate measurement or calculation. It is possible, of course, that an employer may create irrelevant or unnecessary strata in an attempt to explain away the appearance of discrimination, but the existence of real strata beyond the reach of analysis is pervasive and, once again, undercuts the simple random sampling model.

In a typical hiring situation there may be some aspects of clustering and some of stratification. Taking these considerations into account (as well as others previously mentioned), we must reject the proposition that hiring is a random selection process. Although the facts of a given case may indicate that there are gross departures from random selection (e.g., resulting from an affirmative action plan, as in *Washington v. Davis*), the absence of such an indication does *not* ensure that the departure from random selection is trivial or negligible.

·   ·   ·

Relevance

As the Supreme Court implicitly notes, the consideration of statistics bearing on a charge of discrimination must begin with the question of what should reasonably be expected in a situation where discrimination is absent. In *Teamsters,* the Court states:

> absent explanation, it is ordinarily to be expected that nondiscriminatory hiring practices will in time result in a work force more or less representative of the racial and ethnic composition of the population in the community from which employees are hired. Evidence of longlasting and gross disparity between the composition of a work force and that of the general population thus may be significant even though §703(j) makes clear that Title VII imposes no requirement that a work force mirror the general population.

One need not call on the special insights of the statistician or the scientist to recognize that the first assertion in this statement is untenable, and it can only be given a reasonable interpretation as a statement of the impartiality with which the Court must approach a case of this kind. Two major effects that preclude an expectation of absolute representativeness in the work force are the *correlation of characteristics* and *self-selection.*

Correlation of characteristics.... In view of long-term social deprivation enforced on some racial groups, it is hardly surprising that for tests requiring high levels of education or extensive familiarity with certain aspects of the dominant culture, performance is less favorable for some groups than for others. Thus, one might well expect average performance in IQ tests to vary among groups, depending on the extent of language acquisition, education, length of residence, and cultural assimilation, although few could predict in any detail the direction of such intergroup differences. (For example, one might predict that the dominant culture group in a country would always outperform any other, but, in fact, Orientals in the United States have, on average, higher IQ scores than do comparably educated Caucasians.)

The point intended under this heading is not that *substantial* differences will always exist between groups but merely that typically *some* differences do, that the relation is often one of association or correlation rather than one of direct causation, and that for that very reason neither the size nor the direction of such differences can usually be reliably predicted.

Selection. A second major limitation on the interpretation of comparisons between hire or promotion rates for different groups is the self selection of individuals in applying for a position.

. . .

The issue arose in *Hazelwood* (did the affirmative action plan of the city of St. Louis deter city black teachers from applying for jobs in the county?), but the opinion deals with it only in a superficial way.

A substantial contribution to self-selection arises from cultural diversity in the population. Thus, a group in which there is general disapproval of women who work in any but a few professions may contribute its most intelligent and able women to those few approved professions—for example, teaching. At the same time, the abilities of male applicants in those fields will be more varied, and thus female applicants might be expected to test better than males.

An additional, perhaps extensive, force for differential selection is the effect of discriminatory practices elsewhere in the labor market. Qualified women finding themselves largely excluded from such professions as engineering will compete for positions in teaching, nursing, and the like, and the quality of female applicants for positions in those professions will therefore be high. A substantial fraction of qualified men, however, will be drained off into engineering, and the average ability of the males applying in the other areas mentioned would be correspondingly reduced.

A pervasive source of selection is simple proximity. If an employer operates from a location central for group A but inconvenient for members of group B, it is plausible that he will find a wide spread of abilities among his applicants from group A but be limited to the less able members of group B—those unable to find employment more conveniently located for them.

Admittedly, conventional expectations of the direction and magnitude of differences do not form a suitable basis for legal adjudication in a case alleging discrimination. Considerations of equity and justice may indeed require a neutral stance on the part of the law. The point we emphasize here, however, is that "neutrality" is not equivalent to an assumption of "no difference." This is distinct from our point about the failure of randomness. If there is a failure of random sampling in the form of clustered sampling, the use of simple statistical tests would incorporate an underestimate of the standard error, possibly by a large factor, but if the groups compared are inherently of equal ability, we would still expect—with a sufficiently large sample—a nondiscriminatory employment test to produce very nearly equal pass rates. The point we catalog under the term "relevance" is that *small differences in characteristics of all kinds, including ability at different tasks between identifiably distinct groups, are the norm and not the exception, and that with very large samples—one so large that sampling error itself is negligible— we should not expect to find exactly equal performance.* All experience points the other way.

Thus, a reasonable allowance for "nondiscriminatory disparities" (i.e., a degree of disparity ordinarily to be expected where no discrimination is at work) cannot reasonably be based on random sampling models, nor is it sufficient to multiply the standard error by some factor to allow for the effects of nonrandom sampling. We must to some degree allow for the pervasive fact that groups do indeed differ from one another, and that a small difference in average performance, albeit a real one, is not reasonably to be regarded as prima facie evidence of prohibited discrimination.

The key issue is most obvious in cases involving large employers; in a case involving thousands of test takers, it is almost certain that the pass rate for blacks and whites will be statistically disparate, simply because the large sample sizes will tend to make *any* difference *statistically* significant. In smaller samples the failure to allow for real but unimportant differences is largely masked, because the standard errors based on the random selection model are large enough to swamp them. In larger samples the issue cannot unfortunately be thus avoided. In a comparison with, say, 2,000 black and 2,000 white applicants a pass rate of 62% for one group and 64% for the other would result in a finding of a statistically significant difference. If the finding is controlling and the lower pass rate goes with whites, no consequences would typically ensue, but if it goes with blacks it would result, under the methodology advanced in *Hazelwood,* in a finding of prima facie evidence of discrimination against blacks. Thus a firm employing large numbers is almost certain to find that, under the *Hazelwood* standard, its tests or hiring criteria show adverse impact against one group or another. It must then be prepared to mount studies to validate these hiring criteria as predictive of employee productivity (and face the enormous obstacles so well described by Lerner) or abandon the hiring criteria or employment tests altogether and operate by quota, hiring and promoting equal proportions—in effect, using different standards for different groups. Whether this results in good or bad policy and whether it conforms to congressional intent in passing the Civil Rights Act are questions we do not address.

In summary: (*a*) The standard statistical models are based on the assumption of random sampling, an assumption that is unjustified in hiring processes, at least in part, because of clustering or stratification. (*b*) Even when there is only a minor departure from the random sampling model, the sole use of statistical significance tests would be inappropriate because it can lead (especially in large samples) to the detection of disparities even when discrimination is absent, because of correlations between individual characteristics and applicant self-selection.

Alternative Outlooks

What should the Court do, then, given this gap between mathematical theory and practical reality? There are two polar positions.

Abolitionists and Strict Constructionists

This position, represented by legal scholar Laurence Tribe and statistician David Freedman, is that one should entirely eschew the use of *inferential statistics* in situations such as employment discrimination cases. Tribe has argued that quantitative methods are easily misused: they often hide unstated assumptions, focus attention on those elements of a case most readily quantified (but not necessarily most important), and imperil the values of our society by making explicit the implicit fallibility of our legal system. Apart from the last objection, which has troubling paternalistic and elitist implications, these are all legitimate concerns, but they are equally applicable to *any* type of expert testimony: experts often make unequivocal assertions later contradicted by other experts, state conclusions based on a large number of theoretical assumptions seldom articulated and often inapplicable, and carry undue weight with the jury. Just as with any form of technical or scientific evidence, the use of statistics calls for caution rather than neglect.

Freedman, coauthor of a recent and influential textbook, argues that statistical methods of inference should only be used when a random sampling model is clearly applicable. There is again much merit in such a position. The academic literature, as Freedman's text amply illustrates, is rife with examples where no model makes sense and the statistical application is dubious or inappropriate. Numbers, like words, must have a definable and relatively precise meaning to inform; statistical levels of significance refer to the frequency with which certain events occur when samples are drawn at random from a prespecified population, and, absent the framework of a genuinely random process, the onus lies on the user of statistical techniques to justify their appropriateness.

The Benthamites

The holders of the opposite position find the sirenlike attraction of mathematical precision too powerful to resist. If we can succeed in framing a question in a form admitting an exact mathematical solution, we will have at least escaped some of the uncertainties and fallibility with which the law is usually afflicted. The difficulty is: In forcing our old problem into this new form, is the resulting question truly relevant?

A closely related position is that decisions have to be made: life is complex and we should take advantage of anything that aids or assists us. Quibbles about the relevance of random sampling models are just that—we are trying to do the best we can. Although in the best of all possible worlds the model assumptions would be met, at least we are using an objective methodology, which is better than nothing. The trouble with such an argument is that when the model departures are serious, one risks giving credibility or undue weight to an erroneous conclusion; when the mathematical abstraction is a caricature rather than a mirror of reality, it is best to simply face up to that fact and acknowledge a situation that does not admit of simple or clean answers.

Our own approach to these questions lies between the two polar positions (although it is certainly much closer to the first than the second). Statistics per se cannot ascertain whether employment discrimination exists. Nor is the question answered by the standard significance test immediately relevant: hiring does not typically proceed by random selection from a pool. But statistical testing is, we would argue, a useful *bench mark*.

Recognizing the difficulties inherent in proving discriminatory intent on an individual basis, the courts have permitted plaintiffs to proceed by impeaching the *process* by which employment takes place. Although hiring is not a process of random selection, it is not unreasonable to compare it to such a bench-mark process. If the disparity between black and white hire rates is so small that it could have arisen by random sampling from an appropriate population, then it seems reasonable to conclude that the statistics, by themselves, provide no evidence of discrimination.

But what if the differences in hire rates are "statistically significant?" As we have pointed out, it would be inappropriate to view this alone as establishing a prima facie case of discrimination. The first reason for being wary of a statistically significant disparity is that the basic assumptions for applicability of the random sampling model do not apply in employment settings, and may cause the perceived significance of the data to be unduly inflated. We have shown how this arises in the discussion of random sampling.... The second reason is that even if sampling were random from an identifiable pool, *statistical* significance does not imply *practical* significance. To prove that *some* difference exists is not to prove that the difference is the result of legally cognizable discrimination. If we roll a carefully balanced pair of dice enough times, we will inevitably find some departure from the expected outcomes, since perfection in the manufacture is impossible. With a large enough number of rolls, such departures may exhibit statistical significance, but they are certainly not of "practical significance." We have noted in the discussion of "relevance" ... why some differences between groups must be expected as the rule and why it is indispensable that some allowance should be made for departures from a model that can only be hypothetically credible....

Statistical Proof of Discrimination: Beyond "Damned Lies"*

KINGSLEY R. BROWNE

Introduction

· · ·

The method of proving discrimination through statistical proof is based upon faulty statistical and factual assumptions, and because of misconceived interpretations of the meaning of statistical evidence, courts have developed evidentiary doctrines that have the effect of improperly shifting the burden of proof to defendants in discrimination cases. It is the thesis of this Article that statistical evidence of intentional discrimination should be abandoned as a primary method of proof and should become, at most, merely an adjunct to evidence that specific persons have been subjected to discrimination.

· · ·

The centerpiece of a plaintiff's proof ... is a demonstration that the observed representation of women or minorities in the employer's work force is lower than the representation that would be "expected" if employment decisions were made randomly with respect to race or sex; that demonstration is, in turn, coupled with an inference that underrepresentations are a consequence of intentional discrimination....

· · ·

* Excerpts from Kingsley R. Browne, "Statistical Proof of Discrimination: Beyond 'Damned Lies,' " *Washington Law Review,* vol. 68, copyright © 1993 by the University of Washington Law Review. Reprinted with permission of the author and the publisher.

The leap from statistical disparity to a prima facie case of discrimination is based on two powerful, necessary, but incorrect, assumptions—one logical and the other factual. The logical assumption, referred to here as the "Statistical Fallacy," [erroneously conflates two different probabilities].

. . .

The first probability is the probability of the observed disparity given random selection; the second is the probability of random selection given the observed disparity. As will be discussed below, there is no direct relationship between these two probabilities, yet courts uniformly interpret the first probability—which is the only one they have—as if it were evidence of the second, which is the one they need.

. . .

The factual assumption upon which the prima facie case of discrimination is founded, referred to here as the "Central Assumption," is that in the absence of discrimination one would expect that the work force of each employer would—with only chance variations—mirror the racial and sexual composition of the relevant labor force. Put another way, courts assume that blacks, whites, males, and females are all equally likely to be qualified and available for—and interested in—each job.

. . .

The Statistical Fallacy

The core of the Statistical Fallacy is the belief that the probability that a given event occurred by chance is the same as the prior probability of observing the event in a random draw.

. . .

The standard statistical analysis in discrimination cases is one that would support findings of liability against thousands of nondiscriminating employers. Assuming for illustrative purposes that there is no discrimination in the workplaces under consideration and that the employer hires randomly—and even assuming that all employees and applicants are fungible—one in twenty statistical comparisons will result in a conclusion that the observed disparity was caused by nonchance factors, and every one of those conclusions will be wrong. More than 5 percent of employers are at risk, however, because for any given employer there can be statistical comparisons for each job, for each department, for the various racial, ethnic, and sex groupings, and for different time periods. All employers of significant size would likely have substantial numbers of jobs for which a statistical disparity could be demonstrated. Yet the true probability that the observed disparities were obtained by something other than chance is, by hypothesis, zero.

The objection to the hypothesis-testing approach is not that it yields only approximate results or even that it occasionally yields incorrect results.... Rather, the objection to hypothesis testing is that it yields meaningless results. A court's conclusion that a difference between the employer's actual work force and the statistically predicted work force demonstrates that the employer's work force probably (but not certainly) is the product of nonrandom factors is logically flawed. This error in analysis has dramatic consequences, for it causes a court faced with a statistically significant disparity to reason, "I'm faced with a disparity that is very unlikely to have occurred by chance; this rare result is suspicious, and the employer ought to explain it," when it should be thinking, "The plaintiff has described statistics that would be true for thousands of nondiscriminating employers; if the plaintiff wants me to suspect discrimination, he'd better give me a lot more than that."

. . .

Treating statistically significant differences as prima facie proof of discrimination—and thereby calling upon employers to prove a systematic, but nondiscriminatory, cause under pain of liability—places an insurmountable burden on many employers in those cases where the disparities are actually due to chance. Chance disparities that are significant at the 5-percent level are ubiquitous, but under current law highly suspect. Nondiscriminatory disparities are therefore very costly for employers, exacerbating the pressures on them to adopt either overt or surreptitious quotas.

. . .

The Central Assumption

... The factual assumption that a non-discriminating employer's work force would (except for chance variations) mirror the race, ethnic, sex, and age profile of the "qualified" population—what I call the Central Assumption—is an essential foundation of a theory that allows an inference of discrimination to be drawn from statistical disparities. Tests of statistical significance are deemed to exclude chance as a cause of the disparities, and the assumption that populations are equally qualified and interested in each job excludes differential qualifications and interest as explanations for the disparities. Courts are then left with discrimination as the only possible explanation.

. . .

The Central Assumption and Other Title VII Doctrine

The Central Assumption is fundamentally inconsistent with assumptions underlying other Title VII doctrine. For example, advocates of affirmative action have long argued that simple compliance with the nondiscrimination mandate of Title VII will not achieve full integration of women and minorities into the work force in the foreseeable future. Because historically disfavored groups—especially blacks—are so disadvantaged by deficits in education and employment, the argument goes, without affirmative action full integration will take generations. Thus, the rationale underlying affirmative action is exactly contrary to the rationale supporting statistical inferences of discrimination. The former posits that proportional representation is not, at least in the near term, the expected consequence of nondiscrimination; the latter posits that it is.

. . .

[A]t least in the absence of applicant-flow data, courts will generally require comparisons between the employer's work force and the "qualified labor force." The statistical analysis of intentional discrimination then assumes that within this "qualified labor force" qualifications and interest are randomly distributed with respect to race and sex. Limiting the statistical comparison to this qualified labor force is thought to control for differences in qualifications between groups.

The assumption that qualifications are randomly distributed by race and sex within the qualified labor force has no more empirical basis than the same assumption with respect to the general population. The qualifications that define the qualified labor force are so generalized as to belie any claim that there is serious control for qualifications. For example, if the employer requires a law degree for a position, then the qualified labor force would be those persons having such a degree, the ostensible assumption being that qualifications are now controlled for. Yet, how many of the law professors who argue for holding employers liable on the basis of such statistics think that all law school graduates are equally qualified to be hired on their faculties? How many believe that the qualifications of a randomly selected graduate of the "worst" law school are likely to be equal to those of a randomly selected graduate of the "best" law school? How many believe that the person who graduates at the top of his class from a given law school is no better than the person who graduates at the bottom of the same class? How many believe—notwithstanding discrimination in education, differences in attitudes toward education, and any other reasons that may cause racial differences in educational achievement—that blacks and whites on average will have equal law school credentials? The tendency of law schools to hire highly credentialed applicants and to hire "affirmative-action candidates" with lesser credentials suggests that most faculty members believe that credentials are important and not uniformly distributed throughout the population. Yet the core principle of the Central Assumption is that those with the minimum qualifications are essentially fungible and that reliance on higher qualifications is likely to have a race- and sex-neutral result.

. . .

The assumption that race and ethnicity are unrelated to productivity is so demonstrably false as to require little refutation. For example, we are constantly told that blacks attend inferior schools, tend to get less education, do less well on standardized achievement tests and, one suspects, although data are not as readily available, do less well in schools even when they finish. . . .

Notes and Questions

1. The hiring, promotion, discharge, and discipline rates of white men frequently differ from those of protected groups. Using a 5 percent confidence level to test whether these disparities are statistically significant means that 5 percent of the time in which the disparities are purely random, one would erroneously reject the hypothesis that the discrepancies were produced merely by chance. A problem exists if plaintiffs' lawyers can simply comb through personnel records to find the 5 percent of disparities that lead to an erroneous rejection of the hypothesis that the racial or other differential was caused by chance, and then use the statistical test as "proof" of discrimination. Of course, the statistical test is invalidated if one has simply selected a given disparity for litigation by mechanically screening cases to find "statistically significant" disparities.

Browne argues that "More than 5 percent of employers are at risk, however, because for any given employer there can be statistical comparisons for each job, for each department, for the various racial, ethnic, and sex groupings, and for different time periods" (p. 489). Browne's statement implicitly assumes that the courts will use a one-tailed test of statistical significance at the .05 confidence level. Although there are differences among scholars and courts on this issue, most courts have followed the position adopted in *Palmer v. Shultz,* 815 F.2d 84, 96 (D.C.Cir.1987) that "a court should generally adopt a two-tailed approach to evaluating the probability that the contested disparity resulted by chance."

If courts use a two-tailed test of statistical significance, then half of the statistically significant, albeit randomly generated, disparities would favor white men and half would favor the protected group. One would imagine that the cases in which the disparities favored the protected group would be far less likely to generate litigation. This factor suggests that the number of disparities that would erroneously give rise to an inference of disparate treatment—albeit still uncomfortably large—is likely to be only half as great as Browne contends.

2. To convey a sense of the percentage of firms that are at risk of litigation by virtue of the existence of statistically significant disparities in the gender or racial composition of their workforce, consider the results of a study that looked at female employment in eating and drinking establishments in Los Angeles County, California, and black employment among office and clerical workers in banks in Cook County, Illinois. Robert Follett, Michael Ward, and Finis Welch, "Problems in Assessing Employment Discrimination," 83 *American Economic Review Papers and Proceedings* 73 (May 1993). The study began by noting that 48.4 percent of the employees in

all eating and drinking establishments in Los Angeles were women. The authors then examined the percentage of establishments that had a statistically significant shortfall in the number of women employees relative to the baseline of 48.4 percent female employment. While purely random selection from fungible male and female employees would lead to 2.5 percent of the firms falling into this category, in fact "14.3 percent of establishments have too few women to an extent that exceeds the two-standard deviation cutoff."

The pattern is even more extreme among the bank workers in Chicago, where "52.2 of all banking establishments feature a statistically significant shortfall in the employment of black clerical workers [relative to the baseline of 15.9 percent black office and clerical employment in all such establishments]." In other words, if hiring for these two types of jobs were completely random in Los Angeles and Chicago, one would expect the test of statistically significant shortfalls in the hiring of women and blacks to "indict" 2.5 percent of the firms, but in fact the statistical test indicts 14.3 percent of the Los Angeles eating and drinking establishments and 52.2 percent of the Chicago banks.

The problem with the bald statistical evidence is that it reveals with a high degree of certainty that the pattern of hiring was not random, but it doesn't tell us what generated the observed shortfalls. Follett, Ward, and Welch conceded that the huge variations in firms in representation by gender and race may be caused by discrimination, but concluded that other nondiscriminatory factors also influenced the observed employment patterns. As a result, different firms—perhaps due to geographic location, the timing of hiring, or the level of wages offered—do not hire from a single, homogeneous pool of potential employees, as the statistical tests implicitly presume. As Browne emphasizes, these factors may make a response to a statistically based prima facie showing of discrimination difficult for an innocent employer to rebut.

If the average number of women or blacks in a certain type of job category within a city is taken to be the appropriate baseline number, why should it matter whether some firms hire more than the average and some hire less? Does this suggest that the Follett, Ward, and Welch study is focused on the wrong comparison? For example, assume that a black plaintiff tried to use statistical evidence to show racial discrimination in the hiring of office and clerical workers at a Chicago bank. The Supreme Court in *Hazelwood* suggested that the appropriate statistical test for discrimination against blacks in such a firm would compare the percentage of black office and clerical workers in that firm with the percentage of qualified workers in the relevant labor market for that Chicago bank who are black. The Follett, Ward, and Welch comparison differs from the *Hazelwood* comparison as long as the relevant labor market for the particular bank in question is not the class of all current office and clerical workers in Cook County. If the relevant labor market were greater than Cook County, it would probably bring in more whites, thereby lowering the percentage of blacks against which any individual bank would be compared. Conversely, if the relevant labor market included all clerical workers in any industry operating within Cook County, then the benchmark percentage could be either substantially higher or lower than the one used by Follett, Ward, and Welch. Would the *Hazelwood* comparison eliminate at least some of the variability owing to nondiscriminatory factors that would be injected in the Follett, Ward, and Welch comparison across all firms?

3. The issue over how high a threshold of reliability should be imposed before courts will accept statistical evidence of discrimination is simply one aspect of the larger problem indirectly touched upon by Alfred Blumrosen in Section 4.1 of Chapter 4, concerning the relative risks and burdens from inappropriately failing to sanction a discriminator versus inappropriately sanctioning a nondiscriminator. Blumrosen uses the illustration of the widespread racial discrimination in the South at the time of the passage of the 1964 Civil Rights Act to argue that the courts wisely established a lower threshold of proof when discrimination was rampant, but appropriately tightened the standard as discrimination waned and the likelihood of wrongfully imposing liability on nondiscriminators grew. If one believes that discrimination is pervasive and that discriminators will respond to the threat of liability, then one would favor a relaxed standard of statistical proof of a prima facie case of discrimination. Conversely, many believe that discrimination is rare, and that the employer response to the threat of liability does little to reduce the amount of discrimination but instead imposes costly and efficiency-reducing changes in the workplace. Those subscribing to this position would favor a more stringent standard of proof of discrimination, whether based on statistical evidence or not.

The ultimate question of interest is whether society benefits by allowing the use of inferential statistics in employment discrimination cases. Would prohibiting this method of establishing discrimination impede plaintiffs and aid defendants? Allowing statistical evidence probably gives employers—both discriminators and nondiscriminators—an incentive to narrow any statistical disparities by increasing their hiring of black workers. Is this an advantage or disadvantage? If an advantage, does it outweigh the costs of erroneous findings of discrimination based on statistical evidence?

4. Statistical proof of discrimination sometimes founders because certain explanatory variables are unknown or unquantifiable. Consider in this regard *EEOC v. Sears, Roebuck & Co.*, 839 F.2d 302 (7th Cir.1988), in which the EEOC charged Sears with sex discrimination in hiring commission salespersons, and Sears defended on the ground that women and men were not equally interested in such positions. To account for this factor, the EEOC incorporated into its statistical analysis an assumption that the proportion of men interested in such jobs was three times greater than the proportion of women so interested. The EEOC noted that, even with this adjustment, the statistical evidence suggested the presence of sex discrimination in hiring. Since the true value of the proportion of male and female workers interested in such jobs was unknown, the question was whether the uncertainty concerning this variable would redound to the benefit of the plaintiff or to Sears. The district court and a majority of the Seventh Circuit Court of Appeals rejected the EEOC's analysis—a result Browne heartily approves—while the dissenting opinion by Judge Cudahy argued that the EEOC's adjustment was reasonable in light of the "skepticism that courts

ought to show toward defenses to Title VII actions that rely on unquantifiable traits ascribed to protected groups." Id. at 361. Was the EEOC's approach a reasonable method of dealing with the uncertainty over this variable? Does it provide a strong enough foundation for a finding of disparate treatment discrimination? For further discussion of the *Sears* case, see the selection by Vicki Schultz in Chapter 13.

5. An example will illustrate the potential value of a statistical study in illuminating conflicting assertions about discrimination. Richard Epstein argues strenuously in *Forbidden Grounds* (Cambridge, Mass.: Harvard University Press, 1992) at 503 that the effort to ban discrimination has merely changed the identity of the victims:

> Anyone who works in academic circles, and I dare say elsewhere, knows full well that *all* the overt and institutional discrimination comes from those who claim to be the victims of discrimination imposed by others. It is a sad day when any effort to defend the traditional norms of a discipline, profession, trade, or craft exposes the defender to withering political attack for a covert form of discrimination under the guise of excellence and neutral standards. In all too many cases honorable people are attacked as racist or sexist when the charges often apply with far greater truth to the persons who make these charges than to the persons about whom they are made.

Interestingly, Epstein's strong prediction that *all* the overt discrimination comes from those who claim to be the victims of discrimination directly conflicts with the prediction of one of the major critical race theorists, Richard Delgado. Consider Delgado's statements, written in dialogue form:

> [T]he informal nature of equality of opportunity allows members of an empowered group to call upon and invoke the many culturally established routines, practices, and understandings that benefit them.... Take our earlier [example] of the law school that can only hire one professor. There are two finalists, a Black and a white. The formal job description contains the standard criteria: potential for scholarship, teaching, and public service. The two finalists seem equally qualified in each of those respects. Equality of results would dictate that the Black applicant get the job because of the small number of African Americans on the faculty. That is, the approach would strive for equality, for proportional representation, or some similar measure. But ... under equality of opportunity *the white will inevitably get the position.* Equality of opportunity only guarantees that both will receive initial consideration. And when both candidates are considered, a myriad of factors, some conscious, some unconscious will come into play: inflection, small talk, background, bearing, social class, and the many imponderables that go into evaluating 'collegiality.' Critical Race Theory argues, and the battle for civil rights demonstrates, that such a regime is exactly the opposite of fair and neutral....
>
> So, equality of opportunity really just amounts to affirmative action for whites.... It builds in a background of unstated assumptions that confer a consistent advantage in all the competitions that matter. If

society were serious about equality, it would abolish this way of doing things and opt for equality of results. But this is something our culture will never do.... It has defined equal opportunity, the approach which permits its members to win, as legal, principled, and just. If one were to devise a system that would, first, produce racially discrepant results, and, second, enable those who manage and benefit from the system to sleep well at night, it would look very much like the present one.

Delgado, "Rodrigo's Fourth Chronicle: Neutrality and Stasis in Antidiscrimination Law," 45 *Stanford Law Review* 1133, 1149–51 (1993) (emphasis supplied).

6. A recent study by Deborah Merritt and Barbara Reskin, which analyzes law school hiring over the period 1986 through 1991, has examined precisely the issue raised by the opposing statements of Delgado and Epstein. Merritt and Reskin, "Sex, Race, and Credentials: The Truth about Affirmative Action in Law School Hiring." (Draft 1994). The study examined the 1094 professors who were hired into their first tenure-track position during these years, and used a regression model to predict the institutional prestige of the first school to hire them based on the traits of the professors—which are referred to as the independent, or explanatory, variables. The explanatory variables employed in the regression were race, sex, prestige of the undergraduate institution and law school, membership on the law review, type of judicial clerkship, possession of a doctorate or master's degree in a field other than law, and whether the individual previously worked for a law firm, used the AALS recruitment process, was hired by his or her own law school, previously had a non-tenure-track job, or imposed a major geographic limit on his or her job search. Merritt and Reskin conclude that men of color did obtain tenure-track positions at significantly more prestigious institutions than the schools that hired comparably credentialed white men. On the basis of their constructed law school prestige scale ranging from a low of –4.81 to a high of 4.03, the authors found that:

> White women and men of color both obtained jobs at significantly more prestigious institutions than did white men with equivalent credentials.... For white women, their sex conferred an advantage of about four-tenths of a prestige point.... To put this another way, the effect of being female was analogous to the effect of having a master's degree in a field other than law, a credential that also conferred an advantage of about four-tenths of a point in institutional prestige.

> The advantage for men of color was somewhat greater—almost seven-tenths of a point in institutional prestige.... The advantage for men of color can also be compared to the advantage conferred by having a doctorate in a nonlaw field. Id. at 12.

Can we use the evidence amassed by Merritt and Reskin to evaluate Epstein's prediction that *all* the discrimination in academic circles will be in favor of the black candidate, and Delgado's prediction that *all* the discrimination in this setting will favor the white candidate? Merritt and Reskin found that if two candidates, a black man and a white man, had equivalent objective credentials, the black man would be hired at a law school that was

.68 prestige points higher (on the roughly 9-point scale) than the white man. Similarly, a white woman could expect to be hired at a law school that was .4 prestige points higher than the law school that would hire an equally credentialed white man.

To put in perspective the .68 and .4 advantages enjoyed by black men and white women, consider some of the other features that generated benefits in law school hiring: the bonus conferred by membership on the law review was .45, for having a nonlaw doctorate was .67, for having a nonlaw master's degree was .40, for clerking on the Supreme Court was 1.28, and for clerking for the Court of Appeals was .65. In addition, each increase of 1 point in the prestige index of the law school that the candidate attended increased the prestige of the hiring law school by .48.

On its face, this study directly contradicts Delgado's speculation that law schools confronted with black and white candidates with equal objective credentials would always hire the white candidate. But although the evidence is strong and statistically significant, one must consider the possibility that some of the explanatory variables could themselves have been influenced by prejudice or affirmative action. For example, if Supreme Court justices were biased against black men, then fewer blacks would have achieved this highly beneficial credential than their merits would dictate. This could lead to a spurious finding of an advantage in black male hiring when in fact it simply implied bias in securing Supreme Court clerkships. Conversely, if affirmative action aids blacks in securing credentials such as admission to law school, college, or graduate school, then the estimated amount of affirmative action in law school hiring could be understated. In sum, the unadjusted regression evidence supports the view that black men benefited from affirmative action in law school hiring during the period of this study. The evidence in support of preferences for white women is less strong, because both the regression estimate of the magnitude of such a preference is smaller than that for black men, and the extent of affirmative action in securing the various schooling credentials is probably more modest for white women than for black men. See the discussion in John Donohue, "The Legal Response to Discrimination: Does Law Matter?" in Bryant Garth & Austin Sarat, eds., *Justice and Power in Socio-Legal Studies* (Evanston: Northwestern University Press, 1997).

7.   Merritt and Reskin also conclude that black women had no statistically significant advantage over white men in the law school hiring process. If we can take this finding at face value in light of the confounding effects of possible discrimination against and preferences for black women in securing the various credentials, then it would be inaccurate to claim that blacks and women are advantaged in law school hiring, since black women appear to get no such advantage. This finding vindicates the concerns expressed by Kimberlé Crenshaw in her article "Demarginalizing the Intersection of Race and Sex: A Black Feminist Critique of Antidiscrimination Doctrine, Feminist Theory and Antiracist Politics," *University of Chicago Legal Forum* 139 (1989), that there is a tendency "to treat race and gender as mutually exclusive categories of experience and analysis." Crenshaw notes that

> Black women can experience discrimination in ways that are both
> similar to and different from those experienced by white women and
> Black men. Black women sometimes experience discrimination in ways
> similar to white women's experiences; sometimes they share very similar
> experiences with Black men. Yet often they experience double-discrimi-
> nation—the combined effects of practices which discriminate on the
> basis of race, and on the basis of sex. And sometimes they experience
> discrimination as Black women—not the sum of race and sex discrimina-
> tion, but as Black women. (p 149)

The finding that black women receive no advantage in seeking law professor
jobs is surprising, particularly because other studies have suggested that
firms that are interested in securing workers that can meet affirmative
action guidelines will be most interested in hiring black women, since one
worker can fill two quota categories. James Smith and Finis Welch, "Affirmative Action in Labor Markets," 2 *Journal of Labor Economics* 269 (1984).
The presence of this effect in the economy at large, coupled with its absence
in the legal academy, may reflect the inapplicability of the federal government contract compliance program to law school hiring. It would be interesting to explore whether the particular pattern of apparent preferences for
black men and white women, but not for black women, is unique to law
school hiring or applies more broadly to hiring of highly educated workers.

8. Should law professors with certain credentials, such as a Ph.D. in a
nonlaw field or a Supreme Court clerkship, be favored in the law school
hiring process? Would such reliance on credentials have a disparate impact
on the hiring of black candidates? If so, would law schools be able to avoid a
disparate impact violation of Title VII by justifying such credentials as
consistent with business necessity? See Norman Redlich, "Law School Faculty Hiring under Title VII: How a Judge Might Decide a Disparate Impact
Case," 41 *Journal of Legal Education* 135 (1991).

> Consider in this regard some evidence presented by Paul Carrington:

> [B]y 1989, there were 1237 women law teachers, up from 39 in 1967.
> This number constituted about 0.9% of the women lawyers in America.
> For the 1986–87 academic year there were 187 African-American law
> teachers in schools other than those primarily serving African-American
> students—up from as few as 10 in 1965. These teachers constituted
> 1.2% of the African-American lawyers in America. By comparison, in
> 1989 there were approximately 3740 nonminority male law teachers,
> constituting about 0.7% of the nonminority male lawyers.

Carrington, "Diversity!" 1992 *Utah Law Review* 1105, 1126 (1992). Carrington also notes that blacks and women were granted tenure in law schools
between 1981 and 1986 at the same high rate as white men—close to 85
percent.

9. Glen Cain argues that "statistical methods are indispensable in the
task of measuring labor market discrimination, but they are still only one
component of the analysis." Cain, "The Uses and Limits of Statistical
Analysis in Measuring Economic Discrimination," in Emily Hoffman, ed.,
Essays on the Economics of Discrimination 115, 132 (Kalamazoo, Mich.: W.

E. Upjohn Institute for Employment Research, 1991). Cain uses statistical evidence to show that the Irish in 1900 and Japanese Americans in 1940 had substantial earnings shortfalls compared with native whites, but that by 1980, the Irish and Japanese Americans outperformed native whites. Cain argues that the Irish in 1900 and Japanese Americans in 1940 were victims of discrimination. But if one reached this conclusion only on the basis of the statistical evidence, then one would be forced to conclude that in 1980 there was discrimination *in favor* of the Irish and Japanese Americans and against native whites, which seems most unlikely. In other words, Cain argues that knowledge about the institutional and historical factors that generated earnings disparities is essential if one is to attribute such earnings disparities to labor market discrimination.

Sex Discrimination

11

Historical and Psychological Perspectives

Measured in terms of the number of cases filed in federal court, race and sex discrimination cases have historically been the two most important types of employment discrimination. Indeed, prior to the passage of the Americans with Disabilities Act, roughly half of all employment discrimination cases raised a race claim and one-third raised a sex claim. Although the first part of this book has predominantly focused on race discrimination, while we will now more specifically address issues of sex discrimination (and later issues of age and disability discrimination), there are obvious overlaps—and differences—in the issues raised by these different categories of prohibited conduct. First, a driving force behind the creation and continued strengthening of employment discrimination law has been the substantial and persistent differences in earnings between blacks and whites, and between men and women. But whether one is trying to explain the black-white earnings differential or the male-female earnings differential, one must probe the contribution of three factors: discrimination on the part of employers, fellow employees, or customers; differences in human capital; and the personal choices of the workers. Of course, the relative contribution of these three factors may well be different for racial differences in earnings than for sex-based differences.

Second, the procedural requirements for filing employment discrimination cases as well as the evidentiary framework and statistical methods for proving discrimination are identical in race and sex cases, and

326

this is true for both disparate treatment and disparate impact cases. Moreover, disparate treatment based on employer animus will be quite similar, and can be similarly analyzed, whether the employer doesn't want to hire blacks or women—or any other protected group for that matter (older workers, the disabled, Hispanics, Jews, etc.). In addition, because of the similar remedies available in race and sex discrimination cases and the similar costs of suing one's current or past employer, the nature of the decision about whether to litigate an employment discrimination case is much the same whether the basis for the discrimination is race or sex. Furthermore, critical race theorists and some feminist scholars contend that race and sex discrimination are central features of the system of domination by which white men oppress white women and all people of color. According to this view, both types of discrimination share a common origin and function, even if the precise impact of these exclusionary mechanisms differs among the various outsider groups.

Yet despite the many similarities, the issues of race and sex discrimination are also profoundly dissimilar in many respects. First, the historical patterns of and reasons for race-based and sex-based restrictions and exclusions from certain jobs and occupations have been quite different. Except for the period of Reconstruction following the Civil War and then again after the early 1960s, governmental measures directed toward blacks were generally invidious, and were universally so in the South, where most blacks lived. The black community, although largely deprived of any effective political power in the South, condemned racially discriminatory governmental conduct with a unified voice. On the other hand, protective legislation imposing employment restrictions on women frequently was benignly motivated—and often was strongly supported by some feminist groups.

Second, while employers who excluded blacks from certain jobs often did so for reasons of pure racial animus, their restrictions on the employment of women were frequently imposed for productivity or profitability reasons relating to pregnancy and child rearing. Third, these same factors, whether reflecting biological or socially constructed differences, also at times influenced the choices and preferences of women in the workplace, thereby adding an additional complexity in sex discrimination cases—that of sorting out when a lopsided pattern in the gender composition of a particular work force should be deemed evidence of employer discrimination, rather than the product of worker preferences.

Finally, Title VII itself explicitly recognizes that in certain, admittedly rare, circumstances—for example, where privacy concerns or biological differences are important—sex, although never race, may actually be a permissible job requirement. Thus, the law permits an employer to make sex a factor in hiring when it is a "bona fide occupational qualification."

The selections in this chapter provide some historical and psychological perspectives concerning sex discrimination in America and introduce the complex issue of determining how a clear, undeniable, and significant biological difference between men and women—the capacity to become pregnant—should shape the definition of impermissible sex discrimination. We have already seen how difficult it can be to identify and establish discriminatory conduct on the basis of race, where no such biological difference exists between blacks and whites. The presence of this distinction further complicates the effort to define the appropriate requirements of sexual equality in the workplace.

Claudia Goldin discusses the evolution of labor market interventions on behalf of women, beginning with protectionist legislation in the middle of the nineteenth century and continuing through the passage of the Equal Pay Act of 1963 and Title VII of the 1964 Civil Rights Act. As this history reflects, there has been enormous and sustained disagreement about what policy measures should be adopted to advance the interests of women. One theme that Goldin emphasizes is that the American workplace has traditionally been characterized by widespread sex segregation across different jobs. While there are those who argue strenuously that such differences constitute sensible responses to the biological differences between men and women, Nancy Chodorow argues that the social construct of near-exclusive female parenting rather than the biological fact of female pregnancy and childbirth is responsible for the patterns of sexual inequality and male dominance in the workplace. As the selections throughout this part of the book repeatedly demonstrate, the contentious issues of biology versus society, and female choice versus male oppression, play a critical role in shaping one's conception of the appropriate law of sex discrimination in employment.

Understanding the Gender Gap: An Economic History of American Women*
CLAUDIA GOLDIN

Origins and Impact of Protective Legislation

Laws regulating the hours, wages, and work conditions of female employees were passed by virtually all states beginning in the mid-nineteenth century. I deal here with the case of maximum hours legislation, the most extensive and probably most significant form of protective legislation, to show why protective legislation was staunchly defended in opposition to equal rights and anti-discrimination legislation.

State laws regulating daily hours of work appeared in the mid-1800's, and by 1919 all but five states had passed hours restrictions at

---

* Excerpts from Claudia Goldin, *Understanding the Gender Gap: An Economic History of American Women,* copyright © 1990 by Oxford University Press. Reprinted by permission of the author and the publisher.

some time in their histories. With few exceptions, all laws applied exclusively to female workers in manufacturing and mercantile establishments, although the precise number of hours and other details differed by state. . . .

By 1909, 20 states had passed enforceable maximum hours laws covering female manufacturing workers, and the vast majority mandated a 10–hour day. Only five states set a maximum below 10 hours. At that time, the average scheduled workday among manufacturing workers, the majority of whom were male and thus not covered by the laws, was 9.5 hours across all states. In 1919, 40 states had maximum hours laws. Of these, 36 had laws mandating no more than a 10–hour day, and eight had laws mandating no more than an 8–hour day. The remaining four states set limits that exceeded 10 hours per day. The average scheduled workday in 1919 was 8.5 hours. The laws, therefore, were rarely extreme in their prohibitions and often coincided with average scheduled hours of all manufacturing workers.

Two contradictory interpretations of protective legislation have emerged. According to one view, the legislation originated in the genuine concerns of reformers about work conditions of all Americans and ultimately benefited women workers. The opposing view is that protective legislation was intended to restrict the employment of female workers and was passed under the guise of reform. Both views find support in the historical narrative.

The Supreme Court, in 1905, found general hours legislation that applied to men and women alike unconstitutional because the laws restricted the right of labor to contract freely (*New York v. Lochner*). Various states had previously struck down hours legislation on the same ground even when the law applied only to women, as in the case of the Illinois 8–hour law passed in 1893. But in a now-famous case, *Muller v. Oregon* (1908), the Supreme Court upheld the constitutionality of maximum hours restrictions for female workers. According to the Supreme Court, states could pass legislation restricting the hours of women but not those of men. The Oregon law was held constitutional, due, in part, to a brilliant legal brief. The brief became, in the decades following, the legal rationale for the differential treatment of women. *Muller v. Oregon* left a legacy that went beyond the decision to uphold the Oregon 10–hour law.

Louis Brandeis, then a young lawyer, and his sister-in-law Josephine Goldmark, working for the National Consumers' League (NCL), wrote the brief for the NCL. Their defense of the 10–hour law rested on the deleterious effects that work had on women and their future offspring. The brief was predicated on inherent differences between men and women; one bore the next generation, and one did not. It has since exemplified the view that women, because they are physically different from men, require protection. State intervention might be justified on the ground that future lives could be injured by the actions of women and their employers, and that the unborn were insufficiently represented in their actions. Further, women themselves could be coerced into working long hours. The Brandeis–Goldmark brief, however, is a considerably more subtle document than is immediately apparent.

Had women been more powerful as individual workers and as a group, the reform movement would not have had to marshal so radical a case for their protection. But women workers were considerably less organized than male workers. Only 6.3% of all female manufacturing workers were unionized in 1914, while 13.7%, or twice as many, male workers were. And ... female workers were often young, poor, foreign-born, transient, and easy to exploit. Social consensus was easily rallied around the need to protect women and their unborn children, and the Supreme Court bought the case as well. Such tactics were fully justified in the minds of many social reformers by the goal of better working conditions for all American workers. After *Lochner,* it was clear that shorter hours could not be won through comprehensive legislation but might be established for certain groups, such as women. The tactic was clearly articulated by many reformers and labor organizers.

The demand for shorter hours was a recurrent feature of labor agitation beginning with the cotton textile mill strikes of the 1830's and 1840's. Despite demands for shorter hours, the work week in manufacturing was long in all states during the nineteenth century. Thus one interpretation of maximum hours laws is that labor saw in it the means to lower hours of work for all workers, and the only constitutional laws were those applying to women....

An opposing rationale for protective legislation is that hours restrictions were supported by native-born white men who feared female workers would usurp their jobs. A mandated limit on the hours of women workers could reduce the demand for their labor. Mechanization in tobacco and canning had reduced the need for skilled male workers, and it was perceived that hours limits would stem the movement from male to female labor in other industries.

· · ·

To assess which of these hypotheses is correct, I explore the impact of protective legislation on hours of work from 1909 to 1919 and on female employment in 1919.... The two opposing views of protective legislation are assessed by estimating the impact of legislation on the hours and employment of women workers in the covered sectors....

Protective legislation ... had virtually no adverse impact on female employment around 1920, and states with more stringent hours laws had greater declines in hours for all workers than those with less stringent laws. Certain women, to be sure, were constrained by the laws. But from the perspectives of a trade-union leader, a reformer, or a laborer who wanted lower hours, the benefits of maximum hours laws and other types of protective legislation were well worth the costs. Many "social feminists," who in the post-1920's era became involved with "women's issues" in the Department of Labor and elsewhere, had been manufacturing operatives in their youth. Protective legislation was, to them, an indispensable substitute for collective action by women workers. They were probably correct that protective legislation was associated with reduced hours for all workers, although the precise mechanism is not yet clear, and that maximum hours laws resulted in only minor employment effects. But the real costs of protective legislation began to mount almost immediately through opposition to a guarantee of true equality between the sexes. The benefits, though, would remain in the minds of many who fought for shorter hours and better working conditions.

Directly following passage of the Nineteenth Amendment, the National Woman's Party was constituted from the radical wing of the National American Woman Suffrage Association. Under Alice Paul's able leadership, the NWP began its long and still unfinished campaign for the Equal Rights Amendment (ERA). The NWP demanded that "women shall no longer be barred from any occupation, but every occupation open to men shall be open to women, and restrictions upon the hours, conditions, and remuneration of labor shall apply alike to both sexes."

The ERA as drafted by Alice Paul read simply: "Men and woman shall have equal rights throughout the United States and every place subject to its jurisdiction." In 1923, it fell three states short of ratification but remained a live issue during the Depression and immediately after World War II. In 1971, the House of Representatives finally passed the ERA, as did the Senate in 1972, but the ERA ultimately failed ratification again after being blocked by opposition groups in various states. Opposition to the ERA since the 1970's is clearly identified with conservative interests, but earlier in its history the detractors were a more varied group. Immediately after the initial ratification failure in 1923, groups that supported protective legislation banded together in opposition to the ERA. The finest legal scholars in the 1920's, including Felix Frankfurter, believed that equal rights and protective legislation were incompatible, and that embracing equal rights meant abandoning protective legislation.

From the 1920's to the 1960's, many liberals opposed the ERA, while conservatives often supported it. Professional and business women, who had the most to gain from true equality and the least to lose from terminating protective legislation, generally defended the ERA, while those in opposition were often "social feminists" who perceived women would suffer by forfeiting protective legislation. Liberals continued to define the female labor force in the same terms as did Progressive era reformers—as young, poor, transient, and unorganizable women workers who needed protection more than they needed equality. The cause of protective legislation served to delay a national policy to combat discrimination against women through its definition of women as marginal workers and through the opposition it raised to real equality.

The Federal Government and the Economic Status of Women

Differential treatment of women was legislated by the states and the federal government and sanctioned by the courts. It was one of the many pillars of social and familial stability and, for other reasons as well, was viewed less as discrimination than as paternalism. Harmful discrimination by race was more intelligible to Americans than was discrimination by sex. Until the 1960's, few Americans realized the magnitude and implications of sex discrimination. . . .

Numerous factors could be marshaled to explain differences by sex. Men and women chose to have families; children required mothers to remain at home for certain periods, and that, in turn, demanded women's occupations be different from men's. Just how much the observed difference was due to choice and how much to differences in opportunity was not clear. Even statistical measures of discrimination . . . cannot precisely resolve the reasons for differences. In the 1960's, the movement for equality by sex needed a document that could demonstrate to even the most skeptical observer that women were treated differently from men and that the differences were not entirely due to their choice. That document was provided by the 1963 President's Commission on the Status of Women.

The President's Commission on the Status of Women, 1963

The President's Commission on the Status of Women issued its long-awaited report in 1963. The commission, first proposed in 1946, was formed in 1961 by President Kennedy . . . to review progress and make recommendations in six areas, including private employment, protective legislation, and government hiring. It produced a final summary report, *American Women,* and six separate reports of its subcommittees. The subcommittee on private employment was headed by economist Richard Lester, also a member of the commission. As an economist, Lester understood that differences in incomes and occupations between men and women did not constitute prima facie evidence of harmful discrimination, just as differences among men did not. Rather, he and other subcommittee chairs realized that only clear and incontrovertible instances of exclusion and differential treatment would establish that there was harmful discrimination against women.

The final report established various areas of indisputable discrimination against women. Discrimination was evident in the civil service's appointment and advancement policies and practices; those in charge could and did specify the sex of the appointment, even if women and men were equally qualified. Various studies demonstrated that equal pay for equal work was frequently violated in the private sector. State laws mandating maximum hours for women clearly hindered those pursuing professional and managerial careers, as night-work laws did for others. State laws prohibiting women from serving on juries and holding property were also discriminatory.

The document was not a radical statement. Its authors, with only one dissent, voted against endorsing legislation to ensure women equality in employment; they did not want to dismantle the apparatus of protective legislation, and they reaffirmed the importance of the family and women's role in it. The commission, like the majority of Americans, viewed sex and race discrimination as different problems: "The consensus was that the nature of discrimination on the basis of sex and the reasons for it are so different that a separate program is necessary to eliminate barriers to the employment and advancement of women."

Yet the report of the President's Commission on the Status of Women established beyond a doubt the existence of harmful discrimination against women in private and public employment and in the laws of various states. The discrimination, moreover, was detrimental to the nation as a whole. The American public needed a statement with force, authority, and clarity to awaken them to age-old discriminatory practices. The commission's report was exactly that.

The 1963 Equal Pay Act and Title VII of the 1964 Civil Rights Act

When first introduced in 1945, the Equal Pay Act was a tactic to defeat the ERA, which had been voted favorably out of the House Judiciary Committee that year. The doctrine of equal pay by sex for equal work was not a new concept in 1963 and had a long and ambivalent history. Equal pay was a frequent demand by unions in peacetime and during both world wars as a guarantee to male workers that their wages would not be depressed by female workers. As early as the 1860's, for example, male printers demanded that their female counterparts receive "equal pay for equal work"—less for the sake of equity than to protect compositors from the low wages of the needle trades. The International Association of Machinists decried the practice during World War I of "exploiting women by paying as small a wage as possible" and demanded "equal pay for equivalent work." During World War II, the National War Labor Board ... went partway in establishing a doctrine of equal pay for equal work, once again to protect the wages of male workers from encroachment by lower-paid females.

Yet the doctrine of equal pay was clearly central to a policy of sexual equality in the marketplace. Many liberals, such as John Kennedy, who could not support the ERA because of its conflict with protective legislation, endorsed the Equal Pay Act, which did not endanger existing laws. The original version of the Equal Pay Act used the term "comparable work," but was later changed to "equal work." Given the extreme segregation of occupations across the entire economy, particularly across firms, an act that guarantees "equal pay for equal work" within firms can have little impact on differences in occupations and earnings between men and women. . . .

Just one year after passage of the Equal Pay Act and the publication of the report of the President's Commission on the Status of Women, the 1964 Civil Rights Act was passed. It has become "the most comprehensive and important of all federal and state laws prohibiting employment discrimination." . . . But until the day before the law was passed, the word "sex" did not appear anywhere in the document. . . .

Interesting parallels can be drawn between the Civil Rights Act of 1964 and passage of the Fourteenth and Fifteenth Amendments. Women were asked at both times to postpone their demands so the cause of racial equality could be furthered. At the close of the Civil War, women suffragists and abolitionists pressed that female suffrage be incorporated into the Fourteenth and Fifteenth Amendments, but their cause was abandoned by even their abolitionist friends. . . . If not for the curious introduction of the word "sex" in the 1964 Civil Rights Act, women might have lost then as well. In 1964, however, women were told that noninterference not only was in the best interests of the civil rights movement, but also was to their advantage. "Liberals and most of the women's organizations in 1964," writes Caroline Bird, "opposed adding sex to the Civil Rights Bill, primarily because they did not want to endanger protection for Negroes, but also because absolute equality between the sexes before the law might endanger rights and immunities favoring women."

. . . Even after Title VII was passed and the Equal Employment Opportunity Commission was set up to receive and investigate charges of employment discrimination, resources devoted to sex discrimination were severely limited. In its early years, EEOC vigorously investigated newspaper want ads that specified race but would not pursue similar cases in which sex was stipulated. EEOC shied away from cases that might challenge state protective legislation, such as prohibitions against night work for women. Indeed, the National Organization for Women was formed in 1966 to pressure EEOC to deal with these and other aspects of sex discrimination.

Mothering, Male Dominance, and Capitalism*
NANCY CHODOROW

Women mother. In our society, as in most societies, women not only bear children. They also take primary responsibility for infant care, spend more time with infants and children than do men, and sustain primary

---

* Excerpts from Nancy Chodorow, "Mothering, Male Dominance, and Capitalism," in Zillah R. Eisenstein, ed. *Capitalist Patriarchy and the Case for Socialist Feminism,* copyright © 1979 by Zillah R. Eisenstein. Reprinted by permission of Monthly Review Foundation.

emotional ties with infants. When biological mothers do not parent, other women, rather than men, take their place. Though fathers and other men spend varying amounts of time with infants and children, fathers are never routinely a child's primary parent. These facts are obvious to observers of everyday life.

Because of the seemingly natural connection between women's childbearing and lactation capacities and their responsibility for child care, and because of the uniquely human need for extended care in childhood, women's mothering has been taken for granted. It has been assumed to be inevitable by social scientists, by many feminists, and certainly by those opposed to feminism. As a result, the profound importance of women's mothering for family structure, for relations between the sexes, for ideology about women, and for the sexual division of labor and sexual inequality both inside the family and in the nonfamilial world is rarely analyzed.

A Note on Family and Economy

... [Anthropologist Gayle] Rubin suggests ... that every society contains, in addition to a mode of production, a "sex-gender system"— "systematic ways to deal with sex, gender, and babies." The sex-gender system includes ways in which biological sex becomes cultural gender, a sexual division of labor, social relations for the production of gender and of gender-organized social worlds, rules and regulations for sexual object choice, and concepts of childhood. The sex-gender system is, like a society's mode of production, a fundamental determining and constituting element of society, socially constructed, and subject to historical change and development....

We can locate features of a sex-gender system and a mode of production in our own society. In addition to assigning women primary parenting functions, our sex-gender system ... creates two and only two genders out of the panoply of morphological and genetic variations found in infants, and maintains a heterosexual norm. It also contains historically generated and societally more specific features: its family structure is largely nuclear, and its sexual division of labor locates women first in the home and men first outside of it. It is male dominant and not sexually egalitarian, in that husbands traditionally have rights to control wives and power in the family; women earn less than men and have access to a narrower range of jobs; women and men tend to value men and men's activities more; and in numerous other ways that have been documented and redocumented since well before the early feminist movement. Our mode of production is more and more exclusively capitalist.

. . .

The distinction ... between the economy ("men's world") and the family ("women's world") ... does not mean that these two systems are not empirically or structurally connected. Rather, they are linked (and almost inextricably intertwined) in numerous ways. Of these ways, women's mothering is that pivotal structural feature of our sex-gender system—of the social organization of gender, ideology about women, and the psychodynamic of sexual inequality—that links it most significantly with our mode of production.

Women's Mothering and the Social Organization of Gender

... [The fact that] women perform primary parenting functions ... is a universal organizational feature of the family and the social organization of gender.

. . .

In all societies there is a mutually determining relationship between women's mothering and the organization of production. Women's work has been organized to enable women to care for children, though childbirth, family size, and child-tending arrangements have also been organized to enable women to work. Sometimes, as seems to be happening in many industrial societies today, women must care for children and work in the labor force simultaneously.

. . .

Michelle Rosaldo has argued that women's responsibility for child care has led, for reasons of social convenience rather than biological necessity, to a structural differentiation in all societies of a "domestic" sphere that is predominantly women's and a "public" sphere that is men's.

. . .

... Women's and men's spheres are distinctly unequal, and the structure of values in industrial capitalist society has reinforced the ideology of inferiority and relative lack of power vis-à-vis men which women brought with them from preindustrial, precapitalist times.

. . .

Women's Mothering and Ideology About Women

... In this society it is ... assumed ... that ... women are ... working only to supplement a husband's income in nonessential ways. This assumption justifies discrimination, less pay, layoffs, higher unemployment rates than men, and arbitrary treatment. In a country where the paid labor force is more than 40 percent female, many people continue to assume that most women are wives and mothers who do not work. In a situation where almost two thirds of the women who work are married and almost 40 percent have children under eighteen, many people assume that "working women" are single and childless.

The kind of work women do also tends to reinforce stereotypes of women as wives and mothers. This work is relational and often an extension of women's wife-mother roles in a way that men's work is not. Women are clerical workers, service workers, teachers, nurses, salespeople. If they are involved in production, it is generally in the production of nondurable goods like clothing and food, not in "masculine" machine industries like steel and automobiles. All women, then, are affected by an ideological norm that defines them as members of conventional nuclear families.

This ideology is not merely a statistical norm. It is transformed and given an *explanation* in terms of natural differences and natural causes. We explain the sexual division of labor as an outgrowth of physical differences. We see the family as a natural, rather than a social, creation.

. . .

[B]iological mothers have come to have more and more exclusive responsibility for child care just as the biological components of mothering have lessened—as women have borne fewer children and bottle feeding has become available. Post-Freudian psychology and sociology has provided new rationales for the idealization and enforcement of women's maternal role, as it has emphasized the crucial importance of the mother-child relationship for the child's development.

This crucial mothering role contributes not only to child development but also to the reproduction of male supremacy. Because women are responsible for early child care and for most later socialization as well, because fathers are more absent from the home, and because men's activities generally have been removed from the home while women's have remained within it, boys have difficulty attaining a stable, masculine gender role identification. They fantasize about and idealize the masculine role, and their fathers and society define it as desirable. Freud first described how a boy's normal oedipal struggle to free himself from his mother and become masculine generated "the contempt felt by men for a sex which is the lesser." Psychoanalyst Grete Bibring argues from her own clinical experience that "too much of mother," resulting from the contemporary organization of parenting and extra-familial work, creates men's resentment and dread of women, and their search for nonthreatening, undemanding, dependent, even infantile women—women who are "simple, and thus safe and warm." Through these same processes, she argues, men come to reject, devalue, and even ridicule women and things feminine. Thus, women's mothering creates ideological and psychological modes which reproduce orientations to, and structures of, male dominance in individual men and builds an assertion of male superiority into the very definition of masculinity.

Women's Mothering and the Reproduction of Capitalism

Women's mothering ... is also pivotal to the reproduction of the capitalist mode of production and the ideology which supports it.

. . .

[Today, women] ... are responsible for the daily reproduction of the (by implication, male) adult participant in the paid work world. These responsibilities are psychological and emotional as well as physical: sociologist Talcott Parsons claims that the "stabilization and tension-management of adult personalities" is a major family function.... [T]he wife/mother is her family's "expressive" or "social-emotional" leader; [she] does the tension-managing and stabilizing and the husband/father is thereby soothed and steadied.

Socialist-feminist theorists [elaborate that women]'s role in the family ... serves as an important siphon for work discontent and works to ensure worker stability. It also removes the need for employers themselves to attend to such stability or to create contentedness....

... Theorists of the Frankfurt Institute for Social Research and Parsonsians have drawn on psychoanalysis to show how the relative position of fathers and mothers in the family produces men's psychological commitment to capitalist domination: the internalization of subordination to authority, the development of psychological capacities for participation in an alienated work world, and achievement orientation.

Parsonsians start from the mother's intense, often sexualized, involvement with her male infant. In middle-class American families, where mothers tend not to have other primary affective figures around, a mutual erotic investment between son and mother develops, an investment the mother can then manipulate. She can love, reward, and frustrate him at appropriate moments in order to get him to delay gratification and sublimate or repress erotic needs. This close, exclusive pre-oedipal mother-child relationship ... thus creates in sons a personality founded on generalized achievement orientation rather than on specific goal orientations. These diffuse orientations can then be used to serve a variety of specific goals—goals not set by these men themselves.

In an earlier period of capitalist development, individual goals were important for more men, and entrepreneurial achievement as well as worker discipline had to be based more upon inner moral direction and repression. Earlier family arrangements, where dependency was not so salient nor the mother-child bond so exclusive, produced ... greater inner direction....

Slater extends Parsons' discussion. People who start life with only one or two emotional objects, he argues, develop a "willingness to put all [their] emotional eggs in one symbolic basket." Boys who grow up in American middle-class nuclear families have this experience. Because they received so much gratification from their mother relative as compared to what they got from anyone else, and because their relationship to her was so exclusive, it is unlikely that they can repeat such a relationship. They relinquish their mother as an object of dependent attachment, but, because she was so uniquely important, retain her as an oedipally motivated object to win in fantasy. They turn their lives into a search for success.

This situation contrasts with that of people who have had a larger number of pleasurable relationships in early infancy. These people are more likely to expect gratification in immediate relationships and maintain commitments to more people and are less likely to deny themselves now on behalf of the future. They would not be the same kind of good worker, given that work is defined (as it is in our society) in individualist, noncooperative ways.

Max Horkheimer and theorists of the Frankfurt Institute ... emphasize the decline in the father's role—his distance, unavailability, and loss of authority....

... Fathers, with the growth of industrialization, became less involved in family life. They did not simply leave home physically, however. As more fathers became dependent wage laborers, the material base for their familial authority was also eroded. Horkheimer suggests that in reaction fathers have developed authoritarian modes of acting, but because there is no longer a real basis for their authority there can be no genuine oedipal struggle. Instead of internalizing paternal authority, sons engage in an unguided search for authority in the external world. In its most extreme form, this search for authority creates the characterological foundation for fascism. More generally, however, it leads to tendencies to accept the mass ideological manipulation characteristic of late capitalist society and the loss of autonomous norms or internal standards as guides for the individual....

Thus woman's mothering role and position as primary parent in the family, and the maternal qualities and behaviors which derive from it, are central to the daily and generational reproduction of capitalism. Women resuscitate adult workers, both physically and emotionally, and rear children who have particular psychological capacities which capitalist workers and consumers require. Most of these connections are historical and not inevitable....

[W]hile [women's mothering] contributes to the reproduction of sexual inequality, the social organization of gender, and capitalism, it is also in profound contradiction to another consequence of recent capitalist development—the increasing labor force participation of mothers. We cannot predict how or if this contradiction will be resolved. History, ideology, and an examination of industrial countries which have relied on women in the labor force for a longer period and have established alternate childcare arrangements suggest that women will still be responsible for child care, unless we make the reorganization of parenting a central political goal.

Notes and Questions

1. During the first-half of the twentieth century, social feminists fought for protective legislation for women and against the Equal Rights

Amendment, which threatened to outlaw such legislation. These feminists thought that young, poor, and unorganized female workers needed protection more than they needed equality. Throughout this century, a battle has been continuously fought between those believing that women and men should be treated identically and those believing that, given their biological and/or socially imposed differences from men, women should be protected or accommodated. Numerous articles explore the differences of these competing symmetrical and asymmetrical models of equality. See the Littleton excerpt in Chapter 12, the Issacharoff and Rosenblum selection in Chapter 15, and Mary Becker, "Prince Charming: Abstract Equality," *The Supreme Court Review* 201 (1987).

2. Chodorow believes that society should strive "to overcome the sexual division of labor in which women mother ... so that primary parenting [can be] shared between men and women." Chodorow, *The Reproduction of Mothering: Psychoanalysis and the Sociology of Gender* 214–15 (Berkeley: University of California Press, 1978). Is this a desirable social goal? Do you accept Chodorow's argument that the current gendered system of childrearing creates severe dysfunctional psychological patterns in children that will plague them throughout their lives, harm their future relationships, and potentially threaten their society? Can families that wish to adhere to the approach of co-parenting choose to do so? In other words, is this a problem that individuals can solve, or is Chodorow correct that it requires some fundamental societal reorganization? Could a married woman who wanted the greater "access to the prestige and power that come from control over extra-domestic distribution networks" simply bargain with her husband to achieve this goal? Has the psychology of male dominance created a need to be superior to women that would make such a bargain untenable?

Victor Fuchs speculates that women are at a disadvantage in bargaining with men over the division of child-rearing burdens because, on average, they "have a stronger demand for children than men do, and have more concern for their children after they are born. In short, there is a major difference on the side of preferences, and this difference is a major source of women's economic disadvantage." Fuchs, *Women's Quest For Economic Equality* 68 (Cambridge, Mass.: Harvard University Press, 1988).

Do you think that men desire children less and care less about their welfare? As evidence that they do, Fuchs notes that a large number of children are born to and live with single women (with 30 percent of these births to women age 25 or older), women pursue full custody of their children dramatically more frequently than fathers do, and paternal abandonment of children is far more pervasive than maternal abandonment. A recent study of dozens of countries around the world found no society in which fathers spent as much time with children as mothers did, and very few in which fathers had regular close relationships with their young children. Judith Bruce, Cynthia Lloyd, and Ann Leonard, *Families in Focus* (New York: Population Council, 1995). Fuchs notes that if men wanted children more and cared more about them and women were more indifferent, then "the present hierarchy of power would be reversed" because men would have to pay dearly for women's services. Does this suggest that we have a rough balance of utilities where women get more satisfaction from their children, and men get more satisfaction from their jobs and money? Or might it mean that men have manipulated the process of preference formation in a way that enables their advantage to persist?

3. The Family and Medical Leave Act of 1993 (FMLA) provides for parental leave on a gender-neutral basis, thereby at least facially addressing Chodorow's concern that childrearing is improperly viewed as the exclusive responsibility of women. As Samuel Issacharoff and Elyse Rosenblum point out in Chapter 15, however, the FMLA has not changed childrearing patterns to the extent that its supporters had hoped. In general, the FMLA has received two major criticisms: first, that it excludes many working women from coverage; and second, that although the statute is gender-neutral, it does not do enough to deconstruct patterns of gendered childrearing that have forced women to choose between work and family.

First, the FMLA covers only employers with fifty or more employees, leaving many female workers, who disproportionately work in small businesses, unprotected. Second, because the FMLA only requires unpaid leaves, lower income workers—many of whom are again, disproportionately women—cannot afford to take advantage of the law. Moreover, the fact that the leaves are unpaid also means that in dual-career families in which both spouses are eligible to take leave, it is much more likely that the woman will take leave, given that on average they earn less than men. Finally, the key employee exemption also reduces the likelihood that men will take parental leave. Under this exemption, workers who are in the highest paid ten percent of the employer's work force are not guaranteed restoration of their jobs upon returning from leave. In practice, this provision forces working wives of highly-paid men to take leave instead of their husbands in order to ensure the men's job security. See Angie K. Young, "Assessing the Family and Medical Leave Act in Terms of Gender Equality, Work/Family Balance, and the Needs of Children," 5 *Michigan Journal of Gender and Law* 113 (1998). According to some surveys conducted between 1994 and 1995, women did, indeed, take more leaves under the FMLA (58.2 percent for women compared to 41.8 percent for men). Michael Selmi, "The Limited Vision of the Family and Medical Leave Act," 44 *Villanova Law Review* 395 (1999).

4. Rhona Mahony develops Fuchs's point in question 2 above by showing that women make numerous choices throughout their lives that weaken their bargaining position vis-à-vis their husbands, and therefore they are pressed into greater household and child-rearing service, even if that is not their preference. According to Mahony, women will achieve real equality with men only "when there are roughly as many househusbands as housewives and roughly as many female breadwinners as male breadwinners." To make this happen, women must strengthen their negotiating position by investing more in their skills, their education, and their jobs and avoiding higher earning romantic partners (who would have to bear higher economic sacrifices by staying home with children). Mahony, *Kidding Ourselves: Breadwinning, Babies, and Bargaining Power* 5 (New York: Basic Books, 1995).

5. Chodorow contends that the "sex-gender system" is male dominant and not sexually egalitarian, as reflected in the fact that women earn less than men and have access to a narrower range of jobs. A critical issue that must be addressed is whether women voluntarily restrict their employment options—perhaps to be close to home or to limit their hours of work—because of their personal preferences, such as the desire to spend more time with their children. As we will see in Chapter 13, it is clear to Richard Posner both that they do and that we should respect their individual choices. But if the choices are voluntary in the sense that they reflect women's preferences once the effect of socialization has fully acted on any inherent biological predispositions, is it clear that they should necessarily be respected? Amartya Sen has stressed that the chronically deprived often learn to keep their desires in check, which can keep them from striving for much more than they have. Sen notes that there is little widespread dissatisfaction with gender inequality among rural Indian women, "since persistent inequality and exploitation often thrive by making passive allies out of the mistreated and the exploited." Sen, "Individual Freedom as a Social Commitment," *New York Review of Books* 49 (June 14, 1990).

6. Have women in America become the passive allies of their oppressors? Unquestionably, they have been burdened by political and economic discrimination and by their current relative underachievement in the paid labor market. Indeed, according to Catharine MacKinnon, "the women's movement exposed and documented the exploitation and subordination of women by men economically, socially, culturally, sexually, and spiritually." MacKinnon, "Reflections on Sex Equality under Law," 100 *Yale Law Journal* 1281, 1286 (1991). Yet numerous studies have found virtually no difference between men and women in average job satisfaction. See studies cited in David Chambers, "Accommodation and Satisfaction: Women and Men Lawyers and the Balance of Work and Family," 14 *Law and Social Inquiry* 251, 255 (1989), and U.S. Department of Labor, *Report of the Glass Ceiling Initiative* (1995) (discussing a study funded by the Department of Labor's Women's Bureau that found that female executives had levels of job satisfaction and job stress similar to those of their male peers).

As Cass Sunstein has argued,

> a social or legal system that has produced preferences, and has done so by limiting opportunities unjustly, can hardly justify itself by reference to existing preferences. The satisfaction of private preferences, whatever their content and origins, does not respond to a persuasive conception of liberty, welfare, or autonomy. The notion of autonomy should refer instead to decisions reached with a full and vivid awareness of available opportunities, with relevant information, and without illegitimate or excessive constraints on the process of preference formation. When there is inadequate information or opportunity, decisions and even preferences should be described as unfree or nonautonomous.

Sunstein, "The Anticaste Principle," 92 *Michigan Law Review* 2410, 2420 (1994).

But, at least in some dimensions, the status of white women in America would seem to be far from the level of exploitation that makes a clear case for disregarding expressed preferences as a measure of personal well-being. For example, Sen himself developed a Human Development Index—based on longevity, educational attainment, and access to resources—that was designed to measure "people's ability to live a long and healthy life, to communicate and to participate in the life of the community and to have sufficient resources to obtain a decent living." United Nations Development Programme, *Human Development Report* 104 (1993). Yet, on this admittedly crude measure of human welfare, white women in America—the primary beneficiaries of sex discrimination law—come out ahead of not only every other demographic group in the United States but also of the citizens of every other country *in the world*. Thus, white women in the United States stand at the top of the list with an HDI ranking of 1.0, whereas white men in the United States, with a ranking of only .975, are surpassed by the citizens of Japan, Canada, Norway, Switzerland, and Sweden. By comparison, black women have an HDI of only .9, which puts them on a par with the citizens of Greece, and black men have an HDI just above .85, placing them at about the level of the citizens of Bulgaria. See Donohue, "Employment Discrimination Law in Perspective: Three Concepts of Equality," 92 *Michigan Law Review* 2583 (1994). Do these findings have any implications for which demographic groups are most in need of the benefits of affirmative action? See note 6 in Section 3.2 of Chapter 3 for survey evidence that the public more heavily supports preferences in hiring for women than for blacks.

7. Francine Blau's study of trends in the economic well-being of American women throughout the late twentieth century offers a nuanced perspective on women's progress. Blau, "Trends in the Well–Being of American Women, 1970–1995," NBER Working Paper No. W6206, October 1997. She observes that for virtually all ages and education groups, there was an increased gender equality in labor market outcomes (including labor force participation, wages, occupational distributions, and self-employment). She also finds that the share of housework performed by husbands has increased relative to that of their wives, indicating greater gender equality among married couples. However, Blau notes that the gender wage gap, albeit reduced, still persists, and that the challenges of balancing work and family are still greater, on average, for women than for men. Blau also notes that the labor market outcome of less educated and black women have been deteriorating, signaling a growing inequality among women.

12

Feminist Theory

No one doubts that taking time off from work to give birth or to nurture children can be disruptive to a career and can therefore lower earnings. Since 90 percent of women will become pregnant, it is extremely likely that a woman must confront at least one career challenge that no man will have to experience. How the law should deal with this difference in determining the demands of sex discrimination law has been a major concern of feminist literature.

John Donohue has argued that the initial goal of antidiscrimination law was to ensure that a woman (or indeed any worker from a protected class) would be hired and compensated on the basis of her productive contribution to an unbiased employer. Donohue, "Employment Discrimination Law in Perspective: Three Concepts of Equality," 92 *Michigan Law Review* 2583 (1994). In this view, the law was designed to guarantee that the female employee will receive a wage that equals her intrinsic value to the employer. Indeed, if labor markets were as perfectly competitive as financial markets, there would probably be no need for an antidiscrimination law to guarantee "intrinsic equality," since the highly competitive market would furnish it. But labor markets are not as perfect as capital markets for a variety of reasons. First, changing employers involves much higher transaction costs than changing stock ownership, so employees cannot so readily flow to their highest valued use. Second, the benefits from properly assessing the true value of any one of a few thousand financial securities is immensely greater than the benefits of assessing the true value of any one of 120 million workers, so valuations are far more precise in capital markets. While thousands of market analysts spend considerable money and effort in trying to assess the true value of individual corporate securities, potential employers can spend only a minute fraction of such resources in evaluating the productivity of individual potential employees. For this reason, employers rely on proxies of race and sex to aid them in their valuation decisions, and therefore assessments about what the average man and woman will do in terms of their career and family choices can substantially impact the market's valuation of those workers who don't conform to the norm. In other words, statistical discrimination will thrive in the labor market because race and sex will be used to furnish inexpensive information to employers about classes of workers. Conversely, statistical discrimination is unknown in major capital markets because it is far more profitable to know the exact value of a corporate security than to know the exact value of a single worker.

But if all employers hire and compensate female employees on the basis only of their contributions to the firm—which is what *intrinsic equality* is meant to deliver—then women will predominantly suffer from the productivity reduction and attendant earnings disadvantage that flow from the typical pattern in which women bear the burden of childbirth and child rearing. This certainly may be entirely fair from the employer's perspective—an employer who follows the command of the law and provides his workers with wages equaling their intrinsic productive value is not "discriminating" against anyone. But is the mere guarantee of intrinsic equality fair from a societal perspective? Many modern feminists argue that society must compensate women on the basis not only of their value to employers, but also of their value to society—and this the unfettered market will not do.

This unwillingness to accept the goal of intrinsic equality prompts Catharine MacKinnon to ask provocatively: "Why should anyone have to be like white men to get what they have, given that white men do not have to be like anyone except each other to have it?" MacKinnon, "Reflections on Sex Equality Under Law," 100 *Yale Law Journal* 1281, 1287 (1991). To those who believe that antidiscrimination law is designed to promote intrinsic equality, MacKinnon's view seems uninformed. A substantial portion of the earnings differential between men and women could be closed if women pursued their careers as vigorously—through human capital development, continuous attachment to the labor market, and longer hours of work—as men do. For example, white men vary greatly in what they earn, and their earnings are highly correlated with how much time they work per year. Since women work considerably fewer hours in the paid labor force than men, one would similarly expect their earnings to be lower. As Victor Fuchs notes,

> In 1986, among those women ages 25–64 who were working during the week of the Current Population Survey, more than 20 percent worked fewer than thirty hours. Among men, only 7 percent were in that situation. . . . Not only are women more likely to work part time, but even those who have full-time

jobs are much less likely than men to work more than 40 hours per week. Among white married women with eighteen years or more of schooling and at least one child under twelve at home, only *one in ten* works more than 2,250 hour per year. By contrast, *half* of their husbands do, and one-third of the men work more than 2,500 hours.

Fuchs, *Women's Quest for Economic Equality* 44–48 (Cambridge, Mass.: Harvard University Press, 1988).

But MacKinnon's question makes perfect sense given the larger social conception of fairness to women. Rather than looking to what a woman deserves because of her contribution to an employer, many modern feminists wish to replace the goal of intrinsic equality with the more expansive demands of what Donohue has termed constructed equality. Christine Littleton attempts to "reconstruct sexual equality" in a way that assures that biological and cultural differences between men and women do not lead to women receiving fewer resources than men do. Whether antidiscrimination law is the appropriate, or sufficiently powerful, tool to achieve Littleton's goal will be addressed throughout the remainder of this book.

The selection by Martha Chamallas documents the great evolution that feminist theory has undergone over the last three decades, from the now-disfavored work of Matina Horner, which found that women could indeed succeed in the highest levels of the workplace if they would only shed their socially ingrained fear of success, to the more currently popular views that see women's lack of labor market success as the product of structural impediments or the unwelcoming ideology of the culturally dominant groups. Chamallas demonstrates how the development of a more structuralist interpretation of difficulties experienced in the workplace by nondominant groups is directly influencing Title VII litigation and judicial decisions.

Reconstructing Sexual Equality*
CHRISTINE A. LITTLETON

Feminist legal theory has been primarily reactive, responding to the development of legal racial equality theory. The form of response, however, has varied. One response has been to attempt to equate legal treatment of sex with that of race and deny that there are in fact any significant natural differences between women and men; in other words, to consider the two sexes symmetrically located with regard to *any* issue, norm, or rule. This response, which I term the "symmetrical" approach, classifies asymmetries as illusions, "overbroad generalizations," or temporary glitches that will disappear with a little behavior modification. A competing response rejects this analogy, accepting that women and men

* Excerpts from Christine A. Littleton, "Reconstructing Sexual Equality," *California Law Review*, vol. 75, copyright © 1979 by California Law Review Inc. Reprinted by permission of the author and publisher.

are or may be "different," and that women and men are often asymmetrically located in society. This response, which I term the "asymmetrical" approach, rejects the notion that all gender differences are likely to disappear, or even that they should.

Symmetrical Models of Sexual Equality

... There are two models of the symmetrical vision—referred to here as "assimilation" and "androgyny." Assimilation, the model most often accepted by the courts, is based on the notion that women, given the chance, really are or could be just like men. Therefore, the argument runs, the law should require social institutions to treat women as they already treat men—requiring, for example, that the professions admit women to the extent they are "qualified," but also insisting that women who enter time-demanding professions such as the practice of law sacrifice relationships (especially with their children) to the same extent that male lawyers have been forced to do.

Androgyny, the second symmetrical model, also posits that women and men are, or at least could be, very much like each other, but argues that equality requires institutions to pick some golden mean between the two and treat both sexes as androgynous persons would be treated.... In order to be truly androgynous within a symmetrical framework, social institutions must find a single norm that works equally well for all gendered characteristics. Part of my discomfort with androgynous models is that they depend on "meeting in the middle," while I distrust the ability of any person, and especially any court, to value women enough to find the "middle." Moreover, the problems involved in determining such a norm for even one institution are staggering. At what height should a conveyor belt be set in order to satisfy a symmetrical androgynous ideal?

. . .

Asymmetrical Models of Sexual Equality

Asymmetrical approaches to sexual equality take the position that difference should not be ignored or eradicated. Rather, they argue that any sexually equal society must somehow deal with difference, problematic as that may be. Asymmetrical approaches include "special rights," "accommodation," "acceptance," and "empowerment."

The special rights model affirms that women and men *are* different, and asserts that cultural differences, such as childrearing roles, are rooted in biological ones, such as reproduction. Therefore, it states, society must take account of these differences and ensure that women are not punished for them.... Elizabeth Wolgast, a major proponent of special rights, argues that women cannot be men's "equals" because equality by definition requires sameness. Instead of equality, she suggests seeking justice, claiming special rights for women based on their special needs.

The second asymmetrical model, accommodation, agrees that differential treatment of biological differences (such as pregnancy, and perhaps breastfeeding) is necessary, but argues that cultural or hard-to-classify differences (such as career interests and skills) should be treated under an equal treatment or androgynous model. Examples of accommodation models include Sylvia Law's approach to issues of reproductive biology and Herma Hill Kay's "episodic" approach to the condition of pregnancy. These approaches could also be characterized as "symmetry, with concessions to asymmetry where necessary." . . .

My own attempt to grapple with difference, which I call an "acceptance" model, is essentially asymmetrical. While not endorsing the notion that cultural differences between the sexes are biologically determined, it does recognize and attempt to deal with both biological and social differences. Acceptance does not view sex differences as problematic per se, but rather focuses on the ways in which differences are permitted to justify inequality. It asserts that eliminating the unequal consequences of sex differences is more important than debating whether such differences are "real," or even trying to eliminate them altogether.

Unlike the accommodationists, who would limit asymmetrical analysis to purely biological differences, my proposal also requires equal acceptance of cultural differences. The reasons for this are twofold. First, the distinction between biological and cultural, while useful analytically, is itself culturally based. Second, the inequality experienced by women is often presented as a necessary consequence of cultural rather than of biological difference. If, for instance, women do in fact "choose" to become nurses rather than real estate appraisers, it is not because of any biological imperative. Yet, regardless of the reasons for the choice, they certainly do not choose to be paid less. It is the *consequences* of gendered difference, and not its sources, that equal acceptance addresses.

If, as it appears from Gilligan's studies, women and men tend to develop somewhat differently in terms of their values and inclinations, *each* of these modes of development must be equally valid and valuable. In our desire for equality, we should not be forced to jettison either; rather, we should find some way to value both. . . . Thus, if women currently tend to assume primary responsibility for childrearing, we should not ignore that fact in an attempt to prefigure the rosy day when parenting is fully shared. We should instead figure out how to assure that equal resources, status, and access to social decisionmaking flow to those women (and few men) who engage in this socially female behavior.

The focus of equality as acceptance, therefore, is not on the question of whether *women* are different, but rather on the question of how the social fact of gender symmetry can be dealt with so as to create some symmetry in the lived-out experience of all members of the community. I do not think it matters so much whether differences are "natural" or not; they are built into our structures and selves in either event. As social facts, differences are created by the interaction of person with person or person with institution; they inhere in the relationship, not in the person. On this view, the function of equality is to make gender differences, perceived or actual, costless relative to each other, so that anyone may follow a male, female, or androgynous lifestyle according to their natural inclination or choice without being punished for following a female lifestyle or rewarded for following a male one.

As an illustration of this approach, consider what many conceive to be the paradigm difference between men and women—pregnancy. No one disputes that only women become pregnant, but symmetrical theorists analogize pregnancy to other events, in order to preserve the unitary approach of symmetrical theory. Such attempts to minimize difference have the ironic result of obscuring more fundamental similarities.

. . .

The foregoing asymmetrical models, including my own, share the notion that, regardless of their differences, women and men must be treated as full members of society. Each model acknowledges that women may need treatment different than that accorded to men in order to effectuate their membership in important spheres of social life; all would allow at least some such claims, although on very different bases, and probably in very different circumstances.

A final asymmetrical approach, "empowerment," rejects difference altogether as a relevant subject of inquiry. In its strongest form, empowerment claims that the subordination of women to men has itself constructed the sexes, and their differences. For example, Catharine MacKinnon argues:

> [I]t makes a lot of sense that women might have a somewhat distinctive perspective on social life. We may or may not speak in a different voice—I think that the voice that we have been said to speak in is in fact in large part the 'feminine' voice, the voice of the victim speaking without consciousness. But when we understand that women are *forced* into this situation of inequality, it makes a lot of sense that we should want to urge values of care, because it is what we have been valued for. We have had little choice but to be valued this way.

A somewhat weaker version of the claim is that we simply do not and cannot know whether there are any important differences between the sexes that have not been created by the dynamic of domination and subordination. In either event, the argument runs, we should forget about the question of differences and focus directly on subordination and domination. If a law, practice, or policy contributes to the subordination of women or their domination by men, it violates equality. If it empowers women or contributes to the breakdown of male domination, it enhances equality.

The reconceptualization of equality as antidomination, like the model of equality as acceptance, attempts to respond directly to the concrete and lived-out experience of women. Like other asymmetrical models, it allows different treatment of women and men when necessary to effectuate its overall goal of ending women's subordination. However, it differs substantially from the acceptance model in its rejection of the membership, belonging, and participatory aspects of equality.

The Difference that Difference Makes

Each of the several models of equality discussed above, if adopted, would have a quite different impact on the structure of society. If this society wholeheartedly embraced the symmetrical approach of assimilation—the point of view that "women are just like men"—little would need to be changed in our economic or political institutions except to get rid of lingering traces of irrational prejudice, such as an occasional employer's preference for male employees. In contrast, if society adopted the andro-gyny model, which views both women and men as bent out of shape by current sex roles and requires both to conform to an androgynous model, it would have to alter radically its methods of resource distribution. In the employment context, this might mean wholesale revamping of meth-ods for determining the "best person for the job." Thus, while assimila-tion would merely require law firms to hire women who have managed to get the same credentials as the men they have traditionally hired, androgyny might insist that the firm hire only those persons with credentials that would be possessed by someone neither "socially male" nor "socially female."

If society adopted an asymmetrical approach such as the accommo-dation model, no radical restructuring would be necessary. Government would need only insist that women be given what they need to resemble men, such as time off to have babies and the freedom to return to work on the same rung of the ladder as their male counterparts. If, however, society adopted the model of equality as acceptance, which seeks to make difference costless, it might additionally insist that women and men who opt for socially female occupations, such as child-rearing, be compensat-ed at a rate similar to those women and men who opt for socially male occupations, such as legal practice. Alternatively, such occupations might be restructured to make them equally accessible to those whose behavior is culturally coded "male" or "female."

The different models also have different potential to challenge the phallocentrism of social institutions. No part of the spectrum of current-ly available feminist legal theory is completely immune to the feminist critique of society as phallocentric. We cannot outrun our history, and that history demonstrates that the terms of social discourse have been set by men who, actively or passively, have ignored women's voices.... Nevertheless, the models do differ with respect to the level at which the phallocentrism of the culture reappears.

Under the assimilationist approach, for example, women merit equal treatment only so far as they can demonstrate that they are similar to men. The assimilation model is thus fatally phallocentric. To the extent that women cannot or will not conform to socially male forms of behavior, they are left out in the cold. To the extent they do or can conform, they do not achieve equality *as women,* but as social males.

Similarly, empowerment and androgyny (an asymmetrical and a symmetrical approach, respectively) both rely on central concepts whose current meaning is phallocentrically biased. If "power" and "neutrality" (along with "equality") were not themselves gendered concepts, the empowerment and androgyny approaches would be less problematic. But our culture conceives of power as power used by men, and creates androgynous models "tilted" toward the male. . . .

Equality as acceptance is not immune from phallocentrism in several of its component concepts. However, these concepts are not necessarily entailed by the theory and may be replaced with less biased concepts as they reveal themselves through the process of equalization. For example, in discussing employment-related applications of the model, I use the measures already existing in that sphere—money, status, and access to decisionmaking. These measures of value are obviously suspect. Nevertheless, my use of them is contingent. Acceptance requires only that culturally coded "male" and "female" complements be equally valued; it does not dictate the coin in which such value should be measured. By including access to decisionmaking as part of the measure, however, the theory holds out the possibility that future measures of value will be created by women and men *together.* Thus, acceptance strives to create the preconditions necessary for sexually integrated debate about a more appropriate value system.

Equality and Difference

Equality as Acceptance

The model of equality as acceptance [insists] that equality can in fact be applied *across* difference. It is not, however, a "leveling" proposal. Rather, equality as acceptance calls for equalization across only those differences that the culture has encoded as gendered complements. The theory of comparable worth provides one example of this. . . .

Most proponents of comparable worth have defined the claim along the following lines: jobs that call for equally valuable skills, effort, and responsibility should be paid equally, even though they occur in different combinations of predominantly female and predominantly male occupations. Thus, when an employer has defined two job classifications as gendered complements, the employer should pay the same to each. Equality as acceptance makes the broader claim that *all* behavioral forms that the culture (not just the employer) has encoded as "male" and "female" counterparts should be equally rewarded. Acceptance would thus support challenges to the overvaluation of "male" skills (and corresponding undervaluation of "female" ones) by employers, rather than limiting challenges to unequal application of an existing valuation or to the failure to make such a valuation.

.   .   .

The model of equality as acceptance makes difference less costly by equalizing the resources "merited" by gendered complements—that is, by related "male" and "female" attributes or actions. The choice of which resources to equalize is contingent, and has been made on pragmatic, rather than theoretical, grounds. For the present, the model will hold constant the coin in which gendered complements are to be measured—money, status, and access to decisionmaking.

These measures and their application are themselves subject to feminist critique. First, both the value of money and the meaning of status are artifacts of a phallocentric culture. Given the choice, women might choose to value things in nonmonetary form or to define status in a radically different way. Positing alternative currency, however, will have to await a time when women have equal access to the mint. Second, my insistence that male and female job categories be equally paid implicitly accepts the validity of commodification of many forms of labor, which feminists have critiqued in other contexts as arising from a phallocentric desire for control. Finally, the model of equality as acceptance also envisions application within, as well as across, spheres of human activity. But from a radical feminist perspective, even that is problematic. For example, a feminist might argue that equalizing across difference only among workers legitimizes the socially constructed division between professional and personal, paid and unpaid, public and private work—a division strongly contested by feminists.

Symmetrical equality theorists have argued that because biological sex is no longer a strong predictor of social sex, it is harder to maintain the fiction that biological males are "naturally" better at such things as legal practice. Acceptance goes further, holding that once the social sex of a worker no longer accurately predicts that worker's pay, status, or access to decisionmaking, it will become harder and harder to maintain the fiction that socially male behaviors are "naturally" more valuable than their socially female counterparts. This in turn will make it harder to ignore the value of socially female labor in the "private sphere," while at the same time allowing massive infusion of "private" sphere interests into the "public" arena of employment.

In this respect, then, it does not matter that some elements of the acceptance model reflect the phallocentrism of our culture (as they inevitably must do). If socially male pay scales, status, and access to decisionmaking processes are open, not only to socially male women but also to socially female women and men, women's voice *as it is now* will be admitted to the dialogue that constructs social meaning.

. . .

Structuralist and Cultural Domination Theories Meet Title VII: Some Contemporary Influences*
MARTHA CHAMALLAS

Motivational Explanations in Social Science and Legal Discourse

When Title VII was first enacted and throughout the 1960s, research in the social sciences often focused on identifying psychological characteristics of women and racial minorities that would explain why these groups did not achieve "success" in the workplace. In its most simplified form, the motivational line of scholarship asked what there was about outsiders—what were the traits, qualities, and dispositions—that prevented them from attaining positions of power and status.... Posing the question in this way was apt to elicit a victim-blaming response that held the outsider responsible for his or her own predicament.

A classic example of motivational research that was used to explain women's lack of representation in professional or high-status careers is Matina Horner's work on women's "fear of success" in the late 1960s. Horner argued that highly educated women often undermine their own prospects for achievement in the outside world because of internal conflicts about their potential success. According to Horner, women's ambivalence about success arises both from their fears that intellectual achievement would result in a loss of femininity and from a deep-seated, unconscious association of success with loneliness, societal rejection, and despair. The construct of the fear of success was hypothesized as a static property, acquired in early childhood and activated later to stifle career goals. Horner envisioned the fear of success as something that most women brought with them into college classrooms or the workplace and that could not readily be changed by the actions of employers or other institutional decisionmakers....

The implication of Horner's research was that success is within the reach of individual women, if only their psychological makeup would allow them to attain it. Further, because patterns of women's psychological development are unlikely to change quickly, it was reasonable to expect sexual integration of jobs to proceed very slowly. The practical implications of the motivational theory posed no substantial threat to existing organizations or professions. Congruent with Horner's own career as president of Radcliffe College, the best antidote for fear of

* Excerpts from Martha Chamallas, "Structuralist and Cultural Domination Theories Meet Title VII: Some Contemporary Influences," *Michigan Law Review,* vol. 92, copyright © 1994. Reprinted by permission of the author and publisher.

success promised to be the counseling of individual women at elite schools to help them reevaluate their career aspirations.

.   .   .

In its contemporary version in the mass media, the motivational explanation for women's occupational status has tended to shift from fear of success and fear of loss of femininity to an emphasis on women's choice to subordinate their careers to accommodate family obligations. Tokenism and segregation is now typically explained by women's lack of geographic mobility, their need to interrupt careers to have children, and their desire to spend less time at work—the "mommy track." Like the earlier motivational explanations, however, the central feature of these "family conflict" theories of women's occupational status was to locate the principal cause of tokenism and segregation in the choices that individual women make and to imply that women's psychology is highly relevant to those choices.

Motivational explanations have also been prominent in the rhetoric and reasoning of courts deciding Title VII cases, exerting a significant influence on how courts view patterns of segregation and tokenism. The most well-established theory of liability—the theory of intentional disparate treatment—is premised on the motivation of individuals. Under the disparate treatment theory, courts conceptualize discrimination as the outcome of discrete, biased acts of individuals. Statistical proof of patterns of segregation and exclusion do not as such constitute violations of the law for these courts. Rather, they require courts to interpret the origins of those patterns. The critical question is whether to draw from these patterns an inference of discriminatory motivation on the part of the employer or to infer that the patterns result from choices made by members of the underrepresented groups themselves.

.   .   .

Structuralist Theory and Workplace Equality

By the mid-1970s, the psychological model of Horner and others was challenged by research that tended to blame "the system" rather than individuals and sought explanations for racial and sexual imbalances in the structures of institutions. One of the most prominent structuralist scholars of this era was Rosabeth Moss Kanter. Her famous ethnology of a large firm—*Men and Women of the Corporation*—focused on the dynamics of segregation and tokenism as they affect women in the corporation. Kanter's structuralism started from the premise that "the job makes the person," such that, for example, employees with little opportunity to advance will respond by lowering their aspirations and by seeking satisfaction outside the job. The structuralist orientation also located discrimination outside the minds of individuals who make discrete decisions. Kanter reframed and enlarged the concept of discrimination to make it a byproduct of structure, "a consequence of organizational pressures as much as individual prejudice."

. . . The structuralist account of the workplace is that of a highly politicized site where informal encounters often have more importance than formal meetings—where success on the job is measured more by peer acceptance than by competence in performing the tasks found in the formal job description.

Numbers are very important in structuralist analyses of the workplace. A major theme of Kanter's work is the self-perpetuating nature of tokenism. Kanter investigated what she called the "skewed" group, in which there is a large predominance of men—roughly eighty-five percent or more. She believed that the men in skewed groups typically control the work culture, such that it is fair to describe the men as "dominants" and the women as "tokens." Stereotyping is also likely to flourish in skewed settings that lack a critical mass of women.

. . . The tipping point for Kanter is located somewhere between fifteen and thirty-five percent, in groups she described as "tilted." In these tilted groups, the hypothesis is that tokens will become "minorities" and will be able to form coalitions and engage in other effective strategies to influence the culture of the organization. Although Kanter regarded her theory as applicable to any minority group in the workplace, it most directly addressed the predicament of women—and perhaps only white women—because women are the only minority group large enough to reach the percentages Kanter suggested for moving beyond token status.

. . . One very important theme in Kanter's work, for example, is her explication of the social construction of tokens in the workplace. Her research contested the notion that stereotypes of a group would break down in the face of the counterexample of a real person who did not fit the mold. Instead, in a skewed group it often is easier to make the person fit the generalization about the group than to change the generalization. Professional women in the corporation are individually noticed; people know their names and watch their actions. But because women are known primarily because of their sex, they are not known as individuals. The phenomenon of selective perception means that women are noticed and rated on a scale for women only, with focus on their style of dress, their appearance, their bodies, their social graces, and other nonability traits.

Selective perception combined with typecasting can distort everyday encounters with women at work. The behavior of token women is apt to be assimilated and reduced to patterns associated with women outside the workplace. Women are trapped into roles: they can be likened to a mother, a little sister (or pet), or a sexual object (seductress, mistress), or cast as a militant (iron maiden, virgin aunt). Each of these role traps is an obstacle to women's advancement. Mothers might be appreciated for their emotional work, but emotional work is not highly valued in the corporate arena. Little sisters are not taken seriously enough to be considered leaders. Because men tend to compete for the attention of a sexual object, her presence is thought to cause divisions. The militant is looked upon with suspicion from a distance and left to manage on her own.

The structuralist analysis of typecasting emphasizes its dynamic, interactive nature. There is a "feedback loop" between the dominant group's perception of the token and the token's behavior. It is often easier for token women to gain an "instant identity" by conforming to one of the preexisting stereotypes. Even those who resist the feminine stereotypes can be placed into a position of continual alertness to their own behavior, to make sure they do not unwittingly exhibit stereotypically feminine traits. Either strategy results in a measure of self-distortion, with the token holding back whatever fits or does not fit into the preconceived roles. In this way, stereotyping and typecasting—processes over which the employer has some measure of control—actually shape the behavior and identity of employees.

The implication of the structuralist position is that "organizations—not people—[have] to change" to break down the patterns of tokenism and segregation. Kanter's prescription for change was batch or cluster hiring: hire more than one woman at a time and concentrate them, rather than scatter them, throughout the organization. This "critical mass" strategy was thought to maximize women's potential to influence the culture in their specific working groups. The strategy also implied that if women are involved in making decisions about women, that will make a difference. Stereotyping is most prevalent when male-only committees sit in judgment of women....

Because the structuralist account emphasizes the internal dynamics of the organizations, it is not grounded in the common assumption that women's maternal and sexual roles determine their career aspirations and the way they function at work....

As an intellectual force, structuralism found its way into legal discourse through Catharine MacKinnon's work on sexual harassment. Her influential text, *Sexual Harassment of Working Women*, published in 1979, reframed sexual harassment as a structural abuse that was a byproduct of women's inferior position in the workplace. MacKinnon's analysis deprivatized the injury of sexual harassment. She sought to dispel the commonly held view that on-the-job harassment is a personal matter produced by sexual attraction or office flirtation.

Connecting sex segregation with harassment, MacKinnon argued that sexual harassment was facilitated by two structural forces: horizontal segregation, which meant that vast numbers of women were employed in pink-collar, feminized jobs; and tokenism, which severely limited the number of women working in male-defined jobs. For Mac-

Kinnon, the capacity to be sexually harassed was an informal job qualification for women in feminized jobs. Drawing on Kanter and other sociologists, MacKinnon described secretarial work as "sex-defined" work in which secretaries are required to be deferential, pleasing, supportive, wifelike, receptive, and willing to project sexual availability, even if they have no desire for sexual attention from men at work. Particularly because women in female-dominated jobs were most likely to have male supervisors, the structure of the workplace replicated and reinforced a gender hierarchy that placed women in the double bind of needing to appear compliant while successfully resisting sexual overtures. For token women in male-dominated jobs, MacKinnon theorized that they were singled out for harassment because they were highly visible, marked by their sex, and an easy target for male co-workers who resented the invasion of their territory.

· · ·

From an antidiscrimination law perspective, moreover, structuralism is an optimistic theory because it opens up possibilities for effective legal intervention. Under Title VII, the principal defendant is the organization; employers, not individual supervisors or co-employees, are typically held liable.... The structuralist account provides a solid rationale for holding employers accountable because it traces the origin of segregative patterns to the demographics of the workplace and to the opportunity structures within which employees make choices. An employer's hiring decisions, for example, take on an interactive quality; when an employer hires a particular applicant, the employer does not simply recognize the applicant's abilities or talents but, over time, actively shapes the new employee's behavior and contributes to the employee's success or failure. In the structuralist account, the individual employee is an active agent who makes strategic choices within constraints and enabling structures provided by the employer. The employer and the employee each share responsibility for the results.

· · ·

Cultural Domination Theory and the Containment of Equality

The newest orientation to address workplace equality issues—the cultural domination approach—has been most thoroughly developed by critical race and feminist legal scholars. As embodied in the work of Derrick Bell, cultural domination theory posits that dominant groups will find various ways to maintain their position in society. A major theme of this scholarship is that oppression can be reproduced and progress is not inevitable. Cultural domination theorists are alert to the prospect that racial and gender hierarchies may remain intact, even if specific structures or forms of oppression change. In the cultural domination account, even policies such as affirmative action, designed to integrate the workplace, can backfire if they fail to address "culturally ingrained responses" that deny legitimacy to any situation in which white men are not in a "clearly dominant role."

. . .

The somber message implicit in cultural domination theory is that institutions will resist change simply because they cannot believe that high quality is consistent with diversity. The cultural explanation is alert to numbers, particularly as it focuses on the question of why the dominant group feels threatened and resists the introduction of a critical mass of minorities in the workplace. But unlike Kanter, Bell does not assume that the problem lies mainly *in* the numbers. Hiring more women or more minorities may not be enough. In the cultural account, the relationship between numbers and ideological impact is not symmetrical. There is no guarantee that stereotypes and negative images about others will disappear once their representation reaches beyond a certain point.

Under Bell's cultural domination theory, institutions follow a policy of containment—both ideologically and in terms of numbers—by adopting culturally slanted notions of merit and, when necessary, by changing the definition of merit to assure that the white racial status of the institution is maintained. Cultural domination theorists tend to regard "merit" as a moving target. When there is integration in one sector—for example, law school admissions—it is likely that another credential that far fewer minorities or women possess—for example, a Ph.D. in economics or a Rhodes scholarship—will emerge as the new indicator of excellence. This shift rarely results from a conscious conspiracy among those in power to select the standard with the most exclusionary impact. It is rather the cultural association of whiteness (or maleness) with merit and value that leads people to believe that exclusionary sites are the most prestigious. Cultural domination theory, for example, explains the phenomenon of job shifting—the lowering in prestige when a particular job or occupation shifts over time from male-dominated to female-dominated, such as the job of secretary or bank teller. It also supports a major tenet of the comparable worth campaign: that men's work is valued more highly than women's work, regardless of the inherent tasks of the job.

. . .

Perhaps because the cultural account of workplace discrimination emphasizes ideology and deemphasizes numbers, it has been more attentive to discrimination against women of color and other people who are the minorities within minority groups. By the late 1980s, back feminist scholars and lesbian theorists had developed a strong critique of progressive discourses, citing their failure to take account of diversity within minority groups. Institutions were charged with showcasing black men and white women as visible tokens, ignoring women of color and members of other ethnic and racial groups. Kimberlé Crenshaw's theory of intersectionality, for example, asserted that the most privileged within a minority group—heterosexual white women, minority men—were the most likely to benefit from legal intervention and voluntary affirmative action. Patricia Cain forcefully argued that the agenda of contemporary feminist legal scholars often excluded lesbians and their experiences and concerns.

. . .

Although individual scholars tend to emphasize one or perhaps two dimensions of personal identity, cultural domination theory has the potential to respond to multiple differences. The inclusive quality of cultural domination theory comes from the premise that at some point all nondominant social groups will be contained. In contrast to structural accounts like Kanter's, cultural domination theorists do not assume that the predicament of all social groups is fundamentally the same. They tend, instead, to acknowledge that the specific impact of exclusionary mechanisms on different social groups will inevitably differ, with some groups suffering more than others. The common ground is the oppressive nature of the dominant ideology—the myths that support domination of the many by the few.

. . .

An important feature of the cultural domination orientation is the assumption that there are few or no limits on the ability of the dominant group to maintain its position. If reality depends on the version of reality that gets accepted, only what is unimaginable for those in power is off limits. This chimerical quality of culture is disconcerting in that it means that the Big Lie can be accepted as truth. It also means that progress can be undone and that there is no assurance that race or sex discrimination will subside, rather than increase. The narrative of gradual progress implicit in many of the structural accounts is absent in cultural domination theory.

Cultural domination theorists, however, are not relentlessly pessimistic. The chimerical quality of culture also means that there is nothing natural or inevitable about cultural beliefs and patterns. Even the most settled meanings can be changed, and alternative perspectives are possible. . . .

To a greater extent than structuralists, cultural domination theorists stress the importance of perspective and regard knowledge as situated, acknowledging the possibility of multiple truths and realities. In this respect, the cultural domination orientation, as I describe it, shares a common theme with feminist jurisprudence. The emphasis on perspective and the corresponding critique of objectivity and universal truth have been the hallmark of much of the feminist legal scholarship of the past decade. Unmasking the hidden male viewpoint underlying seemingly neutral laws and policies has become a central method of feminists who claim that the law is unresponsive to women's needs and experiences. Feminists embracing various schools of thought—whether labeled as liberal, radical, or relational—agree that women's difference from men has been used to justify disadvantage and that the concept of difference itself needs to be unpacked and examined.

The feminist investigation of difference has yielded two related insights: that the neutral concept of difference tends to obscure the power of those who are able to label others as different, and that even an acknowledged difference, without more, is no justification for unfavorable treatment. Martha Minow's scholarship exemplifies this critical approach to difference and to the connection between difference and domination. Minow argues for a relational concept of difference that challenges the prevailing view of difference as some intrinsic and objective quality of certain groups. In her work, Minow seeks to dislodge the oppressive meaning of difference as deviation from the norm and to question the reference point by which the comparison of difference is made. By showing the social constructedness of the concept of difference, Minow's theory contrasts sharply with motivational research that is premised on the search for intrinsic difference. Her focus on conceptual categories and ways of thinking also differs from the more materialist orientation of structuralists. Like Bell's, Minow's critique of difference locates discrimination in hard-to-displace habits of mind, unlikely to be undone by changes in the organizational chart or even the demographics of the organization.

The strategies linked to the cultural domination orientation are less obvious than those implied by the motivational or structural orientation. The importance placed on ideological containment assumes that piece-meal reforms, such as hiring a few more minorities or installing an affirmative action officer, will be co-opted by the dominant culture unless accompanied by a shift in the meaning of blackness or femaleness in the broader society. Rather than focusing solely on the internal dynamics of the organization, cultural domination theory suggests that contradictions and myths in the larger culture need to be addressed and explored. The awareness that short-term victories can turn out to be long-term losses means that winning a grievance or a lawsuit may not always be the best strategy. The situation may instead call for conscious-ness-raising programs or cultural criticism through the mass media. Cultural domination theorists are more likely to believe that only sus-tained political pressure, rather than organizational self-interest, can be relied upon to stimulate progressive changes....

The Influence of Structuralist Theories in the Courts

In the courts, structuralist influence has been felt mainly in cases involving sexual stereotyping and sexually hostile work environments. In two major cases, Dr. Susan Fiske, a social psychologist of the Kanter school, has presented expert testimony designed to expand legal notions of causation and harm beyond the traditional motivational framework. Both cases involved the treatment of token women in male-dominated workplaces. In both cases the critical question was whether a woman's claim to discriminatory treatment would be judged against a comparative standard that implicitly makes men's experience the measure of fair treatment in the workplace. *Hopkins v. Price Waterhouse* challenged the sex bias resulting in a negative evaluation of a professional woman by her male peers. *Robinson v. Jacksonville Shipyards, Inc.* dealt with harassment of female blue-collar workers in a highly sexualized work environment. The plaintiffs won in each case, and each court cited Fiske's testimony as a factor influencing its decision. The structuralist orientation of Fiske's testimony, however, has not yet found its way securely into the legal doctrine. Instead, structuralist theory has been used selectively to bolster judgments for plaintiffs, without displacing the basic motivational framework.

Biased Evaluations, Causation, and Workplace Demographics: Price Waterhouse v. Hopkins

Price Waterhouse involved the denial of partnership in a Big Eight accounting firm to a female manager who had been especially successful in bringing in clients and racking up billable hours. The partners voted against Anne Hopkins because they did not like her aggressive style and unladylike personal manner; a few partners were incautious enough to couch their objections in explicitly gendered comments—for example, they claimed she was too "macho" and needed "a course in charm school." The courts used the occasion to refine motivational analysis in those disparate treatment cases in which it is clear that the plaintiff's gender influenced the employer's decision to some degree.

In individual disparate treatment cases, a standard formulation for determining causation is the familiar "but for" test: the inquiry is whether the unfavorable treatment of the plaintiff would not have occurred "but for" her sex. In practice, this often means that a female plaintiff must come forward with comparative evidence of a similarly situated man who secured more favorable treatment. This showing is particularly complicated when the measures upon which employees are judged are highly subjective: whether, for example, the plaintiff gets along well with others, presents herself well to clients, or treats subordinates decently.

In *Price Waterhouse,* the causation question boiled down to whether Anne Hopkins was denied the partnership because of her lack of interpersonal skills or because she was a woman. Using what is known as a mixed-motivational framework, the courts tried to predict whether Hopkins's lack of social graces would have been tolerated in a man who possessed the same ability to attract clients and perform the technical aspects of the job. So framed, the comparative question led to a search for the true or objective assessment of the plaintiff's personality: Was Hopkins really as obnoxious as some of the partners said she was, or were their views tainted by gender bias? Was the denial of the partnership caused by Hopkins's personality, or was it the product of the partners' prejudice against women?

Under the motivational framework, there are only two possible sources for a plaintiff's disadvantage; the harm is caused either by the plaintiff's deficiencies or by the intentionally biased attitudes of the evaluators. The dichotomous conceptualization of causation leaves little room to consider how structural features may affect the way a plaintiff's personality and performance is perceived by others in the workplace. The motivational framework does not focus directly on the dynamics of tokenism because it presumes that the structural position of male and female workers in skewed working groups is the same.

In contrast to the motivational approach, Fiske's structural analysis assumed that Hopkins's status as a token woman was of paramount importance. In her testimony, Fiske explained that when women are dramatically underrepresented in organizations, they are especially vulnerable to stereotyping and typecasting. Based on her review of the partners' comments, Fiske concluded that it was likely that Hopkins was scrutinized more closely than her male peers on nonperformance measures often associated with women. Fiske believed that once Hopkins was cast as an "iron maiden," this image might have obscured those aspects of her personality that did not fit the preconceived mold.

Fiske's analysis cast doubt on the neutrality of the partners' view that Hopkins was overbearing and aggressive. Even those partners who thought they were being fair and objective were likely influenced by the skewed demographics of the workplace. . . .

.   .   .

The comparative standard in motivational analysis presupposes that a judge can discover whether there are salient differences about the person being judged—besides a difference in gender—that might justify treating her unfavorably. The question is approached simply as a question of fact. The structuralist account assumes that differences are socially constructed and shifts the focus from the factual inquiry about whether difference exists to an inquiry into how perceptions of difference originate and are maintained. Causation in the structuralist account is complicated by the assumption that a token's personality is shaped and sometimes distorted by her outsider status in the workplace. Under Fiske's analysis, even those partners who did not employ explicitly gendered statements to evaluate Hopkins's performance might be said to have judged her "as a woman," rather than in a truly gender-neutral fashion.

The Supreme Court in *Price Waterhouse* did not rely on Fiske's testimony to disavow the comparative, motivational approach but instead used it to refine the burden of proof in mixed-motivation cases. The crucial test remains whether a plaintiff would have been treated more favorably if she were a man. The burden shifts to the employer to prove lack of causation only in those instances in which the plaintiff produces direct evidence that sexism or sexual stereotyping was a "motivating factor" in the adverse decision.

Unlike the holding in *Price Waterhouse,* a doctrine fashioned along structuralist lines would not turn on whether the plaintiff could adduce some direct evidence of sex-based motivation. Instead, I interpret the structuralist approach as implying that employers should be responsible for counteracting the dynamics of tokenism if they wish to rely on subjective assessments of employee performance. I imagine that under a structuralist approach the plaintiff's prima facie case would consist of a showing of dramatic underrepresentation of the plaintiff's group, satisfactory performance by the plaintiff on objective measures, and evidence of a subjective, largely standardless selection process. In such a case, an employer would be held liable unless it could show that it had taken adequate measures to guard against stereotyping. For example, employers might avoid liability by giving decisionmaking authority to a sexually integrated group or by instituting a structured evaluation process that specified as precisely as possible the criteria to be used in making the decision.

· · ·

Reconceiving Legal Injury: Robinson v. Jacksonville Shipyards, Inc.

The second way structuralism has influenced Title VII litigation involves the important question of what counts as legally cognizable harm. More than other types of claims, suits for sexually hostile work environments highlight the extent to which the basic concept of injury itself is derived from the experience of the dominant group. The type of sexual harassment first recognized by the courts—the claim for quid pro quo harassment—was easily assimilated to an injury that could also be experienced by men. Quid pro quo harassment most often takes the form of employer retaliation against a plaintiff for refusing to comply with sexual demands. A woman who is fired for refusing to sleep with the boss, for example, has suffered the kind of tangible economic harm that is not so different from the harm a man might suffer if he stood up to the unreasonable demands of his boss. When the claim is that of a sexually hostile environment, however, it is more difficult to see the injury suffered by women as analogous to what happens to men in the workplace.

Robinson presents a classic instance of the conflict that arises when a small number of women integrate an intensely male-dominated workplace. At the Jacksonville shipyards, sexualized images of women were so commonplace that they went unnoticed. Pornographic photographs and plaques hung on the walls, and vendors routinely distributed advertising calendars with "pinups" to employees. The management and the male workers believed that it was their right and part of their tradition to display this material, even though several of the pictures very explicitly demeaned women and women's bodies. The female employees were subjected to repeated verbal abuse and humiliation. The conflict escalated when plaintiff pressed her objection to the displays. She was then singled out for retaliatory harassment, and the pornographic displays intensified.

. . .

One important issue in *Robinson* was whether behavior that did not target a specific individual, particularly the pornographic displays, should be held to constitute a legal injury. The plaintiffs had to articulate why material that was innocuous and even pleasurable for the men was injurious to the women. Then they faced the further challenge of demonstrating to the court why their discomfort with the pornography amounted to employment discrimination.

Fiske's structuralist account of pornography's effect on the status of the women as token employees provided this important link. As in *Price Waterhouse,* Fiske started her analysis by explaining how the dramatic sexual imbalance at the shipyards was a precondition for a form of stereotyping known as " 'sex role spillover,' " or the tendency to regard women in terms of their sexuality and their worth as sex objects, rather than as competent co-workers. Fiske theorized that the presence of pornography at the worksite set in motion a process called "priming," which encouraged men to think about women in categorical, sexually objectified terms. Because men controlled all the positions of power at the shipyards, Fiske also noted that women were powerless to have their complaints taken seriously. Fiske cited research explaining that a common response to an outsider's complaint of injustice is to treat the outsider as the source of the problem, rather than to scrutinize the dominant group's behavior. Fiske thus was able to show how the demographics of the workplace affected the grievance process and made it unlikely that the men's behavior would easily be checked.

Fiske's structuralist account of the harassment at the Jacksonville shipyards stressed how harassment functioned as a tool of exclusion—a device to keep down the number of women in skilled jobs and to retard their advancement on the job.... Fiske's testimony in *Robinson* uncovered the job-related consequences of a sexually hostile environment. Fiske was able to recast the injury to the plaintiffs as economic and systemic, rather than as personal and intangible. So deployed, structuralist theory described a gender-specific injury: sexual material that posed no problem for male employees could nevertheless harm the employment status of token women.... The nondominant position of the women was underlined and exacerbated by the sexualized, nonprofessional ambience that pervaded the shipyards....

The district court's ruling in *Robinson* embraced structuralist theory to a greater degree than did the courts in *Price Waterhouse*. The court held that Fiske's testimony "provided a sound, credible theoretical framework from which to conclude that the presence of pictures of nude and partially nude women, sexual comments, sexual joking, and other behaviors previously described creates and contributes to a sexually hostile work environment." This holding in *Robinson* made clear that gender baiting and sexual denigration, as well as sexual propositioning, were actionable forms of sexual harassment. Moreover, the structuralist account of the harmful effects of harassment on the status of token women justified holding the employer liable, although much of the sexual material had not been displayed for the purpose of harming women and had predated the entry of women in the workplace. The court's holding made explicit what is implicit in structuralist theory: that employers have the responsibility to change the prevailing tone of the workplace to make it hospitable to newcomers. The court also accepted Fiske's testimony as a "reliable basis" for concluding that a "reasonable woman" would be harmed by the sexually hostile environment, thus employing structuralist theory to validate the plaintiff's subjective claim of injury.

Notes and Questions

1. Christine Littleton seeks to articulate a vision of equality—called equality as acceptance—that can undermine male-dominated social institutions. According to this vision, male and female job categories should be equally paid and endowed with status by implementing a policy of comparable worth. But unlike the resort to aggressive enforcement of antidiscrimination law to open up traditionally male jobs to women, the adoption of comparable worth would likely reinforce sex segregation among occupations, since the higher wages would make these jobs all the more attractive to women. Conceivably, men might be drawn to such jobs as well, but with increased demand for these jobs by women and shrinking job opportunities as employers cut back employment in response to the higher wages, this is an unlikely route to declining occupational segregation. Comparable worth would only cause such segregation to decline to the extent that the increased wages in "women's" jobs would reduce total employment in those jobs, thereby involuntarily excluding women from their preferred occupations. Does this suggest that comparable worth might strengthen the phallocentric division of labor within the workforce?

As discussed later in Chapter 15, adopting comparable worth would likely narrow the women's wage gap by a few percentage points. Jane Friesen has noted that if comparable worth increased women's earnings sufficiently it might undermine the current structure of gender relations in the home, thereby changing women's preferences. She concludes, however, that traditional antidiscrimination policies would probably achieve this goal more effectively, since they would not reinforce occupational segregation. Friesen, "Alternative Economic Perspectives on the Use of Labor Market Policies to Redress the Gender Gap in Compensation," 82 *Georgetown Law Journal* 31, 63 (1993).

2.   Littleton asserts that the value of money, the meaning of status, and commodification of labor are all artifacts of a phallocentric culture. Is the goal of the theory of equality as acceptance to establish a new hierarchy of values, or simply to assist women to amass more of what is currently valued?

3.   Littleton states that "since pregnancy almost always results in some period of disability for the woman, making the sex difference costless with respect to the workplace requires that money, status, and opportunity for advancement flow equally to the womb-donating woman and the sperm-donating man" (p. 1327). Does this mean that employers should provide paid maternity leave and restore women to the place they would have been had they been men? Would it be preferable to fund the maternity benefits out of general tax revenues? (See Chapter 15, note 7.)

4.   Martha Chamallas discusses the work of Rosabeth Moss Kanter, which seeks to demonstrate that workforce demographics explain which groups exercise power and how employees from nondominant groups are likely to be regarded. Kanter argues that groups need from 15 to 35 percent of the workforce to be able to form coalitions and influence the culture of the organization. Does this suggest that employment discrimination law might harm blacks if it encouraged proportional representation of from 10 to 12 percent in all firms, since bunching of black employees might help to consolidate their power? Would it be better to have no blacks in half the firms, and from 20 to 25 percent black in the other half? (Evidence of such racial bunching in Chicago banks was presented in Chapter 10, note 2). If, as Crenshaw argues, black women—who comprise less than 7 percent of the labor market—should be treated as a separate group (see Chapter 10, note 7), is there any realistic hope that they can muster sufficient numbers to avoid the tokenism that Kanter laments?

5.   Chamallas's discussion of the widespread acceptance of crude sexual photographs and plaques at the Jacksonville Shipyards dramatically reveals that structural change in the workplace is often needed before women can be comfortable in certain occupations. Even though much of the objectionable material was in no way designed to harm the new female employees—it had been there long before women ever entered the shipyards—the federal district court ruled that the preferences of the male workers needed to be subordinated to the preferences of female workers. While the male workers are no doubt distressed by this holding, the Coase theorem suggests that, even though the entitlement to be free of the sexually explicit pictures is now possessed by the female employees, the presence or absence of such material should be unaffected by the legal rule. According to this view, if the male employees desired the offensive pictures more than the female employees wanted to be free of them, the males could purchase from the women the right to maintain the pictures. Although the transaction costs do not appear

to be particularly high in this context, there is no evidence of male workers attempting to purchase this right from female employees. Does this mean that the men don't really care that strongly about the ability to have the pictures? If so, then the court's decision seems efficient: the women more strongly prefer to be rid of the pictures than the men prefer to have them.

Do you think male and female employees ever bargain over such conditions of employment? One possibility is that they don't perceive such Coasean bargaining opportunities. See Donohue, "Opting for the British Rule, or If Posner and Shavell Can't Remember the Coase Theorem, Who Will?" 104 *Harvard Law Review* 1093 (1991). Another possibility, discussed in the Donohue selection in Chapter 13, is that the value of certain rights is compromised if one must bargain to secure them. If so, the female workers could not hope to achieve equality by trying to purchase the right to be free of offensive materials in the work place, and the male workers might feel that the value of displaying sexually explicit material is impaired if they must purchase the right from women. Alternatively, the problem could be that any deal that was struck would be subject to revocation on the hiring of a new female worker, who would be in a position to enjoin the offensive conduct regardless of any prior agreement between the male and female workers. Does the fluidity of the firm's labor force create a high-transaction-cost bargaining situation?

13

Sex Segregation

Almost half of all women work in occupations that are at least 80 percent female. In 1995, the Federal Glass Ceiling Commission reported that women comprised only 6.6 percent of high-level managers at Fortune 1000 companies (minorities were only 2.6 percent of the total). As we have already seen, even highly educated married women who work full time but have children tend to work substantially fewer hours in the paid labor market than their husbands. Are the broad patterns of substantial sex segregation and clustering of women in lower wage positions the product of discrimination or of an efficient and beneficial sexual division of labor? Judge Richard Posner strongly subscribes to the latter view, arguing that many of the employment patterns that are sometimes taken to reflect sexual inequality are the product of reasonable choices by women, given their biological differences from men. It may well be that sex-differentiated practices developed over hundreds of thousands of years in furtherance of the survival of the species—when life was tenuous and short, mature males may have needed to hunt, while pregnant females attended to children. The affluence of modern America, however, enables greater malleability of social organization. Posner believes that such adjustments are occurring naturally without the aid of law.

In contrast, John Donohue argues that, while much of sex segregation has undoubtedly emanated from women's choices, there is evidence that animus-based discrimination is partly responsible for keeping women out of some upper-level positions. He also raises the question of whether antidiscrimination law can improve the quality of the work environment in a way that stimulates beneficial demand and supply shifts for female workers. Moreover, Donohue questions Posner's confidence that the economic integration of men and women is so complete and the check of the market on various types of employer and employee misconduct so powerful that we can dispense with the assistance of the legal prohibitions of employment discrimination.

Finally, Vicki Schultz strongly rejects all notions about women's choice in explaining sex segregation. She argues that women would desire the high-paid, high-pressure jobs that have traditionally been filled largely by men if employers structured the jobs and the workplace environment in a way that would not be threatening to women. More specifically, Schultz believes that women's ostensible lack of interest in certain types of traditionally male employment is not some fixed prelabor market characteristic, but rather is contingent upon the nature of the work environment that awaits them. She therefore favors changes in institutional structures that will draw women into these traditionally male jobs. In this way, Schultz's position embraces and exemplifies the structuralist view that was introduced in the selection by Chamallas in Chapter 12.

An Economic Analysis of Sex Discrimination Laws*
RICHARD A. POSNER

. . .

The Legal Background

A complex set of laws regulates sex discrimination in employment.... The Equal Pay Act of 1963 requires employers to pay their employees the same wages for "equal work" regardless of sex. Equal work is narrowly defined, and unequal pay for equal work is permitted if the employer can show that the inequality is due to something other than the sex of the employees. Title VII of the Civil Rights Act of 1964 forbids sex discrimination in employment—in hiring, firing, promotion, and working conditions. Discrimination in pay is also included, so Title VII overlaps with the Equal Pay Act. "Discrimination" as used in Title VII essentially means disadvantage, but the employer can defend against a charge of sex discrimination by showing that the discrimination is necessary to its business. This is the "BFOQ" (bona fide occupational qualification) defense. A standard example is refusing to consider male actors for female acting parts. Finally, Executive Order No. 11246, as amended in 1967, forbids discrimination on the basis of sex by federal contractors, under pain of loss of their contracts.

* Excerpts from Richard A. Posner, "An Economic Analysis of Sex Discrimination Laws," 56 *The University of Chicago Law Review* 1311, copyright © 1989. Reprinted by permission of the publisher.

... In the Pregnancy Discrimination Act of 1978, Congress, repudiating the Supreme court's decision in *General Electric Co. v Gilbert*, further amended Title VII to forbid discrimination based on pregnancy, with the result that an employer's refusal to classify pregnancy as a disability or to include the medical costs of pregnancy in a health benefits plan for employees is now unlawful discrimination. And the courts have interpreted Title VII discrimination to include sexual harassment. Although Title VII has been held not to require employers to adopt "comparable worth," several states have required it of their public employers. California has in addition required its private as well as its public employers to give female workers maternity leave; recently the Supreme Court held that such a requirement does not violate the Pregnancy Discrimination Act.

The Equal Protection and Due Process Clauses have been held to forbid various forms of governmental sex discrimination, both state and federal. For example, the Equal Protection Clause has been interpreted to require the "degendering" of pension plans for public employees and to forbid differentiating spousal pension and fringe benefits on the basis of the employee's sex. It can be taken for granted that laws excluding women from particular occupations, with narrow exceptions such as jobs involving military combat, are unconstitutional, and almost all such laws have in fact been repealed. On the other hand, in the *Feeney* decision the Supreme Court rejected a complaint by women that a state's policy of giving veterans a preference in public employment denied women equal protection because only a minuscule number of women are veterans.

. . .

Some Economics of Sex Discrimination

Before the economic effects of sex discrimination law can be evaluated, one must get a grip on the economics of sex discrimination. This section lists the basic assumptions of the analysis, then examines the causes of sex discrimination, and finally makes a stab at estimating what our labor markets would be like today without any sex discrimination laws.

Assumptions

I assume that all people—men and women alike—are rational in the usual economic sense. That is, they consistently act to maximize the excess of their private benefits over their private costs. It is consistent with this model, as we shall see, that some—or, for that matter, many or even most—men are misogynistic, exploitative, or ill-informed. I further assume that even if there is no discrimination against women, women will, on average, invest less than men in human capital, both general and job-specific. The qualification that it is only *on average* that women will invest less is important. The characteristics that are related to productive employment are unevenly distributed within each sex, so that even if the means of the distributions differ, the distributions themselves overlap, with the result that many women invest more in their human capital than many men invest in their own human capital. Nevertheless, the *average* woman expects to take more time out of the work force than the average man to raise children, which makes the expected lifetime earnings of the average woman, and hence return to human capital, lower than those of the average man. The average woman will therefore invest less in her human capital, causing her wage to be lower than the average man's, since a part of every wage is repayment of the worker's investment in human capital.

It is possible that the greater propensity of women than men to take time out of the labor force is itself a product of sex discrimination, but I am skeptical of that proposition—I think child-rearing is an area where nature dominates culture—and I do not accept it for purposes of my analysis. However, I will not try to defend this assumption. It is also possible that the propensity will in time disappear, but again I am skeptical, and for the same reason. Even if it does eventually disappear, there can be little doubt that women's *current* wages are depressed because today's working women did not invest heavily in their human capital when they were young. Table 7–3 in the 1987 *Economic Report of the President* shows, for example, that while in 1968 only 27.5 percent of young white women expected to be working when they were 35 years old, in 1985 more than 70 percent of these women *were* working. The table also shows that, by 1979, young women had changed their expectations: almost exactly the same percentage of young women expected to be working at age 35 as were in fact working at that age in 1985. Since women now have more realistic expectations concerning their labor force participation, we can expect them to invest more heavily in their human capital and therefore earn higher wages in the future. Thus, although the fact that the average woman earns substantially less than the average man is often taken to be prima facie evidence of sex discrimination, it is not, and in any case the differential is likely to decline for reasons unrelated to sex discrimination law.

Finally, I assume that men's and women's utility functions are interdependent, and specifically that women derive a benefit from an increase in the income of a husband or other male relative (son, father, brother, etc.), even if no part of the increased income is consumed by the woman. This qualification is necessary because of the importance of joint consumption in the household. Normally if one spouse's income rises, the other spouse will benefit because so much of the consumption in a household is joint. We thus have separate interdependencies: the "pure" interdependency that results from altruism (the satisfaction that most people experience from an increase in the happiness of a close relative), and the interdependency resulting from joint consumption within the household. . . .

It is important to note that the interdependencies between spouses often persist after divorce or the death of a spouse. If a widow's or divorcée's standard of living is a function of her husband's income, increases in that income will increase the wife's welfare. This increase will persist even after a woman is widowed, since her standard of living remains tied to her husband's former income; similarly, a divorced woman's standard of living often remains tied to her former husband's current income. Thus the large percentage of women who are unmarried exaggerates the economic independence of women from men. The vast majority of women marry at some time during their lives, and this is all that is necessary to establish a pervasive economic interdependence between the sexes.

The relationship between majority and minority groups is not characterized by interdependence of either the joint-consumption or altruistic varieties, if only because racial intermarriage remains rare. Interdependence gives the economics of sex discrimination a distinctive cast. To take the extreme case, suppose that all workers were married and that all consumption within the household were joint. Then discrimination against women in the labor force would be compensated for completely in the home, for while wives' wages would be lower than in a nondiscriminatory regime, wives would benefit dollar for dollar from the correspondingly higher wages of their husbands. Of course these assumptions are too strong, and they ignore the fact a woman's earning power may affect her influence over household expenditure decisions, but they point to an important difference between sex discrimination and the other forms of discrimination with which sex discrimination is often, but perhaps facilely, linked.

The Meaning and the Causes of Sex Discrimination

To avoid building a normative assessment into the word "discrimination," I shall follow the lead of Title VII and define sex discrimination as treating a woman differently from a man because she is a woman, without worrying at the definitional stage about whether the discrimination is invidious on the one hand, or justified or even beneficent on the other. This definition is more problematic than it may appear to be, because it leaves unresolved the question whether it is discriminatory (in a sense pertinent to public policy) to treat a woman differently because of a characteristic that no men but only some women have, such as the capacity to bear children. The Supreme Court in *Gilbert* held that such differentiation was not discriminatory, but the Court was overruled by Congress. I shall follow Congress's approach and assume that discrimination based on pregnancy is a form of sex discrimination—which is not to say, of course, that it necessarily is inefficient.

When discrimination is defined as broadly as I am defining it, the causes are multifarious. Here are the main ones, in (roughly) descending order of invidiousness....

Misogyny. By this I mean an elemental distaste on the part of men for associating with women at work not founded on any notions of productivity or efficiency. The misogynist, as I am using the word, is not someone misinformed about either the average or individual quality of female employees—he just doesn't like them in the workplace, maybe because he has traditional views of "the woman's place." Misogyny may appear to be a taste like any other, and therefore ethically neutral from an economic standpoint—a given. But this is not so clear. Insofar as it is expressed in hostile behavior, it may be more akin to a taste for assault than to a taste for chocolate ice cream. Perhaps misogyny is in between a harmless taste and an actual externality like rape or theft.... To further complicate the picture I note that a disinclination to associate with women in the workplace need not reflect a dislike of women and could in fact reflect something nearly opposite to dislike—a desire, not necessarily insincere, to protect women from the hardships of the workplace.

Physical or psychological aggression. A straightforward case of exploitation, more clearly akin to theft or rape than to misogynistic refusal to accept women workers, is sexual harassment conduct designed to elicit sexual favors from women against their will. This phenomenon is related to the "conduit" type of discrimination discussed below, because ordinarily it is not the employer himself (more often, itself) who harasses women, but male employees. The employer merely doesn't want to go to the expense of preventing harassment by its employees. More precisely, the required expense would exceed the potential benefit to the employer from not having to compensate female employees for the disutility of being sexually harassed.

Ignorance about the average working woman. A man who is not a misogynist may nevertheless labor under serious misconceptions concerning the abilities of working women. This is especially likely if there are few women in the workplaces with which the man is familiar. This ignorance may be rational, but that is not to say that it is admirable. Indeed, it may be rational for the entire market to be misinformed, because of the well-known externality problems with information. Whom would it pay to develop information about the working qualities of women in general? How would the social benefits of such information be translated into private benefits for the producer of the information? The pioneer in hiring women in a particular segment of the work force may simply be paving the way for his competitors to learn from his mistakes....

Monopsony. Married women have high relocation costs when the husband earns more than the wife, as is usually the case. In areas where competition for labor among local employers is weak, these employers may be able to set a monopsonistic wage for female employees, so long as such women represent a large fraction of the female labor force or the employer is able to discriminate among women, paying less to those he believes would have difficulty relocating. Monopsony wage-setting is exploitation of female labor in a straightforward economic sense, although it is less invidious than certain other forms of discrimination because it does not rest on any premise that women are inferior workers to men.

Conduit of discrimination. In many cases of discrimination the discriminator is merely reflecting the tastes of customers, employees, government agencies, or others with whom the discriminator has a commercial or regulatory relationship. If male employees don't like working with women, or if customers don't like female workers, the employer will perceive these aversions as additional costs of hiring women and will hire fewer of them, or will pay the women a lower wage to compensate the employer for their greater cost.

Statistical discrimination. Even if employers and their male employees and customers have no discriminatory feelings *and* are perfectly well informed concerning the average characteristics of women in the various types of job, it may be rational for employers to discriminate against women because of the information costs of distinguishing a particular female employee from the average female employee.

... Discussions of statistical discrimination normally assume that, while it would not be efficient to ascertain individual qualifications, it would be *possible* to do so—that is, the cost would not be infinite. But in the case of women, the cost sometimes *would* be infinite, because the uncertainty is inherent and ineradicable. For example, when an employer hires two 21–year-old workers, one male and one female, he knows that the former, being male, has a shorter life expectancy than the latter, but he doesn't know and ordinarily couldn't discover whether *this* female will outlive *this* male.... [H]e doesn't know whether these two workers will track the *average* experience of male and female workers. If differentiations are to be made, they must be made on a statistical basis.

Three things should be noted about my list of the causes of sex discrimination. The first is that it describes a world without sex discrimination laws; for example, we shall see that the problem of "rational ignorance" would be less serious if there were no Equal Pay Act. The second thing to note is the importance of information costs. Half the causes I have identified are based on such costs: ignorance of the average qualities of women workers, statistical discrimination, and inherent uncertainty. Third, only half the causes reflect market failure in a clear economic sense: monopsonistic exploitation of higher relocation costs, aggression against women, and ignorance of the average qualities of women due to information exter-nalities. The other forms of discrimination are, or at least may be, efficient—which does not necessarily make them good from an ethical standpoint. Misogyny, for example, is a morally unattractive trait, but from an economic standpoint it *may* be no different in character from having an aversion to cabbage or rutabaga, though then again it may.

Of the three causes of sex discrimination in employment that clearly reflect a market failure, one has little or no contemporary importance: ignorance of the average qualities of women workers. So many women are employed in so many and diverse fields that few employers can be ignorant any longer concerning women's abilities as workers.... Another cause, high relocation costs conferring monopsony power on employers, has probably never been very important.... The third cause, sexual harassment in the workplace, probably is largely self-correcting. As more and more women are employed, the employer's self-interest in curbing intrigue and harassment, which lower productivity, grows apace.

I conclude that there is no strong theoretical reason to believe that sex discrimination, even if not prohibited by law, would be a substantial source of inefficiency in American labor markets today. If I am correct, then the costs of administering that law will be largely a deadweight loss, from an economic standpoint. That does not make the law immoral or unjust, but any deadweight losses from law enforcement must be considered in deciding whether a particular law or set of laws furthers the public interest.

Discrimination Trends, Ex Law

How much sex discrimination of any sort could we expect today if there were no sex discrimination laws or other pertinent governmental interventions (for example, subsidies for day care)? Some, surely; for we have just seen that some, perhaps most, forms of differential treatment are efficient. But sex discrimination would probably be declining, perhaps steeply, even in the absence of any laws against sex discrimination.

· · ·

Women began working in large numbers long before sex discrimination in the workplace was widely criticized, let alone prohibited, and certainly long before sex discrimination ceased to be rampant (some believe it is still rampant). The percentage of the labor force that is female has grown steadily since 1947, and the primary causes of this growth could not be anti-discrimination laws. The other causes of the increased female participation in the work force are by now well-known. With the decline in infant and child mortality, with improved techniques of contraception, and with the advent of inexpensive household labor-saving devices, women spent less time pregnant and raising children and doing household chores, so their opportunity costs of working in the market fell. At the same time, work was becoming less strenuous, in part because the entrance of large numbers of women into the work force increased the demand for services, hence for service workers, who do lighter work than industrial workers. So the demand for female workers rose, and hence their wages rose. As their wages rose, the opportunity costs of pregnancy and child raising rose too, reinforcing the trend toward fewer pregnancies. This in turn reduced the benefits of marriage to both men and women. The improvement in female job opportunities also reduced women's dependence on men. For both reasons, marriage rates fell and divorce rates soared: the former trend increased women's incentive to invest in their human capital, because they were working more; the latter increased the pressure on women to work, both as insurance against divorce and to maintain their standard of living after divorce.

Assuming that the increased female participation in the labor force is largely independent of the laws forbidding sex discrimination, one may ask what effect the increase is likely to have had on the incidence of sex discrimination (still *ex* law). It should reduce that incidence. First, as more women enter the work force, misconceptions concerning the average qualities of female workers should become less common. . . .

Second, as more wives and daughters enter the work force, we can expect misogyny to decline. Men who love their wives and daughters and empathize with their wives' and daughters' efforts to find work and to cope with misogynistic coworkers or supervisors are less likely to be misogynists in the workplace than if they lacked this family experience. Third, as more women enter the work force misogynistic employers are placed at a competitive disadvantage: their labor costs are higher than non-misogynists' because their employment decisions are constrained by misogyny. Fourth, with more and more women workers, sexual harassment becomes more costly. Apart from the impact on productivity noted earlier, a larger fraction of the work force is offended by it, so the total compensating differential that the employer must pay its female employees rises.

. . .

Because economic analysis predicts that sex discrimination would have declined and the wage gap between men and women narrowed since 1963, when the first federal sex discrimination law—the Equal Pay Act— was passed, these trends cannot automatically be attributed, even in part, to law. Law may have had little or even nothing to do with improvements in women's status in the labor force. This suggestion may seem paradoxical: if the law penalizes certain conduct, the economist's "Law of Demand" implies that the conduct will become less frequent. This assumes, however, that the law is effective, and it may not be, for reasons to be examined in the next section.

The effect of sex discrimination laws on discrimination is ultimately an empirical question—and a difficult one. As argued above, discrimination would have declined without those laws—indeed *was* declining, before those laws were enacted—and it is difficult to isolate the effect of one variable from the others pushing in this direction. Victor Fuchs remarks:

It is easy enough to find particular instances where these laws opened up jobs that were previously closed to women or resulted in a realignment of women's pay scales, but it is difficult to see any major effects on broad trends in women's wages or employment. . . .

This is painting with a pretty broad brush; other scholars have found that sex discrimination law *has* helped to break down barriers to the employment of women in traditionally male occupations. Here is Morley Gunderson's cautious summary: "Clearly, the evidence does *not* unambiguously indicate that the EEO [Equal Employment Opportunity] initiatives of Title VII were a resounding success, although there is some evidence of a positive effect on the earnings and occupational position of women. There is also some evidence that the legislation is more effective when it is strictly enforced and when the economy is expanding." There is no evidence of *large* effects—and we shall see that sex discrimination law may not have improved the net *welfare* of women even if it has somewhat reduced the amount of sex discrimination.

Moreover, the costs of administering the sex discrimination laws must be factored into any attempt at an overall evaluation of those laws. No laws are costless to enforce, not even ineffectual ones. The burdens that sex discrimination laws place on the courts are substantial, and are growing even as discrimination is declining. John Donohue and Peter Siegelman have shown in a recent paper that declining discrimination may be associated with a rise rather than (as one might expect) a fall in the number of cases brought, because as more women are employed in better-paying jobs the gains from suit rise, and because women working side by side with men have a benchmark for proving unequal treatment.

An Economic Examination of Specific Laws and Doctrines

Having sketched the basic sex discrimination laws and the basic economics of sex discrimination, I am prepared to analyze those laws from an economic standpoint. The highly tentative character of the analysis should be self-evident.

Equal Pay Act

At first glance this is the least problematic of the sex discrimination laws. If work is really equal . . . , then it would seem that unequal pay could not be efficient—it must reflect price discrimination. But it is more correct to say that it *may* reflect price discrimination. If the employer is able to pay its female employees a monopsonistic wage because of their high relocation costs, then it is discriminating in the economic (price discrimination) sense. Another possibility, however, is that while the work is nominally equal, the men do it better—are more productive—on average than the women, yet the employer is unable to prove this "factor other than sex" (which, as mentioned above, is a defense under the Act).

A third possibility is that the employer pays its female employees less because the employer's male owners, male managers, or male employees have an aversion to women in the workplace. Then the Act will operate as a tax on misogyny. Such a tax is not objectionable in itself, but we must consider the employer's likely reaction. He ... will try to reduce the tax, by hiring fewer female employees, creating working conditions that are not attractive to them, or—the simplest strategy—placing women in jobs where they are doing work that is not equal to men's work. These would not be feasible strategies if Title VII were totally effective, for virtually all the measures that an employer might take to avoid the mandate of the Equal Pay Act would be a form of sex discrimination forbidden in principle by Title VII. Even substituting computers for secretaries might violate Title VII if the employer's motive were to reduce the number of *female* employees. But if we assume, realistically, that the Equal Pay Act is easier to enforce than Title VII, then the Act will result in fewer women being employed even if the average wage of those women who are employed is higher. And the average wage may not be higher if the employer responds to the Act by shifting women to jobs where their work is not equal to men's. In addition, the Act will prevent women from attempting to overcome any information barriers to hiring them that may exist by offering to work for a lower wage than men.

Even if the employer does not try to avoid or evade the Equal Pay Act there may be a disemployment effect. The Act operates as a payroll tax, and the tax is higher the more workers employed. The employer may raise price in an effort to offset the tax, but unless he faces a totally inelastic demand curve—which no seller does—the increase in his price will reduce the demand for his goods, leading him to curtail his output and hence inputs, including labor inputs. He will employ fewer women as well as fewer men.

.   .   .

To the extent that unequal pay reflects differences in productivity that the equal work standard of the Act is insufficiently sensitive to pick up, the Act's distributive consequences are complicated by the interdependencies between men and women noted earlier in this article. If employers must pay a single wage to workers of different average productivity (i.e., men and women), that wage will be lower than that which the more productive workers would command but for the prohibition of "discrimination." So both men (by hypothesis, the more productive group) and their wives will be worse off. By the same token, the husbands of married women whose pay rises as a result of the Equal Pay Act will be better off. But if women are more altruistic on average than men, the increase in men's welfare resulting from an increase in their wives' income will be less than the decrease in women's welfare resulting from a decline in their husbands' income, even if the increase and decrease are identical in dollar terms. In addition, since more married men than married women work, the transfer of welfare to married women will be larger. When this consideration is added to the Equal Pay Act's potential disemployment effect on women, it becomes a plausible speculation ... that the Act makes women as a group worse off.

Title VII

Two different types of Title VII sex discrimination cases should be distinguished. In a *disparate impact* case, the employee challenges a practice (for example, a height requirement, or a prohibition, as part of an "anti-nepotism" rule, on hiring employees' spouses) that has a disproportionate exclusionary effect on women, though it was not intended to exclude them. Traditionally, such a practice was unlawful unless the employer could show that it was a business necessity; in practice such a showing was difficult to make. Disparate impact litigation has been important in eliminating personnel practices that tended to exclude blacks (i.e., requiring a high-school diploma), but has not been very important in the area of sex discrimination. Most practices challenged under disparate impact theories involve tests and credentials, and these are rarely sex-biased....

The other, and more common, type of sex discrimination case is the *disparate treatment* case. This requires proof that the employer intentionally treated the female employee (or applicant) less favorably than it would have treated a similarly situated male employee. The practical difficulties in such litigation are great. First, it is difficult to prove a complex counterfactual (for example, what would have happened if the employee had been male rather than female). Second, it often does not pay the plaintiff to invest in the necessary proof—which involves looking at similarly situated males to show that the plaintiff's inadequacies were not responsible for her being fired or otherwise mistreated. The stakes are small. They consist of backpay minus whatever the plaintiff has earned in a substitute job (for the employee has a duty to mitigate her damages) plus reinstatement. But reinstatement will rarely be sought, since usually the plaintiff will have gotten another job while the litigation was pending and will be reluctant to go back to work for an employer who mistreated her and whom she sued. Finally, bringing an employment suit impairs the plaintiff's earning capacity: employers are reluctant to hire people who sue employers!

Although the plaintiff's costs in bringing successful sex discrimination litigation under Title VII may well outweigh her gains, there is an important qualification. If class action treatment is possible, as where a large employer is alleged to be discriminating against all or most of its female employees, then plaintiffs will find safety in numbers and it will be feasible for them to develop statistical evidence of discrimination. Yet such evidence often is inconclusive. It usually comes down to an unexplained difference in the wages or number of men and women employed, and it is always possible for the employer to argue that the statistical methodology is insufficiently sensitive to identify all noninvidious explanatory variables.

To the extent that disparate treatment suits do succeed, it is uncertain whether they increase the net welfare of women. Since some forms of unlawful sex discrimination are efficient, Title VII litigation will reduce the efficiency with which employers use labor, and this will result in lower average wages and higher product prices. The direct costs of Title VII litigation—lawyers' fees, executive time, and so forth—will work in the same direction. Full-time housewives will bear a disproportionate share of these costs, since their husbands' wages will fall and the prices they and their husbands pay for goods and services will rise. Conversely, single working women will tend to benefit, except to the extent that employers are reluctant to hire women in the first place out of fear that Title VII will restrict their ability to fire an unsatisfactory female employee without inviting a lawsuit.

. . .

Sexual Harassment

When efforts were first made to attack sexual harassment under Title VII they seemed an exotic extension of the statute, in part because of the strange implication that a bisexual harasser couldn't be liable under the Act, since his conduct was sex neutral. However, the case for prohibiting sexual harassment may actually be stronger from an economic standpoint than the case for prohibiting conventional sex discrimination. Sexual harassment, properly defined to exclude mere flirtations and solicitations, is a coercive practice related to such plainly inefficient practices as rape and extortion. Sexual harassment is unlikely, save for the costs of prevention, to be in the employer's interest. While, in principle, granting a "license" to male supervisory employees to harass female employees would enable the employer to pay a lower wage to those male employees, the reduced cost of hiring supervisors is unlikely to offset: (1) the higher wage the employer will have to pay its female employees to compensate them for being exposed to sexual harassment; (2) time lost by employees in harassing or warding off harassment; (3) distortion in promotions; and (4) adverse selection of employees (the employer would be a magnet for male employees wanting to harass females and for female employees desiring to use their wiles to gain advancement). The problem is that, like other antisocial behavior in the workplace (embezzlement, for example), the costs of prevention are high; and this is an argument for public enforcement—depending of course on *its* costs.

The novelty in the legal concept of sexual harassment is that the usual defendant in a Title VII sexual harassment case is not the harassing male employee, but the employer. It is as if banks were the defendants in cases involving embezzlement by bank employees. The proper analogy, however, is to the tort doctrine of respondeat superior. The most efficient method of discouraging sexual harassment may be by creating incentives for the employer to police the conduct of its supervisory employees, and this is done by making the employer liable. Because "employer" is broadly defined in Title VII, the supervisory employee himself can be and sometimes is made a defendant in a Title VII sexual harassment case. . . .

Pregnancy Discrimination Act

The requirement that the employer not differentiate among its employees on the basis of pregnancy is analytically the same as a requirement that the employer pay the same retirement benefits to male and female employees despite women's superior longevity, or a requirement that the employer grant maternity leave (in other words, agree to reinstate female employees who take time off to have or take care of their babies). In all three cases, the law compels the employer to ignore a real difference in the average cost of male and female employees. The result is inefficient, but a more interesting point is that it may not benefit women as a whole. The employer is required in effect to pay them greater fringe benefits than men (since health care for pregnancy is a benefit men do not require). The employer cannot recoup by reducing women's wages—that would violate the Equal Pay Act—but he can minimize his costs by employing fewer women (as by automating secretarial work faster and more completely). To the extent that this succeeds, women will be hurt. To the extent it does not succeed, the employer will experience a rise in his average cost of labor, causing him to reduce the average wage he pays.

Women will lose not only directly, but also indirectly, in their role as the wives of men who will now be paid less. The clearest loser will be a married but childless working woman. Her wage and that of her husband will fall, and she will not recoup the loss in higher fringe benefits, because the additional benefits are of value only to women with children. And even if the aggregate income of the household is higher, women may have less power within the household if their paychecks are smaller. This, however, is pure speculation—it is far from clear that women's consumption within the household depends on the relative size of the woman's paycheck, as distinct from her relative contribution to the full (nonpecuniary as well as pecuniary) income of the household. Housewives will also suffer from the Pregnancy Discrimination Act because their husbands' wages will fall. The point can be generalized: housewives, being economically identified with their husbands, are hurt by efforts to reduce sex discrimination. The clearest beneficiaries of sex-neutral fringe benefits are unmarried working women with many children—a small group.

This analysis, by illustrating the possibility of deep conflicts of interest among women, may help explain why many women are not feminists. Depending on age, marital status, number and age of children, and other factors, women may gain or lose from measures ostensibly designed to eliminate discrimination "against women." Indeed, women are so heterogeneous a group that it is hard to imagine what public policies would benefit them as a group—except policies designed to maximize social wealth by maintaining and strengthening free markets.

Equal Protection

The interpretation of the Equal Protection Clause as prohibiting sex discrimination in employment unless the discrimination is justified by an important governmental interest has thus far had little effect. Much of the prohibition overlaps Title VII. Many cases have been brought by men rather than women, although women's groups generally support these cases on the ground that they combat stereotypes harmful to women's aspirations for job equality. Many cases have the usual ambiguous effects. Consider the requirement that spousal benefits under social security programs be equalized regardless of the sex of the spouse, so that a widower is entitled to the same social security death benefit as a widow. If the total benefits payable under social security are assumed to be fixed, the result of this entitlement will be to benefit the better off at the expense of the worse off, since widowers are on average wealthier than widows. The *Feeney* decision, upholding Massachusetts' policy of giving veterans a preference in public employment, illustrates the possibility that the optimal ideology for the women's movement may well be a libertarian one. Veterans' benefits programs, which of course systematically benefit men over women, are redistributive measures that are contrary to the principles of efficiency and limited government.

Conclusion

What has been the net effect of the cascade of laws and lawsuits aimed at eliminating sex discrimination in employment? This is maddeningly difficult to say, but it is possible that women as a whole have not benefited and have in fact suffered. Because of the heterogeneity of women as an economic class and their interdependence with men, laws aimed at combating sex discrimination are more likely to benefit particular groups of women at the expense of other groups rather than women as a whole. And to the extent that the overall effect of the law is to reduce aggregate social welfare because of the allocative and administrative costs of the law, women as a group are hurt along with men. Sex discrimination has long been on the decline, for reasons unrelated to law, and this makes it all the more likely that the principal effect of public intervention may have been to make women as a group worse off by reducing the efficiency of the economy. The case for ambitious extensions of sex discrimination law—for example in the direction of comparable worth—is therefore weak.

These suggestions should not be surprising, in light of the extensive, and largely negative, economic literature on regulation. There is a tendency to suppose that laws forbidding discrimination are somehow exempt from the critique of regulation. This position is difficult to sustain.

It is possible that the economic costs of sex discrimination law are offset by gains not measured in an economic analysis—gains in self-esteem, for example. But it is not clear that, if the canvass is broadened in this fashion, the picture brightens. For example, if by reducing the wages of men sex discrimination law propels more wives into the job market, with the result that (since they still bear the principal burden of household production) they work harder, have fewer children, and have less stable marriages, it is not clear that they are better off on balance than they were when their husbands had higher wages and they stayed home. The social, like the economic, consequences of sex discrimination law are murky, and not necessarily positive. In any event it is important to know what the sex discrimination laws cost; the price tag for an increase in women's self-esteem, if known, might be thought too high by society.

Prohibiting Sex Discrimination in the Workplace: An Economic Perspective*

JOHN J. DONOHUE III

Much has changed in the 25 years since conservative Southern congressmen attempted to derail Title VII of the 1964 Civil Rights Act by offering an amendment that would extend its prohibitions to employment discrimination against women. It is difficult to capture in the dry text the mocking condescension with which Congressman Smith of Virginia offered the amendment as his supporters chortled their approval:

> Mr. Chairman, this amendment is offered to the fair employment practices title of this bill to include within our desire to prevent discrimination against another minority group, the women, but a very essential minority group, in the absence of which the majority group would not be here today.
>
> Now, I am very serious about this amendment ... I do not think it can do any harm to this legislation; maybe it will do some good. I think it will do some good for the minority sex.

To the delight of his supporters, Congressman Smith then quoted from a letter he claimed to have received from a female constituent disturbed by the numerical superiority of women to men, which undermined "our spinster friends in their 'right' to a nice husband and family." Congressman Smith concluded,

* Excerpts from John J. Donohue III, "Prohibiting Sex Discrimination in the Workplace: An Economic Perspective," *The University of Chicago Law Review*, vol. 56, copyright © 1989. Reprinted by permission of the publisher.

I read that letter just to illustrate that women have some real grievances and some real rights to be protected. I am serious about this thing. I just hope that the committee will accept it. Now, what harm can you do this bill that was so perfect yesterday and is so imperfect today—what harm will this do to the condition of the bill?

Despite the absence of any hearings or even a single word of testimony on the issue of sex discrimination, the House accepted the amendment, which was subsequently retained by the Senate. Thus was born the law forbidding employment discrimination against women.

Attitudes—on Women, Discrimination, and Law

This story reflects a set of attitudes—that women in the workplace are not to be taken seriously, that they are more concerned with achieving financial security through obtaining husbands than through work—that thankfully has lost currency in the last two and a half decades. All the boors have not been rousted, from Congress or elsewhere, but attitudes toward women in the workplace have changed enough that a current congressional discussion of employment discrimination against women would be unlikely to include the same sneering spectacle that Congressman Smith staged. This is all to the good, and I venture that the passage of Title VII accelerated this shift in attitudes.

All the attitudinal changes concerning women in the workplace certainly are not attributable to federal law, and one should not exaggerate the extent of the improvement. The sorry truth is that most working women today—even with the protection of law—do not feel that they are treated as equals in the workplace, and survey data indicate that they have reason for this belief.

In a recent nationwide random sample, for example, 55% of 483 women with full-time jobs indicated that "at work, most men don't take women seriously." Of course, one cannot know whether this response indicates that most men in fact don't take women seriously or whether a majority of working women merely labor under this misconception, but the results of a study of the beliefs of business executives in 1965 and 1985 seem consistent with the women's perceptions. In 1965, 27% of male business executives said they would feel comfortable working for a woman; by 1985 the percentage had risen, but only to 47%. The comparable figures for female executives were 75% in 1965 and 82% in 1985. Clearly, a significant number of managerial employees would not like to work for a woman.

If Judge Posner is correct that "few employers can be ignorant any longer concerning women's abilities as workers," it is difficult to attribute these findings to anything but misogyny. Judge Posner notes that as more women enter the labor market, we can expect misogyny to decline because male workers will sympathize with the plight of their wives and daughters. But the improvement from 1965 through 1985, even aided by the law, has not been so complete that women can now expect equal treatment in the workplace.

. . .

Judge Posner raises three basic arguments against sex discrimination laws: (1) social welfare will be diminished if their goals are met; (2) the laws are ineffective in meeting their goals; and (3) to the extent that they have been successful in meeting their goals, these laws have actually harmed their intended beneficiaries. This essay will evaluate this collection of attacks, and offer additional views on some aspects of sex discrimination law.

. . . [Judge Posner argues] that it is socially harmful to override the preferences of discriminators and to prohibit employers from engaging in statistical discrimination. I will attempt to refute this argument by showing that Title VII can promote efficiency in a number of ways: by more rapidly eliminating discriminators, by inducing beneficial productivity and supply curve shifts, and by reducing the inefficiencies associated with statistical discrimination. [I] then [address] a number of the specifics of Judge Posner's attack on the practical aspects of sex discrimination laws—namely that the law is costly to enforce, is often unnecessary, and has not enhanced the welfare of women. [I] conclude with an evaluation of the relative importance of equity and efficiency considerations in assessing the desirability of antidiscrimination laws.

Judge Posner's Two Major Theoretical Objections to Antidiscrimination Laws

Overriding Preferences

The first element of Judge Posner's theoretical attack on Title VII's prohibition of sex discrimination in employment is that it interferes with economically efficient behavior by overriding the preferences of employers who discriminate. For example, if some men prefer being treated by male doctors, it would certainly interfere with their preferences—and thus reduce economic efficiency—for the government to require them to choose doctors without regard to sex. Title VII, which focuses only on employment relationships, does not prohibit individuals from choosing doctors in accordance with their preferences; but the law could still be interpreted to abridge choice in ways that many would lament. For instance, Title VII might prohibit a men's college from refusing to hire a woman to fill its only position for a staff physician, despite a preference for male doctors among some of its students. This is probably the strongest case for Judge Posner's position: the discriminatory preference here seems reasonable, and it implicates issues of privacy that are simply lacking when, say, a manager in a manufacturing plant refuses to hire women for the assembly line because, in Judge Posner's words, "he has traditional views of 'the woman's place.' "

In fact, however, the courts have distinguished between these two types of preferences, granting exceptions to the antidiscrimination laws when significant privacy interests are at stake. Thus, "same sex" employment rules have in certain circumstances been upheld as bona fide occupational qualifications permitted by Section 703(e) of Title VII. Furthermore, Title VII's inapplicability to firms with fewer than 15 employees also represents an attempt by lawmakers to accommodate privacy and associational concerns. Thus, a bunch of law school chums who simply want to get together and form a small, clubby, and male law firm are free to exclude female attorneys as long as the firm employs fewer than 15 workers and is not a federal government contractor. Note that in both these instances federal law is more tolerant of discrimination on the basis of sex than on the basis of race: there is no bona fide occupational qualification exception for race under Title VII, and employers in small firms may not discriminate against blacks.

· · ·

The simple, static efficiency argument against Title VII

If one honors all preferences (even the misogynists'), simple economic models support Judge Posner's theoretical position that the law is inefficient. Figure 13.1 depicts the supply and demand for female labor in a simple static model. By comparing social welfare with and without the antidiscrimination law, one can measure the effect of the laws on short-run social welfare. The demand curve D_1 represents the actual productivity of female workers, which by assumption equals that of similarly qualified male workers. The supply curve S_1 represents the wage that women must be paid in order to supply their labor. In a perfectly nondiscriminatory world, then, the market equilibrium wage and quantity of female labor hired would occur at point C, which is the intersection of D_1 and S_1. Since social welfare is depicted as the area below the demand curve and above the supply curve—in this case area FJC—social welfare is maximized at this market equilibrium.

Because many employers are not indifferent to the applicant's sex in making hiring decisions, even when there is no productivity based reason for doing so, outcome C will not be attained under laissez faire. Instead, the laissez-faire equilibrium occurs at the intersection of D_1 and S_2 (point A). This is because demand curve D_1 reflects the marginal benefit from hiring additional female workers and supply curve S_2 reflects the marginal cost (including both monetary and psychic costs). As long as the marginal benefit is greater than the marginal cost (as is the case for any point to the left of point A), then the employer will benefit from hiring more female workers. If the employer were to hire female workers past point A, however, the supply curve would lie above the demand curve, indicating that the costs from additional hiring would outweigh the benefits.

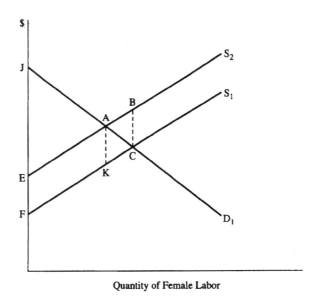

Figure 13.1. The Supply and Demand for Female Labor With and Without Discrimination

The vertical distance BC between supply curves S_2 and S_1 represents an estimate in dollars of the psychic cost to employers of hiring a woman when misogynistic tastes would lead them to prefer a man. Because of these discriminatory preferences, the monetary wage and employment level of women have fallen from point C to point K (the distance AK representing "psychic wages" paid by the employer, but of course of no benefit to the employee), and social welfare has fallen to area EJA. But while discrimination against women unambiguously lowers social welfare, legal intervention can only make matters worse in this simple static model: if society honors all preferences, welfare is still greater under laissez faire than with an antidiscrimination law. The new supply curve S_2 has replaced the nondiscriminatory supply curve S_1, both in determining the free market outcome *and* in determining maximum social welfare. If the passage of an antidiscrimination law increased female employment to point C, social welfare would fall from area EJA to area (EJA–CAB) because the psychic costs to the employer represented by distance BC and triangle CAB cannot be avoided. As long as the costs, both monetary and psychic, embodied in S_2 are taken into account, any interference with the market equilibrium at point A will only reduce short-run social welfare.

Economic arguments in favor of antidiscrimination legislation

THE DYNAMIC EFFICIENCY OF ELIMINATING DISCRIMINATORS. The [preceding] analysis ... has always struck me as incomplete, and I have argued elsewhere that, in a dynamic context, antidiscrimination laws can indeed be wealth-maximizing. This argument, which does not rely upon the implicit social condemnation of discrimination and accepts the legitimacy of discriminatory preferences goes like this: Employers who discriminate because of misogyny are not profit-maximizers, and therefore will ultimately be driven from the market. As the discriminators are forced out of business, social welfare will rise from area DJA to area FJC because the psychic cost of employing women has been eliminated. Consequently, there is a social benefit to be obtained by driving discriminators out of business.

In fully articulating this dynamic efficiency argument, I showed that a law penalizing discrimination will succeed in driving out the discriminators—thereby reducing the psychic costs of discrimination—even more quickly than would occur under laissez faire. The law will be efficient if the following condition holds: the social benefits of more rapidly eliminating discriminators must outweigh the short-run social cost of overriding the discriminators' preferences.

Judge Posner has correctly emphasized that if the market is operating perfectly this condition should not hold, since the market should discipline the discriminators at the optimal rate. But while competitive market forces generally tend to move economic actors in the right direction, these market forces do not always operate at the optimal speed. This seems particularly true in the case of employment discrimination. In such cases, when the government knows that the ultimate equilibrium will involve the elimination of all discriminators from the market, steps taken to overcome the market frictions that retard or even prevent the attainment of the optimal nondiscriminatory outcome can be welfare-enhancing.

THE VALUE OF IMPROVED WORKING CONDITIONS AND ENHANCED SELF-ESTEEM. . . .
[T]he simple static analysis . . . implicitly assumes that the underlying supply and demand curves for female labor are unaffected by the passage of an antidiscrimination law. In other words, while the law may artificially accelerate the attainment of the nondiscriminatory market equilibrium C in Figure 13.1, the "true" social costs and benefits derived from the employment of female labor are still given by demand curve D_1 and supply curve S_2. Ultimately, when all the discriminators have been eliminated, there will be no more psychic cost associated with hiring women. At this point, S_1 will be the "true" supply curve. But the societal pronouncement that women are equal to men, as well as legislated protections against harassment and other indignities, may elevate women's self-esteem and improve life on the job to such a degree that both the demand and the supply curves for female labor shift. In other words, improved working conditions generated by the law can: (1) enhance labor productivity, thereby causing an upward shift in the demand curve; and (2) diminish the onerousness of work, resulting in a downward shift in the supply curve.

To simplify the discussion, I will illustrate this argument in Figure 13.2 under the assumption that only the supply curve shifts, because the showing that the law can generate benefits exceeding its costs applies a fortiori if the demand curve also shifts outward. The laissez-faire equilibrium in a world with some misogyny occurs at the intersection of demand curve D_1 and supply curve S_3. The spacing on D_1 supply curve in the absence of discrimination against women would be S_2, which implies that the psychic cost from hiring an additional female employee is the vertical distance between supply curves S_2 and S_3 (DE). In the analysis presented ... above, passage of the antidiscrimination law simply induced the achievement of the nondiscriminatory equilibrium—here, the intersection of D_1 and S_2 at point E—leading to a reduction in social welfare from the laissez-faire state because the costs of hiring additional female labor beyond point A (as given by S_2) exceed the benefits of their production (given by D_1).

Now suppose that the law simultaneously induces an improvement in working conditions and self-esteem for female employees, which causes a downward shift in the supply curve of labor. The downward shift of the supply curve implies that as working conditions improve more women will be willing to work for any offered wage. To further simplify the graphical analysis, assume that the fall in the supply curve is equal in distance to the size of the per-employee psychic cost of discrimination. This indicates that the new nondiscriminatory market equilibrium that the law tries to enforce is the intersection of D_1 and S_1 at point F, although the total (monetary plus psychic) social cost of hiring these workers is the supply curve S_2 (since $GF = DE$ by assumption). Thus, social welfare under the new law is now measured by area (HBE–EGF). As long as area HACE is greater than area EGF, the law has increased social welfare. The social benefits derived from the downward shift in the supply curve, which are based on an improvement in working conditions for women, outweigh the inefficiency of overriding the preferences of discriminatory employers.

If social welfare would be increased by enacting the law, why wouldn't the employer have an incentive to prohibit discrimination and thereby capture some of the increased wealth? Before answering this question, I must emphasize that in this particular example there is no direct incentive for the employer to act because his welfare after the introduction of the law (which generates equilibrium point F) is actually lower than in the laissez-faire state (which generates equilibrium point C). Of course, the Coase Theorem suggests that female employees will simply bribe employers to enforce a contractual nondiscrimination agreement. But transaction costs in coordinating employees to make such bribes might prevent the attainment of the efficient outcome. More importantly, the very act of bribing the misogynistic employers confirms the absence of equality that is required to generate the favorable supply curve shift. It hardly instills a profound sense of equality for an employer to announce that he will hire the number of women who would be employed in the absence of discrimination (equilibrium point F), so long as these female employees compensate him for relinquishing his discriminatory practices. In other words, the very act of paying a bribe to the employer to move to point F will undermine the self-esteem that is necessary to make the move to point F welfare-enhancing. If the positive supply curve shift can only be generated by treating female employees identically to similarly productive male employees, then it cannot be obtained through a Coasean bribe paid by female employees.

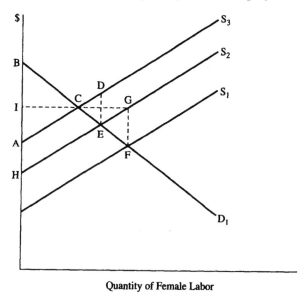

Quantity of Female Labor

Figure 13.2. Beneficial Supply Shifts Induced By Sex Discrimination Laws

Moreover, even if employers privately prohibited discrimination against women, a legal prohibition might still be warranted since public enforcement of Title VII may be superior to private enforcement of contractual promises of nondiscrimination and nonharassment. It is not a persuasive argument against the passage of Title VII that employers will have an incentive to curb the proscribed behavior anyway whenever it is efficient to do so. Certainly we do not require employers to privately enforce rules against embezzlement without the assistance of public law enforcement, though in the absence of criminal laws they would almost surely try to limit such behavior. Public enforcement of rules preventing sex discrimination and harassment may be as efficient as public enforcement of laws prohibiting embezzlement.

It is also conceivable that the effect of a public declaration of equality on the morale and self-esteem of women is far greater than the mere articulation of nondiscrimination policies by individual firms. Certainly, self-esteem is an important element of happiness. Consequently, the costs of Title VII would have to be quite high indeed before they would outweigh any significant increase in women's self-esteem. Moreover, there are both public good and externality elements to the elevation of women's self-esteem. If all firms strongly assert the value of women, then women's self-esteem and quite likely their productivity will rise. If one firm fails to join the chorus of respect, it may still benefit from the productivity enhancements of the general elevation of self-esteem without incurring the expense of monitoring and disciplining its misogynistic male employees. Consequently, government may be needed to prevent such free-riding by firms. Similarly, women outside the workforce may gain from the generalized affirmation of women's equality, and no firm would have an incentive to consider this benefit in deciding how strong a commitment to the equal treatment of women it wished to make.

If the law generates beneficial shifts in the supply and/or demand curves for female labor that cannot otherwise be achieved through private action, then the simple, static efficiency analysis above is incomplete because it does not incorporate such shifts. Depending upon the magnitude of any such shifts, the antidiscrimination law may well be welfare-enhancing. But is there any evidence of beneficial shifts in the supply and demand curves following the passage of Title VII? The matter is difficult to resolve since so many other factors were affecting these curves, but I have already noted Leonard's finding that female productivity rose relative to white men in the period between 1966 and 1977. In addition, the supply curve for female labor shifted outward quite dramatically after 1964 (in other words, the size of the female labor force grew substantially), and the law may have played at least some role in this development. Moreover, the extent of the supply curve shift, whatever its cause, has doubtless contributed to the rather small increase in the wages of women in the last two decades. Judge Posner takes this as a sign of the ineffectiveness of the law. Nonetheless, an increase in the quantity of labor supplied in the aftermath of the law's enactment would be expected to depress the monetary wage, even though the net wage would increase since the burden of working would have fallen.

One of the most important things to realize about the possible supply and demand shifts which may have flowed from the passage of Title VII is that even slight shifts yield extremely large benefits. If the *combined* size of the upward shift in the demand curve (increased productivity) and the downward shift in the supply curve (reduced onerousness of work) is only 1%, then the law has generated annual benefits of roughly $6.66 billion. Certainly, this figure dwarfs the [likely costs of] enforcing the law.

SEXUAL HARASSMENT. Although he is somewhat equivocal on the issue, Judge Posner also appears to believe that laws prohibiting sexual harassment are unnecessary since the problem "is largely self-correcting." Judge Posner argues that employers have an incentive to curb harassment because it lowers productivity: "[W]ith more and more women workers, sexual harassment becomes more costly. Apart from the impact on productivity . . ., a larger fraction of the work force is offended by it, so the total compensating differential that the employer must pay its female employees rises." Though this argument has some force, it fails to account for the severe informational problems associated with sexual harassment. Certainly if women knew in advance that taking a particular job would expose them to harassment, the employer would be harmed because women would either shun the firm or demand higher wages sufficient to compensate for the burden of harassment. In either event, the labor costs of the employer would rise. But it is unlikely that complete information will be available. The molesters rarely begin their assaults before the female worker is hired, nor do they advertise what is to come. Moreover, victims of sexual harassment have little or no incentive to furnish information about their plight to current or potential fellow workers. Disclosure may be embarrassing or bring censure from others. In the absence of legal protection, the response to sexual harassment will frequently be either to quietly endure or to quietly leave—neither of which would provide useful information to the employer or to prospective workers. Therefore, while Judge Posner is quite correct that in a world of perfect information the market will discipline firms that permit the harassment of female workers, the law will certainly be a welcome ally when the lack of perfect information undermines the protection afforded by the market.

Barring Statistical Discrimination

Judge Posner also portrays the prohibition of statistical discrimination as inefficient. There are statistical differences between men and women workers—for example, women live longer but miss more time due to illness each year. Because these factors are relevant to worker productivity and compensation, it is inefficient for employers to ignore them. Certainly, if an employer knew that a particular applicant for a job would be likely to miss more time from work than another, we would not expect her to deem the two applicants equal. Efficiency would require that she pay them differently to reflect their different values. Does this suggest then that women should receive lower salaries, since statistical evidence indicates that they have a lower value on average than male workers?

Not necessarily. When two individual workers are contracting for employment, the one who is known to require more sick leave can take measures to enhance her health; presumably, the worker would take these precautions since doing so would yield greater benefits through higher wages. But when a worker is offered a lower wage because "women take more sick leave," this is not an option. The employer has determined that women are more prone to sickness, and therefore will be paid less. Since compensation is based not on individual but group characteristics, workers will lack incentives to take the optimal health measures. Individual investments in human capital will therefore be distorted. Similarly, if employers do not want to train women for top corporate positions because they will "quit to have children," the incentive to invest in human capital will be inefficiently impaired for women who do not plan to leave their jobs. This inefficiency will exist even if the firm is correct on average in relying upon its statistical information. Thus, while acting on statistical information may be profit-maximizing for the firm, it may still be inefficient for society.

. . .

The Law in Practice

Judge Posner stresses that even if sex discrimination would in theory produce the socially optimal result, there are many reasons to be concerned about the way the laws work in practice. I will turn, then, from the desirability of the goals of sex discrimination laws to a discussion of the means selected to achieve these goals and the extent to which the goals have been realized.

Enforcement Costs

In arguing above that laws forcing employers to disregard the sex of applicants and workers would increase social welfare, I assumed that the laws were costlessly enforced. When these costs are introduced, the possibility exists that the social benefits of achieving gender-neutral employment decisions will be outweighed by the costs.

. . .

The Law Has Not Enhanced the Welfare of Women

Under the analysis outlined above, if the theoretical benefits of a sex discrimination law outweigh the theoretical costs by more than the estimated implementation costs, ... then the theoretical basis for such legislation has been established. But theory and practice at times diverge, and Judge Posner marshals evidence that the theoretical benefits have not been secured. There are several dimensions to his attack.

The laws don't enhance the wages and employment levels of women

Judge Posner argues that the law has not moved us significantly closer to the nondiscriminatory equilibrium (in other words, point C in Figure 13.1). While the evidence on this point is mixed, I agree with Gunderson's summary, which Judge Posner quotes: "Clearly, the evidence does *not* unambiguously indicate that the EEO [Equal Employment Opportunity] initiatives of Title VII were a resounding success, although there is some evidence of a positive effect on the earnings and occupational position of women. There is also some evidence that the legislation is more effective when it is strictly enforced and when the economy is expanding." Judge Posner concludes from this statement that we would be better off without Title VII. Others will conclude that we need stronger enforcement. From the evidence that Judge Posner presents, it is uncertain which conclusion is justified.

Table 13.1   Representation of Protected Groups in Firms
Reporting to the EEOC*

	1966	1970	1974	1978	1980
Black Men	91.8	112.5	123.1	128.4	126.4
Black Women	91.5	118.7	141.2	144.8	154.4
White Women	90.1	93.4	95.8	97.6	96.7

*Figures are percentages of protected workers in EEO-1 reporting firms divided by the corresponding percentages for white men. Ratios are multiplied by 100. Black women were almost 10% less likely to work in reporting compared to non-reporting firms in 1966, and were almost 55% more likely to work in reporting firms in 1980. Welch, *Affirmative Action and Discrimination*.

The position that more enforcement is needed is tenable only if additional enforcement—which is certainly costly—is likely to improve labor market conditions for women. Some recent information compiled by economist Finis Welch is illustrative. Firms with at least 100 workers are required by law to file detailed annual reports—called EEO-1 reports—with the EEOC. The EEOC uses this information in conducting its enforcement activities by targeting firms that seem to have low ratios of "protected" workers in comparison to the available labor pool. Welch has shown that between 1966 and 1980 the representation of black and female workers increased significantly more in firms subject to the EEO-1 reporting requirement than in the non-reporting sector. This increased flow of protected workers to the EEO-1 firms is most dramatic for black women but is also significant for white women, as shown in Table 13.1.

Table 13.1 demonstrates that proportionally more blacks and women have entered firms subject to EEO-1 reporting requirements, presumably because of the increased governmental scrutiny of hiring in these firms. Indeed, Jonathan Leonard has shown that among firms reporting to the EEOC, there is greater hiring of "protected" workers the greater the federal monitoring. Thus, government contractors—who are subject to additional scrutiny by the OFCCP—hire a still greater percentage of blacks and women. These results clearly suggest that more intense government enforcement does increase the demand for black and female labor.

One might wonder whether this conclusion is consistent with the finding that Title VII has generated only modest employment and wage gains for women. It is. Since the sector that is not subject to EEO-1 reporting is so large, the enforcement efforts have tended merely to shift employment patterns by moving blacks and women into the covered sector. But the move by female workers into the EEO-1 reporting sector is evidence that government enforcement has improved the status of female workers in those firms, since presumably women would not have gone to these firms unless lured by more attractive working conditions or compensation. Moreover, if women's wages have not risen, then their conditions of employment must have improved. This is precisely the condition that I argued above must be satisfied for the law to induce beneficial productivity and supply curve shifts. The evidence of the flow of protected workers into EEO–1 firms at least raises the possibility that discriminatory managers and employers are flowing in the opposite direction, into the increasingly white male non-reporting sector. This exodus would both enhance the working conditions of women and reduce the psychic costs of discrimination to the misogynistic employers— perhaps the best of all possible worlds from Judge Posner's perspective. . . .

Women don't benefit from having their wages and employment levels increased

Judge Posner argues that "sex discrimination law may not have improved the net *welfare* of women even if it has somewhat reduced the amount of sex discrimination." This view is premised on the conclusion that these laws are inefficient, and therefore to the extent that they elevate women's wages, they simultaneously depress men's wages. If the laws are efficient, however, as I have argued they are, the unpleasant tradeoff between the welfare of men and women that Judge Posner envisions is unlikely to exist—there should be more for everyone. But even if the tradeoff is real, I still question the view that women do not benefit.

Judge Posner argues that the economic interdependence of men and women implies that "women derive a benefit from an increase in the income of a husband or other male relative (son, father, brother, etc.), even if no part of the increased income is consumed by the woman' " He states that if all workers were married and all consumption within the household were joint, "[t]hen discrimination against women in the labor force would be compensated for completely in the home, for while wives' wages would be lower than in a nondiscriminatory regime, wives would benefit dollar for dollar from the correspondingly higher wages of their husbands." But even if Judge Posner's admittedly extreme assumptions were universally true, his conclusion might not follow. The women in Judge Posner's hypothetical may be married only because sex discrimination makes them financially dependent upon men. If the elimination of sex discrimination removed the financial burden, a greater number of women might not choose to marry (or remain married) and Judge Posner's assumed interdependence would at least to some degree be undermined.

Moreover, even if all men were married and all consumption were joint, wives would not necessarily have the same preferences about consumption as their husbands. The husband may want a hunting lodge in Maine while the wife would prefer a cottage on the Cape. And even though both parties will get enjoyment from either purchase, my guess is that the couple is more likely to end up hunting if the husband controls greater financial resources. Thus, women will not be indifferent to whether sex discrimination increases men's wages at the expense of women's wages.

Judge Posner goes on to suggest that, "if women are more altruistic on average than men, the increase in men's welfare resulting from an increase in their wives' income will be less than the decrease in women's welfare resulting from a decline in their husbands' income, even if the increase and decrease are identical in dollar terms." In other words, the law may not only be needless because men and women have interdependent utilities, but it may be harmful because women are altruistic. But this argument is puzzling. Even if women are more altruistic, their husbands may not be the targets of their generosity. Instead, their greater altruism may be manifested by spending more on their children than their husbands would wish. If such is the case, then by lowering women's wages, sex discrimination will hurt not only working mothers, but their children as well. Furthermore, even if women's bountiful altruism does extend to the welfare of their husbands, there is still no reason to believe that wives would be harmed by a law that increases their wages at the expense of their husbands' wages, for wives can always give the surplus back to their spouses. In this way a wife would experience the altruistic pleasure of giving far more immediately than she would if she simply perceived that her husband earned more money than she did. On the other hand, if wives do not in fact donate their excess earnings to their husbands, it shows that they are happier with the higher earnings that prohibitions on sex discrimination can bring them. In either case, the utility of working wives would seem to be unambiguously elevated by their increased wage.

Judge Posner concludes by observing that, "if by reducing the wages of men sex discrimination law propels more wives into the job market, with the result that (since they still bear the principal burden of household production) they work harder, have fewer children, and have less stable marriages, it is not clear that they are better off on balance than they were when their husbands had higher wages and they stayed home." Moreover, Judge Posner states that "housewives, being economically identified with their husbands, are hurt by efforts to reduce sex discrimination." But if married working women, housewives, and all working men are hurt by sex discrimination laws, one would imagine that groups would be organizing to repeal the laws against sex discrimination, which seems hardly the case. Perhaps the answer is that the antidiscrimination laws have generated efficiency gains sufficient to enhance the welfare of working women without reducing that of other groups.

. . .

While my discussion has held out the possibility that Title VII's prohibition of sex discrimination enhances both equity and efficiency, Judge Posner believes that there is an efficiency price that must be paid. But vague assertions of efficiency losses will not likely overcome the now deeply ingrained notion in American jurisprudence, indeed in the very concept of modern day America, that every individual should be free to advance as far as her talents will permit—a view quite at odds with the notion that discriminatory males should be able to close off employment opportunities for women because of misogynistic preferences. While such equitable concerns would not likely overcome an efficiency loss measured in the hundreds of billions of dollars, I have never seen any evidence to suggest the cost of prohibiting sex discrimination could impose a burden anywhere near this amount.

Telling Stories About Women and Work: Judicial Interpretations of Sex Segregation in the Workplace in Title VII Cases Raising the Lack of Interest Argument*
VICKI SCHULTZ

Introduction

How do we make sense of that most basic feature of the world of work, sex segregation on the job? That it exists is part of our common understanding. Social science research has documented, and casual observation confirmed, that men work mostly with men, doing "men's work," and women work mostly with women, doing "women's work." We know also the serious negative consequences segregation has for women workers. Work traditionally done by women has lower wages, less status, and fewer opportunities for advancement than work done by men. Despite this shared knowledge, however, we remain deeply divided in our attitudes toward sex segregation on the job.... Why does sex segregation on the job exist? Who is responsible for it? Is it an injustice, or an inevitability?

In *EEOC v. Sears, Roebuck & Co.*, the district court interpreted sex segregation as the expression of women's own choice. The Equal Employment Opportunity Commission (EEOC) sued Sears under title VII of the Civil Rights Act of 1964. The EEOC claimed that Sears had engaged

* Excerpts from Vicki Schultz, "Telling Stories about Women and Work: Judicial Interpretations of Sex Segregation in the Workplace in Title VII Cases Raising the Lack of Interest Argument," *Harvard Law Review*, vol. 103, copyright © 1990. Reprinted by permission of the author and publisher.

in sex discrimination in hiring and promotion into commission sales jobs, reserving these jobs mostly for men while relegating women to much lower-paying noncommission sales jobs. Like most employment discrimination plaintiffs, the EEOC relied heavily on statistical evidence to prove its claims. The EEOC's statistical studies showed that Sears had significantly underhired women sales applicants for the more lucrative commission sales positions, even after controlling for potential sex differences in qualifications.

Although the statistical evidence exposed a long-standing pattern of sex segregation in Sears' salesforce, the judge refused to attribute this pattern to sex discrimination. The judge concluded that the EEOC's statistical analyses were "virtually meaningless," because they were based on the faulty assumption that female sales applicants were as "interested" as male applicants in commission sales jobs. Indeed, the EEOC had "turned a blind eye to reality," for Sears had proved that women sales applicants preferred lower-paying noncommission sales jobs. The judge credited various explanations for women's "lack of interest" in commission sales, all of which rested on conventional images of women as "feminine" and nurturing, unsuited for the vicious competition in the male-dominated world of commission selling. In the court's eyes, Sears had done nothing to segregate its salesforce; it had merely honored the preexisting employment preferences of working women themselves.

Few recent cases have received more attention—or provoked more controversy—than *Sears*. The extraordinary attention given the case suggests that it was somehow unusual and therefore noteworthy. . . .

In fact, neither the issues nor the outcome in *Sears* are new. For almost two decades, employers have argued successfully that they had no role in creating sex segregation in their workforces. "It's not our fault," they say. "We don't exclude women from men's jobs. In fact, we've been trying to move women into those jobs. The trouble is, women won't apply for them—they just aren't interested. They grow up wanting to do women's work, and we can't force them to do work they don't want to do." Almost half the courts to consider the issue have accepted this explanation and attributed women's disadvantaged place in the workplace to their own lack of interest in more highly valued nontraditional jobs.

. . .

Title VII promised working women change. But, consciously or unconsciously, courts have interpreted the statute with some of the same assumptions that have historically legitimated women's economic disadvantage. Most centrally, courts have assumed that women's aspirations and identities as workers are shaped exclusively in private realms that are independent of and prior to the workworld. By assuming that women form stable job aspirations before they begin working, courts have missed the ways in which employers contribute to creating women workers in their images of who "women" are supposed to be. Judges have placed beyond the law's reach the structural features of the workplace that gender jobs and people, and disempower women from aspiring to higher-paying nontraditional employment.

. . .

In *EEOC v. Sears, Roebuck & Co.*, for instance, the statistical studies showed that women were severely underrepresented in higher-paying commission sales jobs compared to their representation among all sales applicants. Nonetheless, the court berated the EEOC for failing to produce individual victims of discrimination. "It is almost inconceivable," said the judge, "that, in a nationwide suit alleging a pattern and practice of intentional discrimination for at least 8 years involving more than 900 stores, EEOC would be unable to produce even one witness who could credibly testify that Sears discriminated against her."

. . .

The Conservative Story of Choice

The conservative story of choice is the familiar one told by the *Sears* court: women are "feminine," nontraditional work is "masculine," and therefore women do not want to do it. The story rests on an appeal to masculinity and femininity as oppositional categories. Women are "feminine" because that is the definition of what makes them women. Work itself is endowed with the imagined human characteristics of masculinity or femininity based on the sex of the workers who do it. "Femininity" refers to a complex of womanly traits and aspirations that by definition precludes any interest in the work of men. Even though the story always follows the same logic, the story changes along class lines in the way it is told. Cases involving blue-collar work emphasize the "masculinity" of the work, drawing on images of physical strength and dirtiness. Cases involving white-collar work focus on the "femininity" of women, appealing to traits and values associated with domesticity....

In such cases, conservative courts did not bother to question whether the work fit the gendered characteristics ascribed to it. Indeed, employers did not assert that being male was a bona fide occupational qualification for these jobs. Although some of the jobs may have required considerable physical strength, the courts made no inquiry into whether this was true and if so, whether only men had sufficient strength to perform them. Similarly, although some of the settings may have been dirty, a tolerance for dirt is surely not a "job qualification" possessed only by men. Within the story of coercion, nontraditional work is simply reified, endowed with characteristics typically thought of as masculine, as though there were a natural connection between heavy, dirty work and manhood itself. Ironically, courts associated such work with masculinity even in some cases where the employer's traditionally female jobs involved equally dirty and physically demanding work.

Once the court described the work in reified, masculine terms, women's lack of interest followed merely as a matter of "common sense." "The defendant manufactures upholstered metal chairs," said one court. "Common sense tells us that few women have the skill or the desire to be a welder or a metal fabricator, and that most men cannot operate a sewing machine and have no desire to learn." Or, as another court put it: "Common practical knowledge tells us that certain work in a bakery operation is not attractive to females.... The work is simply not compatible with their personal interests and capabilities" In these blue-collar cases, courts almost never state their specific assumptions about women workers' traits or attitudes.

· · ·

While in blue-collar cases, the story begins by describing the work as "masculine," in white-collar cases, it begins instead by describing women as "feminine." In the white-collar context, courts invoke social and psychological characteristics rather than physical images. In particular, employers invoke women's domestic roles to explain their lack of interest in traditionally male white-collar work, and conservative courts accept these explanations. In *Gillespie v. Board of Education,* the court explained why women teachers did not want to be promoted to administrative positions as follows:

> [M]ales who are pursuing careers in education are often the principal family breadwinners. Women ..., on the other hand, have frequently taken teaching jobs to supplement family income and leave when this is no longer necessary or they are faced with the exigencies of raising a family. We regard this as a logical explanation and find as a matter of fact that there has been no discrimination in the North Little Rock School District.

In some cases the appeal to women's domestic roles is less direct, and even broader in its implications. In *Sears,* for example, the court invoked women's experience in the family as the underlying cause of a whole host of "feminine" traits and values that lead them to prefer lower-paying noncommission sales jobs. According to the court:

> Women tend to be more interested than men in the social and cooperative aspects of the workplace. Women tend to see themselves as less competitive. They often view noncommission sales as more attractive than commission sales, because they can enter and leave the job more easily, and because there is more social contact and friendship, and less stress in noncommission selling.

· · ·

The Liberal Story of Coercion

Like their conservative counterparts, liberal courts assume that women form their job preferences before they begin working. This shared assumption, however, drives liberal courts to a rhetoric that is the opposite of conservative rhetoric. Whereas the conservative story has a strong account of gender that implies a preference for "feminine" work, the liberal story has no coherent account of gender. To the contrary, liberal courts suppress gender difference, because the assumption of stable, preexisting preferences means that they can hold employers responsible for sex segregation only by portraying women as ungendered subjects who emerge from early life realms with the same experiences and values, and therefore the same work aspirations, as men.

The liberal story centers around the prohibition against stereotyping. Courts reject the lack of interest argument by reasoning that "Title VII was intended to override stereotypical views" of women. "[T]o justify failure to advance women because they did not want to be advanced is the type of stereotyped characterization which will not stand." This anti-stereotyping reasoning is the classic rhetoric of gender neutrality: it invokes the familiar principle that likes are to be treated alike. The problem lies in determining the extent to which women are "like" men. On its face, the anti-stereotyping reasoning seems to deny the existence of group-based gender differences and assert that, contrary to the employer's contention, the women in the proposed labor pool are no less interested than the men in nontraditional work. Below the surface, however, this reasoning reflects a basic ambiguity (and ambivalence) about the extent of gender differences. For the anti-stereotyping rule may be interpreted to admit that women are *as a group* less interested than men in nontraditional work, and to assert only that some *individual* women may nonetheless be exceptions who do not share the preferences of most women. Under such an individualized approach, the employer is forbidden merely from presuming that *all* women are so "different" from men that they do not aspire to nontraditional work.

This individualized approach finds support in a number of cases, which emphasize the exceptional woman who does not "share the characteristics generally attributed to [her] group." Some courts condemn employers who raise the lack of interest argument for "stereotyping" all women as being uninterested in nontraditional work. Other courts reject the interest argument by observing that although some women do not desire nontraditional jobs, others do. These courts reason that "Title VII rights are peculiar to the individual, and are not lost or forfeited because some members of the protected classes are unable or unwilling to undertake certain jobs." Logically, however, this reasoning does not suffice to refute the lack of interest argument. The employer is not asserting that no individual woman is interested in nontraditional work, but rather that, within the pool of eligible workers, the women are as a group sufficiently less interested than men to explain their under-representation.

The focus on individual women thus serves a largely symbolic function. The liberal story invokes the image of the victim, the modern woman who comes to the labor market with a preexisting interest in nontraditional work, to signify the presence of a new social order in which the sexes are equal and ungendered. In this brave new world free of gender, women emerge from pre-work realms with the same life experiences and values, and therefore the same work aspirations, as men. The liberal story suppresses gender difference *outside* the workplace to attribute sex segregation *within* the workplace to employer coercion. Insofar as women approach the labor market with the same experiences and values as men, they must have the same job preferences as men, and to the extent that women end up severely underrepresented in nontraditional jobs, the employer must have discriminated.

The symbolic use of the victim, however, does not resolve the underlying issue of how representative of other women the victim is. This poses no practical difficulty when the only women who testify are the plaintiff's witnesses, who say that the employer prevented them from realizing their preferences for nontraditional jobs. But when employers present testimony from other women, who say that they are happier doing traditionally female jobs and that they would not take more highly rewarded nontraditional jobs even if offered, the liberal story confronts a dilemma. Often, liberal courts have simply characterized these women as unrepresentative of the larger group of women in the labor pool. But they have no way of explaining why these women should be considered less representative of most women than the victims, or how they came to have more gendered job aspirations than other women. Because liberal courts have no coherent explanation for gender difference, more conservative courts can easily portray the victims, rather than those satisfied with traditionally female work, as the anomalous, unrepresentative group....

The EEOC's position in *Sears* illustrates this dynamic. The EEOC emphasized that contrary to the district court's findings, it had *not* assumed that female sales applicants were as interested as males in commission sales jobs. Instead, the EEOC had recognized that the women were less interested than the men, and it had controlled for sex differences in interest by isolating the subgroup of female applicants who were similar to the males on a number of different background characteristics and who therefore could be presumed to be equally interested in commission sales. The EEOC argued that "men and women who are alike with respect to [these] ... characteristics ... would be similar with respect to their interest in commission sales." Judge Cudahy, in a dissent from the Seventh Circuit's opinion, agreed. Although he condemned the majority and the district court for "stereotyping" women, his acceptance of the EEOC's argument suggests that the only women whose job interests were being inaccurately stereotyped were those whose earlier life experiences resembled men's. Judge Cudahy's and the EEOC's position assumed that the women had formed specific preferences for commission or noncommission saleswork before they applied at

Sears. Indeed, Judge Cudahy expressed this assumption explicitly, emphasizing that the EEOC's case would have been much stronger if it had produced "even a handful of witnesses to testify that Sears had frustrated their *childhood dreams* of becoming commission sellers." Once this assumption was accepted, it was impossible to analyze seriously the extent to which *Sears* had shaped its workers' preferences. The only alternative was to identify the illusive group of women whose personal histories were so similar to men's that one might safely presume that they had been socialized to prefer the same jobs. . . .

The Need for a New Story

The story one tells about women and work has profound implications for the power of law to dismantle sex segregation in the workplace. Both the conservative and liberal stories are stories about women and work; they are not explicitly about law. But intertwined with their portrayals of women and work are implicit messages—or "morals"—about the constitutive and transformative power of title VII. The conservative story implies that law does not and cannot influence women's work aspirations. There is a natural order of gender and work that even "an Act of Congress cannot overcome."

The liberal story is an inadequate alternative. Indeed, the liberal story's suppression of gender leaves plaintiffs vulnerable to the conservative explanation for sex segregation at work. The partial truth of the conservative story is that people and jobs are gendered. But they are not naturally or inevitably so. To provide an adequate explanation for sex segregation, one must account for how employers arrange work systems so as to construct work and work aspirations along gendered lines. The liberal story fails to develop such an account because it shares the conservative assumption that women form their work preferences exclusively in early pre-work realms. This assumption, in turn, leads the liberal approach to adopt an overly restrictive view of the role title VII can play in dismantling sex segregation in the workplace. If women have already formed their job preferences before seeking work, the most the law can do is to ensure that employers do not erect formal barriers to prevent women from realizing their preexisting preferences.

There is a need for a new story to make sense of sex segregation in the workplace. Gender conditioning in pre-work realms is too slender a reed to sustain the weight of sex segregation. To explain sex segregation, the law needs an account of how employers actively construct gendered job aspirations—and jobs—in the workplace itself.

. . .

The Construction of Gender in the Workplace

An emerging perspective in the sociological literature provides an alternative to the pre-labor market explanation for sex segregation in the workplace. This alternative perspective begins from the premise that people's work aspirations are shaped by their experiences in the work-world. It examines how structural features of work organizations reduce women's incentive to pursue nontraditional work and encourage them to display the very work attitudes and behavior that come to be viewed as preexisting gender attributes.

The central insight of this perspective is that adults' work attitudes and behavior are shaped by the positions they occupy within larger structures of opportunity, rewards, and social relations in the workplace. Perhaps for this reason, this perspective has been coined "the new structuralism." But it should not be mistaken for deterministic theories that portray people as having no capacity for agency, for it emphasizes that people act reasonably and strategically within the constraints of their organizational positions in an effort to make the best of them.... People's work aspirations and behavior are "the result of a sense-making process involving present experiencing and future projecting, rather than of psychological conditioning in which the dim past is a controlling force."

This perspective sheds light on the workplace dynamics that limit women's ability to claim higher-paid nontraditional work as their own. Women's patterns of occupational movement suggest that there are powerful disincentives for women to move into and to remain in non-traditional occupations. The mobility studies show that women in high-er-paying, male-dominated occupations are much less likely to remain in such occupations over time than are women in lower-paying female-dominated occupations, who are more likely to stay put. Thus, just as employers appear to have begun opening the doors to nontraditional jobs to women, almost as many women have been leaving those jobs as have been entering them. To the extent that women have been given the formal opportunity to do nontraditional work, something is preventing them from realizing that opportunity.

The new structuralism perspective instructs us to look beyond formal labor market opportunity and to ask what it is about the workplace itself that disempowers women from permanently seizing that opportunity. Research in this tradition directs us toward the "culture-producing" aspects of work organizations, examining whether there is "something in the relations of employment, in work culture, the way jobs are defined and distinguished from each other, that conspires to keep women from even aspiring to [nontraditional] work." I analyze below two structural features of work organizations that discourage women from pursuing nontraditional work. These two structural fea-tures interact dynamically to construct work and workers along gen-dered lines—the first on the "female" side and the second on the "male" side....

[First,] female-dominated jobs tend to be on distinct promotional ladders that offer far less opportunity for advancement than do those for male-dominated jobs. In light of these unequal mobility structures, "[w]omen in low-mobility ... situations develop attitudes and orientations that are sometimes said to be characteristic of those people as individuals or 'women as a group,' but that can more profitably be viewed as universal *human* responses to blocked opportunities."

. . .

If women's work orientations are attributable not to their individual "feminine" characteristics, but rather to the structures of mobility and rewards attached to jobs, then the solution is to change the work structures. Classwide title VII suits challenging sex discrimination in promotion hold the promise to do just that. In alleging that women on the female job ladder are systematically being denied promotion into better jobs on the male job ladder, plaintiffs seek to restructure internal career ladders to create new paths up and out of entry-level female jobs for all women (and not just an exceptional few). Courts can order remedies that will prompt employers to restructure those ladders in ways that will infuse women workers with new hopes and aspirations. In doing so, they may also stimulate employers to redefine the content of entry-level jobs traditionally done by women in less stereotypically feminine terms.

Unfortunately, the courts all too often fail to respond, and in the process, they reproduce the very rationalizations for the two-tier system that keeps so many women in their place. When courts accept employers' arguments that women in female jobs lack interest in being promoted, they reinforce the sexist notion that there is something about womanhood itself that endows women with a penchant for low-paying, dead-end jobs. By refusing to intervene, they permit employers to continue to structure career ladders in ways that will encourage women to develop the depressed aspirations that can later be identified as "proof" that they preferred to be stuck at the bottom all along. Through their statements and their actions, these courts undercut women's ability to form and exercise the very choice they purport to defend.

. . .

Harassment is a [second] structural feature of the workplace that sex segregation engenders. It creates a serious disincentive for women to enter and remain in nontraditional jobs. Even overtly sexual harassment is widespread. Furthermore, women in male-dominated occupations are more likely to be subjected to harassment than are women in other occupations. Women in female jobs understand that they will be likely to experience harassment if they attempt to cross the gender divide; they may conclude that the price of deviance is too high. Harassment is also driving the small number of women in nontraditional jobs away. Blue-collar tradeswomen report that women are leaving the trades because they cannot tolerate the hostile work cultures, and there are signs that this is occurring in male-dominated professions as well.

One of the most debilitating forms of harassment is conduct that interferes with a woman's ability to do her job. In nontraditional blue-collar occupations, virtually all training is acquired informally on the job. Thus, a woman's ability to succeed depends on the willingness of her supervisors and co-workers to teach her the relevant skills. Yet women's stories of being denied proper training are legion. Indeed, it is sometimes difficult to distinguish inadequate training from deliberate sabotage of women's work performance, both of which can endanger a woman's physical safety. To the extent that foremen and co-workers succeed in undermining women's job performance, they convert the notion that women are not cut out for nontraditional work into a self-fulfilling prophecy.

In nontraditional white-collar occupations, male workers—including elite professionals—also guard their territory against female incursion. Their conduct, too, runs the gamut from overtly sexual behavior, to discriminatory work assignments and performance evaluations, to day-to-day personal interactions that send women the message that they are "different" and "out of place." The white-collar equivalent of work sabotage may lie in evaluating women's work by differential and sexist standards, a practice which occurs even within the upper echelons of professional life.

Whatever men's motivations or sources of insecurity, harassment is a central process through which the image of nontraditional work as "masculine" is sustained.

. . .

This analysis of the relationship between harassment and the "masculinity" of nontraditional work makes clear why many women are reluctant to apply for such work. Women understand that behind the symbolism of masculinized job descriptions lies a very real force: the power of men to harass, belittle, ostracize, dismiss, marginalize, discard, and just plain hurt them as workers. The legal system does not adequately protect women from this harassment and abuse. Courts have erected roadblocks to recovery, abandoning women to cope with hostile work environments on their own. The general attitude of the legal system seems to mirror that held by many male workers and managers: if women want to venture into a man's workworld, they must take it as they find it.

The legal system thus places women workers in a Catch-22 situation. Women are disempowered from pursuing or staying in higher-paid nontraditional jobs because of the hostile work cultures. The only real hope for making those work cultures more hospitable to women lies in dramatically increasing the proportion of women in those jobs. Eliminating those imbalances is, of course, what title VII lawsuits challenging segregation promise. But when women workers bring these suits, too often the courts tell them that they are underrepresented in nontraditional jobs not because the work culture is threatening or alienating, but rather because their own internalized sense of "femininity" has led them to avoid those jobs.

And so the cycle continues. A few women continue to move in and out the "revolving door," with little being done to stop them from being shoved back out almost as soon as they enter. The majority of working women stand by as silent witnesses, their failure to enter used to confirm that they "chose" all along to remain on the outside. There is no need for a sign on the door. Women understand that they enter at their own risk.

Conclusion: The Implications of the New Account for the Law

.   .   .

The new account [of gender and work] ... demands deeper judicial scrutiny of the way employers have structured their workplaces. Once the assumption that women approach the labor market with fixed job preferences is abandoned, it will no longer do to conceptualize discrimination in terms of whether the employer has erected specific "barriers" that prevent individual women from exercising their preexisting preferences. Employers do not simply erect "barriers" to already formed preferences: they create the workplace structures and relations out of which those preferences arise in the first place. Thus, in resolving the lack of interest argument, courts must look beyond whether the employer has provided women the formal opportunity to enter nontraditional jobs. Judges should be skeptical about employers' claims to have made efforts to attract women to nontraditional work. Such efforts are likely to be ineffective unless they enlist the participation of community organizations that serve working women and employ creative strategies to describe the work in terms that will appeal to women. Moreover, even extensive recruiting efforts will fail if the firm manages only to convey an all too accurate picture of organizational life that serves more as a warning than a welcome to women. Through its hiring criteria, training programs, performance evaluation standards, mobility and reward structures, response to harassment and its managers' and male workers' day-to-day attitudes and actions, the firms may have created an organizational culture that debilitates most women from aspiring to nontraditional jobs. These sorts of work cultures can be changed, but only if courts recognize that the firm's practices create a disempowering culture for women.

.   .   .

The new account of gender and work thus reminds judges that they, too, are the authors of women's work aspirations. This awareness should bring a new sensitivity to the way judges exercise their responsibility to resolve the factual determination of whether women lack interest in nontraditional jobs.... Courts can acknowledge their own constitutive power and use it to help create a workworld in which the majority of working women are empowered to choose the more highly rewarded work that title VII has long been promising them. To create that world, they must refuse to proclaim that women already have that choice.

Notes and Questions

1. Posner begins with the assumption that all individuals "consistently act to maximize the excess of their private benefits over their private costs." Would Nancy Chodorow agree with this statement? (See Chapter 11.) Might she say that even if it is true, the social forces have been arrayed in such a fashion that women are simply left with unappealing choices?

Consider in this regard the following statement from Catharine MacKinnon:

> Americans are accustomed to thinking of themselves as freely choosing rather than as determined by social imperatives. Personality or character is defined largely in terms of this opposition. Becoming a person is thought to involve overcoming social determinants, forces which are impediments to individual choice, hence individual self. Women have little choice but to become "women" in the sense of having to become those persons who will then freely choose women's roles. Equally important, and pulling toward change, they struggle against this condition. Once having determined to equalize economic opportunities by sex, the law's role is not to try to overthrow these constructs but to support women who wish to resist the sexualization of their economic insecurity.

MacKinnon, *Sexual Harassment of Working Women: A Case of Sex Discrimination* 217 (New Haven, Conn.: Yale University Press, 1979). Does MacKinnon mean that social forces make it very difficult for a women not to act in a stereotypically female manner? If so, how should this fact affect the obligations imposed on *employers* by antidiscrimination law?

2. Posner stresses that sex discrimination is fundamentally unlike race discrimination in terms of its effects and burdens because men and women are so thoroughly interdependent. This means that if men are advantaged relative to women in the labor market, at least some of the advantage will redound to the benefit of women in their capacities as mothers, wives, daughters, or receivers of alimony or child-support payments. Conversely, if whites are advantaged relative to blacks because of the existence of race discrimination in the labor market, the lack of economic interdependence implies that all of the burden falls on blacks. Clearly, this offsetting tendency arising from the economic interdependence of men and women renders sex discrimination less burdensome on its victims than an otherwise equal amount of race discrimination. Is this fact relevant to the issue of which group is most deserving of affirmative action programs? (See Chapter 3,

Section 3.2.) Do you accept Posner's belief that the economic interdependence between men and women is so great that there is little social cost from sex discrimination?

3. How would Posner explain the survey data, cited by Donohue, suggesting that more than half of male business executives in 1985 said they would not be comfortable working for a woman? Is this evidence of a "lingering trace" of irrational preference for male workers? (The phrase is Christine Littleton's—see her selection in Chapter 12.) Is irrational prejudice against female workers as uncommon as Posner and Littleton assume? Do you think that the male executives simply don't like the "style" of female management, in much the same way that some employers don't like the accents of certain workers? (See the discussion of Mari Matsuda's article concerning accent discrimination in notes 9 through 14 in Chapter 2.)

Claudia Gordon has developed a "pollution" model of sex discrimination, which posits that sex segregation in the workplace occurs as a result of men's desire "to maintain their occupational status or prestige, distinct from the desire to maintain their earnings." Goldin, "A Pollution Theory of Discrimination: Male and Female Differences in Occupations and Earnings," NBER Working Paper No. W8985, June 2002. In this model, sex segregation in certain sectors arises from the male view that women are "polluting" their occupation and diluting its prestige. Goldin's proposed solution is to increase credentialization of segregated occupations, which will purportedly allow women to avoid being perceived as polluters. If deep-seated hostilities towards women exist in traditionally male occupations, is it likely that credentializing women workers will change these attitudes? Is that exactly what employment discrimination law is trying to do anyway?

4. Donohue notes that if antidiscrimination laws enhance the self-esteem and lower the burdensomeness of work in ways that promote productivity, they will generate very large social benefits as measured by the beneficial shifts in the supply and demand for labor. Do you believe that a significant percentage of women are made more productive or feel less burdened by work because of the existence of laws prohibiting sexual harassment and sex discrimination?

If billions of dollars in greater productivity from female workers were attainable, why wouldn't employers take the measures to achieve these gains, as the Coase theorem indicates they would? Donohue suggests that one Coasean mechanism to achieve the efficient outcome—women could bribe their employers to treat them equally—is unavailing since the very act of bribing the employers in this context would underscore the absence of the desired equality. It may be impossible to purchase equality. If Donohue is correct, the law may need to intervene to reach the efficient solution that is unavailable through normal bargaining channels. Still, the job of entrepreneurs is to discover ways to expand production, and it may be too pessimistic to think that they could not find ways to tailor their employment practices so as to make women feel comfortable if that would be profitable.

5. Schultz argues that courts have properly rejected the lack of interest argument in race discrimination cases, but have often, and improperly,

found the argument compelling in sex discrimination cases. Are race and sex cases truly analogous in terms of the likelihood that personal preferences about desirable jobs explain race-and sex-based differences in the patterns of employment?

6. Schultz believes that the pattern of sex segregation in the workplace is wholly socially determined, and that employers should be compelled by antidiscrimination law to move women into the higher paid, traditionally "male" jobs. She notes that "women in higher-paying, male-dominated occupations are much less likely to remain in such occupations over time than are women in lower-paying female-dominated occupations, who are more likely to stay put" Schultz at 1825. To what extent does this phenomenon result from the behavior of firms and male employees in the male-dominated occupations, as opposed to women's preferences?

David Chambers has sought to shed light on this issue in examining the careers of female lawyers. Chambers, "Accommodation and Satisfaction: Women and Men Lawyers and the Balance of Work and Family," 14 *Law and Social Inquiry* 251 (1989). This study of graduates of the University of Michigan Law School from the late 1970s finds that women lawyers with children bear the principal responsibility for the care of children, but are also more satisfied with their careers and with the balance of their family and professional lives than other women and than men. In examining the accommodations made by the women, Chambers notes that "a high proportion of the Michigan mothers seem to have deliberately chosen settings in which they believed they could sustain a rational balance of their family and professional lives. Many seem to have avoided or left private practice because they believed it would place extraordinary demands on their time. And some of those who chose private practice report having sought and selected firms where their needs as parents were recognized and accepted." Id. at 283.

Similarly, Victor Fuchs found in surveys among hundreds of Stanford University undergraduates that

> when asked what changes they would make in their paid employment if they had young children, more than 60 percent of the women but less than 10 percent of the men say they would substantially reduce their hours of work or quit work entirely for several years. . . . When queried about the results, the women explain that they define "successful career" differently from the men—with more emphasis on personal satisfaction than on making money or achieving power.

Fuchs, *Women's Quest for Economic Equality* 47 (Cambridge, Mass.: Harvard University Press, 1988).

7. Do you share Schultz's belief that observed female employment patterns would change dramatically if firms made structural changes that rendered the work environment less problematic for women, such as changing job promotion ladders and eliminating sexual harassment? Would such structural changes alter the observed propensity of women to work part-time? For the view that one must directly accommodate the demands of pregnancy if one is to enable women to pursue nontraditional careers, see the Issacharoff and Rosenblum selection in Chapter 15. Evidence from the

experience in Europe may suggest that women's behavior is not easily changed by even major governmental initiatives. Victor Fuchs writes:

> Sweden has gone much further than the United States in designing private and public policies to promote economic equality between women and men. Employment rates of Swedish women are higher than in the United States, their wages are much closer to men's, and childcare allowances are more generous; nevertheless, a large proportion of Swedish women work part time. The female/male ratio of part-timers is almost six to one in Sweden, much higher than in the United States.

Id. at 47. Fuchs also notes that, although the parental leave laws in Sweden cover both parents, the man takes the leave only 20 percent of the time. Moreover, in Sweden, women spend five times as much time on child care as men; the ratio in the United States is about 3.5 to 1. Id. at 73.

8. A controversial new book by Kingsley Browne, *Biology at Work: Rethinking Sexual Equality* (Piscataway, New Jersey: Rutgers University Press, 2002) argues that there is an evolutionary basis for the lower earnings of women and the scarcity of female CEOs in Fortune 500 companies. For the contrary view that a glass ceiling is holding back women from securing more high level jobs, see the review of a number of recent empirical studies in Jolls, "Is There A Glass Ceiling?" 25 *Harvard Women's Law Journal* 1 (2002). Jolls cites an interesting study by Claudia Goldin and Cecelia Rouse, which found that the shift to blind auditions for major symphony orchestras (so that judges could not see the auditioning musicians) led to a substantial increase in the likelihood that the female candidate would be selected. As Jolls points out, some of this discrimination can be rational: the orchestra might have believed that current members of the orchestra (mostly male) would play better as a group if they played with other "like" (male) musicians or that female musicians would take more leaves of absence, incurring more personnel costs. Nevertheless, as Jolls argues, these rational calculations are still prohibited by antidiscrimination laws. For further evidence of sex discrimination despite women's increased labor force participation and the narrowing of the gender pay gap, see Francine D. Blau and Lawrence M. Kahn, "Gender Differences in Pay," 14 *Journal of Economic Perspectives* 75 (2002).

14

Sexual Harassment

Published accounts of sexual harassment against working women date back to as early as colonial times. Louise F. Fitzgerald, "Sexual Harassment: Violence Against Women in the Workplace," 48 *American Psychologist* 1070 (1993). The Supreme Court, however, did not recognize sexual harassment as a form of sex discrimination under Title VII until 1986 in *Meritor Savings Bank v. Vinson*, 477 U.S. 57 (1986). Since then, highly publicized charges of sexual harassment against prominent public figures, such as Clarence Thomas and former President Bill Clinton, have led to heightened public awareness about the issue. Perhaps reflecting this growing awareness, the number and proportion of sexual harassment claims filed with the Equal Employment Opportunity Commission (EEOC) has been steadily rising. In 1992, there were 10,532 claims of sexual harassment, reflecting 48 percent of all sex-based charges; by 2001 that number had grown to 15,475, reflecting 62 percent of all sex-based charges. During the same period, the proportion of sexual harassment charges filed by men also increased, from 9 percent to 14 percent. Even with this rapid growth in charges, numerous commentators have noted that most victims of sexual harassment do not file charges against the perpetrator.

Title VII prohibits employers from discriminating against employees on the basis of their "sex" with respect to compensation, terms, conditions, or privileges of employment. However, Title VII does not expressly proscribe sexual harassment, nor does the legislative history of Title VII provide any guidance. Indeed, the legislative history of Title VII provides little guidance on the prohibition against sex discrimination in general,

412

as this provision was added at the last minute by an opposing senator in an attempt to block the bill's passage. The legal recognition of sexual harassment as a form of sex discrimination is thus a product of judicial construction, which gained recognition as such only because of the gradual acceptance of seminal theories of feminist legal scholars such as Catherine MacKinnon. MacKinnon argued that sexual harassment involved systematic and invidious discrimination against women as a group, not merely trivial, isolated, or personal occurrences. In the selection from her work that appears in this chapter, MacKinnon conveys a sense of the numerous obstacles that have been surmounted in the development of the legal prohibition of sexual harassment, as well as the continuing obstacles that individual victims of such harassment still must confront. She claims that the body of law that she did so much to create is deinstitutionalizing misogyny step by step, and on the whole is serving the interests of women remarkably well.

In the two decades since sexual harassment emerged as a legally cognizable claim under Title VII, however, courts have been forced to constantly adjust the doctrine in order to address a diverse array of claims falling outside the traditional male-female harassment paradigm conceptualized by MacKinnon. In particular, claims by men who have been harassed by women and same-sex harassment claims have tested the usefulness of the male-female harassment paradigm. The Supreme Court, for its part, attempted to provide some guidance on these issues, although with uncertain success. For example, the Court held in *Oncale v. Sundowner Offshore Services, Inc.*, 523 U.S. 75 (1998), that same-sex harassment was actionable under Title VII but implied that only a narrow range of circumstances would qualify, as evidenced by the limited evidentiary routes the Court suggested plaintiffs could use to prove sex discrimination. In response to these new challenges, legal scholars have tried to re-theorize and re-articulate the definition of sexual harassment and to ask anew why sexual harassment should be treated as a form of sex discrimination. Katherine Franke, Vicki Shultz, and Kathryn Abrams are three prominent scholars who have undertaken this task and generated innovative theories about sexual harassment that are reinvigorating the debate. David Schwartz, in the following excerpted selection, summarizes and critiques each of these scholars' theories. Underlying these debates is the tension between the need to universalize the harm of sexual harassment, and the intuition to particularize it to the experience of women given its historical roots.

In addition to reconsidering the theoretical framework of sexual harassment (the "why" of the law, as Kathryn Abrams writes), courts have faced other challenging issues in adjudicating sexual harassment cases. One of the crucial questions that continues to trouble the courts is whether they should apply the reasonable person or reasonable woman standard (or for that matter, a number of other standards proposed by scholars, such as the reasonable victim or rational women standard) in determining whether the harassing conduct was sufficiently "severe or pervasive." In answer to this question, Anita Bernstein proposes what she calls the respectful person standard. Bernstein argues that the harm of sexual harassment is ultimately dignitary in nature, which is not amenable to the kind of ratiocination subsumed in the variations of the reasonableness standard. The premise of Bernstein's new standard is that "Respect in the sense of recognition [of an individual's inherent worth] is owed to all persons, and thus workplace sexual harassment betrays the ideal of recognition respect. . . ." Anita Bernstein, "Treating Sexual Harassment with Respect," 111 *Harvard Law Review* 445, 452 (1997). In the following excerpted article, Kathryn Abrams argues that Bernstein's respectful person standard is fraught with vulnerabilities and uncertainties of its own; Abrams advocates instead for a renewed understanding and application of the reasonable person standard. The debate between Bernstein and Abrams highlights many of the central concerns at stake in this area of the law.

The uncertainties in sexual harassment law and the wide variety of approaches adopted by different jurisdictions have led some scholars to conclude that courts are becoming susceptible to the "I-know-it-when-I-see-it-ness" idea. Rosa Ehrenreich, "Dignity and Discrimination: Toward a Pluralistic Understanding of Workplace Harassment," 88 *Georgetown Law Journal* 1 (1999). Thus although the problems of vagueness and contradictions in sexual harassment law have generated much legal commentary on the law itself, they have also diverted attention away from the broader question: Has the introduction of the federal legal remedy for sexual harassment reduced the incidence of this misconduct? Large-scale surveys of federal workers in 1980, 1987, and 1994 revealed that the problem of sexual harassment continued to be widespread. In 1994, roughly 43 percent of women and 19 percent of men said that during the previous two years they had experienced uninvited and unwanted sexual attention on the job, similar but slightly higher than the figures for 1980 and 1987. U.S. Merit System Protection Board, *Sexual Harassment in the Federal Workplace* (1995). In the private sector, the prevalence of sexual harassment appears to be comparable to, if not even higher than, the rate in the public sector, according to some surveys. Joseph J. Begany and Michael A. Milburn, "Psychological Predictors of Sexual Harassment: Authoritarianism, Hostile Sexism, and Rape Myths," 3 *Psychology of Men & Masculinity* 119 (2002). Such a high prevalence rate might indicate that the developing law of sexual harassment has had no effect on harassing behavior; but these numbers must be interpreted in light of the likely increase in the awareness and labeling of conduct as sexually harassing prompted by the law, which in turn increased the likelihood that such behavior would be reported in surveys as harassment. Conceivably, the increased reporting might have simply offset a decline in the prevalence of this conduct, thereby obscuring a potentially modest improvement generated by the law (or by heightened public consciousness of the problem).

The even broader issue of whether sexual harassment law has created greater gender equality at work, as MacKinnon has posited, is another complex question that will require continuing evaluation in the context of rapidly evolving sexual harassment law.

Sexual Harassment: Its First Decade in Court (1986)*

CATHARINE A. MACKINNON

Sexual harassment, the event, is not new to women. It is the law of injuries that it is new to. Sexual pressure imposed on someone who is not in an economic position to refuse it became sex discrimination in the midseventies, and in education soon afterward. It became possible to do something legal about sexual harassment because ... [f]eminists ... took women's experience seriously enough to uncover this problem and conceptualize it and pursue it legally.

. . .

The law against sexual harassment is a practical attempt to stop a form of exploitation. It is also one test of sexual politics as feminist jurisprudence, of possibilities for social change for women through law. The existence of a law against sexual harassment has affected both the context of meaning within which social life is lived and the concrete delivery of rights through the legal system. The sexually harassed have been given a name for their suffering and an analysis that connects it with gender. They have been given a forum, legitimacy to speak, authority to make claims, and an avenue for possible relief. Before, what happened to them was all right. Now it is not.

This matters. Sexual abuse mutes victims socially through the violation itself. Often the abuser enforces secrecy and silence; secrecy and silence may be part of what is so sexy about sexual abuse. When the state also forecloses a validated space for denouncing and rectifying the victimization, it seals this secrecy and reenforces this silence. The harm of this process, a process that utterly precludes speech, then becomes all of a piece. If there is no right place to go to say, this hurt me, then a woman is simply the one who can be treated this way, and no harm, as they say, is done.

. . .

* Excerpts from Catharine A. MacKinnon, *Feminism Unmodified: Discourses on Life and Law,* copyright © 1987 by the President and Fellows of Harvard College. Reprinted by permission of the publisher.

... The legal claim for sexual harassment made the events of sexual harassment illegitimate socially as well as legally for the first time.

. . .

... Sexual harassment, the legal claim, is a demand that state authority stand behind women's refusal of sexual access in certain situations that previously were a masculine prerogative. With sexism, there is always a risk that our demand for self-determination will be taken as a demand for paternal protection and will therefore strengthen male power rather than undermine it. This seems a particularly valid concern because the law of sexual harassment began as case law, without legislative guidance or definition.

Institutional support for sexual self-determination is a victory; institutional paternalism reinforces our lack of self-determination. The problem is, the state has never in fact protected women's dignity or bodily integrity. It just says it does. Its protections have been both condescending *and* unreal, in effect strengthening the protector's choice to violate the protected at will, whether the protector is the individual perpetrator or the state. This does not seem to me a reason not to have a law against sexual harassment. It is a reason to demand that the promise of "equal protection of the laws" be *delivered upon* for us, as it is when real people are violated. It is also part of a larger political struggle to value women more than the male pleasure of using us is valued. Ultimately, though, the question of whether the use of the state for women helps or hurts can be answered only in practice, because so little real protection of the laws has even been delivered.

The legal claim for sexual harassment marks the first time in history, to my knowledge, that women have defined women's injuries in a law.

. . .

It is never too soon to worry about this, but it may be too soon to know whether the law against sexual harassment will be taken away from us or turn into nothing or turn ugly in our hands. The fact is, this law is working surprisingly well for women by any standards, particularly when compared with the rest of sex discrimination law. If the question is whether a law designed from women's standpoint and administered through this legal system can do anything for women—which always seems to me to be a good question—this experience so far gives a qualified and limited yes.

It is hard to unthink what you know, but there was a time when the facts that amount to sexual harassment did not amount to sexual harassment. It is a bit like the injuries of pornography until recently. The facts amounting to the harm did not socially "exist," had no shape, no cognitive coherence; far less did they state a legal claim. It just happened to you. To the women to whom it happened, it wasn't part of anything, much less something big or shared like gender. It fit no known pattern. It was neither a regularity nor an irregularity. Even social scientists didn't study it, and they study anything that moves. When law recognized sexual harassment as a practice of sex discrimination, it moved it from the realm of "and then he ... and then he ...," the primitive language in which sexual abuse lives inside a woman, into an experience with a form, an etiology, a cumulativeness—as well as a club.

The shape, the positioning, and the club—each is equally crucial politically. Once it became possible to do something about sexual harassment, it became possible to know more about it, Now we know, as we did not when it first became illegal, that this problem is commonplace. We know this not just because it has to be true, but as documented fact. Between a quarter and a third of women in the federal workforce report having been sexually harassed, many physically, at least once in the last two years. Projected, that becomes 85 percent of all women at some point in their working lives. This figure is based on asking women "Have you ever been sexually harassed?—the conclusion—not 'has this fact happened? has that fact happened?' " which usually produces more. The figures for sexual harassment of students are comparable.

When faced with individual incidents of sexual harassment, the legal system's first question was, is it a personal episode? Legally, this was a way the courts inquired into whether the incidents were based on sex, as they had to be to be sex discrimination. Politically, it was a move to isolate victims by stigmatizing them as deviant.

. . .

[T]he presumption that sexual pressure in contexts of unequal power is an isolated idiosyncrasy to unique individual victims has been undermined both by the numbers and by their division by gender. Overwhelmingly, it is men who sexually harass women, a lot of them. Actually, it is even more accurate to say that men do this than to say that women have this done to them. This is a description of the perpetrators' behavior, not of the statistician's feminism.

Sexual harassment has also emerged as a creature of hierarchy. It inhabits what I call hierarchies among men: arrangements in which some men are below other men, as in employer/employee and teacher/student. In workplaces, sexual harassment by supervisors of subordinates is common; in education, by administrators of lower-level administrators, by faculty of students. But it also happens among coworkers, from third parties, even by subordinates in the workplace, men who are women's hierarchical inferiors or peers. Basically, it is done by men to women regardless of relative position on the formal hierarchy. I believe that the reason sexual harassment was first established as an injury of the systematic abuse of power in hierarchies among men is that this is power men recognize. They comprehend from personal experience that something is held over your head if you do not comply. The lateral or reverse hierarchical examples suggest something beyond this, something men don't understand from personal experience because they take its advantages for granted: gender is also a hierarchy. The courts do not use this analysis, but some act as though they understand it.

Sex discrimination law had to adjust a bit to accommodate the realities of sexual harassment. Like many other injuries of gender, it wasn't written for this. For something to be based on gender in the legal sense means it happens to a woman as a woman, not as an individual. Membership in a gender is understood as the opposite of, rather than part of, individuality. Clearly, sexual harassment is one of the last situations in which a woman is treated without regard to her sex; it is because of her sex that it happens.

. . .

Sex discrimination law typically conceives that something happens because of sex when it happens to one sex but not the other. The initial procedure is arithmetic: draw a gender line and count how many of each are on each side in the context at issue, or, alternatively, take the line drawn by the practice or policy and see if it also divides the sexes. One by-product of this head-counting method is what I call the bisexual defense. Say a man is accused of sexually harassing a woman. He can argue that the harassment is not sex-based because he harasses both sexes equally, indiscriminately as it were. Originally it was argued that sexual harassment was not a proper gender claim because someone could harass both sexes. We argued that this was an issue of fact to be pleaded and proven, an issue of did he do this, rather than an issue of law, of whether he could have. The courts accepted that, creating this kamikaze defense. To my knowledge, no one has used the bisexual defense since.

. . .

Once sexual harassment was established as bigger than personal, the courts' next legal question was whether it was smaller than biological. To say that sexual harassment was biological seemed to me a very negative thing to say about men, but defendants seemed to think it precluded liability. Plaintiffs argued that sexual harassment is not biological in that men who don't do it have nothing wrong with their testosterone levels. Besides, if murder were found to have biological correlates, it would still be a crime. Thus, although the question purported to be whether the acts were based on sex, the implicit issue seemed to be whether the source of the impetus for doing the acts was relevant to their harmfulness.

Similarly structured was the charge that women who resented sexual harassment were oversensitive. Not that the acts did not occur, but rather that it was unreasonable to experience them as harmful. Such a harm would be based not on sex but on individual hysteria. Again shifting the inquiry away from whether the acts are based on sex in the guise of pursuing it, away from whether they occurred to whether it should matter if they did, the question became whether the acts were properly harmful. Only this time it was not the perpetrator's drives that made him not liable but the target's sensitivity that made the acts not a harm at all. It was pointed out that too many people are victimized by sexual harassment to consider them all hysterics. Besides, in other individual injury law, victims are not blamed; perpetrators are required to take victims as they find them, so long as they are not supposed to be doing what they are doing.

Once these excuses were rejected, then it was said that sexual harassment was not really an employment-related problem. That became hard to maintain when it was her job the woman lost. If it was, in fact, a personal relationship, it apparently did not start and stop there, although this is also a question of proof, leaving the true meaning of the events to trial. The perpetrator may have thought it was all affectionate or friendly or fun, but the victim experienced it as hateful, dangerous, and damaging. Results in such cases have been mixed. Some judges have accepted the perpetrator's view; for instance, one judge held queries by the defendant such as "What am I going to get for this?" and repeated importunings to "go out" to be "susceptible of innocent interpretation." Other judges, on virtually identical facts, for example, "When are you going to do something nice for me?" have held for the plaintiff. For what it's worth, the judge in the first case was a man, in the second a woman.

That sexual harassment is sex-based discrimination seems to be legally established, at least for now. In one of the few recent cases that reported litigating the issue of sex basis, defendants argued that a sex-based claim was not stated when a woman worker complained of terms of abuse directed at her at work such as "slut," "bitch," and "fucking cunt" and "many sexually oriented drawings posted on pillars and at other conspicuous places around the warehouse" with plaintiffs' initials on them, presenting her having sex with an animal. The court said: "[T]he sexually offensive conduct and language used would have been almost irrelevant and would have failed entirely in its crude purpose had the plaintiff been a man. I do not hesitate to find that but for her sex, the plaintiff would not have been subjected to the harassment she suffered." "Obvious" or "patently obvious" they often call it. I guess this is what it looks like to have proven a point.

Sexual harassment was first recognized as an injury of gender in what I called incidents of quid pro quo. Sometimes people think that harassment has to be constant. It doesn't; it's a term of art in which once can be enough. Typically, an advance is made, rejected, and a loss follows. For a while it looked as if this three-step occurrence was in danger of going from one form in which sexual harassment can occur into a series of required hurdles. In many situations [, however,] the woman is forced to submit instead of being able to reject the advance. The problem has become whether, say, being forced into intercourse at work will be seen as a failed quid pro quo or as an instance of sexual harassment in which the forced sex constitutes the injury.

. . .

... If sexual harassment is not to be defined only as sexual attention imposed upon someone who is not in a position to refuse it, who refuses it, women who are forced to submit to sex must be understood as harmed not less, but as much or more, than those who are able to make their refusals effective.

Getting recoveries for women who have actually been sexually violated by the defendant will probably be a major battle. Women being compensated in money for sex they *had* violates male metaphysics because in that system sex is what a woman is for. As one judge concluded, "[T]here does not seem to be any issue that the plaintiff did not desire to have relations with [the defendant], but it is also altogether apparent that she willingly had sex with him." Now what do you make of that? The woman was not physically forced at the moment of penetration, and since it is sex she must have willed it, is about all you can make of it. The sexual politics of the situation is that men do not see a woman who has had sex as victimized, whatever the conditions. One dimension of this problem involves whether a woman who has been violated through sex has any credibility. Credibility is difficult to separate from the definition of the injury, since an injury in which the victim is not believed to have been injured *because she has been injured* is not a real injury, legally speaking.

The question seems to be whether a woman is valuable enough to hurt, so that what is done to her is a harm. Once a woman has had sex, voluntarily or by force—it doesn't matter—she is regarded as too damaged to be further damageable, or something. Many women who have been raped in the course of sexual harassment have been advised by their lawyers not to mention the rape because it would destroy their credibility! The fact that abuse is long term has suggested to some finders of fact that it must have been tolerated or even wanted, although sexual harassment that becomes a condition of work has also been established as a legal claim in its own right.

. . .

The more aggravated an injury becomes, the more it ceases to exist. Why is incomprehensible to me, but how it functions is not. Our most powerful moment is on paper, in complaints we frame, and our worst is in the flesh in court. Although it isn't much, we have the most credibility when we are only the idea of us and our violation in their minds. In our allegations we construct reality to some extent; face to face, their angle of vision frames us irrevocably. In court we have breasts, we are Black, we are (in a word) women. Not that we are ever free of that, but the moment we physically embody our complaint, and they can see us, the pornography of the process starts in earnest.

I have begun to think that a major reason that many women do not bring sexual harassment complaints is that they know this. They cannot bear to have their personal account of sexual abuse reduced to a fantasy they invented, used to define them and to pleasure the finders of fact and the public. I think they have a very real sense that their accounts are enjoyed, that others are getting pleasure from the first-person recounting of their pain, and that is the content of their humiliation at these rituals. When rape victims say they feel raped again on the stand, and victims of sexual harassment say they feel sexually harassed in the adjudication, it is not exactly metaphor. I hear that they—in being publicly sexually humiliated by the legal system, as by the perpetrator— are pornography. The first time it happens, it is called freedom; the second time, it is called justice....

A woman can be seen in these terms by being a former rape victim or by the way she uses language. One case holds that the evidence shows "the allegedly harassing conduct was substantially welcomed and encouraged by plaintiff. She actively contributed to the distasteful working environment by her own profane and sexually suggestive conduct." She swore, apparently, and participated in conversations about sex. This effectively made her harassment-proof. Many women joke about sex to try to defuse men's sexual aggression, to try to be one of the boys in hopes they will be treated like one. This is to discourage sexual advances, not to encourage them. In other cases, judges have understood that "the plaintiffs did not appreciate the remarks and ... many of the other women did not either."

The extent to which a woman's job is sexualized is also a factor. If a woman's work is not to sell sex, and her employer requires her to wear a sexually suggestive uniform, if she is repeatedly sexually harassed by the clientele, she may have a claim against her employer. Similarly, although "there may well be a limited category of jobs (such as adult entertainment) in which sexual harassment may be a rational consequence of such employment," one court was "simply not prepared to say that a female who goes to work in what is apparently a predominantly male workplace should reasonably expect sexual harassment as part of her job." There may be trouble at some point over what jobs are selling sex, given the sexualization of anything a woman does.

Sexual credibility, that strange amalgam of whether your word counts with whether or how much you were hurt, also comes packaged in a variety of technical rules in the sexual harassment cases: evidence, discovery, and burden of proof. In 1982 the EEOC held that if a victim was sexually harassed without a corroborating witness, proof was inadequate as a matter of law.

· · ·

... A woman's word, even if believed, was legally insufficient, even if the man had nothing to put against it other than his word and the plaintiff's burden of proof. Much like women who have been raped, women who have experienced sexual harassment say, "But I couldn't prove it." They mean they have nothing but their word. Proof is when what you say counts against what someone else says—for which it must first be believed. To say as a matter of law that the woman's word is per se legally insufficient is to assume that, with sexual violations uniquely, the defendant's denial is dispositive, is proof. To say a woman's word is no proof amounts to saying a woman's word is worthless. Usually all the man has is his denial. In 1983 the EEOC found sexual harassment on a woman's word alone. It said it was enough, without distinguishing or overruling the prior case. Perhaps they recognized that women don't choose to be sexually harassed in the presence of witnesses.

The question of prior sexual history is one area in which the issue of sexual credibility is directly posed. Evidence of the defendant's sexual harassment of other women in the same institutional relation or setting is increasingly being considered admissible, and it should be. The other side of the question is whether evidence of a victim's prior sexual history should be discoverable or admissible, and it seems to me it should not be. Perpetrators often seek out victims with common qualities or circumstances or situations—we are fungible to them so long as we are similarly accessible—but victims do not seek out victimization at all, and their nonvictimized sexual behavior is no more relevant to an allegation of sexual force than is the perpetrator's consensual sex life, such as it may be.

So far the leading case, consistent with the direction of rape law, has found that the victim's sexual history with other individuals is not relevant, although consensual history with the individual perpetrator may be. With sexual harassment law, we are having to deinstitutionalize sexual misogyny step by step. Some defendants' counsel have been demanded that plaintiffs submit to an unlimited psychiatric examination, which could have a major practical impact on victims' effective access to relief. How much sexual denigration will victims have to face to secure their right to be free from sexual denigration? A major part of the harm of sexual harassment is the public and private sexualization of a woman against her will. Forcing her to speak about her sexuality is a common part of this process, subjection to which leads women to seek relief through the courts. Victims who choose to complain know they will have to endure repeated verbalizations of the specific sexual abuse they complain about. They undertake this even though most experience it as an exacerbation, however unavoidable, of the original abuse. For others, the necessity to repeat over and over the verbal insults, innuendos, and propositions to which they have been subjected leads them to decide that justice is not worth such indignity.

Most victims of sexual harassment, if the incidence data are correct, never file complaints. Many who are viciously violated are so ashamed to make that violation public that they submit in silence, although it devastates their self-respect and often their health, or they leave the job without complaint, although it threatens their survival and that of their families. If, on top of the cost of making the violation known, which is painful enough, they know that the entire range of their sexual experiences, attitudes, preferences, and practices are to be discoverable, few such actions will be brought, no matter how badly the victims are hurt. Faced with a choice between forced sex in their jobs or schools on the one hand and forced sexual disclosure for the public record on the other, few will choose the latter. This cruel paradox would effectively eliminate such progress in this area.

Put another way, part of the power held by perpetrators of sexual harassment is the threat of making the sexual abuse public knowledge. This functions like blackmail in silencing the victim and allowing the abuse to continue. It is a fact that public knowledge of sexual abuse is often worse for the abused than the abuser, and victims who choose to complain have the courage to take that on. To add to their burden the potential of making public their entire personal life, information that has no relation to the fact or severity of the incidents complained of, is to make the law of this area implicitly complicit in the blackmail that keeps victims from exercising their rights and to enhance the impunity of perpetrators. In effect, it means open season on anyone who does not want her entire intimate life available to public scrutiny. In other contexts such private information has been found intrusive, irrelevant, and more prejudicial than probative. To allow it to be discovered in the sexual harassment area amounts to a requirement that women be further violated in order to be permitted to seek relief for having been violated. I also will never understand why a violation's severity, or even its likelihood of occurrence, is measured according to the character of the violated, rather than by what was done to them.

In most reported sexual harassment cases, especially rulings on law more than on facts, the trend is almost uniformly favorable to the development of this claim. At least, so far. This almost certainly does not represent social reality. It may not even reflect most cases in litigation. And there may be conflicts building, for example, between those who value speech in the abstract more than they value people in the concrete. Much of sexual harassment is words. Women are called "cunt," "pussy," "tits"; they are invited to a company party with "bring your own bathing suits (women, either half)"; they confront their tormenter in front of their manager with, "You have called me a fucking bitch," only to be answered, "No, I didn't. I called you a fucking cunt." One court issued an injunction against inquiries such as "Did you get any over the weekend?" One case holds that where "a person in a position to grant or withhold employment opportunities uses that authority to attempt to induce workers and job seekers to submit to sexual advances, prostitution, and pornographic entertainment, and boasts of an ability to intimidate those who displease him," sexual harassment (and intentional infliction of emotional distress) are pleaded. Sexual harassment can also include pictures; visual as well as verbal pornography is commonly used as part of the abuse. Yet one judge found, apparently as a matter of law, that the pervasive presence of pornography in the workplace did not constitute an unreasonable work environment because, "For better or worse, modern America features open displays of written and pictorial erotica. Shopping centers, candy stores and prime time television regularly display naked bodies and erotic real or simulated sex acts. Living in this milieu, the average American should not be legally offended by sexually explicit posters." She did not say she was offended, she said she was discriminated against based on her sex. If the pervasiveness of an abuse makes it nonactionable, no inequality sufficiently institutionalized to merit a law against it would be actionable.

When Is Sex Because of Sex? The Causation Problem in Sexual Harassment Law*

DAVID S. SCHWARTZ

Introduction

In 1991, Lois Robinson, a female welder who had worked in a mostly male shipyard for over a decade, won a judgment against her employer for sexual harassment. Robinson proved that the work atmosphere was infested with pornographic pictures and graffiti, which constituted a "visual assault on the sensibilities of female workers." Male co-workers frequently made graphic sexual comments in front of Robinson, referring to this plentitude of pornography. They put misogynistic sexual graffiti on the walls in her working areas and made her the object of sexual comments. Robinson did not allege that any of this abusive sexual conduct was in the nature of a sexual "overture," or that the harassers had a particular sexual interest in her. Yet the court had no trouble concluding that the harassment was "because of sex": "Sexual behavior directed at women will raise the inference that the harassment is based on their sex."

In July 1997, in *Doe v. City of Belleville*, an appellate court ruled that a sixteen-year-old boy, whose male co-workers had subjected him to sexual epithets, grabbed his testicles, and even threatened him with rape, had sufficiently established "discrimination because of sex" to proceed to trial on his sexual harassment claim under Title VII. According to the court, there would have been no question that this was sexual harassment had the plaintiff been a woman, and the court found it clear

* David S. Schwartz, "When Is Sex Because of Sex? The Causation Problem in Sexual Harassment Law," *University of Pennsylvania Law Review*, vol. 150, copyright © 2002. Reprinted by permission of the publisher.

that this too was a case of "discrimination because of sex," notwithstanding that the harassers and the victim were both male. In a striking example of plain good sense, the court stated: "Frankly, we find it hard to think of a situation in which someone intentionally grabs another's testicles for reasons entirely unrelated to that person's gender."

. . .

In the year following *Doe*, the law of sexual harassment underwent major development in both doctrine and academic theory. Four leading theoretical articles on sexual harassment by progressive "second generation" feminist scholars "sought to reconceptualize the wrong of sexual harassment so as to correct conspicuous errors and set the claim on a sound future course." As the last of these was being published, at the end of the 1997—1998 Term, the U.S. Supreme Court issued three opinions on workplace sexual harassment. One of these, *Oncale v. Sundowner Offshore Services, Inc.*, held that a Title VII plaintiff could state a claim for sexual harassment notwithstanding that the harasser was of the same sex. The coincidence of these Supreme Court decisions and the related works of scholarship suggested "the arrival of a jurisprudential moment characterized by reinvigorated theorizing about the appropriate legal response to sexual harassment." . . .

Ironically, in the aftermath of these significant developments it is no longer clear—as it was prior to 1998—that a man or a woman who experiences severe or pervasive sexual epithets, crotch-grabbing, or even threatened rape has experienced "discrimination because of sex." In attempting to reconceptualize sexual harassment, both the second generation theorists and the Court reopened the question of causation and disturbed, if not rejected, the unquestioned assumption that sexual conduct in the workplace is per se "because of sex."

. . .

The "Sex Per Se" Rule and the Causation Inquiry in Sexual Harassment Doctrine

What I call the "sex per se" rule is a doctrine, developed both in the courts and in public understanding, that sexual conduct in the workplace, if it is sufficiently severe or pervasive, is discrimination because of sex. The sex per se rule does not mean that sexual conduct is automatically sex discrimination. Rather, it is addressed only to the causation element of a sexual harassment claim. Under a sex per se rule, sexual conduct in the workplace is always, without more, "because of sex."

The sex per se rule has functioned, therefore, as an evidentiary and conceptual shortcut to a detailed inquiry into discriminatory intent (called "causation" in antidiscrimination law)—an inquiry made problematic by inherent ambiguities in the relevant statutory language and in the concept of discrimination itself. The sex per se rule, which has only ever gained partial acceptance in the courts, in effect lightens a plaintiff's burden of producing evidence on the causation element.

. . .

The Feminist Case Against a Sex Per Se Rule

The second generation sexual harassment scholarship has been aimed at moving sexual harassment doctrine forward through a variety of crosscurrents and pressures that developed since the Supreme Court recognized the cause of action in 1986.... The work of Schultz, Franke, and Abrams, either recently published or in final editorial stages just before the *Oncale* decision was announced at the end of the 1997–1998 Supreme Court Term, are prominent examples of theoretical efforts to deal with these issues. A theme running through all three works is the effort to broaden the understanding of sexual harassment, either to include nonsexual forms of harassment or cases of male-on-male harassment targeting men who fail to conform to traditional masculine gender roles; while at the same time promoting women's sexual agency by rejecting the stereotypical notion that male sexual conduct automatically victimizes women. In this Section, I examine the work of each of these theorists to show how each either expressly rejects the sex per se rule (in the cases of Schultz and Franke) or implicitly abandons it (Abrams), based on the perceived need to address these issues. However, as I go on to argue, the sex per se rule is not part of the problem and its rejection is not necessary to the solution.

Sexual Harassment Reconceptualized

Desexualizing Sexual Harassment

Vicki Schultz has argued for many years that "overtly sexual behavior" is "only the tip of a tremendous iceberg" of harassment of working women through nonsexual behavior. In *Reconceptualizing Sexual Harassment*, Schultz argues that the bulk of that iceberg has been submerged because a "sexual desire-dominance paradigm governs" the law of sexual harassment. According to then-current legal doctrine (pre-*Oncale*, when Schultz wrote her article), sexually harassing conduct was understood to consist of unwanted heterosexual advances. Such conduct was recognized as a violation of Title VII because it came to be seen as motivated either by sexual desire or an intent to exploit women sexually: "Either way, [the harasser's] actions are an abuse of his power and an abuse of her sex," and therefore properly understood as discrimination because of sex. The doctrine grew out of the radical feminist argument that "sexual desire and domination were inextricably linked in the institution of heterosexuality." According to Schultz, the sexual desire-dominance paradigm represented an advance when courts first adopted it, for it overcame their previous refusal to recognize sexual harassment claims at all. However, the paradigm had inherent problems that would eventually undermine its utility. The judicial interpretation of the paradigm falls into the error—which Schultz also attributes to the first feminist theorists of sexual harassment, including MacKinnon—of conflating sexual exploitation and sex inequality.

Schultz argues that the desire-dominance paradigm's insistence on sexual conduct as the defining characteristic of sexual harassment claims has led courts to disregard nonsexual conduct that also creates hostile work environments for women. The focus on sexual conduct in both judicial and popular understandings tends to distract from the inequality-producing harm fundamental to placing sexual harassment as a wrong within Title VII, and instead creates the misleading impression that sexual misconduct is the primary evil. More significant, according to Schultz, is what she calls the "disaggregation" by the courts of sexual and nonsexual harassing conduct. In some instances, courts have separated sexual and nonsexual harassing conduct into factually and legally distinct claims, and in others have dismissed the nonsexual claims altogether. Thus, as Schultz shows, in case after case, courts would artificially split into sexual and nonsexual components a single course of harassing conduct that undermined a woman employee. In *Harris v. Forklift Systems*, for example, the lower courts considered only the sexual misconduct directed at the plaintiff Theresa Harris and failed to give weight to such facts as her being the only manager at the company to be denied an individual office, company car, and allowance and that she was required to serve coffee to the other managers at meetings. One result of such disaggregation is that the plaintiff's burden of proof is unreasonably heightened. Because a sexual harassment plaintiff must show the hostile environment to have been severe or pervasive, disaggregation would tend to make the two separate pieces of the case each seem less severe. Moreover, because the plaintiff must also prove the harassing conduct was "because of sex," courts would often dismiss the nonsexual part of the claim as lacking in proof of sex bias.

Schultz's corrective to this pervasive error by the lower courts is to reconceptualize sexual harassment by replacing the sexual desire-dominance paradigm with what she calls a "competence-centered" paradigm. Sexual harassment should be understood as any conduct, whether or not sexual, "that has the purpose or effect of undermining the perceived or actual competence of women (and some men) who threaten the idealized masculinity of those who do the work." Such a broader understanding better captures the reality of workplace harassment of women, which is not necessarily motivated by "men's desire to exploit or dominate women sexually," but always has "the form and function of denigrating women's competence for the purpose of keeping them away from male-dominated jobs or incorporating them as inferior, less capable workers." The competence-centered account would recognize the full range of harassing conduct that "subverts a woman's perceived or actual competence," including nonsexual verbal denigration as well as such common nonsexual harassing techniques as denial of adequate training and mentoring, assigning unfair or impossible tasks, ostracism, and sabotage. For Schultz, then, not all workplace sexual conduct is discrimination because of sex, and more importantly not all discriminatory harassment because of sex is sexual conduct. In essence, Schultz views the idea of a direct causal nexus between sexual conduct and sex discrimination as a mistake; it is the competence-undermining effect of sexual harassment that mediates and causally connects sexual conduct to "sex."

Heteropatriarchy as Discrimination Because of Sex

Whereas Schultz's reconceptualization of the law is driven by the need to correct the mistake of disaggregating sexual from nonsexual harassing conduct, Katherine Franke's analysis is driven primarily by the failure of sexual harassment law to provide a coherent or principled resolution of same-sex harassment cases. In *What's Wrong With Sexual Harassment?*, Franke suggests that it is necessary to return to first principles in order to resolve such cases....

Although Franke begins with the provocative assertion that the time has come to make a new effort to answer the "seemingly simple" question "why is [sexual harassment] sex discrimination?," it emerges that the real focal point of her analysis is the causation element of sexual harassment claims. Hence the question she poses could properly be restated as "why is sexual conduct because of sex?" Franke sees the existing answers to this question as falling into three categories: "(1) the equality principle: the conduct would not have been undertaken but for the plaintiff's sex; (2) the anti-sex principle: the conduct was discriminatory precisely because it was sexual; and (3) the antisubordination principle: the conduct subordinated women to men." To Franke, these approaches, developed by feminist theorists and litigators, were beneficial in overcoming the initial judicial hostility to recognizing sexual harassment as a violation of Title VII, but each is flawed and incomplete as a theoretical account....

The problem with the formal equality approach, according to Franke, is that it begs the question of why sexual conduct directed by a man toward a woman in the workplace is because of sex. The explanation, often unstated, is that (hetero) sexual desire is only and always directed at the opposite sex, and a man's sexual advance on a woman therefore establishes that her sex is a "but for cause" of his harassing conduct. This explanation fails to explain why cases of sexual conduct not motivated by sexual desire are deemed "because of sex" in male-female harassment cases. Moreover, when a sexual-desire account is used in same-sex cases, the result is that actionable same-sex harassment is typically limited to harassment perpetrated by homosexuals. Harassment motivated by the impulse to coerce conformity with heterosexist gender norms usually escapes liability.

· · ·

The "anti-sex principle" identified by Franke proves to be nothing more than a vacuous version of the third argument—the "antisubordination principle"—which offers a more robust account of the idea that workplace sexual conduct amounts automatically to sex discrimination. Franke identifies antisubordination theory with that articulated by feminist theorists who were instrumental in the development of sexual harassment doctrine in the 1970s and 1980s, particularly Catharine MacKinnon and Susan Estrich. MacKinnon has argued, for example, that a discriminatory "sex stereotype is present in the male attitude, expressed through sexual harassment, that women are sexual beings whose privacy and integrity can be invaded at will, beings who exist for men's sexual stimulation and gratification." MacKinnon, according to Franke, has devoted her career to demonstrating that "male sexual behavior is, in some sense, fundamentally sexist" and "is the principal form and means of women's domination." Franke, for her part, rejects these ideas. The "impulse to collapse sexism with sex," as she calls it, reduces female sexuality to passive victimization. Moreover, says Franke, by reducing sexuality and sexual harassment to something that men do to women, MacKinnon's antisubordination theory fails to recognize the oppressive process of creation and reinforcement of gender roles that results from sexual harassment.

. . .

Franke offers a revised antisubordination account to replace both the theoretically vacuous formal equality theory and MacKinnon's "sex equals sexism" antisubordination theory. According to Franke, "one of the ultimate goals of antidiscrimination laws is, and I believe it should be, to provide all people more options with respect to how they do their gender." Therefore, it is necessary to account for same-sex harassment in cases such as one where the victimized man is subordinated for failing to conform to the norm of the sufficiently masculine, heterosexual male. For Franke, sexual harassment comprises those practices that police or enforce "hetero-patriarchal gender norms." Franke's argument about sexual harassment follows from her argument made elsewhere, that sex discrimination law has committed a fundamental error by assuming the existence of two immutable biological sexes, each of which carries an inextricable gender. Once biological sex and gender are disaggregated, it becomes (relatively) plain that the discriminatory pattern evident in sexual harassment cases is not biological men subordinating biological women, but rather hetero-masculine men subordinating everyone else.

. . .

Broadening Traditional Antisubordination Theory

In *The New Jurisprudence of Sexual Harassment*, Kathryn Abrams takes issue with reconceiving sexual harassment in ways that shift the primary focus away from the subordination of women, a flaw which she finds in the two theoretical accounts she discusses, by Franke and Anita Bernstein. Nevertheless, Abrams agrees that sexual harassment doctrine needs to be fixed: "If we hope to modify or reconstruct sexual harassment doctrine, we need a coherent account of where existing doctrine is going wrong, and, perhaps more importantly, a reconceptualization of the real problem to be remedied through sexual harassment litigation."

Abrams further elaborates the antisubordination theory of sexual harassment that she has developed over several years. For example, she has argued that sexual harassment is:

> either a form of gender discrimination against women—derision of some of the qualities that make women targets for sexual harassment—or a form of gender discrimination against men that disciplines not the group but a distinct subset for abandoning the qualities associated with men for the more socially stigmatized characteristics associated with women.

According to Abrams, sexual harassment "has emerged as a means of preserving male control over the workplace." Abrams's revised antisubordination theory is designed to broaden the understanding of sexual harassment so that it can recognize various forms of harassing behavior and the complex identities of sexual harassment claimants. This broader understanding would include recognition of male-on-male harassment claims, even though the understanding is grounded on a theory of sex discrimination as subordination of women: Although most sexual harassment is aimed at women, male-on-male harassment also can be sexist by "asserting the primacy of male prerogatives or norms in the workplace."

Although she moves the understanding of sexual harassment beyond MacKinnon's male-sexuality-as-domination view, Abrams, unlike Franke or Schultz, does not appear at all invested in a rejection of MacKinnon. According to Abrams, it is not that MacKinnon wrongly conflates sexism with sex (as Franke contends), but rather that the social conditions have changed since MacKinnon wrote in 1979. "As more women have begun to claim equal status in society and have sought access to a wider range of jobs, male control over the workplace is no longer so hegemonic that sexualization and sexual availability are built uncontroversially into women's job descriptions," as MacKinnon had argued.

. . .

The Lack of Necessity to Abandon the Sex Per Se Rule

For Franke and Schultz, the sex per se rule is inextricably associated with MacKinnon's theory that male sexuality is inherently subordinating, making male sexual conduct in the workplace per se discrimination "because of sex." Thus, they assert that the sex per se rule must be abandoned because it interferes with the goals they seek to advance: for Schultz, to include nonsexual claims of harassment, and for Franke (and secondarily for Schultz), to move to an understanding of harassment as gender subordination more broadly conceived. Further, both believe that a sex per se rule demeans women's sexual agency: it necessarily conceives of women as automatic victims of sexual conduct. Abrams does not find it necessary to reject MacKinnon, yet at the same time she perceives no particular need to defend a sex per se rule; moreover, she seems in accord with Schultz and Franke's perceived need to restructure the causation inquiry to address the problems of female sexual agency, nonsexual harassment, and same-sex harassment. On closer examination, however, it appears that the sex per se rule is not to blame for these problems, and getting rid of it is not necessary to address them.

The Problem of Female Sexual Agency

Both Franke and Schultz express the concern that relying on sexual conduct as a touchstone for the sex-discriminatory quality of sexual harassment—equating sexuality with sexism—will repress benign sexual expression and undermine female sexual agency. Schultz argues that "sexual relations (heterosexual or otherwise) do not inherently enact male dominance over women," thus aligning herself with the modern trend of "feminist scholarship that criticizes earlier feminist thought for conflating gender inequality and (heterosexual) sexual relations." But the sexual desire-dominance paradigm, by equating sexuality with sexism, results in both an unduly paternalistic concern for women's sexual sensibilities and unduly oppressive efforts to purge all traces of sexuality from the workplace. Such efforts, Schultz further asserts, are doomed to fail, and only will succeed in generating resistance to sexual harassment laws and give feminism a bad name....

The persuasive force of these criticisms should not keep us from looking carefully at the real identity of their target. If the target is the courts or prevailing legal doctrine, then their criticism may be somewhat misplaced. Prevailing doctrine has not, in fact, seriously attempted to banish all sexual expression from the workplace....

On closer examination, the Franke and Schultz argument about female sexual agency is an argument not with the courts but with MacKinnon's antisubordination theory. Given MacKinnon's stature both as a founder of sexual harassment doctrine and as a major figure in feminism, this is certainly a worthwhile argument to have. But is the sex per se rule inextricably bound up with MacKinnon's conflation of sexism and sexuality?

I think not. What I refer to as the "sex per se" rule is not MacKinnon's theory, but rather an evidentiary shortcut to a causation finding. To the extent that it has gained a foothold in doctrine, that does not provide evidence of judicial acceptance of MacKinnon. Franke and Schultz both underestimate the possibility that the sex per se rule represents a judicial intuition reaching toward the broader notion that sexuality in the workplace is sufficiently likely to be, in Franke's phrase, a "technology of sexism" that it is worthwhile to shift the factual inquiry beyond "causation" to the other elements of a sexual harassment claim.

It is worth restating some basics at this point. A claim of sexual harassment that violates Title VII has a number of elements, of which "because of sex" is only one. The plaintiff in a hostile environment case must show not only that the conduct was "because of sex," but also that it was "unwelcome" and "sufficiently severe or pervasive 'to alter the conditions of [the victim's] employment and create an abusive working environment.'" The environment must be both subjectively hostile, meaning that the victim "subjectively perceived the environment to be abusive," and objectively hostile, meaning "an environment that a reasonable person would find hostile or abusive."

. . .

The Problem of a Sexual-Desire-Based Causation Theory

Sexual desire as a touchstone for the causation inquiry has very little to recommend it. . . . Sexual-desire-based causation makes lust the critical motivation rather than motivations that have more to do with discrimination, such as an intent to subordinate women or to preserve hetero-male control over workplaces. This, as discussed above, opens the door to intrusive and ugly inquiries into the sexuality of the parties that should be irrelevant in a case of sex-based employment discrimination. Moreover, it lends itself to the deplorable "homosexuals only" rule in which gay harassers become target defendants of Title VII, whereas non-gay men can harass gender nonconforming men with impunity. Finally, a sexual-desire based understanding of sexual harassment contributes to the "disaggregation" error—the marked tendency to focus on sexual conduct to the exclusion of nonsexual forms of harassment—convincingly documented by Schultz.

Starting with the latter point, is it necessary to abandon a sex per se rule in order to solve the disaggregation problem? Schultz, in essence, argues that when she criticizes what she calls a "two-tiered structure of causation" in harassment cases. In this "two-tiered structure," causation (because of sex) is presumed in sexual conduct cases, but must be proven with additional evidence in other cases. Schultz contends that this double standard for required proof is part and parcel of the courts' relative inattention to nonsexual harassing conduct. The solution Schultz appears to advocate is that sexual conduct cases should not be privileged in any way over nonsexual ones in terms of proof. . . .

Schultz's attack on the sex per se rule is less persuasive than her central insights about the need for courts to overcome their failure to recognize nonsexual harassment. The two-tiered structure of proof is not necessarily either cause or effect of the problem of sexual conduct overshadowing nonsexual conduct in the perception of unlawful sex-based harassment. Instead, it may be nothing more than a recognition that some evidence more clearly reveals its sex basis for Title VII purposes than other evidence, in the same way that berating a female employee as "dumb" is less obviously "because of sex" than berating her, as in *Harris*, as a "dumb-ass woman." . . . Eliminating two-tiered causation in effect by requiring similar comparative or sex-specific evidence in sexual conduct cases may accomplish nothing other than to decree that more proof of causation will be required in all cases. . . .

. . . the EEOC has long taken the position that "sexual harassment is one type of harassment based on sex. However it is not the only type of unlawful harassment which is sex-based or which stems from sex discrimination." Thus, the ends advocated by Schultz may be attainable by strengthening the recognition of this basic insight articulated by the EEOC, that any sort of harassment directed at women is discrimination because of sex, and that sexual harassment is merely a subset of this larger category of sex-based harassment. In other words, the disaggregation error can be corrected without abandoning a sex per se rule.

Nor, more generally, does it seem necessary to abandon a sex per se rule in order to disabuse courts of a desire-based theory of causation. A sex per se rule is not the same thing as assuming that sexual conduct must be based on desire or attraction in order to be because of sex. Since sexual conduct may be motivated by various reasons—including the motivations implicit in the notion that sexual harassment is a "technology of sexism"—to treat sexual conduct as per se "because of sex" would treat all sexual conduct in the workplace as more likely than not because of sex, without distinguishing between harassers motivated by desire and those motivated to preserve the workplace as a male domain. It would, in effect, make the harasser's specific motivation irrelevant to the causation issue and thereby solve the problem of messy inquiries into the harasser's state of mind.

Same-Sex Harassment

A concern very much in the foreground for Franke and Abrams, and secondarily for Schultz, is to solve the conundrum of same-sex harassment cases. These cases have produced perverse results. On the one hand, courts that would probably never rely on an antisubordination theory to reject, say, a challenge to an affirmative action plan by a reverse discrimination plaintiff, seem to rely on antisubordination selectively to reject same-sex claims: Sexual harassment doctrine, they say, was designed to protect women, who traditionally have been subordinated in the workplace, not men. On the other hand, a sexual-desire-based understanding of harassment would tend to allow heterosexual males to sue gay harassers, but not the other way around. Thus, bolstered by the current exclusion of sexual orientation from Title VII protection, a class of marginalized and subordinated employees—gender nonconformists—could be targeted as defendants but left largely unprotected as plaintiffs. This type of "reverse discrimination" approach to same-sex harassment is arguably indicated by the *Oncale* decision.

A sex per se rule does not produce such a result, however. Again, the culprit is a theory based on sexual desire. Plaintiffs in the gender nonconformist cases, such as *Doe v. City of Belleville*, are almost invariably subjected to sexualized forms of abuse. They would all be able to show their harassment was "because of sex" under a sex per se rule. To be sure, so would the heterosexual plaintiff claiming unwanted sexual attention from a gay harasser. In that sense, the sex per se rule might be overinclusive (which is no doubt why Franke wants to get rid of it), although it would still be necessary for the plaintiff to show that the sexual attention was severe. However, that sort of problem—the recognition of reverse discrimination claims by members of the dominant group—would seem to be inherent in Title VII cases so long as courts follow a formal equality approach rather than an antisubordination approach to the statute.

. . .

Conclusion

Both the Supreme Court and the second generation theorists of sexual harassment have discredited the sex per se rule, not out of any conscious intent to make proof more difficult for Lois Robinson, but rather to address other issues. For feminist theorists, the challenge was to find a unifying antisubordination theory that could at the same time bring both H. Doe and Lois Robinson under the same protective Title VII umbrella. For the Supreme Court, however, the agenda seems to have been to make proof more difficult for H. Doe in order to prevent Title VII from drifting toward prohibition of harassment because of sexual orientation. But abandonment of the sex per se rule would seem to leave the Lois Robinsons standing out in the rain—a result intended by neither feminist theorists nor indeed the Court.

. . . The sex per se rule has helped combat the subordination of women in the workplace by easing otherwise potentially difficult problems in proving causation, particularly in cases like Robinson, and it could function in the same way to combat subordination based on gender more broadly conceived. After *Oncale*, the first order of business for theorists of sexual harassment law should be to rehabilitate the sex per se rule by showing courts that it has a theoretical and textual basis. . . .

The New Jurisprudence of Sexual Harassment*
KATHRYN ABRAMS

The Respectful Person: Depoliticizing Sexual Harassment

Anita Bernstein's article, *Treating Sexual Harassment with Respect*, exemplifies the shift in sexual harassment jurisprudence from a focus on "how" we litigate claims to a focus on "why" sexual harassment is a wrong. The first target of her analysis is the great bugbear of recent

* Kathryn Abrams, "The New Jurisprudence of Sexual Harassment," *Cornell Law Review*, vol. 83, copyright © 1998. Reprinted by permission of the publisher.

sexual harassment scholarship: the reasonableness standard for assessing sexual harassment in the workplace. According to Bernstein, reasonableness as "ratiocination"—the exercising of the powers of reason—is inherently unsuited to evaluate a harm whose basis of offense is indignity. It also fails to acknowledge the centrality of emotion in sexual harassment injuries and evokes age old, stereotypic questions about whether women are capable of directing themselves according to reason. More centrally, "reasonableness as average or typical thinking" is defeated by a series of problems that emerge, hydra-like, as the standard is amended or modified.

According to Bernstein's analysis, the "reasonable person" perpetuates subtly gendered understandings under the guise of neutrality. The "reasonable woman," its most widely defended replacement, manifests even greater difficulties. It can essentialize those it seeks to protect, transforming their distinct perceptions into fragility, and their experiences of coercion into inevitable victimization. It can create problems for both male triers of fact, who must embrace a perspective they have never experienced, and male victims, who may be considered, in relation to their female counterparts, to be impervious to workplace coercion. Finally, more particularized standards, such as the "reasonable person of the same gender and race or color as the plaintiff," threaten the goal of an objective measure and make prospective legal guidance difficult....

Reasonableness must be replaced, Bernstein argues, with the term "respect." Respect has historically been linked to reason through the Kantian framework in which the capacity for reason makes human beings worthy of respect. Yet respect, according to Bernstein, has been immured in none of the sexist controversies over the differential capacities of men and women. More importantly, "recognition respect," a form of respect elaborated in philosophical literature, seems promisingly germane to the problems presented by sexual harassment. Unlike appraisal respect, which is rendered for excellence, recognition respect involves " 'taking account of the fact that [the individual] is a separate person, [and] that his is the only life he has.' " It is "premised on the ideas that all human beings have respect-warranting traits in common and that each person is uniquely free." These "respect-warranting traits" have been interpreted by philosophers as imposing on others three "duties to refrain": from treating another person only as means of achieving one's ends; from humiliating another person; and from denying the personhood and self-conception of another person. According to Bernstein, these obligations create a framework from which a respectful person could assess harassing conduct in the workplace.

The respectful person contributes by helping us assess claims of sexual harassment. But it also helps us think about the wrong itself and about the means through which we might correct it. The wrong of sexual harassment, according to this view, is a fundamental lack of respect. It is a failure to forebear, for example, in the ways that the three duties require; it results in an injury the basis of which is offense, indignity, or humiliation....

... As a call for reconceptualization and redirection of the sexual harassment claim, however, Bernstein's argument has serious drawbacks.

Reasoning About Reasonableness

The first difficulty lies in Bernstein's critique of reasonableness. The alleged incompatibility between ratiocination and the claim for sexual harassment is far more contingent than Bernstein suggests. Bernstein seems initially to forget the question that the reasonable person standard was enlisted to answer: whether the harassing behavior was sufficiently pervasive as to "unreasonably interfere" with plaintiff's employment and create an environment that was hostile, intimidating, or abusive. Although it is true that some elements of this question have an emotional component, questions regarding the pervasiveness of the harm and the interference with employment are susceptible to the ratiocinative faculties. Moreover, this alleged incompatibility rests heavily on Bernstein's claim that sexual harassment must be understood as a dignitary harm—a feature, I will argue, that captures only part of the wrong. If sexual harassment is also understood as a barrier to women's professional progress, or, as a denial of their capacity for self-definition or self-direction, it seems quite capable of being apprehended by the faculties of reason.

Furthermore, the implication of reason in a series of stigmatizing, gendered dichotomies is neither inevitable, nor necessarily dispositive, if the standard is otherwise workable. Feminists and other theorists have developed sophisticated conceptions of reason that are more inclusive and less stigmatizing to women and minorities. One virtue of a properly elaborated reasonableness standard is that it would demonstrate that joining women, sex, and reason need not be oxymoronic. Not only does Bernstein eschew this revisionary strategy, but her insistence on the emotional character of the harm of sexual harassment threatens to replicate the dichotomy: to say that sexual harassment is an emotional injury that cannot be apprehended by reason risks reinforcing the all-too-prevalent belief that it is a women's injury that cannot be apprehended by the rest of the population.

There are comparable problems with Bernstein's critique of reason as average thinking. Although she is meticulous in documenting the analytic problems that reasonableness standards have produced, she is less persuasive in arguing that these problems inhere in reason as a substantive standard. The gender-inflected problems that have dogged the reasonable person, the reasonable woman, and their even more particularized counterparts arise not so much from the nature of reasonableness, as from the fact that the term has been leached of virtually all substantive content when applied in these contexts. Defining reasonableness as averageness or typicality has made the "reasonable" part of the standard a cipher. . . .

The movement toward prototypes may be countered by offering a fuller explanation of what is meant by the critical term "reasonable." Courts and commentators using the reasonable woman standard, for example, have sought to specify the perception possessed by the average woman that the average person, characteristically male, lacks. If this approach to what is reasonable does not overcome all of the difficulties Bernstein addresses, it at least points toward a promising strategy: one could attempt to define "reasonable" rather than the noun that it qualifies. If reasonable is not understood as average, but is taken to be the object of explanation itself, we can move away from prototypes toward more contextualized understandings.

Consider the following possibility. A reasonable person is defined by more than ratiocinative faculties. In order to reason competently about a particular phenomenon, a person needs information about that phenomenon—it would hardly be reasonable to make a judgment without information germane to the question to be decided. So a reasonable person could be understood to be a well informed person, a person armed with context-specific information about the question to be resolved. What should a person be expected to know about how sexual harassment operates in the workplace in order to render a reasonable judgment about whether a particular problem has become pervasive? In a recent article, for example, I identified four categories of things that a reasonable trier of fact should know about sexual harassment in order to assess its pervasiveness in a particular case. The factors range from the barriers that women have faced and continue to face in the workplace to the effects sexual harassment has on the work lives of its targets. Although the content of the list might be debated, such context-based elaboration can reduce the scope within which dominant norms operate. It can be done, moreover, without replacing the existing standard.

Whether respect will be less entangled in gendered controversies is not at all clear. . . .

Respect is likely to be translated by triers of fact as a kind of decency. It connotes both civility and, as Bernstein suggests in her model instructions, giving a person his or her due. . . . Although one would not describe a person as being worthy of reason, we can and do debate whether particular persons are worthy of respect. Bernstein attempts to downplay this aspect of respectfulness by arguing that sexual harassment implicates "recognition respect," a form of respect which is due people as human beings, rather than "appraisal respect," a form of respect which reflects "admiration" for certain distinctive qualities. However, this distinction between forms of respect that apply uniformly to human beings (recognition respect) and forms of respect that discriminate among them (appraisal respect), is not likely to be as easily maintained as Bernstein suggests.... While recognition respect is, in theory, applicable to all of us as humans, it has proven persistently difficult, in practice, for most of us to treat all humans with an even hand. Estimations of the level of respect that is due persons as human beings are almost inevitably tied to our assessment of what kinds of human beings we believe they are. These judgments of respectability, in turn, are often deeply influenced by assumptions regarding gender, race, class, and other group based characteristics. Two examples of recent legal scholarship analyzing the social meanings of respectability make this clear.

The first emerges from Mary Louise Fellows's analysis of women and the provision of childcare in the late-nineteenth and twentieth centuries. Hiring domestic workers was one of the ways that members of the emerging middle class expended their discretionary income, in large part because it helped them to realize the norms of respectability that characterized urban capitalism of that time. Respectability, in this setting, was associated with "good character, ... sobriety, chastity, and dedication to family," and, in the important context of the home, with "cleanliness, orderliness, and ornateness of children, things, and rooms."

A careful analysis of this notion of respectability reveals that it was deeply inflected with notions of gender, race, and class. The middle class wife, who was constantly at risk of falling from respectability because of women's association with the primitive and the bodily, was obliged to keep an immaculate, orderly household but also was required "to be above the dirty work of scrubbing floors and changing babies." These conflicting pressures led to the transformation of homemaking and child rearing into a profession in which the respectable woman supervised others who removed the inculpatory dirt. The creation of the homemaking and caregiving professions both reflected and exacerbated distinctions in respectability among women. Those deemed appropriate to perform this domestic labor were largely nonwhite, working class women. However, the employment of these women in homemaking and child rearing positions resulted in their further degradation.

· · ·

The second example of the group-inflected meanings of the term respectability emerges from Randall Kennedy's *Race, Crime, and the Law*. In this book, Kennedy describes a "politics of respectability" that he hopes will encourage advocates of equality for African–Americans to consider his approach of race-neutrality in criminal law. The main tenet of this politics is that "freed of crippling, invidious racial discriminations, blacks are capable of meeting the established moral standards of white middle-class Americans." One of its principal strategies is "to distance as many blacks as far as possible from negative stereotypes used to justify racial discrimination against all Negroes." ... The politics of respectability, thus described, helps advocates of black equality decide which blacks should be the focus of legal and political reform (black victims) and which should not (blacks who are accused of crimes). It also helps black reformers decide which initiatives should be undertaken (those that are "extra-careful in order to avoid the derogatory charges lying in wait in a hostile environment") and which should not (those that "singe the sensibilities of many, particularly whites").

In both these examples, concern with respectability reflects and perpetuates intricate hierarchies based on race, gender, class, and other attributes. It reflects a desperate "politics of the margin," in which relatively privileged members of a devalued group degrade other members of their own group in order to demonstrate their worth to those in power. In addition to dividing those who might make common cause for change, the pursuit of respectability naturalizes, or renders invisible, the power arrangements that created centrality and marginality in the first place.

. . .

The Neutered Wrong of Disrespect

Interestingly, Bernstein appears to concur in many of these conclusions. Her own argument offers a critique of current sexual harassment doctrine and is strongly concerned with a reconceptualization of the wrong. The great advantage of the respect standard, according to Bernstein, is that it is "a standard that measures action rather than reaction." The respect standard offers not only a standpoint from which to assess legal claims but also an affirmative account of what is wrong with harassing behavior. Harassment, in this view, is a failure of respect: it is a dignitary injury that offends, humiliates, and denies the equal human status of the object. However, the value of this dual role for respect depends on its account of the wrong. A legal standard, however practical, that is linked to an erroneous or incomplete description of the wrong has little value. Herein lies my final and most pressing reservation about Bernstein's argument. Her account of the wrong seems accurate but disturbingly underspecified.

There is no doubt that sexual harassment is a failure of respect. Although her use of putative synonyms such as "offensiveness" or "in civility" risks trivializing the wrong, Bernstein's description of harassment as a dignitary injury that humiliates and denies the equal personhood of the target seems wholly accurate. Moreover, Bernstein's sensitive discussions of the impact of this injury on the lives of women suggest that she fully appreciates the dignitary dimension of the harm. The problem with her account, however, is not with what it says but with what it fails to say. First, it is not central to Bernstein's conceptualization of the wrong that sexual harassment occurs in the workplace. Bernstein reflects in passing on the meaning of being humiliated at work and argues that respect should entail an appreciation of the community that connects the harasser and the target. But the indignity that she defines as harassment's central harm could occur anywhere—on the street, in a social institution, in one's home. Bernstein neglects important dimensions of the injury specifically attributable to the fact that it occurs in the workplace. The absence of these work-specific dimensions affect the completeness of her account. The humiliation of sexual harassment occurs in a setting where it has the potential to thwart the earning of one's livelihood and to prevent the achievement of one's professional fulfillment or self-definition. It also occurs in a setting where women have historically been marginalized or relegated to distinct and limited roles and where they continue to face hostility and systematic obstacles to professional progress.

This latter observation raises a second difficulty that goes not simply to the completeness of Bernstein's account but to its political valence. It is not central to Bernstein's account that the humiliation of sexual harassment is perpetrated by more powerful members of a gendered hierarchy against the less powerful members. This is a hierarchy that shapes not only the workplace but also a range of institutions and attributes of our social and cultural life. What is relevant, and obscured by Bernstein's account, is that the humiliation of sexual harassment parallels a number of other humiliations suffered by women through their sexual coercion, their reduction to two-dimensional stereotypes, the devaluation of their abilities, and the discounting of their critical perspectives on discriminatory practices in many walks of life....

... Yes, harassment is a dignitary injury, but if we do not appreciate that this dignitary injury is a function of, and connected to, other injuries within an unequal, hierarchial relationship, we miss much of what is morally and politically significant about the wrong....

First, failing to highlight the fact that this humiliation arises from a context of systematic gender inequality individualizes the wrong and diminishes the imperative for responding to it Correcting a nonsystematic problem of disrespect is a far less urgent matter than curtailing a practice of gender discrimination, which imposes consequences on women's economic and personal well-being and which has parallels throughout society. This is not simply an abstract point but an issue with ramifications for public education, legal enforcement, and private efforts at prevention. The public will better understand the need for concerted enforcement efforts, and employers will better comprehend the need for strong affirmative obligations of prevention and response, if they understand that they are remedying a longstanding, often entrenched problem.

Second, and perhaps more importantly, failing to highlight the political or gendered character of sexual harassment will make it more difficult, as a practical matter, to assess and prevent. If I am right about

Bernstein's pragmatic remedial focus, disrespect operates as a noninf-lammatory proxy for the sexist devaluation of the less powerful by the more powerful members of a sex and gender hierarchy. Because the term and the helpful instructions that accompany it do not begin to capture the varied, intricate dynamics of that devaluation, they are unlikely to enable triers of fact and employers to recognize all of the problematic conduct they need to act against. Triers of fact may not recognize the gendered forms that disrespect takes. Employers charged with preven-tion may not recognize the subtly stereotypic or devaluative attitudes that increasingly fuel harassment as women move into the workplace in greater numbers and as competition becomes more intense. Employees asked to modify their behavior prospectively may not grasp the range of conduct that is forbidden or the underlying attitudes that need to be re-examined. Declining to identify the gendered character of sexual harass-ment both effects a moral and political neutering of the problem and imposes an unnecessary impediment to remedying or preventing it.

Notes and Questions

1. The hostility that women employees have faced on entering certain traditionally male-dominated positions is well documented. For example, one case of egregious sex discrimination against a promising female employee at the Central Intelligence Agency, which led to a settlement for the plaintiff of $410,000, alleged that the agency's directorate of operations was plagued by "a pervasive atmosphere of machismo and sexual discrimination." Tim Weiner, "C.I.A. to Pay $410,000 to Spy Who Says She Was Smeared." *The New York Times* A1 (December 8, 1994). Moreover, Elvia Arriola has documented how pioneering female construction workers in New York City met with virulent harassment and sabotage from co-workers. Arriola argued that women recognize that "behind the symbolism of masculinized job descriptions lies a very real force: the power of men to harass, belittle, ostracize, dismiss, marginalize, discard, and just plain hurt them as work-ers." Arriola, " 'What's the Big Deal?' Women in the New York City Construction Industry and Sexual Harassment Law, 1970–1985," 22 *Colum-bia Human Rights Law Review* 21 (1990).

Richard Epstein would likely concede the deep antagonism but would conclude from these examples that coercing interactions through antidis-crimination laws is unwise. Is the antagonism likely to be a transitional problem until the presence of women throughout the economy is widely accepted, or will the antagonism persist? This is one of the central questions of all employment discrimination law, which tends to be premised on the view—articulated in the excerpt from Gunnar Myrdal in Chapter 1—that enforced interaction causes prejudices and antagonisms to soften, while segregation tends to cause attitudes and biases to harden.

2. Richard Epstein has complained that there is no need to apply the law of employment discrimination to the problem of sexual harassment, because the existing law of tort is sufficiently encompassing to prohibit all of the offensive conduct. See Epstein, *Forbidden Grounds* (Cambridge, Mass.:

Harvard University Press, 1992). But under the existing law of employment discrimination, a complaint to an employer triggers potential employer liability if the firm does not prevent further harassment. Isn't the ability to enlist the support of the employer likely to be a far more immediate, more effective, and less costly approach to the problem than requiring victims to file a civil suit in state court complaining of offensive touching (battery) or intentional infliction of emotional distress?

Consider the case of J. P. Bolduc, the chief executive officer of W. R. Grace & Co., who liked to pat female employees on the buttocks and

> occasionally would lick his finger and put it in a female employee's ear. One friend and former executive says Mr. Bolduc would sometimes run his hand up a female employee's leg, or put his arm around her, adding, "More of this later." . . . [W]hen Mr. Bolduc was scheduled to visit . . . , some women called in sick.

Does Epstein's suggestion of a state court tort claim for battery seem like the best way to address such conduct? How would Epstein respond to the argument that MacKinnon made in her book in 1979, that common-law tort remedies are not adequate because they fail to recognize the wrong as "group harm" against women: "By treating the incidents as if they are outrages particular to an individual woman rather than integral to her social status as a woman worker, the personal approach on the legal level fails to analyze the relevant dimensions of the problem." Catherine MacKinnon, *Sexual Harassment of Working Women: A Case of Sex Discrimination* 88 (New Haven: Yale University Press, 1979).

Mark Hager and Ellen Paul reject MacKinnon's characterization of sexual harassment as "group harm." They both advocate an individualized tort approach to sexual harassment because "it gets the federal courts out of what is essentially a personal matter between individuals . . . it places fault where fault truly lies—with the perpetrator." Ellen Paul, "Sexual Harassment as Sex Discrimination: A Defective Paradigm," 8 *Yale Law and Policy Review* 333, 364–65 (1990). See also Mark Mclaughlin Hager, "Harassment as a Tort: Why Title VII Hostile Environment Liability Should be Curtailed," 30 *Connecticut Law Review* 375 (1998). For further discussion of the doctrinal tensions in this area, see Mary Ann Case, "Disaggregating Sex From Gender and Sexual Orientation: The Effeminate Man in the Law and Feminist Jurisprudence," 105 *Yale Law Journal* 1 (1995).

Rosa Ehrenreich, on the other hand, recognizes the link between sexual harassment and the socio-historical subjugation of women as a group, but she argues (in the same vein as Anita Bernstein) that fundamentally, sexual harassment is wrong because it imposes dignitary harm to workers, regardless of the gender of the harasser or the harassed. Thus she argues that because Title VII emphasizes discrimination at the expense of dignity, exclusive focus on Title VII as a tool of redressing sexual harassment is deeply misguided. Rosa Ehrenreich, "Dignity and Discrimination: Toward a Pluralistic Understanding of Workplace Harassment," 88 *Georgetown Law Journal* 1 (1999).

3. The decision in *Robinson v. Jacksonville Shipyards*, which was discussed in the selection from Chamallas in Chapter 12, indicated that the pervasive presence of pornography in the workplace creates a sexually hostile work environment. Kingsley Browne contends that this holding violates the First Amendment, and argues that only harassment targeted at specific individuals should be considered impermissible sex discrimination. Kingsley Browne, "Title VII as Censorship: Hostile–Environment Harassment and the First Amendment," 52 *Ohio State Law Journal* 481 (1991).

Eugene Volokh has also argued that the use of harassment law to sanction expression in the work place creates a serious First Amendment issue in that it actually bars and certainly chills some core-protected speech. He writes:

> The EEOC has charged a company with harassing a Japanese–American employee by using images of samurai, kabuki, and sumo wrestling in its ad campaign to refer to its Japanese competitors, and by referring to the competitors as "Japs" and "slant-eyed" in its internal reports.... A district court has characterized an employee's hanging "pictures of Ayatollah Khomeini and a burning American flag in Iran in her own cubicle as 'national-origin harassment' " of an Iranian employee who saw the pictures. A Massachusetts trial court has held that it was sexual harassment for a worker to attach pictures of a female union candidate to two Hustler centerfolds and circulate them to some of his coworkers. The court awarded the woman $35,000 plus costs and attorney's fees, to be paid personally by the offending worker.

Eugene Volokh, "How Harassment Law Restricts Free Speech," 47 *Rutgers Law Review* 563, 565–66 (1995). See also Eugene Volokh, "What Speech Does 'Hostile Work Environment Harassment Law Restrict?' " 85 *Georgetown Law Journal* 627 (1997) (noting that employers will restrict individual statements even when they are not severe or pervasive enough to create a hostile environment because employers fear that in the aggregate, they may be actionable).

Denouncing what she deems a "transparent ploy to continue the bigoted abuse and avoid liability," Catharine MacKinnon strongly criticizes the view that dehumanizing displays of pornography in the workplace merit the protection of the First Amendment, as the defendants argued in *Jacksonville Shipyards*. MacKinnon, *Only Words* (Cambridge, Mass.: Harvard University Press, 1993).

Underlying the debate about the role of the First Amendment in the context of harassment law is a fundamental question about why workplaces should be treated any differently than other forums in which speech is protected. In this vain, Volokh asks, "If it's permissible to restrict sexually suggestive speech at work because it 'communicates to male coworkers that it is acceptable to view women in a predominantly sexual way,' why is it improper to restrict such expression on television, which doubtless causes much more harm to sexual equality? If paintings of nudes can be taken down wherever there are employees present, why can't they be banished from all public places given that there will always be some employees in any public place?" Volokh, "Thinking Ahead about Freedom of Speech and Hostile Work Environment Harassment," 17 *Berkeley Journal of Employment & Labor Law* 305, 319 (1996). In response, David Oppenheimer argues, "Women and minority group members in the workplace are a captive audience in much the same way as school students, medical patients, or employees facing a union election. For example, unlike the targets of street harassment, they cannot simply walk away from on-the-job-harassment." Oppenheimer, "Workplace Harassment and the First Amendment: A Reply to Professor Volokh," 17 *Berkeley Journal of Employment & Labor Law* 321, 323 (1996). See also J.M. Balkin, "Free Speech and Hostile Environments," 99 *Columbia Law Review* 2295, 2307 (1999) (elucidating the captive audience theory).

For more general discussions about cases involving conflicts between antidiscrimination laws and the First Amendment, see David E. Bernstein, "Antidiscrimination Laws and the First Amendment," 66 *Missouri Law Review* 83 (2001) (supporting the recent Supreme Court ruling in *Boy Scouts of America v. Dale* that for the first time privileged the First Amendment over an antidiscrimination law).

4. A regrettable feature of advanced capitalist societies seems to involve the use of sexualized images of women as a means of advertising products of all kinds, and particularly the sale of addictive substances such as alcohol and tobacco. Indeed, certain Communist regimes, such as Maoist China, have tried to limit this exploitive practice as a means of promoting gender equality. For example, Mao sought to improve the status of women when he took power in 1949 by prohibiting prostitution, child marriages, the use of concubines, and the sale of brides. Moreover, women and men wore shapeless gray tunics and cosmetics were effectively banned. During a tour of China in 1959, W. E. B. DuBois commented favorably on these changes: "The women of China are becoming free. . . . They are not dressed simply for sex indulgence or beauty parades. . . . [T]hey are strong and healthy and beautiful not simply of leg and false bosom, but of brain, brawn and rich emotion." David Levering Lewis, ed., *W. E. B. DuBois: A Reader* 435 (New York: Henry Holt, 1995).

Yet, as China has moved in the direction of a market economy, the highly sexualized use of women in advertising has proliferated, which raises issues of exploitation that are in some fundamental ways different from racial subordination. Pornography and bride selling have reemerged, and while the grinding poverty that led to mass starvation in China at about the time of DuBois's visit is giving way to growing prosperity—a trend reflected in substantial recent health improvements for women—the economic gains of men are far outstripping those of women. As one article noted:

While some discrimination . . . existed even during the Maoist era, women in those days were not regarded as sex objects—because femininity was essentially banned. Now, the return of short skirts and the rise of the advertising industry have nurtured a wolf-whistle culture.

In many cases, the new emphasis on economic efficiency and making money has also made women less desirable as employees. Employers say women run home early to look after the children or take days off to take children to the doctor. Moreover, employers complain that generous maternity benefits make women more costly as workers: after giving birth, Chinese women receive 90 days to one year of leave at full or partial salary.

Sheryl WuDunn, "With Focus on Profits, China Revives Bias against Women," *New York Times* A1 (July 28, 1992).

Does the experience in China suggest that true sexual equality can be generated only through massive governmental restrictions on personal freedom? Do such restrictions inevitably impair the health and material wealth of the population, as they did in China and Eastern Europe?

5. Refusing to make Title VII a "general civility code," the Supreme Court in *Oncale* held that "male-on-male horseplay or intersexual flirtation" does not constitute severe or pervasive behavior. As to what constitutes innocuous sexual behaviors at work, the Court stated, "Common sense, and an appropriate sensitivity to social context, will enable courts and juries to distinguish between simple teasing or roughhousing among members of the same-sex, and conduct which a reasonable person in a plaintiff's position would find severely hostile or abusive." *Oncale*, 523 U.S. at 82. But does this mean that in blue-collar workplaces where there is more rough horseplay in general, workers should be less protected because the work climate is already infused with sexual innuendos?

Is the Supreme Court's common-sense approach problematic in light of the emerging empirical studies on how men and women perceive and label sexual harassment? According to these studies, women are much more likely to find social-sexual behavior offensive and harassing than men. Studies also conclude that many men who sexually harass are not aware that their actions are inappropriate. Fritz Strack, "Attractiveness of the Underling: An Automatic Power? Sex Association and Its Consequences for Sexual Harassment and Aggression," 68 *Journal of Personality and Social Psychology* 768 (1995).

Consider Susan Estrich's radical and controversial solution to the problem of sexual harassment at work:

> As things stand now, we protect the right of a few to have 'consensual' sex in the workplace (a right most women, according to studies, do not even want), at the cost of exposing the overwhelming majority to oppression and indignity at work. Is the benefit to the few so great as to outweigh the costs to so many more? I think not. For my part, I would have no objection to rules which prohibit men and women from sexual relations in the workplace, at least between those who worked directly for the other.

Estrich, "Sex at Work," 43 *Stanford Law Review* 813, 860 (1991).

6. As discussed above, Anita Bernstein's respectful person standard is only one of the many alternatives proposed by scholars who wish to do away with the reasonable person standard. Gillian Hadfield's rational women standard is an interesting alternative. It purportedly moves away from troubling normative judgments about what harassment is offensive enough

to constitute discrimination, and focuses on the economic impact of sexual harassment on women. According to this standard, "sex-based harassment is defined as sex-based, non-job related workplace conduct that would lead a rational woman to alter her workplace behavior—such as by refusing overtime, projects, or travel that will put her in contact with a harasser, requesting a transfer, or quitting—if she could do so at little or no cost to her." Hadfield, "Rational Women: A Test for Sex–Based Harassment," 83 *California Law Review* 1151, 1157 (1995). Thus a fact finder applying Hadfield's standard would simply ask, would a hypothetical rational woman alter her workplace behavior to her detriment in order to eliminate the risk of conduct in question if she could do so costlessly? If so, sexual harassment has occurred.

There are, however, at least two problems with this standard. First, as Hadfield claims, "the test uncovers the merest hint of discrimination in women's employment decision-making by identifying conduct that introduces a factor into women's employment decisions that is absent from men's employment decisions." Hadfield at 1180. While Hadfield's test is designed to provide corrective remedies for even the slightest unequal treatment at work, the courts have often pointed out that hostile environment sexual harassment law prohibits only "severe or pervasive" conduct, not any and all conduct that distorts women's employment behavior. Second, despite Hadfield's claims to the contrary, it is not clear how this standard will avoid troublesome normative judgments any more than the reasonable person standard. In order to apply the rational women standard, a fact finder must imagine a hypothetical rational woman and how she would make certain employment decisions; this is a process that will be inevitably infused with that particular fact finder's normative evaluations about whether certain sexual conduct at work should result in economic costs to the woman.

7. Employer liability is a crucial issue in sexual harassment cases. According to a recent survey study of federal court decisions on sexual harassment between 1986 and 1995, employer liability was one of the three most commonly cited reasons by courts for finding against the plaintiff. Ann Juliano and Stewart J. Schwab, "The Sweep of Sexual Harassment Cases," 86 *Cornell Law Review* 548 (2001). In the aftermath of *Meritor*, lower courts uniformly agreed that employers were strictly liable for the conduct of supervisors in *quid pro quo* cases. In hostile environment cases, however, lower courts have applied widely varying rules. In 1998, the Supreme Court addressed this confusion, holding that employers were vicariously liable for the conduct of supervisors even if there was no "tangible employment action" against the employee. However, the Court created a new affirmative defense in those cases, in which the employer must show that it had "exercised reasonable care to prevent and correct promptly any sexually harassing behavior," and that the plaintiff had "unreasonably failed to take advantage of any preventive or corrective opportunities provided by the employer." *Faragher v. City of Boca Raton*, 524 U.S. 775 (1998); *Burlington Industries, Inc. v. Ellerth*, 524 U.S. 742 (1998).

According to some commentators, this affirmative defense creates perverse incentives for employers. That is, "employers attempting to limit their liability should exercise reasonable care, but not *too much* care because employers can be punished when employees feel comfortable enough to use the procedures." David Sherwyn, Michael Heise, and Zev J. Eigen, "Don't Train Your Employers and Cancel Your '1–800' Harassment Line: An Empirical Examination and Correction of the Flaws in the Affirmative Defense to Sexual Harassment Charges," 69 *Fordham Law Review* 1265, 1294 (2001). Another commentator has noted that employers face another dilemma in attempting to take advantage of this affirmative defense: Employers must act promptly to eliminate sexually hostile environment, but the consequences of acting too promptly or firmly may very well expose them to lawsuits by the accused *harassers*. Estelle D. Franklin, "Maneuvering through the Labyrinth: The Employers' Paradox in Responding to Hostile Environment Sexual Harassment," 4 *Fordham Law Review* 1517 (1999).

8. Studies have shown that the majority of victims of harassment at work do not report it due to a fear of reprisal or loss of privacy. According to one study, reporting may worsen the harassed individual's job, psychological, and health outcomes. Some studies have found that reporting mechanisms are structurally male-biased, further preventing women from reporting harassing conduct. Louise F. Fitzgerald, "The (Un)reasonableness of Reporting: Antecedents and Consequences of Reporting Sexual Harassment," 87 *Journal of Applied Psychology* 230 (2002). Given these findings, is it fair to require harassment victims to report sexually harassing incidents before courts will recognize their claims of hostile environment harassment?

According to Juliano and Schwab, who studied 650 federal court opinions before the Supreme Court created the affirmative defense discussed above, two critical factors for successful cases were: (1) that the victims complained within the organization; and (2) that there was no formal mechanism to deal with sexual harassment issues. Thus these authors predict that the Supreme Court's new affirmative defense will not significantly change the plaintiff success rate. Juliano and Schwab at 592.

9. Under *Faragher* and *Ellerth*, the affirmative defense is available only in cases in which there is no tangible job detriment. The underlying assumption of the Court appears to be that employers are much more likely to be on notice when tangible job detriment is involved, justifying the imposition of strict liability with no affirmative defenses. However, in reality, employers may be more likely to be alerted to openly and persistently harassing conduct that creates a hostile general working environment, rather than *quid pro quo* cases in which a supervisor makes personal and private advances to an employee for illicit sexual favors.

10. Some courts acknowledge claims of same-sex harassment if the harasser is a homosexual under the theory that the harassment occurred because of sexual attraction, and the "but for . . . victim's sex" element is satisfied. Most courts, on the other hand, deny relief in such cases, holding that a homosexual worker who had been harassed because of his sexual orientation is not discriminated because of his sex. Under the "but for" reasoning often employed by courts, however, one could argue that the harassment would not have occurred if the homosexual male worker had

been female, since in that case her sexual attraction to men would not have been stigmatizing. Moreover, as one commentator points out, an allegation of antimiscegenation discrimination by an employer can state an actionable Title VII claim under the theory that "the plaintiff was discriminated against on the basis of his race because his race was different from the race of the people he associated with." In much the same way then, courts should find that homosexual plaintiffs who had been harassed because he expressed his sexual desire for someone of the "wrong sex" should have an actionable claim under Title VII. E. Gary Spitko, "He Said, He Said: Same-Sex Harassment Under Title VII and the 'Reasonable Heterosexist' Standard," 18 *Berkeley Journal of Employment & Labor Law* 56 (1997). Are these arguments convincing?

11.   In the absence of state antidiscrimination law that explicitly bars employment discrimination based on sexual orientation, homosexual workers who had been sexually harassed have no recourse in many jurisdictions. Do you think some courts are partly animated by an implicit recognition of this reality when they find that harassment due to sexual orientation falls within Title VII? If so, are they engaging in judicial lawmaking, especially given that Congress has refused to prohibit discrimination based on sexual orientation on numerous occasions? Consider this statement made by Justice Scalia in *Oncale*: "As some courts have observed, male-on-male sexual harassment in the workplace was assuredly not the principal evil Congress was concerned with when it enacted Title VII. But statutory prohibitions often go beyond the principal evil to cover reasonably comparable evils, and it is ultimately the provisions of our laws rather than the principal concerns of our legislators by which we are governed." *Oncale* at 523 U.S. at 79.

12.   Bisexual harassment or "equal opportunity" harassment is another sexual harassment claim that does not fit comfortably into the traditional male-female harassment paradigm. Under the formal equality principle, if a bisexual supervisor sexually harasses both male and female workers, no one is being treated differently, and thus no discrimination has occurred within the meaning of Title VII. Does this mean that an employer can escape liability by displaying posters of naked men if he fears that posters of naked women will expose him to liability? Should harassing conduct cease to be legally actionable if both men and women are being subjected to it? In *Vinson v. Taylor*, 760 F.2d 1330, 1333 n. 7 (D.C.Cir.1985), Judge Bork wrote in his dissent: "Had Congress been aiming at sexual harassment, it seems unlikely that a woman would be protected from unwelcome heterosexual or lesbian advances but left unprotected when a bisexual attacks. That bizarre result suggests that Congress was not thinking of individual harassment at all but of discrimination in conditions of employment because of gender."

13.   There are a number of interesting evidentiary problems that arise in sexual harassment cases, which have their parallels in rape cases. For example, should the defendant be allowed to introduce plaintiff's prior consensual sexual relationship with the defendant or her past sexual history in the process of determining whether the conduct in question was welcome? Should the fact finder be allowed to consider the plaintiff's dress and use of sexually oriented language in determining the unwelcomeness of the alleged

sexually harassing conduct? Some defendants try to introduce evidence of past sexual abuse or other psychological problems in the plaintiff's medical history in order to show that the sexual harassment was not the main cause of the plaintiff's emotional distress. Should the defendant be allowed to introduce this evidence? Consider the following findings of a recent empirical study focusing on the question of whether a history of childhood sexual abuse makes a woman more vulnerable to sexual harassment in adult life: "there are no scientific grounds for claiming that women with a history of sexual abuse are per se any more reactive to sexual material than other women. Despite being directly and repeatedly exposed to escalating examples of sexually suggestive, sexually offensive, and sexually aggressive material, the abuse victims in this sample had reactions that were virtually identical to the nonabused women." Louise F. Fitzgerald, et al., "Junk Logic: The Abuse Defense in Sexual Harassment Litigation," 5 *Psychology, Public Policy, and Law* 730, 742 (1999).

15

Alternative Proposals for Creating Sexual Equality in the Workplace

This book has focused on the two labor market interventions that have been widely advocated as remedies for the problem of race and sex discrimination—an antidiscrimination law, including both its disparate treatment and disparate impact components, and an affirmative action program in employment. We saw in Chapter 7 Robert Cooter's suggestion of using market incentives to encourage the hiring of certain workers—a policy that could be implemented on behalf of blacks or women with equal ease, but this approach has yet to be adopted. Because of the unique issues that confront women in the workplace and the strong sex differentiation that is found there, some have argued that additional measures to combat sex discrimination are needed.

For example, the clustering of women in low-paying occupations, such as clerical work, teaching, and nursing, has important implications when trying to craft a public policy that can narrow the male-female wage differential. The considerable degree of sex segregation by occupation undermines the ability of the Equal Pay Act to elevate women's wages, because it applies only to wage differences that exist between men and women in the *same* job at the same firm. Indeed, as Sidney Webb noted in 1891, the problem with this limited notion of equal pay is "the impossibility of discovering any but a very few instances in which men and women do precisely similar work, in the same place and at the same epoch." (Quoted by Claudia Goldin, *Understanding the Gender Gap* (New York: Oxford University Press, 1990).) Strict enforcement of sex discrimination law can open up opportunities in high-paying occupations, but for women in their forties and fifties, the prospect of retraining and reeducating to pursue such opportunities may be unrealistic or impossible. Given this reality, some scholars have looked for an alternative method to enhance the welfare of women.

The policy prescription that has been advanced as a means to elevate the income of a large number of women workers quickly is the adoption of a requirement that employers pay employees in female-dominated occupations a wage that is equal to that paid to workers in higher paid male-dominated jobs of "comparable worth." Mark Killingsworth provides an excellent analysis of the difficult issues that have to be confronted in trying to implement a wage policy that disregards the full array of supply and demand conditions that influence market-determined wages, and shows that, even in a world without discrimination, there is no reason to believe that occupations that require comparable skills will pay similar wages. A policy of comparable worth is also potentially problematic because it would encourage or reinforce women's tendencies to gravitate toward traditionally female occupations. Killingsworth suggests that antitrust enforcement might be a more effective tool to address the problem of low wages in some fields in which women are clustered.

Samuel Issacharoff and Elyse Rosenblum are interested in devising a governmental policy that not only will provide women with the *opportunity* to achieve career-wage profiles that are comparable to those of men, but will also increase women's attainment of higher paid employment more effectively than a mere removal of discriminatory bars to such employment. Thus, they reject the current antidiscrimination model as the best way to deal with the predictable career interruptions caused by pregnancy. They also reject the efficacy of the Family and Medical Leave Act of 1993, which is based on what they call the "individual free choice model," rather than the antidiscrimination model. The solution that Issacharoff and Rosenblum offer is an insurance compensation scheme that they argue will better protect the ability of women to continue their career development. In so doing, Issacharoff and Rosenblum side with the branch of feminism that holds that to promote sexual equality, one must recognize and accommodate the sex-based biological differences that adversely impact working women.

The Economics of Comparable Worth: Analytical, Empirical, and Policy Questions*
MARK R. KILLINGSWORTH

... Many discussions of comparable worth provide a reasonably clear statement of the general nature of the standards that would be used to

---

* Excerpts from Mark R. Killingsworth, "The Economics of Comparable Worth: Analytical, Empirical, and Policy Questions," in Heidi I. Hartmann, ed., *Comparable*

determine comparability: two jobs would be deemed comparable if they are found to require the same skill, effort, and responsibility and to involve the same working conditions. For example, to gauge skill requirements one might analyze the educational attainment and training of the persons in the two jobs in question; likewise, one might use formal job evaluations to derive measures of the effort and responsibility requirements and working conditions of the two jobs. The worth of any given job would then be computed as a weighted sum of the scores it receives for its working conditions and its skill, effort, and responsibility requirements. Two jobs would be deemed comparable if one job's worth, calculated in the manner just described, is the same as (or within a few points of) the other job's worth.

In a superficial sense, the job evaluations that would be used in determining the worth of different jobs would therefore be similar to those currently used by employers. However, there is one crucial difference between the kind of job evaluation that would be used with comparable worth policies and the kind of job evaluation typically used by employers: the latter are typically based explicitly on market considerations. For example, commercial job evaluation firms often benchmark wages for key jobs on the basis of labor market surveys and use procedures such as regression analysis of existing salary structures to determine the weights that the marketplace itself gives to the different factors considered. In contrast, some analysts of comparable worth question such a market-oriented approach on the grounds that the wage relationships that currently exist are likely to be distorted by discrimination. Some comparable worth proponents advocate the use of bias-free job evaluations, i.e., ones that are derived independently of the existing wage structure and in which the weights given to the different factors considered (skill, effort, responsibility, and working conditions) would be determined on an a priori—or to put it less charitably, ad hoc—basis.

· · ·

Discussions of comparable worth usually do not specify clearly which jobs would be covered under a comparable worth requirement. In principle, the notion of comparable worth might be applied to literally all jobs, in which case coverage would be universal. In practice, however, most discussions of comparable worth present it as a remedy for sex discrimination. This suggests a simpler, partial rule: two jobs that are found to be comparable (in the sense defined above) would be required to pay the same wage only if women are a greater proportion of the workers in the low-paying job than in the high-paying job.

· · ·

One coverage question, however, does have an explicit answer. Contrary to the complaints of many critics who have charged that comparable worth would amount to government wage fixing on a national basis, most advocates of comparable worth have emphasized that comparable worth would be implemented on an employer-by-employer (or even an establishment-by-establishment) basis. Thus, although comparable worth might require a given employer to pay tool mechanics and secretaries the same wage (so long as the two jobs were found to be comparable at the firm in question), it would not establish a uniform national wage for secretaries (or tool mechanics) and would not necessarily require even that any other employer pay identical wages to tool mechanics and secretaries. That would depend on whether, at any other such firm, the jobs of tool mechanic and secretary were found to be comparable.

· · ·

The Conceptual Basis of Comparable Worth: An Economic Analysis

From the standpoint of economic analysis, the concept of comparable worth has two fundamental flaws. First, contrary to what many of its proponents assume, there is nothing inherently discriminatory in *unequal* pay for jobs of "comparable worth," and there is no reason why a nondiscriminatory labor market would necessarily entail *equal* pay for jobs of "comparable worth." Second, although proponents of comparable worth are correct in implicating employer discrimination as an important demand-side factor responsible for male-female pay differentials, they typically pay insufficient attention to the role of employee choices, which is an important supply-side factor that also contributes to such pay differentials.

Should Comparable Worth Necessarily Mean Equal Pay?

The first difficulty with comparable worth is its central premise: that unequal pay for jobs deemed to be of comparable worth is inherently discriminatory or, equivalently, that jobs deemed to be of comparable worth should receive the same wage. Unfortunately, this notion betrays a fundamental misunderstanding of the way in which labor markets (even nondiscriminatory ones) operate and of how employer discrimination harms women. *Unequal pay for jobs of comparable worth is not inherently discriminatory. Even in a sex-neutral labor market*—one in which sex is entirely irrelevant to market outcomes—*there is no reason why individuals in jobs of comparable worth should necessarily receive the same wage.*

The basic reason for this is simple. Individual tastes and preferences differ; comparability is in the eye of the beholder. Suppose that a given individual considers jobs A and B to be equally acceptable—i.e., would have no preference for one over the other if both jobs paid the same wage. Is there any reason to suppose that all other individuals would feel the same way? Would it be at all surprising if, at given wages, at least some individuals preferred A to B, while at the same time still other persons preferred B to A? Obviously not. Thus, even if the two jobs are found to be comparable according to a formal job evaluation scheme, there is no reason to suppose that all individuals will in fact view them as comparable. There is likewise no reason to suppose that supplies and demands for the two jobs would be equal if the two jobs paid the same wage. Hence, there is no reason to suppose that jobs that are comparable in the eyes of a given individual or job evaluation firm would in fact pay the same wage—even in a sex-neutral labor market.

. . .

To many this point will be obvious. Of course, individual tastes and preferences differ, so perhaps some illustration may be worthwhile. Following is one example: an employer asks us to evaluate the comparability of the jobs of Spanish–English translator and French–English translator. A priori, it would seem difficult to argue that either of these two jobs requires more skill, effort, or responsibility than the other, and it would be surprising if, at a given firm, the working conditions for the two jobs were appreciably different. Presumably, then, most job evaluation schemes would conclude that these two jobs are comparable in terms of their working conditions and skill, effort, and responsibility requirements; and so, presumably, a comparable worth policy would require an employer to pay the same wage to persons in each of the two jobs.

But would pay for these two jobs necessarily be equal, even in a sex-neutral labor market? Perhaps, but now suppose we learn that the employer in question is located in Miami. Would it be reasonable to expect that Spanish–English translators in Miami would get the same pay as French–English translators in Miami? Almost certainly not. Would it even be possible to predict which job would receive the higher wage? Again, almost certainly not. True, one would expect that in Miami the supply of qualified Spanish–English translators would be greater than the supply of qualified French–English translators. Other things being equal, that would mean that the latter job would pay more than the former. However, other things are not necessarily equal, even in a sex-neutral labor market. In particular, Miami's demand for Spanish–English translators might well be greater than its demand for French–English translators. Other things being equal, that would mean that the latter job would pay less than the former.

As this example indicates, even in a labor market in which sex is irrelevant, wages are determined by market supplies and demands rather than by comparability—which may have little or nothing to do with wage determination. The reason is that supplies and demands summarize the tastes and preferences of all individuals, whereas comparability merely indicates the tastes and preferences of one individual or of a single entity (e.g., a job evaluation firm).

. . .

Economic Consequences of Comparable Worth and Other Remedies for Discrimination

Whatever the merits or defects of the conceptual basis for comparable worth, to many the most important question about comparable worth has to do with whether it would be a suitable remedy for discrimination. This section compares comparable worth and other antidiscrimination measures and evaluates the consequences of each.

. . . The conventional approach to employer discrimination as such is to break down discriminatory barriers that keep women out of high-paid jobs and to require equal pay for equal work. Eventually such measures will completely counteract the effects of employer discrimination: women's relative representation in high-paying jobs will rise, and sex differentials within the same job will be erased. However, the full impact of such measures may not be felt for some time to come.

Moreover, in this view, conventional antidiscrimination measures cannot realistically be expected to do much for older cohorts of women workers; these women entered low-paying jobs some years ago (either because societal discrimination induced them to choose such jobs or because employer discrimination prevented them from entering other jobs), and they are now locked in. Providing access to high-paying jobs can do little for such women; they do not have the training required for such jobs (and at midcareer it usually makes little sense to get such training), and now, if only because of their initial socialization and the development of habits over time, such women might not even want to be in other jobs, despite the higher pay. A policy of requiring wage increases for predominantly female, low-paying jobs would provide immediate benefits for such women—who, in this view, have little to gain from conventional antidiscrimination measures.

Unfortunately, requiring wage increases for predominantly female low-paying jobs is likely to have serious, albeit unintended, adverse side effects, not merely for women as a whole but for older cohorts of women workers in particular.

To see why, [consider a] simple two-job economy [in which women predominate in the low-wage job, A, and men predominate in the high-wage job, B].

. . . [I]ncreasing the A wage in accordance with a modified comparable worth policy will obviously raise the A wage and reduce the differential between the A wage and the B wage (of either men or women). However, the policy will also have some unfortunate side effects:

1. The number of workers in job A will fall and unemployment of workers formerly in job A will rise.

2. Wages for both men and women in job B will fall.

3. The wage differential between men and women in job B will widen.

4. Employment and output will fall and consumer prices will rise.

Thus, in the short run, some women (and men) workers in job A will gain, but everyone else—all men and all women in job B and all other women (and men) in job A—will lose. The notion that raising wages in low-paid, predominantly female jobs will help older cohorts of women who are locked into those jobs is at best half true: such a policy will certainly benefit some of these women but, by reducing the total demand for such jobs, will necessarily harm the rest of them.

Now consider the effects of increasing the wage in job A in the long run, i.e., allow for the fact that, given sufficient time, supplies of labor to the two jobs will adjust to the changed wages prevailing for those jobs. As in the short-run case, the comparable worth policy will raise the A wage both absolutely and relatively to the B wage (of men or women). Again, then, the comparable worth policy raises wages in the low-wage, predominantly female jobs and narrows the pay gap between low-wage and high-wage jobs.

However, in the long run as in the short-run, the policy of raising pay for job A will also have several adverse side effects. First, as in the short-run case, firms' demands for workers for job A will fall as the A wage rises. This will reduce employment of workers in job A, leading to unemployment for some individuals who would otherwise be in job A. (Since women are overrepresented in job A, this unemployment will hit women harder than men.) Second, the increase in the A wage relative to the wage for both men and women in job B attracts workers toward job A and away from job B. This reduces employment of both men and women in job B. In the absence of any restraint on the A wage, this increase in the supply of labor to job A would drive the A wage back to its original level. However, the comparable worth policy prevents the A wage from falling; instead, the increased supply to job A turns into more unemployment. Finally, since total employment in job A declines and employment of both men and women in job B also declines, production drops. The drop in production results in an increase in the price level.

Are these predictions about the effects of comparable worth policies supported by any empirical evidence?

The United States has not implemented comparable worth strategies to any considerable extent, but Australia's experience with its policy of enforcing equal pay for work of equal value is illuminating. Under the policy, which began in 1972, Australia's federal and state wage tribunals have set the same rate of pay (regardless of the gender of the majority of incumbents) for all jobs judged to be comparable in terms of skill, effort, responsibility, and working conditions. The tribunals fix minimum rates (not actual levels) of pay and have considerable latitude in determining comparability. These potential loopholes notwithstanding, Australia's comparable worth policy apparently had a substantial effect on the aggregate female:male earnings ratio: that ratio (for full-time nonmanagerial adult workers in the private sector) rose from .607 in 1971 to .766 in 1977.

For purposes of this discussion, however, the most interesting aspect of Australia's experience is that the policy's side effects appear to have been generally adverse. Gregory and Duncan found that increases in women's wages attributable to the policy reduced the rate of growth of female employment (below the rate that would otherwise have prevailed), relative to the rate of growth of men's employment, in (1) manufacturing, (2) services, and (3) overall (i.e., in all industries combined). Comparable worth had a negligible effect on the relative employment growth rate of women only in the public authority and community services sector. Their overall estimates imply that, as of 1977, the cumulative effects of the policy served to reduce the rate of growth of women's employment, relative to that of men, by almost one-third....

Gregory and Duncan also analyzed the impact of the policy on female joblessness. Their estimates imply that the policy's cumulative impact as of 1977 was an increase in the female unemployment rate of about 0.5 of a percentage point. (The actual female unemployment rate in August 1976 was 6.2 percent.)

In sum, the Gregory and Duncan study indicates that Australia's "equal pay for work of equal value" policy adversely affected both the rate of relative employment growth for women and the female unemployment rate, as implied by the analysis in this section.

The Gregory and Duncan findings that Australia's comparable worth policy had no appreciable effect on women's relative employment in the public authority and community service sector highlight two potential exceptions to the general propositions presented above: the government sector and nursing.

Much of the impetus for comparable worth seems to have come from public-sector employees, notably the American Federation of State, County, and Municipal Employees (AFSCME). This may well be no accident. In contrast with the private sector, the government sector will have little or no difficulty (at least in the short run) in maintaining the demand for its "output" at existing levels, despite policy-induced increases in its labor costs. To cover the increased labor costs, government can simply compel the rest of the economy to pay higher taxes, keeping its real revenues unchanged. (The private sector will try to cover policy-induced increases in labor costs by raising its prices, but it cannot compel the rest of the economy to go on purchasing the same amount of its output at the higher prices.)

. . .

Antitrust laws and the problem of employer cartels.... Many comparable worth advocates point to nursing as a particularly dramatic example of the failure of wages to respond to supply and demand. Although wages in nursing are said to be low, hospitals and other employers of nurses are said to suffer from severe shortages. Yet these shortages are alleged not to have led to wage increases for nurses; about all that has happened is a step-up in recruiting efforts, either of foreign nurses or via one-time-only inducements (a year's country club membership, a few months' paid rent, and so on) for first-time domestic recruits. Unfortunately, most comparable worth advocates have simply pointed out the seeming paradox inherent in situations of this kind without asking how and why such situations could have arisen or what can be done about them.

The paradox begins to make sense, however, once one considers the possibility that markets for some kinds of predominantly female jobs (e.g., nursing) have been cartelized—that, for example, hospitals and other large employers of nurses in major metropolitan areas have agreed not to compete with each other by offering higher wages to attract nurses. In effect, such cartelization amounts to a set of informal or formal areawide wage-fixing agreements. If this accurately describes the labor market for nurses, then it explains not only the alleged low pay of nurses, but also the alleged shortages of nurses, the failure of nurses' wages to rise, and the almost exclusive reliance on nonwage forms of competition for new recruits. With wages held at an artificially low level, it is not surprising that individual hospitals would like more nurses than they are able to attract (i.e., face shortages); that individual hospitals do not raise pay in an attempt to attract more nurses; or that competition in the nursing market takes the form of foreign recruitment, one-time-only sign-up bonuses, and so forth, rather than higher wages—just as competition in air travel centered on nonprice matters (seating, food, etc.), when airfares were regulated.

Is there any evidence (as opposed to mere conjecture) that markets for nurses and other predominantly female jobs have in fact been cartelized? The nursing labor market is literally a textbook example of a cartelized (or, in economic jargon, "monopsonized") labor market. According to one witness at recent congressional hearings, hospital administrators in Denver have colluded to fix wages. Similarly, another witness testified that employers of clerical workers in cities such as Boston and San Francisco have formed organizations, euphemistically known as consortia or study groups, whose true purpose is to engage in wage fixing in much the same way that producer cartels engage in collusive price fixing.

To the extent that labor markets are indeed cartelized—and I should emphasize that this is something about which, in general, there is very little hard evidence—then forcing wage increases in such markets need not have any adverse impact on employment. However, none of this has anything to do with whether the jobs in question are comparable to predominantly male jobs, be they pharmacist, tree trimmer, or parking lot attendant. . . .

What the possibility of labor market wage fixing—cartelization—does suggest is the advisability of a remedy that is quite different from both conventional antidiscrimination measures and comparable worth: enforcement and, if need be, amendment of the antitrust laws to ensure that employers cannot collude to depress wages.

Women and the Workplace: Accommodating the Demands of Pregnancy*

SAMUEL ISSACHAROFF AND ELYSE ROSENBLUM

The Travails of Working Women and Maternity

. . .

Wages and Continuous Workplace Participation

. . .

Beginning in the 1970s, economists began to apply econometric tools to National Longitudinal Surveys data of the demographic characteristics of the population. . . . [T]he initial studies indicated quite strongly that "[d]ifferences in work history patterns accounted for a considerable portion of the wage gaps between white men and white and black women, largely because women acquired less tenure, completed less training, and were more likely to work part time."

. . .

In light of the strong effects that childbearing has on women's participation in the work force, it would be simply astounding if there were no corresponding effect on the experience of women in the labor market during early career stages. As Professor McCaffery suggested,

> It is almost certain that the firm will guess that women, and especially married women, will have an average tenure with the firm shorter than that of men. The reason, of course, is that firms believe that these women will have children and leave the work force, at least temporarily.

The expectation of shorter female job tenure is reflected in the behavior of women who are in the work force and those who are entering it. It is also reflected in the actions taken by firms in anticipation of sex-differentiated participation patterns in the work force. Women may logically respond to the expectation of leaving the work force by reducing their investment in training or pre-work force education, what economists term human capital formation. Firms may similarly face incentives to track women away from certain career ladders:

> If there are large personnel investment costs associated with job turnover, an employer attempting to earn a normal rate of return on a fixed personnel investment is not inclined to pay women the same wage as is paid to equally productive men who are expected to remain on their jobs longer.

The presumption that women are more likely to leave employment creates an incentive for a form of "statistical discrimination" among employers who have neither the resources nor the wherewithal to determine which women are likely to quit and which are likely to stay. This form of statistical discrimination falls most heavily on those women who have a genuine commitment to the work force.... Because of the difficulty of "signaling" for women who intend to stay in the work force, all women of childbearing age will be presumed to be at high risk for early departure from the workplace—particularly since close to ninety percent of all women do conceive at some point in their lives.

. . .

It is therefore entirely predictable that interruption of work force participation would have adverse effects on expected earnings of working women, as well as on their overall career trajectory. While this propensity for career interruption has not been shown to account for the entire wage disparity between working men and women, some estimates attribute at least half the disparity in wages to different patterns of participation. If the objective of a regulatory intervention into the employment market is to allow women the opportunity for career-wage profiles comparable to those of men, the antidiscrimination model is inherently insufficient. Rather, the predictable mid-career interruptions caused by pregnancy must be accommodated under a regulatory scheme aimed at protecting the ability of women to continue their career work force participation through the predictable periods of fertility.

. . .

Pregnancy and Antidiscrimination Law

. . .

Congress's initial consideration of pregnancy and female work force participation treated the issue of sex-based differences purely as a simple matter of invidious or volitional discrimination. The Pregnancy Discrimination Act [PDA], passed in 1978, amended Title VII of the Civil Rights Act of 1964 to make plain that discrimination based on pregnancy was included under the general prohibition against sex discrimination in the workplace....

Congress enacted the PDA in response to the Supreme Court's decision in *General Electric Co. v. Gilbert.* In *Gilbert,* the Court held that the exclusion of pregnancy and related conditions from otherwise comprehensive disability insurance plans did not constitute sex discrimination in violation of Title VII. Justice Rehnquist reasoned that since pregnancy is not a condition that affects all women, the exclusion of pregnancy from the insurance plan did not constitute gender discrimination. The majority explained that:

> As there is no proof that the package is in fact worth more to men than to women, it is impossible to find any gender-based discriminatory effect in this scheme simply because women disabled as a result of pregnancy do not receive benefits; that is to say, gender-based discrimination does not result simply because an employer's disability-benefits plan is less than all-inclusive. For all that appears, pregnancy-related disabilities constitute an *additional* risk, unique to women, and the failure to compensate them for this risk does not destroy the presumed parity of the benefits....

The exact converse of Justice Rehnquist's reasoning in *Gilbert* has held true. Justice Stevens's dissent identified the strained reasoning of the majority opinion: "[b]y definition, such a rule discriminates on account of sex; for it is the capacity to become pregnant which primarily differentiates the female from the male." As Justice Stevens properly argued, it is precisely because pregnancy is a condition unique to women that the exclusion of pregnancy from disability coverage is a sex-based classification that should trigger the protections of Title VII.

Congress agreed with the dissent and enacted the PDA.... The PDA amended the definition of sex discrimination in Title VII to include discrimination based on pregnancy, childbirth, and related medical conditions. The PDA goes on to require the same treatment of similarly situated pregnant and non-pregnant persons.

The congressional debate and committee reports confirm that the intent of Congress was to prevent discrimination on the basis of pregnancy by forbidding employers from treating pregnant employees differently from other, similarly situated, ones. Representative Hawkins, one of the initial sponsors of the PDA in the House, said the Act attempts to "insur[e] the equal treatment of men and women in the work-place, especially with respect to fringe benefit programs." The mandate of equal treatment was coupled with repeated disclaimers that the bill did not require employers to instigate any special benefit programs for pregnancy; rather, the bill simply required pregnancy to be treated the same as any other disability.... This is consistent with Congress's desire to overturn *Gilbert,* which upheld the exclusion of pregnancy from a general package of disability benefits. Neither *Gilbert* nor its congressional repudiation through the PDA addressed the broader issue of the affirmative need for disability benefits for pregnancy, even in the absence of generally available employee leave.

The Supreme Court took its first look at whether the PDA permits special treatment of pregnancy in *California Federal Savings & Loan Ass'n v. Guerra*. In *Guerra*, the Court addressed a challenge from businesses and business associations to a California state statute requiring employers to provide unpaid leave and reinstatement to pregnant employees. *Guerra* exposed the heart of the problem with the PDA because the California statute singled out pregnancy as the basis for an express classification, yet did so in order to grant preferential treatment to pregnant employees.

. . .

The heart of the majority opinion is the interpretation of equality to mean equal opportunity in the workplace. Under the majority's view, the California preferential treatment law enabled women to have children and return to work, thus putting them on equal footing with men who routinely have children and remain in the workplace. By reading the PDA to encompass equality in the sense of equal opportunity, as opposed to equal treatment, [the Court concluded] that the PDA was " 'a floor beneath which pregnancy disability benefits may not drop—not a ceiling above which they may not rise.' " Thus, the majority held that the PDA permitted the accommodation of pregnancy.

. . .

Following *Guerra*, one might have expected that the Supreme Court would continue to interpret the PDA in a way that would permit special treatment of pregnancy. That expectation was not realized when the Court next confronted a special treatment policy in *UAW v. Johnson Controls, Inc.* In *Johnson Controls*, the Court struck down the employer's fetal protection policy, which prohibited women of childbearing age from having significant workplace exposure to lead, as a violation of the PDA. That the Court struck a fetal protection policy which broadly excluded women from desirable positions without any substantial documentation of the extent of the health hazard was not particularly surprising or problematic. What was surprising and somewhat problematic was that the Court relied quite heavily on the language and legislative history of the PDA to mandate unequivocal equal treatment of pregnancy. . . .

The holdings in *Johnson Controls* and *Guerra* can be reconciled if they are seen as seeking to protect the employment opportunities of working women. The facts of these cases differed significantly. The special treatment in *Guerra* was clearly beneficial to women's capacity to remain in the work force once they were employed. In contrast, the special treatment of pregnancy in the Johnson Controls policy was detrimental to women because it excluded them from certain high-paying jobs, even to the extent of removing working employees from the positions they held. While the exclusion could also be thought of as beneficial because it prevented exposure to high levels of lead, it did so at an appreciable cost to women's careers. Because the Johnson Controls policy excluded women from certain jobs, it fit more neatly within the anticipated scope of the PDA—preventing discrimination against women based on pregnancy.

. . .

The Family and Medical Leave Act

An alternative statutory model that seeks to provide actual benefits rather than simply to prohibit discrimination is found in the Family and Medical Leave Act of 1993 (FMLA). This much-heralded legislation was designed in large part to provide some accommodation to working women for the time of childbirth and recovery. The FMLA allows permanent employees to take unpaid leave for serious domestic emergencies, including not only pregnancy but also such family crises as the illness of a close family member.

Although working women were the intended primary beneficiaries, the FMLA was designed to be "non-discriminatory" in its provision of benefits; accordingly, the FMLA does not specifically focus on women. Instead, pregnancy is addressed as part of a broad pattern of leave provisions for family-related emergencies. An examination of the FMLA reveals that it does not address the particular disabilities faced by women in the work place in terms of the likely early career interruption of employment, nor does it address the costs associated with pregnancy leave.

It is therefore not surprising that the FMLA has serious limitations in providing benefits for working women. First, the FMLA covers only those firms with more than fifty employees. This limitation means that ninety-five percent of firms and more than half the work force is unaffected by the legislation. The smaller firms that are not covered by the law are the ones that are least likely to offer such benefits currently. Even among covered employers, the FMLA threatens to have adverse economic consequences among smaller firms where disproportionate numbers of women are employed. A large percentage of major companies have already adopted some or all of the benefits established by the FMLA. Among Fortune 500 corporations, an estimated eighty percent were said to provide parental leave. During the debates on the FMLA, therefore, while there was some discussion of the aggregate costs of the bill in terms of benefits offered to employees during periods of leave, much of the testimony and discussion centered on the impact of the FMLA on small businesses. Small business owners were concerned that after they paid the costs of having an employee take leave and holding a position open, the employee would not return to work. . . .

The FMLA therefore has two potentially serious adverse consequences. First, although leave is unpaid, it is still costly to the employer. The FMLA provides that the employer must continue payments of benefits during the period of leave. In addition, there are likely to be search and training costs associated with replacement of permanent employees, who likely have a high degree of knowledge of the particular work demands of a specific firm, with generally skilled temporary employees. Moreover, to the extent that the work of a firm is not routinized but depends on personal client connections or specific employee skills, temporary labor is likely to be far less efficient. As one goes higher up the professional and managerial ladder, there is also the problem that employees available on a temporary basis are not likely to be as skilled as those in permanent positions—even leaving aside firm-specific capabilities.

By assigning the costs of leave to firms, particularly smaller firms, the FMLA reintroduces an incentive to discriminate against women at the hiring stage. For example, during testimony in 1989, the House Subcommittee on Labor–Management Relations was told in no uncertain terms: "Faced with mandated parental leave, a business owner choosing between two qualified candidates—one male and one female—would be tempted to select the male. Direct and hidden costs to employers will compel them to think twice before hiring additional employees."

Second, the FMLA fails to alleviate the plight of working women facing a temporary pregnancy-occasioned departure from the work force, but who are without any means of economic support. By contrast to the European model we discuss below, the FMLA does not provide for a single penny of direct funding to women during their time away from the work force. In other words, the FMLA leaves women as the primary insurers of their own periods of unemployment occasioned by pregnancy.

· · ·

An Insurance Model for Pregnancy Leave

We now turn ... to a proposal for accommodating the specific needs of pregnancy that does not turn primarily on an antidiscrimination model, like the PDA, or on an individual free choice model, like the FMLA, both of which fail to address the specific needs of pregnancy and its associated costs. Our proposal will try to account for four concerns: 1) that some special accommodation is needed in order for women to have the choice of continuous work force participation through pregnancy; 2) that in order to secure the opportunity for continuous work force participation, women must be guaranteed the right to return to their previous employment following a limited period of pregnancy leave; 3) that working women should not be the exclusive or perhaps even the primary cost bearers of their pregnancy leaves; and 4) that risk pooling should be used to make individual firms as indifferent to gender as possible when faced with similar male and female candidates for jobs, in situations where there is a substantial risk of demands for pregnancy leave if the female applicant is hired.

These considerations point to the development of an insurance system for pregnancy leave. Here too there are several features that must be considered. First, the overriding concern is to create a system of compensation for the necessary and predictable costs of pregnancy that will limit the incentives of individual firms to engage in statistical discrimination. In other words, the cost calculus must be undertaken in a way that will achieve the objective of making firms as indifferent as possible in deciding to hire men and women of similar capabilities. Second, there is a normative belief on our part that reproduction is a societal good and therefore working women, either individually or as a group, are not the appropriate cost-bearers for what is at bottom a social and biological imperative. Put slightly differently, there is something rather disturbing in having a wealthy society maintain economically-compelled divisions between women who fully join the labor force and women who serve primarily on the reproductive front. Third, and as a direct consequence, our goal is to find a way to allow women to get over the hurdle of pregnancy, *if they so choose,* and to maintain a career or life-cycle employment profile through the period of fertility. Finally, we seek to accomplish this through an administratively simple system that will neither drain resources nor provide its own disincentive to employers hiring women.

· · ·

Our proposal has five parts, incorporating many of the central features of unemployment insurance:

1. *Uniform employer contributions based on payroll.* This feature corresponds to the central risk pooling strategy of unemployment insurance. In order to induce indifference among employers as to the hiring of comparably credentialed men and women, the costs associated with pregnancy have to be moved away from the employing firm to the greatest extent possible. Therefore employers would be obligated to contribute to such a system regardless of whether or not any specific firm employed women of childbearing age. The amounts necessary to fund a specific pregnancy benefits program should be far less than the average 2.4 percent of taxable payroll required to fund state unemployment insurance programs in 1988.

2. *Fixed term of payments to women who receive pregnancy benefits.* Insurance benefits, unlike traditional welfare payments, are for fixed terms. Unemployment insurance is set at twenty-six weeks with occasional supplemental benefits awarded by Congress. Effective in 1994, the European Community will require all member nations to provide at least sixteen weeks of paid mater-

nity leave, including two weeks off prior to the expected date of birth. Canada provides for fifteen weeks of pregnancy leave, which may be extended by one week for each week that a newborn is hospitalized. Our proposal would be for twelve weeks post-partum, a practice that seems to correspond to many maternity leave programs in place in the corporate sector, with pre-partum complications treated under normal disability programs.

3. *Payout as percent of prepartum earnings.* There is little that can be put forward as a matter of principle in setting forth pregnancy benefits. We would propose a formula based on the generous side of established unemployment insurance programs. Our proposal would be for benefits equal to two-thirds of average taxable earnings for the past twenty-six weeks of employment. The amount would be capped at $382 per week, the unemployment benefits level in Massachusetts as of 1993 and apparently the highest in the country.

4. *Minimum eligibility periods.* In the unemployment compensation system in the United States, the receipt of benefits is conditioned upon layoffs from a firm. Since the firm's experience rating is affected by layoffs, there is little risk of collusive behavior between firms and individuals desirous of receiving benefits. Moreover, since the triggering event is a layoff, there is little that an employee can do unilaterally to secure receipt of benefits. By contrast, a nonworking woman in the early stages of pregnancy, or intending to become pregnant, may use a pregnancy insurance system as a form of welfare-type subsidy simply by finding employment. In such a case, the insurance system would provide a welfare subsidy to an individual who had not contributed to the insurance pool through her employer. We therefore must concede the greater capacity for abuse of this system than of unemployment insurance in general. We are also mindful that the insurance pool is funded through payments diverted from other firm expenditures, including increased salaries to those employed. It would be inequitable to allow individuals to come into the risk pool under conditions in which they had not contributed to building the corpus of the pool, yet were certain to draw upon its resources.

In Canada, this problem was partially addressed through the rule of the "magic ten" weeks of work pre-conception, which were required from pregnant women receiving benefits. These additional weeks insured that the woman was already employed at the time of conception. . . .

5. *Partial Payment to Employers.* We save the most difficult issue for last. Pregnancy leave is fundamentally different from unemployment insurance in one critical respect: whereas unemploy-

ment insurance is designed to assist laid off workers in circumstances where the employer either temporarily or permanently does not wish to utilize the employee's labor, pregnancy is an employee-initiated separation from the worksite during a time when the employee's work is desired. In the case of a laid-off employee, the firm is not suffering any dislocation as a result of that employee receiving an alternative source of compensation. In contrast, in the case of an employee out on maternity leave, the firm suffers the costs associated either with a lack of production or with the need to pay for temporary labor. We therefore turn to a proposal to ease the dislocation costs on the firm as part of a pregnancy leave package in order to satisfy the important condition that firms be made as indifferent as possible when choosing between men and women of comparable credentials for purposes of hiring or promotion.

In order to reduce employers' disincentive to hire female employees, we propose that a portion of the pregnancy benefits be paid to the employer rather than to the employee. The purpose is to recognize that firms do incur costs associated with the absence of an employee on pregnancy leave and to adjust the payment of benefits from the normal unemployment insurance model to reflect the additional firm costs. Our proposal is that between fifteen and forty percent of the pregnancy benefits be paid to the firm to underwrite the costs of continuing benefits and securing temporary replacements. The greater the specialization of job skills, the greater the proportion of benefits that would go to the firm to reflect the presumptively greater costs of temporary replacements; the less the specialization, as with fast food employees, for example, the less would go to the firm. There are several ways of calibrating the amount of specialization required for a position, such as a ratio based on the amount of schooling and experience necessary for entry into the position. The administratively simplest mechanism would be to base the percentage going to the employer on the level of taxable income: the higher the income, the greater the percentage recaptured by the employer.

. . .

Notes and Questions

1. In a competitive market, wages are determined by both supply and demand. The policy of comparable worth tries to set wages without fully considering the influence of these market forces. In so doing, it will tend to drive up the wages in traditionally female jobs but lower the total employment in these jobs—much in the fashion of an increase in the minimum wage. Killingsworth argues that conventional antidiscrimination measures are superior to a policy of comparable worth because they will lead to steadier (albeit slower) gains in *both* female wages and employment. A recent study examining the effects of comparable worth legislation in Ontario,

Canada offers additional support for Killingsworth's doubts about this doctrine. Michael Baker and Nicole Fortin find that while Ontario's comparable worth legislation had virtually no effect on aggregate wages in female jobs or the gender wage gap in the long-run, it suppressed the wage growth for women in male jobs and men in female jobs. Baker and Fortin, "Does Comparable Worth Work in a Decentralized Labor Market?" NBER Working Paper No. W7937, October 2000. For a more favorable assessment of comparable worth, see the Littleton selection in Chapter 12.

2. While the case for comparable worth as a general approach to dealing with sex discrimination seems questionable, there is an argument that it might be an appropriate transitional policy. In Chapter 13, Posner cites evidence showing that in 1968 young white women had unrealistically low expectations of the probability that they would be working at age 35. As a result, it is not surprising that they invested less in a career than they would have had they more accurately anticipated the future. (In 1950, 13.6 percent of men and only 5.2 percent of women aged 20 to 24 were enrolled in college, but by 1980 23.7 percent of men and 21.4 percent of women in this age group were enrolled. Larry Barnett, *Legal Construct, Social Concept: A Macrosociological Perspective on Law* 58 (New York: Aldine De Gruyter, 1993).) The more realistic expectations of today's young women will undoubtedly translate into more career investment and higher earnings, but the transitional phase for women who made career choices on the erroneous belief that their economic security would come through marriage was a very difficult one.

If one assumes that sex discrimination limited the opportunities of women, who later had to fend for themselves in the workplace, one could imagine that the remedy of allowing a school teacher or secretary at age 40 to go back to school to study law or engineering is not very attractive. While using antidiscrimination law to break down barriers is clearly the preferable long-run remedy, it might offer little hope to these older women whose opportunities were foreclosed by employment discrimination that existed at the time they were making their educational and career choices. Providing a comparable worth remedy for these women might appropriately give more money to a group with strong equitable claims, and the strategy would be particularly effective to the extent that the induced disemployment effects would fall on younger women who were freer to pursue the more abundant menu of opportunities that now exist for women. (Seniority-based reductions in employment might preserve the jobs of the older women, who had the strongest equitable claims to a comparable worth remedy, although one could not be sure that the employment reductions would in fact be made in this way.) This constellation of factors might explain the increased demand for comparable worth in the late 1970s and early 1980s.

3. Note that comparable worth would attempt to eliminate wage disparities between women and men *within* the same firm. Because most of the sex differential in earnings is *between industries* and *between firms* in the same industry, however, comparable worth cannot be expected to eliminate the bulk of the wage gap. A study by George Johnson and Gary Solon in 1978 concluded that if every employer implemented comparable worth, the

then-existing earnings differential of 34 percent would have been reduced by 3 to 8 percentage points. If, as is more likely, comparable worth were applied only in the public sector and to large private firms, then the improvement would be only 2 to 3 percentage points. Johnson and Solon, "Estimates of the Direct Effects of Comparable Worth Policy," 76 *American Economic Review* 1117 (December 1986). For citations to studies suggesting a somewhat higher wage increase for women, and corresponding greater loss of female jobs, see Jane Friesen, "Alternative Economic Perspectives on the Use of Labor Market Policies to Redress the Gender Gap in Compensation," 82 *Georgetown Law Journal* 31, 64 (1993).

4. In addition to the disincentives created by the FMLA for men to take or even ask for parental leave (discussed in Chapter 11, question 3), there are widespread social norms that discourage childcare by male workers. Consider the case of Kevin Knussman, a Maryland State Trooper, whose request for state and federal mandated leaves were summarily rejected by his superiors:

> In anticipation of his daughter's birth, Knussman sought leave from work under both the federal Family and Medical Leave Act of 1993 and a Maryland law that offers thirty days paid leave to state employees serving as "primary care provider" to a newborn or newly adopted child. State officials rebuffed both requests. "Only women can breast feed the baby," the Maryland State Police (MSP) personnel chief said, and so only a woman can be an infant's primary care provider. And although Trooper Knussman applied for FMLA leave more than a year after the Act took effect and purportedly was implemented by the MSP, he was told by a supervisor there was "no way" he would be allowed more than two weeks of leave. Even after his wife suffered pregnancy complications that left her bedridden, police rejected Trooper Knussman's reapplication for family leave under Maryland's primary care law. "God decided only women can give birth," the personnel chief told a stunned Mr. Knussman. "So unless your wife is in a coma or dead, you can't be a primary care provider."

Robin R. Cockey and Deborah A. Jeon, "The Family and Medical Leave Act at Work: Getting Employers to Value Families," 4 *Virginia Journal of Social Policy & the Law* 225 (1996).

Should the law accept these deeply-entrenched gendered views about childcaring and provide specialized benefits only to women, as Issacharaoff and Rosenblum advocate, rather than trying to bring about transformations in underlying societal norms, which might prove to be futile? For example, one survey of 218 workers (conducted in 1992 and again in 1998) showed that there were no changes in gender-role attitudes about childcaring before and after the enactment of the FMLA. Rosemarie Feuerbach Twomey and Gwen E. Jones, "The Family and Medical Leave Act of 1993: A Longitudinal Study of Male and Female Perceptions," 3 *Employee Rights and Employment Policy Journal* 229 (1999).

5. There are empirical debates about the reasons for the lack of effectiveness of the FMLA. For example, one of the reasons Issacharoff and

Rosenblum cite is the inability of many workers to afford unpaid leave. Indeed, according to the 1995 report issued by the Commission on Family and Medical Leave, 63.9 percent of the surveyed employees who needed leave did not take it because they could not afford to do so. Joseph Willis, "The Family and Medical Leave Act of 1993: A Progress Report," 36 *Journal of Family Law* 95 (1997/1998). But while Issacharoff and Rosenblum argue that the costs of paying out benefits to employees on leave while also holding their positions open might be prohibitive for many small businesses, Lisa Bernstein contends that the empirical evidence concerning the FMLA shows that "Since the implementation of family and medical leave, businesses have reported lower absenteeism and higher employee morale, have found the law easy and costless to administer, and have eliminated the costs associated with permanently replacing workers who needed leave." Bernstein, "Inclusion and Exclusions in Work–Family Policy: The Public Values and Moral Code Embedded in the Family and Medical Leave Act," 10 *Columbia Journal of Gender and Law* 77 (2000).

6. Issacharoff and Rosenblum would like to see the United States import some of the social welfare measures, prevalent in Europe, that assist childbearing among working women. The more advanced attitude on this dimension in Europe may be surprising, since many believe that "feminists have less influence [in Europe] than they do in the United States"—as evidenced in part by the fact that the very concept of sexual harassment was made in America and exported, somewhat slowly, across the Atlantic. Anita Bernstein, "Law, Culture, and Harassment," 142 *University of Pennsylvania Law Review* 1227, 1231 (1994). But the patterns of female employment and child rearing have not changed as sharply as some might expect in the European countries that have adopted the type of benefits that Issacharoff and Rosenblum advocate. (See chapter 13, note 7.)

7. Lamenting the utter absence of political support at present in the United States for what might be their preferred financing scheme, Issacharoff and Rosenblum reject the approach to maternity benefits used in most European countries: a governmental program funded through general revenues. Clearly, funding the maternity leave program through a broad-based progressive tax scheme is more equitable and efficient than a payroll tax scheme. Are Issacharoff and Rosenblum too quick to reject this proposal? With roughly 4 million babies born each year, at most 3 million mothers would be subject to some compensation during leave from work. If the program paid around $400 per week for twelve weeks to these mothers or their employers, the cost would be around $15 billion per year. This is a significant amount of money, but only about the size in 1994 of federal agricultural subsidies, which have virtually no social justification. (See Chapter 3, Section 3.2, note 8.)

8. Assume that the Issacharoff and Rosenblum proposal would stimulate market work effort by women, and stimulate childbearing by working women. Are these desirable consequences?

9. Victor Fuchs argues that in contemporary America, the greatest barrier to women's attainment of economic equality is not employer preju-

dice or exploitation but women's stronger preference, whether biologically or culturally induced, for having and nurturing children. (See Chapter 11, note 2.) He argues in favor of universal child allowances funded out of general revenues, because children

> are the group that has been most adversely affected by recent social and economic trends. The "feminization" of poverty ... is largely illusory, at least for white women. But the "juvenilization" of poverty is very real for children of all races.
>
> I also believe that policies that help children have significant positive externalities for society as a whole. When children are stunted physically, mentally, or emotionally, we all pay a price, and we all ought to be willing to bear some of the cost of raising the potential of the next generation. Even modest child allowances would move substantial numbers of children out of poverty.

Fuchs, *Women's Quest for Economic Equality* 147 (Cambridge, Mass.: Harvard University Press, 1988). Fuchs's program would impose lower social costs than a scheme that both interfered with labor market decisions and burdened employers. Moreover, it would directly benefit *all* women and their children—not just those women who worked a sufficient period of time before becoming pregnant. Is there some risk that providing fixed monetary awards to any woman who has a child would encourage poor women to have more children, thereby increasing the number of children in poverty rather than decreasing it as Fuchs projects?

10. Edward McCaffery embraces the view, similar to that of Vicki Schultz in Chapter 13, that there are structural impediments that are skewing the employment choices of women. McCaffery, "Slouching towards Equality: Gender Discrimination, Market Efficiency, and Social Change," 103 *Yale Law Journal* 595 (1993). But while Schultz argues that these impediments stem from the conduct of employers and fellow workers, and the environment that their conduct establishes, McCaffery contends that aspects of public policy—in particular tax policy—accentuate the sexual division of labor. McCaffery states that in response to the birth of a child,

> we might conclude that [the] mother would look for part-time work [and] that *both* spouses would cut back on their labor force participation to share in the joys and stresses of child-rearing, while each contributed money income and maintained workplace skills. But neither of these patterns develops very often in America.... Most of the growth in part-time employment over the last twenty years has been involuntary ... Relatively few married mothers avail themselves of the part-time employment option, and the two part-time earner household is exceedingly rare.

Id. at 620. Accordingly, he advocates: (1) repealing the equal wage requirement of federal sex discrimination law, which would make labor markets more fluid; and (2) creating a differential tax scheme to alter the sexual division of labor that encourages women to be the primary caretakers of children. Noting that optimal tax theory suggests that workers with elastic labor supply should have lower tax rates than workers with inelastic supply, he would increase tax rates on married men and decrease those on married women.

McCaffery contends that the structure of work for women has changed little. But what about the development of the so-called "mommy-track"? Isn't this work option precisely what McCaffery suggests women want—a less pressured, less time-consuming work option that will enable them to juggle work and family obligations? Isn't this just what Schultz concludes women do not want? (See Chapter 13.) Does the push to part-time work in Sweden, which has very active governmental measures to promote sex equality, suggest that McCaffery is right? (See Chapter 13, note 7.)

McCaffery advocates repeal of the equal-pay requirement for women because he believes—as do Issacharoff and Rosenblum—that the primary cause of sex discrimination in the workplace is rational statistical discrimination based on the shorter expected tenure that female workers will spend in the labor market. Repealing the equal pay provision might well provide greater flexibility to employers to deal with this ostensible difference between male and female workers. Might the repeal also exacerbate problems of animus-based or taste-based discrimination against women? Would courts be able to sort out pay differentials that were permissible because they were based on statistical discrimination and those that were impermissible because of nonrational discrimination? McCaffery would maintain the prohibition on failure to hire women, but one way employers might violate this provision is simply by offering unreasonably low wages. The equal-pay provision would at least provide a benchmark for assessing a discriminatory wage—the wage paid to men performing substantially similar work. Could courts prevent employers from circumventing the requirement of equal hiring opportunities by offering unreasonably low wages to women?

The repeal of the equal-pay requirement would eliminate some labor market distortions, but the higher tax rates on married men would presumably impose distortions on two margins—the decision of men to marry and their labor-leisure trade-off. Do you think that many men would be deterred from marrying or would work significantly less because of the higher tax rates? If work effort fell, would they spend more time with their children? Would the differential tax rates be a constant irritant that could not be salved by reference to the ideology of equality that justifies antidiscrimination law?

11. Kristin Mammen and Christina Paxson ask whether the role of women in the labor force varies with the level of country's economic development. In their cross-country study of women's economic status, Mammen and Paxson find that economic development results in initial declines in women's labor force participation, followed by a steady rise in their labor force participation:

> Taken as a whole, . . . there may be a U-shaped relationship between women's labor force participation and economic development. For very poor countries, female labor force participation is high, and women work mainly in farm or non-farm family enterprises. Development initially moves women out of the labor force, partly because of the rise in men's

market opportunities and partly because of social barriers against women entering the paid labor force. However, as countries continue to develop, women's education levels rise, and women move back into the labor force as paid employees holding mainly white-collar jobs.

Mammen and Paxson, "Women's Work and Economic Development," 14 *Journal of Economic Perspectives* 141 (2000).

There is evidence that women's labor force participation does alter power relationships between husbands and wives and resource allocation within the family. In a study of working-class families, one husband's comments revealed this changed dynamic; he complained that his wife "doesn't know how to give respect ... Because she's working and making money, she thinks she can argue back whenever she feels like it." Dora L. Costa, "From Mill Town to Board Room: The Rise of Women's Paid Labor," 14 *Journal of Economic Perspectives* 101 (2002). See Chapter 11, note 6 for how women in different countries rate on the Human Development Index, which measures longevity, educational attainment, and access to resources.

12. Perhaps what is needed for greater sexual equality in the workplace is not an alternative scheme to the existing antidiscrimination mandate, but a better implementation of it. Robert Nelson and William Bridges argue that courts have too often uncritically accepted employers' claim that they were following the market when they set lower wages for predominantly female jobs compared to predominantly male jobs. Nelson and Bridge, *Legalizing Gender Inequality: Courts, Markets, and Unequal Pay for Women in America* (New York: Cambridge University Press, 1999). However, what Nelson and Bridges find is that a substantial portion of the pay differential is not market-based at all; rather, it is a product of "employers' own actions in setting internal pay scales to suit their organizations' needs and values." But won't employers who set pay scales at less than the market rate find that they cannot attract or retain female workers?

16

Age Discrimination

Americans witnessed a dramatic increase in the elderly population throughout the twentieth century as improving health generated substantial increases in longevity. Coupled with a declining birth rate, census and population experts predict that this rise in the elderly population will translate into twenty-two percent of Americans being over the age of sixty-five by 2030. This unprecedented demographic shift—what many refer to as the "graying of America"—raises important social, political, and economic questions about how aging and working should be conceptualized and what policy measures should be implemented. In general, the conflict between an increasingly consumerist, youth-oriented culture and the considerable political power and wealth of older Americans has been shaping public policy in the realm of social security, medical insurance, property and income taxes, school finance, and, of course, the employment arena. While the elderly have traditionally been economically disadvantaged relative to the rest of society, there have been dramatic advances made by the elderly over the last few decades. Indeed, some argue that the balance may actually be shifting too far in *favor* of the elderly today. In the employment setting, as chronological age loses its ability to predict functionality and productivity of older workers, the project of formulating specific policies and programs for older workers becomes increasingly difficult.

State legislative efforts to regulate arbitrary discrimination against older workers can be traced to the beginning of the twentieth century. Preceding federal legislation by over six decades, Colorado passed the first legislation prohibiting age discrimination in employment in 1903.

The Colorado statute stated that no employer "shall discharge any individual between the ages of eighteen and sixty years, solely and only upon the basis of age," as long as the employee was "well versed in the [employer's] line of business" and was "qualified physically, mentally, and by training and experience, to satisfactorily perform and does satisfactorily perform the labor." Lawrence M. Friedman, *Your Time Will Come: The Law of Age Discrimination and Mandatory Retirement* 124, note 6 (New York: Russell Sage Foundation, 1984). By 1966 (on the eve of the enactment of the federal age discrimination law), twenty-three states had adopted statutes that prohibited age discrimination in the workplace. Most of these statutes protected workers between the ages forty and sixty-five, although some states, such as Colorado (covering ages eighteen to sixty) and Oregon (covering ages twenty-five to sixty-five) also made their statutes applicable to discrimination because of youth. Foreshadowing the yet-to-come federal legislation, most state statutes generally prohibited discriminatory practices in hiring, discharge, and terms or conditions of employment by private sector employers, labor organizations, and employment agencies. Remedies available under the state statutes included criminal penalties and/or civil suits, as well as administrative remedies in some states. "Age Discrimination in Employment: the Problem of the Older Worker," 41 *New York University Law Review* 383 (1966).

At the federal level, however, no law made age discrimination illegal. There were, on the other hand, federal programs that trained, educated, and assisted in placing older workers. The Department of Labor, for example, had a program that engaged in research, education, placement, and counseling of older workers to address the problem of their unemployment. There were also federal programs that were designed to generally aid the elderly, or viewed in a less altruistic light, shift the burden of caring for the elderly from people middle-aged and younger to the government. Beginning with the New Deal's Social Security Act of 1935, an array of federal laws was enacted to ensure "social security" for the elderly, including the landmark benefits program for the elderly, Older Americans Act of 1964, and the Medicare and Medicaid amendments to the Social Security Act in 1965.

By the 1950s, however, there were nagging complaints about job discrimination that many older workers seemed to face—complaints that people over the age of forty could not get jobs. Thus when the Civil Rights Act of 1964 was being drafted, age was originally considered among Title VII's protections. In the end, however, the proposal was dropped and what emerged was a Congressional directive to the Secretary of Labor to undertake a study of age discrimination in employment. In June of 1965, Secretary W. Willard Wirtz submitted his report, *The Older American Worker: Age Discrimination in Employment,* which focused on the pervasive tendency of employers to set age limits in the hiring process. The report cited statistical data that showed that nearly one-half of the job openings in the private sector arbitrarily disqualified applicants over the age of fifty-five, while a quarter were closed off to workers over forty-five. In addition to the moral wrong of seemingly arbitrary discrimination, Congress also was concerned with the economic advantages of keeping older workers in the workforce, as their unemployment would heavily tax the economy and the federal government. In responding to these concerns, Congress enacted the Age Discrimination in Employment Act (ADEA) in 1967. Modeled after Title VII of the 1964 Civil Rights Act, the stated purpose of the ADEA was to "promote employment of older persons based on ability rather than age; to prohibit arbitrary age discrimination in employment; to help employers and workers find ways to meeting problems arising from the impact of age on employment." The Act initially provided protection for workers between the ages of forty and sixty-five, which was subsequently raised to age seventy in 1978 and eliminated altogether in 1986.

In the three decades following its enactment, the ADEA has produced certain unintended consequences. First, although the statute was drafted with a clear legislative intent to curb discrimination in hiring practices, less than nine percent of ADEA cases filed during the 1980's involved a refusal to hire. Instead, a majority of ADEA cases (76 percent) involve unlawful termination. Second, far from assisting older workers who would otherwise become dependent on the state if they were unemployed, typical litigants in ADEA cases are overwhelmingly white male professionals and managers who earn high salaries. Finally, although the primary concern of the ADEA was to improve the general long-term employment of older workers as a group, there appears to be little evidence that the ADEA has alleviated the unemployment problem of older workers. For more detailed recent empirical data on ADEA litigants and ADEA litigation, see Howard C. Eglit, "The Age Discrimination in Employment Act at Thirty: Where It's Been, Where It Is Today, Where It's Going," 31 *University of Richmond Law Review* 579 (1997).

These findings have galvanized heated debates about the efficacy, efficiency, and moral legitimacy of the ADEA. In the first excerpted article, Samuel Issacharoff and Erica Worth Harris argue that the ADEA should not have been based on an antidiscrimination model, as ageism in the employment context is driven more by economic calculations that flow from the life-cycle employment model than by invidious prejudice. In their view, the analogy between race or sex discrimination and age discrimination is all the more flawed because the elderly constitute one of the most affluent and politically powerful groups in the United States. Indeed, the reason why the ADEA has become one of the most far reaching antidiscrimination statutes, they argue, is precisely because it has been captured by the "gray lobby." Richard Posner is also critical of what he considers the misguided aims of the ADEA. He argues first, that the ADEA is inefficient because it prohibits statistical discrimination that allows employers to cost-effectively use age as a proxy for ability to perform. Second, Posner argues that the ADEA is ineffective in achieving its stated goals, in that it harms both older workers and the society as a whole.

Although Lawrence Friedman would agree with Issacharoff, Harris, and Posner that age discrimination is different—less invidious—than race or sex discrimination, he believes that the concerns with the burdens of prejudice and stereotyping that the elderly face are more significant than these other authors acknowledge. Thus, even though he appears ambivalent about the efficiency and efficacy of the ADEA, he is more willing to entertain the question of whether age discrimination can be analogized to race and sex discrimination. As to arguments that the ADEA is economically inefficient, Christine Jolls offers a number of counterarguments to Issacharoff, Harris, and Posner. Based on the age-wage model that is well described in the Issacharoff and Harris excerpt, Jolls argues that the ADEA serves a useful "hand-tying" function, which prevents employers from firing older workers just when they should be reaping benefits of higher than marginal value wages that they had foregone in their earlier work careers.

Is Age Discrimination Really Age Discrimination? The ADEA's Unnatural Solution*
SAMUEL ISSACHAROFF & ERICA WORTH HARRIS

Aging Under Employment Contracts

The Original Understanding

In 1967, half of all private job openings were barred to applicants over fifty-five, and a quarter to those over forty-five. This "Elders Need Not Apply" attitude was found to be the cause of a growing problem among America's elderly: long-term unemployment. Relying on a Department of Labor report, Congress found that the burden of unemployment was falling disproportionately on older workers, that employers were operating under mistaken assumptions about the effects of aging, and that age barriers to hiring were the root of the unemployment problem. The Department of Labor's Commissioner on Aging reported that, although older workers were "frequently preferred over the younger" workers when it came to promotions and treatment within the workplace, older applicants were treated with disdain. Testimony before Congress condemned this type of age discrimination as inhumane, unjust, and cruel. This testimony called for legislation to break down stereotypes used by employers and to open opportunities to older workers. Although there was some variation amongst the proposed bills, there was broad agree-

---

* Samuel Issacharoff and Erica Worth Harris, "Is Age Discrimination Really Age Discrimination?: The ADEA's Unnatural Solution," *New York University Law Review*, vol. 72, copyright © 1997. Reprinted by permission of the publisher.

ment that antidiscrimination legislation was the answer. At its most basic, the argument ran: "To prohibit age discrimination in employment is so plainly and unarguably right, that to belabor it is to dull it, ... nobody defends such discrimination, and ... there is general agreement that it ought to be stopped."

Thus, after little debate and even less public attention, Congress passed the Age Discrimination in Employment Act of 1967. Modeled on Title VII of the Civil Rights Act, the ADEA made it illegal for an employer "to fail or refuse to hire or to discharge any individual or otherwise discriminate against any individual with respect to his compensation, terms, conditions, or privileges of employment, because of such individual's age."

From the ADEA's inception, however, an unmistakable current recognized that, despite tracking the statutory form of Title VII, the Act addressed something other than traditional discrimination. The legislative history reflects Congress's understanding that "age discrimination in employment [is] a complex phenomena [sic] based on many interrelated factors." Unlike the victims of traditional forms of discrimination, aging employees confront a question of "economics; it is not discriminatory or malice [sic], it is simply that it costs more money to employ [older workers]." As one individual explained:

> The problem of age discrimination is a complex one because it is seldom a matter of blind or arbitrary prejudice which often exists for reasons of race, creed, color, national origin, or sex. Age discrimination is a more subtle series of problems based upon a combination of institutional factors and stereotyped thinking.

Because age discrimination was considered to be independent of other forms of discrimination, Congress declined to place enforcement of the Act with the Equal Employment Opportunity Commission (EEOC). As originally codified, the ADEA applied to individuals aged forty to sixty five and was administered by the Department of Labor.From the very beginning, the most striking feature of the ADEA as applied, rather than as intended, was the marked disparity between the stated congressional aim of redressing barriers to job acquisition by older employees and the actual effect of the statute. While the Act had an immediate impact on formal barriers to employment, such as maximum age listings for job openings, the removal of these barriers failed to solve, or even reduce, the problem of long-term unemployment. At the 1976 "Impact of the ADEA" hearings, the clear weight of the testimony was that the 1967 Act had no discernible impact on the long-term unemployment problem for older employees. Despite the growing number of ADEA suits, long-term unemployment amongst the elderly had in fact increased by 2.8% between 1967 and 1976. *The Life–Cycle Model*The ADEA failed in its stated objective because it rested on a misunderstanding of the sources of employment barriers for older workers. Employers' reluctance to hire older workers was not necessarily attributable to an inaccurate assumption of older workers' capabilities based on animus or lack of familiarity with a socially isolated group of potential employees. Rather, the barriers to employment stemmed from an accurate understanding of the relation between wages and age, borne out by the actual workplace experience of employers. That relationship is most accurately depicted by the life-cycle model of career employment. . . .

Employment markets have a unique feature that sets them apart from the neoclassical economic depiction of supply and demand curves dictating price. The typical long-term employment relationship that emerged in the American workplace after World War II featured a steady pattern of wage increases for employees up until the moment of retirement. These wage increases persisted in cases where identifying any increase in productivity was impossible and even in circumstances where one could establish that productivity either leveled off earlier in the employee's career or was actually falling. The life-cycle model was developed to explain the paradox of what economists would term the absence of wage elasticity, or simply, the failure of wages to fluctuate in response to the actual productivity of employees. If wages rise without a corresponding increase in productivity, what explains the willingness of employers in the late stages of an employee's career to pay more than the cost of obtaining cheaper substitute labor from a younger employee? In the absence of some external constraint introducing a monopoly-like distortion in the labor market, no employer could pay wages above employee productivity without inviting market challenge from more efficient competitors. So long as one focuses exclusively on wages and productivity at a particular point or even a single day in the career of a senior employee, the paradox of apparent overpayment is unresolvable. Shifting the focus to the entire worklife of a career-term employee, however, exposes that wages and marginal productivity are separated not only at the late stages of employment, but throughout a typical employees' career. An illustration of the career-wage model helps clarify the issue:

Figure 1.

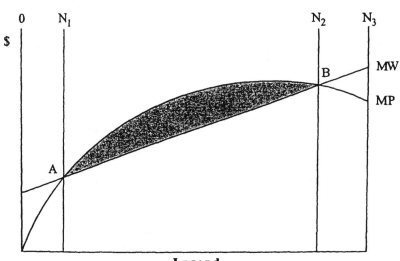

Legend

MW:	Marginal Wage of Employee
MP:	Marginal Product of Employee
Shaded Area:	Period in mid-career where employee's wage is less than employee's marginal productivity
0–N_1:	Training Period
N_1–N_2:	Mid-Career
N_2–N_3:	Later Career
A & B:	Cross Points

In simple economic terms, the model depicts the employee receiving a wage premium during the training stages of employment and again at the end stages of his or her career. During the middle stages, however, the employer is actually paying the employee less than the employees' marginal productivity. Accordingly, in order to ensure an increasing wage structure, employer's paid workers more than their worth during the beginning and ending phases of their careers. They were willing to suffer this loss in exchange for an intermediate period of superprofitability from the employee's services. This exchange depended on two further steps. First, the employer had to resist the temptation to discharge the employee in the late stages of employment. This discharge would be opportunistic because the employer would have already received the benefits of the bargain during the middle stages of employment. Furthermore, the employee would be in no position to recapture his or her legitimate late-stage compensation from any other employer. Second, the system of mandatory retirement made the exchange possible by providing the necessary endpoint to the bargain. The mandatory retirement age allowed for a predesignated moment at which the employment relationship could be revisited.... Viewed in this way, mandatory retirement provided not so much the compelled endpoint of employment but rather a prearranged point of renegotiation. This prearranged negotiation provided career employees some security against constant reviews of productivity and some dignitary protection should their skills begin to ebb later in their careers. For employers, mandatory retirement afforded a point at which employees could be reevaluated without imposing the stigma of having been singled out for potential termination as nonperforming individuals. Mandatory retirement also enabled employers to avoid the corresponding costs to overall employee morale if employees were seen to be "picked upon" in their later years....

. . .

... [T]he life-cycle employment model ... illustrates the vulnerability of older employees and explains why employers do not want to hire older workers, independent of any matter of discrimination. An employee in an arrangement that holds out pay in excess of productivity in the later stages of an employee's career faces distinct risks. The primary risk is that an employer under financial stress may come to see an expensive senior employee as an unaffordable luxury, regardless of implicit contractual obligations.... A second risk directly tied to the first is that if an employee were to lose her employment, there would be a strong disincentive to any subsequent employer hiring her. Any new employer hiring a senior employee at her then-current wage scale would be assuming a wage premium for service delivered to another employer.... Thus, the 1967 Act, which set its sight on express age discrimination in hiring, was insufficient to solve the problem of long-term unemployment. The "No Elders Need Apply" signs came down, but the reluctance to hire older workers remained.

Antidiscrimination With a Difference

... [T]he shifting of the burden of production upon a relatively minimal plaintiffs' showing, which is known as the *McDonnell Douglas* approach in Title VII law ... [cannot be justified in] age discrimination. First, and most simply, the ADEA is not concerned with a constitutionally protected class. Unlike race and sex, age is not a suspect classification and no credible claim has ever been made that older Americans are subject to arbitrary state laws inspired purely by animus. In *Massachusetts Board of Retirement v. Murgia*, the Supreme Court explained that "old age does not define a 'discrete and insular' group ... in need of 'extraordinary protection from the majoritarian political process.' Instead, it marks a stage that each of us will reach if we live out our normal span." As summarized by Professor Rutherglen, the ADEA "cannot be justified in terms of opening opportunities to a historically disfavored group."

Second, in age cases, as opposed to racial discrimination claims, the alternative explanation is everpresent. In simple doctrinal terms, courts have been forced to recognize that cost-based discrimination may serve as a defense to an age-based classification in circumstances in which comparable defenses would be unavailing were the challenged classification to be triggered by race or sex. For example, several courts have held that a legitimate business reason or economic purpose could justify a differentiation in benefits based on age. The question of the relation between age and seniority-sensitive employee rights came to the fore in *Hazen Paper Co. v. Biggins*, in which the Supreme Court ruled that "there is no disparate treatment under the ADEA when the factor motivating the employer is some feature other than the employee's age"—even if that feature happens to correlate with age. *Hazen* seemed to doom attempts to prove a prima facie case of age discrimination by showing that employer reliance upon a proxy for age—such as seniority, income level, or pension status—was sufficient to establish the discriminatory intent necessary for liability under the Act.

This result in turn exposes the paradox of the ADEA. Concern about employer opportunism against older employees is well founded. As demonstrated by the life-cycle model, employers have a significant incentive to breach their part of the implicit bargain. Having enjoyed the period of superprofits during the middle stages of employee careers, employers in economic straits may seek to evade the obligations that underlie the career-wage relationship. By providing older employees a legal remedy for an opportunistic breach, the ADEA has been recast from a statute providing access to the workplace for older Americans into the most dramatically far reaching of the antidiscrimination statutes. As a result, ADEA claims in the federal courts are mushrooming. In 1988, they accounted for more than 25% of the work of the EEOC, and between 1989 and 1993 the number of claims filed with the EEOC jumped 34%.

While the ADEA may indeed serve the purpose of providing legal redress to one sector of the older workforce, whether antidiscrimination legislation is the proper vehicle for redressing this concern remains unclear. If the source of the risk to older workers is economics, in general, and opportunistic breaches, in particular, a real question emerges as to why this problem should be folded into the antidiscrimination rubric. Professor Jolls defends the Act as "hands-tying" by which employers are deterred from cheating on their implied contractual obligations. Not only is this explanation a rather significant departure from the original stated purpose of the Act, but it constitutes a peculiar use of the antidiscrimination model. Protection of long-term employees could be accomplished by recognizing the important role of common law actions, as described by Professor Schwab; by relaxing the at-will presumption found in the common law, as proposed by Professors Estlund and Kamiat; by creating a statutory abrogation of employment at will, as has already been done in Montana; by creating compulsory arbitration over the termination of long-term employees, as proposed by the Model

Employment Termination Act; or by establishing administrative mechanisms to deter employer misconduct. Using the ADEA to substitute for a "for cause" rule of employment law provides only patchwork protection to a handful of successful plaintiffs. Additionally, those few plaintiffs who do succeed tend to be drawn disproportionately from the ranks of the most privileged employees.

Furthermore, the expense of this solution may very well overwhelm any stopgap protection that is obtained. The 1984 transfer of enforcement power over the ADEA from the Department of Labor to the EEOC should not obscure the significant advantages available to ADEA plaintiffs over other antidiscrimination complainants. Unlike pre–1991 Title VII plaintiffs, ADEA plaintiffs received the right to jury trials and liquidated damages. Although these changes were hardly noticed at the congressional hearings, they proved to be highly significant in the subsequent onslaught of litigation. The ADEA emerged as the most potent of the antidiscrimination statutes with remedies that included injunctive relief, reinstatement, front pay, and reasonable costs and attorneys' fees. Moreover, unlike the pre–1991 version of Title VII, the ADEA's right to back pay is not discretionary, it is a matter of right. Liquidated damages provide double recoveries where the employer committed a willful violation of the statute, and awards of back pay include damages for lost wages, pension benefits, insurance benefits, profit sharing benefits, and accrued sick leave.

More critically, the relaxed reliance on the antidiscrimination model as a panacea for all employment problems served as an invitation to other forms of opportunistic behavior—this time by the beneficiaries of the ADEA statutory scheme.

Reforms and Capture

The Emergence of an Interest Group Strategy

The ADEA has had a long and complex history. Since 1967, there have been several series of initiatives, some successful, some not. The first significant amendment to the Act came as Congress began to examine seriously the condition of an aging workforce. In the early 1970s, Congress not only approved significant increases in Social Security benefits and passed the Employee Retirement Income Security Act of 1974, but also extended the ADEA to cover employees of federal and state governments. By 1976, the Gray Lobby and its allies in Congress moved to eliminate the age cap of the ADEA altogether in both the public and private sectors. In fact, one group wanted not only the end of mandatory retirement, but also affirmative action programs "comparable to those contained in Title VII." More moderate proposals simply would have raised the statutory age cap from sixty-five to seventy, a position that finally won out in the 1978 amendments to the Act. In 1984, Congress transferred enforcement to the EEOC, the enforcement agency for Title VII legislation, and held additional hearings on eliminating the age cap for private sector employees. In 1986, these objectives were realized as all workers over the age of forty were brought under the statutory umbrella and, notably, virtually all mandatory retirement was eliminated. Finally, in 1990, Congress passed the Older Workers Benefits Protection Act (OWBPA), a far ranging statute prohibiting the use of many targeted retirement inducement programs. . . .

These amendments to the ADEA did not occur in a vacuum. Over the same twenty-five-year period, the number of older Americans increased, their percentage of the national wealth soared, and they brought a steadily increasing number of cases under the ADEA. Interestingly, there is a stunning mismatch between the expansion of ADEA litigation and the dramatic improvement in the economic status of the elderly. For example, between 1970 and 1984, the median real income of households comprised of persons over sixty-five rose by 35%, compared to less than 1% for those comprised of persons aged twenty-five to sixty-four. This increase reflects a steady and dramatic rise in individual income for senior citizens; between 1957 and 1990, the median income of persons in the over-sixty-five category more than doubled, a pace far outstripping the rate of the rest of the population. With older Americans living longer and having more wealth and disposable time, we now confront a concern noted by Judge Posner:

> [Our] concern is that the increase in nonworking life expectancy associated with the growing fraction of elderly people implies a decline in the ratio of productive to consuming years over the life cycle, and that the elderly will use their political muscle to force the productive young to support the consuming old.

This opportunity for capture by a specific group is significant given the power of the elderly in this country. Older persons are more likely than any other group to vote, to write members of Congress, and to join public interest organizations. As summarized by Representative Claude Pepper, the enthusiastic champion of ever greater benefits for senior citizens, "they have money and they have power." The result has been that, since the 1970s, "the elderly have reaped a steadily increasing proportion of governmental benefit programs." From Medicare to Social Security, today's elderly comprise one of the most favored groups in the country with respect to legislative entitlements. Unsurprisingly, that power clearly can be seen at play in the expansion of the ADEA.

Most central has been the evolution of thinking about the problem of aging in the workforce. As we set out above, the image of the Act has changed from a reflection of a concern over entry barriers to a vehicle for addressing concerns at the end of an employee's worklife. No discussion of this transformation is possible, however, without addressing the critical role played by interest group pressures organized through the American Association of Retired Persons (AARP). Although reforms of the ADEA may not appear as serious a problem as the viability of the

Social Security system or the state of medical insurance, the reforms of the Act had every bit as much to do with an intergenerational struggle over societal goods. Moreover, while the changes in the Act's focus brought the ADEA in closer step with the problems identified by the life-cycle model, they also introduced the prospect of a direct financial benefit to an identifiable group of people.

Bad Statutes and the Invitation to Capture

Although the initial ADEA vision may have been misguided, there is no evidence that it offered direct financial benefits to its proponents. The original legislation was primarily an attempt to eliminate the offensive categorical restrictions on hiring older workers. As is so often the case in the antidiscrimination context, that which appeared as undoubtedly necessary to the eradication of a societal wrong proved over time to be insufficient to accomplish the task alone. Nonetheless, as the Secretary of Labor testified in 1967, there was no Gray Lobby to motivate the original Act. Because of that absence, the original Act was considered a measured approach, and its framers predicted that it would result in fewer than 1000 charges annually. In stark contrast, the legislation that evolved during the 1986 and 1990 reforms was clearly aimed to benefit a discrete group that served, not coincidentally, as its chief champion.

. . .

The Capture of the ADEA

If, as we propose, the conceptual shortcomings of the ADEA's antidiscrimination scheme made it a walking invitation to capture, the missing ingredient was the agent that would accept that invitation. That agent proved to be the American Association of Retired Persons (AARP). Although the organization had been founded in 1958, the AARP did not emerge as the pivotal agent for older Americans until the early 1980s. During the 1976 congressional hearings on the ADEA, for example, the AARP was still a secondary player. The incremental change in the age cap from sixty-five to seventy was mainly the result of efforts by other organizations such as the National Council on Aging (NCOA) and the Council on Aging (COA).

The radical transformation of ADEA legislative reforms is inseparable from the corresponding transformation of the AARP. After experiencing financial difficulties in the late 1970s, the AARP began a vigorous marketing campaign to increase its membership. In 1983, the AARP dropped its minimum membership age requirement from fifty-five to fifty, instantaneously adding thousands to its membership rolls. By 1984, the AARP claimed "15% of the U.S. adult population." That membership was quickly parlayed into a huge trust fund, which in turn was used to build "a public policy institute, [a team of] professional lobbyists, [and] a legal staff." The AARP has grown to become the largest private, non-profit, and nonpartisan membership organization in the world. Today, its annual budget is over $386 million, $86 million of which comes from government funding, and its membership includes nearly one of every five voters in the United States.

As its membership grew, the AARP became a serious political presence with an agenda to transform the ADEA. By 1983, the AARP had announced its "global initiatives," which included its opposition to mandatory retirement. In 1984, it began to pursue aggressively its political interests, while advertising itself as "[a] strong, effective voice in Washington, . . . committed to opposing age discrimination in employment, modifying negative attitudes towards older persons and protecting our members' right to work."

The power of "the nation's largest special-interest group" has not gone unnoticed by Congress. Despite increasing budgetary constraints in the 1980s and 1990s, the AARP has been at the forefront of a successful capture of an ever-increasing share of government welfare benefits and has made entitlement programs like Social Security and Medicare political sacred cows. Today's elderly, "who make up about 12.5% of the population, receive 60% of federal social spending." The AARP's growth in power coincides neatly with the changing focus of the ADEA and the expansion of its statutory initiatives.

· · ·

Conclusion

. . . The ADEA emerged from the 1986 and 1990 amendments as the most potent of antidiscrimination laws. Through relentless effort by special interest lobbyists, the antidiscrimination model was captured for the benefit of a group that is not socially reviled, not penurious, neither discrete nor insular, not cut off from the mainstream of society, and not marked by the unmistakable badge of social opprobrium. The ADEA amendments forced a self-conscious wealth transfer not to society's victims or even its unfortunates, but to some of its most advantaged and secure. We cannot escape the conclusion that the use of antidiscrimination law and rhetoric to accomplish this aim is simply deplorable.

Age Discrimination by Employers and the Issue of Mandatory Retirement*
RICHARD A. POSNER

. . . I argue that the age discrimination law is largely ineffectual but that to the extent it is effective it has a perverse impact both on the welfare of the elderly and on the equality of income and wealth across the entire population. The age discrimination law is at once inefficient, regressive, and harmful to the elderly.

The Nature and Consequences of Age Discrimination in Employment

Animus discrimination. The justification offered for the law [ADEA] was that people over 40 are subject to a form of prejudice, "ageism," that is analogous to racism and sexism.... [W]e can posit two kinds of ageism, only one plausible. The implausible is a systematic undervaluation, motivated by ignorance, viciousness, or irrationality, of the value of older people in the workplace. This is sometimes referred to as "animus discrimination." I do not deny that there is resentment and disdain of older people in our society, or widespread misunderstandings, some disadvantageous to the old....

But the present chapter is about the work place....

... [T]he kind of "we-they" thinking that fosters racial, ethnic, and sexual discrimination is unlikely to play a large role in the treatment of the elderly worker. Not because a young person will (in all likelihood) someday be old; to put much weight on the continuity of personal identity would slight the multiple-selves issue. But because the people who do the hiring and firing are generally as old as the people they hire and fire and are therefore unlikely to mistake those people's vocational abilities.

. . .

Statistical discrimination. The form of ageism (if it should be called that) that is more plausible and better substantiated than animus discrimination against the old consists of attributing to all people of a particular age the characteristics of the average person of that age. It is an example of what economists call statistical discrimination and non-economists "stereotyping": the failure or refusal, normally motivated by the costs of information, to distinguish a particular member of a group from the average member....

This phenomenon does not, however, make age discrimination in employment inefficient any more than the substitution in some other field of activity of a rule (for example, do not drive faster than 65 miles per hour) for a standard (do not drive too fast for conditions) need be inefficient. A rule is simpler to administer than a standard and therefore cheaper, and the cost savings may exceed the loss from disregarding circumstances that may make the rule disserve the purposes behind it in a particular case.

. . .

Whether this procedure should be viewed as a form of "discrimination" in an invidious sense may be doubted, unless it is somehow unfair to judge a person as a member of a group rather than as an individual. Is it unfair? We do it all the time, and could hardly act otherwise. Lacking unmediated access to the "inner man" or complete knowledge of his life history, we relentlessly "type" people and base our judgments on this typing. . . . If employers are forbidden to use efficient methods of evaluation, their labor costs will rise, and it is now generally accepted that increases in payroll taxes or other labor costs are borne largely by the workers themselves, in the form of reduced wages or benefits.

. . .

The argument that statistical discrimination is inefficient in the case of age is unpersuasive. When the costs of making individualized assessments of employee's performance are prohibitive, as they often are, prohibiting the use of the age proxy will lead to the substitution of other proxies. The problem of underinvestment will be shifted, not solved. Whoever is "unfairly" disadvantaged by the new proxy, in the sense that it does not measure *his* abilities accurately . . . will lack the incentive to make the optimal investment in his human capital. And if the new proxies are less efficient than age—as they probably will be, because otherwise they would in all likelihood have been adopted without government prodding—wages will fall because employers' labor costs will be higher, and with lower wages there will be less incentive for workers to invest in their human capital.

The Effects of the Age Discrimination in Employment Act

The previous section questioned the need for a law against discrimination on the grounds of age. But we have the law, and we must now consider more carefully its probable effects both on elderly workers and on the rest of the society.

. . .

Hiring cases. We know that, wholly apart from any laws, employers are reluctant to hire older workers. The cost of training an older worker is higher than that of training a younger one because of the age-related decline of fluid intelligence, while the expected return to the investment in training is lower because the older worker has a shortly working life expectancy. The age discrimination law adds to the costs of employing older workers, and hence to the reluctance of employers to employ them, by giving them more legal rights against their employer than younger workers have. By thus reducing the hiring prospects of older people, the Act adversely impairs the incentive of the exceptional old to invest in their human capital, by reducing the expected return on such an investment.

The Act does forbid age discrimination in hiring as well as in firing, demotions, wages, and so forth. But it is largely ineffective against hiring discrimination because of the extreme difficulty of proving substantial damages in such cases. Damages are not the only relief available in a suit under the Act; injunctive relief is also possible. But the disappointed applicant is unlikely to be satisfied with an order requiring the employer to hire him; he would be entering upon the employment under most inauspicious circumstances.

. . .

So it is no surprise that a large sample of litigated age discrimination cases contained no hiring cases; more than two-thirds of the cases involved termination (discharge or involuntary retirement), with most of the others involving promotion or demotion. A more recent study, of age discrimination complaints lodged with the Equal Opportunity Commission, finds that 87.9 percent of the complaints in which no other form of discrimination was alleged besides age discrimination involved termination, only 8.6 percent hiring.

. . .

... A point made even by scholars who support the laws against employment discrimination is that the more likely a member of a protected group is to bring a termination suit and the less likely he or she is to bring a hiring suit, the greater will be the disincentive of employers to hire the member of such groups.

Firing (and other discharge) cases. I have said that only if the employee is let go is an age discrimination case likely to get as far as an award of damages or any other remedy. And yet the merits of awarding substantial damages even in such cases could be questioned, on the following ground which has not, however, so far as I am aware, even been advanced by an employer, although it is firmly rooted in the basic human-capital model. We recall from chapter 3 that part of a wage that reflects the greater value to the firm of an employee who has firm-specific human capital may be generated by the *employer*'s contribution to that capital. The employee himself pays for employer's investment in the employee's *general* human capital—skills that he can employ elsewhere in the economy—by accepting a lower wage. The employer would have no protection against the employee's using that capital to obtain a higher wage from another employer, and he therefore will not pay for it. But the employer will pay for a share, possible a very large share, of the employee's firm-specific capital, because the employee by definition cannot obtain a return on that capital from another employer. The greater the share of this capital that the employer pays for, the lower will be the turnover of employees (for they will have a higher salary) and hence the likelier will the employer be to reap the benefit of its investment.

The analysis argues for allowing the employer to deduct from damages in an age discrimination firing case that portion of the difference between the wage he paid the employee, and the lower wage that the employee would command in his best alternative employment, that represents a return on specific human capital for which the employer paid. The employer loses this investment in the employee's human capital by losing the employee, and should not have to pay twice—first by swallowing the loss of the investment, and then by in effect "buying" the investment back by having to pay damages measured by its value.

The argument is sound, but it is too exotic, and the computations required by it are too difficult, to be likely to command itself to the courts. Its real significance to an evaluation of the effects of the Age Discrimination in Employment Act lies in directing attention to the fact that employers have their own incentives, unrelated to law, to avoid firing competent employees of any age, even if replacements are available. The employer has invested in the employee, and if the employee is still productive the employer is continuing to earn a return on the investment.

The analysis to this point suggests that insofar as the age discrimination law forbids discrimination against individual employees, as distinct from discrimination against age-defined classes of employees (mainly through mandatory retirement at fixed ages, about which more later), it may, like ERISA, have little effect. The abuse against which it is directed, the arbitrary treatment of older workers, would be rare, at least in private markets, even without the law. It would be rare because, as with ERISA, employers have market incentives to avoid the abuse. . . .

So age discrimination against individual workers in whom the employer has invested significant firm-specific human capital is unlikely, at least by private employers, while age discrimination against other workers, and against older persons seeking jobs, is unlikely to be rectified by the age discrimination law because plaintiffs drawn from these categories are unlikely to have a substantial financial stake in suing.

. . .

So: age discrimination against individual workers in whom the employer has invested significant firm-specific human capital is unlikely, at least by private employers, while age discrimination against other workers, and against older persons seeking jobs, is unlikely to be rectified by the age discrimination law because plaintiffs drawn from these categories are unlikely to have a substantial financial stake in suing.

Further evidence of the likely inefficacy of the law is the very poor win rate of plaintiffs in age discrimination cases. . . . In my sample, while plaintiffs won 47.7 percent of the 20 percent of the cases that went to verdict, 74.7 percent of the cases were disposed of by summary judgment, meaning that there was no triable issue; and plaintiffs won only 1.6 percent of those cases.

Why do most age discrimination plaintiffs do so poorly? . . . In the absence of smoking-gun evidence of age discrimination, now difficult to come by, a plaintiff must as a practical matter show than an equally competent but younger employee was treated better. Such proof is difficult because of the intangible elements in evaluating a worker's performance other than in the simplest jobs—and the simplest jobs do not generally generate the plausibly high damage claims that repay the costs and uncertainties of litigation. The simplest jobs require little human capital, whether general or specific, and (partly for that reason) pay low wages.

Moreover, a firm that wants to get rid of an older employee can often so with near impunity by cashiering a young employee at the same time. One hears rumors that this is a common practice. It may be feasible because there is high turnover among young employees anyway and the firm may not yet have invested much in the young employee's firm-specific human capital (a principal reason why turnover of young employees is high) and so has little to lose from firing him, though concern with reputation must inhibit this Machiavellian strategy to some and perhaps to a great extent. The "RIF" (reduction in force) is a related strategy; victims of RIFs who complain on age discrimination grounds do very poorly. . . .

Another thing that makes it hard for the employee to win an age discrimination case is that older employees tend to be more costly to a firm than younger ones, by virtue of receiving a larger package of wages and benefits. The more costly they are, the more difficult it is to ascribe their discharge to age, as distinct from their expense. The older employee may be more productive by reason of his greater experience, or he may be paid a higher wage either to discourage shirking in his last period of employment or as a reward for not having shirked previously. If he is more productive, then he is not in fact more costly to the firm than a younger, less well paid, but also less productive worker. And if he is being paid a so-called "efficiency" wage either to discourage shirking or to repay the "bond" that he posted as a young employee by accepting a lower salary in exchange for an implicit promise of compensation later if he behaved, he is merely receiving the benefit of his bargain. But a court is not apt to tumble to the reason why the older employee is not really being "overpaid" and to see therefore that the employer is reneging on an implicit contract. All the court can see is that the employer had a reason unrelated to age for firing the older worker—he was more expensive.

Courts could try to deal with this problem by treating "discrimination" based on salary as a form of age discrimination, since age and salary tend to be positively correlated. But maybe because this would make it difficult for firms to take rational steps to reduce their costs then they find, for whatever reason, that they are paying wages in excess of the market, the Supreme Court has rejected this approach.

. . .

What kind of worker brings an age discrimination suit? ... [M]ost age discrimination suits are brought by professional or managerial employees, who have high salaries; and most plaintiffs are in their fifties, and so have accumulated a lot of specific capital and therefore have a substantial damages claim. In my study, 234 cases of 388 cases were brought by professional, managerial, or sales employees—more than 60 percent. This figure is greatly disproportionate to the share of these classes of workers in the working population as a whole....

The largest number of plaintiffs in the sample were in the 55 to 59 age group and the second largest in the 50 to 54 and 60 to 64 groups; only 24.3 percent were younger than 50. Young people would not have accumulated as much firm-specific human capital and therefore would have lower damages. Elderly people (only 8.6 percent of the plaintiffs were 65 or older) would be either retired, and therefore no longer protected by a statute protecting employees (unless they had been involuntarily retired), or close to retirement, in which event their expected damages would be low, just as in the case of young workers.

As other studies have shown, blacks and women are underrepresented as plaintiffs in age discrimination cases. One explanation is that blacks and women don't "need" to file an age discrimination suits as much as white males, because they have other civil rights statutes to base a suit on.... A more likely explanation is that blacks and women tend to have smaller investments in human capital, including firm-specific human capital, than white males. The smaller that investment, the less the expected gain from bringing an age discrimination suit.

Given who the plaintiffs are, the Age Discrimination Act cannot realistically be characterized as progressive legislation. To the extent that the employer must factor into his labor costs the expected costs of damages judgments or settlements along with all the other costs of complying with (or violating) the Act, he will pay lower wages. He will try to lower the wages of those classes of workers most likely to bring and win age discrimination suits, but a perfect match-up cannot be expected, and this means that the costs of the Act will be borne in part at least by average workers. The Act's effect is thus to redistribute wealth from younger to older workers, or, after it has been in effect for many years, from the same workers' youth to their middle age; and, to a lesser extent, from average workers to members of professional and managerial class ... who account for most age discrimination cases.

The effects on the economy summarized. I have emphasized the extent to which the goals, at least the ostensible goals, of the Age Discrimination in Employment Act appear to have been subverted as a result of rational profit-maximizing conduct by employers. But it would be a mistake to conclude that the Act's effect on the economy has been negligible (although probably it has been small), even if costs of litigation and of legal counseling are ignored. The transition costs, both the costs of gearing up for compliance with the new law and the costs of revising the terms of employment in order to reestablish the employer's desired age profile, should not be ignored because they are transitional. They can, however, be minimized by advance notice of the law. . . .

It is possible that the Act, rather than raising the average retirement age . . . has, by encouraging offers of early retirement some of which are accepted by employees whom the employer does not want to lose, reduced the average retirement age, inducing an inefficient substitution of leisure for work. . . . Another way in which the Act may have hurt elderly workers is by discouraging contracts in which a worker agrees to work for a reduced wage, because of his diminished capacity, in lieu of being discharged. . . .

The law causes another distortion. . . . [N]ew firms are likely to have a younger age distribution than old ones, because they do more hiring and most hires are of young workers; older workers tend to be locked into their existing employments by their firm-specific human capital and also to be less adaptable to new situations. This suggests that the age discrimination law discriminates in favor of new firms because a smaller proportion of their employees are in the protected class . . . and because, as I have pointed out, the law is far more effective against discrimination in firing than in hiring. A possibly offsetting factor, however, is economies of scale in compliance with complex laws. These economies would tend to disfavor new firms relative to old ones because the former would be on average smaller.

The Economics of Mandatory Retirement

I want to examine more closely the effects of the 1986 amendment to the Age Discrimination in Employment Act that abolished mandatory retirement at any age in most occupations. A mundane but important point is that most workers want to retire when they reach what has been the normal retirement age. A few must want to stay on; otherwise firms would never have imposed mandatory retirement. But many who do want to stay on can negotiate mutually satisfactory terms with employers for doing so. And if not, they can, as we have seen, be gently pried out, even after mandatory retirement has been abolished, by means of offers of early retirement on advantageous terms.

. . .

Let us take a closer look at the history and rationale of mandatory retirement. It did not become common until after World War II. Its advent coincided with the provision of pension benefits on a systematic basis by large firms to all their long-time employees. The combination of a pension plan with mandatory retirement protects the worker against penurious old age and the employer against having to pay a wage to a worker who is no longer productive yet may actually be receiving a wage premium in order to counteract his incentive to slack off in his last period. Even if the worker is not receiving an incentive wage premium, and even if there is no contractual impediment to a reduction in his wage, age-related decline in capability may have reduced his productivity to the point where the employer would be better off replacing him. The employer could discharge the worker or force him to retire. But in the absence of mandatory retirement at a fixed age the employer would have to make a costly and (to the worker) humiliating determination that the worker had ceased to be sufficiently productive to justify retention. Because of its relation to incentive wage premia, union protections, and concern with avoiding stigma, mandatory retirement at fixed ages, rather than being a symptom of the exploitation of older workers or the operation of a mindless ageism, is correlated with employment terms and practices that favor older workers.

Mandatory retirement may also reduce an employer's agency costs (the costs of aligning employees' incentives with those of the employer). When involuntary retirement is at the discretion of the employer, employees who want to work past the normal retirement age will have an incentive to forge alliances with their supervisors that may undermine the loyalty of both sets of employees, the supervised and the supervisory, to the employer. This concern may help explain why the federal civil service was one of the earliest institutions to adopt mandatory retirement. The goal was to sever the "personal ties and informal bonds" that continued to characterize relationships within the civil service long after the formal abolition of the spoils system.

ADEA and ADA Assessed*
LAWRENCE M. FRIEDMAN

... "Age" is not an inborn characteristic that sharply sets off group against group. It is, rather, a part of the life cycle. We all get old (if we live long enough), whereas we are born white or black, male or female; the matter is settled at birth, once and for all. But where does this reasoning lead us? It is true that, for all of us, our time will come. Does this mean that people empathize more easily with old people than with other "minorities"? Not necessarily. Most white males a century ago were sure that blacks were racially inferior and that God and biology put women under men. These opinions are far from dead, but they are less prevalent than they used to be, one hopes. Most people (including some old people) think of old people, too, as inferior—weaker, less quick of mind, and so on. Since we all wear out in the end, these prejudices are plausible and persistent. "Negative stereotypes" abound; even the old come to accept them. But the basis for these stereotypes is much weaker than most people think. The question is: how can the facts about age be gotten across in a meaningful way, to as large an audience as possible?

* Lawrence M. Friedman, *Your Time Will Come: The Law of Age Discrimination and Mandatory Retirement*, copyright © 1984 by Russell Sage Foundation. Reprinted by permission of the publisher.

There is no easy answer. Racism is taboo, and sexism may be following close behind. "Ageism" still has a long way to go. Jokes about old people are still acceptable in circles that would not dare make jokes about race.

Old people are, generally speaking, objects of pity or derision. If you live long enough, people will consider you a freak, even when you act quite normally ("she's over 90, and she still does sit-ups"; "he's 85 and still goes to the office twice a week"). When somebody over 80 (say) rides a bicycle, starts piano lessons, goes to college, or in general behaves like an ordinary human being, he is thought to be at least unusual, and (alas, most likely) rather eccentric. These attitudes are slow to change.

There is, however, some sign that change is coming. Neugarten and Hagestad, writing in 1976, saw society moving in two quite opposite directions. On the one hand, "age segregation" was growing. "Bureaucracy" was "bringing with it the increasing use of chronological age in sorting and sifting people"; age was also becoming significant factor in politics. But, on the other hand, society was getting accustomed to a blurring of age categories: "70–year-old students ... 60–year-olds and 30–year-olds wearing the same clothing styles," and so on. This suggested a movement "in the direction of what might be called an age-irrelevant society."

The "age-irrelevant" society is, of course, a long way off. For one thing, certain social criteria will have to change. Here one might take a hint from the black pride movement. For blacks, it was important to insist that "black is beautiful"; this meant rejecting standards set by whites and for whites. Blackness could hardly be "beautiful" (in all sorts of senses) if beauty meant looking as much like white people as possible. Similarly, for old people to be "beautiful" or "strong" or whatever, they may have to evolve their own standards. If the standards are how fast you can run or how you look in a bathing suit, the old will come out in last place.

In one regard, race, sex, and age prejudice *can* be compared. Attitudes on each of these start out, historically, heavily laden with biological mumbo jumbo. Scientists in the nineteenth century, and even later, gathered "evidence"—now totally discredited—to prove that blacks were inferior to whites. (One natural history, published in 1883, claims that the "Ethiopian or Negro race" was "unendowed with mental faculties or moral perceptions"; all "civilized nations were Caucasian.") Most people think of race as a biological category. Actually, this is far from clear-cut. There are biological differences between races, but they are trivial. There is no *biological* reason why society should emphasize skin color and related physical traits, rather than height, hair color, or body shape. Race, as people use the term, is a social concept—as social as "class" or "nationality." The child of a black and white is defined in America as black, not white. This is certainly not a *biological* definition.

Similarly, feminists have had to confront "evidence" that women are by birth unfit for male pursuits, and not meant to be equal in politics, arts, and business. Most men—and women?—firmly believed this. (Many men and some women still do.) The difference between men and women are certainly important, unlike inborn differences of race. But these differences have to do with sex and babies, not with whether women make good accountants, doctors—or prime ministers.

With the elderly, too, we start with a biological fact: many people slow down when they reach high old age. Eventually they stop living altogether—the ultimate BFOQ is staying alive. The task is to unpack biology from mythology. Old people are probably much more capable than society is willing to grant. And the aging process is extremely variable; some people are hale and hearty at 70; others have broken down or are downright dead. When stereotypes about race and sex began to weaken, unfair patterns and practices began to get weaker, too. This will have to happen for the elderly as well.

.   .   .

Age Consciousness

Not that these laws [ADA and ADEA] are necessarily the right vehicles or the best vehicle to advance, or smooth out, social change. They may be bad; or they may be flawed but as good as can be expected, for political reasons. Perhaps any law would pose problems. The statutes try to put muscle behind a subtle and difficult campaign. Enforcement agencies have to carry out the program; their staffs consist neither of geniuses nor of angels. The governing laws are vague in spots. They have to be fleshed out, interpreted, implemented. Workers in the field need guidance. Rules and regulations proliferate; courts spin out new doctrines.

Still, age law cannot be wrapped up in a net of rules. The point is to change people's minds, to alter culture and influence behavior. The *mechanism* is a blunt, dense tissue, enforced by ordinary people. The process, then is far from perfect. Private litigation has a role to play. It gives the public a direct voice, an outlet; but it adds, of course, a layer of irrationalities; and there is never any guarantee that the "right" people sue.

Whether the campaign to alter minds will succeed is hard to say. Prejudice can be a powerful emotion. Discrimination originates in a frame of mind. Discriminatory *behavior* is another story. It may have one or more of three causes. First, it may be emotionally charged. Second, some discriminatory behavior is structural; third, some based on ignorance. For these last two, *structural* change or *informational* investment may bring about important changes in behavior. There is prejudice against old people; but it is, on the whole, not rooted in deeply irrational emotions as the prejudice against black people or against "women's liberation"; it is rather more structural and informational.

This conclusion gets a certain degree of support from an interesting little study. The subjects were some 300 MBA students in Pittsburgh, most of them men. They were shown lists, which described traits of a hypothetical employee. The lists were all the same, except for the age of the employee, which was 35, 50, 60, or 70, depending on the list. Generally speaking, students did not react strongly to age differences (although the exceptions were always unfavorable to older workers); they showed no deep prejudice against the elderly. But when asked "Would you hire this person?" fewer than a quarter said yes for the 70–year-old, and only 38 percent said yes for the 60–year-old; 61 percent agree to hire the 50–year-old, 67.6 percent the 35–year-old. Why was this so? The authors suggest "structural barriers (such as mandatory retirement) and concern as to whether or not the person will stay on the job." These considerations might convince managers that "older workers are more costly to hire." It is this sort of discrimination that legal reform has the best chance of curing. In other words, structural change (an end to mandatory retirement) and better information about older workers could change people's minds, and perhaps their behavior. No amount of information can touch prejudice grounded in ideology or hate.

Hands–Tying and the Age Discrimination in Employment Act*
CHRISTINE JOLLS

I accept, for the most part, the premise that the ADEA cannot be justified on traditional distributive or rights-based grounds. The project is then to meet the challenge posed by the concluding passage of a recent empirical analysis of the ADEA: "[The ADEA] cannot be justified in terms of opening opportunities to a historically disfavored group.... It is therefore necessary to turn to other justifications for the ADEA. These have yet to be supplied...." I examine the possibility of an efficiency-based argument in favor of the ADEA, one that links the Act to a market failure potentially remedied by it....

The efficiency argument developed below arises out of the difficulty of achieving desirable "hands-tying" in the employer-employee relationship. Hands-tying refers to a commitment not to engage in behavior that is attractive in the short term but ultimately destructive of long-term goals. Such a commitment may be desirable in the employment setting for several reasons, some familiar and others less so, and, as explained below, may be facilitated by legal limits on age discrimination in employment. An important theme in the analysis to follow is the role of labor market mobility in an efficiency-based analysis of the ADEA. I suggest that whatever one believes about the need for legal intervention to remedy shortcomings of private contracting between employers and employees known to be in long-term relationships—the focus of much of the contemporary literature in employment law—job mobility creates an independent and possibly more broadly compelling basis for legal involvement.

.   .   .

The Age–Wage Relationship

ADEA Cases

The paradigmatic ADEA claim arises from an employer's decision to replace an older worker with a younger, cheaper employee capable of performing the same job. Thus, for example, in *Metz v. Transit Mix, Inc.*, the court held that an employer violated the ADEA when, in seeking to cut its costs, it replaced the fifty-four-year-old plaintiff with a forty-three-year-old employee earning little more than half the plaintiff's salary. Judge Easterbrook, in dissent, strenuously disputed the majority's conclusion: "It is hard to imagine how the use of wages could not be [a valid business measure]; wages correspond precisely to the costs of doing business, and hence to profitability."

.   .   .

Implications

If, as the cases and the empirical evidence suggest, older workers have higher wage-productivity ratios than younger employees, how could it ever be efficient to force an employer to stick with its older employees? At first glance, such an outcome would appear to be at odds with any plausible notion of efficiency. Employers would be holding onto older workers to perform jobs that younger, cheaper candidates could do as well or better relative to their cost. Society would pay more for goods and services, and younger workers would sacrifice more in their early years than they would gain later on. Plants would be shut down, the need for cost-cutting policies would be frustrated, and the options of governmental bodies seeking to deal with shrinking budgets would be severely limited.

This gloomy view, however, fails to consider why it might be that older workers are paid so generously. Wages are determined in the market, not handed down from above. Thus, if employers and employees are opting for age-based wages, presumably there is some reason for their doing so. The sensibility of prohibiting cost-based decisions about older workers cannot be assessed without consideration of the parties' reasons for getting themselves into the high-wage situation in the first place. . . .

Explanations for Age–Based Wages

The view that forcing firms to retain older, more expensive workers is necessarily inefficient reflects a purely static conception of efficiency. From a static perspective, paying an input more than its marginal revenue product is clearly inefficient; neoclassical theory predicts that firms will hire workers up to the point at which marginal revenue product just equals the wage. But the world is more complicated than this. The analysis below explains that once we move beyond the static perspective, age-based wages may be desired by market actors either as a response to incentive problems in the employment relationship or due to employees' psychological preference for increased earnings over time. . . .

Incentive Problems in the Employment Relationship

A classic problem in the employment setting is that workers may tend not to work hard when they are paid on the basis of time worked rather than performance. This moral hazard problem is potentially serious because almost ninety percent of employees in the United States are paid on time-worked basis. Direct oversight of workers can alleviate the problem, but such oversight often imposes substantial costs of its own. . . .

A widely-noted solution to the moral hazard problem involves offering workers delayed rewards for good behavior. Even if detailed monitoring of employees' effort or output levels is prohibitively costly (so that performance-based wages are not realistic), detecting the simple fact of "shirking" of some sort, with some probability, may be feasible. Alternatively, assuming the infeasibility of cost-effective monitoring on a day-by-day or month-by-month basis, it may nevertheless be possible to infer something about employees' devotion and loyalty from their behavior over a longer period. In either case, back-loading employees' wages reduces their incentive to shirk by increasing the potential punishment associated with such behavior. With back-loaded wages, much of the reward from not shirking comes later in the employee's working life. Thus, shirking may be punished—severely—by firing the wayward employee and depriving him or her of the back-loaded reward. The potential cost of shirking at any point is therefore higher than it would be if wages did not rise over time.

· · ·

Psychological Preference for Increased Earnings Over Time

A second possible explanation for age-based wages is a psychological preference for improvement in earnings over time. Human beings appear to prefer increasing quantities of good things over time, as compared to constant streams or decreasing quantities. This may reflect in large part a tendency to evaluate options based on whether they represent upward movement from an initial status quo. Thus, for example, earning $20,000 one year, $22,000 the next, and $24,000 the year after that would typically be preferred to earning $22,000 each year. The former path entails repeated upward movement relative to the previous year's benchmark and is more attractive on that account.

Evidence from experimental economics studies suggests the existence of just this type of preference for improvement over time. In the context of job earnings specifically, one study found that individuals asked to choose between wage profiles that declined over time and wage profiles that increased over time overwhelmingly preferred the latter, even though the discounted present value of wage payments was higher with the former. This preference existed despite discounting of future events (which would imply a preference for declining profiles) in other contexts. Subjects asked why they preferred increasing wage profiles gave, as the most common explanation, "pleasure from increase," followed by "aversion to decrease." The preference for increasing profiles was less pronounced, although still present, in the case of rental income earned from ownership of an apartment building, a context in which improvements to the status quo are less likely to be attributed to actions taken by the individual. These results may reflect what psychologists have called "mastery"—the idea that people derive satisfaction from the perception that they have mastered their environment, and for this reason prefer steady improvements to a flat path over time.

. . .

The Role of the Law: Hands–Tying

The preceding Part described two theories of age-based wages that, individually or together, seem to provide at least a partial account of the wage pattern suggested by the ADEA cases and the empirical evidence. One question raised by these theories is whether legal limits on cost-based decisions about older workers might contribute to private parties' ability to make use of age-based wages. If parties are readily able to reach their preferred solution on their own, then legal involvement is probably unnecessary. As this Part explains, however, private parties may be limited in their ability to rely on age-based wages in a world in which individuals often change jobs at least once over the course of their working lives. Labor market mobility, though certainly valuable on balance, creates a species of inter-employer externality that interferes with parties' ability to use contracts or other market mechanisms to commit to age-based wages. Commitment is essential because employers will be tempted to renege on their side of the bargain when wages rise above marginal revenue product, as illustrated by the claims of cost-based decisionmaking under the ADEA.

Legal limits on cost-based decisions about older workers represent a possible solution to the inter-employer externality problem arising from labor market mobility. They facilitate commitment by tying employers' hands and preventing them from reneging on age-based wages when the back-loaded portion of those wages comes due. The law may thus play a desirable hands-tying role in a setting in which the unregulated market is unable to ensure the satisfaction of employers' and employees' preferences for age-based wages.

. . .

Hands-Tying Through Legal Rules

The limits on market mechanisms for committing to age-based wages lead to the question whether legal rules could conceivably help to mitigate the failure of the private market....

Legal Limits on Cost–Based Discharge of Older Workers—A threshold question about legal limits on cost-based discharge of older workers concerns the appropriate scope of such limits. Would employers be permitted to substitute lowering the wages of expensive older workers for discharging these individuals on cost grounds? In theory, this is an important question, but in practice it is relatively unimportant for the simple reason that employers are extremely reluctant to cut their workers' pay, fearing adverse consequences for dedication and morale. Thus, the important issue in practice is the degree to which cost-based discharge of older employees is limited by legal rules. I assume in what follows that older workers will not be vulnerable to wage cuts, either because of the practical considerations militating against such action or because of legal rules against it.

Legal limits on cost-based discharge of older workers address the central problem emphasized above with contractual means of commitment to age-based wages. As described above, labor market mobility impedes parties' ability to rely on contractual means of commitment because of the infeasibility of contracting in advance for protection against cost-based discharge with every potential future employer. The inability to contract in advance in this way means that an employee who has changed jobs has no contractual entitlement to continued employment once wages have risen above marginal revenue product. Legal limits on cost-based discharge of older workers respond to the limits on contractual solutions by reaching beyond the limits of any single employment relationship. Unlike contracts, they commit employers that have not entered into contracts with particular employees. In effect, legal rules replicate the contractual terms parties would bargain for were they contracting in advance with all potential future employers. Legal limits on cost-based discharge thus mitigate the job-mobility barrier to contractual means of commitment and effectively tie the parties' hands where contracts cannot.

Legal Limits on Cost-Based Failure To Hire—The hands-tying argument for legal limits on cost-based decisions about older workers applies not only to decisions to discharge older workers but also to decisions not to hire these individuals. Legal limits on cost-based failure to hire provide the mobile employee with an entitlement to age-based wages at a new firm—assuming the employer does not have an independent ground for refusing to hire the individual. Legal rules thus replicate the arrangement the parties would have bargained for were ex ante contracting feasible. The only qualification of the previous argument is that legal protection against wage cuts may be more important in the case of hiring than in the case of discharge, as in the latter case employers' reluctance to impose wage cuts may be greater. Apart from this distinction, the argument for legal limits on cost-based failure to hire tracks that for limits on cost-based discharge. In both instances, legal rules tie the parties' hands where contracts cannot....

Richard Posner has argued that legal limits on failure to hire older workers are unlikely to have much practical force because of the insubstantial economic damages suffered by disappointed job applicants, as distinguished from workers who are discharged after having accumulated significant relationship-specific human capital. As described above, however, older workers appear to be paid more than younger ones simply because of their age—at least up to some point. It follows that an older worker who is refused a job at a wage greater than marginal revenue product has in fact suffered substantial economic damages as a consequence of the employer's behavior.

Empirical Confirmation

The hands-tying argument for legal limits on cost-based decisionmaking suggests that imposing such limits will increase the feasibility, and therefore the use, of age-based wages. This prediction is one that is testable in principle. For example, if certain states were to adopt legal limits on cost-based decisionmaking during a particular period while other states did not adopt such limits, then the relative change in the use of age-based wages in the two groups of states might provide some insight into the effect of the legal change. If, however, legal limits on cost-based decisionmaking are imposed at the national level (as with the ADEA), then empirical confirmation of the hands-tying argument is difficult....

Indirect means of corroborating the hands-tying argument are somewhat more promising. One means of testing the argument is to look to the wages negotiated by unions—institutions that may help to address the inter-employer externality problem that arises with job mobility. Whereas an employee who changes jobs at a point at which wages exceed marginal revenue product may be unlikely to earn age-based wages at a nonunionized firm, a unionized firm needing experienced workers may find it difficult to employ them except at the wage level specified by the union. The union thus in effect mimics the ex ante contracting that would enable the parties to solve the inter-employer externality problem. In this way, unions may help to mitigate the shortcomings of private contracting—which of course persist to some degree in a market with imperfect restraints on employer behavior, such as those imposed by the ADEA. Whether unions actually perform this function is another question. It is, however, empirically true that unionized employees are more likely to have pensions, and were more likely to be subject to mandatory retirement, than their nonunionized counterparts, consistent with the suggestion of greater feasibility of age-based wages in the unionized sector.

As a final observation, the fact that job mobility plays an important role in the hands-tying analysis developed above does not imply that only highly-mobile employees should avail themselves of legal protection against cost-based discharge or failure to hire. Given the existence of such protection, employees in long-term relationships, who might otherwise rely on contract terms for protection, may find it easier (less costly) to rely on legal rules. The off-the-shelf approach economizes on negotiating, drafting, and other transaction costs, and it permits the employee to capture the benefits, such as predictability, of using terms that have already been extensively litigated and interpreted by courts. The empirical evidence indicates that many ADEA plaintiffs have been with their current employers for substantial periods, suggesting that employees who are not highly mobile do indeed rely on legal means of protection.

ADEA Implications

This Part focuses on the doctrinal implications of the hands-tying analysis developed [earlier]. An important threshold issue is the degree to which the efficiency considerations underlying that analysis properly influence the project of interpreting the ADEA.

. . .

Disparate Impact Liability Under the ADEA

The Case for Imposing Disparate Impact Liability—The "disparate impact" rubric in antidiscrimination law applies to employment practices that disproportionately burden a protected group but are not directly motivated by the protected characteristic. Disparate impact analysis originated under Title VII, and its application in the ADEA context remains uncertain. The Court in *Hazen Paper* expressly reserved the question of the availability of disparate impact analysis under the ADEA, and appeals courts since then have split on the question. The hands-tying analysis offered above provides a possible policy argument for imposing disparate impact liability: cost-based decisions about older employees—which the disparate treatment rubric cannot reach—may reflect a market failure remediable by legal involvement. Hands-tying thus argues in favor of disparate impact liability for cost-based decision-making.

Judge Easterbrook's *Metz* dissent ironically provides support for imposing disparate impact liability on hands-tying grounds. The dissent notes, "The distressed or shrinking firm may try to dispose of higher paid, older employees, cheating them out of the high compensation at the end of their careers. A disparate impact approach under the ADEA might help to curtail this opportunism." Judge Easterbrook did not pursue this suggestion because he found it inapplicable to the facts of the case. However, the suggestion—though difficult to reconcile with the tenor of his opinion as a whole—is squarely in line with the hands-tying analysis developed above. Judge Posner has similarly recognized the possible desirability of limiting cost-based decisions about older workers, but he goes on to reject the idea out of hand, reasoning that "maybe because [it] would make it difficult for firms to take rational steps to reduce their costs when they find, for whatever reason, that they are paying wages in excess of the market, the Supreme Court has rejected this approach." *Hazen Paper* is cited in support of the concluding assertion, but, as noted above, the implications of that decision for disparate impact liability under the ADEA are somewhat murkier than Posner suggests. From a policy perspective, hands-tying considerations provide an argument in favor of the approach of circuits that have upheld disparate impact liability under the ADEA.

The "Discrimination" Label and Other Caveats—On first glance, labeling a cost-based discharge or refusal to hire "age discrimination" may seem incongruous. After all, the employer is acting not on the basis of age but on the basis of cost. The observation has particular salience in the case of discharge of a recently-hired older employee or refusal to hire an older candidate, as here the employer has not benefited from payment of low wages early on. On the other hand, these are precisely the situations in which private contracts are least effective (as job movement has occurred) and, thus, in which the hands-tying argument for legal involvement has the greatest force.

Several considerations support labeling cost-based discharge or failure to hire "age discrimination." First, the employer's behavior is based on the simple fact of the employee's position on the wage trajectory, which in turn is directly related to the employee's age. Second, in a world in which (because of legal or other constraints) employers typically do not engage in cost-based decisionmaking even as to older employees on whom they have not capitalized during low-wage periods, an employer that does engage in such decisionmaking will in effect reap the benefits of low wage payments without paying the full costs.

Apart from the labeling concern, imposition of disparate impact liability for cost-based decisions about older workers raises serious issues of implementation and may entail considerable administrative and other costs. To begin, courts may often be unable to distinguish between cases of cost-based discharge or refusal to hire an older worker and cases in which the worker is unattractive on independent grounds. Second, the behavior targeted by legal limits on cost-based decisionmaking is a deviation from the age-based wages desired by market participants. Identifying departures from a benchmark that is not itself easily identifiable presents obvious difficulties.

Courts might respond to the latter problem by looking to other firms in an employer's industry or in other industries to formulate rough age-wage benchmarks against which to assess the employer's behavior. Yardstick competition of this sort is used routinely by utility regulators seeking to uncover firms' underlying cost structures, much as courts here must seek to uncover underlying age-wage relationships. Yardstick competition can also be used to guard against the imposition of liability for adverse decisions on an employer to whom, for some reason, older workers tend to flock—a response that is desirable on both fairness and efficiency grounds.

These observations hardly suffice (and in some cases do nothing) to dispel the concern that courts applying disparate impact analysis to cost-based decisions about older workers impose costs greater than any conceivable benefit. My argument is simply that hands-tying considerations provide a possible argument for imposing disparate impact liability. Contrary to the suggestion of several courts and commentators, imposition of liability for cost-based decisionmaking is not inefficient as a matter of basic economics. Instead, imposition of such liability may facilitate the use of age-based wages and is potentially desirable on that ground.

Why the ADEA?

An important question is whether the ADEA is likely to be a better means of achieving desirable hands-tying than other legal doctrines potentially suited to that function. The most obvious alternative to the ADEA, and the alternative on which I focus here, is the law of wrongful discharge, which, as its name suggests, imposes limits on employers' ability to discharge employees without cause. Wrongful discharge law looks much like the ADEA in terms of the demographic characteristics of plaintiffs. Moreover, several commentators on wrongful discharge law have focused on the precise features of wages and productivity emphasized above in the analysis of the ADEA.

I offer two arguments about the suitability of the ADEA on hands-tying grounds, one comparative (involving the ADEA and wrongful discharge law) and the other a purely affirmative argument for the ADEA. As to the comparative issue, I want to suggest that, in two specific respects, the ADEA provides a better fit with the underlying problem than does wrongful discharge law. First, wrongful discharge law applies only to discharge, and not to refusal to hire an older candidate. Thus, wrongful discharge law does nothing to facilitate contract-like protection for employees who find it necessary to search for new jobs during the life-cycle. Second, tenure with a particular firm may be a significant factor in an employee's ability to prevail on a wrongful discharge claim (which will often rest on a notion of implied contract). Thus, again, wrongful discharge law fails to protect many of the individuals—this time, individuals who have recently joined new firms—who would be protected by the ADEA. These gaps in protection under wrongful discharge law are problematic because, as documented above, it is age, not tenure at a particular firm, that produces the wage-productivity disparity that in turn drives cost-based decisions about older workers. Wrongful discharge law is incomplete because it is fundamentally predicated upon the model of the employment relationship as a long-term relationship between employer and employee—a model that, as described above, has animated much of the existing literature but fails to account for the conceptually and practically important phenomenon of job mobility.

The affirmative argument for the ADEA is in some sense just a recasting of the comparative argument. The affirmative version of the argument is that the ADEA makes pivotal the precise feature of an employee that makes contract-like protection desirable. According to the hands-tying analysis developed above, it is age, not time with a particular employer, that gives rise to a need for protection, and it is age that gives rise to protected status under the ADEA.

Notes and Questions

1. Contrary to the initial expectations of those who drafted the ADEA, age discrimination cases have secured a significant presence among antidiscrimination lawsuits. For example, age discrimination claims accounted for fifty-one percent of the monetary damages obtained in employment discrimination cases brought by the EEOC between 1984 and 1988, representing about twenty-five percent of the EEOC's caseload over that period. Moreover, the EEOC witnessed a thirty-four percent growth in the number of ADEA claims filed between 1989 and 1993. Jolls at 1814. While the number of claims filed with the EEOC dipped slightly over the latter half of the 1990's, some predict that the aging of the Baby Boomer generation will engender a steep increase in the number of age discrimination claims in the years to come. Lisa Stansky, "New Age Woes," *American Bar Association Journal* 66 (January 1997).

2. Much of the debate about whether age discrimination should be compared to race or sex discrimination arises from diverging perceptions about the American elderly. Providing support to the portrayal of the elderly that Issacharoff, Harris, and Posner depict, Peter Schuck offers the following litany of legislations that the elderly were able to procure as a powerful lobbying group: "By 1975 their successes included Medicare and Medicaid, which together pay for over two-thirds of the health-care costs of the elderly; rapidly rising Social Security benefits indexed against inflation; the Supplementary Security Income program, which established a minimum federal

income for the elderly, blind, and disabled and also is indexed against inflation; special housing programs; pension reform; the Age Discrimination in Employment Act of 1967; and preferential tax treatment." Schuck, "The Graying of Civil Rights Law: The Age Discrimination Act of 1975," 89 *Yale Law Journal* 27, 41–42 (1979). In terms of economic power, Peter Uhlenberg points out that between 1959 and 1987, the notion that the elderly were economically disadvantaged became obsolete, as the proportion of the elderly with income below the poverty line dropped from 35 percent to 12 percent. Uhlenberg, "Population Aging and Social Policy," 19 *The Annual Review of Sociology* 449, 458 (1992). Older Americans now have lower poverty rates than young Americans.

This view is strenuously opposed by another group of scholars, such as George Alexander, who suggest that the elderly are often victims of stigmatizing stereotypes, which make them vulnerable to getting involuntarily replaced by younger workers. These scholars further argue that the elderly are among the poorest and politically vulnerable groups, unable to counteract or effectively respond to this kind of involuntary unemployment. In 1975, Robert Butler wrote, "Older people begin to face age discrimination as early as age 45, even if highly qualified. . . . They are denied the right to work and thus, one important ingredient in the right to survive. They are restricted in the control of their own lives because they are captives of their economic history—first depression, now inflation—and their previous thrift is meaningless, for life savings are gobbled up by the caprice of the marketplace. The price of retirement leisure is the loss of one-fourth to one-half of their income." Butler, *Why Survive? Being Old in America* 66 (New York: Harper & Row, Publishers, 1975). In the words of Niall Paul, writing in 1989, "Throughout recent history older employees have been forced to leave work, live in poverty, and seek government subsidies." Paul, "Reduction in Force Early Retirement Incentives and the Age Discrimination in Employment Act," 3 *Detroit College of Law Review* 987, 1037 (1989).

Lawrence Friedman tries to steer a middle course between the polar characterizations of the elderly in contemporary America, stating that: "The elderly may not be disadvantaged as a group; but when they stumble and fall, they fall very far, and irreversibly. Most old people are reasonably active and strong; when they are badly off, they are badly off indeed. To die slowly, miserably, in poverty and pain; to lose everything in the end: this is a recurrent social nightmare, and its strength helps to run the benefit machine." Friedman at 70.

3. Similarly, competing notions of the consequences of retirement fuel the debate on whether mandatory retirement is an appropriate social policy for older workers. In some commentators' view, early retirement (which will inevitably be the result of mandatory retirement for some workers who are not ready to retire at a fixed age) forces capable workers from giving up their jobs with very real negative emotional and economic consequences on individual retirees. Moreover, early retirement incentives (even if implemented in a noncoercive manner) may reinforce the ageist stereotypes of faltering productivity that impact the entire class of older workers. Paul at 996. In contrast, scholars such as Issacharoff and Harris point out that there

are important dignitary benefits to mandatory retirement: "Because mandatory retirement is imposed by society on all members of society, at least potentially, it entails neither the stigmatization nor victimization associated with the imposition of constraints on discrete and insular groups." Issacharoff and Harris at 820. In this view, retirement is generally conceptualized as a boon for older workers: "A retired American today is probably the freest human being ever to walk the earth. Assuming that basic needs are met by a pension, Social Security, Medicare and investment income, the retiree lives in a perpetual paradise of leisure and recreation. If the retiree stays healthy, this special status can be enjoyed for 15 to 20 years. There is time to fish all day and golf every afternoon." Kingsley Davis, "Our Idle Retirees Drag Down the Economy," *New York Times* A31 (October 18, 1987).

Which of these two opposing views is more convincing?

4.   There is no specific rationale for why the age of forty was chosen as the lower threshold for protection under the ADEA. Robert Coulson notes the possibility that the designation was attributable to the experience of Congressman Pucinsky who made a fact-finding "undercover" mission to several factories. "The employment office didn't even ask for his name; instead, they took a look at his gray hair and asked him how old he was.... They were not interested in his experience, but simply complied with a company policy not to hire anyone over 40." Coulson, *Empowered at Forty* (New York: Harper Collins, 1990). The ADEA's designation of forty, like the assignation of sixty-five as the traditional retirement age under Social Security, is essentially arbitrary. Under the terms of protection set forth by the ADEA, employers would not be prohibited from engaging in age discrimination against someone who is thirty-eight or thirty-nine, for instance. Is it equitable to deny a thirty-eight or thirty-nine year old worker means of legal recourse while affording redress to workers past a certain arbitrarily designated age? Echoing this sentiment, John Blackburn argues that Congress should reduce the lower age limit of the ADEA to age 18. Blackburn, "Charting Compliance under the Age Discrimination in Employment Act," 57 *Chicago-Kent Law Review* 559 (1981). Taking this logic even further, one commentator proposes an elimination of all age restrictions under the ADEA. Bryan B. Woodruff, "Unprotected Until Forty: The Limited Scope of the Age Discrimination in Employment Act of 1967," 73 *Indiana Law Journal* 1295 (1998). Interestingly, the Age Discrimination Act of 1975, which prohibits age discrimination by all entities receiving federal funding, does protect all persons of all ages. Peter Schuck points out, however, that this all-inclusive provision is critically flawed because virtually all action taken by the entity receiving federal assistance will have a disparate effect on different age groups, and thus some will always be more adversely affected than others. Schuck, "The Graying of Civil Rights Law: The Age Discrimination Act of 1975." 89 *Yale Law Journal* 27, 50 (1979).

5.   The ADEA does not create an absolute prohibition against all age-based employment decisions. Indeed, it is not unlawful for employers to discriminate on the basis of age "where age is a bona fide occupational qualification reasonably necessary to the normal operation of the particular business" (usually referred to as "BFOQ") or "where the differentiation is based on reasonable factors other than age" (otherwise known as the

"RFOA" exception). The ADEA also allows employers "to observe the terms of a bona fide seniority system [or] to observe the terms of a bona fide employee benefit plan" when such plans are not used as a pretext or subterfuge for age discrimination. And finally, employers are allowed to "to discharge or otherwise discipline an individual for good cause."

The legislative history does not provide much guidance on how courts should construe these exceptions. However, following the judicial construction of the BFOQ defense in Title VII cases, courts have delineated the following BFOQ test for ADEA cases. The employer must show: (1) the qualification is reasonably necessary to the essence of the employer's business; and (2) that all or substantially all workers in the protected category are unable to perform the job or that individualized assessment is highly impractical. The second prong of this test can be satisfied by statistical employment profiles correlating age and job performance, either within the employer's workforce or industry. Isn't allowing this kind of statistical performance data based on age directly contradictory to the aim of the ADEA to protect older workers from stigmatizing stereotypes? After all, in its preamble, the ADEA declares that the purpose of the ADEA is "to promote employment of older persons based on their *ability* rather than age." (emphasis added)

The RFOA exception also presents thorny issues. For example, if an employer terminates older employees and claims that the decision was based on their health, not age, should the employer escape liability even though the decision has a disparate impact on older workers? (For further discussions on the applicability of the disparate impact theory in ADEA cases, see question 7 below.) With respect to the use of health as a reasonable factor other than age, courts have generally accepted the employer's argument, finding that the "age statute was not meant to prohibit employment decisions based on factors that sometimes accompany advancing age, such as declining health or diminished vigor and competence." *Loeb v. Textron, Inc.*, 600 F.2d 1003, 1016 (1st Cir.1979). In these cases, however, the terminated employees may still have a cause of action under the Americans with Disabilities Act, which requires employers to provide reasonable accommodation to disabled employees. Constance Kleiner Hood, "Age Discrimination in Employment and the Americans with Disabilities Act: A Second Bite at the Apple," 6 *Elder Law Journal* 1 (1998). Considering this potential interaction between the ADEA and the Americans with Disabilities Act, Posner notes, "The ADA may succeed in helping older workers where the ADEA has been ineffective." Posner at 339. See also Alison Barnes, "The Americans with Disabilities Act: Envisioning a Future for Age and Disability Discrimination Claims," 35 *Michigan Journal of Law Reform* 263 (2002).

Finally, the bona fide seniority or benefits plan exception also raises problematic issues of its own. Courts have struggled to decide whether early retirement incentive plans that became popular after mandatory retirement was abolished constituted the kind of bona fide employee benefit plan covered by this exception. In these cases, question of voluntariness became central, especially as many employers required that employees who accepted the incentive waive all claims that might arise under the ADEA. In 1990,

Congress enacted the Older Workers Benefit Protection Act (OWBPA) to ensure that workers who released age discrimination claims did so in a "knowing and voluntary" manner. Thus Title II of OWBPA sets forth specific threshold requirements for procuring a valid waiver of ADEA rights. Since its enactment, however, the OWBPA has been criticized by scholars as compromising the antidiscrimination goals of the ADEA. See, e.g., Richard J. Lussier, "Title II of the Older Workers Benefit Protection Act: A License for Age Discrimination? The Problem Identified and Proposed Solutions," 35 *Harvard Journal on Legislation* 189 (1998); Michael C. Harper, "Age–Based Exit Incentives, Coercion, and the Prospective Waiver of ADEA Rights: The Failure of the Older Workers Benefit Protection Act," 79 *Virginia Law Review* 1271 (1993).

6.   Before *Hazen Paper Co. v. Biggins*, 507 U.S. 604 (1993), a number of courts had held that factors such as retirement eligibility or seniority are so closely and invariably correlated with age that decisions based on those factors constitute unlawful age discrimination. However, in *Hazen Paper*, the Supreme Court narrowed the age proxy doctrine by holding that decisions based on age-related factors do not necessarily amount to age discrimination. In *Hazen Paper*, the plaintiff was a sixty-two year old worker who alleged that his employer had fired him in order to prevent his pension benefits from vesting. The court held that because the pension status of the plaintiff was "analytically distinct" from his age (albeit closely correlated with age), the plaintiff had no recourse under the ADEA. In the aftermath of *Hazen Paper*, it appears that in order to prevail under the ADEA, the plaintiff must show that the employer used an age-related factor in order to mask a discriminatory animus against the plaintiff's age. But as one commentator points out, an employer "rarely waves a red flag announcing his or her discriminatory intent." Toni J. Querry, "A Rose by Any Other Name No Longer Smells as Sweet: Disparate Treatment Discrimination and the Age Proxy Doctrine after *Hazen Paper Co. v. Biggins*," 81 *Cornell Law Review* 530, 554 (1996).

7.   *Hazen Paper* explicitly left open the question whether the disparate impact doctrine was applicable to claims arising under the ADEA. However, some courts have interpreted *Hazen Paper* as implying that intentional discrimination is a prerequisite for ADEA liability and thus disparate impact theory is no longer applicable for ADEA cases. The disparate impact theory, as developed in Title VII cases, holds that even facially neutral employment practices that are not motivated by discriminatory intent are prohibited if it has a disproportionate effect on a protected group. As applied to older workers, for example, the disparate impact theory would hold that when an employer fires all employees with more than five years of experience at a firm because it costs more to pay those workers (many of whom are older), they may have a discrimination claim even if the employer did not have the motive of discriminating against older workers per se. In 2002, the Supreme Court was expected to settle this question in *Adams v. Florida Power Corporation*, which involved allegations of disparate impact surrounding an employer's decision to terminate workers as part of a reorganization effort. After hearing oral arguments, however, the Court declined to rule on the

issue. As a result, the question of the applicability of the disparate impact theory in ADEA cases remains unresolved.

Many scholars argue against extending the disparate impact theory to ADEA cases on the basis that the ADEA's legislative history only evinces an intent to allow disparate treatment, that age discrimination is fundamentally different from race/sex discrimination, and that any other construction would render the RFOA provision superfluous. See, e.g., Evan H. Pontz, "What a Difference ADEA Makes: Why Disparate Impact Theory Should Not Apply to the Age Discrimination in Employment Act," 74 *North Carolina Law Review* 267 (1995); Douglas C. Herbert and Lani Schweiker Shelton, "A Pragmatic Argument Against Applying the Disparate Impact Doctrine in Age Discrimination Cases," 37 *South Texas Law Review 625* (1996). Other scholars argue that disparate impact theory is crucial for upholding the broad aim of the ADEA, that there are important parallels between age and race/sex discrimination, and that practically it is very difficult for plaintiffs to prove intentional discrimination in ADEA cases. See, e.g., Brendan Sweeney, " 'Downsizing' the Age Discrimination in Employment Act: The Availability of Disparate Impact Liability," 41 *Villanova Law Review* 1527 (1996); Mack A. Player, "Wards Cove Packing or Not Wards Cove Packing? That Is Not the Question: Some Thoughts on Impact Analysis Under the Age Discrimination in Employment Act," 31 *Richmond Law Review* 819 (1997).

In addition to the disparate impact theory, commentators have raised the possibility of importing other theories of discrimination from Title VII to ADEA. For example, should hostile environment cause of action be available under the ADEA? See Julie Vigil, "Expanding the Hostile Environment Theory to Cover Age Discrimination: How Far Is Too Far?" 23 *Pepperdine Law Review* 565 (1998).

8. According to Issacharoff and Harris, the special interest group for the elderly has been relentless in widening the scope of the ADEA, and that it has even advocated an affirmation action policy for the elderly. Indeed, one commentator notes that in recent years, many companies are implementing preferential hiring policies for older workers. Barry Bennett Kaufman, "Preferential Hiring Policies for Older Workers under the Age Discrimination in Employment Act," 56 *Southern California Law Review* 825 (1983). Does this violate the age-neutrality mandates of the ADEA? For example, when the ADEA was being considered by the Senate vote in 1967, Senator Yarborough summed up the Act this way: "this is a bill to give every American the opportunity to be equally considered for employment and promotional opportunity. It would not give preference to an older worker over a man who is 35 years old, but it gives him the right to be equally considered...." 113 Cong. Rec. 31, 253 (1967).

Consider the following questions that Lawrence Friedman raises:

> Billions and billions of dollars are paid out every year for old-age pensions, Medicare, housing for the elderly, services under OAA [Older Americans Act], to mention only the largest of the age-based programs.... The number of programs is growing all the time, along with

other special benefits, large and small—including such local ones as lower bus fares for senior citizens. All of these convey a social message, which might be a wrong message, a stereotyped message, even a "discriminatory" message. (Compare the attitude staunch feminists take toward old-fashioned laws for "protecting" women.) How can one explain this rapid movement in opposite directions—*for* benefits, and yet *for* age neutrality? Are benefits some sort of reparation or payoff? If so, for what?

Friedman at 12.

9.   The "same actor inference" is a controversial doctrine that originated with an ADEA case, *Proud v. Stone*, 945 F.2d 796 (4th Cir.1991). In *Proud*, the Fourth Circuit held that a strong inference of nondiscrimination arises when the same person both hires and fires the plaintiff. Citing work by Donohue and Siegelman, the Court reasoned, "It hardly makes sense to hire workers from a group one dislikes ... only to fire them once they are on the job." Since the 1991 decision in *Proud*, the same actor doctrine has been adopted by other courts and in other types of antidiscrimination claims. One commentator, however, points out that this doctrine can be problematic if not carefully applied. For example, the hiring official's relationship with the employee may change over time, leading to a termination decision motivated by prohibited animus (e.g., a hiring official may tolerate an older worker at an entry-level position but object to her insistence on being considered for promotion). Julie S. Northup, "The 'Same Actor Inference' in Employment Discrimination: Cheap Justice?" 73 *Washington Law Review* 193 (1998).

17

Disability Discrimination

The first major piece of federal legislation designed to prevent discrimination against the disabled was the 1973 Rehabilitation Act, which applied only to entities receiving federal funds. Seventeen years later, Congress sought to extend this prohibition on discrimination against the disabled to employers in the private sector, places of public accommodation, and state and local governments, when it adopted the Americans with Disabilities Act (ADA). The ADA was initially hailed as a comprehensive civil rights law that would transform the lives of disabled individuals by fully integrating them into every facet of American economic, political, and social life. The law garnered unprecedented bipartisan support in the House and Senate, as well as a vocal endorsement from President George Bush, who had previously resisted the expansion of other types of civil rights laws.

Despite this initial political support, the ADA generated a strong judicial backlash. According to the American Bar Association's 1998 study of all published federal district court decisions on ADA Title I cases (pertaining to employment discrimination), plaintiffs lost 92 percent of the time. Ruth Colker's comprehensive study of all federal district and appellate ADA Title I cases between 1992 and 1998 generally confirmed this finding. According to Colker, defendant-employers prevailed in more than 93 percent of all reported cases at the trial court level, and of those cases that were appealed, defendants prevailed 84 percent of the time. Based on these outcomes, she concluded, "These results are worse than results found in comparable areas of the law; only prisoner rights cases fare as poorly." Colker, "The Americans with

Disabilities Act: A Windfall for Defendants," 34 *Harvard Civil Rights–Civil Liberties Law Review* 99, 100 (1999).

Some scholars, such as Richard Scotch, argue that the failure of the ADA to live up to the expectations of its supporters lies in the continuing judicial reliance on an inappropriate conception of disability. Scotch, "Models of Disability and the Americans with Disabilities Act," 21 *Berkeley Journal of Employment and Labor Law* 213 (2000). According to Scotch, courts have mistakenly "employed a traditional medical model of disability based on incapacity that focuses on the limitations of plaintiffs with disabilities...." Id. at 218. In contrast, the correct interpretation of the ADA views disability "not as a physical or mental impairment, but as a social construction shaped by environmental factors, including physical characteristics built into the environment, cultural attitudes and social behaviors, and the institutionalized rules, procedures, and practices of private entities and public organizations." Id. at 214. Thus for example, under this socio-political model, what disables an individual in a wheelchair is not necessarily her physical impairment, but rather, a set of social choices that created an environment that confines her to her home. While Scotch contends that the drafters of the ADA envisioned that courts would examine the attitudinal and structural environments confronting a disabled individual, he argues that courts have myopically focused on the impairment in a way that improperly locates the problem within the individual.

Many critics of the judicial backlash further point out that courts have narrowed the potential reach of the statute by narrowly interpreting the definition of disability under the ADA. In the recent trilogy of Supreme Court cases decided in 1999, for example, the Court held that plaintiffs with severe myopia (*Sutton v. United Air Lines*, 527 U.S. 471), hypertension (*Murphy v. United Parcel Service*, 527 U.S. 516), and monocular vision (*Albertson's v. Kirkingburg*, 527 U.S. 555) failed to show that they were disabled or regarded as disabled. To disability rights advocates, these results appear inconsistent with the broad aim of the ADA, as reflected in its sweeping definition of disability, which includes persons with "a physical or mental impairment that substantially limits one or more of the major life activities," "a record of such an impairment," or "being regarded as having such an impairment." Mary Johnson argues that what courts have done, in effect, is to limit the ADA's protection to "only those people deemed 'disabled enough' to have the 'special privilege' of using the law—as if, in the 1960s, companies had successfully argued that only people who were of 100 percent African–American heritage could use the Civil Rights Act." Johnson, "Disabling a Civil Right," *The Nation* 20 (February 11, 2002).

Issacharoff and Nelson argue that this kind of controversy about what constitutes disability under the ADA is a reflection of the tension between the ADA's antidiscrimination command and the redistributive mandate (as embodied in the reasonable accommodation provision). They argue that the ADA is radically different from other civil rights laws, in that while it purports to be an antidiscrimination statute, it is in fact, a statute that unevenly imposes an unspecified amount of redistribution on employers. In their view, the Court in *Sutton*, *Murphy*, and *Kirkingburg* was using a narrow definition of disability as a gatekeeper in order to avoid reaching the problematic concept of redistribution. They recommend that Congress should directly address the cost implications of the ADA's reasonable accommodation mandate. In contrast, Samuel Bagenstos generally views the ADA as similar to other types of civil rights laws, in that its foremost aim is to protect an identifiable and disadvantaged class of people who share a common experience of systematic prejudice. He thus argues that what courts need is an "antisubordinationist approach" to understanding the ADA, which will allow them to properly construe what constitutes disability.

Another controversy surrounding the ADA involves its potential social and economic impact. One of the most vexing fears about the ADA is that it may have adversely impacted the employment level of disabled workers, as employers may simply refuse to hire disabled workers in order to avoid potentially burdensome obligations of reasonable accommodation. In one of the excerpted articles in this chapter, Susan Schwochau and Peter Blanck challenge empirical studies that have advanced this conclusion, exploring some of the salient alternative explanations for the apparent or actual decline in the employment of the disabled. Michael Stein shares Schwochau and Blanck's skepticism of the theory that the ADA has done more harm than good, and he critiques what he considers to be the flawed assumptions of the neoclassical model of the labor market. In particular, he offers a critical look at the set of arguments advanced by scholars such as Richard Epstein, who believe that the potential benefits associated with reasonable accommodations are inherently less than the costs they impose.

Whatever the empirical evidence on the ADA's role in incorporating disabled individuals into the workforce, what remains clear is that on all measures of socio-economic well being, individuals with disabilities lag substantially behind those without disabilities. For example, in 1997 the employment rate for people between the ages 21 and 64 with no disability was 84.4 percent, compared with 82 percent for those with a non-severe disability, and 31.4 percent for those with a severe disability. Moreover, disabled workers generally earn substantially less than workers without disability. In 1997, among men between the ages 21 and 64 with no disability, median earnings were $23,654, compared with $20,457 for those with a non-severe disability, and $13,272 for those with a severe disability. There is also a sharp disparity in educational achievement between the non-disabled and the disabled. Among individuals between the ages 25 and 64 with no disability, only 10.7 percent had not finished high school, compared with 32.6 percent among the severely disabled. These and other indicators point to the reality that disability

remains closely associated with poverty and dependency in the United
States.

Discrimination With a Difference: Can Employment Discrimination Law Accommodate the Americans With Disabilities Act?*

SAMUEL ISSACHAROFF AND JUSTIN NELSON

Introduction

All employment discrimination laws carry forth a dual objective. These
laws embody both a straightforward anti-discrimination command and a
redistributive norm.

. . .

What then is the relation between the two objectives of employment
discrimination law? Or, put another way, how much redistribution is
proper under the rubric of nondiscrimination? The core of this Article
will be an exploration of this question with regard to the Americans with
Disabilities Act (ADA or the "Act"), particularly in light of the troubling
decisions of the Supreme Court during the 1998–1999 term in the ADA
accommodation trilogy, *Sutton v. United Air Lines, Inc.*, *Albertson's, Inc.
v. Kirkingburg*, and *Murphy v. United Parcel Service, Inc.* . . .

Our argument is that because of the inherent uncertainty in the
obligation to provide "reasonable accommodation," the ADA trilogy
reveals more starkly than prior employment discrimination case law the
tension between the nondiscrimination command and the redistributive
side of employment opportunity law. The Title VII cases required neither
an independent normative justification for their redistributive impact
nor an independent measure of how much redistribution was appropriate. The redistribution in early discrimination case law flowed directly
from the prohibition on discrimination simpliciter and the measure of
required redistribution followed tort-based principles of making whole
the victims of that discrimination. In the ADA context, by contrast, the
overwhelming sweep of cases concern not discrimination simpliciter, but
a claimed failure to redistribute in the form of accommodation. The ADA
cases, therefore, require an independent normative command for the
obligation to redistribute or accommodate and some measure of how
much redistribution should ensue.

. . .

* Samuel Issacharoff and Justin Nelson, "Discrimination With a Difference: Can
Employment Discrimination Law Accommodate the Americans With Disabilities Act?"
North Carolina Law Review, vol. 79, copyright © 2001. Reprinted by permission of the
publisher.

Differential Treatment and Discrimination

The choice of the anti-discrimination model for the ADA was certainly not an oversight. The Act proclaims its primary purpose as being "a clear and comprehensive national mandate for the elimination of discrimination against individuals with disabilities." . . . Unlike other major employment discrimination statutes, however, the ADA runs into immediate difficulty in identifying the protected class.

Title VII presents a paradigmatic model of the relation of the anti-subjugation command to anticipated redistribution. In its original application, Title VII addressed forcible occupational segregation by race such that black employees were held to the lowest paying and most unattractive jobs. The presumption was that, but for discrimination, black employees, just as their white counterparts, would prefer to work as over-the-road truck drivers instead of local delivery drivers or would prefer to move into skilled trades in the steel industry rather than serve in the dirty and dangerous position of coal shovelers. Title VII's removal of the discriminatory barriers proved this assumption absolutely correct; black employees did indeed move into the more desirable positions. The perfectly predictable consequence was a corresponding redistribution of income and opportunity. Indeed, the smooth interrelation between the anti-subjugation command and the ensuing redistribution may explain the unparalleled success of Title VII in its immediate post-enactment period.

The key to these early Title VII cases was the ease of the syllogism that, but for the improper discrimination, blacks and whites would be similarly situated and would obtain an equitable distribution of social opportunities. The simplicity of that syllogism breaks down as the anti-discrimination norm becomes more venturesome and attempts to subsume differences that are not merely the product of societal construction, but that draw substantially from different sets of employees who are differently situated, as with distinctions according to pregnancy or age. What is unique about the ADA is precisely that it is the first employment discrimination law that does not attempt, even as a formal matter, to derive its redistributive objective from the anti-subjugation command. Rather, the concept of discrimination is defined in terms of the failure to redistribute initially. Put another way, the core of the antisubjugation command is that similarly situated persons should be treated similarly. The ADA's reasonable accommodation standard, however, starts this unique statutory inquiry with the claim that differently situated persons should be treated differently. Whether both sets of claims can coexist under the same anti-discrimination rubric is, we shall propose, at the heart of the current interpretive controversies surrounding the ADA.

Moreover, the ADA marks a further departure from even the extended discussions about the use of facially-neutral criteria. In challenges to standardized admissions tests in higher education, for example, a common critique is to question the ability of the selection mechanism to accurately measure either ability or likely performance. Yet the basic accommodation claim under the ADA accepts the propriety of the employer's ability to measure productivity while simultaneously arguing that there is an intervening duty to alter the work environment, even if a disabled employee may never be as productive as a non-disabled potential employee. Thus, the claim, at least in part, is not that employers are enslaved to irrational preconceptions, but that even if the preconceptions reflect actual productivity, there is an independent duty to accommodate a disabled candidate.

Whereas definitions based on race, sex, or age are in the broad run of cases self-defining, the definition of a disability for purposes of employment is inherently problematic. The statute defines "disability" as "(A) a physical or mental impairment that substantially limits one or more of the major life activities of such individual; (B) a record of such an impairment; or (C) being regarded as having such an impairment." Each of these terms leaves open critical definitional questions and the interpretive guidelines issued by the Equal Employment Opportunity Commission (EEOC) do little beyond redefining the terms at even greater levels of abstraction. Not only have these threshold definitional questions consumed ADA litigation, but they seem deliberately aimed at foreclosing the emergence of a predictable regulatory regime. As expressed by the EEOC, "the determination of whether an individual is substantially limited in a major life activity must be made on a case-by-case basis."

The difficulty of defining the scope of the class and activities protected by the statute is compounded by a similar ambiguity in defining the scope of the employer's corresponding obligation. The difficult issues in any system of redistribution or costly accommodation arise from determining the proper parties to bear the cost burden and the proper level of cost that must be borne. In other anti-discrimination contexts, however, the cost burdens are to greater or lesser extents constrained by the underlying equality norm. In other words, the costs imposed result from the failure to treat like candidates for employment in like fashion. The ADA eschews this formal equality command by directing that the finding of a disability affecting a major life activity triggers a duty of reasonable accommodation.

The use of the formal discrimination model allowed Congress to disclaim the clear cost consequences of the burden of accommodation it shifted onto employers. The "unfunded mandate" quality of the obligation was magnified by the undefined scope of the ensuing responsibility to accommodate. The problem with the statute is that once a person is deemed disabled, the parties then must litigate at substantial cost the issues of reasonable accommodation, business necessity, and qualification standards.

. . .

Major Life Activities Versus Reasonable Accommodation: The ADA Trilogy

If, as we have set out thus far, the ADA delivers courts into a regulatory environment bereft of clear markers for regulating potentially costly market activity, then the Supreme Court's recent ADA trilogy may be viewed as just the latest effort in the Court's ongoing attempt to define defensible and administrable boundaries for disability accommodation claims. Under this view, the Court's decisions in *Sutton v. United Air Lines, Murphy v. United Parcel Service*, and *Albertson's, Inc. v. Kirkingburg* are best understood as an attempt to create a gatekeeping mechanism within an inherently ambiguous legislative standard. . . .

. . . Under this approach, courts would avoid the ensuing envelopment into the minute factual details of each individual accommodation claim by raising the barriers to entry into ADA litigation.

. . .

Courts in the Regulatory Abyss

A Social Insurance Model of Discrimination

. . . Karlan and Rutherglen propose a normative justification by casting the ADA into the model of an implicit insurance arrangement. To do so, they posit a world of individuals in an original position in which their particular attributes could not be known at the time the social policy had to be created. By asking what the world would look like behind such a Rawlsian veil of ignorance, Karlan and Rutherglen can posit that because people would have no way of knowing whether they would become disabled, everyone would want some form of accommodation for the possibility of having a disability. Consequently, they argue, the ADA could properly be seen as a form of workplace insurance against the common risk that anyone could have been the individual suffering a disabling misfortune.

While the Karlan and Rutherglen insurance model presents a useful starting point for analysis, ultimately it does not completely capture the true nature of the employer's liability under the ADA. Under a veil of ignorance, not only is it impossible to know whether one will actually be disabled, it is also impossible to guess whether any particular person will bear the primary burden of paying for this insurance. In other words, their model answers only half of the question. An insurance scheme not only must avoid the adverse selection problem, it also must have the capacity to smooth the risk pool over the entire class. While Karlan and Rutherglen neatly capture the first part, they barely address the lack of risk-spreading in the ADA. In any insurance program, the insurer must be able to spread its risk across a sufficient number of people to reduce the potential that chance alone will cause costs and liabilities to soar dramatically.

It is the lack of risk-spreading that distinguishes the ADA from a true insurance pooling arrangement. The ADA's accommodation standards are triggered first by the fact that a potential employee selected one employer rather than another to apply to for a job. Thus, any individual employer may be subject to costs of unknown dimensions while her competitors are not. In turn, the extent of the accommodation standard is defined not by a uniform obligation across all employers, but by the ability of any employer to pay, regardless of fault or ensuing competitive disadvantage. By contrast, a true insurance model would tax employers either on a standard scale, or perhaps on some experience-rated scale, and then pay off the ensuing costs out of the insurance pool. The key to a genuine insurance view of employer costs is that costs either become an across-the-board feature of doing business for all employers (as with the minimum wage) or they provide some other mechanism to pool risk (as with unemployment insurance).

Another member of the emerging Virginia school of statutory remediation, Professor Verkerke, tries to fill in the gap left by Karlan and Rutherglen. Professor Verkerke argues that the ADA could properly be viewed as equitably spreading risk if, instead of imposing costs on all employers, it directed disabled employees to those employers who were best able to accommodate them in a cost-effective fashion. This approach to the ADA might not fully resolve the inter-employer equity problem, but it would claim great social utility because it would efficiently allocate the societal costs of accommodation. If Professor Verkerke is right, there would be a strong normative justification for the regulatory processes of the ADA as achieving a maximum of accommodation by the cheapest cost providers of that accommodation. Unfortunately, this argument also has a fundamental shortcoming: Nothing in the ADA, its case law, or its regulations explains how the ADA will provide for the most effective accommodation.

The ADA specifies that once an employee qualifies as disabled, the employer has the duty to accommodate unless such accommodation proves unduly burdensome. That inquiry, in turn, is not a comparative one that would allow proof that another employer exists that could provide accommodation at a lesser price, at least not under the current positive case law of the ADA. Under the reasoning of the Court in *Sutton*, for example, an employee would not even be classified as disabled in the first instance if she could transition into any other job within a broad category of employment. But even if we carve out the recent ADA trilogy, it is still not clear what the mechanism is that avoids a liability determination until the least costly accommodator is found. Not only does Professor Verkerke admit that there is no tie-in to the case law at present, but it is also unclear what legal standards he would like to see emerge. Certainly no other area of employment discrimination law has evolved a defense to discrimination on the basis of a rival firm being a cheaper alternative for an unwanted employee.

Professor Verkerke's argument also might create perverse incentives for employers to fight all forms of accommodation for their current employees. Under current law, many cases that make it past the first hurdle of proving a disability and the potential for reasonable accommodation settle because of the uncertain nature of both recovery for monetary damages and injunctive relief. Consequently, many employees and employers accept a compromise when the employer makes some form of minimal accommodation in exchange for the employee returning to the job and dropping the lawsuit. Professor Verkerke's plan would discourage even this minimal amount of accommodation because once an employer made some type of accommodation, that employer would become a magnet for other disabled employees. Under a comparative accommodation approach, even a marginal difference in accommodation would permit other employers to use the first employer as evidence that someone else could better accommodate the disabled employee. Thus, more disabled employees would "match" with employers who already accommodated either through settlement or coercion, or simply because the employer thought it was the right thing to do. Employers might shy away from making any affirmative or voluntary steps toward accommodation if they thought that it would require them to employ a heavier concentration of disabled workers with attendant higher costs. Indeed, the workplaces that would best match disabled workers might be those workplaces that happened through chance to accommodate first, thus not resolving the fundamental point about the ADA's lack of risk pooling.

The Costs of Redistribution

... The odd quality of the ADA is that risk is not pooled through the broad market, but through the random act of a prospective employee applying for a job, a feature that is only somewhat offset by the requirement that the employer have at least fifteen employees to fall under the statute's mandates. By itself, however, that lone number is not a fully satisfactory definition of an ability to avoid adverse selection or arbitrary bad luck. A workplace with fifteen employees does not command a sufficient market presence to pass off the cost to consumers or have a presumptive surplus from other employees.

Moreover, the ADA is fundamentally different from other statutes such as the Sherman Act, the Clean Air Act, and the Endangered Species Act. In almost all other statutes in which Congress uses vague terms, it does so within the overall aim of the statute itself. For example, courts know that poorly defined words in environmental regulation statutes still fit under the general goal of improving the environment, even if their cost-benefit contours are hazy. Indeed, in almost all of these statutes, Congress and the implementing agencies have expressly acknowledged the wealth-redistributive aspect of the statute. The fundamental distinction between these statutes and the ADA is that the latter forces the inquiry within the poorly-fitted context of a "but for" discrimination model. With regard to the Sherman Act, for example, courts are able to confer a meaning on a broad and vaguely-worded statute because both the courts and Congress have recognized the long common-law tradition of judicial involvement in this area. If Congress does not like a decision, it can enact a statute overturning the ruling; both Congress and the courts work under a shared understanding of the basic meaning of the terms, even if they might disagree on the result in any given case. When Congress disagrees with the Court's interpretation of the Sherman Act under say, a rule of reason standard, Congress knows exactly how to overrule the Court's decision.

Yet the resolution is not so clear cut in the ADA cases. Fundamentally, the ADA is distinct from statutes like the Sherman Act because the ADA runs counter to the common law, rather than supplementing it. The history of the courts' involvement in antitrust law lends itself relatively well to judicially-crafted rules. By contrast, courts have traditionally been extremely wary of crafting rulings when it receives so little guidance from Congress in areas that have a profound effect on private market ordering and wealth redistribution. The courts' common-law experience with discrimination statutes is centrally within the realm of "but for" discrimination. Courts have the competence to decide whether the government or a private actor is discriminating against a person based solely upon that person's skin color or sex. Courts tread on more precarious turf when the "but for" discrimination aspect becomes secondary to the unstated wealth redistribution goal of the statute.

Even the analogy to tort law development is fundamentally distinct from the ADA. In tort cases, courts are able to balance the risks versus the benefits and do so classically, even within the employment relationship. As Karlan and Rutherglen point out, "negligence law places the loss on the party, either plaintiff or defendant, who could have reduced the risk that caused the harm to the plaintiff at the least cost." The ADA, by contrast, does not rely on efficiency per se; rather, it looks to equalize the workforce without giving substantive guidance or effect to the meaning of terms like "reasonable accommodation" and "undue hardship."

The problem with the ADA is a combination of factors yielding a series of concerns, the first two of which are most apparent, while the third is potentially the most problematic. First, the statute poorly confronts its core concern with accommodation by invoking time-tested anti-discrimination norms. Second, the statute does not confront the costs that must be borne to meet the redistribution it impliedly envisions. These two concerns yield some failure of political accountability for the trade-off in using societal resources for access as opposed to other goals. While troubling, these concerns are present in large areas of the regulatory landscape and do not set apart the ADA. By contrast, the third concern, the failure of the statute to insure that costs are borne equitably across the class of affected employers, may be addressed independently.

. . .

Conclusion

Our goal is to show that behind the odd interpretations in the latest round of ADA employment cases lies a difficult problem of judicial administration of a poorly-crafted statute. The seeming inconsistencies of the recent ADA trilogy stem from the fact that while the ADA purports to be a statute attacking "but for" discrimination, it is really a statute inviting an unspecified amount of redistribution. Although other statutes since Title VII have had to balance the anti-discrimination command with an implicit commitment to redistribution, only the ADA finds its primary statutory concern in the anticipated shift of resources to its intended beneficiaries. No doubt a wealthy and benevolent society may direct substantial resources to facilitate the integration of the disabled or any other disadvantaged group. But while such societal objectives are entirely noble, there is insufficient political responsibility in passing statutes that are only marginally related to their true objectives. The ADA is not just another anti-discrimination statute, and it was incumbent on Congress to address how it was to be implemented and at what cost.

Subordination, Stigma, and "Disability"*
SAMUEL R. BAGENSTOS

"Disability" as a Subordinated Group Status

... I attempt to shed light on the proper interpretation of the ADA's "disability" category by developing a particular conception of the problem to which the ADA should be seen as responding. Drawing on the congressional findings in the text of the ADA, as well as the writings of a number of disability studies scholars, I suggest that the statute can be seen as responding to a problem of impairment-based subordination: Through prejudice, stereotypes, and widespread neglect, society's attitudes and practices attach systematic disadvantage to particular impairments. By so doing, disability rights scholars have persuasively argued, society in fact creates an identifiable class of "people with disabilities." Disability rights law can therefore be seen as providing members of that subordinated class with the means (antidiscrimination and reasonable-

* Samuel R. Bagenstos, "Subordination, Stigma, and 'Disability,'" *Virginia Law Review,* vol. 86, copyright © 2000. Reprinted by permission of the publisher.

accommodation requirements) to challenge the practices that enact and enforce their subordinated status.

· · ·

Stigma as a Key Concept. Erving Goffman's notion of stigma is a useful tool here. Although "stigma" refers colloquially to animus and prejudice, Goffman used the term to refer to a broader problem. He described the condition as an "undesired differentness" from what society deems to be "normal" or expected. Under Goffman's approach, the core aspect of stigma occurs when prevailing social practices treat particular "undesirable" traits as universally discrediting. As Goffman emphasized, those who deal with stigmatized persons "tend to impute a wide range of imperfections on the basis of the original one." As a result, people with stigmatized traits are not considered to be among the "normals" for whom society, and its institutions, are designed. This stigma is as much about social attitudes as about the traits themselves; even if an individual can "cure" a stigmatized trait, she may still not be accepted in the community of "normals."

Goffman's construct of "stigma" provides a useful tool in giving content to my subordination-based understanding of disability rights law for at least two reasons. First, Goffman's analysis strongly influenced the thoughts of many of the disability rights activists on whose work I rely. Second, that analysis provides a way of connecting the animus-and stereotype-based discrimination experienced by many people with disabilities with their more systemic neglect in the design of the environment. It therefore provides a way of treating the three basic manifestations of disability discrimination under a single rubric, and it provides a way of predicting which types of impairments are likely to be associated with systematic deprivation of opportunities. Because Goffman wrote primarily about individual interactions between "the normals" and "the stigmatized," his notion of stigma most directly helps to describe the prejudice and stereotypes people with disabilities experience in such interactions. It is especially useful in explaining the "spread effect," under which an impairment to a particular life function is seen as universally disabling. But Goffman's analysis of stigma helps to describe the society-wide neglect of people with disabilities as well. In particular, it helps to explain why people with some impairments are likely to be systematically neglected by social decisions, and why those people are likely to be the same people as those who experience animus and stereotyping. If stigma means that an individual is not considered to be one of "the normals," then people with stigmatized impairments are likely not to be a part of the social "norm" considered by those who design the social and physical environment. Even if the environment's "designers" do not harbor prejudiced or stereotyped thoughts about people with stigmatized conditions, they are likely not to consider their needs in the same way that they consider the needs of those who are "normal."

Disability rights advocates have long made this precise point about "disability." They have argued that "the entire physical and social organization of life" is frequently structured as though everyone were physically strong, as though all bodies were shaped the same, as though everyone could walk, hear, and see well, as though everyone could work and play at a pace that is not compatible with any kind of illness or pain, as though no one were ever dizzy or incontinent or simply needed to sit or lie down.

This phenomenon is most obvious in the built environment. Architects design structures with a model of the "normal" user in mind, and that model has typically been a person without any discernible impairments. This "assumption of able-bodiedness as the norm" can be seen in buildings with unnecessary stairs, doorways that are too narrow to accommodate wheelchairs, and entrances that fail to provide any detectable warning for people with visual impairments. But the phenomenon of neglect extends beyond the decisions that have constructed our physical architecture. It affects our patterns of social organization as well. Among other things, it affects the structure of jobs and the means by which businesses and governments deliver services.

. . .

. . . Whatever the underlying reason for its persistence . . . that stigma can help us to understand the means by which disability-based subordination is transmitted. More importantly, stigma can serve an evidentiary function: It can help us identify cases where impairments are likely to be associated with systematic deprivation of opportunities. Seen in this light, the "disability" category embraces those people who experience impairment-based stigma—that is, those people who, because of present, past, or perceived impairments, are considered by society to be outside of the "norm." As Carol Gill puts it, "disability is a marginalized status that society assigns to people who are different enough from majority cultural standards to be judged abnormal or defective in mind or body." Although I would argue that stigma identifies and explains—but does not necessarily define—disability-based subordination, Gill's analysis substantially overlaps my own.

In this view, "disability" is a group status, but it is not one defined by anything inherent in the members of the group. Rather, the attitudes and practices that exclude people with "disabilities" from many opportunities to participate in society are the very ones that create the "disability" category. Although individuals embraced by the category have vastly different impairments and limitations (indeed, some have no impairment or limitation at all), what is crucial is that society treats them as essentially similar. In Wendell's words, "widespread perceptions that people with disabilities are similar in very significant ways create the category, 'people with disabilities.' " The widespread acts of "discrimination, segregation, and denial of equal opportunity" directed at people with disabilities have effectively marked that group as a "dependent caste."

Subordination-Focused Approach to the ADA

General Framework

 Defining the Approach

How might we use this understanding of disability as subordination to inform interpretation of the ADA's "disability" definition? The foregoing discussion should suggest one polestar: The statutory "disability" category should embrace those actual, past, and perceived impairments that subject people to systematic disadvantages in society. And the concept of stigma should play an important evidentiary role. Impairments that are stigmatized—that type people who have them as "abnormal or defective in mind or body"—are particularly likely to meet the systematic disadvantage standard. This basic orientation can help to develop a principled framework to guide interpretation of the ADA's ambiguous definition of its protected class.

· · ·

Applications

Mitigating Measures

 Properly Taking Account of Mitigating Measures

The principal question before the Court in *Sutton* and *Murphy* involved what has come to be known as the "mitigating measures" issue: Should the "substantial limitation" inquiry take account of whatever mitigating measures (such as medicines or prosthetics) an individual uses to reduce the limiting effects of his or her impairment? Or, should the impairment be considered in its untreated state? In accord with specific language in the committee reports accompanying the ADA, the EEOC and the DOJ had stated (in "interpretive guidance") that courts should ignore mitigating measures when making the "substantial limitation" decision.... In *Sutton*, the Court resolved a conflict in the circuits and rejected the administrative interpretation.

 The Court found it apparent that if a person is taking measures to correct for, or mitigate, a physical or mental impairment, the effects of those measures—both positive and negative—must be taken into account when judging whether that person is "substantially limited" in a major life activity and thus "disabled" under the Act. The Court echoed this conclusion in *Murphy*.

 The Court's conclusion seems entirely sound, both as a matter of basic statutory interpretation and as a means of implementing an antisubordination principle. Showing off its facility with grammatical categories, the *Sutton* Court noted one crucial textual point: "The phrase 'substantially limits' appears in the Act in the present indicative verb form." If a person has uncorrected vision of 20/800 (well beyond the threshold of "legal blindness") but can correct her vision to 20/20 simply by wearing contact lenses or glasses, it is hard to say that her visual impairment "substantially limits" anything. To be sure, it would substantially limit the major life activity of seeing—if we lived in a world without corrective lenses. But corrective lenses are a readily available, easy to use mechanism that will eliminate the limiting effect of the impairment at no appreciable cost. Nor are corrective lenses—or the condition of being unable to see without them—stigmatized in society at large to the degree that they frequently result in the denial of opportunities to people who wear them.

. . .

Thus, the Court was correct to hold that the identical-twin plaintiffs in *Sutton* had no "actual" disability. Although their uncorrected vision was 20/200 in the right eye and 20/400 in the left, their vision in both eyes was correctable to 20/20. United Airlines rejected their applications for pilot positions because the airline required uncorrected vision of 20/100 or better in both eyes. Because their impairment was so readily correctable, and imposed so little societal disadvantage once corrected, it is hard to say that the *Sutton* plaintiffs experienced any substantial limitation on major life activities.

Taking Proper Account of Mitigating Measures

Notwithstanding the conventional wisdom, however, it is important to note that the *Sutton* opinion did not reject the core of the EEOC/Justice Department interpretation. As the Court explained, the "use of a corrective device does not, by itself, relieve one's disability. Rather, one has a disability under subsection A if, notwithstanding the use of a corrective device, that individual is substantially limited in a major life activity." Indeed, the measures taken to mitigate the effects of an impairment may themselves impose substantial limitations. My discussion of infertility illustrates both points. Medical treatments may allow a person with infertility to have a child, but that fact alone does not necessarily relieve the substantial limitation in the major life activity of reproduction. When gestation can occur only through a burdensome and stigmatizing course of treatment, a person's medically generated ability to reproduce will not eliminate the substantial limitation on reproduction.

. . .

Remembering the "Record" Prong

Perhaps more important, the *Sutton* and *Murphy* decisions did not at all address the "record" prong of the ADA's "disability" definition, which protects people from discrimination based on a "record of" a substantially limiting impairment. *Sutton* and *Murphy* would have been particularly poor cases for invocation of the "record" prong: There appears to have been no suggestion in either case that the plaintiffs spent a substantial amount of time with their impairments before they began to use the mitigating measures at issue. The plaintiffs therefore could have had no "record" of a substantially limiting impairment, because their impairments were essentially always "controlled" and hence never (under the Court's assumption) in fact substantially limiting.

Many people with now-controlled medical conditions were at some point substantially limited, however. A person may have been hospitalized for tuberculosis but have fully recovered. Another might have recovered after a year-long battle with cancer. Still others might have experienced significant, limiting effects from diabetes or seizure disorders before their physicians discovered the appropriate treatment. If an employer denies a job to one of these individuals because of their prior diagnoses—whether by disqualifying them for all time or by disqualifying them until they have shown no symptoms for an arbitrarily fixed period—it seems clearly to have discriminated based on the individual's "record of" a substantially limiting impairment. If courts begin to recognize the potential of the "record" prong, the statute can still provide protection to people who face prejudice and stereotypes based on the lingering stigma of a once-active condition. It can do so, however, without ignoring the effects of all corrective measures.

Substantial Limitation in Working

   "Working" as a Major Life Activity

The notion of stigma helps to explain why substantial limitations on working are properly treated as "disabilities." Working is a major part of being "normal" in our society. It is "a means of proving yourself worthy in your own eyes and in the eyes of others," it "shapes individual identities in ways both general and particular," and it provides the arena for significant social integration. Since our nation's founding, work has been "a medium through which a free man might demonstrate that he was a citizen." People who cannot work because of their impairments are therefore likely to experience prejudice, and they are particularly likely to be ignored when others decide how to construct the physical environment and attendant social structures. Such prejudice and neglect may result in even further deprivation of employment opportunities which may in turn promote additional prejudice and neglect. People with "work disability" are therefore likely to need the ADA's protections against systematic disadvantage.

This stigma-based justification for extending the ADA's protection to people with "work disability" can help to frame a proper inquiry into what "substantial limitation" means in the "working" context. To begin with, it seems clear that the inability to perform a single position with a single employer ought not constitute a "substantial limitation." For a variety of idiosyncratic reasons, many people are unable to perform particular jobs—even jobs they want very much. The employer may need to have someone on the job immediately, for example, and the applicant may be unable to start for another two weeks. Whether the reason is a prior commitment to another employer, the need to take care of a sick relative, or the applicant's own recovery from minor surgery, the inability to take a particular job immediately is neither unusual nor stigmatized, and there is no reason to assume that the applicant is likely to suffer systematic disadvantage as a result. If the exclusion from a single position with a single employer did constitute a "substantial limitation" in working, moreover, then the *Sutton* Court's concern about circularity would be quite apt: The employer's very act of rejecting the plaintiff would be the sole basis for affording the plaintiff protection against the rejection. (This, recall, is the cover-everyone position).

Things are very different when an individual's impairment results in disqualification from a large number of jobs. Such individuals do experience systematic disadvantage as a result of their impairment. And there is nothing circular about protecting people against individual acts of discrimination on the ground that they are subjected to repeated exclusion by many employers. Thus, the Court was quite correct to say in *Sutton* that people whose impairments disqualify them from "a broad class of jobs" are substantially limited in working.

. . .

It is difficult to make the same defense of *Murphy*. There, high blood pressure (at least as perceived by UPS) rendered Murphy unable to work in any job that required driving a commercial motor vehicle in interstate commerce. The ability to drive a commercial motor vehicle is hardly a highly specialized skill like the ability to fly an international airliner. Indeed, as the Government's brief in *Murphy* pointed out, over seven million people had commercial driver's licenses in 1994, the year Murphy was fired. And the inability to drive a commercial motor vehicle would not disqualify Murphy from "only a particular job" as the Court stated. Rather, it would disqualify him from literally millions of jobs: mechanic's jobs that, like his position at UPS, required some test-driving of trucks; an enormous number of truck and bus driving jobs; and other jobs that involve incidental driving of commercial motor vehicles. Given his education and experience (he had worked over 22 years as a mechanic), it seems unlikely that Murphy would have had a fair chance of obtaining any other position as rewarding as that of a mechanic. And his blood pressure limited him to a subset (and presumably a less highly valued subset) of mechanic's jobs. It is not much of a stretch to say that Murphy "possessed an attribute that made him different from others in the category of persons available for him to be, and of a less desirable kind." A reasonable person whose prospects were so limited would experience that systematic limitation as meaningful, and the Court should have concluded that it was "substantial."

. . .

A focus on subordination suggests that the Court's restrictive interpretation of the substantial limitation requirement—even if limited to the major life activity of working—is an inappropriate way of giving content to the ADA's "disability" category. As in *Murphy*, the Court's approach denies protection to some people whose impairments lead to a stigmatizing loss of status. At the same time, it stigmatizes those people it protects. Under the Court's inability-to-work approach, plaintiffs who argue that they were wrongfully denied a job must begin by demonstrating that their impairment makes it virtually impossible for them to work. Even if that initial showing does not doom the plaintiff's subsequent attempt to establish that she is "qualified" for the position at issue, the requirement that the plaintiff make such a showing replicates the disempowering effects of the "truly disabled" approach. Because the Court's restrictive approach seems to be limited to the major life activity of "working," it may not have much practical effect. A subordination-focused analysis nonetheless suggests that the Court was wrong to adopt such an approach, even in that limited context.

"Regarded As" Substantially Limited in Working. The Court did not purport to decide whether the plaintiffs in *Sutton* and *Murphy* were actually substantially limited in the ability to work. Rather, it focused only on whether they were "regarded" by the defendants as substantially limited. In *Sutton*, the "regarded as" posture seems to have had a significant effect on the Court's analysis. In particular, the Court expressed great discomfort with the notion that an employer's adoption of a generally applicable physical standard for its employees could compel the conclusion that the employer "regarded" an individual screened out by the requirement as substantially limited in working. The approach I have sketched in this paper suggests that the Court's discomfort was misplaced.

As the Court approached the issue, a "regarded as" claim requires "that a covered entity entertain misperceptions about the individual" plaintiff—misperceptions of a kind that "often 'result from stereotypic assumptions not truly indicative of . . . individual ability.' " But United had no misperception about the *Sutton* plaintiffs. It rejected them because it correctly concluded that they could not satisfy a generally applicable standard that required "uncorrected visual acuity of 20/100 or better." That the airline maintained such a vision requirement, the Court concluded, did not in and of itself "establish a claim that respondent regards petitioners as substantially limited in the major life activity of working." The plaintiffs had argued that United "regarded" them as substantially limited in working, because they would in fact have been substantially limited in working if all global airlines had used United's criteria. The Court, however, found it improper to speculate whether United's vision requirements, if imposed by all global airlines, would make the plaintiffs "substantially limited" in the ability to work. The Court explained that "an otherwise valid job requirement, such as a height requirement, does not become invalid simply because it would limit a person's employment opportunities in a substantial way if it were adopted by a substantial number of employers." A contrary ruling, the court suggested, would call into question employers' ability "to prefer some physical attributes over others and to establish physical criteria" for their employees; such a ruling would therefore override Congress's decision to allow employers "to decide that some limiting, but not substantially limiting, impairments make individuals less than ideally suited for a job."

Aside from the fact that it was unnecessary to the Court's decision, this analysis is flawed. To begin with, actions speak louder than words. The best evidence of what an employer regards to be necessary to perform a job is the set of minimum requirements it actually imposes on those who seek that job. If an employer disqualifies all people with asthma from bicycle courier positions, for example, one can rationally infer that the employer regards asthma as sufficiently interfering with an individual's ability to perform that job to disqualify her from all bicycle courier positions. If disqualification from all bicycle courier jobs amounts to a substantial limitation on working, it should not matter whether asthma is in fact substantially limiting. The "regarded as" analysis should be satisfied by the fact (inferred from the employer's imposition of the job requirement) that the employer regards asthma as imposing a limitation that would be substantial.

For the same reason, the employer's job criteria ought to be imputed to all other employers for purposes of the "regarded as" analysis. In a "regarded as" case where the plaintiff alleges that the defendant regarded her as disabled, it should be irrelevant whether other employers have adopted similarly disqualifying criteria. The issue should instead turn on whether the defendant believed that the plaintiff's impairment was incompatible with the safe and economical performance of a sufficient number of jobs to constitute a substantial limitation. Unless the employer acknowledges that its selection criteria are irrational—that they do not serve the purpose of screening out those who are incapable of performing the job safely and economically—there is every reason to believe that the employer regards applicants who fail its criteria as unable to perform similar jobs for all other employers.

Despite the Court's concerns, a decision to allow unsuccessful applicants to satisfy the "regarded as" prong by demonstrating that they failed the employer's physical standards would not necessarily render those standards "invalid." It would merely subject them to scrutiny under the ADA's substantive provisions. If the criteria in issue were "job related for the position in question" and "consistent with business necessity," and if the plaintiffs who failed those criteria were unable, "with or without reasonable accommodation, [to] perform the essential functions of the employment position," then the employer would be free to maintain them. The "regarded as" finding has only a limited effect: It requires the employer to justify general physical criteria that disqualify people with impairments without regard for their individual abilities. Such a result directly advances the central purposes of the ADA.

· · ·

Although the *Sutton* Court's analysis of the "regarded as" issue was wrong, it should not be overread. In particular, the Court's decision continues to allow a "regarded as" claim where the defendant rejects the plaintiff because it "entertains misperceptions about [her as an] individual," rather than rejecting her because it correctly perceives that she cannot satisfy generally applicable physical standards it imposes for the job. The Court favorably quoted an EEOC release that "explained that the purpose of the regarded as prong is to cover individuals 'rejected from a job because of the "myths, fears and stereotypes" associated with disabilities.' " Where an employer, on discovering an applicant's impairment, rejects that applicant because of an unproven "myth, fear, or stereotype" about its effects on the applicant's ability to perform the job safely and economically, there remains strong reason to conclude that the employer "regarded" the applicant as substantially limited in a major life activity. In such cases, the employer entertains an individually inaccurate perception of the applicant's impairment....

Sutton, with its focus on individualized misperceptions, suggests that courts should give great weight to the employer's reliance on "myths, fears, and stereotypes." By emphasizing that the hallmark of a "regarded as" claim is stereotyping—the "primary cognitive component" of stigma—the Court made clear that stigma counts in the "regarded as" analysis. It is unfortunate, however, that the Court did not seem to recognize that systematic exclusion can be transmitted by general physical criteria as well as individualized misperceptions.

· · ·

Conclusion

... I have tried to demonstrate the value of a subordination-based approach to the ADA's "disability" definition. The vague and open-ended statutory language requires courts to look to some broader principle in interpreting that definition, and the notion of subordination seems a promising candidate for the honor. A subordination-based approach seems to work on an abstract level: It makes sense of the statute's substantive provisions, accords with the basic goals of the disability rights movement, and meshes well with diverse normative arguments for the ADA. It also provides a fruitful and attractive way of approaching concrete controversies that arise under the Act. To be sure, my proposed approach does not provide determinate answers in hard cases. But it does provide a framework within which courts can make the difficult decisions such cases require. And it provides a principle that, elaborated over time in a case-by-case manner, can make the "disability" determination far more determinate and predictable than it is now. That may not be the most profound achievement, but it may be all that we can expect from a statute that is as ambiguous as the ADA.

The Economics of the Americans With Disabilities Act, Part III: Does the ADA Disable the Disabled?*

SUSAN SCHWOCHAU AND PETER DAVID BLANCK

Economic Models of the Effects of the ADA

Basic Labor Market Models

Effects of ADA Title I

Because the ADA focuses on decisions made by firms, most of the models developed to assess its effects deal primarily with predicting the law's effects on labor demand. In general, employers will hire an individual only if the marginal benefits of doing so at least equal the marginal costs. This is true for both disabled and nondisabled individuals. Employers will incur additional hiring costs (those associated with medical insurance, life insurance, and pensions, for instance) only if the benefits of so doing outweigh the costs incurred in hiring. If, for example, employers find that providing fringe benefits makes the attracting and retaining of employees cheaper and productivity greater, then they will supply fringe benefits.

Similarly, in the absence of the ADA (or any other comparable legislation), the standard models suggest that if an employer's providing a disabled individual with particular tools or a particular work setting yields net profits, the employer would make these accommodations. As in the case of fringe benefits, however, disabled individuals provided with such accommodations should expect their wages to be reduced to the extent of the costs of accommodating them. If no such reduction occurs, the net gain to the employer of hiring the disabled individual who needs accommodation will clearly be less than the net gain of hiring an individual needing no such accommodation, and the employer will maximize profits by hiring the nondisabled individual. Under such a conceptualization of the employer's decision making, the chronic unemployment of the disabled is due in part to the fact that they cost more, causing employers to prefer nondisabled individuals.

---

* Susan Schwochau and Peter David Blanck, "The Economics of the Americans With Disabilities Act, Part III: Does the ADA Disable the Disabled?" *Berkeley Journal of Employment and Labor Law*, vol. 21, copyright © 2000. Reprinted by permission of the publisher.

The above description does not account for any possible differences in productivity between the disabled and the nondisabled. Within most models, an individual's disability is expected to reduce productivity on a particular job, or to restrict the individual's ability to be productive in a variety of jobs. Because profits may only be realized if pay given to employees is less than or equal to what the sale of their output yields, the pay of disabled workers will be less than that given to nondisabled workers if, even without needing accommodation, individuals with disabilities are less productive. Thus, disabled persons' wages are less than the wages of nondisabled individuals for two primary reasons: (1) lower productivity and (2) increased marginal costs due to accommodation. Disabled individuals for whom the lower pay does not justify participation in the labor market will drop out of that market, or never enter it.

Note that these principles yield the conclusion that the ADA is not necessary. Employers do, without the ADA, what is economically rational and efficient. Disabled individuals are hired, with or without accommodations, to the extent that doing so is profitable. They are matched to jobs throughout the economy in ways that maximize both firm profits and individual utility.

. . .

With this picture of employer behavior as a starting point, predictions of the effects of the ADA are developed by focusing on what the law forces employers to do differently. Viewing the pre-ADA environment as efficient overall, it should be no surprise that the ADA is predicted to lead to inefficiencies and generally to the imposition of costs on all, or virtually all, affected. Economists often focus on the effects of two of the ADA's provisions: the "equal pay" requirement, and the reasonable accommodation requirement. Each is predicted to have deleterious effects on disabled and nondisabled individuals, on firms and on the economy.

. . .

Empirical Tests of the ADA's Effects on Employment

Given the relative newness of the law, empirical studies of the effects of ADA Title I are understandably few in number. In this Part, we review two studies of the ADA's effects that have received attention: one conducted by Daron Acemoglu and Joshua Angrist, and another by Thomas DeLeire.

DeLeire employs seven panels of SIPP [Survey of Income and Program Participation] data for men ages 18–64 to test which of two models is supported by those data. The first model is one developed using the standard theories of supply and demand described above. The predictions derived from that model were that the ADA would lead to reduced employment and increased wages of disabled individuals, with disemployment effects greatest for workers who were less skilled, less educated, and younger. The latter prediction is based on arguments relating to the characteristics of disabled individuals who would receive accommodations without the ADA. In essence, because an employer would provide accommodations voluntarily only if the benefits of doing so outweighed the costs, individuals who would produce the greatest marginal benefit for the employer per accommodation dollar would be the individuals most likely to be employed and provided accommodations. Greater returns to an accommodation expenditure are realized by accommodating more highly skilled, experienced workers with disabilities who require only inexpensive modifications of the work environment. Thus, DeLeire's prediction amounts to an expectation that the ADA's mandates will have the greatest marginal effects on those who would not be voluntarily accommodated. The second model purportedly tested is one based on Becker's theory of discrimination.

Acemoglu and Angrist use CPS [Current Population Survey] data for men and women ages 21–58 for the 1988 to 1997 period to test a model that is based on standard economic theories that incorporate concepts of hiring and firing costs. Within that model, the ADA imposes not only accommodation costs per disabled employee, but also hiring and firing costs associated with disabled applicants and employees. Hiring costs come about as firms reject disabled applicants, who with some probability challenge those decisions in court. Firing costs are comparably defined and apply to firms' decision to layoff or terminate disabled workers. Because firms can avoid hiring costs by employing disabled individuals, Acemoglu and Angrist's model allows the prediction that the ADA may lead to increases in employment levels. However, because firing costs and accommodation costs are likely to be larger, the law is predicted to have the overall result of reducing employment. The "equal pay" provision is expected to increase wages for disabled employees, creating involuntary unemployment.

Perhaps not surprisingly, both studies report findings that they argue support the models' general predictions. DeLeire summarizes his findings as indicating that the ADA has led to an eight percent decrease in the relative employment of disabled individuals, and to a three percent increase in relative wages. In part because effects were found to be larger for those individuals who had mental disabilities, were younger, and had less education, DeLeire concludes that the ADA's influences are the result of forcing firms to provide more accommodation than they voluntarily would. Acemoglu and Angrist conclude that the ADA has had substantial disemployment effects on disabled men aged 21–58, and on disabled women under the age of 40. They too attribute this finding to the accommodation costs of the ADA.

Behind the Numbers and Conclusions

With two empirical studies attributing findings of lower employment among disabled individuals to the ADA in large national samples, are we to conclude that the law has failed in achieving its goals? For a number of reasons, we believe the answer to this question is no.

. . .

Have the Reasonable Alternatives Been Eliminated?

To attribute the effects reported to the ADA, both studies' authors consider a number of possible alternative explanations for their results. What is not generally considered, however, are explanations that are tied to the characteristics of individuals with disabilities represented in the samples.

Critics of the ADA have spoken at length of the ambiguities within the law's provisions, identifying myriad difficulties associated with determining who falls into the ADA's definition of disabled. What constitutes a disability is not always clear. Individuals with disabilities vary in degree to which their impairments affect their abilities to do various tasks, and in the nature of the accommodations necessary to perform essential job functions. Thus, unlike Title VII, the argument goes, whether an individual is covered by the ADA is not unambiguous—disability is not as easily determined as gender, race, or national origin. Also unlike the case with gender, race, or national origin, we cannot make assumptions regarding individuals with disabilities being as productive as those without disabilities.

In light of the ink devoted to describing the uncertainty associated with the definition of the disabled, and the variation that exists within the population of individuals with impairments that affect work, it is somewhat surprising to find empirical tests using the same types of measures as are used in studies focusing on the wages and employment of women versus men, and of whites versus blacks. Both DeLeire and Acemoglu and Angrist employ indicator variables for the presence of a disability—a single variable that measures whether an individual has a disability or not—as their primary measures of interest. This type of measure treats those with disabilities as a relatively homogenous group, particularly given that a number of other individual characteristics are left unmeasured.

The use of an indicator variable is unfortunate in part because it prevents analysis of the effects of the ADA on various subgroups within the group of those with disabilities. Title I protects *qualified* individuals with disabilities. It does not provide coverage to all persons with physical or mental limitations, or even to all persons with "disabilities" as the ADA defines that term. The law divides individuals with impairments into three groups: individuals with impairments that do not substantially limit a major life activity, individuals with substantial limitations who are qualified (as the law defines that term), and individuals with substantial limitations who are not qualified. The law provides protection to those in the second group, but not to those in the first or third group. Instead of recognizing in empirical work the fact that these three groups receive different treatment under the ADA, DeLeire and Acemoglu and Angrist treat them as equivalent.

The definition of disability used also deviates from that employed in the ADA. DeLeire divides his sample of individuals into the disabled and nondisabled through the use of a question that asks respondents whether they have a physical, mental, or other health condition that limits the kind or amount of work that they can do. This is the standard SIPP-based item used in tabulating broad indicators of labor force participation of individuals with work-limiting impairments. The item Acemoglu and Angrist use to categorize the disabled comes from the March CPS Income Supplement and asks whether individuals "have a health problem or disability which prevents [them] from working or which limits the kind and the amount of work [they] can do."

Both definitions are narrower than the ADA's definition of disability in that they focus on impairments that limit working activity (rather than any major life activity), and fail to incorporate individuals with a record of a substantial limitation on a life activity, or those perceived to have a substantial limitation. . . .

Within the category of disabled individuals, the problem is not one of miscategorization per se, but one of including individuals clearly not qualified under the ADA. DeLeire and Acemoglu and Angrist include in the category of disabled individuals those persons whose impairments prevent them from working at all. Individuals whose disabilities prevent them from working are considered not qualified, and therefore do not receive the protection of the ADA. . . .

Acemoglu and Angrist's indicator of disability explicitly combines individuals whose impairments prevent them from working with those whose disabilities limit, but do not prevent work. . . . Because the studies rely on comparisons of the disabled and the nondisabled, inclusion in the category of the disabled individuals who cannot work at all would depress coefficients associated with disability and make differences more likely to be found.

Although the inclusion of those unable to work in a single disabled category depresses the estimate of the average effect of having a work disability, it would not necessarily explain Acemoglu and Angrist's findings of differences between the disabled and nondisabled for years after 1992. To explain this pattern, changes in the proportion of individuals within the disabled category who were unable to work would have to have been realized. For example, if the "prevented from working" subgroup increased in size over the period of interest relative to the "not prevented from working" subgroup, the change could be reflected in findings of significant differences between the disabled and those not disabled. In both studies, it is recognized that, as a percentage of the population, the number of disabled individuals increased over the time periods under investigation. What researchers do not consider, however, is evidence suggesting that the percentage of those with work disabilities who are unable to work also increased over the period of interest. The increase in the percentage of those unable to work has been greatest for individuals between the ages of 18 and 44, though a general trend upward is discernible for older workers.

Where researchers do consider changes within the disabled population, it is generally to eliminate the possibility that the results reflect changes in the degree to which individuals report themselves to be disabled. This concern reflects the possibility that individuals had a greater tendency to report themselves as disabled after passage of the ADA to gain the benefits of the law, or because disability "became more socially acceptable." In each study, the authors attempted to address this concern by estimating models for individuals reporting the same disability status in both pre-and post-ADA periods. DeLeire does not report results of this analysis, stating in a footnote that results "do not differ substantially from those reported in the table." Acemoglu and Angrist do report their findings. The authors' results differ significantly from previously reported results.

The first difference is revealed in results that seek to replicate previous findings. Whereas use of a multi-year dataset suggested significant disemployment effects for young men, this result is not repeated when data for a one-year period are used. The second difference appears when observations are restricted to those for which individuals reported the same disability status in both years. Here, results suggest statistically significant differences in the number of weeks worked only for the subsample of men aged 40–58. There are no significant differences in weeks worked for young men, young women, or older women. One is left with the possibility that prior results reflect in part that individuals who are disabled for a period of less than a year work fewer weeks in that year than those who are not disabled. Although questions remain as to why in prior results differences emerged after 1993 for young men and women, it is with less ease that the pattern may be attributed to the ADA's equal pay and accommodation provisions.

Such changes in findings underscore the problems associated with not considering the characteristics with respect to which individuals classifying themselves as disabled differ, and how those characteristics may translate into differences in employment patterns. Given evidence that characteristics of the disabled—such as whether they report themselves to be disabled in two consecutive periods—are associated with differences in findings, the attribution to the ADA of results not taking those characteristics into account is highly suspect.

There are other reasons to believe that attribution of disemployment results to the ADA is premature. One possible explanation for the results of both papers is that disabled individuals experienced during the post-1990 period a continuation of a downward trend in employment that began at an earlier time. DeLeire, for example, presents a figure based on one [of] his models that reflects a downward trend in relative employment that appears to have begun prior to the ADA's enactment. Acemoglu and Angrist control for a disability-specific trend—the possibility that over the entire period examined, weeks worked or wage rates for disabled individuals exhibited an increasing or decreasing trend. When the trend variable is included, many of the negative coefficients are no longer statistically significant. The overall results suggest that once trends over time are controlled for, differences in weeks worked in specific years between disabled and nondisabled individuals existed only for young men and young women. The fact that the meaning of results changes with the inclusion of an additional variable suggests that those results may not be attributable to the ADA.

Labor Markets, Rationality, and Workers with Disabilities*

MICHAEL ASHLEY STEIN

The Paradigm of Rational Market Decisions and the Puzzle of Unemployed Workers With Disabilities

... The assumption that informs Title I, as well as more traditional prohibitions against discrimination in employment, is that imposing these regulations will equalize employment opportunities for targeted groups. But empirical studies of post-ADA employment effects highlight a phenomenon that is puzzling. Although analyses suggest that employing workers with disabilities can be cost effective, and despite a burgeoning economy in which the unemployment rate for most categories of workers has plummeted, unemployment of working-age individuals with disabilities appears not to have similarly diminished. From the point of view of scholars applying the neoclassical labor market paradigm to Title I, the clearest explanation of this phenomenon seems to be that the studies reporting the cost effectiveness of employing the disabled are incorrect (even if only overstated). Following from this explication is the conclusion that selecting workers with disabilities over nondisabled workers is an inefficient practice.

· · ·

Flawed Assumptions

The neoclassical economic model of the labor market begins from the premise that markets for goods and services operate rationally. As part

* Michael Ashley Stein, "Labor Markets, Rationality, and Workers with Disabilities," *Berkeley Journal of Employment and Labor Law*, vol. 21, copyright © 2000. Reprinted by permission of the publisher.

of this postulate it is assumed that markets set their own prices, free bargaining is the norm, and knowledge is completely and symmetrically disseminated, resulting in correct end values for commodities. Under this theory, market forces discipline employers and their self-destructive tastes against particular groups by driving those employers from the market. This economic Darwinism occurs because employers' discriminatory practices of declining to hire particular types of employees despite their greater utility adds to business costs, and thus diminishes their profit margins. Exercising distaste also raises the net-product margin of nondiscriminatory competitors who engage same-group employees at reduced wage levels.

Resting on this foundation, the neoclassical economic paradigm posits that in the context of a rational labor market employers hire workers with the greatest net productivity. This utility is calculated by subtracting total labor cost from total production benefit. Since workers with disabilities require costly inputs in the form of accommodations, an employer, if sufficiently unconstrained so that she can act of her own rational preference, would logically choose non-disabled employees.

The most thorough criticism of Title I from a law and economics perspective was published by Richard Epstein after passage of the ADA, but prior to promulgation of its regulations. Although therefore somewhat precipitous, because successive literature closely follows Epstein's position in applying the neoclassical economic labor market model, elucidating his arguments will yield an understanding of how those who utilize similar assumptions assess Title I. For facility of reference, these views (with his courteous permission) will be attributed directly to Epstein. At the same time, however, my criticisms of Epstein are apropos to other law and economics practitioners to the extent that they adopt normative assumptions common to the neoclassical economic model, for example the belief in an existing rational marketplace for labor services.

Epstein advances three main reasons for believing that the potential benefits associated with reasonable accommodations are inherently less than the costs they engender. First, it is in the nature of disability that those individuals are less productive than their able-bodied counterparts. Second, providing accommodation—that is, giving a disabled worker something her able-bodied peers do not receive as a means of ameliorating her impairments—must be costly. Third, the employment of workers with disabilities extracts yet a further cost when co-workers and customers respond with "awkward" and "unpleasant" feelings, which as "preferences should not be blithely condemned as irrational."

When employers are forced to hire disabled employees against their own considered judgment, these employers are made to internalize costs that they would not have otherwise borne. Consequently, according to Epstein, Title I accommodations are inherently inefficient because they reduce the utility the employer is able to achieve. Title I's requirements are also unfair because they compel private employers to bear the costs of an inefficient social policy. Epstein therefore concludes that the current exclusion of people with disabilities from the employment sphere is the result of rational decisionmaking, not of prejudice or statistical discrimination.

According to Epstein, a better solution towards achieving the same end of altering historical imbalances in the labor market would be to abrogate the ADA so as to allow the market to function normally. In this circumstance, employees with disabilities could underbid the true value of their services or decline health insurance coverage as a way of offsetting their accommodation costs. If necessary, the state could create incentives for accommodating disabled workers by spreading those costs through the tax structure or by directly issuing vouchers to employers. Finally, Epstein maintains that specific industries and plant locations could be chosen as "centers" of accommodation. By concentrating workers with disabilities at such sites, there is increased likelihood that physical plant or equipment accommodations will see repeated usage. According to Epstein, this last option "far from being seen as handicap ghettoization, will be regarded as a sensible effort to economize on public funds."

Four principal theoretical flaws undermine Epstein's application of neoclassical economic principles to Title I. . . .

Over-Reliance on the Neoclassical Model

The first flaw in Epstein's account is his unqualified approbation of the neoclassical economic model. As set forth above, this paradigm posits that employers acting rationally will hire and maintain workers with the greatest net productivity, while employees who act irrationally will be disciplined by market forces and ultimately driven from competition. This premise, which is taken as a standard economic assumption by many law and economics practitioners, has questionable factual and normative elements as applied to the reality of disabled workers' experiences in the labor market. In explaining this assertion, the scholarship of Cass Sunstein and John Donohue is instructive.

There is a factual objection to applying the neoclassical labor market model to disabled workers. To begin with, the standard neoclassical economic model is premised on complete and symmetrical distribution of information to all actors within a given market. Yet not all markets function equally in this respect. Accordingly, although the neoclassical economic account of information dissemination might be true of financial markets whose extensive "reporting" requirements are rigorously enforced by the Securities and Exchange Commission, no parallel structure exists in the labor market. Similarly, the liquidity of financial market commodities does not extend to the market for employment services, where the value of individual workers is difficult to disaggregate.

Next, contrary to the neoclassical labor market account, empirical studies conducted both before and after passage of the ADA clearly demonstrate the persistence of employment discrimination as an obstacle to labor market opportunities for workers with disabilities. In analyzing the effects of employer practices, these studies, which assume information asymmetry in the labor market, glean the effects of non-statistical (or economically rational) behavior from that caused by prejudice. In other words, they separate the consequences of decisions arising from the use of indicators which substitute reliable generalizations about group characteristics from those which either wrongly assume or overestimate the existence of those characteristics. In the case of workers with disabilities, existing misconceptions about disabled workers that substitute for less easily obtainable accurate information tend to sway estimates of indicators that are meant to signal appraisals of productivity and accommodation cost. Additionally, even if economically rational indicators were substituted for biased ones, a market failure would continue because employers' discriminatory behavior would be rewarded as efficient (and conversely, a system requiring economically empowered employers, rather than economically disempowered employees, to bear cost differentials incurred by disregarding rational economic discrimination may arguably be more efficient from a social welfare standpoint). Thus, the baseline assumption that employers act in a rational manner while seeking to maximize their own profits appears empirically invalid.

Moreover, the neoclassical economic model asserts that once discriminatory practices are observed, employers who exercise distaste are disciplined by market forces that reduce their profit margins while increasing those of their nondiscriminatory competitors. As with the first premise, this theory has not been empirically demonstrated. Indeed, logical application of the neoclassical economic paradigm would recount that prior to 1964, when federal antidiscrimination laws injected inefficiency into the dynamics governing private employment relationships, discriminatory firms would have been either penalized or driven from competition. I am unaware of any empirical evidence that supports this position. To the contrary, United States markets have historically evinced various forms of unpunished discriminatory behavior. Consequently, there is no proof for a belief in the self-corrective force of competitive market pressures in the labor field.

There is also a normative objection to utilizing neoclassical economic principles to examine the dynamics of disabled participation in the labor market. Accepting this paradigm would not discipline irrational behavior and restore the employment market to a nondiscriminatory equilibrium. Instead, reliance on competitive pressure as advocated in neoclassical economic analyses would perpetuate market failure by reinforcing the stereotypes Title I was meant to counteract. This is because the neoclassical economic paradigm uses as its baseline a status quo designed by an empowered majority that has already absorbed existing prejudices and made them endogenous to future decision making. Hence, any analysis that assumes market neutrality has reflexively erected obstacles to antidiscrimination principles that are entrenched in the same stereotypes those civil rights statutes seek to alter. Whether embracing these stereotypes is an unconscious, semi-conscious, conscious, or cognitively biased decision remains hotly debated, as does the issue of whether preferences are fixed or malleable. For now, however, it is sufficient to say that accepting the neoclassical economic model's view that existing prejudicial preferences built into the marketplace are neutral will only serve to continue those stereotypes.

. . .

Miscalculating Productivity

The second systemic flaw in Epstein's account is his tripartite assumption that because disabled employees are by nature less productive than their non-disabled counterparts, they require accommodations, and that these accommodations are inherently costly. Empirical studies have not established the prevalence of the need for accommodation among disabled workers across the labor market. It is reasonable to assume that some percentage of employees with disabilities will require accommodations. The size of this group will depend upon the individual circumstances of present or prospective employees, the degree to which an employer's worksite and processes are already accessible, and how the term "disabled" is conceived or measured. There is, however, no reason to suspect that every employee with a disability requires an accommodation, and counterexamples to any such broad generalization are abundant.

Moreover, although the area needs greater and more representative study, available empirical data suggest that accommodating workers with disabilities engenders little or no cost. For example, a study examining 500 accommodations made by Sears, Roebuck & Co. over the twenty-year period 1978–96 found that nearly all of the accommodations were made at minimal cost. Results of the Sears Study are corroborated by those of the Job Accommodation Network, which reported the typical cost of accommodation as $200, and by other appraisals showing similarly moderate costs. Another analysis concluded that the cost of accommodating disabled workers was equal to that of acclimating nondisabled workers. Nevertheless, the fact that these studies report the activities of only a minority of corporations, when similar practices would compel more widely spread efficient corporate planning, evidences a market failure.

Lastly, it is not accurate to assume that disabled workers are by nature less productive than their counterparts free of disabilities, although this may be true for some individuals with disabilities, just as some nondisabled workers are less productive than the majority of disabled ones. In terms of statutory protection, a disabled worker is not considered "qualified" under Title I unless she can perform the essential job functions of her chosen occupation, either with or without accommodation. A disabled employee who satisfies the requirements of her position without accommodation is equally as productive as her non-disabled peers. When she needs accommodations to accomplish integral activities, the existence and degree of her relatively lower net productivity is affected by her ability to accomplish nonessential job functions, as well as the value of those supplementary services to her employer. It bears noting, however, that forty years of pre-ADA empirical studies indicate comparable overall productivity levels between disabled and non-disabled workers. For example, statistics from the U.S. Office of Vocational Rehabilitation indicate that 91% of disabled workers were rated either "average" or "better than average," the same rating given to non-disabled workers. Judging from the shortage of disability awareness and management programs instituted by corporations as part of their business practices, human resource managers seem unaware of this information. This scarcity further denotes an information asymmetric; under a neoclassical economic model, companies with access to this information would act on these favorable economic incentives and promote greater employment among the disabled.

Weighting Distaste

A third systemic flaw in the Epstein view is its account of co-worker and client distaste when calculating the costs of employing people with disabilities. Although law and economics assessments are expected to account for all possible costs and benefits when assessing efficiency, it is atypical when calculating social good to give weight to preferences arising from socially undesirable criteria (for example, illegal tastes). Consequently, deferring to prejudicial irrationalities about disabled workers is a controversial method of applying conventional law and economics criteria. Such inclusion would also result, as was shown above, in continuation of the same biases that Title I was meant to counteract. At the very least, Epstein needs to justify such atypical accession to irrational preferences. Furthermore, his focus on disability as the exclusive cause of distaste felt by one worker for another posits a depth of ignorance about human reactions, as well as the kind of information void that Epstein claims does not exist in a rational workplace.

An information asymmetry also exists as to the distastes of employers and third parties towards workers with disabilities. While empirical surveys of Fortune 500 executives, senior executives, and co-workers uniformly report favorable attitudes to employing disabled individuals, available data fails to evince significant increases in the relative employment rate among disabled individuals. Two alternative conclusions can be drawn from this apparent paradox: either cognitive dissonance causes the individuals surveyed to believe they favor disabled employment when in reality they do not, or those interviewed truly do espouse prodisabled sentiments, but because of an information asymmetry this preference does not manifest itself when these individuals act aggregately as corporations.

. . .

The Utility of Employing Workers With Disabilities

There are positive external benefits to consider when assessing the potential economic effect of a disabled worker on a given firm. These externalities are not all readily quantifiable. Considering the impact of these benefits will not result in all accommodations being seen as economically efficient, but should render a more balanced calculus.

The most immediately quantifiable benefits are those internalized by employers due to savings in recruitment, training, and replacement expenses. One federally funded agency found that for every dollar spent on accommodation, companies saved an average of fifty dollars in net benefits. Another survey reported that 60% of disabled workers remained with their job placement as opposed to only 40% of able-bodied workers, and that the average cost of each job turnover was $2,800. Moreover, empirical evidence corroborates that workers with disabilities have absenteeism rates equal to or lower than their nondisabled peers. The rational economics of hiring workers with disabilities is also validated by anecdotal accounts.

In addition, according to Peter Blanck, many accommodations produce desirable "ripple effects." Among such desirable consequences are higher productivity, greater dedication, better identification of qualified candidates for promotion, fewer insurance claims, reduced post-injury rehabilitation costs, improved corporate culture, and more widespread use of available technologies.

Among the external benefits to employers that are less immediately quantifiable are public cost savings, including reduction of disability-related public assistance obligations estimated at $120 billion annually. Hiring people with disabilities has also been shown to be beneficial to taxpayers' burdens and the national economy. These economic benefits, which were clearly a Congressional concern when passing the ADA, are recognized by a minority of companies.

Finally, intangible benefits also flow from the extension of employment sphere protection to disabled individuals. Although the effects of such protections upon individual employers are more difficult to quantify, these advantages may nonetheless maximize the collective good. These benefits include placing people with disabilities in a position to exercise all the responsibilities of citizenship, acknowledging that capable individuals have a "right" to work, permitting the disabled to achieve dignity through labor and productivity, and realizing the value of a diverse society. The value of these gains, as well as what any of them is worth to individual employers, is not necessarily negligible even if it is unclear. The expenses extracted for achieving these benefits must therefore be closely evaluated in any determination of whether to place such costs upon employers rather than spread them through taxes or other state-governed devices. Nevertheless, employers arguably benefit individually from a collective climate in which citizens value the identities they achieve from being productive more than they do the relief of being excused from productivity.

How and when to allocate the costs of maintaining a culture of productivity raises a host of issues, including criticisms of those law and economics studies utilizing wealth as a value, the continuing debate surrounding commodification, questions about the perspective of policymakers, and differences of opinion on the advantages of investing in human capital. Regardless of how these issues are resolved, an account that educates both employers and economists about some of the difficult-to-quantify benefits listed above is far more consistent with our traditional thinking about the personal and social value of productivity than a narrow construction of social motivation which it assumes, counterfactually, that the statute "would not be necessary if these [accommodations] were beneficial to employers, as they automatically act in ways that promote their self interests."

Notes and Questions

1.   Chai Feldblum argues that the ADA should not have offered any definition of disability. Feldblum, "Definition of Disability Under Federal Anti–Discrimination Law: What Happened? Why? And What Can We Do About It?" 21 *Berkeley Journal of Employment and Labor Law* 91, 94 (2000). He reasons that just as Title VII does not provide a definition of race or sex or religion but relies on the limiting factor of plaintiff's showing that discrimination was *based* on such characteristics, the ADA could have covered *any* impairment and relied on the limiting factor of plaintiff's showing that discrimination occurred *because of* such an impairment. In effect, "A possible legislative determination in a civil rights law could then have been that no impairment, whether mildly limiting or severely limiting, should be the basis for decision-making in employment or society generally, except when such an impairment makes an individual unqualified for a job or ineligible for a service." Id. at 102.

This universal approach goes too far for Samuel Bagenstos, who advocates an "antisubordinationist approach" to understanding the ADA's aim, as described in his excerpt. If, as he points out, the primary operating principle of the ADA is to prevent creation of a permanent class of a stigmatized or subordinated group, mild impairments that are not stigmatizing and discriminatory actions that affect only certain individuals on a nonsystematic basis do not merit government intervention because societal costs outweigh individual benefits. Are there arguments against interpreting the ADA and other civil rights laws as establishing a general prohibition against arbitrary or irrational treatment regardless of whether such treatment creates a stigmatized group? The California city of Santa Cruz adopted such a prohibition in 1993, when it banned all discrimination based on, among other characteristics, personal appearance, including a person's height, weight, and other physical attributes. It is hardly the case that, say, persons who are tall form a historically stigmatized group and yet the ordinance prohibits using height as a basis of discrimination, presumably because it aims to promote rational decision-making in general. Is this type of ordinance theoretically desirable and practically enforceable? For discussions on the relationship between workers' physical appearance and their earning levels, see John Cawley, "Body Weight and Women's Labor Market Outcomes," NBER Working Paper No. W7841, August 2000 (finding that higher body weight lowers wages for white women); Ciska M. Bosman, et al., "Business Success and Businesses' Beauty Capital," NBER Working Paper No. W6083, July 1997 (suggesting that wage differentials associated with employees' "beauty" might be due to differences in their productivity and not merely due to discrimination).

2. Certain disorders are explicitly excluded from coverage under the ADA. For example, drug addiction, transvestism, transsexualism, pedophilia, exhibitionism, voyeurism, compulsive gambling, kleptomania, and pyromania, among other mental and sexual disorders are excluded. For some of these disorders, such as drug addiction and pyromania, public or workplace safety and health concerns reasonably dictate their exclusion. Other disorders, however, such as transvestism and transsexualism, raise no obvious public health or safety issues. Exclusion of these types of disorders perhaps reflects a collective moral judgment that they fall outside the acceptable social norm and thus should not be sanctioned with legal protection. To the extent that that moral judgment is based on an assumption of individual choice that is absent in consideration of more "morally deserving" physical or mental disabilities, there is uncertainty about the law's ability to delineate this distinction equitably. For example, should the law make a distinction between a paraplegic at birth and someone who becomes a paraplegic because of his decision to engage in an unreasonably risky behavior? Should the growing class of Americans who are becoming obese fall within the morally undeserving category or should one explore whether the obesity stems from a genetic predisposition or from a lack of self-control?

For a related discussion on how the ADA should treat "voluntary" disabilities—disabilities that are "caused, continue to exist, or are being worsened as a result of [disabled individuals'] own voluntary conduct"—see Lisa E. Key, "Voluntary Disabilities and the ADA: A Reasonable Interpretation of Reasonable Accommodations," 48 *Hastings Law Journal* 75 (1996).

3. The third prong of the ADA's definition of disability—"regarded as having such an impairment"—has been vulnerable to varying interpretations. Courts generally have construed this provision narrowly to hold that "such an impairment" refers to the first prong of the definition, which requires that the disability substantially limit one or more major life activities. Under this literalist reading, a disability is covered under the third

prong only if the defendant regards the plaintiff as having a type of impairment that substantially limits a major life activity. Disability rights advocates, however, argue that the legislative history of the ADA dictates a much broader reading. They claim that if the plaintiff experiences a limitation in a major life activity because of others' attitudes and discriminatory actions in response to the plaintiff's impairment, that impairment should be covered under the ADA. This broader reading is somewhat circular (because as Chai Feldblum points out, "it is the defendant's action itself that creates the coverage for the plaintiff"), but the literalist reading of the "regarded as" prong also raises knotty issues: for example, should a defendant be allowed to argue that, while he did not regard the plaintiff's impairment as substantially limiting a major life activity, he found it to be salient enough to be the basis of his discriminatory action? Would a negative answer to this question effectively eviscerate the ADA's threshold designed to prevent claims based on *de minimis* impairments? Is there a rationale for holding that someone with a very serious impairment should not be denied a job on that basis but someone with a far less serious impairment can be denied the job on that basis?

4. Courts have tried to make a clear distinction between mere "medical conditions" and true disabilities. For example, courts have found in some cases that individuals with such conditions as breast cancer, multiple sclerosis, stroke, lymphoma, brain tumors, heart disease, diabetes, hemophilia, and epilepsy were merely suffering from a medical condition, not disability. Is this distinction a principled one or purely pragmatic? Under the Family and Medical Leave Act of 1933 (FMLA), employees are entitled to twelve weeks of unpaid leave for their own "serious health condition," which is defined as "an illness, injury, impairment, or physical or mental condition that involves (A) inpatient care ... ; or (B) continuing treatment by a health care provider." This means that an employee who might not be considered disabled under the ADA may still have a cause of action under the FMLA if the employer refuses to grant her twelve weeks of leave for her condition. Conversely, an employee with a disability may not have a "serious health condition" that entitles her to the twelve weeks mandated by the FMLA. For example, an employee with a permanent hearing loss may be considered to have a disability that substantially limits a major life activity, but unless the condition requires inpatient care or continuing medical treatment, it will not be considered a serious health condition under the FMLA.

There are interesting questions that arise at the intersection of these two statutes. For example, if an employer grants twelve weeks of leave to an employee under the FMLA, can that employer take into consideration the financial effects of having granted that leave in deciding whether to provide reasonable accommodation under the ADA to the same employee? Lisa J. Gitnik, "Will the Interaction of the Family and Medical Leave Act and the Americans with Disabilities Act Leave Employees with an 'Undue Hardship?'" 74 *Washington University Law Quarterly* 283 (1996). The ADA generally prohibits medical inquiries of employees unless the inquiry is "job-related and consistent with business necessity." On the other hand, the FMLA permits an employer to require an employee to provide medical certification to support her request for a leave. Should an employee requesting a leave of absence be allowed to argue that the medical certification requirement violates the ADA restriction on the type of medical information that the employer is entitled to? James A. Passamano, "Employee Leave under the Americans with Disabilities Act and the Family and Medical Leave Act," 38 *South Texas Law Review* 861 (1997).

5. Employers are required to scientifically and medically assess the risks to public or workplace health and safety that a potential employee's disability might pose before excluding her from the job on safety grounds. In addition, to exclude a disabled individual, the employer must show that she poses a "direct threat"—i.e., a significant risk of substantial harm—to the health or safety of others and that such a risk cannot be eliminated by reasonable accommodations. These mandates try to obviate the potential that irrational perceptions of danger associated with certain disability will harm disabled workers. But is the burden of making this type of showing too onerous for employers? For example, it has been well documented that clinical assessments by psychologists and results of psychological personality tests are notoriously inaccurate in predicting whether an individual with a mental disorder will become violent on the worksite. What other types of scientific assessment can employers turn to in such cases?

6. Some scholars have pointed out that the ADA's conception of equality that mandates accommodation rather than mere equal treatment may be a form of affirmative action. This attempt to analogize the ADA to other types of affirmative action may have political significance because if successful, the same conservative attacks that have galvanized significant resentment and hostility towards traditional affirmative action programs might be deployed against the ADA. Underlying the opposition to affirmative action is a popular belief that such programs simply grant special privileges to selected groups. And as Michael Wald, points out, "Americans consistently emphasize that they do not want to be a redistributional society." Wald, "Moving Forward, Some Thoughts on Strategies," 21 *Berkeley Journal of Employment and Labor Law* 473, 474 (2000).

On the other hand, advocates of affirmative action have been able to reframe the debate to invoke notions of corrective justice, and the same strategy has been used to defend the reasonable accommodation requirement. That is, "the reasonable accommodation requirement is not a means of giving people with disabilities a special benefit or advantage; rather, it is a means of equalizing the playing field so that people with disabilities are not disadvantaged by the fact that the workplace ignores their needs." Matthew Diller, "Judicial Backlash, the ADA, and the Civil Rights Model," 21 *Berkeley Journal of Employment and Labor Law* 19, 41 (2000). Are there other ways in which the reasonable accommodation requirement can be analogized or distinguished from traditional types of affirmative action?

7. The problem with Title I, according to some scholars, is that it redistributes wealth while unevenly imposing costs of accommodation on certain employers. As Samuel Issacharoff and Justin Nelson point out in the excerpted selection above, only those employers forced to hire disabled

workers must expend extra resources to accommodate them; the rest of the employers remain unaffected. In addressing this concern, Issacharoff and Nelson point to the German model, which spreads the cost of alleged redistribution more evenly through its "pay or play" regime. The basic mandate of the German model is that all employers with more than fifteen workers must hire one severely disabled person for every sixteen job slots or pay a monthly fee of two hundred deutsche marks, which is collected by the state welfare agency and the federal employment office.

Although the German model does appear to have the advantage of more equitably spreading the cost of accommodation, it has been criticized as potentially stigmatizing its intended beneficiaries. Does the German market-based approach advance fairness to employers and improve employment prospects for the disabled more effectively than the ADA's civil rights regime that seeks to avoid such stigmatization? For an empirical discussion of the impact of the German model, see Mary C. Daly, "Who Is Protected by the ADA? Evidence from the German Experience," 549 *The Annals of The American Academy of Political and Social Science* 101 (1997).

Is it clear that the costs of accommodation are high? According to a recent study commissioned by Sears, for example, of the 436 reasonable accommodations provided by the company between 1978 and 1992, 69 percent cost nothing, 28 percent cost less than $1,000, and only 3 percent cost more than $1,000. In addition, employers enjoy considerable tax breaks for costs associated with providing accommodations to disabled workers. If employers are really choosing not to hire certain disable workers because of concerns about the costs of reasonable accommodation, should the penalties for refusals to hire on these grounds be elevated? Conversely, if such disemployment effects are real, would this be an argument for repeal of the ADA?

8. Another problem with the reasonable accommodation mandate might be that in some cases, it causes some employers to violate certain provisions of collective bargaining agreements, which is governed by another regulatory scheme, the National Labor Relations Act. For example, when an employer reassigns a disabled employee in order to comply with the reasonable accommodation provision of the ADA, that reassignment might violate the seniority provisions of a collective bargaining agreement. A majority of courts that have considered the conflict between the ADA and collective bargaining agreements have adopted a per se rule that an employer does not have to reassign disabled workers in violation of a collective bargaining agreement. This approach has been criticized by some scholars. See Brian P. Kavanaugh, "Collective Bargaining Agreements and the Americans with Disabilities Act: A Problematic Limitation on 'Reasonable Accommodation' for the Union Employee," *University of Illinois Law Review* 751 (1999). How should courts resolve these types of conflicts?

9. Christine Jolls offers a rigorous economic analysis of accommodation mandates that target specific group of workers, such as the disabled. Jolls, "Accommodation Mandates," 53 *Stanford Law Review* 223 (2000). Jolls shows that the Summers model, which is a framework for analyzing man-

dates targeting workers as a whole, is inadequate for analyzing accommodation mandates because it ignores the constraints imposed by the presence of
antidiscrimination law. When antidiscrimination restrictions against not
hiring or giving less pay to accommodated workers are binding on employers,
accommodation mandates have a greater scope for benefiting their intended
beneficiaries than the Summers model of universal mandates would suggest.
Jolls concludes, however, that with respect to the ADA, restrictions on
employment differentials are unlikely to be binding, while restrictions on
wage differentials are likely to be binding. Her analysis therefore predicts
that the ADA will reduce the relative employment rate of disabled workers
while either increasing or leaving unchanged their wage levels. For analysis
of Jolls' framework and its application to analyzing sexual harassment and
disparate impact liability, see John J. Donohue, "Understanding the Reasons
for and Impact of Legislatively Mandated Benefits for Selected Workers," 53
Stanford Law Review 897 (2001).

Ascertaining the impact of any law is a very tricky enterprise, so it is
not surprising that different scholars have reached different conclusions
about the impact of the ADA as they develop new theoretical frameworks
and parse the data using different statistical models. One potentially confounding issue in empirical studies of the ADA is that in addition to the
passage of the ADA, the late 1980s and 1990s was a period of another
important change impacting the employment of disabled workers. Specifically, "between 1984 and 2000, the share of non-elderly adults receiving
benefits from the Social Security Disability Insurance (DI) and Supplemental
Security Income (SSI) programs rose from 3.1 to 5.3 percent" due to the
interaction of reduced screening stringency and a rising earnings replacement rate from these governmental benefits programs. David Autor and
Mark Duggan, "The Rise in Disability Recipiency and the Decline in Unemployment," NBER Working Paper No. W8336, June 2001. See also Richard
V. Burkhauser, "Post-ADA: Are People with Disabilities Expected to Work?"
549 *The American Academy of Political and Social Science* 71 (1997). This
very dramatic increase in the number of non-elderly adults receiving disability benefits has the potential to confound estimates of the employment effects
generated by the passage of the ADA, as it can both reduce the relative
employment levels of the disabled and may increase average earnings of the
remaining workers if the lowest-wage workers are the ones to shift to
governmental income maintenance. At the same time, it shows that our
society has substantially increased its financial commitment to the disabled
through monetary grants over the last two decades.

†